LOEB CLASSICAL LIBRARY

FOUNDED BY JAMES LOEB 1911

EDITED BY

JEFFREY HENDERSON

VELLEIUS PATERCULUS

LCL 152

VELLEIUS PATERCULUS

EDITED AND TRANSLATED BY

A. J. WOODMAN

HARVARD UNIVERSITY PRESS
CAMBRIDGE, MASSACHUSETTS
LONDON, ENGLAND
2024

Copyright © 2024 by the President and Fellows
of Harvard College
All rights reserved

First published 2024

LOEB CLASSICAL LIBRARY® is a registered trademark
of the President and Fellows of Harvard College

Library of Congress Control Number 2024003697
CIP data available from the Library of Congress

ISBN 978-0-674-99763-9

Composed in ZephGreek and ZephText by
Technologies 'N Typography, Merrimac, Massachusetts.
Printed on acid-free paper and bound by
Maple Press, York, Pennsylvania

CONTENTS

PREFACE	ix
INTRODUCTION	xi
ABBREVIATIONS	xlv
GENERAL BIBLIOGRAPHY	xlvii

VELLEIUS PATERCULUS

BOOK I	2
BOOK II	50
DIRECTORY OF PEOPLES AND PLACES	351
INDEX OF NAMES	365

To Dorothy
in memoriam

PREFACE

This edition and translation of Velleius Paterculus replaces that of F. W. Shipley, which first appeared a century ago. I am most grateful for the honor of being invited to join the Loeb Classical Library series and to General Editor Jeffrey Henderson and Managing Editor Michael B. Sullivan for their expertise and advice throughout. Every care has been taken to ensure that the book complies with the stylistic and presentational conventions prescribed by the Loeb series.

For various kinds of help I am greatly indebted to S. Audano, S. Bartera, A. Chahoud, C. H. George, J. E. Lendon, D. S. Levene, M. V. McGuiness, R. Maltby, E. A. Meyer, J. Nelis-Clément, T. Rood, F. Santangelo, D. B. Saunders, Z. Stamatopoulou, C. L. Whitton, and P. J. Woodman. I am also glad to have the opportunity of repeating my gratitude for inheriting the Velleian *Nachlass* of John Prater. That Velleius' history might prove a promising topic for research was first suggested to me by G. B. A. Fletcher, who presented me with his copy of Rhenanus' *editio princeps* one Christmas as a gift and his copy of Kritz' rare edition on the occasion of my wedding. For these and many other reasons I am extremely grateful to him.

To my great profit the Introduction was read and com-

ix

PREFACE

mented on by I. M. Le M. Du Quesnay. The whole of the book was read by R. G. Mayer and J. W. Rich, who devoted an enormous amount of time and energy to correcting mistakes, supplying information, answering follow-up emails, and generally providing me with invaluable advice of every sort. I am very greatly in their debt, and, if any errors have escaped their acuteness, I alone am responsible.

The first volume of my commentary on Velleius was published on the day that I married my wife, to whose memory the present book is lovingly dedicated.

A. J. WOODMAN
Durham
Autumn 2022

INTRODUCTION

Velleius Paterculus, soldier and senator, wrote a brief history down to his own day at Rome and published it in AD 30 in honor of the consul of that year, Marcus Vinicius, to whom the work was dedicated. Although the history has often been criticized or even ignored on account of its positive portrayal of the emperor Tiberius, under whom Velleius served in his army days, a reappraisal began in the 1970s and has continued into the twenty-first century.

CAREER AND QUALIFICATIONS

The various stages of Velleius' life must be inferred from the narrative of his history, in which he provides us with an unusual amount of personal information. We know that in AD 6 he was designated as one of the quaestors, the office that brought with it membership of the senate (111.3):[1] since a man was eligible for the quaestorship in his mid-twenties, it is thought that Velleius was born in or a little before 20 BC. His birthplace is unknown. In his

---

[1] It is conventional to see Velleius' work as consisting of two "books," comprising, respectively, 18 and 131 "chapters," and to omit the book number from references later than chapter 18 of Book 2.

xi

INTRODUCTION

only reference to his parentage, he says that when he was sent to Germany as a cavalry officer with Tiberius in AD 4, he succeeded his father in that position (104.3); he also says that in 43 BC his father's brother, the senator Velleius Capito, formally supported the charges brought against Cassius, one of the killers of Julius Caesar (69.5). Likewise, Velleius makes a single reference to the father of these two men, his paternal grandfather C. Velleius, "a man second to none in Campania," who killed himself at Naples in 41 BC when the infirmities of age prevented him from accompanying his great friend Ti. Claudius Nero, father of the future emperor Tiberius, on his flight from the armed forces of Octavian, the future emperor Augustus (76.1). The historian also tells us a little about his maternal ancestors. His great-grandfather was Minatius Magius from the Campanian town of Aeculanum, whose sterling service on behalf of Rome in the Social War of 91–89 BC received political reward: his two sons eventually became praetors (2.16.2–3). Minatius' distant ancestor was Decius Magius from Capua (2.16.2), who had similarly shown loyalty to Rome during the Hannibalic War (Livy 23.7–10).

Around 2 BC Velleius began his soldier's life by serving as military tribune under the father of his dedicatee in Thrace and Macedonia; he then moved south into mainland Greece and from there traveled east to the Hellespont, the shores of the Black Sea, and the provinces of Asia Minor as far as the River Euphrates, the easternmost point of the Roman Empire where it bordered the vast territories of Armenia and Parthia (101.3). At some stage in this journey he joined the staff of Gaius Caesar, Augustus' grandson and an exact contemporary, and is our sole wit-

xii

INTRODUCTION

ness for the spectacular meeting between Gaius and the Parthian king that took place on an island in the middle of the river in perhaps AD 1 or 2. Well might the historian say, nearly thirty years later, that he had "a very pleasant memory of so many events, places, peoples, and cities" (101.3). Subsequently, in AD 4, Velleius accompanied Tiberius when he went north into Germany, where the reception of their old commander by his troops is movingly described (104.3–4). Velleius in fact wonders whether readers will believe his description, but, as we know from modern parallels such as Field Marshal Montgomery,[2] this is how troops respond to a much loved leader: compare the Greek historian Xenophon on the admiral Teleutias in the fourth century BC, "it seems to me that it is well worth a man's while to consider what sort of conduct it was that enabled Teleutias to inspire the men he commanded with such a feeling toward himself" (*Hell*. 5.1.3–4). The next year Tiberius advanced to the Elbe, and once again Velleius captures the moment of Roman success by an iconic river scene, as an anonymous German elder seeks permission to cross the River Elbe and approach Rome's future emperor (107.1–2). In AD 6 Tiberius was planning to attack the German chief Maroboduus, but he was prevented by revolt in Pannonia and Dalmatia, which drew him and Velleius to the western Balkans for the next three years;

[2] "Anyone not in England at the time might find it almost impossible to imagine the degree of adulation which Monty received in 1944 . . . It meant that he could get his troops, American as well as British, to do anything for him" (A. Horne with D. Montgomery, *The Lonely Leader: Monty 1944–1945* [London, 1994], 76).

xiii

INTRODUCTION

in the winter of AD 7–8 Tiberius placed Velleius in charge
of one of the winter camps (113.3). When the Pannonians surrendered in AD 8, Tiberius turned his attention
to Dalmatia, where the distinguished service of Velleius'
brother, Magius Celer Velleianus, was recognized by both
Augustus and Tiberius (115.1). The brother's name indicates that he was adopted by a member of the Magius
family, perhaps their maternal grandfather. By AD 9, as a
result of the disaster to Varus in that year, Velleius was
back in Germany for his final tour of duty.

When Velleius returned to Rome in (probably) AD 12
after more than a dozen years abroad, nine of them in the
continuous service of Tiberius (104.2), he had visited
much of the Roman Empire along a vast arc that stretched
from the Elbe to the Euphrates. The extraordinary nature
of this traveling invites reflection. Most Italians would
never visit Rome: indeed the great majority of them would
spend their entire lives within the confines of their own
village, a mode of existence that survived for centuries
after the Roman Empire had passed into history. In the
premodern world it was generally a struggle just to survive, and, even if a man had the desire, curiosity, energy,
and resources to explore beyond his own locality, conditions of travel made such exploration extremely difficult.[3]
Yet Velleius, thanks to his family background, was not only
familiar with the capital of the empire but had traveled the
length and breadth of that empire itself. When the poet
Catullus in the 50s BC pledged loyalty to his friends by

---

[3] "Even a visit to the neighboring market town could be something of a momentous event" (P. Thompson, *The Edwardians*
[London, 1975], 45, of early twentieth-century Britain).

INTRODUCTION

saying that he would accompany them either to the distant north of the known world or to the far southeast (11.1–12), the far-flung alternatives were deliberately chosen for their very implausibility; yet Velleius had traveled to both extremes, and to all the lands in between.

The scale of Velleius' traveling is mirrored in the number of geographical references in his work. The foundation of towns and other places across the Mediterranean world constitutes one of the principal themes at the start of Book 1 (1.1–2, 1.4, 2.3, 3.1, 3.3, 4.1–3, 6.4–5, 7.2–4, 8.4), while in a lengthy digression at the end of that book (1.14–15) he records and dates the foundation of forty-nine separate Roman colonies. A corresponding digression in Book 2 (38–39) records and dates the establishment of roughly two dozen Roman provinces, from Gaul in the north to Africa and Egypt in the south, from Spain in the west to Cappadocia and Syria in the east. Now foundation stories of one sort or another were common in Greek and Latin poetry and prose: for example, the elder Cato's *Origines*, written in the second century BC, described the origin of Rome and of "each Italian community" (Nep. *Cato* 3.3). Velleius was familiar with the *Origines*, since he takes issue with Cato's dating of the foundation of Capua and Nola (1.7.2–4), and it is obviously possible that his interest in colonization is to be explained by his reading of Cato and other so-called "ktistic" authors (the Greek *ktisis* means "foundation"). However, since Velleius' early references to foundations are pre-Roman and they stretch from Cadiz in the far west (1.2.3) to Asia Minor in the east (e.g., 1.4.1), it may be that the reason for his interest is more experiential and that his unusually extensive travels across Europe and Asia awak-

xv

INTRODUCTION

ened in him an intellectual curiosity about his many destinations.

It is true that Velleius' responses to the inhabitants of foreign countries are conventional and that, even when his personal experience is invoked, he seems to describe only what he expected to find, as in the case of the Germans (118.1): "But—and this is scarcely credible unless one has experienced it—they are highly cunning despite their extreme wildness, a race of born liars." There is nothing unusual in this: as is well known, no one would guess from Sallust's description of Africa in his history of the Jugurthine War (*Iug.* 17–19) that in the mid-40s BC he had lived in Africa as the first governor of the province of Africa Nova. Nevertheless, there was a close relationship between geography and historiography, as Cicero insisted (*De or.* 2.63, *Orat.* 66), and we may speculate that Velleius' evident interest in history was an indirect but fortunate consequence of the time he spent abroad.

On his return from settling affairs in Germany, Tiberius celebrated a triumph in (almost certainly) AD 12 for his achievements in the Balkans. Participating in the triumph were Velleius and his brother (121.3), who are next heard of at the time of Augustus' death two years later, when we are told that each of them was standing for the praetorship (124.4): since both were "candidates of Caesar," they were guaranteed to be elected. This is the last occasion on which Velleius makes an appearance in his own history: since it is difficult to believe that so individualistic a writer would have kept silent about further service or commissions, the most plausible explanation for his silence seems to be that his public life was thereafter restricted to meetings of the senate, his attendance at which

INTRODUCTION

is suggested by his enthusiastic summary of the years 17 to 21 (129.3), which reveals some interesting correspondences with Tacitus' account of the same period in his *Annals*.[4]

The 20s were dominated by the rise to power of Tiberius' minister, Sejanus, whose role Velleius discusses in a digressive passage toward the end of his work (127–28). Many scholars have seen the passage as a "eulogy" of Sejanus and have speculated that, as a result of having written it, Velleius was one of the many individuals who lost their lives after Sejanus' disgrace and fall in AD 31. But this is to misread the passage in question, which, so far from being a eulogy of Sejanus, is a defense of Tiberius' elevation of him. Of course this may not have saved Velleius from becoming a victim; yet no punishment befell M. Terentius, whose self-defense in AD 32 rested on similar grounds (Tac. *Ann.* 6.8.1–9.1), and the public career of M. Vinicius, to whom Velleius dedicated the allegedly offending history, continued from strength to strength for another sixteen years. The most that can be said is that nothing more is heard of Velleius after the appearance of his work: he never became consul, although two sons reached the consulship thirty years later (AD 60 and 61).

The second-century BC historian Polybius laid it down that historiography is a tripartite activity (12.25e.1): the historian needs to consult and compare the relevant sources; he must have had "sight of cities, places, rivers" and other geographical features; and, finally, he requires experience of political activity. Polybius is often regarded as a model historian, and it is very striking indeed that, if

---

[4] See the relevant annotations to this passage.

xvii

INTRODUCTION

we leave aside for the moment the matter of sources, Velleius more than fulfills the second and the third of Polybius' criteria. During the three decades of which we know (ca. 1 BC–AD 29), Velleius spent the first dozen years in acquiring a personal familiarity with the Roman Empire that was significantly greater than that of most of his contemporaries; and, once returned to the capital, he spent the remaining time near the pinnacle of political power. He was ideally placed to write a history.

VELLEIUS' HISTORY

Velleius' work comprises a single "volume" (131.1) divided into two parts (1.14.1), which are conventionally referred to as Book 1 and Book 2. The first book, which goes from mythical times to the Romans' destruction of Carthage and Corinth in 146 BC, begins in midsentence, since the preface and opening narrative, together with any title, are missing. Also missing is the text of six hundred years' narrative between 1.8.6 (the foundation of Rome) and 1.9.1 (168 BC). These significant losses mean that the present shortness of Book 1 is deceptive, that its original length is unknown, and that it is very difficult to know what the precise scope and nature of its narrative would have been. The narrative of Book 2 continues that of Book 1. After dealing with the expected high points—such as the Gracchi brothers (2.2.1–7.1), Julius Caesar (41–58), the civil war (49–87), the death of Cicero (66.2–5), the battle of Actium (84–86), the establishment of the Augustan principate (89–123), and the disaster to Varus (117–20)—the narrative ends in the year AD 29 (130.4–5). The space allocated to Tiberius' reign is relatively circumscribed

xviii

INTRODUCTION

(126–30), but Velleius' hero has been the focus of the narrative for far longer (94–130). The final chapter consists of a prayer, in which the author asks the gods to ensure the future of Rome and its emperor (131.1–2); the work ends as it began, in midsentence, since the last few words of the prayer are missing.

A striking feature of the work is the frequency with which Velleius addresses M. Vinicius (1.8.1, 1.8.4, 1.12.6, 1.13.5, 2.7.5, 49.1, 65.2, 96.2, 101.3, 103.1, 104.2, 113.1, 130.4), whose term of office as consul in AD 30 is often used as a point from which to date other events. From these addresses, which usually take the form of Vinicius' name in the vocative case, scholars reasonably infer that there will have been a further address in the preface and that the work as a whole was formally dedicated to Vinicius. Such a dedication would be by no means unique in the Roman historiographical tradition, but the loss of Velleius' preface means that we are deprived of any explanation for it.

The Vinicii, whose home town was Cales in Campania, had become an important family during the course of Augustus' reign. M. Vinicius, the grandfather of Velleius' dedicatee, rose to a suffect consulship in 19 BC and possibly to the proconsulship of Asia in 12–10 BC; as legate of Augustus he held commands in Illyricum in 13 BC (cf. 96.2) and later on the Rhine (AD 1–4), where his exploits were rewarded by "a most impressive inscription" and the so-called "triumphal insignia" (cf. 104.2). It was under this man's son, P. Vinicius, that Velleius began his military career in Thrace and Macedonia (101.3); P. Vinicius became consul in AD 2 and was almost certainly proconsul of Asia around the end of the decade. According to the

xix

INTRODUCTION

elder Seneca, he was a noted orator and a great lover of Ovid (*Controv.* 7.5.11, 10.4.25), an author of whom Velleius also approved (36.3).

When in AD 20 the former consul Cn. Calpurnius Piso was accused of causing the death of Germanicus, Tiberius' nephew and adopted son, the trial resulted in a senatorial decree, the famous *Senatus Consultum de Cn. Pisone Patre*: one of the seven witnesses to the official transcription of this document was M. Vinicius, P. Vinicius' son and Velleius' dedicatee, who was quaestor at the time (*SCPP* 4). Subsequently, the younger M. Vinicius, an accomplished orator like his father (Tac. *Ann.* 6.15.1), continued the incremental importance of his family. After his consulship in AD 30, he was chosen by Tiberius in 33 as husband for Julia Livilla, daughter of Germanicus and Agrippina; half a dozen or so years later he too became proconsul of Asia, and in 45 was consul for a second time, before dying in the following year. No doubt Velleius' military service under M. Vinicius' father, as well as the Campanian background of both families, will have provided him with reasons for his choice of dedicatee; but, in the absence of a preface to the work, the details must remain unknown.

Scholars usually see Velleius' dedication as being related to three other striking features of his work, of which the first is the number of times that he refers, in more or less explicit terms, to its *brevity* (1.16.1, 29.2, 38.1, 48.6, 52.3, 55.1, 66.3, 86.1, 89.1, 96.3, 99.4). Equally distinctive are his references to the *speed* with which he is writing (1.16.1, 41.1, 108.2, 124.1) and to his intention of writing *a major history in the future* (48.5, 89.1, 96.3, 99.3, 103.4, 114.4, 119.1). These three sets of references have long been regarded as complementary, and from them scholars

xx

INTRODUCTION

have inferred the following hypothetical scenario: Velleius had been collecting material for a major history of sizable proportions when, sometime in the middle of AD 29, the younger M. Vinicius was elected to the consulship of 30; wishing to recognize the honor thus done to his friend, Velleius interrupted work on his major history and, writing against the clock and using the materials he had already collected, produced within roughly six months a shortened history that he could dedicate to Vinicius on his assumption of office on 1 January 30.

Others have argued that this scenario is mistaken. It is suggested that Vinicius' election to the consulship of 30 will have been known well in advance (perhaps even some years in advance) and that no reliance can be placed on Velleius' references to a planned major history, since authors' references to future work(s) are a literary commonplace that cannot always be taken at face value. Velleius, it is argued, embarked in the mid-20s on writing a one-volume miniature history and his references to brevity and speed are not to be explained by his having to write hastily within the space of a few months but are to be understood as programmatic allusions to the restricted nature of his work. In the 30s BC, when Sallust in his history of the Jugurthine War declined to write in detail about Carthage "because time warns me to hasten elsewhere" (*Iug.* 19.2), he was not operating under any time constraint but, as the author of a monograph, was claiming the same virtue as Velleius. Selectivity was a recognized literary virtue, and all the more important for a self-professed proponent of brevity, for whom only the most significant matters came within his scope. In his work on the writing of history, the second-century AD writer Lucian says that "speed (τάχος)

xxi

INTRODUCTION

is always useful, especially when there is a lot of available material . . . That is, pass over the trivia and less essential topics, but give adequate treatment to important matters. You can actually omit a great deal" (*Hist. conscr.* 56).

Readers will make up their own minds whether they prefer the first or the second of these scenarios (or some variation thereon), but, if Velleius were really pressed for time during the process of composition, it seems odd that his work is so digressive. The most striking example is the double digression that he introduces as a way of separating Book 1 from Book 2 (1.14–18). The first of these digressions, as we have already seen, is an extensive list of colonial foundations (1.14–15), which Velleius defends on the grounds that a focused survey is more memorable than a narrative account (1.14.1); to this digression he tacks on a second, in which he discusses (in a somewhat leisurely fashion) the phenomenon whereby the great Greek and Latin writers in any one genre have tended to cluster together at the same period (1.16–17), a discussion that leads him to end the book by tacking on yet another point—analogous but essentially tangential—about the literary supremacy of Athens (1.18). The digression on colonization is matched in Book 2 by another on the establishment of provinces (38–39), which Velleius defends on the same grounds as before, and in so doing acknowledges that he is repeating material that he has already covered in his narrative (38.1); conversely, later in Book 2, he inserts a final digression, whose explicit purpose is the recording of affairs that he has omitted in their proper place (68).

The digression on the provinces is preceded almost immediately by a digressive passage of literary history

xxii

INTRODUCTION

(36.2–3), which in its turn looks back to a previous digression on earlier Latin writers (2.9). In Book 1 a discussion of Homer (1.5) is quickly followed by another of Hesiod (1.7.1), which leads first into a dispute with the elder Cato concerning the foundation dates of Capua and Nola (1.7.2–4) and then into a paragraph on the Olympian Games (1.8.1–2).

It is difficult to imagine that any of these cultural passages would have been incorporated by a historian who was rushed for time; but, whether or not that was the case, they contribute significantly to the distinctive character of Velleius' history. That ancient historians, like poets, allude to other texts, both verse and prose, is well known, and Velleius is no exception: he shows himself especially familiar with the works of Cicero, Sallust, and Livy, and he echoes or imitates their phraseology throughout his history. But it is not at all usual for ancient historians to spend so much time *discussing* literary figures: if the Curtius Rufus and Petronius who appear in Tacitus' *Annals* are the authors of the same names (11.21, 16.18–19), as scholars often believe, Tacitus makes no mention of it. Yet Velleius not only goes out of his way to name a whole range of authors from Homer (1.5) to Ovid (36.3) but does so in such a way that he seems to be familiar also with the scholarship that those great names had attracted. Just as Virgil is known to have read the *Iliad* and the *Odyssey* with the aid of commentaries on Homer, so it is arguable that Velleius had been dipping into the critical works of Greek scholars such as Aristonicus of Alexandria, his contemporary. Velleius' whole manner bespeaks the scholar-critic.

This manner is particularly evident in his concern for chronology and dating, a preoccupation that his other di-

xxiii

INTRODUCTION

gressions share with those on literature. The very mention of Thessaly leads to critical remarks on anachronism in Greek tragedy (1.3.2), which are followed by a defense of Homer's equally anachronistic use of the name Corinth rather than Ephyre (1.3.3). Homer himself is dated relative to the Trojan War and then in relation to Hesiod (1.5.3, 1.7.1); the list of colonies gives rise to a succession of dates of various types, including interval dating (e.g., 1.14.2), consular dating (e.g., 1.14.6) and dating from Velleius' own day (e.g., 1.14.7); the whole point of the digression on generic synchronisms is the narrowness of the timeframes involved (1.16.2, 5; 1.17.4); the earlier period of Latin literature is first identified (2.9.1) and then has its stages calibrated (2.9.2–6), while the relative nearness of the later period is emphasized twice (36.2–3); and, finally, the list of provinces displays another succession of various types of dates.

Velleius' concern for chronology is not restricted to the digressions but extends throughout his work. Straightforward dating is particularly evident in the surviving portions of Book 1 (e.g., 1.2.1, 3.3, 6.1–2, 6.4–5, 8.1–2, 13.1) and is sometimes elaborate: the foundation of Rome and the destruction of Carthage, for example, are each dated three different ways (1.8.4, 1.12.5). Such dating continues in Book 2 (4.5, 7.5, 44.4, 49.1, 65.2, 90.1, 100.2, 103.3) but coexists with contrasts or continuities between "then" and "now." It is interesting to be told that the house of Sisenna Statilius Taurus formerly belonged to Marcius Censorinus and before him to Cicero (2.14.3); elsewhere Velleius' temporal reflections are motivated by city walls (1.4.2) or porticoes (1.11.3, 2.8.3) or statuary (1.11.3, 61.3), or an inscription (25.4) or aqueduct (81.2), or even the cost of

xxiv

INTRODUCTION

renting (2.10.1). Analogous is his interest in family generations (2.10.2, 2.11.3; cf. 2.8.2, 21.5), particularly if the latest member is contemporary with himself (43.4, 72.3, 112.2). His eagerness to correct Cato's chronology (1.7.2–4) is followed by anonymous chronological challenges elsewhere (1.17.4, 2.4.7, 53.4), all of them passages that, regardless of whether he is right, symbolize his preoccupation with time.

Although there is no certainty about the sources Velleius used when composing his work,[5] it seems likely that he will have derived much, if not all, of his chronological information from two authors writing in the middle years of the first century BC: Catullus' dedicatee Cornelius Nepos and Cicero's friend Atticus, although neither the *Chronica* of the former nor the *Liber Annalis* of the latter is now extant; all that survives is a few so-called "fragments," none of them verbatim. We may reasonably assume that each author will have given priority to political and military matters, but a notable feature of both works is that they included literary or cultural material: Atticus evidently mentioned that Livius Andronicus was the first to put on a play (fr. 6C/5P), while Nepos referred to Homer and Archilochus (fr. 1C/2P, 4C/4P). Although Velleius' incorporation of literary topics is unusual for a work of classical historiography, as we have seen, it is pos-

---

[5] The only source he names is the elder Cato (1.7.3–4), in a passage that seems to show him in the act of consulting a synchronizing work; elsewhere he implies or refers to an anonymous plurality in the manner of other Roman historians (1.4.1, 1.8.5, 1.15.3, 2.4.6, 27.5, 53.4). He refers by name to the (now lost) historian Q. Hortensius, although not as a source (2.16.3).

XXV

INTRODUCTION

sible that he found some precedent in Nepos and Atticus. If that is so, Velleius may also have derived from these authors the notion that his work should be brief: Catullus famously praised the *Chronica* of Nepos, his dedicatee, for embracing "the whole of time" in only three volumes (1.6), while Atticus' work, like that of Velleius, comprised only a single volume, as we are told by Nepos in his *Life of Atticus*. In fact, Nepos' description of Atticus' work could almost be taken as a description of Velleius' (18.1–2):

> He was a first-class representative of ancestral custom and lover of antiquity, with which he had so diligently familiarized himself that it was the totality of it that he set out in the volume where he listed the magistrates: there is no law, peace, war, or illustrious achievement of the Roman people that is not noted there at its proper time, and (something that was very difficult) he wove in the origin of families in such a way that we can know from it the generations of distinguished men.

Whether Atticus also incorporated events from Greek history is unknown but thought very likely; Nepos himself certainly mentioned Alexander in his *Chronica* (fr. 6C/6P), and, since we know from a stray fragment on the Greek politician Cimon (1.8.6) that Velleius referred to people and events of Greek history at least into the fifth century, it may be that here too we have a further link between him and these two chronographic authors.

If monographs and specialist works like those of Nepos and Atticus are excluded, we can detect in Latin histori-

xxvi

INTRODUCTION

ography a trend toward ever greater scale: Valerius Antias (cf. 2.9.6) seemingly wrote a history in at least seventy-five volumes, and when Livy died, probably in AD 17, he left as his monument a history of Rome in one hundred and forty-two volumes (cf. 36.3). It is therefore perhaps not surprising that Velleius should want to write a history characterized by brevity, a literary virtue that may well have had contemporary appeal in other genres. Valerius Maximus, writing shortly after Sejanus' disgrace in AD 31, likewise claimed brevity for his book of examples collected from history (*praef.*, 4.1.12, 6.4 *init.*); a little earlier the Augustan architect Vitruvius had claimed brevity in the preface to his fifth book (5 *praef.* 2–5), while later in the century the fabulist Phaedrus several times refers to his brevity (2 *prol.* 11ff., 3.7.1, 3.10.2, 3.10.59–60, 3 *epil.* 8, 3 *epil.* 14, 4 *epil.* 7).

Cicero's mouthpiece in his *De oratore*, the orator Antonius, is made to disparage the early Roman historians for thinking that "brevity is the only virtue" (2.53): "they transmitted, without any elaboration, only plain notices of dates, persons, places and events." It was this circumstance that led Cicero, who believed that the history of Rome deserved a literary treatment suited to its greatness, to transpose from forensic oratory to historiography the rhetorical technique of "invention," whereby the inherent possibilities of a given situation could be given imaginative literary treatment, regardless of whether the resulting account was factually true (*De or.* 2.62–64). A by-product of Velleius' brevity is that his work scarcely allows for invention; only in his narrative of the disaster to Varus and its aftermath in AD 9–10 (117–20) does he even approach the

xxvii

INTRODUCTION

kind of dramatic episode that we expect to find in a historian such as Livy.[6] It may seem strange of Velleius to choose a notorious Roman defeat for narrative elaboration, but he does so in order to praise by contrast the effective response of his hero, Tiberius (120.1–2): "the perennial patron of the Roman Empire took up the cause to which he was accustomed."[7]

Many scholars have said that in its later chapters Velleius' work has become an encomium of Tiberius, but those making such remarks seem not to have realized that Velleius was in fact adopting the conventions of formal encomium and that their adoption was entirely deliberate. Now it was recognized in antiquity that historiography was very close to epideictic oratory (Cic. *Orat.* 66), the genre to which encomium belonged,[8] but the apparent merging of history and encomium in Velleius invites some broader explanation. According to Dionysius of Halicarnassus, an

---

[6] Direct speech is brief and relatively infrequent (2.4.4, 2.7.2, 2.14.2–3, 32.1, 67.4, 70.3, 83.3, 86.3, 104.1, 104.4, 107.2).

[7] Compare the emperor Verus writing to the historian Fronto in AD 165/6 (p. 108.23–6 vdH²): "You should dwell for a long time on the initial causes of the war, and even on the things that went badly in my absence; take your time in coming to my role. In fact I think you should make clear how superior the Parthians were before I arrived, so that the extent of my achievements will be evident."

[8] The phenomenon is not restricted to antiquity: in the Middle Ages and the Renaissance "all literature became subsumed under epideictic, and all writing was perceived as occupying the related spheres of praise and blame" (B. Vickers, *In Defence of Rhetoric* [Oxford, 1988], 54).

xxviii

INTRODUCTION

older contemporary, historians "ought first of all to choose noble and elevated subjects," to which they could respond with admiration and enthusiasm (*Ant. Rom.* 1.1.2). This is something that he has done in his own work (*Ant. Rom.* 1.2.1):

> That I have indeed chosen a noble and elevated . . . subject will not in my opinion require any lengthy argument, at least for those who are not utterly unacquainted with universal history. For if anyone turns his attention to the successive supremacies both of cities and of nations . . . , he will find that the supremacy of the Romans has far surpassed all those that are recorded from earlier times, not only in the greatness of its empire and the splendor of its achievements—which no account has as yet worthily celebrated—but also in the length of time during which it has endured down to our own day.

Velleius has simply adopted toward his subject the enthusiastic attitude expected of patriotic historians: the difference is that the collectivism of republican days has been replaced by a focus on the emperor, upon whose wellbeing and success the state now depended. It was natural that an imperial historian—especially a veteran who had participated in Tiberius' imperialist campaigns and had personal experience of him as his general—should write in an encomiastic manner.

How, then, is one to sum up Velleius' work? It is a *"tour de force of brevity"* in which he "compressed history from the beginning of mythical time to the present moment within a single volume" and "made the whole of world

xxix

INTRODUCTION

history lead up first to the empire of Rome and then to the consul of the day and his imperial master."[9]

MODES OF EXPRESSION

It is something of a paradox that a writer of self-proclaimed brevity should be so wordy. The historian's summary of Gaius Gracchus (2.6.3, "He left nothing undisturbed, nothing tranquil, nothing peaceful, nothing, in short, in the same state") says the same thing four times; on the other hand, the pleonasm provides the opportunity for a quadruple anaphora and, in the original Latin, a threefold assonance based on the letters *qu*. Or take Velleius' introduction of Pompey the Great (29.2–4):

> He was born to Lucilia (his mother was of senatorial stock) and was outstanding in appearance, *yet not the kind by which* the flower of one's youth is enhanced but, being based upon his dignity and consistent with his famous prestige and fortune, it accompanied him to the last day of his life. He was exceptional in integrity, a model of scrupulousness, average in eloquence, highly desirous of *the kind of power that* might be conferred on him as an honor and not seized by him through violence, the most skilled of leaders in war, in a toga the most restrained of citizens (*except when* he was afraid of having an equal), tenacious in friendships, placable when affronted, loyal in reestablishing goodwill, compliant when receiving satisfaction, never (*or*

[9] Rich, 87.

xxx

INTRODUCTION

only rarely) becoming power-mad from power, and devoid of almost every flaw—*unless* it be counted among the greatest flaws in a free community, mistress of the world's peoples, to resent seeing anyone level in rank while at the same time regarding all citizens as equal in law.

Typical of Velleius are the repeated superlative expressions (e.g., "outstanding," "exceptional," "most skilled," "most restrained") and the repeated antitheses ("not . . . but . . . ," "leaders . . . citizens," "power-mad . . . power," "level in rank . . . equal in law"), all of which in the original Latin are enhanced by alliteration, assonance, chiasmus, and variation. But in this passage there is an additional element: on several occasions (identified by italics) Velleius adds a qualification, as if there are considerations that he cannot bear to omit. This feature, quite antithetical to the ideals of brevity and "speed," is especially evident in his use of parentheses.

The impression created by many of Velleius' parentheses is that he cannot bear to leave anything out (e.g., 1.12.4, 2.13.2, 28.2, 70.1, 112.4). This impression is intensified when there are two parentheses in quick succession (e.g., 2.18.3–4), and even more so when there is one parenthesis within another (e.g., 52.2 and 58.2). A very striking example of this latter type is 43.3–4, a single sentence on Julius Caesar that is framed by its subject at the beginning ("As for his remaining activities in the City") and its main verb at the end ("their need of my pen is less"); in between is a long and essentially parenthetical list of Caesar's domestic activities that itself is rounded off by a parenthetical clause on the Antistii Veteres, whom Velleius

xxxi

INTRODUCTION

cannot bear to omit on account of the contemporary members of the family. Likewise, when Velleius is dealing with the delicate subject of Tiberius' retirement to the island of Rhodes in 6 BC (99.1–2), the subject of the long sentence is once again fronted ("Ti. Nero") and the main verb comes, after a series of parenthetical remarks, at the very end ("asked"); slightly different is 128.1–3, where the fronted subject ("The ancients") is separated from the main verb ("thought") not so much by parenthetical remarks as by a sequence of seven historical precedents (*exempla*) arranged in five relative clauses.

Velleius cultivates rhythmical clausulae at the ends of many of his sentences and is fond of producing aphorisms or *sententiae* (e.g., 67.2, "so true is it that men find it difficult to defer their hopes, however conceived"). His antithetical manner of expression can incorporate metaphor, such as those of journeying at the start of Book 2 (2.1.1):

> The earlier Scipio had *opened up* the Romans' *road* to power, the later *opened up their road* to luxury: with the dread of Carthage removed and the empire's rival eliminated, it was *not step by step but at a headlong pace* that there was a defection from virtue and a transfer to vice. The old discipline was abandoned, the new introduced: the community turned from vigilance to somnolence, from weapons to pleasures, from action to inactivity.

Although the English translation in its last four words reproduces the wordplay *a negotiis in otium*, it cannot replicate the sentence's closural rhythm ($-\cup-\cup-$, one of Velleius' favorites), and it fails entirely to represent the

xxxii

INTRODUCTION

numerous examples of alliteration and assonance with which the Latin of this opening passage is tricked out. This is a real problem for the reader of the English translation, since Velleius' stylistic effects are by no means restricted to particular passages but are in evidence throughout. Consider his brief and utterly routine notice on the foundation of Naples and Capua (1.4.2):

> *u*triusque *u*rbis eximia semper in Romanos *f*ides *f*acit eas nobilitate atque *amoeni*tate sua *d*ignissi-mas; sed *illis dili*gentior *rit*us *p*a*tr*ii *man*sit *cus*todia, *Cumanos Os*ca *m*uta*v*it *v*icinia. *v*ires autem *v*eteres earum urbium hodieque *m*agnitudo ostentat *moe-ni*um.

> The *e*xceptionally *e*nduring loyalty of both cities toward the Romans means that they well deserve their noble fame and picturesque aspect; but the latter has *r*etained more diligently its ancestral *r*itu-als, whereas the Cumans were changed by their Oscan surroundings. As for the cities' *p*owerful *p*ast, it is still visible today in their *for*midable *for*ti-fications.

The Latin contains eight cases of alliteration (most of them initial) and several examples of assonance (three of them of different types), of which *amoenitate* ~ *moenium* suggests a translinguistic etymology involving a Greek alpha privative, as if natural beauty were associated with the absence of fortifications (*a-moenitate*). As on countless other occasions throughout Velleius' work, no English translation will ever be able to reproduce such an accumulation of stylistic features, yet this inability means that

xxxiii

INTRODUCTION

readers of the translation will be deprived of most of Velleius' manner of expression and hence will have little idea of the consummate care that has gone into the production of his narrative. The above translation captures the alliteration of the final sentence and substitutes one alliteration for another in the first and second sentences; but the rest—including (very unfortunately) the "etymology," with its implied antithesis between nature and culture— has perforce escaped.

A similar effect seems to be in evidence in Velleius' account of the Social War, where the Italians are complaining that they do not receive their due from the Romans for supporting and protecting the latter's empire (2.15.2):

> per eos in id ipsum pervenisset *fasti*gium ex quo homines eiusdem et gentis et sanguinis ut externos alienosque *fasti*dire posset.

> which, thanks to them, had reached the very height from which it could slight persons of the same family and blood as if they were foreigners and aliens.

The Italians' homoeoarchon is not simply an example of assonance, here represented by "height . . . slight," but suggests that there is an etymological connection between the height that the empire has reached and the contempt with which it looks down on its allies, a connection that seems impossible to catch. Sometimes there is a felicitous correspondence between translation and original: Maroboduus is "a barbarian in *kind* rather than in *mind*" (108.2, "*nātione* magis quam *rătione* barbarus"), and Tiberius took the initiative "in going on the *offen*sive in a war

xxxiv

INTRODUCTION

that his father and fatherland had been content merely to have *fen*ded *off*" (120.2, "*ar*ma infert quae *ar*cuisse pater et patria contenti erant"). More often, however, one is confronted with a passage such as the death of Scipio Aemilianus (2.4.6):

> eiusque corpus ve*lato capite elatum est* cuius opera super totum terrarum orbem Roma *extulerat caput.*

> and they *lifted away, fitted* with a shroud over his *head*, the body of one by whose efforts Rome had *lifted* her *head* above the whole world.

It is straightforward to retain in English the literal and the metaphorical senses of the noun "head," but how is a translation to suggest that Velleius not only puns on two different senses of the same verb (*elatum est* = "lifted away," *extulerat* = "lifted") but also involves *elatum* in an assonance with *velato* ("lifted . . . fitted")?

It must be borne in mind that in the ancient world the writing of history was a *literary* activity, quite different from modern-day historiography. Historians were assessed for their style, which came within the province of literary critics: it is difficult to imagine a modern historian being praised as "mouthpiece of the Muses," as Xenophon was by Cicero (*Orat.* 62) and Quintilian (10.1.33). Rhetorical effects are evidence of the care that goes into the work of a serious historical writer. From the two occasions on which Velleius apologizes for his choice of words (41.3, 52.4) it is clear that his aim throughout, like that of Tacitus in his *Annals* (13.31.1), was to sustain a level of linguistic dignity that was consistent with what was to be expected in the formality of Latin historiography. It has been con-

xxxv

INTRODUCTION

ventional among scholars, should they spot some of the mannerisms described above, to regard them with a pitying condescension and to compare Velleius' manner of expression unfavorably with that of a "proper" historian like Tacitus. Yet such a comparison is refuted by the evidence of Tacitus' own text, which, when analyzed without preconceptions, shows that Tacitus is at least as concerned with wordplay and similar features as is Velleius.

"Men and dynasties pass, but style abides." The famous last words of Syme's *Tacitus* seem more provocative than they are often taken: they imply that, when all is said and done, it is style that elevates Tacitus above other Latin historians. Many readers, perhaps all, will undoubtedly prefer Tacitus' mode of expression to that of Velleius, but a stylistic preference is no basis for denigrating, still less rejecting, the evidence of one who wrote from long experience as a military man and had served as a magistrate and senator, experiencing at firsthand many of the events about which he would later write.

NOTE ON TRANSLATION

There are almost as many theories of translation as there are translators, but it is surely desirable that the translation gives at least some idea of the ways in which the translated author differs from other authors. We have already seen some of the difficulties of representing Velleius' Latin in an English translation, but there are others. The word "tract" in English is much more usually used of place than of time, yet Velleius uses *tractus* rather more often of time (1.6.4, 1.7.2, 1.15.3, 2.9.1, 2.10.2, 78.1, 94.1) than of place

xxxvi

INTRODUCTION

(69.2, 94.4, 104.3, 110.2, 126.3); since the idiolect is so characteristic of the author, who on one occasion has each usage in quick succession (94.1, 4),[10] it seems worth retaining "tract" for time as well as place. Another idiolect is *praediximus*, which on fourteen occasions Velleius uses quasi-parenthetically with *ut* but frequently elsewhere with a relative pronoun (e.g., 2.15.3, 98.1): this too is so characteristic—and, in combination with *ut*, almost unique in classical Latin[11]—that one wants to translate it consistently throughout, but, since consistency would sometimes result in a misleading banality, both "as we mentioned earlier" (e.g., 21.1) and "as we just mentioned" (e.g., 25.3) have to be adopted according to the context.

Since Velleius sees historical events principally in terms of the individuals involved, his work is replete with character sketches: these not only illustrate his volubility particularly well but, in keeping with the general thrust of his work, are presented primarily in moral terms. Moral terminology is particularly difficult to render consistently in English. The classic example is the word *virtus*, which Velleius uses more than sixty times: ideally, one would wish to translate *virtus* by the same English word on every occasion, but this is impossible, since different aspects of *virtus* seem intended in different contexts; and the same

[10] *hoc tractu temporum* (Vell. 1.6.4, 78.1, 94.1) is imitated in the *Chronica* of Sulpicius Severus (1.13.6, 2.5.1, 2.9.3; cf. 2.12.1, 2.33.4), one of the authors who show familiarity with his work (E. Klebs, "Entlehnungen aus Velleius," *Philologus* 49 [1890]: 285–312, at 290n14).

[11] The only other example is Suet. *Aug.* 90.1.

xxxvii

INTRODUCTION

difficulty arises with much of the historian's other moralizing vocabulary. Also difficult to translate consistently is political terminology. Few if any problems arise from translating *res publica* as "commonwealth" throughout, but the same cannot be said for *imperium* and (especially) *princeps*: Velleius uses the latter over forty times, applying it to persons as different as authors (1.17.3, Cicero; 36.3, Virgil), enemy leaders (118.2, Sigimerus; 129.3, Sacrovir), prominent Romans (e.g., 19.4, Marius; 53.2, Pompey), and, of course, emperors (e.g., 89.4, Augustus; 128.1, Tiberius). Ideally, one wants to render *princeps* in a way that will illustrate Velleius' view of the evolution from republic to principate, an aspect of his work that is seen as being important. As a general rule (there are inevitable exceptions), I have used "principal figure" when *princeps* refers to persons other than the emperor, but I have retained the Latin word itself when reference is being made to the emperor.

TEXT

Velleius' text depends ultimately on a now lost manuscript, seemingly written in a minuscule script in the late eighth or early ninth century, which was discovered by Beatus Rhenanus, a friend of Erasmus, in the Benedictine monastery at Murbach, Alsace, some time between March and August 1515. The manuscript, called (M), was seen to be extremely corrupt, difficult to read, lacking both punctuation and word divisions, and variously lacunose: Velleius' preface and the greater part of Book 1 were missing. Rhenanus quickly arranged for the manuscript to be copied by a friend, whom he does not name: this copy, which

xxxviii

INTRODUCTION

is also lost, is known as (R).[12] Three or four years later Rhenanus began to prepare for the first edition of Velleius' text to be printed by Johann Froben in Basel. The *editio princeps*, known as P, was based on (R) and was mostly completed by 15 November 1520, but one of Rhenanus' scribes, J. A. Burer, noticed a discrepancy between (M), which Rhenanus had submitted to the printer along with (R), and P: this led Burer to collate P with (M), and this collation, known as B, is printed as a ten-page appendix to P.

The latest date in the *editio princeps* is 13 December 1520, but we know that the book—a most elegant and attractive A4-sized volume—was still not published by 13 January 1521, and indeed the earliest reference to its appearance is 11 March of that year. Since in several places different copies of P have different readings, it follows that the first printing of the edition was not the final printing; moreover, the copy of the *editio princeps* that belonged to Rhenanus himself, whose library is preserved at Sélestat to this day, shows that he continued his attempts to improve the text even after the edition was published: the copy displays marginal emendations in his own hand that sometimes anticipate those of later scholars.

In the early nineteenth century, J. C. Orelli discovered in the Academy in Basel a manuscript of Velleius that had been written by Bonifacius Amerbach, a young friend of Rhenanus, and is dated 11 August 1516.[13] Since A (as

[12] So called by K. Halm, "Ueber die handschriftliche Ueberlieferung des Velleius Paterculus," *RhM* 30 (1875): 534.

[13] It is now MS AN II 38 in the Öffentliche Bibliothek of Basel University.

xxxix

INTRODUCTION

Amerbach's apograph is known) was evidently written at speed, it seems unlikely to derive directly from (M), which was so difficult to read; and since A also lacks the first eight chapters of Book 1 as extant, Orelli decided that it was not identical with the copy of (M) on which the *editio princeps* was based and which evidently contained those first eight chapters. Nevertheless the discovery of A generated considerable interest, and some scholars were persuaded that the apograph—perhaps simply on the grounds of its being a manuscript and of a slightly earlier date than P—was of more value than the text printed by Froben. This view was countered by Woodman (1977), who argued that the readings of (M) could best be reconstructed by P as regulated by B, and these arguments, accepted by L. D. Reynolds in a standard work,[14] underlie the present edition.[15]

BIBLIOGRAPHICAL NOTE

General

Commentaries and Editions

The nineteenth-century interest in Velleius' text manifested itself in the publication of numerous commentaries, including those of J. C. H. Krause (1800) and F. Kritz

[14] L. D. Reynolds, "Velleius Paterculus," in id., ed., *Texts and Transmission: A Survey of the Latin Classics* (Oxford, 1983), 431–33.

[15] The textual notes in the present edition, though ample, are confined to variants and conjectures that significantly affect the translation or interpretation, and exclude the countless mistakes in A, whose readings are cited only if they seem preferable, diag-

xl

INTRODUCTION

(1840), which remain invaluable. The last decades of
the twentieth century saw a resurgence of such interest.
F. Portalupi's annotated text of 1967 was followed by two
volumes of commentary on chapters 41 to 131 of Book 2
by Woodman (1977; 1983). The Budé edition of J. Hellegouarc'h (1982) was followed by a new Teubner edition from W. S. Watt (1988; rev. 1998), and there have
been commentaries from M. Elefante (1997) and A. Ruiz
Castellanos (2014).

Translations

During the past hundred years there have been translations of Velleius into various languages, including Russian
and Catalan.[16] The two principal translations into English
are those by F. W. Shipley (1924), which has minimal an-
notation, and J. C. Yardley and A. A. Barrett (2011), which
is equipped almost with a background narrative;[17] the
notes in the present Loeb edition are aimed in particular
at providing dates, identifying individuals, and clarifying

---

nostic, or in agreement with B; in the interest of economy, variants or emendations of only text-critical significance are passed
over in silence. For further details the reader is referred to the
critical editions.

[16] А. И. Немировский, М. Ф. Дашкова, *"Римская История"
Веллея Патеркула* (Voronezh, 1985); J. J. Castelló, *Vel·lei Patèr-
cul: Història Romana* (Barcelona, 2015).

[17] Yardley and Barrett misleadingly begin their translation at
1.8.4, relegating 1.1.1–1.8.3 to an appendix. The fragment at 1.8.6
is omitted from its place before 1.9.1 and appears as another appendix; omitted altogether is the fragment of Aemilius Sura that
has found its way into Velleius' text at 1.6.6.　　　　•

xli

INTRODUCTION

obscurities. Much earlier there was the translation of J. S. Watson (1852).[18]

Scholarship

In the twenty-first century Velleius continues to attract considerable scholarly attention, which is well represented by the volumes edited by E. Cowan (2011) and A. Valvo and G. Migliorati (2015). Both volumes include helpful bibliography, but note too the extensive bibliography to be found in the edition and commentary of Ruiz Castellanos (2014, esp. pp. 132–98).

Topics

Life

The reappraisal of Velleius' work started with G. V. Sumner, "The Truth about Velleius Paterculus: Prolegomena," *Harvard Studies in Classical Philology* 74 (1970): 257–97; for the Campanian background, see Elefante in Cowan, 59–72.

Genre

Questions relating to Velleius' brevity and genre were raised by A. J. Woodman, *Classical Quarterly* 25 (1975): 275–82 (= *From Poetry to History: Selected Papers* [Oxford, 2012], 204–13); there is an excellent, more recent discussion by Rich, with further bibliography.

[18] The Reverend Watson, an experienced translator, murdered his wife in 1871 and died in prison in 1884.

xlii

INTRODUCTION

Literary-Historical Digressions

Standard older works are F. A. Schöb, *Velleius Paterculus und seine literar-historischen Abschnitte* (PhD diss., Tübingen, 1908), and J. Gustin, *Les péricopes littéraires dans l'ouvrage de Velleius Paterculus* (PhD diss., Louvain, 1944); more recent are Schmitzer, 72–100; F. Russo, *Florentia Iliberritana* 19 (2008): 293–312, and Manzoni, all with further references.

Time, Chronology, Scholarship

Excellent discussion by Bispham; note too R. Rau, *Zur Chronologie und Quellenfrage bei Velleius Paterculus* (PhD diss., Tübingen, 1921).

Tiberius

Discussion and analysis by H. J. Steffen, *Die Regierung des Tiberius in der Darstellung des Velleius Paterculus* (PhD diss., Kiel, 1954), and C. Kuntze, *Zur Darstellung des Kaisers Tiberius und seiner Zeit bei Velleius Paterculus* (Frankfurt/Bern/New York, 1985); commentary on Velleius' Tiberian narrative by Woodman (1977).

Style

Comprehensive discussion by S. P. Oakley, "Point and Periodicity: The Style of Velleius Paterculus and Other Latin Historians Writing in the Early Principate," in *Seneca the Elder and His Rediscovered "Historiae Ab Initio Bellorum Civilium": New Perspectives on Early-Imperial Roman Historiography*, ed. M. C. Scappaticcio (Berlin, 2020),

xliii

INTRODUCTION

199–234; for individual features see H. J. W. Verhaak, *Velleius Paterculus en de rhetoriek van zijn tijd* (Grave, 1954). For "wordiness" see P. Freitag, *Stilistische Beiträge zu Velleius Paterculus: Pleonasmus und Parenthese* (PhD diss., Vienna, 1942), and, for clausulae, T. Keeline and T. Kirby, *"Auceps syllabarum*: A Digital Analysis of Latin Prose Rhythm," *Journal of Roman Studies* 109 (2019): 161–204, esp. 170 and 188–89.

Text

The lost manuscript (M) is discussed by S. Persson, "A Note on Reading Velleius Paterculus," *Classica et Mediaevalia* 59 (2008): 99–115, and L. Calvelli, "Novità sulla fortuna del *codex unicus* di Velleio Patercolo," *Rivista di Cultura Classica e Medioevale* 58 (2016): 357–72; the *editio princeps* by G. von der Gönna, "Beatus Rhenanus und die editio princeps des Velleius Paterculus," *Würzb. Jahrb. f. d. Altertumsw*, n.f. 3 (1977): 231–42. For the relationship between the various witnesses see, in addition to Woodman (1977, 3–27), Watt, v–x.

Reputation

Velleius' harshest critic in the twentieth century was the most distinguished Roman historian of modern times, Sir Ronald Syme (e.g., "Mendacity in Velleius," *American Journal of Philology* 99 [1978]: 45–63 [= *Roman Papers* (Oxford, 1984): 3.1090–1104]); for a survey of other opinion see Schmitzer, 14–23, and for a recent study of various aspects see A. Domainko, "The Conception of History in Velleius Paterculus' *Historia Romana*," *Histos* 9 (2015): 76–110.

ABBREVIATIONS

BA	*Barrington Atlas of the Greek and Roman World*, ed. R. J. A. Talbert (Princeton, 2000)
CIL	*Corpus Inscriptionum Latinarum*
cos.	consul
cos. des.	consul designate
cos. suff.	suffect consul
FRHist	*The Fragments of the Roman Historians*, vols. 1–3, ed. T. J. Cornell (Oxford, 2003)[1]
OLD	*Oxford Latin Dictionary*
pr.	praetor
qu.	quaestor
SCPP	*Senatus Consultum de Cn. Pisone Patre.* See A. E. Cooley, *The Senatus Consultum de Cn. Pisone Patre. Text, translation, and commentary* (Cambridge, 2023)
trib. pleb.	tribune of the plebs

[1] References to the fragmentary historians are given according both to this edition and to the earlier edition of H. Peter.

GENERAL BIBLIOGRAPHY

Works mentioned more than once are referred to by author's name only (accompanied by a date in cases of potential ambiguity); full details are found in the following list.

Beard, M. 2007. *The Roman Triumph.* Cambridge, MA/London.

Bispham, E. 2011. "Time for Italy in Velleius Paterculus." In Cowan, 17–57.

Cowan, E., ed. 2011. *Velleius Paterculus: Making History.* Swansea.

Elefante, M. 1997. *Velleius Paterculus: Ad M. Vinicium consulem libri duo.* Hildesheim/Zurich/New York.

Hellegouarc'h, J. 1982. *Velleius Paterculus. Histoire romaine.* Vols. 1–2. Budé ed., Paris.

Krause, I. C. H., ed. 1800. *C. Velleii Paterculi quae supersunt ex Historiae Romanae libris duobus recensere et illustrare coepit C.D. Iani continuavit I.C.H. Krause.* Leipzig.

Kritz, F., ed. 1840. *M. Vellei Paterculi quae supersunt ex historiae Romanae libris duobus. Ad editionis principis, collati a Burerio Codicis Murbacensis, apographique amerbachiani fidem, et ex doctorum hominum coniecturis recensuit accuratissimisque indicibus instruxit Fridericus Kritzius.* Leipzig.

GENERAL BIBLIOGRAPHY

Manzoni, G. E. 2015. "Cronologie letterarie greche in Velleio." In Valvo and Migliorati, 115–29.

Portalupi, F. 1967. *Velleio Patercolo: Storia Romana*. Turin.

Rich, J. W. 2011. "Velleius' History: Genre and Purpose." In Cowan, 73–92.

Ruiz Castellanos, A. 2014. *Veleyo Patérculo: Historia de Roma*. Madrid.

Schmitzer, U. 2000. *Velleius Paterculus und das Interesse an der Geschichte im Zeitalter des Tiberius*. Heidelberg.

Shipley, F. W. 1924. *Velleius Paterculus; Res Gestae Divi Augusti*. Loeb Classical Library 152. London/Cambridge, MA.

Syme, R. 1958. *Tacitus*. Oxford.

———. 1986. *The Augustan Aristocracy*. Oxford.

Valvo, A., and G. Migliorati, eds. 2015. *Ricerche storiche e letterarie intorno a Velleio Patercolo*. Milan.

Watson, J. S. 1852. *Sallust, Florus, and Velleius Paterculus*. London.

Watt, W. S. 1988, [2]1998. *Velleius Paterculus: Historiarum Libri Duo*. Leipzig/Stuttgart.

Woodman, A. J. 1977. *Velleius Paterculus: The Tiberian Narrative*. Cambridge

———. 1983. *Velleius Paterculus: The Caesarian and Augustan Narrative*. Cambridge.

Yardley, J. C., and A. A. Barrett. 2011. *Velleius Paterculus: The Roman History*. Indianapolis/Cambridge, MA.

VELLEIUS PATERCULUS

LIBER PRIOR

1.[1] *** tempestate[2] distractus a duce suo Nestore Metapontum condidit. Teucer, non receptus a patre Telamone ob segnitiam non vindicatae fratris iniuriae, Cyprum adpulsus cognominem[3] patriae suae Salamina constituit. Pyrrhus, Achillis filius, Epirum occupavit, Phidippus Ephyram in Thesprotia. at rex regum Agamemnon, tempestate in Cretam insulam reiectus, tres ibi urbes statuit, duas a patriae nomine, unam a victoriae memoria, Mycenas, Tegeam, Pergamum. idem mox scelere patruelis fratris Aegisthi, hereditarium exercentis in eum odium, et facinore uxoris oppressus occiditur. regni potitur Aegisthus per annos septem. hunc Orestes matremque socia consiliorum omnium sorore Electra, virilis animi femina, obtruncat. factum eius a diis comprobatum spatio vitae et felicitate imperii apparuit: quippe vixit annis XC, regnavit LXX. quin[4] se etiam a Pyrrho, Achillis filio, virtute vindi-

---

[1] *initium textus non exstat*
[2] *ante* tempestate *suppl.* Epeus *Puteanus*
[3] cognominem *Gelenius*: -e *P*
[4] quin *Wopkens*: qui *P*

BOOK ONE

1. ⟨Epeus,⟩ separated from his leader, Nestor, by a storm, founded Metapontum. Teucer, not welcomed back by his father Telamon because of his negligence in failing to avenge the wrong done to his brother,[1] sailed to Cyprus and established Salamis, named after his fatherland. Epirus was occupied by Pyrrhus, Achilles' son, and Ephyra in Thesprotia by Phidippus. Agamemnon, king of kings, cast ashore on the island of Crete by a storm, set up three cities there, two named after his fatherland, one in memory of his victory (respectively Mycenae, Tegea, and Pergamus); subsequently, succumbing both to the crime of his cousin, Aegisthus, who was indulging an hereditary hatred of him, and to the wickedness of his wife, he was slain. Aegisthus took charge of the kingdom for seven years, but Orestes, whose sister Electra was his ally in all his plans, a woman with a man's spirit, butchered him and their mother. That his deed was approved by the gods was apparent from the length of his life and the happiness of his rule: he lived ninety years and reigned for seventy. Moreover he also took valiant vengeance on Pyrrhus, Achilles'

---

[1] Teucer's half brother, Ajax, had not been awarded the arms of Achilles after the latter's death and as a result had gone mad and killed himself.

VELLEIUS PATERCULUS

cavit: nam, quod pactae ei[5] Menelai atque Helenae filiae Hermiones nuptias occupaverat, Delphis eum interfecit.

4 Per haec tempora Lydus et Tyrrhenus fratres cum regnarent in Lydia, sterilitate frugum compulsi sortiti sunt uter cum parte multitudinis patria decederet. sors Tyrrheno[6] contigit: pervectus in Italiam et loco et incolis et mari nobile ac perpetuum a se nomen dedit.

Post Orestis interitum filii eius Penthilus et Tisamenus regnavere triennio.

2. Tum fere anno octogesimo post Troiam captam, centesimo et vicesimo quam Hercules ad deos excesserat, Pelopis progenies, quae omni hoc tempore pulsis Heraclidis Peloponnesi imperium obtinuerat, ab Herculis progenie expellitur. duces recuperandi imperii fuere Temenus, Cresphontes, Aristodemus, quorum abavus[7] fuerat. eodem fere[8] tempore Athenae sub regibus esse desierunt, quarum ultimus rex fuit Codrus, Melanthi filius, vir non praetereundus. quippe cum Lacedaemonii gravi bello Atticos premerent respondissetque Pythius quorum dux ab hoste esset occisus, eos futuros superiores, deposita veste regia pastoralem cultum induit, immixtusque castris hostium, de industria ⟨inter⟩ imprudentes[9] rixam ini-

---

[5] ei *Aldus*: eius *P, secl. Hottinger*: sibi *Heinsius*

[6] Tyrrheno *Ellis*: -um *P*

[7] abavus *Scaliger*: atavus *P*

[8] fere *B*: ferme *P*

[9] ⟨inter⟩ imprudentes *Woodman*: imprudenter *P*: ⟨cum⟩ imprudente *Cornelissen* (ab imprudente *Ursinus*)

BOOK 1.1–2

son: he killed him at Delphi for preempting marriage to Hermione, the daughter of Menelaus and Helen, to whom he had been betrothed.

During these times, when the brothers Lydus and Tyrrhenus were reigning in Lydia, they were compelled by a crop failure into drawing lots to see which of them should leave their fatherland along with some of their people. The lot fell to Tyrrhenus: traveling to Italy, he gave his own familiar and noble name in perpetuity to the place, its inhabitants, and the sea.[2]

After the passing of Orestes, his sons Penthilus and Tisamenus reigned for three years.

2. Then, in about the eightieth year after the capture of Troy, the one hundred and twentieth after Hercules had departed to the gods, Pelops' progeny, who had held power all this time in the Peloponnese after the expulsion of the Heraclidae, were expelled by the progeny of Hercules. The leaders in this recovery of power were Temenus, Cresphontes, and Aristodemus; their great-great-grandfather had been Hercules. At about the same time Athens stopped being subject to kings, the final king being Codrus, Melanthus' son, a man not to be passed over. For, when the Lacedaemonians were pressing the people of Attica in a grueling war, and the Pythian oracle had declared that the winners would be those whose leader had been killed by the enemy, Codrus laid aside his regal clothing and dressed himself like a shepherd, and, mingling in the camp of the enemy and deliberately provoking

[2] The Tyrrhenian Sea lies off the west coast of Italy; "Tyrrhenia" and "Tyrrhenian" are alternative terms for Etruria and Etruscan.

5

VELLEIUS PATERCULUS

2 ciens[10] interemptus est. Codrum cum morte aeterna gloria, Atheniensis secuta victoria est. quis ⟨enim⟩[11] eum non miretur qui iis artibus mortem quaesierit quibus ab ignavis vita quaeri solet? huius filius Medon primus archon Athenis fuit; ab hoc posteri apud Atticos dicti Medontidae, sed hic[12] insequentesque archontes usque ad Charopem, dum viverent, eum honorem usurpabant. Peloponnesii digredientes finibus Atticis Megaram, mediam Corintho Athenisque urbem, condidere.

3 Ea tempestate et Tyria classis, plurimum pollens mari, in ultimo Hispaniae tractu, in[13] extremo nostri orbis termino, ⟨in⟩[14] insula circumfusa Oceano, perexiguo a continenti divisa[15] freto, Gadis condidit. ab iisdem post paucos annos in Africa Utica condita est.

Exclusi ab Heraclidis Orestis liberi iactatique cum variis casibus tum saevitia maris quinto decimo anno sedem cepere circa Lesbum insulam.

3. Tum Graecia maximis concussa est motibus. Achaei ex Laconica pulsi eas occupavere sedes quas nunc obtinent. Pelasgi Athenas commigravere, acerque belli iuvenis nomine Thessalus, natione Thesprotius, cum magna

[10] rixam iniciens *Rhenanus*: rixam.ncies *B*: rixanincies *P*: rixam ciens *Burer*
[11] *suppl. Ruhnken (cf. 1.16.2, 36.2, 122.1)*
[12] hic *Susius*: hii *P*
[13] *secl. Ruhnken*
[14] *suppl. nescioquis*
[15] circumfusa . . . divisa *Lipsius*: -am . . . -am *P*

BOOK 1.2–3

a quarrel among some men unsuspicious of him, was killed. Codrus' death was followed by eternal glory for himself as well as by victory for the Athenians. For who could not admire a man who sought death by means of the very techniques by which cowards customarily seek survival?[3] His son Medon was the first archon at Athens; it was from him that his successors were called Medontidae by the people of Attica. He and the following archons up as far as Charops held that honorable office for life. The Peloponnesians, on withdrawing from Attic territory, founded Megara, a city halfway between Corinth and Athens.

That was also the time when the Tyrian fleet, preeminently powerful at sea, founded Gades in the furthest tract of Spain, at the extreme boundary of our world, on an island surrounded by Ocean and separated from the mainland by a very narrow strait.[4] The same people founded Utica in Africa a few years later.

The children of Orestes, excluded by the Heraclidae and having been tossed about by various misfortunes and especially by the savagery of the sea, took up residence around the island of Lesbos in the fifteenth year.

3. Then Greece was shaken by the greatest tremors. The Achaeans, driven from Laconia, seized the abodes that they hold now. The Pelasgians migrated to Athens, and a warlike young man by the name of Thessalus, Thesprotian by nationality, along with a considerable company

---

[3] Namely, disguise.   [4] Cadiz is described very similarly by the geographer Pomponius Mela (3.46), a younger contemporary of V. Ocean is the name of the sea that in the ancient imagination encircled the world.

VELLEIUS PATERCULUS

civium manu eam regionem armis occupavit quae nunc ab eius nomine Thessalia appellatur, ante Myrmidonum vocitata civitas. quo nomine mirari convenit eos qui Iliaca componentes tempora de ea regione ut Thessalia commemorant. quod cum alii faciant, tragici frequentissime faciunt, quibus minime id concedendum est: nihil enim ex persona poetae, sed omnia sub eorum qui illo tempore vixerunt dicunt.[16] quod si quis a Thessalo Herculis filio eos appellatos Thessalos dicet, reddenda erit ei ratio cur numquam ante hunc insequentem Thessalum ea gens id nominis usurpaverit.

Paulo ante Aletes, sextus[17] ab Hercule, Hippotis filius, Corinthum, quae antea fuerat Ephyre, claustra Peloponnesi continentem, in Isthmo condidit. neque est quod miremur ab Homero nominari Corinthum: nam ex persona poetae et hanc urbem et quasdam Ionum colonias iis nominibus appellat quibus vocabantur aetate eius, multo post Ilium captum conditae.

4. Athenienses in Euboea Chalcida ⟨et⟩[18] Eretriam colonis occupavere, Lacedaemonii in Asia Magnesiam.[19] nec multo post Chalcidenses, orti (ut praediximus) Atticis, Hippocle et Megasthene ducibus Cumas in Italia condiderunt. huius classis cursum esse directum alii columbae

[16] dicunt *Cludius*: dixerunt *P*
[17] sextus *P*: quintus *Lipsius*
[18] *suppl. Gelenius*
[19] Asia Magnesiam *Rhenanus*: Asiam ac Nesiam *P*

---

[5] V. seems to be echoing the regular Greek literary-critical expression "in his own person," used by the scholiast on Hom. *Il.*

BOOK 1.3–4

of citizens, seized by force of arms the region that is now called Thessaly after his name but was previously styled the community of the Myrmidons. For this reason it is right to be surprised at those who, in their compositions about Trojan times, record that region as being Thessaly. Although others do this, tragedians do it very frequently and it is they who should least be given this concession, since they say nothing in their own person, as poets, but everything through the persons of those who lived at that time. And if anyone says that those men were called Thessalians after Hercules' son Thessalus, he will have to explain why that people never adopted that particular name before the subsequent Thessalus.

A little while before, Aletes, Hippotes' son in the sixth generation from Hercules, founded Corinth on the Isthmus (it had been Ephyre and is the gateway to the Peloponnese); and we have no need to be surprised that Corinth is named by Homer, because it is in his own person, as a poet,[5] that he calls both this city and some Ionian colonies by the names by which they were styled in his lifetime, founded as they were long after the capture of Troy.

4. The Athenians through their colonists occupied Chalcis and Eretria in Euboea, and the Lacedaemonians likewise Magnesia in Asia. And not long afterward the Chalcidians, descended (as we just mentioned) from the people of Attica, founded Cumae in Italy under the leadership of Hippocles and Megasthenes. Some say that their fleet was guided on its voyage by a dove flying in front of

2.570 when noting that the poet uses the name Corinth there but Ephyre at *Il.* 6.152. See below, 1.5.3n.

9

VELLEIUS PATERCULUS

antecedentis volatu ferunt, alii nocturno aeris sono, qualis
2 Cerealibus sacris cieri solet. pars horum civium magno
post intervallo Neapolim condidit. utriusque urbis eximia
semper in Romanos fides facit eas nobilitate atque amoenitate sua dignissimas; sed illis[20] diligentior ritus patrii
mansit custodia, Cumanos Osca mutavit vicinia. vires autem veteres earum urbium hodieque magnitudo ostentat
moenium.

3 Subsequenti tempore magna vis Graecae iuventutis,
abundantia virorum[21] sedes quaeritans, in Asiam se effudit. nam et Iones duce Ione profecti Athenis nobilissimam
partem regionis maritimae occupavere, quae hodieque
appellatur Ionia, urbesque constituere Ephesum, Miletum, Colophona, Prienen, Lebedum, Myuntem,[22] Erythras, Clazomenas, Phocaeam, multasque in Aegaeo atque
Icario occupavere insulas, Samum, Chium, Andrum, Te
4 num, Parum, Delum aliasque ignobil‹ior›es.[23] et mox
Aeolii eadem[24] profecti Graecia longissimisque acti erroribus non minus inlustres obtinuerunt locos clarasque urbes[25] condiderunt, Smyrnam, Cymen, Larissam, Myrinam
Mytilenenque et alias urbes quae sunt in Lesbo insula.

5. Clarissimum deinde Homeri inluxit ingenium, sine
exemplo maximum,[26] qui magnitudine operis et fulgore
2 carminum solus appellari poeta meruit; in quo hoc maximum est quod neque ante illum quem ipse[27] imitaretur
neque post illum qui eum imitari posset inventus est. ne-

---

[20] illis *Ruhnken*: aliis *P*   [21] virorum *Burman*: virium *P*:
civium *Damsté*   [22] Myuntem, ‹Teum› *Vossius*

[23] ignobil‹ior›es *Woodman*: ‹non› ignobiles *Watt*

[24] ‹ex› eadem *Madvig*   [25] urbes *secl. Ruhnken*

[26] sine exemplo maximum *secl. Bothe*

[27] ipse *Halm*: ille *P, secl. Gruter*

BOOK 1.4–5

it, others by the sound of bronze cymbals at night, like that which is customarily produced in the rites of Ceres. After a long interval some of these citizens founded Neapolis. The exceptionally enduring loyalty of both cities toward the Romans means that they well deserve their noble fame and picturesque aspect; but the latter has retained more diligently its ancestral rituals, whereas the Cumans were changed by their Oscan surroundings. As for the cities' powerful past, it is still visible today in their formidable fortifications.

In a subsequent period a great force of young Greeks, seeking settlements because of the numbers of their men, poured into Asia. The Ionians for their part set off from Athens under the leadership of Ion and seized the most renowned part of the coastal region, which today is still called Ionia, and they established the cities of Ephesus, Miletus, Colophon, Priene, Lebedus, Myus, Erythrae, Clazomenae, and Phocaea, and seized many islands in the Aegean and Icarian seas, namely Samos, Chios, Andros, Tenos, Paros, and Delos and others not so well known. Later it was the Aeolians who likewise set off from Greece and, after being driven about on the longest of wanderings, took possession of places no less illustrious and founded the distinguished cities of Smyrna, Cyme, Larissa, Myrina, and Mytilene and other cities on the island of Lesbos.

5. Next there shone out, the brightest dawn of all, the incomparably great genius of Homer, who, for the greatness of his work and the radiance of his poems, alone has deserved the name of poet; the greatest thing about him is that no one has been found either before him whom he imitated or after him who had the ability to imitate him;

11

VELLEIUS PATERCULUS

que quemquam alium, cuius operis primus auctor fuerit, in eo perfectissimum praeter Homerum et Archilochum reperiemus. hic longius a temporibus belli quod composuit Troici[28] quam quidam rentur abfuit: nam ferme ante annos DCCCCL floruit, intra mille natus est. quo nomine non est mirandum quod saepe illud ⟨οἷοι νῦν βροτοί εἰσιν⟩ usurpat:[29] hoc enim, ut hominum, ita saeculorum notatur differentia. quem si quis caecum genitum putat, omnibus sensibus orbus est.

6. Insequenti tempore imperium Asiaticum ab Assyriis, qui id obtinuerant annis MLXX, translatum est ad Medos, abhinc annos ferme DCCCLXX.[30] quippe Sardanapalum eorum regem mollitiis fluentem et nimium felicem malo suo, tertio et tricensimo[31] loco ab Nino et Semiramide, qui Babylona condiderant, natum, ita ut semper successor regni paterni foret filius, Arbaces[32] Medus imperio vitaque privavit.

Ea aetate clarissimus Grai nominis Lycurgus Lacedaemonius, vir generis regii, fuit severissimarum iustissimarumque legum auctor et disciplinae convenientissimae [vir],[33] cuius quam diu Sparta diligens fuit, excelsissime[34] floruit.

---

[28] Troici *secl. Damsté*   [29] *illud Homericum fere post* usurpat *suppl. edd.*   [30] DCCCLXX *Lipsius*: DCCLXX *P*
[31] tricensimo *B*: trecentesimo *P*
[32] Arbaces *Fabricius*: Pharnaces *P*
[33] vir *P, secl. Acidalius*: viris *Lipsius*: iis *Scrinerius*: *alii alia*
[34] excellentissime *Cludius*

---

6 Archilochus (ca. 670–640), associated especially with the invention of iambic poetry, was often coupled with Homer.

BOOK 1.5–6

nor shall we discover anyone else, apart from Homer and Archilochus, who reached perfection in the genre of which they were the first founder.[6] He was far more distant than some think from the times of the Trojan War about which he composed, since he flourished about 950 years ago and was born less than a thousand. For this reason we should not be surprised that he often repeats his "such as men now are," for it marks a difference in epochs just as much as in men.[7] Anyone who thinks Homer was blind from birth is lacking all his senses.

6. In the following period the Asian empire passed from the Assyrians, who had held it for 1,070 years, to the Medes, about 870 years ago. The Assyrian king Sardanapalus—whose birth in the thirty-third generation from Ninus and Semiramis, the founders of Babylon, was one in a continuous succession of sons to their fathers' kingdom—exuded softness and, his excess of good fortune being his undoing, he was deprived of his empire and his life by Arbaces the Mede.[8]

At that time the most distinguished person of Greek nationality was Lycurgus the Lacedaemonian, a man of royal lineage, who was the originator of very severe and just laws and a discipline to match: as long as Sparta adhered to it, she flourished to the highest degree.

[7] This Homeric formula, seemingly quoted only here in all of Latin literature, occurs four times in the *Iliad* (5.304, 12.383, 12.449, 20.287). V.'s point is found in commentators on Homer and may have been conventional.

[8] Sardanapalus (Assurbanipal) was proverbial for his luxury and effeminacy, with which "softness" was conventionally associated (see also 88.2).

13

VELLEIUS PATERCULUS

4   Hoc tractu temporum, ante annos quinque et sexaginta quam urbs Romana conderetur, ab Elissa Tyria, quam qui-
5 dam Dido autumant, Carthago conditur. circa quod tempus Caranus, vir generis regii,[35] undecimus[36] ab Hercule, profectus Argis regnum Macedoniae occupavit; a quo Magnus Alexander, cum fuerit septimus decimus, iure materni generis Achille auctore, paterni Hercule gloriatus est.

6   [Aemilius Sura de annis populi Romani: Assyrii principes omnium gentium rerum potiti sunt, deinde Medi, postea Persae, deinde Macedones. exinde duobus regibus Philippo et Antiocho, qui a Macedonibus oriundi erant, haud multo post Carthaginem subactam devictis summa imperii ad populum Romanum pervenit. inter hoc tempus et initium regis Nini Assyriorum, qui princeps rerum potitus est, intersunt anni MDCCCCXCV.][37]

7. Huius temporis aequalis Hesiodus fuit, circa CXX annos distinctus ab Homeri aetate, vir perelegantis ingenii et mollissima dulcedine carminum memorabilis, otii quietisque cupidissimus, ut tempore tanto viro, ita operis auctoritate proximus. qui vitavit ne in id quod Homerus

---

[35] vir generis regii *secl. Lipsius*
[36] undecimus *Scaliger*: sextusdecimus *P*
[37] *haec omnia ut aliena secl. Delbenius*

---

9 Philip V of Macedon was defeated by T. Quinctius Flamininus (cos. 198) at Cynoscephalae in 197; Antiochus III the Great, ruler of the Seleucid Empire, was defeated in 190 (38.5n): the "taming of Carthage" must therefore refer to the ending of the Second Punic War in 201.

BOOK 1.6–7

During this tract of time, sixty-five years before the City of Rome was founded, Carthage was founded by Tyrian Elissa, benamed Dido by some. And it was around this time that Caranus, a man of royal lineage and in the eleventh generation from Hercules, set off from Argos and seized the kingdom of Macedonia; since Alexander the Great was in the seventeenth generation from him, he gloried in having Achilles as progenitor thanks to his mother's side and Hercules thanks to his father's.

[Aemilius Sura, *On the Years of the Roman People*: The Assyrians were the first of all nations to hold power, then the Medes, next the Persians, and then the Macedonians. Subsequently, on the defeat of the two kings Philippus and Antiochus (who were descendants of the Macedonians) and not long after the taming of Carthage,[9] supreme command devolved upon the Roman people. Between this moment and the beginning of the Assyrians' king Ninus, the first to hold power, there is an interval of 1,995 years.[10]]

7. A contemporary of this period was Hesiod, separated from Homer's time by about 120 years, a man of the most fastidious talent and memorable for the smooth sweetness of his poems, desirous of peace and quiet, and very close to the great man not only in period but also in the prestige of his work. Avoiding the error into which

[10] The deleted section is an interpolation and constitutes the only remaining fragment of Aemilius Sura, of whom nothing is known (*FRHist* 1.616–17, where there is bibliography on the theory of the succession of empires); whether the italicized words are in fact Sura's title is unclear. Ninus is perhaps to be identified with Tukulti-Ninurta I (r. 1244/43–1208/7).

15

VELLEIUS PATERCULUS

incideret, patriamque et parentes testatus est, sed patriam, quia multatus ab ea erat, contumeliosissime.

2 Dum in externis moror, incidi in rem domesticam maximique erroris et multum discrepantem auctorum opinionibus: nam quidam huius temporis tractu aiunt a Tuscis Capuam Nolamque conditam ante annos fere

3 DCCCXXX. quibus equidem adsenserim, sed M. Cato quantum differt! qui dicat Capuam ab eisdem Tuscis conditam ac subinde Nolam; stetisse autem Capuam, ante-

4 quam a Romanis caperetur, annis circiter CCLX. quod si ita est, cum sint a Capua capta anni CCXL, ut condita est, anni sunt fere D. ego (pace diligentiae Catonis dixerim) vix crediderim tam mature tantam urbem crevisse, floruisse, concidisse, resurrexisse.

8. Clarissimum deinde omnium ludicrum certamen et ad excitandam corporis animique virtutem efficacissimum Olympiorum initium[38] habuit ⟨et⟩[39] auctorem Iphitum Elium. is eos ludos mercatumque instituit ante annos

2 quam tu, M. Vinici, consulatum inires DCCCXXIII. (hoc sacrum eodem loco instituisse fertur abhinc annos ferme MCCL Atreus, cum Pelopi patri funebres ludos faceret; quo quidem in ludicro omnis[que][40] generis certaminum Hercules victor extitit.)

[38] Olympiorum initium *secl. Watt*: initium *secl. Bothe*
[39] *suppl. Acidalius*
[40] omnis[que] *Gelenius*: cuiusque *Gurlitt*

---

[11] The two most famous poems of Hesiod (fl. ca. 700), born in Ascra in Boeotia, are the *Theogony* and *Works and Days*. From the latter we learn that when Hesiod and his brother Perses quarreled over their inheritance, Perses relied on corrupt authorities

BOOK 1.7–8

Homer fell, he testified to his fatherland and parents, but very insultingly in the case of his fatherland, because it had punished him.[11]

While I was lingering in foreign territory, I stumbled upon a domestic matter, the source of very great error and much disputed in the opinion of authors. Some say that it was during this tract of time that Capua and Nola were founded by the Etruscans, about 830 years ago; and I would agree with them, but how different is Marcus Cato! He says that Capua and subsequently Nola were indeed founded by the Etruscans, but that Capua had stood for only around 260 years before it was captured by the Romans.[12] If that is so, then because there are only 240 years since the capture of Capua, there are roughly 500 years since it was founded. For my part, speaking with all due respect for Cato's diligence, I can scarcely believe that so great a city grew, flourished, fell and revived so quickly.

8. Next, the most distinguished sporting contest of all, and the most effective in bringing out the best in body and mind, the Olympian Games, had its beginning at the instigation of Iphitus from Elis. He established them and their fair[13] 823 years before you, Marcus Vinicius, embarked on your consulship. (It is said that this festival was established in the same place about 1,250 years ago by Atreus, when he was conducting the funeral games for his father, Pelops. In this sporting event Hercules proved the winner in contests of every type.)

for a settlement (Hes. *Op*. 27–41). Whether Homer was in fact earlier than Hesiod, as V. says, was disputed in antiquity.

[12] Cato, *Orig*. fr. 52C/69P.

[13] Cf. Cic. *Tusc*. 5.9.

17

VELLEIUS PATERCULUS

3   Tum Athenis perpetui archontes esse desierunt, cum fuisset ultimus Alcmaeon, coeperuntque in denos annos creari; quae consuetudo in annos LXX mansit ac deinde annuis commissa est magistratibus res publica. ex iis qui denis annis praefuerunt primus fuit Charops, ultimus Eryxias, ex annuis primus Creon.

4   Sexta Olympiade, post duo et viginti annos quam prima constituta fuerat, Romulus, Martis filius, ultus iniurias avi urbem Romam[41] Parilibus in Palatio condidit. a quo tempore ad vos consules anni sunt DCCLXXXI;[42] id actum

5 post Troiam captam annis CCCCXXXVII. id gessit Romulus adiutus legionibus Latinis[43] avi sui: libenter enim iis qui ita prodiderunt accesserim, cum aliter firmare urbem novam tam vicinis Veientibus aliisque Etruscis ac Sabinis cum imbelli et pastorali manu vix potuerit, quamquam

6 eam asylo facto inter duos lucos auxit. hic centum homines electos appellatosque patres instar habuit consilii publici. hanc originem nomen patriciorum habet. [raptus virginum Sabinarum][44]

---

[41] Romam urbem *P, transpos. Woodman*   [42] DCCLXXXI *Vossius:* D.CCCC.LXXX.L *P*   [43] Latinis *Lipsius:* -i *P*
    [44] raptus . . . Sabinarum *secl. Vossius*

---

[14] V. is following the version of Romulus' story according to which his mother was Rhea Silvia, the daughter of Numitor, who was thwarted of his inheritance—the kingship of Alba Longa—by his younger brother Amulius. Romulus and his twin brother, Remus, eventually overthrew Amulius and reinstated Numitor.

[15] The Palatine Hill is the central of the Seven Hills of Rome and from the time of Augustus was the site of the imperial residence; the Latin *Palatium* can be used both for the residence and for the hill itself. The traditional date of the founding of Rome

BOOK 1.8

Then at Athens there stopped being perpetual archons (the final one was Alcmaeon) and they began to be appointed for ten years at a time; this custom remained for seventy years, and thereafter their commonwealth was entrusted to annual magistrates. Of those who were in charge for ten years, the first was Charops, the last Eryxias; of the annual ones the first was Creon.

In the sixth Olympiad, twenty-two years after the first had been established, Romulus, the son of Mars, after avenging the wrongs done to his grandfather,[14] founded the City of Rome on the Palatine on the Parilia.[15] There are 781 years from that moment to your two consulships,[16] and the event was 437 years after the capture of Troy. Romulus was helped in his achievement by the Latin legions of his grandfather. (I gladly agree with those who have handed down this version, since otherwise, given the proximity of the Veientines and of other Etruscans and the Sabines, he could hardly have consolidated his new city with the help only of an unwarlike group of shepherds, although he increased its population by making an asylum between the two groves.[17]) As an official council he had a hundred selected men called "fathers," from whom the name "patricians" originates. [The rape of the young Sabine women][18]

---

was 21 April, when the ancient agricultural festival of the Parilia was celebrated. [16] Referring both to Vinicius and to his consular colleague, L. Cassius Longinus.

[17] Describing an area of the Capitoline Hill as it was in V.'s own day; cf. Livy 1.8.5. [18] The bracketed phrase seems to be a marginal gloss that not only has survived the loss of the text with which it was associated but has actually supplanted that text.

19

VELLEIUS PATERCULUS

*** nec minus clarus ea tempestate fuit Miltiadis filius Cimon.[45]

9. *** quam[46] timuerat hostis expetit. nam biennio adeo varia fortuna cum consulibus conflixerat ut plerumque superior fuerit magnamque partem Graeciae in socie-
2 tatem suam perduceret. quin[47] Rhodii quoque, fidelissimi antea Romanis, tum dubia fide speculati fortunam proniores regis partibus fuisse visi sunt; et rex Eumenes in eo bello medius fuit animo: neque fratris initiis neque suae
3 respondit consuetudini. tum senatus populusque Romanus L. Aemilium Paulum, qui et praetor et consul triumphaverat, virum in tantum laudandum in quantum intellegi virtus potest, consulem creavit, filium eius Pauli qui ad Cannas quam tergiversanter perniciosam rei publicae
4 pugnam inierat, tam fortiter in ea mortem obierat. is Per-

[45] nec minus . . . Cimon *servavit solus Prisc. (2.248.4K)*

[46] quam *hic incipit* A; *de lacuna quae in ed. pr. est inter* Sabinarum *et* quam *Rhenanus aliquamdiu disserit ad loc.*

[47] quin *Gelenius*: quibus *BPA*

---

[19] The grammarian Priscian (fl. AD 500) attributes these words to "Book 1" of V. (2.248.4K). Miltiades was the victorious Athenian general at the battle of Marathon (490 BC); Cimon enjoyed a checkered career as politician and general, dying in 450/49.   [20] Apart from the words quoted by Priscian, the whole of V.'s narrative between the foundation of Rome (1.8.4–6) and 168 BC (1.9.1), a period of almost six hundred years, has been lost: see Rich, 76–80. The first sentence here coincides with the start of Amerbach's apograph (pp. xxxix–xl); its lacunose state means that we know neither whether *quam* means "than" or "which" nor whether *hostis* (the enemy) is the subject of *timuerat* (had feared) or of *expetit* (demanded).

20

BOOK 1.8–9

*** and no less distinguished at that time was Miltiades' son, Cimon.[19]

9. *** *quam timuerat hostis expetit*.[20] For during a two-year period he had engaged with the consuls with such varied fortune that on most occasions he was the winner and was bringing over a large part of Greece into alliance with himself.[21] Moreover the Rhodians too, formerly extremely loyal to the Romans, were now wavering in their loyalty and, keeping the king's fortunes under observation,[22] seemed to have been more inclined to his side. King Eumenes remained neutral in the war, responding neither to the start made by his brother nor to his own custom.[23] That was the moment at which Lucius Aemilius Paullus—who had triumphed as both praetor and consul, a man whose claim on praise is as great as one can conceive courage to be, and son of the Paullus whose bravery when facing death at Cannae matched his reluctance at entering a fight that was so calamitous for the commonwealth—was appointed consul by the senate and Roman people.[24] He

[21] The subject of the sentence is Perseus, king of Macedon and son of Philip V, with whom the Romans had been at war since 171.

[22] The Latin may also mean "keeping the situation under observation" or "looking out for the right moment."

[23] Eumenes II was king of Pergamum and elder brother of Attalus II, his successor, both of them traditionally friends of Rome.

[24] In 168, having been praetor in 191 and consul in 182; he triumphed (from Liguria) after his first consulship, but the tradition that he had also triumphed after his praetorian command in Further Spain is false. Paullus' father, also L. Aemilius Paullus, had been consul in 219 and 216, the year of the battle of Cannae.

VELLEIUS PATERCULUS

sen[48] ingenti proelio apud urbem nomine Pydnam in Macedonia fusum fugatumque castris exuit deletisque eius copiis destitutum omni spe coegit e Macedonia profugere, quam ille linquens in insulam Samothraciam profugit[49] templique se religioni supplicem credidit. ad eum Cn. Octavius, praetor qui classi praeerat, pervenit et ratione magis quam vi persuasit ut se Romanorum fidei com-
5   mitteret. ita Paulus maximum nobilissimumque regem in triumpho duxit. quo anno et Octavii praetoris navalis et Anicii regem Illyriorum Gentium ante currum agentis[50]
6   triumphi fuere celebres. quam sit adsidua eminentis fortunae comes invidia altissimisque adhaereat etiam hoc colligi potest, quod cum Anicii Octaviique triumphum nemo interpellaret, fuere qui Pauli impedire obniterentur.[51] cuius tantum priores excessit vel magnitudine regis Persei vel specie simulacrorum vel modo pecuniae ut bis miliens centiens sestertium aerario contulerit [his][52] et omnium[53] ante actorum comparationem amplitudine vicerit.

---

48 Persen *Vossius*: Persam *PA*   49 perfugit *Crusius*
50 agentis *Gelenius*: -ium *PA*   51 adniterentur *tent. Acidalius*   52 *secl. Gelenius*   53 pecuniae (bis . . . contulerat) ut omnium *Haase olim: alii alia*

---

25 In 168.   26 The island was famous for its local cult and temple, where Perseus was seeking asylum.
27 Cn. Octavius (cos. 165) was currently propraetor, for which V. uses the term *praetor*.
28 The consular year 167.
29 L. Anicius Gallus (cos. 160), propraetor in Illyria. For the chariot see 30.2n.
30 If V., like Diodorus Siculus (31.8.10), is following a tradition

22

BOOK 1.9

routed Perseus and put him to flight in a mighty battle near a city called Pydna in Macedonia,[25] and, divesting him of his camp, and with the man's forces destroyed, he compelled him, now destitute of all hope, to flee Macedonia, from where he departed in flight to the island of Samothrace and entrusted himself as a suppliant to the sanctity of the temple.[26] The praetor Gnaeus Octavius, who was in charge of the fleet,[27] went to him and, more by reason than by force, persuaded him to commit himself to the Romans' good faith. Thus it was that Paullus led the greatest and noblest of kings in triumph. In the same year[28] there were the celebrated triumphs both of Octavius, the naval praetor, and of Anicius, who drove Gentius, king of the Illyrians, before his chariot.[29] How assiduously envy accompanies the peaks of fortune, and how it attaches itself to the most exalted, can be gathered also from the fact that, although no one objected to the triumphs of Anicius and Octavius, there were those who strove to prevent that of Paullus, which so far exceeded the earlier ones[30]—owing to the importance of King Perseus or to the impressiveness of its images[31] or to the amount of money— that he contributed to the treasury two hundred million sesterces and by comparison surpassed in grandeur all those held previously.

in which the triumphs of Octavius and Anicius preceded that of Paullus, he is in error; but the Latin may have a less specific meaning: the sentence as a whole is not at all clear and may be corrupt.

[31] The triumphal procession would feature representations of the victorious general's battles and of the landscape in which he fought them (cf. Ov. *Ars am.* 1.217–28; Tac. *Ann.* 2.41.2, where the same word, *simulacrum*, is used). See also 56.2n.

23

VELLEIUS PATERCULUS

10. Per idem tempus, cum Antiochus Epiphanes, qui Athenis Olympieum[54] inchoavit, tum rex[55] Syriae, Ptolemaeum puerum Alexandriae obsideret, missus est ad eum legatus M. Popilius Laenas, qui iuberet incepto desis-

2 tere. mandataque exposuit, et regem deliberaturum se dicentem circumscripsit virgula iussitque prius responsum reddere quam egrederetur finito harenae circulo. sic cogitationem[56] regiam Romana disiecit constantia oboeditumque imperio.

3 L. autem Paulo magnae[57] victoriae compoti quattuor filii fuere: ex iis duos natu maiores, unum P. Scipioni P. Africani filio, nihil ex paterna maiestate praeter speciem nominis vigoremque eloquentiae retinenti, in adoptionem dederat, alterum Fabio Maximo. duos minores natu prae-

4 textatos, quo tempore victoriam adeptus est, habuit. is cum in contione extra urbem more maiorum ante triumphi diem ordinem actorum suorum commemoraret, deos immortales precatus est ut, si quis eorum invideret operibus ac fortunae suae, in ipsum potius saevirent quam in

5 rem publicam. quae vox veluti oraculo emissa magna parte eum spoliavit sanguinis sui: nam alterum ex suis[58] quos in familia retinuerat liberis ante paucos triumphi, alterum post pauciores amisit dies.

---

[54] Olympieum *Sylburg*: Olympicum *PA*
[55] rex *Aldus*: regem *PA*   [56] cunctationem *Acidalius*
[57] Macedonicae *Ruhnken*   [58] his *Gelenius*

---

[32] In fact, in 168.   [33] The protagonists are Antiochus IV, Ptolemy VI Philometor (still a teenager), and C. Popilius Laenas (cos. 172), whom V. seems to have confused with M. Popilius Laenas: the two were brothers, and consuls in adjacent years.

24

BOOK 1.10

10. Around the same time,[32] when Antiochus Epiphanes—who started the Olympieum at Athens and was now king of Syria—was besieging the boy Ptolemy at Alexandria, an envoy, Marcus Popilius Laenas, was sent to order him to desist from his undertaking.[33] Popilius set out the instructions and, when the king said that he would ponder them, traced a circle round him with his staff and ordered him not to emerge from the confines of the circle in the sand until he had given a response. Thus did Roman resolve dispel a king's calculation, and the command was obeyed.

Lucius Paullus, winner of the great victory, had four sons: of these, he had given the two elder into adoption, one to Publius Scipio, son of Publius Africanus but retaining nothing of his father's sovereign authority apart from his impressive name and an energetic eloquence, the other to Fabius Maximus. The two younger sons were in the praetexta[34] at the time of his victory. When before the day of his triumph in a meeting outside the City he was recalling, by ancestral custom, the details of his actions, he begged the immortal gods that, if any of them envied his achievements and good fortune, their savagery should be directed at himself rather than at the commonwealth. These words, as if uttered by an oracle, robbed him of a great part of his bloodline: of the children whom he had retained in his family, he lost one a few days before his triumph, the other even fewer days after.

[34] The *toga praetexta* (again at 59.2) had a distinctive purple border and was worn by young boys until exchanged for the *toga virilis*, or "toga of manhood," in the early teens (29.5, 99.2); the *praetexta* was also worn by certain Roman magistrates (65.3).

25

VELLEIUS PATERCULUS

6   Aspera circa haec tempora censura Fulvii Flacci et Postumii Albini fuit: quippe Fulvii censoris frater, et quidem consors, Cn. Fulvius senatu motus est ab iis censoribus.[59]

11. Post victum captumque Persen, qui quadriennio post in libera custodia Albae decessit, Pseudophilippus, a mendacio simulatae originis appellatus, qui se Philippum regiaeque stirpis ferebat, cum esset ultimae, armis occupata Macedonia, adsumptis regni insignibus brevi temeri-
2 tatis poenas dedit: quippe Q. Metellus praetor, cui ex virtute Macedonici ‹cog›nomen[60] inditum [erat],[61] praeclara victoria ipsum gentemque superavit, et immani etiam Achaeos rebellare incipientis fudit acie.
3   Hic est Metellus Macedonicus qui porticus quae fuerunt circumdatae duabus aedibus sine inscriptione positis, quae nunc Octaviae porticibus ambiuntur, fecerat, quique hanc turmam statuarum equestrium quae frontem aedium spectant, hodieque maximum ornamentum eius loci, ex
4 Macedonia detulit. cuius turmae hanc causam referunt, Magnum Alexandrum impetrasse a Lysippo, singulari talium auctore operum, ut eorum equitum qui ex ipsius

---

> [59] ab iis censoribus *secl. Bothe*
> [60] ‹cog›nomen *edd. plerique*   [61] *secl. Gelenius*

---

[35] Q. Fulvius Flaccus (cos. 179) and A. Postumius Albinus (cos. 180) were censors in 174. Co-owners of inherited property (*consortes*) were often brothers, as here.

[36] That is, Alba Fucens.   [37] Q. Caecilius Metellus Macedonicus (cos. 143) was praetor in 148.

[38] All of the Peloponnese was at this time united in the Achaean League.   [39] Jupiter Stator (built by Metellus him-

26

BOOK 1.10–11

Around this time was the harsh censorship of Fulvius Flaccus and Postumius Albinus: Gnaeus Fulvius, brother of the censor Fulvius and in fact co-heir with him, was removed from the senate by the censors.[35]

11. After the defeat and capture of Perseus, who passed away four years later under house arrest at Alba,[36] one Pseudophilippus—so called because of the false origin that he had pretended (he presented himself as a Philip and of royal stock, although he was of the lowest)—seized Macedonia by armed force and, having assumed the royal insignia, was soon punished for his rashness: for the praetor Quintus Metellus,[37] on whom for his prowess the cognomen Macedonicus was bestowed, overcame the man and his people in a distinguished victory, and in a prodigious battle also routed the Achaeans,[38] who were beginning to rebel.

This is the Metellus Macedonicus who had built the portico surrounding the two temples that were erected without any inscription and are now encircled by the portico of Octavia;[39] he also brought back from Macedonia the present squadron of equestrian statues that face the front of the temples and today are still a very great adornment of the area. People relay the following origin of the squadron: Alexander the Great prevailed upon Lysippus, a singular creator of such works, to make statues of the horsemen from his own squadron who had fallen at the

self) and Juno Regina (preexisting). Octavia was Augustus' sister. Her portico, known as the Porticus Octaviae, replaced that of Metellus and was dedicated to the memory of her son, Marcellus (cf. 93.1); it incorporated a library and a space where the senate could meet. See also 2.1.2n.

27

VELLEIUS PATERCULUS

turma apud Granicum flumen ceciderant expressa similitudine figurarum faceret statuas et ipsius quoque iis inter-
poneret.

5 Hic idem primus omnium Romae aedem ex marmore
in iis ipsis monumentis molitus[62] vel magnificentiae vel
6 luxuriae princeps fuit. vix ullius gentis, aetatis, ordinis
hominem inveneris cuius felicitatem fortunae Metelli
compares. nam praeter excellentes triumphos[63] honores-
que amplissimos et principale in re publica fastigium extentumque[64] vitae spatium et acres innocentesque pro re
publica cum inimicis contentiones quattuor filios sustulit,
omnes adultae aetatis vidit, omnes reliquit superstites et
7 honoratissimos. mortui eius lectum pro rostris sustulerunt
quattuor filii, unus consularis et censorius, alter consularis, tertius consul, quartus candidatus consulatus,
quem honorem adeptus est. hoc est nimirum magis feliciter de vita migrare quam mori.

12. Universa deinde instincta in bellum Achaia, cuius[65]
pars magna, ut praediximus,[66] eiusdem Metelli Macedonici virtute armisque fracta[67] erat, maxime Corinthiis in
arma cum gravibus etiam in Romanos contumeliis insti-

---

[62] *post* molitus *suppl.* huius *Ruhnken*

[63] excellentem triumphum *Lipsius*

[64] extentumque *Gelenius*: extenuatumque *PA*

[65] cuius *Aldus*: cum *PA*   [66] ut praediximus, *post* deinde
traditum, huc transpos. Madvig   [67] fracta *Aldus*: tracta *PA*

---

[40] The scene of Alexander's victory over the Persians in 334.

[41] Metellus triumphed on his return from Macedonia in 146
and may have triumphed after his command in Nearer Spain in
143–142 (2.5.2–3).

BOOK 1.11–12

Granicus River,[40] reproducing the likeness of their features, and to insert his own statue too among them.

It was the same man who first constructed, amid those very monuments, a temple of marble at Rome and was thus a pioneer either of grandeur or of luxury. You would hardly find a man of any people, generation, or rank whose happiness you could compare with the fortune of Metellus. For—quite apart from his outstanding triumphs,[41] the fullest of honors,[42] a pinnacle of preeminence in the commonwealth, an unusually long life, and the bitter but blameless quarrels with his enemies on behalf of the commonwealth—he raised up four sons,[43] saw all of them reach adulthood, and left them all to survive him and very greatly honored. On his death his bier was raised up on the rostra by the four sons, one an ex-consul and ex-censor, the second an ex-consul, the third a consul, and the fourth a candidate for the consulship, an honor that he achieved.[44] Truly this is not so much dying as a happy departure from life.

12. The whole of Achaea was roused to war next (much of it, as we mentioned earlier,[45] had been broken by the courage and arms of the same Metellus Macedonicus), and, the impulse to arms coming particularly from the Corinthians, who in addition seriously insulted the Romans, the

[42] He was consul in 143, censor in 131, and had been an augur since before 140.   [43] A father would pick up a newborn child as a gesture of formal recognition.

[44] Respectively, Q. Metellus Balearicus (cos. 123, cens. 120), L. Metellus Diadematus (cos. 117, cens. 115), M. Metellus (cos. 115), C. Metellus Caprarius (cos. 113, cens. 102).

[45] At 1.11.2.

VELLEIUS PATERCULUS

gantibus, destinatus ei bello gerendo consul ‹ L. ›[68] Mummius.

2 Et sub idem tempus, magis quia volebant Romani quidquid de Carthaginiensibus diceretur credere quam quia credenda adferebantur, statuit senatus Carthaginem 3 excidere. ita eodem tempore[69] P. Scipio Aemilianus, vir avitis P. Africani paternisque L. Pauli virtutibus simillimus, omnibus belli ac togae artibus,[70] ingeniique ac studiorum eminentissimus[71] saeculi sui, qui nihil in vita nisi laudandum aut fecit aut dixit ac sensit, quem Paulo genitum, adoptatum a Scipione Africani filio diximus, aedilitatem petens consul creatus est. bellum Carthagini iam ante 4 biennium a prioribus consulibus inlatum maiore vi intulit (cum ante in Hispania murali corona, in Africa obsidionali donatus esset, in Hispania vero etiam ex provocatione, ipse modicus virium, immanis magnitudinis hostem interemisset) eamque urbem magis invidia imperii quam ulla 5 eius temporis noxia[72] invisam Romano nomini funditus sustulit fecitque suae virtutis[73] monumentum quod fuerat avi eius clementiae. Carthago diruta est, cum stetisset annis DCLXVI,[74] abhinc annos CLXXVII[75] Cn. Cornelio

---

[68] *suppl. Stanger*   [69] eodem tempore *secl. Raphelengius*
[70] artibus *Ruhnken*: dotibus *PA*   [71] ‹cultu› eminentissimus *Cornelissen olim*   [72] ulla . . . noxia *Gruter*: ullius . . . noxiae *PA*: *alii alia*   [73] suae virtutis *PA*: severitatis *Clericus*
[74] DCLXVI *A*: DCLXVII *P*
[75] CLXXVII *B*: CCLXXVII *PA*

---

[46] P. Cornelius Scipio Africanus Aemilianus was consul in 147 (and would be again in 134). See 1.10.3.

[47] The mural crown was awarded to the first man who scaled

30

BOOK 1.12

man designated for waging the war was the consul Lucius Mummius.

It was about the same time that the senate—more because the Romans wanted to believe whatever was said about the Carthaginians than that believable news was arriving—decided to demolish Carthage. So at the same moment Publius Scipio Aemilianus—a man very like the virtues of his grandfather Publius Africanus and of his father Lucius Paullus, with all the skills of war and the toga, the most outstanding of his age for his intellect and literary pursuits, who neither did nor said nor thought anything in his life that was not laudable, whose siring by Paullus and adoption by Scipio, Africanus' son, we have mentioned—was appointed consul while a candidate only for the aedileship.[46] He carried with greater force against Carthage the war that had already been carried against them two years before by earlier consuls (previously he had been presented with the mural crown in Spain and with the siege crown in Africa,[47] and in Spain too, in response to a challenge, he had killed an enemy of prodigious size, though himself being of only average strength), and he razed to the ground a city that was resented by the Roman nation more for its resentment of our empire[48] than for any wrongdoing at the time, and he made it a monument to his prowess as it had been to the clemency of his grandfather. Having survived for 666 years, Carthage was leveled 177 years ago in the consulship of

an enemy wall, the siege crown (most distinguished of all such crowns) to one who rescued a Roman force from destruction. Scipio's awards were in 151 and 149, respectively.

[48] Or, "for our resentment of its power."

31

VELLEIUS PATERCULUS

6 Lentulo L. Mummio consulibus. hunc finem habuit Romani imperii [Carthago][76] aemula, cum qua bellare maiores nostri coepere Claudio et Fulvio consulibus ante annos CCXCVI quam tu, M. Vinici, consulatum inires. ita per annos CXV aut bellum inter eos populos aut belli prae-
7 paratio aut infida pax fuit. neque se Roma iam terrarum orbe superato securam speravit fore si nota[77] usquam stantis maneret Carthaginis: adeo odium certaminibus ortum ultra metum durat et ne in victis quidem deponitur, nec quicquam ante[78] invisum esse desinit quam esse desiit.

13. Ante triennium quam Carthago deleretur, M. Cato, perpetuus diruendae eius auctor, L. Censorino M'. Manilio[79] consulibus mortem obiit.

Eodem anno quo Carthago concidit, [A.][80] Mummius Corinthum post annos DCCCCLII quam ab Alete Hippotis[81] filio erat condita funditus eruit. uterque imperator
2 devictae a se gentis nomine honoratus, alter Africanus, alter appellatus est Achaicus; nec quisquam ex novis hominibus prior Mummio cognomen virtute partum vindicavit.
3 diversi imperatoribus mores, diversa fuere studia: quippe Scipio tam elegans liberalium studiorum omnisque doc-

---

[76] secl. *Woodman* (cf. 2.1.1)   [77] nota *Woodman*: nomen *P*: mo *A* (monitu *A^c*): monimentum *Baiter*

[78] nec quicquam ante *Cludius*: neque ante *PA*

[79] M'. Manilio *Sigonius*: M. Manlio *PA*

[80] secl. *Vossius*   [81] ab Alete Hippotis *Gelenius*: ab elete (*vel* a Belete) Hipponis *PA*

---

[49] In 146.

[50] The First Punic war began in 264.

[51] In the extant narrative, the famous M. Porcius Cato the

32

BOOK 1.12–13

Gnaeus Cornelius Lentulus and Lucius Mummius.[49] This was the end of the Roman Empire's rival, with whom our ancestors began to war in the consulship of Claudius and Fulvius,[50] 296 years before you embarked on your consulship, Marcus Vinicius. Thus, for 115 years, there was either war between the two peoples or preparation for war or a suspicious peace. Despite having overcome the whole world, Rome did not expect to be secure if any trace at all remained of Carthage's survival. So true is it that the hatred arising from contention lasts longer than the dread and is not laid aside even when one party is defeated, nor does something cease to be resented until it has ceased to be.

13. Three years before the destruction of Carthage, Marcus Cato, who had consistently proposed that it should be leveled, died in the consulship of Lucius Censorinus and Manius Manilius.[51]

In the same year that Carthage fell, Mummius razed Corinth to the ground 952 years after it had been founded by Aletes, the son of Hippotes. Each of the two commanders was honored by the name of the people he had defeated, one being called Africanus, the other Achaicus; nor did any new man before Mummius claim a cognomen won for his courage.[52] The commanders had different habits, different enthusiasms. Scipio was so elegant an

Elder (cos. 195, cens. 184) has been mentioned hitherto only at 1.7.3–4 but was presumably given full treatment in the vast lacuna that follows 1.8.6. See also 35.2.

[52] Since Mummius' father had been praetor in 177, the technical expression "new man" is here being used to indicate lack of a consular (as opposed to a senatorial) ancestor (cf. 2.1.4).

33

VELLEIUS PATERCULUS

trinae et auctor[82] et admirator fuit ut Polybium Panae-
tiumque, praecellentes ingenio viros, domi militiaeque
secum habuerit. neque enim quisquam hoc Scipione ele-
gantius intervalla negotiorum otio dispunxit semperque
aut belli aut pacis serviit artibus: semper inter arma ac
studia versatus aut corpus periculis aut animum disciplinis
4 exercuit. Mummius tam rudis fuit ut capta Corintho, cum
maximorum artificum perfectas manibus tabulas ac statuas in Italiam portandas locaret, iuberet praedici condu-
5 centibus, si eas perdidissent, novas eos reddituros. non
tamen puto dubites, ⟨M.⟩[83] Vinici, quin magis pro re publica fuerit manere adhuc rudem Corinthiorum intellec-
tum quam in tantum ea intellegi, et quin hac prudentia illa
imprudentia decori publico fuerit convenientior.

14. Cum facilius cuiusque reī in unum contracta species quam divisa temporibus oculis animisque inhaereat,
statui priorem huius voluminis posterioremque partem
non inutili rerum notitia in artum contracta distinguere
atque huic loco inserere quae quoque tempore post Romam a Gallis captam deducta sit colonia iussu senatus
(nam militarium et causae et auctores ex ipsarum praeful-
gent nomine).[84] huic rei per idem tempus civitatem pro-

---

82 fautor *Lipsius*
83 *suppl. Woodman*
84 ex . . . nomine *Heinsius*: et . . . nomina *PA*

---

53 Rome was taken by the Gauls in 390 BC (on the conventional chronology). The chronological indications in the following
list have some internal inconsistencies and often conflict with the
statements of other sources, especially Livy. For a tabulation of
V.'s chronological framework, see Bispham, 46–47. V. does not
distinguish between colonies founded with full citizen rights and

BOOK 1.13–14

author and admirer of liberal studies and of all learning that he kept Polybius and Panaetius, outstanding intellectuals, by his side at home and on campaign. For no one punctuated their activities more elegantly with interludes of inactivity than did Scipio: he was always devoted to his skills in war and peace, always to be found with his army or with his studies, exercising his body in times of danger or his mind through learning. Mummius was so unrefined that, when he captured Corinth and was contracting for the paintings and statues—products from the hands of the greatest artists—to be transported to Italy, he ordered the contractors to be told that, if they lost or damaged them, they would be replacing them with new ones. Yet I do not think you should doubt, Marcus Vinicius, that it was more to the commonwealth's benefit that appreciation of Corinthian wares should remain unrefined than that they should be appreciated as well as they are, and that that inexperience was more conducive to public seemliness than is the present expertise.

14. Since the impression that is made by something is implanted more easily in the mind's eye by being concentrated in one place rather than split up chronologically, I have decided to separate the earlier part of this volume from the later by listing things in a useful and concentrated manner and to insert at this point the names and dates of the colonies that were settled on the order of the senate after Rome's capture by the Gauls. (The origins and founders of the military colonies are self-evident from their names.)[53] It will not seem inappropriate if we weave

those whose settlers received only the so-called Latin right. By "military colonies" V. refers chiefly to the foundations of Sulla, Caesar, and Augustus.

35

VELLEIUS PATERCULUS

pagatam[85] auctumque Romanum nomen communione iuris haud intempestive subtexturi videmur.

2   Post septem annos quam Galli urbem ceperant,[86] Sutrium colonia deducta est et post annum Setia[87] novemque interiectis annis Nepe, deinde interpositis duobus
3 et triginta Aricini in civitatem recepti. abhinc annos autem CCCL[88] Sp. Postumio Veturio Calvino consulibus Campanis data est civitas partique Samnitium sine suffragio, et eodem anno Cales deducta colonia. interiecto deinde triennio Fundani et Formiani in civitatem recepti, eo ipso
4 anno quo Alexandria condita est. insequentibusque consulibus a Sp. Postumio Philone Publilio[89] censoribus Acerranis data civitas. et post triennium Tarracina[90] deducta colonia interpositoque quadriennio Luceria ac deinde interiecto triennio Suessa Aurunca et Saticula, Interam-
5 naque post biennium.[91] decem deinde hoc munere anni vacaverunt; tunc Sora atque Alba deductae coloniae et
6 Carseoli post biennium. at Q. Fabio quintum[92] Decio Mure quartum[93] consulibus, quo anno Pyrrhus regnare coepit, Sinuessam Minturnasque missi coloni, post qua-

---

85 civitatem propagatam *Lipsius*: -es -as *PA*
86 ceperant *Madvig*: -erunt *PA*
87 Setia *Aldus*: Sentina *PA*
88 CCCLX *Schott*: CCCLXII *Jani*
89 Publilio *Lipsius*: Publio *PA*
90 Tarracina *Lipsius*: -am *PA*
91 quinquennium *Rau*
92 at Q. Fabio quintum *Rhenanus*: ad quintum Fabioque *BPA*
93 quartum *Gelenius*: -o *BPA*

BOOK 1.14

into this the expansion of citizenship during the same period, and the extension of the Roman name by means of the sharing of rights.

Seven years after the Gauls captured the City, Sutrium was settled as a colony, and Setia a year later, and after an interval of nine years Nepe, and then after thirty-two intervening years the people of Aricia were received into citizenship. Three hundred and fifty years ago, in the consulship of Spurius Postumius and Veturius Calvinus,[54] citizenship without the vote was given to the Campanians and some of the Samnites, and in the same year Cales was settled as a colony. After a three-year interval the people of Fundi and Formiae were received into citizenship, the very year that Alexandria was founded; and under subsequent consuls citizenship was given to the people of Acerrae by the censors Spurius Postumius and Philo Publilius.[55] After three years Tarracina was settled as a colony, and after four intervening years Luceria, and then after a three-year interval Suessa Aurunca and Saticula, and Interamna two years later. The next ten years were free of this beneficial responsibility; then Sora and Alba[56] were settled as colonies, and Carseoli two years later. In Quintus Fabius' fifth and Decius Mus' fourth consulship,[57] the year when Pyrrhus began his rule,[58] colonists were sent to Sinuessa and Minturnae, and to Venusia four years later;

[54] In 334.   [55] In 332. Like some other Latin authors, V. frequently transposes a person's gentile name and cognomen, as here with Q. Publilius Philo and, just below, with P. Cornelius Rufinus.   [56] That is, Alba Fucens.   [57] In 295.

[58] Pyrrhus (319–272) was king of Epirus and a famously fierce enemy of Rome in 280 to 275.

37

VELLEIUS PATERCULUS

driennium Venusiam; interiectoque biennio M'. Curio et
Rufino Cornelio consulibus Sabinis sine suffragio data
7 civitas; id actum ante annos ferme CCCXX.[94] at Cosam et
Paestum abhinc annos ferme trecentos Fabio Dorsone et
Claudio Canina consulibus, interiecto<que>[95] quinquen-
nio Sempronio Sopho et Appio Caeci filio consulibus Ariminum <et>[96] Beneventum coloni missi et suffragii fe-
8 rendi ius Sabinis datum. at initio primi belli Punici Firmum
et Castrum colonis occupata, et post annum Aesernia
postque XVII[97] annos Aefula[98] et Alsium Fregenaeque[99]
[anno][100] post biennium proximoque anno Torquato Sem-
pronioque consulibus Brundisium et post triennium Spoletium, quo anno Floralium ludorum factum est initium.
postque biennium <de>ducta[101] Valentia et sub adventum
in Italiam Hannibalis Cremona atque Placentia.

15. Deinde neque dum Hannibal in Italia moratur neque proximis post excessum eius annis vacavit Romanis
colonias condere, cum esset in bello conquirendus potius
miles quam dimittendus et post bellum vires refovendae
2 magis quam spargendae. Cn. autem Manlio Vulsone et
Fulvio Nobiliore consulibus Bononia deducta colonia
abhinc annos ferme CCXVII, et post quadriennium Pisaurum ac Potentia interiectoque triennio Aquileia et Gra-
3 visca et post quadriennium Luna.[102] eodem temporum

94 CCCXX *BA*: CCCXXX *P*
95 interiecto<que> *Madvig*
96 *suppl. Jani*   97 XVII *Sigonius*: XXII *PA*
98 Aefula *Woodman*: Aefulum *A, obelis not. Watt*: Aesulum *P*
99 Fregenaeque *Sigonius*: Fregellaeque *PA*
100 *secl. Gelenius*   101 <de>ducta *Gelenius*
102 Luna *Madvig*: Luca *PA*

38

BOOK 1.14–15

and after a two-year interval, in the consulship of Manius Curius and Rufinus Cornelius,[59] citizenship without the vote was given to the Sabines: that was done about 320 years before now. About three hundred years ago, in the consulship of Fabius Dorso and Claudius Canina,[60] colonists were sent to Cosa and Paestum, and after a five-year interval, in the consulship of Sempronius Sophus and Appius,[61] the son of Caecus, to Ariminum and Beneventum, and the right of casting votes was given to the Sabines. At the start of the First Punic War[62] Firmum and Castrum were taken over by colonists, as were Aesernia a year later and Aefula seventeen years later and Alsium and Fregenae two years later, and in the next year, in the consulship of Torquatus and Sempronius,[63] Brundisium and, three years later, Spoletium, the year in which Flora's Games started.[64] After a two-year period Valentia was settled and, just before Hannibal's arrival in Italy, Cremona and Placentia.

15. Subsequently, neither while Hannibal was loitering in Italy nor in the years immediately following his departure did the Romans have any scope to found colonies, since during the war it was more important to find soldiers than to dispatch them and after the war forces needed to be replenished rather than dispersed. But in the consulship of Gnaeus Manlius Vulso and Fulvius Nobilior[65] Bononia was settled as a colony roughly 217 years ago, and four years later Pisaurum and Potentia, and after a three-year interval Aquileia and Gravisca, and Luna four years

[59] In 290. [60] In 273; V. is alone in giving Fabius' cognomen as Dorso rather than Licinus. [61] In 268. [62] In 264. [63] In 245. [64] The festival of the Floralia was held on 28 April. [65] In 189.

39

VELLEIUS PATERCULUS

tractu, quamquam apud quosdam ambigitur, Puteolos Salernumque[103] et Buxentum missi coloni, Auximum autem in Picenum abhinc annos ferme CLXXXVII, ante triennium quam Cassius censor a Lupercali in Palatium versus theatrum facere instituit, cui in eo moliendo[104] eximia civitatis severitas et consul Caepio[105] restitere, quod ego inter clarissima publicae voluntatis argumenta numeraverim.

4 Cassio autem Longino et Sextio Calvino, qui Sallues[106] apud aquas quae ab eo Sextiae appellantur devicit, consulibus Fabrateria deducta est abhinc annos ferme CLIIII.[107] et post annum Scolacium Minervia,[108] Tarentum Neptunia Carthagoque, ⟨quae⟩[109] in Africa prima (ut praediximus) extra Italiam colonia condita est. de Dertona

5 ambigitur; Narbo autem Martius in Gallia Porcio Marcioque[110] consulibus abhinc annos circiter CXLVIII[111] colonia deducta est. post XVIII[112] annos in Bagiennis

103 Salernumque *Gelenius*: Falernumque *PA*
104 in eo moliendo *Riguez*: in demoliendo *PA*
105 Cepio *P (litura in A)*: Scipio *Aldus*
106 Sallues *BA*: Sallyes *P*   107 CLIIII *E. Thomas*: CLVII *PA*
108 Minervia *Stegmann*: -ium *PA*
109 *suppl. Vossius*   110 Marcioque *Vossius (Q. Marcio iam Gelenius)*: Marcoque *PA*
111 CXLVIII *E. Thomas*: CLIII *PA*
112 XVIII *Aldus*: tres et viginti *PA*

66 The Lupercal was a large cave at the foot of the southern side of the Palatine Hill (1.8.4n) and reputedly the place where Romulus and Remus were suckled by the wolf; the area was renovated by Augustus (*Res Gestae* 19.1). V.'s orientation of the theater is not at all clear.

40

BOOK 1.15

later. During the same tract of time, although there is uncertainty in some authors, colonists were sent to Puteoli, Salernum, and Buxentum, and to Auxinum in Picenum about 187 years ago—three years before Cassius as censor started to build a theater from the Lupercal facing the Palatine,[66] in the construction of which he met resistance from the community's extreme strictness and from Caepio as consul,[67] which I would count among the clearest proofs of the public disposition. When Cassius Longinus and Sextius Calvinus, who defeated the Sallues at the waters that are called Sextiae after him,[68] were consuls,[69] Fabrateria was settled about 154 years ago; and a year later Scolacium Minervia, Tarentum Neptunia, and Carthage in Africa, which was the first colony founded outside Italy, as we mentioned earlier.[70] About Dertona there is uncertainty; but Narbo Martius in Gaul was settled as a colony in the consulship of Porcius and Marcius,[71] around 148 years ago, and eighteen years later Eporedia among the Bagienni

[67] C. Cassius Longinus (cos. 171) and M. Valerius Messalla (cos. 161) as censors in 154 contracted for the building of a stone theater, which would have been the first in Rome, but ca. 151 P. Scipio Nasica (2.3.1n) persuaded the senate to stop its construction (Livy, *Epit.* 48; Val. Max. 2.4.2). V.'s reference to a consul Caepio (whose name Aldus wished to emend to *Scipio*) may result from confusion with a later episode in 106 (App. *B Civ.* 1.28.125), when the consul Q. Servilius Caepio demolished a theater being built by L. Cassius Longinus (cos. 107). See Wiseman in Cowan, 280–82.

[68] That is, Aquae Sextiae (mod. Aix-en-Provence).

[69] In 124.

[70] The reference must have been in a part of the text that is now lost. Cf. 2.7.7, below.   [71] In 118.

41

VELLEIUS PATERCULUS

Eporedia Mario sextum[113] Valerioque Flacco consulibus. neque facile memoriae mandaverim quae nisi militaris post hoc tempus deducta sit.

16. Cum haec particula operis velut formam propositi excesserit, quamquam intellego mihi in hac tam praecipiti festinatione, quae me rotae pronive gurgitis [ac[114] verticis][115] modo nusquam patitur consistere, paene magis necessaria praetereunda quam supervacua amplectenda, nequeo tamen temperare mihi quin rem saepe agitatam animo meo neque ad liquidum ratione perductam signem

2 stilo. quis enim abunde mirari potest quod eminentissima cuiusque professionis ingenia in ean⟨dem⟩[116] formam et in idem artati[117] temporis congruere spatium, et, quemadmodum clausa[118] pascuo[119] aliove[120] saepto diversi generis animalia nihilo minus separata ⟨ab⟩[121] alienis in unum quaeque[122] corpus congregantur, ita cuiusque clari operis capacia ingenia in similitudine et temporum et profectuum semet ipsa ab aliis separaverunt?

3 Una neque multorum annorum spatio divisa aetas per divini spiritus viros, Aeschylum, Sophoclen, Euripiden, inlustravit tragoediam;[123] una priscam illam et veterem sub ·Cratino, Aristophane et Eupolide comoediam; ac

---

[113] Mario sextum *Cludius*: Mario sexiens *BA*: sexies, Mario sexies *P*   [114] ac *PA*: aut *Watt*   [115] ac verticis *PA, secl. Ruhnken* (pronive verticis ac gurgitis *Kritz*)   [116] ean⟨dem⟩ *Rhenanus*: eam *PA*: unam *Lipsius*   [117] artata *Acidalius*: artatum *Watt*   [118] ⟨eodem⟩ clausa (clauso *A*) *Castiglioni*
[119] pascuo *Delz*: capso *BA*: capsa *P*: campo *Watt*
[120] aliove *Acidalius*: alioque *PA*   [121] *suppl. Vascosanus*
[122] quaeque *Lipsius*: quoque *PA*: quodque *Heinsius*
[123] tragoediam *Lipsius*: -as *PA*

42

BOOK 1.15–16

in the consulship of Marius (for the sixth time) and Valerius Flaccus.[72] It would not be easy for me to place on record any settlements after this date apart from military ones.

16. Despite this section of my work having exceeded (as it were) the form of that which I intended, and although I realize that in my present very headlong haste—which like a wheel or waterfall [and whirlpool] does not allow me to stop anywhere—it is almost more important to pass over what is necessary than to embrace what is superfluous, nevertheless I cannot refrain from putting down in writing a matter that I have often tossed around in my mind but of which I have failed to produce a rational clarification. For who can wonder sufficiently that the most outstanding talents of each profession have clustered in the same genre and in the same narrow period of time and that, just as animals of different kinds, when they are shut up in a pasture or other enclosure, still isolate themselves from the alien ones and they each flock together into their own single group, so the capable talents in the various distinguished genres have isolated themselves from others in terms of their similar time and success?

One era, divided off in a period of not many years, lit up tragedy with men of divine inspiration, Aeschylus, Sophocles, Euripides;[73] another did the same for the famous early genre of old comedy under Cratinus, Aristophanes and Eupolis;[74] as for new comedy, Menander, as well

---

[72] In 100.

[73] Aeschylus died in 456, Sophocles and Euripides in 406.

[74] Cratinus died in 422, Aristophanes ca. 386, Eupolis ca. 412.

VELLEIUS PATERCULUS

novam [comicam][124] Menander aequalesque eius aetatis magis quam operis, Philemon ac Diphilus, et invenere intra paucissimos annos neque imitandam[125] reliquere.

4 philosophorum quoque ingenia Socratico ore defluentia omnium, quos paulo ante enumeravimus, quanto post Pla-

5 tonis Aristotelisque mortem floruere spatio? quid ante Isocratem, quid post eius auditores eorumque discipulos clarum in oratoribus fuit? adeo quidem artatum angustiis temporum ut nemo memoria dignus alter ab altero videri nequiverint.

17. Neque hoc in Graecis quam in Romanis evenit magis. nam nisi aspera ac rudia repetas et inventi laudanda nomine, et ut Livium quoque priorum aetati adstruas,[126] in Accio circaque eum <ingeniis>[127] Romana tragoedia est, dulcesque Latini leporis facetiae per Caecilium Teren-

2 tiumque et Afranium subpari aetate nituerunt. historicos

---

[124] comicam *PA, secl. Acidalius*: comoediam *Gruner*

[125] imitandam *Acidalius*: -a *PA*

[126] et ut . . . adstruas, *tradita post* historicos *(1.17.2), huc transpos. Woodman*   [127] *suppl. Woodman*

---

[75] Menander, ?344/3–292/1; Philemon, 368/60–267/63; Diphilus was born in the decade 360–350.

[76] This must have been in a part of the text that is now lost.

[77] Plato died ca. 347, Aristotle in 322.

[78] Isocrates, 436–338. It is strange that Demosthenes (384–322) is not mentioned by name.

[79] This seems to be a reference to Cn. Naevius (280/60–200), regarded as the inventor of *fabula praetexta* (a form of Latin tragedy) and dispraised by Ennius (*Ann.* 206–7 Skutsch).

[80] Livius is Livius Andronicus, if the transposition suggested in the text is accepted (see *Histos* 15 [2021]: 283–88). Livius'

BOOK 1.16–17

as Philemon and Diphilus (his peers in terms of their era rather than their work), invented it within a very few years and left it without imitators.[75] And also the talented philosophers whose source was the mouth of Socrates, all of whom we listed a little earlier[76]—how long did they flourish after the deaths of Plato and Aristotle?[77] Among orators what distinction was there either before Isocrates or after his auditors and their disciples?[78] It was so confined within a narrow band of time that no single memorable individual could not have been seen by another.

17. Nor did this happen more among the Greeks than the Romans. For, unless you go back to the rough crudities that deserve praise only on account of their invention,[79] and if you add Livius too to the generation of earlier writers,[80] Roman tragedy is embodied in Accius and the talents around his time,[81] and the delightful witticisms of Latin humor shone brightly through Caecilius, Terentius, and Afranius in almost the same generation.[82] Historians,

---

dates are usually placed ca. 280/70–200, though he was dated significantly later by Accius (cf. Cic. *Brut.* 72–74). He was dispraised by Cicero (*Brut.* 71) but famous as a literary pioneer (e.g., Cic. *Brut.* 72; Livy 7.2.8; Val. Max. 2.4.4) and is credited with the titles of at least eight tragedies and three comedies. If the transposition is not accepted, Livius will be the historian Livy, and "earlier writers" will be a reference to some of the numerous historians—almost all of them now fragmentary—who preceded him. See 36.2–3.

[81] Accius' dates are 170–86.

[82] Caecilius, 220–166; Terence, 195–159; Afranius flourished in the second half of the second century BC. The omission of Plautus' name (fl. ca. 200) is striking.

VELLEIUS PATERCULUS

praeter Catonem et quosdam veteres et obscuros minus
octoginta annis circumdatum aevum tulit, ut nec poeta-
3 rum in antiquius citeriusve processit ubertas. at oratio ac
vis forensis perfectumque prosae eloquentiae decus, ut
idem separetur Cato (pace P. Crassi Scipionisque et Laelii
et Gracchorum et Fannii et Servii Galbae dixerim) ita
universa sub principe operis sui erupit Tullio ut delectari
ante eum paucissimis, mirari vero neminem possis nisi
4 aut ab illo visum aut qui illum viderit. hoc idem evenisse
grammaticis, plastis, pictoribus, scalptoribus quisquis
temporum institerit notis reperiet, eminentiam cuiusque
operis artissimis temporum claustris circumdatam.
5   Huius ergo recidentis in ‹suum quod›que saeculum[128]
ingeniorum similitudinis congregantisque se et in studium
par et in emolumentum causas cum saepe requiro, numquam reperio quas esse veras confidam, sed fortasse veri
6 similes, inter quas has maxime. alit aemulatio ingenia, et
nunc invidia, nunc admiratio imitationem[129] accendit,
matureque[130] quod summo studio petitum est ascendit in
summum difficilisque in perfecto mora est, naturaliterque

[128] recidentis *Cornelissen,* in ‹suum quod›que saeculum
Madvig: recedentis mq. seculum *B:* praecedentisque seculi *P (Ȧ*
vix legi potest)
[129] imitationem *Acidalius:* incitationem *PA*
[130] matureque *Acidalius:* naturaque *PA*

BOOK 1.17

apart from Cato and some old and obscure figures,[83] were produced in a circumscribed epoch of less than eighty years; similarly neither did the abundant crop of poets spring up in an earlier or nearer season than it did. Oratory and effectiveness in the forum and the glorious perfection of prose eloquence, if Cato may again be set aside (and I speak with all due respect to Publius Crassus, Scipio, Laelius, the Gracchi, Fannius, and Servius Galba),[84] burst forth so completely under Tullius, the principal figure in his genre, that there were very few before him in whom one could take pleasure and no one whom one could admire except who was seen by him or who saw him. Anyone who pauses over the date markers[85] will find that there has been the same phenomenon among grammarians, masons, painters, and sculptors and that outstanding quality in each genre is circumscribed by the narrowest chronological boundaries.

On the many occasions when I seek reasons for this similarity of talents, which each fall into their own particular period and flock together in the same rewarding artistic endeavor, I never find any that I am confident are true, but perhaps some that are plausible, among which there are especially the following. Emulation nourishes talents, and sometimes it is envy, sometimes admiration that fires imitation, and that which has been sought with the highest enthusiasm will rise quickly to the highest point, and, since it is difficult to remain at a level of perfec-

[83] Cato's dates are 234–149.

[84] P. Licinius Crassus Mucianus was consul in 131; the others recur at 2.9.1–2 (nn).   [85] Seemingly a reference to marking special dates on a calendar or tabular chronicle, etc.

47

VELLEIUS PATERCULUS

7 quod procedere non potest recedit. et ut primo ad conse-
quendos quos priores ducimus accendimur, ita ubi aut
praeteriri aut aequari eos posse desperavimus, studium
cum spe senescit, et quod adsequi non potest sequi desinit
et velut occupatam relinquens materiam quaerit novam,
praeteritoque eo in quo eminere non possumus aliquid in
quo niteamus[131] conquirimus, sequiturque ut frequens ac
mobilis transitus maximum perfecti operis impedimen-
tum sit.

18. Transit admiratio ab condicione[132] temporum
[et][133] ad urbium. una urbs Attica pluribus annis[134] eloquentiae operibusque[135] quam universa Graecia floruit,
adeo ut corpora gentis illius separata sint in alias civitates,
ingenia vero solis Atheniensium muris clausa existimes.

2 neque hoc ego magis miratus sim quam neminem Argi-
vum, Thebanum, Lacedaemonium oratorem aut dum vixit
auctoritate aut post mortem memoria dignum existima-
3 tum. quae urbes talium[136] studiorum fuere steriles, nisi[137]
Thebas unum os Pindari inluminaret: nam Alcmana La-
cones falso sibi vindicant.

131 niteamus *Cludius*: nitamur *PA*
132 ad conditionem *PA, corr. Schegk*
133 *secl. Gruner*
134 annis *PA*: <praest>antis *Watt (qui et* hominibus *ante* operibusque *suppl.)*
135 operibusque (*post* Graecia *PA*) *huc transpos. Woodman*
136 talium *P*: et initalia (in Italia *A*) talium *BA*
137 nisi *BA*: ni *P*

48

BOOK 1.17–18

tion, that which cannot proceed will naturally recede. Just as at first we are fired to overtake those whom we consider leaders, so, whenever we despair of being able to overhaul or draw level with them, enthusiasm wilts along with hope, and one stops running after that which one cannot run down, and, leaving the source material as being already appropriated, one searches for new, and, skirting that in which we cannot be outstanding, we seek something in which we can shine, and it follows that frequent and volatile switching is the greatest impediment to generic perfection.

18. Our wonder switches from the situation with periods to that with cities. One Attic city flourished in eloquence for more years and in more works than did the whole of Greece, such that you would think the bodies of that nation were distributed between the different communities but their intellects enclosed within the walls of Athens alone. And I no more wonder at this than at the fact that no Argive, Theban, or Lacedaemonian orator was either esteemed for his influence while he lived or was thought memorable after his death. These cities were barren of such artistic endeavors, were it not that Thebes was lit up by the single voice of Pindar. (The Laconians' claim to Alcman is false.)

49

LIBER POSTERIOR

1. Potentiae Romanorum prior Scipio viam aperuerat, luxuriae posterior aperuit: quippe remoto Carthaginis metu sublataque imperii aemula non gradu sed praecipiti cursu a virtute descitum, ad vitia transcursum; vetus disciplina deserta, nova inducta; in somnum a vigiliis, ab armis ad voluptates, a negotiis in otium conversa civitas. tum Scipio Nasica in Capitolio porticus, tum quas praediximus Metellus, tum in circo Cn. Octavius multo amoenissimam moliti sunt, publicamque magnificentiam secuta privata luxuria est.

3   Triste deinde et contumeliosum bellum in Hispania duce latronum Viriatho secutum est, quod ita varia fortuna gestum est ut saepius Romanorum gereretur adversa. sed interempto Viriatho fraude magis quam virtute Servilii

---

[1] P. Cornelius Scipio Africanus (cos. 205, 194) defeated Hannibal at the battle of Zama (202) and brought the Second Punic War to an end (cf. 1.6.[6]); P. Cornelius Scipio Aemilianus Africanus (cos. 147, 134) destroyed Carthage in 146 (1.12.5–7).

[2] See 2.3.1. The Latin word *Capitolium* is used both for the Capitoline Hill and for the complex of buildings upon it, among them the temple of Capitoline Jupiter (131.1).

[3] See 1.11.3.

50

BOOK TWO

1. The earlier Scipio had opened up the Romans' road to power, the later opened up their road to luxury:[1] with the dread of Carthage removed and the empire's rival eliminated, it was not step by step but at a headlong pace that there was a defection from virtue and a transfer to vice. The old discipline was abandoned, the new introduced: the community turned from vigilance to somnolence, from weapons to pleasures, from action to inactivity. That was when Scipio Nasica constructed his portico on the Capitol,[2] Metellus the one that we mentioned earlier,[3] and Gnaeus Octavius much the most picturesque, in the circus,[4] and public grandeur was followed by personal luxury.

Next there followed a bitter and humiliating war in Spain, with Viriathus leading the bandits, which was waged with such variable fortune that quite often it was waged to the Romans' disadvantage. But, when Viriathus was killed (more by the deceit of Servilius Caepio than by

[4] The portico, known as the Porticus Octavia (and not to be confused with the Porticus Octaviae, mentioned at 1.11.3), was built by Octavius near the Circus Flaminius between 167 and 163 following his naval command (1.9.4–5); its restoration by Augustus (*Res Gestae* 19.1) explains V.'s description of it.

51

VELLEIUS PATERCULUS

4 Caepionis Numantinum gravius exarsit. haec urbs numquam plura quam X ‹milia›[1] propriae iuventutis armavit, sed vel ferocia ingenii vel inscitia nostrorum ducum vel Fortunae indulgentia cum alios duces tum Pompeium (magni nominis virum) ad turpissima deduxit foedera (hic primus e Pompeiis consul fuit),[2] nec minus turpia ac
5 detestabilia Mancinum Hostilium consulem. sed Pompeium gratia impunitum habuit, Mancinum verecundia [quippe non recusando][3] perduxit huc ut per fetiales nudus ac post tergum religatis manibus dederetur hostibus. quem illi recipere se negaverunt, sicut quondam Caudini fecerunt,[4] dicentes publicam violationem fidei non debere unius lui sanguine.

2. Immanem deditio Mancini civitatis movit dissensionem. quippe Ti. Gracchus, Ti. Gracchi clarissimi atque

---

[1] plura quam X ‹milia› *Aldus:* X plura quam *PA*^{c}

[2] hic . . . fuit *secl. ed. Bipont., Kreyssig, fort. recte*

[3] *secl. Krause:* quippe ‹culpam› non recusando *nescioquis: alii alia*

[4] fecerant *Heinsius*

---

[5] Viriathus was the leader of the Lusitani. Successive Roman commanders in Further (i.e., western) Spain campaigned against him from ca. 146 until Q. Servilius Caepio (cos. 140) arranged for him to be killed in 139.

[6] Numantia was a leading town of the Celtiberi, against whom Roman commanders in the province of Nearer Spain campaigned in 155–151 and 143–133.

[7] Q. Pompeius (cos. 141) and C. Hostilius Mancinus (cos. 137) arranged treaties with the Numantines in 139 and 137, respectively, but the senate refused to ratify either of them.

52

BOOK 2.1–2

his bravery),[5] the more serious Numantine War flared up.[6] This city never armed more than ten thousand of its own young men, but, either because of an innate defiance or our leaders' incompetence or the indulgence of Fortune, it reduced our leaders in general and especially Pompeius (a man of great name) to the most disgraceful treaties (he was the first of the Pompeii to be consul), and the consul Mancinus Hostilius to treaties no less disgraceful and execrable.[7] But, whereas popularity or influence kept Pompeius unpunished, a sense of shame [namely, by not refusing] brought Mancinus to the point where, through the agency of the fetials,[8] he was surrendered, naked and with his hands bound behind his back, to the enemy. But, like the Caudini on a previous occasion,[9] they refused to receive him, saying that an official violation of trust ought not to be expiated by the blood of an individual.

2. The surrender of Mancinus caused a prodigious split in the community. Tiberius Gracchus, son of the very distinguished and outstanding Tiberius Gracchus, and grand-

[8] Priests concerned with treaties and declarations of war, one of whose roles was to carry out the surrender to another people of any Roman who had broken a treaty with them or who had violated their ambassadors. The words deleted as an intrusive gloss may rather be evidence of more extensive corruption; it is impossible to know.

[9] In 320 the Caudini, a Samnite tribe, were famously said to have trapped a Roman force at the Caudine Forks, from where it was extricated only by a humiliating treaty, later repudiated (Livy 9.8–11). The tradition is often supposed to be a fiction imitating the events of 137.

53

VELLEIUS PATERCULUS

eminentissimi viri filius, P. Africani ex filia nepos, quo
2 quaestore et auctore id foedus ictum erat, nunc graviter
ferens aliquid a se pactum[5] infirmari, nunc similis vel iudi-
cii vel poenae metuens discrimen, tribunus plebis creatus,
vir alioqui vita innocentissimus, ingenio florentissimus,
proposito sanctissimus, tantis denique adornatus virtutibus quantas perfecta et natura et industria mortalis condicio recipit, P. Mucio Scaevola L. Calpurnio consulibus
abhinc annos CLXII descivit a bonis, pollicitusque toti
3 Italiae civitatem, simul etiam promulgatis agrariis legibus,
omnibus statum[6] concupiscentibus, summa imis miscuit et
in praeruptum atque anceps periculum adduxit rem publicam. Octavioque collegae pro bono publico stanti imperium abrogavit, triumviros agris dividendis coloniisque
deducendis creavit se socerumque suum, consularem
Appium, et Gaium[7] fratrem admodum iuvenem.

5 pactum *Kreyssig*: factum *PA*
6 statum *P, obelis not. Watt*^{2}: factum *A*: statum ‹novum› *Halm*
7 Gaium *Halm*: Gracchum *PA*

---

10 Ti. Sempronius Gracchus (trib. pleb. 133) was son of the
consul of 177 and 163 and Cornelia, daughter of Scipio Africanus
(2.1.1n). He served as quaestor under Mancinus at Numantia.

11 In 133. The expression "the good men" (*boni*), common in
political texts, is used approvingly of those who, usually wealthy,
support the status quo; an alternative term is "optimates" (2.3.2,
20.3, 31.4, 40.5, 47.3), *optimus* being the superlative form of the
Latin *bonus*.

12 Reviving the ban on holding land in excess of 500 *iugera*
(about 330 acres), originally imposed by the Licinian law in 367
(cf. 2.6.3), Tiberius Gracchus proposed a law establishing a com-

54

BOOK 2.2

son of Publius Africanus through his daughter,[10] had had responsibility for striking that treaty during his quaestorship, and he was not only taking it badly that an agreement of his was being disabled but he was dreading the predicament of a similar verdict or punishment. Appointed tribune of the plebs, this man—otherwise of a totally blameless life, fertile in intellect and scrupulous of purpose, equipped, in short, with virtues as great as any allowed by the mortal condition when it is brought to perfection by nature and application—defected from the good men when Publius Mucius Scaevola and Lucius Calpurnius were consuls 162 years ago,[11] and, promising citizenship to the whole of Italy and simultaneously promulgating land laws at a time when everyone craved some standing,[12] he turned everything topsy-turvy and brought the commonwealth into a precipitate and critical danger. He revoked the command of his colleague Octavius, whose stance was that of support for the public good,[13] and, as triumvirs for dividing up land and settling colonies, he appointed himself, his father-in-law (the ex-consul Appius[14]) and his brother Gaius, still just a young man.

mission to recover public land held over this limit and to distribute it in allotments. V.'s claims that Tiberius also promised citizenship to the Italians is supported by no other source and probably arose through confusion with the later activity of his brother Gaius.

[13] M. Octavius as a fellow tribune persisted in using his veto against the land law, which was passed only when Gracchus carried a law deposing him from office.

[14] Ap. Claudius Pulcher (cos. 143).

VELLEIUS PATERCULUS

3. Tum P. Scipio Nasica, eius qui optimus vir a senatu iudicatus erat nepos, eius qui censor porticus in Capitolio fecerat filius, pronepos autem Cn. Scipionis, celeberrimi viri P. Africani patrui,[8] privatusque et togatus, cum esset consobrinus Ti. Gracchi, patriam cognationi praeferens et quidquid publice salutare non esset privato[9] alienum existimans (ob eas virtutes primus omnium absens pontifex maximus factus est), circumdata[10] laevo bracchio togae lacinia ex superiore parte Capitolii summis gradibus insistens hortatus est,[11] qui salvam vellent rem publicam, se 2 sequerentur. tum optimates, senatus, atque equestris ordinis pars melior et maior, et intacta perniciosis consiliis plebs inruere in Gracchum stantem in area cum catervis suis et concientem paene totius Italiae frequentiam. is fugiens decurrensque clivo Capitolino, fragmine subsellii ictus vitam, quam gloriosissime degere potuerat, immatura morte finivit.

---

[8] patrui *Gelenius*: -us *PA*: patrui is *Aldus*
[9] privato *Woodman*: -tim *P*: -tum *A*   [10] circumdata
Puteanus, Aldus: cum data *PA*   [11] est ‹ut› *Novák*

---

[15] The great-grandfather of P. Cornelius Scipio Nasica Serapio (cos. 138) was Cn. Cornelius Scipio Calvus (cos. 222); his grandfather was P. Cornelius Scipio Nasica (cos. 191), who in 204 was judged the best man in the state and hence suitable to receive the Great Mother goddess when she arrived in Italy (Livy 29.14.6–8); and his father was P. Cornelius Scipio Nasica Corculum (cos. 162 and 155, censor 159: see 2.1.2).

[16] The descriptions "private" and "in a toga" both denote someone of merely civilian status, holding no public office, although the toga is about to play a role in the narrative as well.

[17] Scipio's exhortation is expressed in a formula used during a

BOOK 2.3

3. Then, although Publius Scipio Nasica—grandson of the man who had been adjudged "best" by the senate, son of the man who as censor had built the portico on the Capitol, and great-grandson of Gnaeus Scipio, uncle of the celebrated Publius Africanus[15]—was a private person and in a toga[16] and a cousin of Tiberius Gracchus, nevertheless, giving his fatherland precedence over his relationship and believing that whatever was not conducive to the common weal was unworthy of a private person (it was on account of these virtues that he was the first to be made Chief Pontiff in his absence), he wrapped the hem of his toga around his left arm and, standing on the top steps on the upper part of the Capitol, he urged that anyone who wanted the well-being of the commonwealth should follow him.[17] Thereupon the optimates, the senate, the better and greater part of the equestrian order,[18] and those of the plebs who remained untouched by the man's destructive plans, all rushed at Gracchus as he was standing in the precinct with his groups of supporters and stirring up a crowd from almost everywhere in Italy. Running down Capitoline Bank to escape,[19] he was struck with a piece of broken bench and ended by an untimely death a life that he could have spent in the greatest glory.

state of emergency (see, e.g., Kaster on Cic. *Sest.* 128); his deployment of his toga also seems ritualistic, but its significance is disputed.   [18] The term "order" is used technically to denote persons of a particular sociopolitical class, especially the equestrians (as here and at 76.4, 127.3) and the senate (2.13.2, 28.3, 35.3, 69.5); these two are often designated by the expressions "each order" or "both orders" (32.3, 34.3, 50.4, 100.5).

[19] Capitoline Bank was a street that led from the Capitol to the forum.

57

VELLEIUS PATERCULUS

3   Hoc initium in urbe Roma civilis sanguinis gladiorum-
que impunitatis fuit. inde ius vi obrutum potentiorque
habitus prior, discordiaeque civium antea condicionibus
sanari solitae ferro diiudicatae bellaque non causis inita
4 sed prout eorum merces fuit. quod haud mirum est: non
enim ibi consistunt exempla unde coeperunt, sed quamlibet in tenuem recepta tramitem latissime evagando[12] sibi
viam faciunt, et, ubi semel recto deerratum est, in praeceps pervenitur, nec quisquam sibi[13] putat turpe quod alii
fuit fructuosum.

4. Interim, dum haec in Italia geruntur, Aristonicus,
qui mortuo rege Attalo a quo Asia populo Romano here-
ditate relicta erat, sicut relicta postea est a Nicomede Bithynia, mentitus regiae stirpis originem armis eam occupaverat, is[14] victus a M. Perpenna ductusque in triumpho
(sed a M'. Aquilio) capite poenas dedit, cum initio belli
Crassum Mucianum, virum iuris scientissimum, deceden-
tem ex Asia[15] proconsulem interemisset.

2   Et P. Scipio Africanus Aemilianus, qui Carthaginem
deleverat, post tot acceptas circa Numantiam clades crea-

12 evagando *Woodman*: -di *PA*
13 sibi *BA, om. P*
14 [is] *Vossius*
15 Asia *P*: alia *A* (Italia *A^c*)

---

20 Attalus III, the last king of Pergamum, died in 133. Nicomedes' bequest of his kingdom of Bithynia, to which V. refers at
39.2, led to the outbreak of Rome's final war with Mithridates
in 74.

21 P. Licinius Crassus Dives Mucianus (cos. 131) was proconsul of Asia in 130, when he was killed; he was succeeded by M.

BOOK 2.3–4

This was the beginning of civil bloodshed and of license for the sword in the City of Rome. Henceforward right was overwhelmed by might; the more powerful were held to have priority; disagreements between citizens, which previously were accustomed to be healed by pacts, were decided by steel; wars were embarked upon, not for a reason, but depending on their profitability. And no wonder: precedents do not stop at the point from which they start but, no matter how tiny the track on which they gain entrance, they make a way for themselves by roaming widely, and, whenever there is deviation from the right route, a precipice is reached, and no one thinks that something is shameful for himself if it was gainful for another.

4. In the meantime, while these things were happening in Italy, Aristonicus—who on the death of King Attalus (by whom Asia had been left as an inheritance to the Roman people, as was Bithynia afterward by Nicomedes)[20] had falsely claimed descent from the royal stock and had seized the province by arms—was conquered by Marcus Perpenna and, having been led in triumph (but by Manius Aquilius), he was punished with his life, since at the start of the war he had killed Crassus Mucianus, a man very expert in the law, on his departure from Asia as proconsul.[21]

And, after the many defeats experienced around Numantia, Publius Scipio Africanus Aemilianus, who had destroyed Carthage, was appointed consul for a second

Perpenna as consul (130), who himself was succeeded by M'. Aquilius (cos. 129), who returned from his proconsulship of Asia in 126 and celebrated a triumph (11 November).

59

VELLEIUS PATERCULUS

tus iterum consul missusque in Hispaniam fortunae virtutique expertae in Africa respondit in Hispania, et intra annum ac tres menses quam eo venerat circumdatam

3 operibus Numantiam excisamque aequavit solo. nec quisquam ullius gentis hominum ante eum clariore[16] urbium excidio nomen suum perpetuae commendavit memoriae: quippe excisa Carthagine ac Numantia ab alterius nos

4 metu, alterius vindicavit contumeliis. hic, eum interrogante tribuno Carbone quid de Ti. Gracchi caede sentiret, respondit, si is occupandae rei publicae animum habuisset, iure caesum. et cum omnis contio acclamasset, "hostium," inquit, "armatorum totiens clamore non territus, qui possum vestro moveri, quorum noverca est Italia?"

5 reversus in urbem intra breve tempus, M'. Aquilio C. Sempronio consulibus abhinc annos CLX,[17] post duos consulatus duosque triumphos et bis excisos terrores rei publicae mane in lectulo repertus est mortuus, ita ut quae-

6 dam elisarum faucium in cervice reperirentur notae. de tanti viri morte nulla habita est quaestio, eiusque corpus velato capite elatum est cuius opera super totum terrarum orbem Roma extulerat caput. seu fatalem, ut plures, seu conflatam insidiis, ut aliqui prodidere memoriae, mortem obiit, vitam certe dignissimam egit, quae nullius ad id tem-

7 poris praeterquam avito fulgore vinceretur. decessit anno ferme LVI; de quo si quis ambiget, recurrat ad priorem

---

[16] clariore *Burer*: -ori *PA^c*: -orum *A*
[17] CLX *Laurent*: CL *PA*

---

[22] In 134.

[23] C. Papirius Carbo (cos. 120) was tribune of the plebs in 131 or 130.   [24] In 129.

60

BOOK 2.4

time and sent to Spain,[22] and in Spain he repeated the success and prowess he had shown in Africa: within a year and three months of his arrival there he surrounded Numantia with siege works, demolished it, and razed it to the ground. And no one previously of any nationality placed his name on everlasting record for a more brilliant demolition of cities: by demolishing Carthage and Numantia he rescued us from dread in the one case and from humiliation in the other. This was the man who, when the tribune Carbo[23] asked him what he thought about the killing of Tiberius Gracchus, replied that, if the man had intended to seize control of the commonwealth, he was justly slain; and, when the whole meeting protested, he said: "Having been unafraid of the shouting of armed men on so many occasions, how can I be disturbed by yours, for whom Italy is only a stepmother?" Within a short time of his return to the City, in the consulship of Manius Aquilius and Gaius Sempronius,[24] 160 years ago, after two consulships and two triumphs, and having twice demolished frightening threats to the commonwealth, he was found dead in his bed in the morning, such that some marks of crushing of the throat were found on his neck. No investigation was held into the death of so great a man, and they lifted away, fitted with a shroud over his head, the body of one by whose efforts Rome had lifted her head above the whole world. Whether he met his death naturally, as is placed on record by the majority, or whether it was the result of treachery, as by some others, at least he lived the most worthy of lives, the like of which was beaten in brilliance by no one else's up to that time with the exception of his grandfather's. He died in about his fifty-sixth year: anyone uncertain about it should refer back to the first consulship

61

VELLEIUS PATERCULUS

consulatum eius, in quem conlatus[18] est anno XXXVI:[19] ita dubitare desinet.

5. Ante tempus excisae Numantiae praeclara in Hispania militia D.[20] Bruti fuit, qui penetratis omnibus Hispaniae gentibus ingenti vi hominum urbiumque potitus numero, aditis quae vix audita erant, Gallaeci cognomen 2 meruit. et ante eum paucis annis tam severum illius Q. Macedonici in his gentibus imperium fuit ut, cum urbem (Contrebiam nomine) in Hispania oppugnaret, pulsas praecipiti loco quinque cohortes legionarias eodem proti- 3 nus subire iuberet, facientibusque omnibus in procinctu testamenta, velut ad certam mortem eundum foret, non deterritus proposito, quem moriturum miserat militem victorem recepit: tantum effecit perseverantia ducis,[21] mixtus timori pudor spesque desperatione quaesita. hic virtute ac severitate facti, at Fabius Aemilianus Pauli ‹filius›[22] exemplo disciplinae in Hispania fuit clarissimus.

[18] conlatus *Woodman*: creatus *PA*: evectus *nescioquis*

[19] XXXVI *PA*: XXXVII *Kasten*: XXXVIII *Puteanus*

[20] D. *Aldus*: A. *PA*

[21] perseverantia ducis, *quod post* proposito *habent PA, post* effecit *transpos. Kritz, post* foret *E. Thomas (secl. Davies)*

[22] *suppl. Ruhnken*

---

[25] The consulship was in 147 (1.12.3); he was born in 185/4.

[26] D. Iunius Brutus Callaicus (cos. 138), whose activities in his province of Further Spain continued at least until 136.

[27] After the Gallaeci (or Callaeci), a people of northwestern Spain.

[28] See 1.11.2–6. As governor of Nearer Spain in 143–142, Macedonicus campaigned against the Celtiberi.

BOOK 2.4–5

of the man, on whom it was conferred in his thirty-sixth year:[25] then he will desist from doubting.

5. Before the time of Numantia's demolition there was the distinguished campaigning in Spain of Decimus Brutus,[26] who, having penetrated all the peoples of Spain and captured a large force of men and a large number of cities, entering areas that had scarcely been heard of, earned the cognomen Gallaecus.[27] And, a few years before him among those same peoples, the command of the famous Quintus Macedonicus[28] was of such severity that, when he was storming a city in Spain called Contrebia, he ordered five legionary cohorts immediately to ascend the same precipitous place from which they had been beaten back; and, when they were all on standby and making their wills, as if having to go to certain death, he was undeterred from his purpose and welcomed back victorious the soldiery whom he had sent to a likely death: this success resulted from the leader's perseverance, from the mixture of fear and shame, and from hope born of hopelessness. He won distinction in Spain for his prowess and the severity of his action, but Fabius Aemilianus, Paullus' son, for his exemplary discipline.[29]

[29] Q. Fabius Maximus Aemilianus (cos. 145), son of L. Aemilius Paullus (1.9.3n), campaigned against Viriathus as governor of Further Spain in 145–144. He is credited with training raw recruits in Roman discipline (App. *Hisp.* 65), but V. may be thinking rather of his adoptive brother, Q. Fabius Maximus *Servilianus* (cos. 142), who as governor of Further Spain in 142–141 also campaigned against Viriathus and was chosen as an example of military discipline by Valerius Maximus (2.7.11) for amputating the hands of Roman deserters (cf. also Frontin. *Str.* 4.1.42).

63

VELLEIUS PATERCULUS

6. Decem deinde interpositis annis, qui Ti. Gracchum idem Gaium fratrem eius occupavit furor, tam virtutibus eius omnibus quam huic errori[23] similem, ingenio etiam

2 eloquentiaque longe praestantiorem. qui cum summa quiete animi civitatis princeps esse posset, vel vindicandae fraternae mortis gratia vel praemuniendae regalis potentiae eiusdem exempli tribunatum ingressus, longe maiora et acriora petens[24] dabat civitatem omnibus Italicis, exten-

3 debat eam paene usque Alpes, dividebat agros, vetabat quemquam civem plus quingentis iugeribus habere (quod aliquando lege Licinia cautum erat), nova constituebat portoria, novis coloniis replebat provincias, iudicia a senatu transferebat ad equites, frumentum plebi dari instituebat:[25] nihil immotum, nihil tranquillum, nihil quietum, ⟨nihil⟩[26] denique in eodem statu relinquebat; quin alterum etiam continuavit tribunatum.

4 Hunc L. Opimius consul, qui praetor Fregellas exciderat, persecutus armis unaque Fulvium Flaccum, consularem ac triumphalem virum, aeque prava cupientem, quem C. Gracchus in locum Tiberii fratris triumvirum nominaverat ⟨et⟩[27] eum socium regalis adsumpserat po-

5 tentiae, morte adfecit.[28] id unum nefarie ⟨factum⟩[29] ab Opimio proditum, quod capitis non dicam Gracchi, sed

---

[23] hoc errore *Damsté*
[24] petens *Ruhnken*: repetens *PA*
[25] instituebat *Herel*: -uerat *PA*   [26] *suppl. Ruhnken*
[27] *suppl. Krause*   [28] adfecit *Herel*: adficit *PA*
[29] *suppl. Cludius, qui et* nefarium *pro* nefarie *tentavit*

---

[30] Gaius Gracchus was tribune of the plebs in 123 and 122.

64

BOOK 2.6

6. After an interval of ten years, the madness of Tiberius Gracchus now seized his brother Gaius likewise, a similar man in all his virtues as well as in the present derangement, and far more outstanding in intellect and eloquence. Although he could have been a principal figure in the community if he had been of the calmest temperament, it was either to avenge his brother's death or to pave the way for kingly power that he embarked on a tribunate of the same character but sought far greater and more unpalatable ends, giving citizenship to all Italians and extending it almost all the way to the Alps, dividing up land, forbidding any citizen from holding more than five hundred acres (which had once been prescribed by the Licinian law), instituting new customs duties, filling the provinces with new colonies, transferring the courts from the senate to the equestrians, establishing that grain be given to the plebs. He left nothing undisturbed, nothing tranquil, nothing peaceful, nothing, in short, in the same state. Moreover he even followed his tribunate with another.[30]

The consul Lucius Opimius, who as praetor had demolished Fregellae,[31] went in armed pursuit of both him and Fulvius Flaccus, an ex-consul and triumpher[32] whose desires were equally perverted (Gaius Gracchus had nominated him triumvir to replace his brother Tiberius and had enlisted him to be an associate in his kingly power), and had them done to death. The one wicked action of Opimius that has been handed down is that he proposed to

[31] L. Opimius (cos. 121) had been praetor in 125; Fregellae, a Latin colony, had been in revolt.

[32] M. Fulvius Flaccus (cos. 125) had celebrated a triumph in 123 for operations in southeastern Gaul.

65

VELLEIUS PATERCULUS

civis Romani, pretium se daturum idque auro repensurum
6 proposuit. Flaccus in Aventino armatos ad[30] pugnam ciens
cum filio maiore iugulatus est; Gracchus profugiens, cum
iam comprehenderetur ab iis quos Opimius miserat, cervicem Euporo servo praebuit, qui non segnius se ipse interemit quam domino succurrerat. quo die singularis Pomponii equitis Romani in Gracchum fides fuit, qui more
Coclitis sustentatis in ponte hostibus eius, gladio se trans-
7 fixit.[31] ut Ti. Gracchi antea corpus, ita Gai mira crudelitate
victorum in Tiberim deiectum est.

7. Hunc Ti.[32] Gracchi liberi, P. Scipionis Africani nepotes, viva adhuc matre Cornelia, Africani filia, viri optimis ingeniis male usi, vitae mortisque[33] habuere exitum;
qui si civilem dignitatis concupissent modum, quidquid
tumultuando adipisci gestierunt quietis obtulisset res
publica.
2 Huic atrocitati adiectum scelus unicum. quippe iuvenis
specie excellens necdum duodevicesimum transgressus
annum immunisque delictorum paternorum, Fulvii Flacci
filius, quem pater legatum de condicionibus miserat, ab
Opimio interemptus est. quem cum haruspex Tuscus ami-
cus flentem in vincula duci vidisset, "quin tu hoc potius,"

---

[30] armatos ad *Gelenius*: armatus ad *PA*: armatus ac *Kritz*
[31] gladio se ⟨ipse⟩ transfixit *Novák*
[32] Ti. *Gelenius*: C. *PA*   [33] mortisque *fort. secludendum*

---

[33] The Aventine, one of the Seven Hills of Rome, is in the
south of the City.
[34] Pomponius, of whom little is otherwise known, copied the
heroic example of Horatius Cocles, who, according to legend,

66

BOOK 2.6–7

put a price on the head, I will not say of Gracchus, but of a Roman citizen, and to pay it in gold. Flaccus, along with his elder son, was slaughtered on the Aventine while rousing his armed men to fight;[33] when the fleeing Gracchus was already in the process of being apprehended by those whom Opimius had sent, he presented his neck to his slave Euporus, who killed himself as readily as he had helped his master. On that day singular loyalty was shown to Gracchus by Pomponius, a Roman equestrian, who, having held back the man's enemies on the bridge in the manner of Cocles,[34] ran himself through with his sword. As in the case of Tiberius Gracchus earlier, Gaius' body was thrown into the Tiber owing to the astonishing cruelty of the victors.

7. Such were the deaths that ended the lives of Tiberius Gracchus' children, the grandsons of Publius Scipio Africanus, while their mother Cornelia, Africanus' daughter, was still alive—men who misused their very great talents. If they had craved a level of rank that befitted citizens, the commonwealth would have offered them in tranquility whatever they yearned to acquire by their turmoil.

To this atrocity[35] was added a unique crime. A young man of excellent appearance, not yet beyond eighteen years old, and uninvolved in his father's delinquency, the son of Fulvius Flaccus whom his father had sent as an envoy about terms, was killed by Opimius. When an Etruscan soothsayer, who was his friend, saw him being led tearfully to his chains, he said "Why don't you do this

confronted the attacking Etruscans at the Sublician Bridge over the Tiber in the late sixth century BC.

35 Presumably a reference to 2.6.7.

67

VELLEIUS PATERCULUS

inquit, "facis?" protinusque inliso capite in postem[34] lapideum ianuae carceris effusoque cerebro expiravit.

3 Crudelesque mox quaestiones in amicos clientesque Gracchorum habitae sunt. sed Opimium, virum alioqui sanctum et gravem, damnatum postea iudicio publico memoria ipsius saevitiae nulla civilis prosecuta[35] est mise-
4 ricordia. eadem Rupilium[36] Popiliumque, qui consules asperrime in Ti. Gracchi amicos saevierant, postea iudiciorum publicorum[37] merito oppressit invidia. (rei tantae
5 parum ad notitiam pertinens interponatur.[38] hic est Opimius a quo consule celeberrimum Opimiani vini[39] nomen; quod iam nullum esse spatio annorum colligi potest, cum
6 ab eo sint[40] ad te, M. Vinici, consulem anni CLI.[41] factum Opimii [quod[42] inimicitiarum quaesita erat ultio][43] minor secuta auctoritas, et visa ultio privato odio magis quam publicae vindictae data.
7 In legibus[44] Gracchi inter perniciosissima numeraverim quod extra Italiam colonias posuit. id maiores, cum

---

[34] postem *Aldus*: pontem *PA*
[35] prosecuta *Cludius*: persecuta *PA*
[36] Rupilium *Puteanus, Aldus*: Rut- *PA* [37] *post* publicorum *lacunam statuit Watt, opera suppl. Shackleton Bailey*
[38] interponatur *Lipsius*: -etur *PA*
[39] vini A^{mg}, *Gelenius*: vici *P*: vicini *A*
[40] sint *BA, om. P* [41] CL *Aldus*: CLII *Laurent*
[42] quod *PA*: quo *Heinsius* [43] *secl. Krause*
[44] in legibus . . . condita est *huc a fine 2.14.3 transposuit Krause*

---

[36] Although Opimius was prosecuted in 120 for the suppression of Gaius Gracchus and his supporters, he was acquitted;

BOOK 2.7

instead?" and thereupon dashed his head on the stone jamb of the prison door and, as his brain spilled out, expired.

Cruel investigations were later held into the friends and clients of the Gracchi. But Opimius, an otherwise scrupulous and serious man who was afterward condemned at a public trial, was regarded without pity by the citizens because they remembered his own savagery.[36] Likewise Rupilius and Popilius, whose savagery as consuls[37] against the friends of Tiberius Gracchus had been particularly fierce, were deservedly overwhelmed by the resentment in public trials afterward. (An item scarcely relevant to one's knowledge of so important a subject may be inserted. This is the Opimius from whose consulship derives the greatly celebrated name of Opimian wine, of which none can be picked up any longer owing to the years intervening, since from his consulship to yours, Marcus Vinicius, there are 151 years.) Opimius' deed [because retribution was sought for private enmities] was followed by a diminution of prestige: his retributive action was seen as yielding to personal hatred rather than as delivering an official punishment.

Among the most pernicious of Gracchus' laws I would be inclined to count the fact that he established colonies outside of Italy. When our ancestors saw how much more

however, Gracchan sympathies later played a part in his conviction by the special commission inquiring into corrupt dealings with Jugurtha in 110.

[37] In 132. P. Rupilius died soon after his consulship, but P. Popilius Laenas was exiled under a law of Gaius Gracchus in 123 and then recalled in 120.

69

VELLEIUS PATERCULUS

viderent tanto potentiorem Tyro Carthagi-em, Massiliam Phocaea, Syracusas Corintho, Cyzicum ac Byzantium Mileto, genitali solo, diligenter[45] vitaverant, ut cives Romanos ad censendum ex provinciis in Italiam revocaverint. 8 prima autem extra Italiam colonia Carthago condita est; subinde Porcio Marcioque consulibus deducta colonia Narbo Martius.

8. Mandetur deinde memoriae severitas iudiciorum. quippe C.[46] Cato consularis, M. Catonis nepos, Africani sororis filius, repetundarum ex Macedonia damnatus est, cum lis ei HS[47] IIII[48] milibus aestimaretur: adeo illi viri magis voluntatem peccandi intuebantur quam modum, factaque ad consilium dirigebant et quid, non in quantum, admissum foret aestimabant.

2 Circa eadem tempora M. ⟨et C.⟩[49] Metelli fratres uno die triumphaverunt. non minus clarum exemplum et adhuc unicum Fulvii Flacci, eius qui Capuam ceperat, filiorum, sed alterius in adoptionem dati, in collegio consulatus[50] fuit; adoptivus in Acidini[51] Manlii familiam datus.

45 ⟨adeo⟩ diligenter *Castiglioni*
46 C. *Aldus*: COS. *PA*
47 ei HS *Scaliger*: eius *PA*
48 IIII *PA*: XVIII *Lipsius* (*cf. Cic. Verr. 4.22*)
49 M. ⟨et C.⟩ *Pighius* (M. ⟨C.⟩ *Vossius*): M. *PA*: duo *Sigonius*
50 consulatus *Krause*: COS. *PA*
51 in Acidini *Sigonius*: in Acidiani *P*: macidiani *A*

---

38 Respectively, in 122 (Colonia Iunonia) and in 118: see 1.15.5–6.

39 Consul in 114. For the episode see further Cic. *Verr.* 4.22, where similar points are made.

BOOK 2.7–8

powerful Carthage was than Tyre, Massilia than Phocaea, Syracuse than Corinth, Cyzicus and Byzantium than Miletus, in each case than the parental soil, they had been careful to avoid the same, with the result that they recalled Roman citizens from the provinces to Italy to be registered in the census. Nevertheless the first colony to be founded outside Italy was Carthage; subsequently, in the consulship of Porcius and Marcius, the colony of Narbo Martius was settled.[38]

8. The severity of the courts should next be placed on record. The ex-consul Gaius Cato[39]—grandson of Marcus Cato and son of Africanus' sister—was condemned for extortion in Macedonia, although the assessment of damages was only four thousand sesterces: so completely did those men have regard for the willingness to err rather than for the amount; they saw deeds in terms of intention and they assessed what had been perpetrated, not for how much.

About the same time the brothers Marcus and Gaius Metellus triumphed on a single day.[40] A no less distinguished, and so far unique, case was the joint consulship of the sons—one of them given up to adoption—of the Fulvius Flaccus who had taken Capua; the adopted one was given to the family of Acidinus Manlius.[41] As for the

[40] M. Caecilius Metellus (cos. 115) and C. Caecilius Metellus Caprarius (cos. 113) triumphed in 111.

[41] Q. Fulvius Flaccus and L. Manlius Acidinus Fulvianus were consuls together in 179; their father was Q. Fulvius Flaccus (cos. 237, 224, 212, 209), and the adoptive father was L. Manlius Acidinus (pr. 210).

71

VELLEIUS PATERCULUS

nam censura[52] Metellorum patruelium, non germanorum, fratrum fuit, quod solis contigerat Scipionibus.

3   Tum Cimbri et Teutoni transcendere Rhenum, multis mox nostris suisque cladibus nobiles. per eadem tempora clarus eius Minucii[53] qui porticus, quae hodieque celebres sunt, molitus est ex Scordiscis[54] triumphus fuit.

    9. Eodem tractu temporum[55] nituerunt oratores Scipio Aemilianus Laeliusque, Ser. Galba, duo Gracchi, C. Fannius, Carbo Papirius; nec praetereundus Metellus Numidicus et Scaurus, et ante[56] omnes L.[57] Crassus et M. Antonius; quorum aetati ingeniisque successere C. Caesar

2 Strabo, P. Sulpicius. (nam Q. Mucius iuris scientia quam

3 proprio[58] eloquentiae nomine celebrior fuit.) clara etiam per idem aevi spatium fuere ingenia[59] in togatis Afranii, in

[52] censura *Gelenius*: census *PA*
[53] Minucii *Gelenius*: Minici *P*: manici *A*
[54] Scordiscis *Rhenanus*: Cord- *PA*
[55] tractu temporum *BA*: tem- tra- *P*
[56] et ante . . . Antonius *post* Papirius *transpos. Ruhnken*
[57] L. *BA, om. P*
[58] proprio *Heinsius*: -iae *PA*: -ie *Lipsius*
[59] Ennii *suppl. post* ingenia *Bothe, post* magnumque *Orelli, post* locum *Heinsius*

---

[42] These were two different Metelli from the pair just mentioned: Q. Caecilius Metellus Numidicus (cos. 109) and C. Caecilius Metellus Caprarius (cos. 113) were censors in 102.

[43] L. Cornelius Scipio (cos. 350) and P. Cornelius Scipio were censors together in perhaps 340.

[44] M. Minucius Rufus (cos. 110) triumphed in 106.

[45] For P. Cornelius Scipio Aemilianus (185/4–129), see 1.12.3 and elsewhere; C. Laelius Sapiens (ca. 190–128) was consul in

72

BOOK 2.8–9

censorship of the Metelli,[42] they were cousins, not brothers-german, something that had happened only to the Scipios.[43]

Then the Cimbri and Teutoni, later famed for many defeats, both ours and their own, crossed the Rhine. During the same time there was the distinguished triumph over the Scordisci of the Minucius who constructed the portico that is still celebrated today.[44]

9. In the same tract of time there lived the glittering orators Scipio Aemilianus and Laelius, Servius Galba, the two Gracchi, Gaius Fannius and Carbo Papirius; Metellus Numidicus and Scaurus are not to be passed over, and Lucius Crassus and Marcus Antonius above all.[45] Their successors in terms of age and talent were Gaius Caesar Strabo and Publius Sulpicius.[46] (Quintus Mucius was more celebrated for his legal expertise than for eloquence properly so called.[47]) Also distinguished during the same period of time were the talented Afranius in comedies and

---

140; Ser. Sulpicius Galba was consul in 144; Ti. Sempronius Gracchus (2.2.1–3.2) was tribune of the plebs in 133; C. Sempronius Gracchus (2.6.1–7) was tribune of the plebs in 123 and 122; C. Fannius was consul in 122; for Papirius Carbo see 2.4.4n. For Metellus see 2.11.1–3 and 2.8.2 (just above), and for Scaurus see 2.12.2. L. Licinius Crassus was consul in 95, M. Antonius in 99. For what remains of these orators, see G. Manuwald, *Fragmentary Republican Latin: Oratory, Part 1* (LCL 540; Cambridge, MA, 2019).

46 C. Iulius Caesar Strabo was aedile in 90; P. Sulpicius Rufus was tribune of the plebs in 88: for them see G. Manuwald, *Fragmentary Republican Latin: Oratory, Part 2* (LCL 541; Cambridge, MA, 2019).

47 Q. Mucius Scaevola was consul in 95.

73

VELLEIUS PATERCULUS

tragoediis Pacuvii atque Accii, usque in Graecorum ingeniorum comparationem evecti,[60] magnumque inter hos ipsos facientis operi suo locum, adeo quidem ut in illis li-
4 mae, in hoc paene plus videatur fuisse sanguinis. celebre et Lucilii nomen fuit, qui sub P. Africano Numantino bello eques militaverat. (quo quidem tempore iuvenes[61] adhuc Iugurtha ac Marius sub eodem Africano militantes in iisdem castris didicere quae postea in contrariis facerent.)
5 historiarum auctor iam tum Sisenna erat iuvenis, sed opus belli civilis Sullanique post aliquot annos ab eo seniore
6 editum est. vetustior Sisenna fuit Coelius, aequalis[62] Sisennae Rutilius Claudiusque Quadrigarius et Valerius Antias. sane non ignoremus eadem aetate fuisse Pomponium sensibus celebrem,[63] verbis rudem et novitate inventi a se operis commendabilem.

> [60] evecti *Gelenius*: evectis *B*: eius aetatis *PA*
> [61] iuvenes *Burman*: -is *PA*
> [62] aequales *Kreyssig*
> [63] celebrem *PA*: crebrum *Orelli, fort. recte*

---

[48] L. Afranius wrote native Roman comedies (*fabulae togatae*) in the second half of the second century BC; the dates of M. Pacuvius and L. Accius were ca. 220–130 and 170–ca. 86, respectively. Pacuvius was a nephew of Ennius, whose omission from V.'s list has sometimes been considered the result of textual corruption.   [49] *sanguis* (blood) is a common literary-critical metaphor (*OLD* 5b).

[50] C. Lucilius, the inventor of Latin satire, died in old age ca. 102.

[51] L. Cornelius Sisenna was praetor in 78, which does not correspond to a synchronism with the Numantine War (see 2.1.3–

BOOK 2.9

Pacuvius and Accius in tragedy:[48] the latter was even elevated to a comparison with the talented Greeks and made a significant place for his own work in such company, at least to the extent that it almost seems that, though there was more polish in them, there was more blood in him.[49] Celebrated too was the name of Lucilius, who had served as an equestrian under Publius Africanus in the Numantine War.[50] (At this time, in fact, Jugurtha and Marius, still young men, were serving under the same Africanus and they learned in the same camp what they would later put into practice in opposing ones.) Sisenna, the author of histories, was already then a young man, but he published his work on the civil and Sullan wars some years afterward when he was elderly.[51] Older than Sisenna was Coelius, contemporary with Sisenna were Rutilius, Claudius Quadrigarius, and Valerius Antias.[52] Of course we should be aware that belonging to the same generation was Pomponius, celebrated for his ideas, unrefined in vocabulary, and to be commended for the novelty of the genre he discovered.[53]

4). Since he gave his name to a book of Varro's on historiography (Gell. *NA* 16.9.5), he was presumably quite well known. For further information on him and the following historians, together with the surviving fragments of their works, see *FRHist*.

[52] The *floruit* of L. Coelius Antipater was ca. 110; for P. Rutilius Rufus (cos. 105) see 2.13.2. Q. Claudius Quadrigarius and Valerius Antias were also historians, of the early first century BC, but their precise dates are unknown and those of Antias especially controversial.

[53] L. Pomponius (fl. ca. 89) was a writer of farce (*fabula Atellana*), which he is credited with having made a more sophisticated literary production.

75

VELLEIUS PATERCULUS

10. Prosequamur notam[64] severitatem censorum Cassii Longini Caepionisque, qui abhinc annos CLIIII[65] Lepidum Aemilium[66] augurem, quod sex milibus ‹ HS ›[67] aedes conduxisset, adesse iusserunt. at nunc si quis tanti habitet, vix ut senator agnoscitur! adeo mature[68] a rectis [in vitia, a vitiis][69] in prava, a pravis in praecipitia pervenitur.

2 Eodem tractu temporum et Domitii ex Arvernis et Fabii ex Allobrogibus victoria fuit nobilis; Fabio Pauli nepoti ex victoria cognomen Allobrogico inditum. notetur Domitiae familiae[70] peculiaris quaedam et, ut clarissima, ita artata numero felicitas: VIII[71] ante hunc nobilissimae simplicitatis iuvenem Cn. Domitium[72] fuere, singuli[73] omnino[74] parentibus geniti, sed omnes ad consulatum sacerdotiaque, ad triumphi autem paene omnes pervenerunt insignia.

11. Bellum deinde Iugurthinum gestum est per Q. Metellum, nulli secundum saeculi sui. huius legatus fuit

---

[64] nota *Madvig*: notae *Krause*   [65] CLIIII *Aldus*: CLVII *PA*
[66] Aemilium *Aldus*: Aelium *PA*   [67] ‹ HS › *Krause*
[68] mature *P*: natura *A*   [69] in . . . vitiis *secl. Ruhnken*: a rectis in prava, a pravis in vitia, a vitiis . . . *Sterke*
[70] familiae *P*: filiam *A*   [71] VIII *Woodman*: uti *PA: alii alia*
[72] Domitium *PA*: -ii *Pluygers*   [73] singuli *Puteanus*: -is *PA*
[74] omnino *PA*: omnes *Pluygers*

---

[54] L. Cassius Longinus Ravilla (cos. 127) and Cn. Servilius Caepio (cos. 141) were censors in 125; their victim was M. Aemilius Lepidus Porcina (cos. 137).

[55] Cn. Domitius Ahenobarbus (cos. 122) and Q. Fabius Maximus Allobrogicus (cos. 121) were victorious in the years of their consulships.

BOOK 2.10–11

10. We should observe the well known severity of the censors Cassius Longinus and Caepio, who 154 years ago ordered the appearance before them of the augur Lepidus Aemilius, on the grounds that he had rented a house for six thousand sesterces.[54] If anyone were an occupant at such a price nowadays, he would scarcely be recognized as a senator! So swift is the progression from the straight [to vices, from vices] to the perverted and from the perverted to the precipitous.

To the same tract of time belong the famous victories of Domitius over the Arverni and of Fabius over the Allobroges; the cognomen Allobrogicus was bestowed on Fabius, Paullus' grandson, for his victory.[55] With reference to the family of the Domitii, one should note a particular success whose distinction is all the greater for the limited numbers involved: before the present Gnaeus Domitius, a young man of the noblest straightforwardness, there were eight, single sons of their parents overall, who all nevertheless reached the consulship and priesthoods and almost all of them the insignia of a triumph.[56]

11. Next the Jugurthine War was waged by Quintus Metellus, second to none of his generation.[57] His legate

56 Cn. Domitius is V.'s own contemporary, the consul of AD 32 (and father of the emperor Nero), whom he here describes in the same terms as he will use for the man's father at 72.3. Only the consuls of 96 (2.12.3) and 94 (26.2) were brothers. There is a family tree in J. Carlsen, *The Rise and Fall of a Noble Family: The Domitii Ahenobarbi 196 BC–AD 68* (Odense, Denmark, 2006), 10.

57 The war against Jugurtha, king of Numidia, began in 111 and was entrusted to the consul Q. Caecilius Metellus in 109.

VELLEIUS PATERCULUS

C. Marius, quem praediximus, natus equestri loco, hirtus atque horridus vitaque sanctus, quantum bello optimus, tantum pace pessimus, immodicus, gloriae[75] insatiabilis, impotens semperque inquietus. hic per publicanos aliosque in Africa negotiantes criminatus Metelli lentitudinem, trahentis iam in tertium annum bellum, et naturalem nobilitatis superbiam morandique in imperiis cupiditatem effecit ut, cum commeatu petito Romam venisset, consul crearetur bellique paene patrati a Metello, qui bis Iugurtham acie fuderat, summa committeretur sibi. Metelli tamen et triumphus fuit clarissimus et merito virtuteque[76] cognomen Numidici inditum. (ut paulo ante Domitiae familiae, ita Caeciliae notanda claritudo est: quippe intra XII ferme annos huius temporis consules fuere Metelli aut censores aut triumpharunt amplius duodecies, ut appareat, quemadmodum urbium imperiorumque, ita gentium nunc florere fortunam, nunc senescere, nunc interire.) 12. at C. Marius L. Sullam iam tunc ut praecaventibus Fatis copulatum sibi quaestorem habuit et per eum missum ad regem Bocchum Iugurtha rege abhinc annos

---

[75] gloriae *ex* insatiabilis *potius quam ex* immodicus *pendere putavit Burman*

[76] merito virtuteque *Woodman*: meritū: virtutique *P*: meritū & virtutique *A*: meritum virtute[que] *Aldus*: meritum virtute ei *Ortvinius*

---

[58] At 2.9.4; see also 1.15.5.

[59] In 107.

[60] Between 123 and 109 (fifteen years, counting inclusively) Metelli held six consulships, two censorships, and four triumphs. The line *fato Metelli Romae fiunt consules* (Metelli are fated to

BOOK 2.11–12

was Gaius Marius, whom we mentioned earlier,[58] of equestrian rank by birth, shaggy and scruffy, scrupulous in lifestyle, as pernicious in peace as he was fine in war, intemperate, insatiable for glory, impetuous, and always impatient. Using tax collectors and other businessmen in Africa as his agents, he charged Metellus not only with dawdling, dragging out the war now into its third year, but also with the haughtiness innate in the nobility, and with a desire to linger in his command, the result being that, when he arrived in Rome after requesting leave, he was appointed consul[59] and was entrusted with responsibility for a war that had almost been concluded by Metellus, who had routed Jugurtha twice in the battle line. Nevertheless not only was Metellus' triumph extremely distinguished but the cognomen Numidicus was bestowed on him for his service and prowess. (As with the family of the Domitii just before, so the distinction of that of the Caecilii is to be noted: within roughly twelve years at this period Metelli were consuls or censors or triumphers on more than twelve occasions,[60] so it is clear that the fortunes of families, like those of cities and empires, flourish at one moment, languish at another, and die at another.) 12. As for Marius, he already had Lucius Sulla attached to him as his quaestor at that time, as if the Fates were planning ahead,[61] and, by sending him to King Bocchus,[62] he captured King Jugurtha about 134 years ago; and, desig-

become consuls at Rome) was attributed to the third-century BC poet Naevius, fr. 59 Viredaz = Naevius T 5 (LCL 314).

[61] Marius and Sulla were destined to be enemies.

[62] King of Mauretania and a relative and ally of Jugurtha, whom he was induced to betray to the Romans.

79

VELLEIUS PATERCULUS

ferme CXXXIIII[77] potitus est; designatusque iterum consul in urbem reversus secundi consulatus initio Kal. Ianuariis eum in triumpho duxit.

2   Effusa, ut praediximus, immanis vis Germanarum[78] gentium, quibus nomen Cimbris ac Teutonis erat, cum Caepionem Malliumque[79] consules et ante Carbonem Silanumque fudissent fugassentque in Galliis et exuissent exercitu, Scaurumque Aurelium consularem[80] et alios celeberrimi nominis viros trucidassent, populus Romanus non alium repellendis tantis hostibus magis idoneum im-
3   peratorem quam Marium est ratus. tum multiplicati consulatus eius. tertius in apparatu belli consumptus; quo anno Cn. Domitius tribunus plebis legem tulit ut sacerdotes, quos antea collegae sufficiebant, populus crearet.
4   quarto trans Alpes circa Aquas Sextias cum Teutonis conflixit, amplius CL ‹milia›[81] hostium priore ac postero die
5   ab eo trucidata[82] gensque excisa Teutonum. quinto citra Alpes in campis[83] quibus nomen erat Raudiis[84] ipse consul et proconsul Q. Lutatius Catulus fortunatissimo decertavere proelio: caesa aut capta amplius C milia hominum. hac victoria videtur meruisse Marius ne eius nati rem

[77] CXXXIIII *Aldus*: CXXXVIII *PA*
[78] Germanarum *Lipsius*: -orum *PA*
[79] Malliumque *Sigonius*: Manliumque *PA*
[80] consularem *Puteanus, Aldus*: COS. *PA*
[81] *suppl. vulgo*   [82] trucidata *Ruhnken*: -is *PA*: -i *Kritz*
[83] *ante* in campis *suppl.* cum Cimbris *Freudenberg*
[84] Raudiis *Riguez*: Raudis *PA*

---

[63] 1 January 104.   [64] At 2.8.3.
[65] Q. Servilius Caepio (cos. 106) and Cn. Mallius Maximus

BOOK 2.12

nated consul for a second time, on his return to the City he led the king in his triumph at the beginning of his second consulship on the Kalends of January.[63]

A prodigious force of Germanic peoples, whose names were the Cimbri and Teutoni, had streamed out, as we mentioned earlier,[64] and—after they had routed the consuls Caepio and Mallius (and previously Carbo and Silanus) in the Gauls and put them to flight, had stripped them of their army, and had butchered the ex-consul Scaurus Aurelius and other men of celebrated name[65]—the Roman people deemed that no other commander was more suitable to repel such enemies than Marius. Thereupon his consulships multiplied.[66] His third was spent in preparing for war, a year in which Gnaeus Domitius, tribune of the plebs, carried a law that priests (who previously would be appointed by the priestly fellowship) should be elected by the people. In his fourth he engaged with the Teutoni across the Alps near Aquae Sextiae, and more than one hundred and fifty thousand of the enemy were butchered by him over a two-day period, and the people of the Teutoni was eradicated. In his fifth he himself as consul and Quintus Lutatius Catulus as proconsul fought a very favorable battle on this side of the Alps on the Raudian Plains, as they were called: more than one hundred thousand of the enemy were slain or captured. This is the victory by which Marius seems to have earned the commonwealth's

(cos. 105) were crushingly defeated at Arausio (mod. Orange) in 105. Cn. Papirius Carbo was consul in 113 and M. Iunius Silanus in 109. M. Aurelius Scaurus (cos. suff. 108) was killed serving under Mallius in 105.   [66] His next four consulships were in 103 to 100; he was consul for a seventh time in 86.

81

VELLEIUS PATERCULUS

6 publicam paeniteret, ac bonis mala[85] repensasse. sextus consulatus veluti praemium ei meritorum datus. non tamen huius consulatus fraudetur gloria, quo Servilii Glauciae Saturninique Apulei furorem continuatis honoribus rem publicam lacerantium et gladiis quoque et caede comitia discutientium, consularibus[86] armis compescuit hominesque exitiabiles in Hostilia curia morte multavit.

13. Deinde interiectis paucis annis tribunatum iniit M. Livius Drusus, vir nobilissimus, eloquentissimus, sanctissimus, meliore in omnia ingenio animoque quam fortuna
2 usus. qui cum senatui priscum restituere cuperet decus et iudicia ab equitibus ad eum transferre ordinem (quippe eam potestatem nacti equites Gracchanis legibus cum in multos clarissimos atque innocentissimos viros saevissent, tum P. Rutilium, virum non saeculi sui sed omnis aevi optimum, interrogatum lege repetundarum maximo cum gemitu civitatis damnaverant), in iis ipsis quae pro senatu moliebatur senatum habuit adversarium, non intellegentem, si qua de plebis commodis ab eo agerentur, veluti

---

85 bonis mala *Cludius*: bona malis *PA*
86 consularibus *Acidalius*: COS. *PA*

---

67 L. Appuleius Saturninus was tribune of the plebs in 103 and 100; in 100 C. Servilius Glaucia added a praetorship to his tribunate of the plebs in 101.

68 After suppressing the uprising of Saturninus and Glaucia, Marius imprisoned them and their associates in the senate house, where they were lynched by the mob. The republican senate house, or *curia*, in the northwest area of the forum at the foot of the Capitoline Hill, was sometimes called the Curia Hostilia from its supposed establishment by Tullus Hostilius, traditionally the third king of Rome.

BOOK 2.12–13

lack of regret at his birth and to have compensated for his wicked deeds by his good ones. His sixth consulship was given as a kind of reward for his services; yet he should not be cheated of the glory of this consulship, during which, with consular armed forces, he checked the madness of Servilius Glaucia and Saturninus Apuleius, who had been tearing the commonwealth apart with their repeated offices[67] and even disrupting the elections with slaughter and the sword; and he punished these murderous men with death in the Curia Hostilia.[68]

13. Then, after an interval of a few years, Marcus Livius Drusus embarked on his tribunate,[69] the most noble, most eloquent and most scrupulous of men, whose talent and heart were in general better than the fortune he experienced. Although his desire was to restore to the senate its old-fashioned esteem and to transfer the courts from the equestrians to that order (the equestrians, having obtained that power under the Gracchan legislation, had directed their savagery against many distinguished and innocent men and in particular, under the extortion law, had arraigned Publius Rutilius, the best not just of his own generation but of every era, and, to the vocal dismay of the community, had condemned him[70]), he found the senate opposed to him in the very matters on which he was working on the senate's behalf, since it failed to understand that, whatever business it conducted to the plebs' advan-

[69] In 91.
[70] P. Rutilius Rufus (cos. 105) was prosecuted in 92 for extortion and after his condemnation went into exile at Smyrna.

83

VELLEIUS PATERCULUS

inescandae inliciendaeque multitudinis causa fieri, ut mi-
3 noribus perceptis maiora permitteret. denique ea fortuna
Drusi fuit ut malefacta collegarum eius quam[87] optime ab
ipso cogitata senatus probaret magis, et honorem qui ab
eo deferebatur sperneret, iniurias quae ab aliis intende-
bantur aequo animo reciperet, et huius summae gloriae
invideret, illorum *** modicam[88] ferret.

14. Tum conversus Drusi animus, quando bene coepta[89]
male cedebant, ad dandam civitatem Italiae. quod cum
moliens revertisset e foro, immensa illa et incondita[90] quae
eum semper comitabatur cinctus multitudine in atrio[91]
domus suae cultello percussus, qui adfixus lateri eius relic-
2 tus est, intra paucas horas decessit. sed cum ultimum red-
deret spiritum, intuens circumstantium maerentiumque
frequentiam, effudit vocem convenientissimam conscientiae suae: "Ecquandone," inquit, "propinqui amicique,
3 similem mei civem habebit res publica?" hunc finem clarissimus iuvenis vitae habuit, cuius morum minime omittatur argumentum. cum aedificaret domum[92] in Palatio in
eo loco ubi est quae quondam Ciceronis, mox Censorini
fuit, nunc Statilii Sisennae est, promitteretque ei architec-
tus ita se eam aedificaturum ut liber[93] a conspectu immu-

---

87 quam eius *P, transpos. Ruhnken*: quamvis *A*

88 *ante* modicam *lacunam stat. Woodman*: <vim im>modicam
Castiglioni: <im>modicam *Halm*

89 incepta *A*

90 incondita *Acidalius*: incognita *PA*

91 atrio *PA^c*: area *A*

92 domum *BA*: templum *P*

93 liber *Fröhlich*: libera *PA*

84

BOOK 2.13–14

tage, the reason was to bait and beguile the masses so that, if they acquired lesser things, they might allow larger ones. In the end it was Drusus' misfortune that the senate was more approving of his colleagues' malpractice than of the best of intentions from himself; that it spurned the respect that was being conferred by him, while accepting with equanimity the insults that were being aimed by others; and that it resented his great glory, while tolerating their mediocre ***.[71]

14. Since his fine undertakings were proving unsuccessful, Drusus next turned his attention to giving the citizenship to Italy. When he was working on this and had returned from the forum, surrounded by the famously big and chaotic crowd that always accompanied him, in the atrium of his house he was stabbed with a small knife that was left sticking in his side, and within a few hours he passed away. When he was rendering up his last breaths, however, he looked at the numbers of grieving bystanders and uttered words well suited to his self-knowledge: "Relatives and friends," he said, "when will the commonwealth ever have a citizen like me?" So ended the life of this most distinguished young man, evidence of whose moral character should not be omitted. When he was building his house on the Palatine—in the place where stands the one that was formerly Cicero's, then Censorinus', and is now Statilius Sisenna's[72]—and the architect was promising to build it in such a way that he would be free of people's gaze

[71] Something seems required to complete the sense, which, as of the sentence as a whole, is not at all clear.
[72] L. Marcius Censorinus was consul in 39 BC, T. Sisenna Statilius Taurus in AD 16.

85

VELLEIUS PATERCULUS

nisque ab omnibus arbitris esset neque quisquam in eam despicere posset, "Tu vero," inquit, "si quid in te artis est, ita compone domum meam ut quidquid agam ab omnibus perspici possit."[94]

15. Mors Drusi iam pridem tumescens bellum excitavit Italicum: quippe L. Caesare et P.[95] Rutilio consulibus, abhinc annos CXX, universa Italia, cum id malum[96] ab Asculanis ortum esset (quippe Servilium[97] praetorem Fonteiumque[98] legatum occiderant) ac deinde a Marsis exceptum in omnes penetrasset regiones, arma adversus 2 Romanos cepit. quorum ut fortuna atrox, ita causa fuit iustissima: petebant enim eam civitatem cuius imperium armis tuebantur: per omnes annos atque omnia bella duplici numero se militum equitumque fungi neque in eius civitatis ius recipi quae per eos in id ipsum pervenisset fastigium ex quo[99] homines eiusdem et gentis et sanguinis ut externos alienosque fastidire posset.

3 Id bellum amplius CCC milia iuventutis Italicae abstulit. clarissimi autem imperatores fuerunt Romani eo bello Cn. Pompeius, Cn. Pompeii Magni pater, C. Marius, de quo praediximus, L. Sulla, anno ante praetura functus, Q. Metellus, Numidici filius, qui meritum cognomen Pii 4 consecutus erat: quippe expulsum civitate a L. Saturnino tribuno plebis, quod solus in leges eius iurare noluerat,

---

94 *post* possit *PA habent* in legibus . . . condita est (*cf.* 2.7.7–8)
95 P. *Gelenius*: Pompeio *PA*
96 universa Italia cum id malum *A*: cum id malum universa Italia *P*
97 Servilium *Aldus*: Servium *PA*
98 Fontemiumque *BA*
99 ex quo *Ruhnken*: per quod *PA*

BOOK 2.14–15

and safe from all viewers and no one would be able to look into it, he said: "Use all your skill to design my house in such a way that whatever I do can be seen by everyone."

15. The death of Drusus caused the Italian War to break out, which had already been gathering to a head beforehand. In the consulship of Lucius Caesar and Publius Rutilius,[73] 120 years ago, the whole of Italy (the disorder had arisen among the people of Asculum—they had slain the praetor Servilius[74] and his legate Fonteius—and had then been caught by the Marsi and had penetrated into all areas) took up arms against the Romans. Their situation was frightful but their cause very just, since they were attacking the very citizen body whose empire they were protecting by arms: in every year and every war, they said, they were supplying double the number of soldiers and cavalry yet were not admitted to the rights of a community which, thanks to them, had reached the very height from which it could slight persons of the same family and blood as if they were foreigners and aliens.

The war carried off more than three hundred thousand of the Italian youth. The most distinguished Roman commanders in the war were Gnaeus Pompeius,[75] father of Pompey the Great, Gaius Marius, whom we mentioned earlier, Lucius Sulla, praetor in the previous year,[76] and Quintus Metellus, Numidicus' son, who had deservedly acquired the cognomen Pius, since by his piety[77]—and

[73] In 90.   [74] Q. Servilius was praetor in 91.

[75] Cn. Pompeius Strabo (cos. 89).

[76] That is, 91 (as again at 2.17.3), but Sulla was praetor in (probably) 97 and then spent several years as governor of Cilicia.

[77] The reference is to familial devotion.

87

VELLEIUS PATERCULUS

pietate sua, auctoritate senatus, consensu populi Romani[100] restituit patrem. nec triumphis honoribusque quam aut causa exilii aut exilio aut reditu clarior fuit Numidicus. 16. Italicorum autem fuerunt celeberrimi duces Silo Popaedius, Herius Asinius, Insteius Cato, C. Pontidius, Telesinus Pontius, Marius Egnatius, Papius Mutilus.[101] neque ego verecundia domestici sanguinis gloriae quicquam, dum verum refero, subtraham: quippe multum Minatii Magii, atavi mei, Aeculensis,[102] tribuendum est memoriae, qui nepos[103] Decii Magii, Campanorum principis, celeberrimi et fidelissimi viri, tantam hoc bello Romanis fidem praestitit ut cum legione quam ipse in Hirpinis conscripserat Herculaneum simul cum T. Didio caperet, Pompeios cum L. Sulla oppugnaret Compsamque[104] occuparet; cuius de virtutibus cum alii tum maxime dilucideque[105] Q. Hortensius in annalibus suis rettulit. cuius illi pietatis[106] plenam populus Romanus gratiam rettulit ipsum viritim civitate donando, duos filios eius creando praetores, cum seni adhuc crearentur.

2

3

4   Tam varia atque atrox fortuna Italici belli fuit ut per

---

100 populi Romani *Puteanus, Aldus*: Reip. *P*: rei publicae *A*
101 Mutilus *Raphelengius*: -ius *PA*
102 Aeculensis *Cluverius*: Asculensis *PA*
103 <pro>nepos *Sumner*
104 Compsamque *Vossius*: Cosamque *PA*
105 dilucide[que] *Lipsius*
106 pietatis *Kritz*: -i *PA*

---

78 In 100 (see 2.12.6).   79 Consul in 98, Didius was killed on 11 June 89 (Ov. *Fast.* 6.567–68).

80 The orator mentioned at 36.2 and 48.6 (cos. 69); despite

88

BOOK 2.15–16

thanks to the authority of the senate and the consensus of the Roman people—he reinstated his father, who had been banished from the community by Lucius Saturninus when tribune of the plebs[78] because he alone had refused to swear agreement to the latter's laws. And all Numidicus' triumphs and honors brought him no more distinction than did the reason for his exile or the exile itself or his return. 16. The most celebrated Italian leaders were Silo Popaedius, Herius Asinius, Insteius Cato, Gaius Pontidius, Telesinus Pontius, Marius Egnatius and Papius Mutilus. And, given the fidelity of my record, I should not, out of diffidence, take anything away from the glory of my personal family. Great tribute must be paid to the memory of Minatius Magius, my great-grandfather from Aeculanum: he was a descendant of Decius Magius (a principal figure among the Campanians and a most celebrated and loyal man), and in this war he demonstrated such loyalty to the Romans that, with a legion that he himself had conscripted among the Hirpini, he took Herculaneum alongside Titus Didius,[79] besieged Pompeii alongside Lucius Sulla, and seized Compsa. His virtues have been expressed by others but especially, and vividly, by Quintus Hortensius in his annals.[80] The Roman people expressed full thanks to him for his devotion by presenting him as an individual with citizenship and by appointing his two sons as praetors at a time when six were still being appointed.[81]

So variable and frightening were the fortunes of the Italian War that during an unbroken two-year period two

Catull. 95.3, his annals were almost certainly in prose, not verse (*FRHist* 1.338–40).

[81] In 81 Sulla raised the number to eight.

VELLEIUS PATERCULUS

biennium continuum duo Romani consules, Rutilius ac deinde Cato Porcius, ab hostibus occiderentur, exercitus populi Romani multis in locis funderentur, utque ad saga iretur diuque in eo habitu maneretur. caput imperii sui Corfinium legerant, quod[107] appellarunt[108] Italicum.[109] paulatim deinde recipiendo in civitatem qui arma aut non ceperant aut deposuerant maturius vires refectae sunt, Pompeio Sullaque et Mario fluentem procumbentemque rem publicam Romanam[110] restituentibus.

17. Finito ex maxima parte, nisi quae Nolani belli manebant reliquiae, Italico bello, quo quidem Romani victis adflictisque ipsi exanimati[111] quam integris[112] universis civitatem dare maluerunt, consulatum inierunt Q.[113] Pompeius et L. Cornelius Sulla, vir qui neque ad finem victoriae satis laudari neque post victoriam abunde vituperari potest. hic natus familia nobili, sextus a Cornelio Rufino, qui bello Pyrrhi inter celeberrimos fuerat duces, cum familiae eius claritudo intermissa esset, diu ita se gessit ut nullam petendi consulatum cogitationem habere videretur. deinde post praeturam inlustratus bello Italico et ante in Gallia legatione sub Mario, qua eminentissimos duces

107 legerant quod *B*: legerantque *PA*: legerant ‹at›que *Orelli*
108 appellarunt *Burer*: -arent *A (om. P)*: -arant *Lipsius*
109 Italicum *B*: -am *A*: -ani *P*
110 rem publicam Romanam *Kritz*: rem P.R. *BA*: Remp. *P*
111 exanimati *Acidalius*: exarmati *PA*
112 integri *Heinsius*   113 Q. *B*: Cn. *P* (inieruntq. *A*)

---

82 P. Rutilius Lupus was killed on 11 June 90, the year he was consul (Ov. *Fast.* 6.563–66); L. Porcius Cato also died in the year of his consulship (89).

90

BOOK 2.16–17

Roman consuls, Rutilius and then Cato Porcius, were slain by the enemy,[82] armies of the Roman people were routed in many places, military dress was assumed, and for a long time that attire remained in place. As their command headquarters the Italians had chosen Corfinium and called it Italicum.[83] Then, by receiving into citizenship those who either had not taken up arms or had put them down fairly quickly, there was a gradual rebuilding of strength, as Pompeius, Sulla and Marius restored the health of the wilting and prostrate Roman commonwealth.

17. For the most part, except for such remnants of the war as remained around Nola, the Italian War had ended (in which the Romans preferred to give them the citizenship when they were conquered and stricken—and themselves exhausted—rather than when all of them were unimpaired), and there entered upon the consulship Quintus Pompeius and Lucius Cornelius Sulla,[84] a man for whom there cannot be sufficient praise up to the end of his victory nor adequate vituperation after his victory. Born into a noble family, a sixth-generation descendant of Cornelius Rufinus[85] (who had been among the most celebrated leaders in the war with Pyrrhus), it was because his family's distinction had lapsed that for a long time he conducted himself in such a way that he seemed to have no thought of seeking the consulship; but then, having shone in the Italian War after his praetorship, and previously in Gaul in his legateship under Marius,[86] in which he had routed

[83] The name is "Italia" on the insurgents' coinage.
[84] In 88.   [85] Consul in 290 and 277; V. is counting inclusively.   [86] Sulla was praetor in (probably) 97 (2.15.3n) and had been legate in Gaul in 104–103.

91

VELLEIUS PATERCULUS

hostium fuderat, ex successu animum sumpsit petensque consulatum paene omnium civium suffragiis factus est; sed eum honorem undequinquagesimo aetatis suae anno adsecutus est.

18. Per ea tempora Mithridates, Ponticus rex, vir neque silendus neque dicendus sine cura, bello acerrimus, virtute eximius, aliquando fortuna, semper animo maximus, consiliis dux, miles manu, odio in Romanos Hannibal, occupata Asia necatisque in ea omnibus civibus
2 Romanis, quos quidem eadem die atque hora redditis civitatibus litteris ingenti cum pollicitatione praemiorum in-
3 terimi iusserat, quo tempore neque fortitudine adversus Mithridatem neque fide in Romanos quisquam Rhodiis par fuit (horum fidem Mytilenaeorum perfidia inluminavit, qui M'. Aquilium aliosque Mithridati vinctos tradiderunt, quibus libertas in unius Theophanis gratiam postea a Pompeio restituta est), cum terribilis Italiae quoque videretur imminere, sorte obvenit Sullae Asia provincia.
4 Is egressus urbe cum circa Nolam moraretur (quippe ea urbs pertinacissime arma retinebat exercituque Romano obsidebatur, velut paeniteret eius fidei quam om-
5 nium sanctissimam bello praestiterat Punico), P. Sulpicius tribunus plebis, disertus, acer, opibus gratia amicitiis vigore ingenii atque animi celeberrimus, cum antea rectis-

---

87 The minimum age at which a man might be consul was forty-two.   88 Aquilius had been consul with Marius in 101. Sent on a mission to Asia in 90, he had played a part in the outbreak of the war with Mithridates.

89 Theophanes was Pompey's personal historian and accompanied him on his campaign against Mithridates (37.1–5, below).

90 P. Sulpicius Rufus was tribune of the plebs in 88.

BOOK 2.17–18

the enemy's most outstanding leaders, he took courage from his success and, seeking the consulship, was elected by the votes of almost all the citizens; but he achieved the honor only in the forty-ninth year of his life.[87]

18. It was during these times that Mithridates, king of Pontus—a man about whom one must neither keep silent nor speak without concern, very fierce in war, exceptional in prowess, sometimes very successful but always very spirited, in strategy a leader but a soldier in muscle, a Hannibal in his hatred for the Romans—had seized Asia and executed all the Roman citizens there: by the delivery of letters to the various communities, to whom he promised huge rewards, he had ordered them to be killed on the same day and at the same hour. (This was a time when no one matched the Rhodians either in bravery against Mithridates or in loyalty to the Romans, and their loyalty was only highlighted by the disloyalty of the Mytilenaeans, who had bound Manius Aquilius[88] and others and handed them over to Mithridates and whose freedom was afterward restored by Pompey simply to please Theophanes in particular.)[89] When the royal terrorist seemed to be threatening Italy too, the province of Asia fell to Sulla by lot.

When he had left the City and was lingering around Nola (a city that had been stubbornly holding on to its arms and was under siege by a Roman army, as if it regretted the loyalty, more scrupulous than anyone else's, that it had shown in the Punic War), Publius Sulpicius, the articulate and fierce tribune of the plebs,[90] celebrated for his wealth, charm, friendships, and intellectual and emotional energy, and who had previously acquired the highest im-

93

VELLEIUS PATERCULUS

sima voluntate apud populum maximam quaesisset dignitatem, quasi pigeret eum virtutum suarum et bene
6 consulta ei male cederent, subito pravus ‹se›[114] et praeceps C. Mario post septuagesimum annum omnia imperia
et omnis provincias concupiscenti addixit legemque ad
populum tulit qua Sullae imperium abrogaretur, C. Mario
bellum decerneretur Mithridaticum aliasque leges perni-
ciosas et exitiabiles neque tolerandas liberae civitati tulit.
quin etiam Q. Pompeii consulis filium eundemque Sullae
generum per emissarios factionis suae interfecit.

19. Tum Sulla contracto exercitu ad urbem rediit eamque armis occupavit, XII auctores novarum pessima-
rumque rerum, inter quos Marium cum filio et P. Sulpicio,
urbe exturbavit ac lege lata exules fecit. Sulpicium etiam[115]
adsecuti equites in Laurentinis paludibus iugulavere,
caputque eius erectum et ostentatum pro rostris velut
2 omen imminentis proscriptionis fuit. Marius post sextum
consulatum annumque[116] LXX nudus ac limo obrutus,
oculis tantummodo ac naribus eminentibus, extractus
harundineto circa paludem Maricae, in quam se fugiens
consectantes Sullae equites abdiderat, iniecto in collum
loro in carcerem Minturnensium iussu duumviri perduc-
3 tus est. ad quem interficiendum missus cum gladio servus
publicus natione Germanus, qui forte ab imperatore eo

114 se *post* pravus *suppl. Woodman, post* praeceps *Puteanus*
115 etiam *ut iteratum ex* Sulpitium *susp. Orelli*
116 annumque *Vossius*: -oque *PA*: -osque *Puteanus*

BOOK 2.18–19

portance with the people on account of his correct disposition, suddenly, as if he were disgusted with his own virtues and his good intentions were proving unsuccessful, conceived a perverted and precipitate attachment to Gaius Marius, who, though past seventy, was craving any and every command and province. So he carried a law before the people by which Sulla's command was revoked and the war against Mithridates was decreed to Marius; and he carried other pernicious and baleful laws that should not be tolerated by a free community. Moreover, by means of emissaries from his faction, he even killed the man who was son of the consul Quintus Pompeius and son-in-law of Sulla.

19. Thereupon Sulla, having assembled an army, returned to the City and seized it by armed force: he evicted from the City the twelve instigators of the wicked revolution, including Marius along with his son and Publius Sulpicius, and, by a law duly carried, made them exiles. Sulpicius was also slaughtered, in the Laurentine Marshes, by cavalry who had overtaken him; and his head, raised on high and displayed on the rostra, acted as an omen of the imminent proscription.[91] As for Marius, with a sixth consulship and his seventieth year behind him, he was dragged—naked and covered in mud, with only his eyes and nostrils sticking out—from a reed bed near Marica's Marsh, where he had fled to hide from Sulla's pursuing cavalry; and, with a strap thrown around his neck, he was taken to the prison at Minturnae on the order of the duumvir.[92] An official slave, of German nationality, was sent with a sword to kill him, but by chance he had been

---

[91] See 28.3.   [92] A local official.

95

VELLEIUS PATERCULUS

bello Cimbrico captus erat, ut agnovit Marium, magno[117] eiulatu exprimente[118] indignationem casus tanti viri abiecto gladio profugit e carcere. tum cives, ab hoste misereri paulo ante principis viri docti, instructum eum viatico conlataque veste in navem imposuerunt. at ille adsecutus circa insulam Aenariam[119] filium cursum in Africam derexit inopemque vitam in tugurio ruinarum Carthaginiensium toleravit, cum Marius aspiciens Carthaginem, illa intuens Marium, alter alteri possent esse solacio.

20. Hoc primum anno sanguine consulis Romani militis imbutae manus sunt:[120] quippe ⟨Q.⟩[121] Pompeius, collega Sullae, ab exercitu Cn. Pompeii proconsulis seditione, sed[122] quam du⟨x ipse e⟩xcitaverat,[123] interfectus est.

Non erat Mario Sulpicioque[124] Cinna temperatior. itaque cum ita civitas Italiae data esset ut in octo tribus contribuerentur novi cives, ne potentia eorum et multitudo veterum civium dignitatem frangeret plusque possent recepti in beneficio quam auctores benefici, Cinna in omnibus tribubus eos se distributurum pollicitus est:

[117] magno *BA*: cum magno *P*   [118] exprimente *Heinsius*: exprimenti *A*: expromenti *BP*: expromente *Ruhnken*

[119] circa Taenariam *PA, corr. Gruner et Gelenius*

[120] sunt *BA, om. P*

[121] ⟨Q.⟩ *Heinsius*

[122] *an* sed *perperam iteratum ex* seditione?

[123] du⟨x ipse e⟩xcitaverat *Woodman* (excitaverat *iam Burer*): dux creaverat *BPA*

[124] Sulpitioque *A, Rhenanus*: Sulpitio *P*

---

[93] Q. Pompeius Rufus (cos. 88) was distantly related to Cn. Pompeius Strabo (cos. 89).

[94] L. Cornelius Cinna, consul in 87 with Cn. Octavius (22.2),

BOOK 2.19–20

captured by Marius when the latter was in command during the Cimbrian War, and, when he recognized Marius, he cried out loudly in indignation at the fate of so great a man and, casting aside his sword, fled from the prison. Then the citizens, taught by an enemy to pity a man who only a little while previously had been a principal figure, furnished him with travel items and a pile of clothing and put him on a ship. Overtaking his son near the island of Aenaria, however, he set course for Africa and endured a life of poverty in a hut amid the ruins of Carthage—Marius gazing at Carthage, she looking upon Marius, the one able to be a comfort to the other.

20. This was the first year that the hands of Roman soldiery were steeped in the blood of a Roman consul: Quintus Pompeius, Sulla's colleague, was killed by the army of the proconsul Gnaeus Pompeius in a mutiny, but one that the leader himself had stirred up.[93]

Cinna was no more restrained than Marius and Sulpicius.[94] Hence, although citizenship had been given to Italy in such a way that the new citizens would be distributed in only eight tribes (lest their influence and number should infringe the importance of the old citizens, and the recipients of the benefit have more capability than the instigators of the benefit), Cinna promised he would distribute them among all the tribes;[95] for this reason he had sum-

had been elected despite the opposition of Sulla, who had then departed for the war with Mithridates (23.3).

[95] The voting power of the new citizens had been reduced by their being assigned to a limited number of new voting tribes; after his eventual victory Cinna revived a proposal of Sulpicius Rufus in 88 (cf. 2.18.6) to distribute them across the existing thirty-five tribes, and this remained in force.

97

VELLEIUS PATERCULUS

quo nomine ingentem totius Italiae frequentiam in urbem
3 acciverat. e qua pulsus collegae optimatiumque viribus
cum in Campaniam tenderet, ex auctoritate senatus consulatus ei abrogatus est suffectusque in eius locum L. Cornelius Merula flamen dialis. haec iniuria homine quam
4 exemplo dignior fuit. tum Cinna corruptis primo centurionibus ac tribunis, mox etiam spe largitionis militibus, ab
eo exercitu qui circa Nolam erat receptus est. is cum universus in verba eius iurasset, retinens insignia consulatus
patriae bellum intulit, fretus ingenti numero novorum
civium, e quorum delectu CCC amplius cohortes conscrip-
5 serat ac triginta legionum instar impleverat. opus erat partibus auctoritate, gratia, cuius augendae ⟨causa⟩[125] C.
Marium cum filio de exilio revocavit quique cum iis pulsi
erant.

21. Dum bellum autem infert patriae Cinna, Cn. Pompeius, Magni pater, cuius praeclara opera bello Marsico,
praecipue circa Picenum agrum, ut praediximus,[126] usa
erat res publica, quique Asculum ceperat, circa quam urbem, cum in multis aliis regionibus exercitus dispersi forent, quinque et LXX ⟨milia⟩ civium Romanorum, am-
2 plius LX Italicorum una die conflixerant, frustratus spe
continuandi consulatus ita se dubium mediumque parti-

---

[125] *suppl. Laurent* (gratia *post* augendae *transpos. Koch*)
[126] praediximus *Ruhnken*: praescripsimus *PA* (ut praescripsimus *secl. Krause*)

---

[96] The college of pontiffs included fifteen *flamines* (a category
of priest), each assigned to the worship of a single god: the Flamen Dialis, one of the three major *flamines*, was the priest of
Jupiter.   [97] V. is referring to 2.15.3.

98

BOOK 2.20–21

moned into the City a huge crowd from the whole of Italy. But he was banished from the City by the forces of his colleague and of the optimates, and, as he was making his way to Campania, his consulship was revoked on the senate's authority and Lucius Cornelius Merula, the Flamen Dialis,[96] was substituted in his place. This injustice was more worthy of the man than as a precedent. Thereupon Cinna, having first bribed the centurions and tribunes and then the soldiers too with the hope of largesse, was welcomed by the army that was in the vicinity of Nola. When they had all sworn allegiance to him, still retaining the insignia of his consulship he waged war on his fatherland, relying on the huge number of new citizens, from whom he had conscripted more than three hundred cohorts by means of a levy and had filled the equivalent of thirty legions. To increase the authority and influence that his party needed, he recalled from exile Gaius Marius along with his son and those who had been banished with him.

21. But, while Cinna was waging war on his fatherland, Gnaeus Pompeius, Pompey the Great's father—of whose distinguished service in the Marsian War, especially in the area around the territory of Picenum, the commonwealth had availed itself, as we mentioned earlier,[97] and who had taken Asculum, a city where, although armies were scattered across many other regions, seventy-five thousand Roman citizens and more than sixty thousand Italians had engaged on a single day—was cheated in his hope of continuing his consulship[98] and presented himself as a neu-

[98] If V. is right, Pompeius had hoped to proceed straight from his consulship in 89 to a second consulship in 88.

99

VELLEIUS PATERCULUS

bus praestitit ut omnia ex proprio usu agere[127] tempori-
busque insidiari videretur, et huc atque illuc, unde spes
maior adfulsisset[128] potentiae, sese exercitumque deflec-
3   teret. sed ad ultimum magno atrocique proelio cum Cinna
conflixit; cuius commissi patratique sub ipsis moenibus
oculisque[129] urbis Romanae pugnantibus spectantibusque
quam fuerit eventus exitiabilis, vix verbis exprimi potest.
4   post hoc cum utrumque exercitum velut parum bello
exhaustum laceraret pestilentia, Cn. Pompeius decessit.
cuius interitus voluptas amissorum aut gladio aut morbo
civium paene damno repensata[130] est, populusque Romanus quam vivo iracundiam debuerat in corpus mortui con-
5   tulit. (seu duae seu tres Pompeiorum fuere familiae, primus eius nominis ante annos fere CLXXII[131] Q.[132]
Pompeius cum Cn. Servilio consul fuit.)
6   Cinna et Marius haud incruentis utrimque certami-
bus editis urbem occupaverunt, sed prior ingressus Cinna
de recipiendo Mario legem tulit. 22. mox C. Marius pes-
tifero civibus suis reditu intravit moenia. nihil illa victoria
2   fuisset crudelius, nisi mox Sullana esset secuta: neque
licentia gladiorum in mediocres saevitum, sed excelsissimi[133] quoque atque eminentissimi[134] civitatis viri variis
suppliciorum generibus adfecti. in iis consul Octavius, vir
lenissimi animi, iussu Cinnae interfectus est. Merula autem, qui se sub adventum Cinnae consulatu abdicaverat,

---

[127] agere *Vossius*: -et *PA*   [128] adfulsisset *Aldus*: adfuisset
PA   [129] oculisque *Lipsius*: sociisque *PA*

[130] damnum repensa‹re existima›ta *Shackleton Bailey*

[131] CLXXII *Laurent*: CLXVII *BA*: CLXVIII *P*

[132] Q. *Gelenius*: quem *A*: quam *P*   [133] excelsissimi *Gelenius*: -ae *PA*   [134] eminentissimi *Aldus*: -ae *PA*

100

BOOK 2.21–22

tral, uncommitted to any party, such that he seemed to be doing everything for his own advantage and to be lying in wait for the right moment, diverting himself and his army to wherever there gleamed a greater hope of power. But in the end he engaged with Cinna in a great and terrible battle, which was joined and concluded beneath the walls and eyes of the City of Rome; how baleful its outcome was for fighters and spectators can scarcely be expressed in words. After it, when plague was tearing through each army (as if they were insufficiently exhausted by war), Gnaeus Pompeius passed away. The pleasure at his death was almost counterbalanced by the cost of citizens lost to the sword or disease, and the Roman people subjected the dead man's body to the anger that it had owed him when alive. (Whether there were two or three families of Pompeii, the first of that name to be consul was Quintus Pompeius with Gnaeus Servilius, about 172 years ago.)[99]

After staging contests that had shed so much blood on both sides, Cinna and Marius seized the City, but, since Cinna was the first to go in, he carried a law for the recall of Marius. 22. Later Gaius Marius entered the walls, a pestilential return for his fellow citizens. Nothing could have been more cruel than that victory, had not Sulla's followed soon after; nor did the license of the sword direct its savagery only at the average person, but the most exalted and outstanding men of the community were afflicted with various forms of reprisal. One of them was the consul Octavius, a man of the mildest disposition, who was killed on Cinna's order. Merula on the other hand, who had abdicated from the consulship in response to Cinna's

99 In 141. See 2.1.4.

VELLEIUS PATERCULUS

incisis venis superfusoque altaribus sanguine, quos saepe pro salute rei publicae flamen Dialis precatus erat deos,[135] eos[136] in execrationem Cinnae partiumque eius tum precatus optime de re publica meritum spiritum reddidit.

3 M. Antonius, princeps civitatis atque eloquentiae, gladiis militum, quos ipsos facundia sua moratus erat, iussu Marii
4 Cinnaeque confossus est. Q. Catulus, et aliarum virtutum et belli Cimbrici gloria, quae illi cum Mario communis fuerat, celeberrimus, cum ad mortem conquireretur, conclusit se loco nuper calce harenaque perpolito[137] inlatoque igni, qui vim odoris excitaret, simul exitiali hausto spiritu, simul incluso suo, mortem magis voto quam arbitrio inimicorum obiit.

5 Omnia erant praecipitia in re publica, nec tamen adhuc quisquam inveniebatur qui bona civis Romani aut donare auderet aut petere sustineret. postea id quoque accessit, ut saevitiae causam avaritia praeberet et modus culpae ex pecuniae modo constitueretur et qui fuisset locuples fieret [in]nocens,[138] sui[139] quisque periculi merces foret, nec quidquam videretur turpe quod esset quaestuosum.

[135] deos *secl. Krause*
[136] eos *secl. Herel*
[137] perlito *Lipsius*: praelito *Burman*
[138] nocens *Gelenius*
[139] sui‹que› *Acidalius*

---

[100] This is a variant of the story that Antonius charmed the death squad by his oratory and had to be killed by the commanding officer (e.g., App. *B Civ.* 1.72.335).

[101] Cf. Val. Max. 4.3.14b, "Although they [sc. Marius and Cinna] had offered the houses of those they proscribed for plun-

BOOK 2.22

arrival, sliced open his veins and, pouring his blood on the altars, cursed Cinna and his party in a prayer to the gods to whom, as Flamen Dialis, he had so often prayed for the health of the commonwealth, rendering up his life's breath that had served the commonwealth so well. Marcus Antonius, a principal figure in the community and in eloquence, was stabbed on the order of Marius and Cinna by the swords of soldiers whom he had actually stalled by his fluency.[100] When Quintus Catulus—celebrated for the glory of his virtues in general but especially for that which he had won in the Cimbrian War and had shared with Marius—was being hunted down to be killed, he shut himself up in a place recently given a smooth finish with lime and sand: he had brought in a fire to intensify the strong smell, and, at one moment inhaling the fatal fumes, at another holding in his own breath, he met a death that his enemies had desired but was not of their choosing.

Everything in the commonwealth was collapsing headlong, but no one was yet found who either ventured to make a donation of a Roman citizen's goods or who could bring himself to seek them.[101] Afterward that element too was added: greed provided a motive for savagery, the sum of one's guilt was established by the sum of money involved, those already wealthy became culpable, each person was the reward of his own danger,[102] and nothing seemed shameful if it could be profitable.

der at the hands of the common folk, nobody could be found to seek booty from the mourning of citizens" (trans. Shackleton Bailey).

[102] That is, the wealthy, though blameless, were regarded as legitimate targets, and there was a price on a person's head.

103

VELLEIUS PATERCULUS

23. Secundum deinde consulatum Cinna et septimum Marius in priorum dedecus iniit, cuius initio morbo oppressus decessit, vir in bello hostibus, in otio civibus infes-
2 tissimus quietisque impatientissimus. in huius locum suffectus Valerius Flaccus, turpissimae legis auctor qua creditoribus quadrantem solvi iusserat, cuius facti merita
3 eum poena intra biennium consecuta est. dominante in Italia Cinna maior pars nobilitatis ad Sullam in Achaiam ac deinde post in Asiam perfugit.

Sulla interim cum Mithridatis praefectis circa Athenas Boeotiamque et Macedoniam ita dimicavit ut et Athenas reciperet et plurimo circa multiplices Piraei portus munitiones labore expleto amplius CC milia hostium inter-
4 ficeret nec minus multa caperet. si quis hoc rebellandi tempus, quo Athenae oppugnatae a Sulla sunt, imputat Atheniensibus, nimirum veri vetustatisque ignarus est: adeo enim certa Atheniensium in Romanos fides fuit ut semper et in omni re, quidquid sincera fide gereretur, id
5 Romani Attica fieri[140] praedicarent. ceterum tum[141] oppressi Mithridatis armis homines miserrimae condicionis cum ab inimicis tenerentur, oppugnabantur ab amicis et animos extra moenia, corpora necessitati servientes intra muros habebant.

6 Transgressus deinde in Asiam Sulla parentem ad[142] omnia supplicemque Mithridatem invenit, quem multa-

---

140 ‹ fide › fieri *Freudenberg*   141 ṭum *BA*: cum *P*
142 ad *Ruhnken*: ante *PA*

---

103 On 13 January 86.
104 Of the debt owed.
105 See 24.1.

104

BOOK 2.23

23. Then Cinna entered upon his second consulship and Marius his seventh, to the disgrace of his former six, but at the beginning of it he was overcome by illness and passed away,[103] a man of the utmost hostility to enemies during wartime and to citizens during peacetime, intolerant of any tranquility. The substitute in his place was Valerius Flaccus, instigator of a most shameful law by which he had ordered that only a quarter[104] be paid to creditors, for which action punishment deservedly overtook him within two years.[105] With Cinna master in Italy, the majority of the nobility fled to Sulla in Achaea and after that to Asia.

Meanwhile Sulla's battles with Mithridates' prefects around Athens and in Boeotia and Macedonia had the result that he recaptured Athens and, after expending a great deal of effort around the diverse defenses of the harbor of Piraeus, killed more than two hundred thousand of the enemy and took captive not many less. If anyone blames the Athenians for this period of rebellion, during which Athens was under assault by Sulla, he is evidently ignorant of actuality and antiquity: so sure was the Athenians' loyalty to the Romans that any deed at all, if performed with unblemished loyalty, was always said by the Romans, and in every circumstance, to be done with "Attic loyalty." But on that occasion, overwhelmed by Mithridates' armed forces, the people were in the most wretched condition, since they were being held by their enemies but assaulted by their friends, having their hearts outside the battlements but, bowing to necessity, their bodies inside the walls.

Then, crossing into Asia, Sulla found Mithridates obedient on all counts and in suppliant mode: he punished

105

VELLEIUS PATERCULUS

tum pecunia ac parte navium Asia omnibusque aliis provinciis quas armis occupaverat decedere coegit, captivos recepit, in perfugas noxiosque animadvertit, paternis (id est Ponticis) finibus contentum esse iussit. 24. C. Flavius Fimbria, qui praefectus equitum ante adventum Sullae Valerium Flaccum consularem virum interfecerat excercituque occupato imperator appellatus ⟨sua⟩[143] sponte[144] Mithridaten[145] pepulerat proelio, sub adventum Sullae se ipse interemit, adulescens quae pessime ausus erat fortiter executus.

2 Eodem anno P. Laenas tribunus plebis Sex. Lucilium, qui [in][146] priore anno tribunus plebis fuerat, saxo Tarpeio deiecit, et, cum collegae eius, quibus diem dixerat, metu[147] ad Sullam perfugissent,[148] aqua ignique iis interdixit.

3 Tum Sulla compositis transmarinis rebus, cum ad eum primum omnium Romanorum legati Parthorum venissent, et in iis quidam magi ex notis corporis respondissent caelestem eius vitam et memoriam futuram, revectus in Italiam haud plura quam XXX armatorum milia adversum

---

[143] ⟨sua⟩ *Woodman*   [144] sponte *Halm (cf. App. Mith. 52 αὐτὸν αὐτοκράτορα ἀπέφηνε τοῦ στρατοῦ): fonte PA:* forti *Puteanus*   [145] Mithridaten *P:* -em *A:* Mithridatem ⟨filium⟩ *Shackleton Bailey*   [146] *secl. Gelenius*   [147] metu *Burer:* motu *PA*   [148] perfugissent *Baiter:* pro- *PA*

---

[106] Successful generals were acclaimed by their troops with the honorific title "commander" (*imperator*), the practice modeled here.   [107] Fimbria's suicide and Sulla's settlement with Mithridates took place in 85, but V. here reverts to an event of 86.

[108] The Tarpeian Rock is on the south side of the Capitoline Hill (2.1.2n).   [109] An exile was forbidden to re-enter Roman

106

BOOK 2.23–24

him by the forfeiture of money and of some of his ships, compelled him to withdraw from Asia and all the other provinces that he had seized by armed force, welcomed back captives, took measures against deserters and the guilty, and ordered the king to be content with his ancestral boundaries (that is, those of Pontus). 24. Gaius Flavius Fimbria—who as cavalry prefect before Sulla's arrival had killed the ex-consul Valerius Flaccus and, having seized the latter's army, and hailed as its "commander,"[106] had beaten Mithridates in battle on his own account—killed himself in response to Sulla's arrival, a young man who bravely executed his wicked ventures.

In the same year[107] Publius Laenas, tribune of the plebs, threw Sextus Lucilius, who had been tribune of the plebs in the previous year, down from the Tarpeian Rock,[108] and, when his colleagues (to whom he had issued summonses) fled in fear to Sulla, he forbade them fire and water.[109]

Then Sulla, affairs overseas having been settled (where he had been the first of all Romans to whom there came legates from the Parthians, and certain magi among them had declared from marks on his body that his life and memory would be of a heavenly nature),[110] sailed back to Italy[111] and at Brundisium disembarked no more than

territory and, if he did so, could not legally be offered shelter or sustenance, i.e., his re-entry was on pain of death. The prohibition of "fire and water" came to be used as a formula denoting exile itself. [110] Sulla had received the Parthian embassy ca. 95, when, as governor of Cilicia (2.15.3n), he had been obliged to intervene in the affairs of Cappadocia. Magi were Iranian priests with expertise in magic and astrology. [111] In 83.

107

VELLEIUS PATERCULUS

4 CC amplius hostium exposuit Brundisii. vix quicquam in Sullae operibus clarius duxerim quam quod, cum per triennium Cinnanae Marianaeque partes Italiam obsiderent, neque inlaturum se bellum iis dissimulavit nec quod erat in manibus omisit, existimavitque ante frangendum hostem quam ulciscendum civem, repulsoque externo metu, ubi quod alienum esset vicisset, superare[149] quod erat domesticum.

5 Ante adventum L. Sullae Cinna seditione orta ab exercitu interemptus est, vir dignior qui arbitrio victorum moreretur quam iracundia militum. de quo vere dici potest ausum eum quae nemo auderet bonus, perfecisse quae a nullo nisi fortissimo perfici possent, et fuisse eum in consultando temerarium, in exequendo virum. Carbo nullo suffecto collega solus toto anno consul fuit.

25. Putares Sullam venisse in Italiam non belli vindicem sed pacis auctorem: tanta cum quiete exercitum per Calabriam Apuliamque cum singulari cura frugum, agrorum, hominum, urbium perduxit in Campaniam temptavitque iustis legibus et aequis condicionibus bellum componere; sed iis quibus et pessima[150] et immodica cupiditas 2 erat non poterat pax placere. crescebat interim in dies Sullae exercitus confluentibus ad eum optimo quoque et[151] sanissimo. felici deinde[152] circa Capuam eventu Sci-

---

[149] superare *Ursinus*: -aret *PA*: -andum *Ruhnken*: -avit *Gelenius*　　　[150] ⟨res⟩ pessima *Ruhnken*
[151] et *BA, om. P*　　　[152] deinde *BA*: denique *PA^c*

---

[112] The text of this sentence is uncertain and the meaning unclear.　　　[113] That is, 84. Cn. Papirius Carbo was also consul in 85 and 82 (26.1).

108

BOOK 2.24–25

thirty thousand armed men to face more than two hundred thousand of the enemy. I rather think that scarcely anything among Sulla's achievements is more distinguished than the fact that, when for three years the party of Cinna and Marius had Italy in a state of siege, he neither dissembled that he would wage war on them nor neglected the war that he had on his hands: he reckoned that breaking an enemy should take precedence over exacting revenge on a citizen and that, once an external dread had been repelled, it was only then, when he had conquered what was foreign, that he should overcome what was domestic.[112]

Before Lucius Sulla's arrival Cinna was killed by his army in a mutiny that had sprung up, a man whose death should more properly have resulted from a decision of the victors than the anger of his soldiers. It can truly be said of him that he ventured what no good man would venture, achieved what could be achieved by none except the bravest, and that he was rash in forming plans but a man in their execution. With no colleague substituted for him, Carbo was sole consul for the whole year.[113]

25. You would have thought that Sulla had arrived in Italy not as an avenger in war but as an instigator of peace, such was the lack of disruption with which he led his army through Calabria and Apulia into Campania, having a singular concern for crops, land, persons, and cities, and he tried to settle the war through just laws and on fair terms; but peace could not please those whose desire was one of unrestrained wickedness. Meanwhile Sulla's army was growing by the day, as all the best and soundest men kept converging on him. Then he enjoyed a happy outcome in the vicinity of Capua, when he overcame the consuls

109

VELLEIUS PATERCULUS

pionem Norbanumque consules superat, quorum Norbanus acie victus, Scipio ab exercitu suo desertus ac proditus
3 inviolatus a Sulla dimissus est. adeo enim Sulla dissimilis
fuit bellator ac victor ut, dum vincit, [ac][153] iustissimo[154]
lenior, post victoriam audito fuerit crudelior. nam et consulem (ut praediximus) exarmatum ‹Quintum›que[155] Sertorium (pro quanti mox belli facem!) et multos alios, potitus eorum, dimisit incolumes, credo, ut in eodem homine
duplicis ac diversissimi animi conspiceretur exemplum.
4 post[156] victoriam qua ad [emendes][157] montem Tifata cum
C. Norbano concurrerat, Sulla grates[158] Dianae, cuius
numini[159] regio illa sacrata est, solvit; aquas salubritate
medendisque corporibus nobiles agrosque omnes addixit[160] deae. huius gratae religionis memoriam[161] et in-
scriptio templi adfixa posti hodieque ‹et›[162] tabula tutatur[163] aerea intra aedem.

26. Deinde[164] consules Carbo tertium et C. Marius,
septiens consulis filius, annos natus XXVI, vir animi magis
quam aevi[165] paterni, ‹qui›[166] multa fortiterque molitus

---

153 *secl. Gelenius*   154 iustissimo *PA*: iusto *vel* mitissimo
Lipsius: alii alia   155 ‹Quintum›que *Heinsius*

156 post *Gelenius*: posuit *BPA*

157 qua ad [emendes] *Novák*: qua demendes *BPA*: qua descen-
dens *Gelenius: alii alia*   158 gratis *BA*: -us *P*

159 numini *P*: nomini *BA*

160 addixit *Gelenius*: adduxit *BPA*

161 memoriam *Lipsius*: -ia *BPA*

162 *suppl. Gelenius*   163 tutatur *Woodman*: testatur *PA*

164 intra aedem. deinde *Gelenius*: interea deinde *B*: inter
edeinde *A* (inter edem de *A^c*): intra aedem *P*

165 aevi *PA, obelis not. Watt*: fati *Heinsius*: ingeni *Orelli*

166 *suppl. Gelenius*

110

BOOK 2.25–26

Scipio and Norbanus,[114] of whom Norbanus was beaten in the battle line, while Scipio, deserted and betrayed by his army, was dismissed by Sulla unharmed. For Sulla was so different as warrior and conqueror that, while he was conquering, he was milder than the most just of men, whereas after conquest he was more cruel than anyone had heard of. For he dismissed unscathed the weaponless consul, as we just mentioned, and also Quintus Sertorius (soon, alas, to be the firebrand of a great war!) and many others, despite having them in his power, so that in one and the same man, I believe, there could be witnessed an example of a double and very divided personality. After the victory in which he had engaged with Gaius Norbanus at Mount Tifata, Sulla paid thanks to Diana, to whose divinity that region is sacred: he assigned to the goddess the waters that are famous for good health and bodily remedies, and also all the territory. The memory of this welcome religious gesture is still preserved today both by an inscription affixed to a doorjamb of the temple and by a bronze tablet within the shrine.

26. Then followed[115] the consulship of Carbo, for the third time, and Gaius Marius, son of the seven-times consul, twenty-six years old, a man resembling his father in temperament rather than in age,[116] who, after many coura-

[114] The consuls of 83 were L. Cornelius Scipio Asiaticus and C. Norbanus.

[115] In 82.

[116] The elder Marius had been almost twice his son's age when he first became consul in 107; V. seems to be making an analogous point to that which he made about Sulla at 2.17.3.

111

VELLEIUS PATERCULUS

neque usquam inferior nomine consulis apud Sacriportum pulsus a Sulla acie Praeneste, quod ante natura munitum praesidiis firmaverat, se exercitumque contulit.

2   Ne quid usquam[167] malis publicis deesset, in qua civitate semper virtutibus certatum erat, certabatur sceleribus, optimusque sibi videbatur qui fuerat[168] pessimus. quippe, dum ad Sacriportum dimicatur, Damasippus praetor Domitium,[169] Scaevolam etiam, pontificem maximum et divini humanique iuris auctorem celeberrimum, et C. Carbonem praetorium, consulis fratrem, et Antistium aedilicium velut faventes Sullae partibus in curia

3 Hostilia trucidavit. non perdat nobilissimi facti gloriam Calpurnia, Bestiae filia, uxor Antistii, quae iugulato (ut praediximus) viro gladio se ipsa transfixit. quantum huius gloriae famaeque accessit! nunc virtute ⟨femina⟩[170] eminet propria[171] ⟨nec⟩[172] latet!

    27. At Pontius Telesinus, dux Samnitium, vir animi[173] bellique fortissimus penitusque Romano nomini infestissimus, contractis circiter XL ⟨milibus⟩ fortissimae pertinacissimaeque in retinendis armis iuventutis, Carbone ac Mario consulibus, abhinc annos CXI[174] Kal. Novembri-

---

[167] usquam *Puteanus*: unquam *PA*   [168] fuerat *PA*: foret *Halm*   [169] Domitium ⟨consularem⟩ *Ruhnken*

[170] *suppl. Woodman (iam* ⟨feminae⟩ *Laurent)*

[171] propria *Orelli*: patria *PA*

[172] nec *hic suppl. Woodman, post* eminet *Bothe*

[173] animi *PA*: domi *Rhenanus: alii alia*

[174] CXI *Aldus*: XI *BA*: XL *P*

---

[117] L. Iunius Brutus Damasippus' victims were L. Domitius Ahenobarbus (cos. 94), Q. Mucius Scaevola (cos. 95), C. Papirius

112

BOOK 2.26–27

geous initiatives and in no respect inferior to the name of consul, was beaten by Sulla in the battle line at Sacriportus and betook himself and his army to Praeneste, which, though naturally fortified, he had previously strengthened by defenses.

So that no element should be missing anywhere from the public maladies, there was a competition in crime in the very community where there had always been a competition in virtue, and whoever was worst thought himself best. While the fighting was in progress at Sacriportus, the praetor Damasippus butchered, in the Curia Hostilia, Domitius and also Scaevola, the Chief Pontiff and celebrated author in the areas of divine and human law, and the ex-praetor Gaius Carbo (the consul's brother) and the ex-aedile Antistius, on the grounds that they were supporters of Sulla's party.[117] Calpurnia, daughter of Bestia[118] and wife of Antistius, should not be deprived of the glory of her most noble action: after her husband (as we just mentioned) was slaughtered, she ran herself through with a sword. What an addition to his own glory and fame! Now a woman stands out for her own manly courage and does not stay hidden![119]

27. On the other hand Pontius Telesinus, leader of the Samnites, a man whose brave spirit thrived best in war and who was deeply hostile to the Roman nation, assembled around forty thousand of his bravest young men, still stubbornly holding on to their weapons, and, in the consulship of Carbo and Marius, on the Kalends of November 111

Carbo Arvina (pr. 83?) and P. Antistius (trib. pleb. 88). For the Curia Hostilia see 2.12.6n. [118] L. Calpurnius Bestia (cos. 111). [119] Text and meaning are highly uncertain. Cf. 88.3.

113

VELLEIUS PATERCULUS

bus ita ad portam Collinam cum Sulla dimicavit ut ad summum discrimen et eum et rem publicam perduceret,
2 quae non maius periculum adiit Hannibalis intra tertium miliarium castra conspicata quam eo[175] die quo circumvolans ordines exercitus sui Telesinus dictitansque adesse Romanis ultimum diem vociferabatur eruendam delendamque urbem, adiiciens numquam defuturos raptores Italicae libertatis lupos, nisi silva in quam refugere so-
3 lerent[176] esset excisa. post primam demum horam noctis et Romana acies respiravit et hostium cessit. Telesinus postera die semianimis repertus est, victoris magis quam morientis vultum[177] praeferens, cuius abscisum caput ferri[178] gestarique circa Praeneste Sulla iussit.
4 Tum demum desperatis rebus suis C. Marius adulescens per cuniculos, qui miro opere fabricati in diversas agrorum partis ferebant,[179] conatus erumpere, cum foramine e terra emersisset, a dispositis in id ipsum interemp-
5 tus est. sunt qui sua manu, sunt qui concurrentem mutuis ictibus cum minore fratre Telesini[180] una obsesso et erumpente occubuisse prodiderint; utcumque cecidit, hodieque tanta patris imagine[181] non obscuratur eius[182] memoria. de quo iuvene quid existimaverit Sulla in promptu est:

175 eo *B*: eodem *PA*
176 solerent *Burer*: solent *PA*
177 vultum *Gelenius*: cultum *PA*
178 ferr‹o fig›i *Madvig*
179 ferebant *Burman*: fuerunt *PA*
180 Telesini *Duker*: -o *PA*
181 imagine *PA*: magnitudine *Ruhnken*
182 eius *P*: civis *BA*

114

BOOK 2.27

years ago, fought such a battle with Sulla at the Colline Gate[120] that he brought the utmost of crises upon him and the commonwealth, which faced no greater danger when it spied Hannibal's camp within the third milestone[121] than on that day when Telesinus, flying about the ranks of his army and repeating that for the Romans the final day had arrived, shouted that the City had to be razed and destroyed, adding that the wolves who robbed Italians of their freedom would never become extinct unless the wood in which they were accustomed to take refuge were cut down. At length, after the first hour of the night, the Roman battle line revived and that of the enemy yielded. Telesinus was discovered the next day only half-alive, his expression more that of a victor than of a dying man; Sulla ordered his head to be cut off, carried to Praeneste, and paraded there.

Then finally, his situation desperate, the young Gaius Marius tried to break out through the tunnels that, in an amazing undertaking, had been constructed and led to different parts of the countryside, but, when he emerged from an opening in the ground, he was killed by men deployed there for that very purpose. There are those who have reported that he met his death by his own hand, others that he and Telesinus' younger brother, in whose company he had been besieged and was breaking out, ran at each other with reciprocal blows; but, however he fell, his memory even today is not eclipsed by the image of his great father. What Sulla thought of the young man is self-evident, since it was only when he was finally slain that he

[120] In the northeast of Rome, at the junction of the Via Salaria and Via Nomentana.   [121] That is, from Rome.

115

VELLEIUS PATERCULUS

occiso enim demum eo Felicis nomen adsumpsit, quod[183] quidem usurpasset iustissime, si eundem et vincendi et vivendi finem habuisset.

6   Oppugnationi autem Praenestis ac Marii praefuerat Ofella[184] Lucretius, qui, cum ante Marianarum[185] fuisset partium adiutor,[186] ad Sullam transfugerat. felicitatem diei quo Samnitium Telesinique pulsus est exercitus Sulla perpetua ludorum circensium honoravit memoria, qui sub[187] eius nomine Sullanae Victoriae celebrantur. 28. paulo ante quam Sulla ad Sacriportum dimicaret, magnificis proeliis partium eius viri hostium exercitus[188] fuderant, duo Servilii apud Clusium,[189] Metellus Pius apud Faventiam, M. Lucullus circa Fidentiam.

2   Videbantur finita belli civilis mala, cum Sullae crudelitate aucta sunt. quippe dictator creatus (cuius honoris usurpatio per annos CXX intermissa: nam proximus post annum quam Hannibal Italia excesserat, uti appareat populum Romanum usum dictatoris ut ‹in›[190] metu desiderasse, ita in otio[191] timuisse potestatem) imperio ‹quo›[192]

---

183 quod *P*: quo *BA*   184 Ofella *B*: Afella *A*: Asella *PA[m]*

185 Marianarum *P*: marinarum *BA*   186 adiutor *Woodman (cf. 41.2, 74.3, 76.1)*: praetor *PA, secl. Novák*

187 qui sub *BA*: quibus *P*   188 exercitus *Halm*: -um *PA*

189 Clusium *Gelenius*: Pl- *PA*

190 ut ‹in› *Rosenheyn*: aut *PA*

191 ita in otio *Rosenheyn*: Tulio Co *P (sim. A)*

192 *suppl. Gelenius*

---

122 Felix is the Latin for "fortunate."

123 The games (26 October–1 November) consisted of chariot

BOOK 2.27–28

assumed the name Felix,[122] which he certainly would have been very justified in adopting if the end of his victory had coincided with that of his life.

In charge of blockading Marius in Praeneste was Ofella Lucretius, who, although he had previously been a supporter of the Marian party, had deserted to Sulla. The felicity of the day on which the army of Telesinus and his Samnites was beaten was signalized by Sulla by the perpetual memorial of circus games, which are celebrated as being for "Sulla's Victory" after his name.[123] 28. Shortly before Sulla fought at Sacriportus, men of his party had routed enemy armies in splendid battles—the two Servilii at Clusium, Metellus Pius at Faventia, and Marcus Lucullus in the vicinity of Fidentia.[124]

The evils of the civil war were looking ended, when they were reinforced by the cruelty of Sulla. Created dictator (resort to this office had been in suspension for 120 years: the last was the year after Hannibal had left Italy,[125] from which it is clear that the Roman people desired the use of a dictator in times of dread but feared his power in times of peace), he used his command as a license for

races in the Circus Maximus, culminating on the anniversary day of the battle. With "felicity" V. is playing on Sulla's name Felix.

[124] The identity of the two Servilii is not certain, although one of them may have been P. Servilius Vatia Isauricus (39.2n); the others named are Q. Caecilius Metellus Pius (cos. 80) and M. Terentius Varro Lucullus (cos. 73), brother of the more famous L. Lucullus (cos. 74). [125] Sulla was elected dictator in 82; the last dictator had been appointed in 202, like many of his predecessors, just to hold elections. The last dictator appointed for a military emergency had been Q. Fabius Maximus in 216.

117

VELLEIUS PATERCULUS

priores ad vindicandam maximis periculis[193] rem publicam[194] olim usi erant, eo ‹in›[195] immodicae crudelitatis

3 licentiam[196] usus est. primus ille—et utinam ultimus!—
exemplum proscriptionis invenit, ut in qua civitate petu-
lantis convicii iudicium †historiarum†[197] ex alto[198] reddi-
tur, in ea iugulati civis Romani publice[199] constitueretur
auctoramentum, plurimumque haberet qui plurimos interemisset, neque occisi hostis quam civis uberius foret

4 praemium fieretque quisque merces mortis suae. nec tantum[200] in eos qui contra arma tulerant sed in multos in-
sontes saevitum. adiectum etiam ut bona proscriptorum
venirent exclusique paternis opibus liberi etiam petendo-
rum honorum iure prohiberentur simulque (quod indig-
nissimum est) senatorum filii et onera ordinis sustinerent
et iura perderent.

29. Sub adventum in Italiam L. Sullae Cn. Pompeius,
eius Cn. Pompei filius quem magnificentissimas res in
consulatu[201] gessisse bello Marsico praediximus, XXIII
annos natus, abhinc annos CXIII privatis ut opibus ita

---

[193] prores (proh res *P*) ad vindicandam (-um *P*) maximi periculi *PA, em. Gelenius*   [194] rem p. *Gelenius,* olim *Cludius,* usi
erant *Vossius:* spolia musierant *(vel sim.) PA*   [195] *suppl.
Davies*   [196] licentiam *Burman:* -ae *PA*   [197] historiarum
BA: historiarium *P:* histrioni *Gelenius:* iniuriarum *Pithoeus (locus
desperatus)*   [198] ex alto *BPA:* ex albo *Pithoeus*   [199] Romani
publice *Puteanus:* Reip. *P:* R. publicae *A*   [200] tantum *Pithoeus:*
tamen *PA*   [201] consulatu *BA:* senatu *P*

---

[126] Proscription was the public listing of the names of individuals deemed outlaws and liable for execution, though it was
often used as a means of settling personal scores.

BOOK 2.28–29

unrestrained cruelty, a command that his predecessors had formerly used to rescue the commonwealth from its greatest dangers. He was the first—and would that he had been the last!—to discover a model in proscription,[126] such that remuneration for slaughtering a Roman citizen was officially established in a community where judgment on an aggressive insult is delivered †. . .† from on high;[127] the man rewarded most was the man who had killed the most; the prize for an enemy's slaying was no more valuable than that for a citizen's; and each man became the price of his own death. Nor was the savagery directed only at those who had taken up arms in opposition, but at many who were innocent. Additional factors were that the goods of the proscribed were put on sale, and their children, cut off from their fathers' property, were even prohibited from the right to seek office, and at the same time (something that is quite disgraceful) the sons of senators maintained the burdens of rank while losing its rights.

29. In response to the arrival of Lucius Sulla in Italy, Pompey, son of the Gnaeus Pompeius whose very magnificent achievements as consul in the Marsian War we mentioned earlier,[128] at the age of twenty-three,[129] 113 years

---

[127] The word corruptly transmitted has not been convincingly emended. Some older scholars believed that *ex alto* was a reference to the platform or tribunal from which the verdict would be delivered in a court case (cf. Mart. 11.98.17): if so, V. seems to be contrasting the regular legalism by which a verbal and relatively minor offense is punished and the *ad hoc* system of Sulla, which legalized the act of murder and rewarded the murderer.

[128] At 2.15.3 (cf. 21.1).   [129] Pompey's twenty-third birthday was on 29 September 83 (cf. 53.4).

119

VELLEIUS PATERCULUS

consiliis magna ausus magnificeque conata executus, ad vindicandam restituendamque dignitatem patriae Firmum ex agro Piceno, qui totus paternis eius clientelis re-

2 fertus erat, contraxit exercitum; cuius viri magnitudo multorum voluminum instar exigit, sed operis modus paucis eum narrari iubet.

Fuit hic genitus matre Lucilia stirpis senatoriae, forma excellens, non ea qua flos commendatur aetatis sed ex dignitate constans atque[202] in illam conveniens amplitudinem fortunamque eum[203] ad ultimum[204] vitae comitata est

3 diem; innocentia eximius, sanctitate praecipuus, eloquentia medius, potentiae, quae honoris causa ad eum deferretur, non vi[205] ab eo occuparetur, cupidissimus, dux bello peritissimus, civis in toga, nisi ubi vereretur ne quem haberet parem, modestissimus, amicitiarum tenax, in offensis exorabilis, in reconcilianda gratia fidelissimus, in accipienda satisfactione facillimus, potentia sua numquam aut raro ad impotentiam usus, paene omnium vitiorum[206] ex-

4 pers, nisi numeraretur inter maxima in[207] civitate[208] libera dominaque gentium indignari, cum omnes cives iure haberet pares, quemquam aequalem dignitate conspicere.

5 hic a toga virili adsuetus commilitio prudentissimi ducis,

---

[202] constans atque *Heinsius*: constantiaque *PA^c*: constientiaque *A*: *alii alia*

[203] eum *Lipsius*: eius *PA*

[204] ultimum *BA*: -am *P*

[205] vi *Mommsen*: ut *PA*

[206] vitiorum *Aldus*: votorum *PA*

[207] in *BA*, *om. P*

[208] civitate *BPA^c*: -em *A*

120

BOOK 2.29

ago, ventured great things on his personal initiative and with his personal resources, and, carrying out his enterprise in great style, assembled an army at Firmum from the region of Picenum (all of which was crammed with his father's client networks) in order to rescue and restore the dignity of his fatherland. The man's greatness demands the equivalent of many volumes, but the limitations of my work order him to be described in only a few words.

He was born to Lucilia (his mother was of senatorial stock) and was outstanding in appearance, yet not the kind by which the flower of one's youth is enhanced but, being based upon his dignity and consistent with his famous prestige and fortune, it accompanied him to the last day of his life. He was exceptional in integrity, a model of scrupulousness, average in eloquence, highly desirous of the kind of power that might be conferred on him as an honor and not seized by him through violence, the most skilled of leaders in war, in a toga the most restrained of citizens (except when he was afraid of having an equal), tenacious in friendships, placable when affronted, loyal in reestablishing goodwill, compliant when receiving satisfaction, never (or only rarely) becoming power-mad from power, and devoid of almost every flaw—unless it be counted among the greatest flaws in a free community, mistress of the world's peoples, to resent seeing anyone level in rank while at the same time regarding all citizens as equal in law. From the time of his toga of manhood[130] he had been accustomed to being a fellow soldier

---

[130] The toga of manhood was assumed by Roman boys in their early teens and replaced the *toga praetexta* (1.10.3n).

121

VELLEIUS PATERCULUS

parentis sui, bonum et capax recta discendi ingenium singulari rerum militarium prudentia excoluerat.[209]

***[210] ut a[211] Sertorio Metellus laudaretur magis, Pom-
peius timeretur validius. 30. tum M. Perpenna praetorius,
e proscriptis, gentis clarioris quam animi, Sertorium inter
cenam Oscae interemit Romanisque certam victoriam,
partibus suis excidium, sibi turpissimam mortem pessimo
2 auctoravit[212] facinore. Metellus et Pompeius ex Hispa-
niis[213] triumphaverunt,[214] sed Pompeius, hoc quoque
triumpho adhuc eques Romanus, ante diem quam consu-
3 latum iniret, curru urbem invectus est. (quem virum quis
non miretur per tot extraordinaria imperia in summum
fastigium evectum[215] iniquo tulisse animo C. Caesaris[216]
in altero consulatu petendo senatum populumque Roma-

> [209] prudentia excoluerat *Ruhnken*: prudentiae celeriora *PA*
> [210] *lacunam hic stat. Shackleton Bailey, post* validius *Krause*
> [211] ut a *Gelenius*: et a *PA^c*: aeta *A*
> [212] maturavit *Cornelissen*   [213] Hispaniis *BA*: -nis *P*
> [214] triumphaverunt *BA*: -arunt *P*
> [215] evectum *Heinsius*: vectum *PA*
> [216] Caesaris ⟨absentis⟩ *Krause*

---

[131] Q. Sertorius (pr. 83) had belonged to the Marian party,
whose defeat saw him become a rebel in Spain, where he was
propraetor in 82 and attracted popular support. In 79–78 he inflicted serious defeats on Q. Caecilius Metellus Pius (cos. 80),
proconsul of Further Spain, and in 77 Pompey was made proconsul of Nearer Spain and given the command against Sertorius
jointly with Metellus. V. anticipated Sertorius' intransigence at
29.3 and will recall it at 90.3, yet Sertorius' death in 72 is recorded
in the very next sentence here (30.1) without there having been
any further mention of him apart from the present elliptical refer-

122

BOOK 2.29–30

of that most prudent of leaders, his father, and he had cultivated his fine talent, so capable of learning what was correct, thanks to a singular prudence in military matters.

*** such that Sertorius' praise for Metellus was greater but his fear of Pompey stronger.[131] 30. Then Marcus Perpenna, an ex-praetor and one of the proscribed, whose family was more distinguished than his loyalty, killed Sertorius during a dinner at Osca and by this worst of deeds ensured certain victory for the Romans, destruction for his party, and the most shameful of deaths for himself.[132] Metellus and Pompey triumphed for their achievements in the Spains, but Pompey, who in this triumph too was still a Roman equestrian, entered the City by chariot on the day before he embarked on his consulship.[133] (Who could not be amazed that this man, elevated to the highest pinnacle through so many irregular commands, bore with ill will the fact that the senate and Roman people paid regard to Gaius Caesar in the matter of his seeking a sec-

ence: it seems certain that there is a lacuna in the text, which "was clearly quite substantial" (Rich, 76): the events covered in the missing section will have included Pompey's activities in support of Sulla in Italy, Sicily, and Africa; Sulla's resignation and death; the revolt of Lepidus; and most of the Sertorian War.

[132] He was executed by Pompey.

[133] Pompey triumphed on 29 December 71, the last day of the year (on the pre-Julian calendar). It was his second triumph; his first had probably been in 81 or 80 on his return from Africa. All previous triumphs had been held by senators in or following a magistracy. The chariot symbolized the triumph (again at 1.9.5, 122.1) and distinguished it from the lesser "ovation" (Beard, 62–63).

123

VELLEIUS PATERCULUS

num rationem habere? adeo familiare est hominibus omnia sibi ignoscere, nihil aliis remittere, et invidiam rerum non ad causam sed ad voluntatem personasque dirigere.)

4 hoc[217] consulatu Pompeius tribuniciam potestatem restituit, cuius Sulla imaginem inanem[218] reliquerat.

5 Dum Sertorianum bellum in Hispania geritur, LXIIII fugitivi e ludo gladiatorio Capua profugientes duce Spartaco, raptis ex ea urbe gladiis, primo Vesuvium montem petiere, mox crescente in dies multitudine gravibus va-

6 riisque casibus adfecere Italiam. quorum numerus in tantum adolevit ut qua ultimo dimicavere acie †XLaCCC†[219] hominum se Romano exercitui opposuerint. huius patrati gloria penes M. Crassum fuit, mox rei publicae unum trium[220] principem.[221]

31. Converterat Cn. Pompei persona totum in se terrarum orbem et per omnia maiore vi[222] ‹praeditus›[223] habebatur. qui cum consul perquam laudabiliter iurasset se in nullam provinciam ex eo magistratu iturum idque servas-

2 set, post biennium A. Gabinius tribunus legem tulit ut, cum belli more non latrociniorum, orbem classibus iam

---

217 ‹in› hoc tent. Watt (cf. 44.4)

218 inanem ed. Bipont.: in iure PA   219 XLaCCC PA, obelis not. Watt: XL ‹milia› DCCC Ellis: alii alia

220 unum trium Watt: omnium PA

221 principem PA: -um Watt

222 maiore vi PA: maior civi Heinsius, plerique (sed cf. 31.4 vis)

223 suppl. Woodman

---

134 Pompey was consul in 70 along with M. Licinius Crassus (cos. II 55). Both consuls carried the law restoring the full powers of the tribunes.

124

BOOK 2.30–31

ond consulship? So true is it that men habitually forgive themselves everything, concede nothing to others, and focus their resentment of things not according to the cause but according to their attitude toward the persons involved.) In this consulship Pompey restored the tribunician power, of which Sulla had left only an empty manifestation.[134]

While the Sertorian War was being waged in Spain, sixty-four runaways fled from a gladiatorial school at Capua under the leadership of Spartacus, and, snatching up swords in that city, made first for Mount Vesuvius and then, as their numbers grew by the day, inflicted various serious disasters on Italy. Their total increased so much that, in the final engagement in the battle line, †. . .† men threw themselves against the Roman army.[135] The glory of bringing the episode to a conclusion rested with Marcus Crassus, later one of the three principal figures of the commonwealth.[136]

31. Pompey's character had turned the attention of the entire world in his direction, and in every respect he was regarded as possessed of some greater power. Although when consul he had sworn extremely laudably that he would not go to any province after his magistracy, and had kept his word, two years later[137] the tribune Aulus Gabinius carried a law that, since the pirates were now terror-

[135] Appian attributes to Spartacus variously huge numbers of followers at different points in his revolt, "many tens of thousands" in the final encounter (*B Civ.* 1.117.542–120.559).

[136] Crassus was given the command against Spartacus in 72–71; for the so-called first triumvirate see 44.1–2.

[137] In 67.

125

VELLEIUS PATERCULUS

non furtivis expeditionibus piratae terrerent quasdamque etiam Italiae urbes diripuissent, Cn. Pompeius ad eos opprimendos mitteretur essetque ei imperium aequum in omnibus provinciis cum proconsulibus usque ad quin-
3 quagesimum miliarium a mari. quo scito[224] paene totius terrarum orbis imperium uni viro deferebatur; sed tamen idem hoc ante †biennium†[225] M. Antonio in[226] praetura
4 decretum erat. sed interdum persona ut exemplo ⟨prodest vel⟩[227] nocet, ita invidiam auget aut levat. in Antonio homines aequo animo passi erant: raro enim invidetur eorum honoribus quorum vis non timetur; contra in iis homines extraordinaria ⟨imperia⟩[228] reformidant qui ea suo arbitrio aut deposituri aut retenturi videntur et modum in voluntate habent. dissuadebant optimates, sed consilia impetu victa sunt.

32. Digna est memoria Q. Catuli cum auctoritas tum verecundia. qui cum dissuadens legem in contione dixisset esse quidem praeclarum virum Cn. Pompeium sed nimium iam liberae[229] rei publicae neque omnia in uno reponenda, adiecissetque "si quid huic acciderit, quem in

---

[224] quo scito *Schegk*: quos ĉ A: quo senatus COS. *P*

[225] biennium *PA, obel. not. Woodman*: septennium *Krause*

[226] M. Antonio *(iam Davies)* in *Woodman*: in M. Antoni *PA* (in M. Antonio praetore *Brouhier*)

[227] *suppl. Heinsius*

[228] *suppl. Mommsen*

[229] liberae *Rhenanus*: liber aeret *BA*: liber aere *P*

---

[138] M. Antonius Creticus, father of Antony the triumvir, had held a Mediterranean-wide command against the pirates (either 75–72 or 74–71), but without much success.

BOOK 2.31–32

izing the globe not by mere banditry but as if in a proper war, and not in clandestine raids but with proper fleets, and had even plundered some cities in Italy, Pompey should be sent to crush them and that, in all provinces up to the fiftieth milestone from the sea, he should have a command equal to that of the proconsuls. By this measure command over almost the entire world was being conferred on one man, yet the very same had nevertheless been decreed previously to Marcus Antonius in his praetorship.[138] But sometimes, just as a character can set a beneficial or harmful precedent, so it can increase or lessen resentment. In Antonius' case men had tolerated it with equanimity, since resentment is rarely directed at the honors of those whose power is not feared; on the other hand, men dread irregular commands in the case of those who seem likely to lay them down or retain them at their own discretion and whose wishes determine their limit. The optimates argued against, but their advice was defeated by the momentum.

32. Both the authority and the respectfulness of Quintus Catulus deserve their memorial.[139] When in the meeting[140] he had argued against the law by saying that Pompey was of course a very distinguished man but already too much for a free commonwealth, and that everything should not be made to rest on one man, he had added "If anything happens to him, whom will you substitute in his

[139] Q. Lutatius Catulus had been consul in 78.
[140] That is, of the people, officially summoned to debate the law on Pompey's command.

127

VELLEIUS PATERCULUS

eius locum substituetis?"[230] succlamavit universa contio "te, Q. Catule!" tum ille victus consensu omnium et tam
2 honorifico civitatis testimonio e contione discessit. hic hominis verecundiam, populi iustitiam mirari libet, huius quod non ultra contendit, plebis quod dissuadentem et adversarium voluntatis suae vero testimonio fraudare noluit.
3 Per idem tempus ⟨L.⟩[231] Cotta iudicandi munus, quod C. Gracchus ereptum senatui ad equites, Sulla ab illis ad senatum transtulerant, aequaliter in utrumque ordinem partitus est. Otho Roscius lege sua equitibus in theatro loca restituit.[232]
4 At Cn. Pompeius multis et praeclaris viris in id bellum adsumptis discriptoque in[233] omnes recessus maris praesidio navium, brevi inexsuperabili manu terrarum orbem liberavit praedonesque per multa †a†[234] multis locis victos
5 circa Ciliciam classe adgressus fudit ac fugavit; et quo maturius bellum tam late diffusum conficeret, reliquias eorum contractas in urbibus remotoque ⟨a⟩ mari loco in

230 substituetis *Vascosanus*: -uitis *PA^c*: -utis *A*
231 *suppl. Shackleton Bailey*
232 constituit *Aldus*: instituit *Lipsius*
233 descriptoque in *P*: discripto quos . . . in *(inter* quos *et* in *duae lectiones vix legi possunt) A*
234 a *PA, obelis not. Woodman*: ac *Burer*: ⟨proeli⟩a *Gelenius*: ⟨mari⟩a *ed. Bipont.*: ⟨tempor⟩a *Halm*

---

141 L. Aurelius Cotta (cos. 65) carried out his reorganization when he was praetor in 70; in fact, the *tribuni aerarii*, a lower-ranking class often bracketed with the equestrians, were also included. For the two orders (again at 34.3, below) see 2.3.2n.

128

BOOK 2.32

place?" to which the whole meeting responded with shouts of "You, Quintus Catulus!" Thereupon, defeated by the unanimity and by so honorific an endorsement from the community, he withdrew from the meeting. It is a pleasure to admire here the man's respectfulness and the people's sense of justice, the former because he did not contend further, the plebs because, despite his arguments in opposition to their wishes, they refused to cheat him of his proper endorsement.

During the same period the responsibility of jury service, which Gaius Gracchus had stolen from the senate and transferred to the equestrians, and which Sulla had transferred from them to the senate, was divided by Lucius Cotta equally between each of the two orders.[141] By a law of his own, Otho Roscius restored to the equestrians their own places in the theater.[142]

As for Pompey, having enlisted many very distinguished men for the war and dispatched a naval patrol into every recess of the sea, in a short time he freed the world from an invincible force:[143] having beaten the brigands through many †. . .† in many places,[144] he attacked them with a fleet off Cilicia, routed them, and put them to flight; and in order to conclude all the more quickly so widespread a war, he gathered the remnants of them in cities in an area remote from the sea, establishing them in a fixed

[142] This famous law was passed when L. Roscius Otho was tribune of the plebs in 67.

[143] Or, possibly, "with an invincible force."

[144] It is impossible to know what the right reading should be.

129

VELLEIUS PATERCULUS

6 certa sede constituit. sunt qui hoc carpant, sed quamquam in auctore satis rationis est, tamen[235] ratio quemlibet magnum auctorem faceret: data enim facultate sine rapto vivendi rapinis arcuit.

33. Cum esset in fine bellum piraticum [cum][236] et L. Lucullus, qui ante septem annos ex consulatu sortitus Asiam Mithridati oppositus erat magnasque ac memorabiles res ibi gesserat, Mithridaten saepe multis locis fuderat, egregia Cyzicum liberarat victoria, Tigranen, regum maximum, in Armenia vicerat ultimamque bello manum paene magis noluerat imponere quam non potuerat, quia[237] alioqui per omnia laudabilis et bello paene invictus pecuniae pellebatur[238] cupidine, idem bellum adhuc administraret, Manilius tribunus plebis, semper venalis et alienae minister potentiae legem tulit ut bellum Mithridaticum per Cn. Pompeium administraretur. accepta ea

2 magnisque certatum inter imperatores iurgiis, cum Pompeius Lucullo infamiam pecuniae, Lucullus Pompeio interminatam cupiditatem obiceret imperii neuterque[239] ab

3 altero[240] quod arguebat[241] mentitus argui posset. nam neque Pompeius, ut primum ad[242] rem publicam adgressus

[235] tamen *A*: tum *PA^c*
[236] *secl. Riguez*
[237] quia *Bothe*: qui *PA*
[238] pellebatur *A (cf. Sen. Ep. 75.17)*: exp- *P*: imp- *Heinsius*
[239] neuterque *B*: ne (nec *A*) uterque *PA^c*
[240] altero *Burman*: eo *BPA*
[241] arguebat *Aldus*: -atur *BPA*
[242] ad *BA, om. P*

BOOK 2.32–33

abode. There are those who criticize this, but, although it is perfectly reasonable in the case of its instigator, nevertheless the reasoning would have made any instigator great: for, by giving them the opportunity to live without raiding, he kept them from raids.

33. When the pirate war was in its final stages, Lucius Lucullus was still managing the same war as before (on being allotted Asia after his consulship seven years previously,[145] he had confronted Mithridates and performed great and memorable feats there, had routed Mithridates often and in many places, had liberated Cyzicus in an exceptional victory, had defeated Tigranes—greatest of kings—in Armenia,[146] and had failed to put the finishing touch on the war more for reasons of inclination than ability, because, though otherwise generally praiseworthy and almost undefeated in the war, he was driven by a lust for money); but then Manilius, tribune of the plebs,[147] always venal and abetting the power of another, carried a law that the Mithridatic War should be managed by Pompey. On the acceptance of the law, an extremely quarrelsome dispute arose between the commanders, since Lucullus was charged by Pompey with monetary disreputableness and Pompey by Lucullus with a desire for unlimited command, and neither one of them could be accused by the other of having lied in his accusations. For Pompey, from the moment he entered political life, did not tolerate an

---

[145] According to Plutarch (*Vit. Luc.* 5–6), L. Licinius Lucullus as consul in 74 had been allotted the province of Cisalpine Gaul by sortition but through intrigue exchanged it for Asia, Cilicia, and the renewed war with Mithridates.

[146] See 37.2.   [147] In 66.

131

VELLEIUS PATERCULUS

est, quemquam [animo][243] parem tulit, et in quibus rebus primus esse debebat, solus esse cupiebat (neque eo viro quisquam aut alia omnia minus aut gloriam magis concupiit), in adpetendis honoribus immodicus, in gerendis verecundissimus, et qui eos ut libentissime iniret, ita finiret aequo animo, et quod[244] cupisset arbitrio suo sume-

4 ret,[245] alieno deponeret; et Lucullus, summus alioqui vir, profusae huius in aedificiis convictibusque et apparatibus luxuriae primus auctor fuit, quem ob iniectas moles mari et receptum suffossis montibus in terras mare haud infacete[246] Magnus Pompeius Xerxen Togatum vocare adsueverat.

34. Per id tempus a Q. Metello Creta insula in populi Romani potestatem redacta est, quae ducibus Panare et Lasthene XXIIII milibus iuvenum coactis, velocitate pernicibus, armorum laborumque patientissimis, sagittarum usu celeberrimis, per triennium Romanos exercitus fati-

2 gaverat. ⟨ne⟩[247] ab huius quidem usura gloriae[248] temperavit animum Cn. Pompeius, quin[249] victoriae partem conaretur vindicare. sed et Luculli et Metelli triumphum

[243] animo *PA, secl. nescioquis (cf. 29.3)*: ⟨aequo⟩ animo *Lipsius*   [244] quod *PA*: quos *Kritz*   [245] sumeret *Acidalius*: -ere *PA*   [246] infacete *A*: infectae *P*   [247] *suppl. Gelenius*
[248] usura gloriae *Rhenanus*: usurae gloria *PA*
[249] quin *Gelenius*: qui *PA*

---

[148] That is, the Roman Xerxes. Lucullus was said to have started the fashion for building houses out into the sea and, in a further reversal of the natural order, tunneling under mountains to let in sea water (Sall. *Cat.* 13.1; Plin. *HN* 9.170; Plut. *Vit. Luc.* 39.3). Xerxes the Great, who ruled the Achaemenid Empire in

BOOK 2.33–34

equal and desired to be the only one in those areas in which he should have been merely first (and no one had less desire for anything extraneous, or more desire for glory, than him), being, as he was, unrestrained in seeking honors, respectful in holding them, the kind of man who entered upon them very gladly and ended them with equanimity, who took up at his own discretion whatever he desired, and laid it down at that of someone else; while Lucullus, otherwise the finest of men, was the first to instigate the present profusion of luxury in buildings, dinner parties, and furnishings: it was because he threw piles into the sea and undermined mountains to admit the sea onto land that Pompey the Great used to call him, not without wit, "the Togaed Xerxes."[148]

34. During that period the island of Crete was brought into the power of the Roman people by Quintus Metellus:[149] for three years it had exhausted Roman armies under its leaders Panares and Lasthenes, with twenty-four thousand young men recruited, all of them blessed with agility and speed, undaunted by fighting and toil, and famous for their skill as archers. Pompey could not refrain from enjoying even this man's glory, but tried to appropriate part of his victory.[150] But the favorable reception of Lucullus' and Metellus' triumphs among all the best men

the fifth century BC (486–465), famously dug a canal through the isthmus at Mount Athos and attempted to bridge the Hellespont in trying to invade Greece (Hdt. 7.22–24, 33–36).

[149] Q. Caecilius Metellus (Creticus) was proconsul in Crete and Achaea in the years immediately following his consulship in 69.   [150] See 40.5.

133

VELLEIUS PATERCULUS

cum ipsorum singularis virtus tum etiam invidia Pompeii apud optimum quemque fecit favorabilem.

3 Per haec tempora M. Cicero, qui omnia incrementa sua sibi debuit, vir novitatis nobilissimae et ut vita clarus ita ingenio maximus, qui effecit ne, quorum arma viceramus, eorum ingenio vinceremur, consul Sergii Catilinae Lentulique et Cethegi et aliorum utriusque[250] ordinis virorum coniurationem singulari virtute, constantia, vigilia 4 curaque aperuit.[251] Catilina metu consularis[252] imperii urbe pulsus est; Lentulus consularis et praetor iterum Cethegusque et alii clari nominis viri auctore senatu, iussu consulis in carcere necati sunt.

35. Ille senatus dies quo haec acta sunt virtutem M. Catonis iam multis in rebus conspicuam atque prae- 2 nitentem clarissime inluminavit.[253] hic genitus proavo

---

[250] utriusque *P*: utrius *BA*

[251] aperuit *Gelenius*: eripuit *PA*: eruit *Lipsius*

[252] consularis *BA, om. P*

[253] clarissime *Kreyssig,* inluminavit *Rhenanus*: in altissimo luminavit *PA*: in altissimo ‹culmine›, inluminavit *Haase*: *alii alia*

---

[151] Lucullus triumphed in 63, Metellus in 62.

[152] The expression "noblest newness" is an oxymoron: a "noble" was technically an individual who could boast a consular ancestor; a "new man" (1.13.2n) could make no such boast. Like Agrippa, of whom V. uses the same oxymoron (96.1), Cicero was a new man who by his consulship (in 63) ennobled his family.

[153] V. is echoing such claims as are found in Cic. *Brut.* 254, that because of Cicero the Romans had beaten the Greeks at their own game: eloquence. For Rome's military defeat of Greece, cf. such events as the sack of Corinth in 146 (1.13.1).

134

BOOK 2.34–35

was ensured not only by their own singular prowess but also by resentment at Pompey.[151]

It was during this period that the consul Marcus Cicero—who owed all his advancement to himself alone, being a man of the noblest newness[152] and as distinguished in his manner of life as he was superlative in intellect, and who ensured that we were not beaten intellectually by those whose armed forces we had beaten[153]—exposed the conspiracy of Sergius Catilina, Lentulus, Cethegus, and other men of both orders by means of his singular prowess, resolution, watchfulness, and concern.[154] Catiline, in dread of the consul's power, was driven from the City; Lentulus, ex-consul and second-time praetor, Cethegus, and the other men of distinguished name were executed in prison on the authority of the senate and by order of the consul.[155]

35. The day of the senate on which these transactions took place highlighted very clearly the virtue of Marcus Cato, which in many areas was already conspicuous and shining brightly. Descended from the Marcus Cato who was his great-grandfather and famously the principal fig-

[154] L. Sergius Catilina had been praetor in 68; P. Cornelius Lentulus Sura (cos. 71) had been expelled from the senate in 70 and was currently praetor again (see below); C. Cornelius Cethegus was a senator.

[155] In Cicero's first oration against him on 7 November 63 Catiline was challenged to leave Rome and did so that very night, setting off to join the army of rebels in Etruria. Once the conspiracy had been revealed on 3 December, the other conspirators were executed after the senate meeting on 5 December. See also 35.5 and note.

135

VELLEIUS PATERCULUS

M. Catone, principe illo familiae Porciae, homo[254] Virtuti simillimus et per omnia ingenio diis quam hominibus propior, qui numquam recte fecit ut facere videretur sed quia aliter facere non potuerat, cuique id solum visum est rationem habere quod haberet iustitiam, omnibus humanis vitiis immunis semper fortunam in sua potestate habuit.

3 hic tribunus plebis designatus et[255] adhuc admodum adulescens, cum alii suaderent ut per municipia Lentulus coniuratique custodirentur, paene inter ultimos interrogatus sententiam, tanta vi animi atque ingenii invectus est in coniurationem, eo[256] ardore oris orationem omnium leni-

4 tatem suadentium societate consilii suspectam fecit, sic impendentia ex ruinis incendiisque urbis et commutatione status publici pericula exposuit, ita consulis[257] virtutem amplificavit, ut universus senatus in eius sententiam transiret animadvertendumque in eos quos praediximus censeret maiorque pars ordinis eius Ciceronem[258] pro-

5 sequerentur domum. at Catilina non segnius vita abiit[259] quam sceleris conandi consilia inierat: quippe fortissime dimicans quem spiritum supplicio debuerat proelio[260] reddidit.

36. Consulatui Ciceronis non mediocre adiecit decus natus eo anno divus Augustus abhinc annos LXXXXII,[261]

[254] homo P: non BA
[255] et Rhenanus: est BA, om. P
[256] eo Lipsius: et PA
[257] consulis Rhenanus: consilis B: consilii PA
[258] Ciceronem Hottinger: Catonem PA
[259] vita abiit Aldus: vota (nota B) obiit PAB: conata obiit Acidalius: alii alia   [260] proelio Gelenius: supplicio P, om. A
[261] LXXXXII Aldus: LXXXII PA

136

BOOK 2.35–36

ure in the Porcian family,[156] he was a man very similar to Virtue itself and in every respect closer in temperament to the gods than to men, who never acted correctly in order to be seen so acting but because he had not been able to act otherwise, and to whom the only thing that seemed reasonable was that which was just: immune from all human flaws, he was always in control of his own fate. Currently tribune designate of the plebs and still just a young man, he was almost among the last to be asked for his opinion, and, although others were arguing that Lentulus and the conspirators should be held under guard in various townships, he inveighed against the conspiracy with such force of spirit and intellect—and such was the oratorical fervor with which he raised suspicions of collusion in the oratory of all those arguing for leniency, so well did he set out the dangers threatened by the burning ruins of the City and by the upheaval in public order, to such a degree did he magnify the consul's courage—that the entire senate crossed over to his opinion, voted that measures be taken against those whom we just mentioned, and the majority of the order escorted Cicero to his house. As for Catiline, he took his leave from life as readily as he had taken to plotting his criminal project: fighting bravely, he rendered up in battle the life's breath that he had owed as a punishment.[157]

36. An extraordinary distinction accrued to Cicero's consulship from the birth in that year, ninety-two years

[156] See further 1.13.1 and note.
[157] The battle, early in 62, is traditionally said to have taken place at Campo Tizzoro, a short distance north of modern Pistoia.

137

VELLEIUS PATERCULUS

omnibus omnium gentium viris magnitudine sua inducturus caliginem.

2   Iam paene supervacaneum videri potest eminentium ingeniorum notare tempora: quis enim ignorat diremptos gradibus aetatis floruisse hoc tempore Ciceronem, Hortensium, [saneque[262] Crassum, Catonem,[263] Sulpicium][264] moxque Brutum, Calidium, Caelium, Calvum et proximum Ciceroni Caesarem eorumque velut alumnos Corvinum ac Pollionem Asinium, aemulumque Thucydidis Sallustium, auctoresque carminum Varronem ac Lucretium neque ullo in suscepti[265] operis sui carmine[266] minorem

3   Catullum? paene stulta est inhaerentium oculis ingeniorum enumeratio, inter quae maxime nostri aevi eminent princeps[267] carminum Vergilius Rabiriusque et consecu-

[262] saneque *PA*: anteque *ed. Bipont.*: Antonium *Aldus*
[263] Catonem *PA*: Cottam *Aldus*: *alii alia*
[264] saneque . . . Sulpicium *PA, secl. nescioquis*
[265] suscepti *Lipsius*: suspecti *PA*
[266] carmine *PA*: genere *Halm*: *alii alia*
[267] princeps *BA*: principes *P*

---

[158] That is, of the narrative, as it nears the times of V. and his contemporaries: there is an implied contrast with the literary insertions relating to earlier periods (esp. 2.9).

[159] The text of the bracketed passage will make sense only if "and of course" is emended to mean "and previously," but even then the reference to Cato seems anomalous. Perhaps the words are interpolated on the basis of 2.9.1–2, where the orators Crassus and Sulpicius were already mentioned (and cf. 1.17.3 for Cato).

[160] For the famous orator Q. Hortensius Hortalus (114–49, cos. 69) see 2.16.3, 48.6; for M. Iunius Brutus (85?–42, cos. des. 41) see 58–70 *passim*; and for M. Caelius Rufus (pr. 48) see 68.1–

138   •

BOOK 2.36

ago, of the Divine Augustus, who because of his greatness was destined to put all men of all peoples in the shade.

At this point[158] it can seem almost superfluous to mark periods of outstanding talents, for who is unaware that, separated only by the variations in their ages, there flourished at this time Cicero and Hortensius, [and of course Crassus, Cato, Sulpicius,][159] and later Brutus, Calidius, Caelius, Calvus and (closest to Cicero) Caesar, and their foster children (as it were), Corvinus and Asinius Pollio,[160] and Sallust the rival of Thucydides, or that, as authors of poems, there were Varro and Lucretius and, by no means their inferior in any poem of his own adopted genre, Catullus?[161] It is almost foolish to list talents still in the mind's eye, among whom those of our era that particularly stand out are Virgil, the principal figure in poetry, and

2. M. Calidius (pr. 57) and C. Licinius Calvus (b. 82) do not recur in the narrative; the latter, though well known as an orator, was often paired with Catullus as a famous poet too. The description of M. Valerius Messalla Corvinus (64 BC–AD 8, cos. 31) and C. Asinius Pollio (76 BC–AD 4, cos. 40) as "foster children" of the preceding writers indicates that they are here seen as practitioners of oratory, not historiography, which is represented in this first list of names only by Sallust (ca. 86–35, pr. 46). For what remains of all these orators see G. Manuwald, *Fragmentary Republican Latin: Oratory, Parts 2–3* (LCL 541–542; Cambridge, MA, 2019).

161 Varro is much more likely to be the poet P. Terentius Varro Atacinus (b. 82 BC) than the polymath M. Terentius Varro Reatinus (b. 116 BC), most of whose vast output was in prose. The dates of Lucretius are ca. 94–54, of Catullus ca. 84–54 (though the matter is controversial). What V. means by his description of Catullus, if the text is right, is disputed.

139

VELLEIUS PATERCULUS

tus Sallustium Livius Tibullusque et Naso, perfectissimi in
forma operis sui; nam vivorum ut magna admiratio, ita
censura difficilis est.

37.[268] Dum haec in urbe Italiaque geruntur, Cn. Pompeius memorabile adversus Mithridaten, qui post Luculli
profectionem magnas novi exercitus vires reparaverat,[269]
2 bellum gessit. at[270] rex fusus fugatusque et omnibus exutus
copiis Armeniam Tigranemque soc<ium atque eundem
gen>erum[271] petit,[272] regem eius temporis, nisi qua[273]
3 Luculli armis erat infractus, potentissimum. simul itaque
duos persecutus Pompeius intravit Armeniam. prior filius
4 Tigranis, sed discors patri, pervenit ad Pompeium; mox
ipse supplex et praesens se regnumque dicioni eius per-
misit, praefatus neminem alium neque Romanum neque
ullius gentis virum futurum fuisse cuius se potestati[274]
commissurus foret quam Cn. Pompeium: proinde omnem
sibi vel adversam vel secundam, cuius auctor ille esset,
fortunam tolerabilem futuram: non esse turpe ab eo vinci
quem vincere esset nefas, neque inhoneste aliquem sum-
5 mitti huic quem Fortuna super omnes extulisset. servatus
regi honos imperii, sed multato ingenti pecunia, quae

[268] *Cap. 37 post cap. 39 transpos. Haase*
[269] [re]paraverat *Ruhnken*
[270] at *BA*: ac *P*   [271] soc<ium atque eundem gen>erum
Woodman (iam socium *Herel,* generum *Aldus):* socer <gener>um
Heinsius   [272] petiit *Halm*   [273] qua *Gruter*: quia *PA*
[274] potestati *Aldus*: societati *PA*

---

[162] It is striking that there is no place for Horace, author of
the *Carmen saeculare* (17 BC), in a list consisting of Virgil (70–19
BC), Rabirius (a contemporary of the others but precise dates

BOOK 2.36–37

Rabirius and, following on from Sallust, Livy, and Tibullus and Naso, both the height of perfection in the form of their work.[162] As for the living, while there is great admiration for them, assessment is difficult.

37. While these things were happening in the City and in Italy, Pompey waged a memorable war against Mithridates, who, after Lucullus' departure, had rebuilt his great military strength in the form of a new army. But the king was routed and put to flight, and, stripped of all his forces, he made for Armenia and his ally (who was also his son-in-law) Tigranes, the most powerful king of the time (except where he had been broken by the army of Lucullus).[163] So, in simultaneous pursuit of the two of them, Pompey entered Armenia. The first to approach Pompey was a son of Tigranes, who was rebelling against his father; but later it was the man himself who, as a suppliant and in person, handed over himself and his kingdom to Pompey's jurisdiction, having stated as a preliminary that there would have been no one else, neither Roman nor of any other people, to whose power he would entrust himself apart from Pompey: accordingly, he said, any fortune that Pompey dictated, whether adverse or favorable, would be tolerable to him; there was no disgrace in being conquered by one whom it was impious to conquer, nor was it dishonorable for anyone to submit to the man whom Fortune had elevated above everyone. The king's imperial honor was preserved, but he was punished by forfeiting a huge

unknown), Livy (59 BC–AD 17, or possibly 64 BC–AD 12), Tibullus (d. 19 BC), and the exiled Ovid (43 BC–AD 17).

163 See 33.1. V.'s account of affairs in the east is a misleading simplification.

141

VELLEIUS PATERCULUS

omnis, sicuti Pompeio moris erat, redacta in quaestoris
potestatem ac publicis descripta litteris. Syria aliaeque
quas occupaverat provinciae ereptae, et aliae restitutae
populo Romano, aliae tum primum in eius potestatem
redactae, ut Syria, quae tum primum facta est stipendiaria. finis imperii regii[275] terminatus Armenia.

38. Haud absurdum videtur propositi operis regulae
paucis percurrere quae cuiusque ductu gens ac natio redacta in formulam provinciae stipendiaria facta[276] sit, ut
quae partibus notavimus facilius[277] simul universa conspici
2 possint. primus in Siciliam traiecit exercitum consul Claudius, sed[278] provinciam eam post annos ferme LII captis
Syracusis fecit Marcellus Claudius; primus ⟨in⟩[279] Africam Regulus nono ferme anno primi Punici belli, sed post
CVIIII[280] annos P. Scipio Aemilianus eruta Carthagine
abhinc annos CLXXVII[281] Africam in formulam redegit
provinciae. Sardinia inter primum et secundum bellum
Punicum ductu T. Manlii consulis certum recepit imperii
3 iugum. (immane bellicae civitatis argumentum quod se-

275 regii *Heinsius*: regi *PA*
276 stipendiaria facta *A*[c]: stipendia pacta *PA*
277 notavimus facilius ut quae partibus *PA, transpos. Acidalius*
278 sed *Mommsen* (set *Sauppe*): et *PA*
279 *suppl. Gelenius, alii suppl. verbum finitum ut* intravit
280 CIX *ed. Bipont.*: CCIIII *PA*
281 CLXXVII *ed. Bipont.*: CLXXXII *PA*

164 Appius Claudius Caudex was consul in 264.
165 In 211; however, V.'s statement is true only for southeastern Sicily, formerly the kingdom of Hiero. The rest of the island
was under Roman control from the end of the First Punic War in

142

BOOK 2.37–38

amount of money, all of which, as was Pompey's custom, was brought under the control of the quaestor and recorded in the official documents. Syria and the other provinces that he had seized were wrested from him: some were returned to the Roman people, others were brought under its control for the first time, like Syria, which then became taxable for the first time. The boundary of the king's empire ended with Armenia.

38. It does not seem discordant with the principle of the present work to run through in a few words the peoples and nations that were reduced to provincial status and became taxable, and under whose leadership, so that what we have noted piecemeal can be seen more easily all together at the same time. The first to transport an army to Sicily was Claudius in his consulship,[164] but it was made a province about fifty-two years later by Marcellus Claudius on the capture of Syracuse;[165] first into Africa was Regulus in roughly the ninth year of the First Punic War,[166] but it was 109 years later that Publius Scipio Aemilianus razed Carthage and 177 years ago reduced Africa to provincial status.[167] Sardinia assumed the lasting yoke of empire between the First and Second Punic Wars under the leadership of the consul Titus Manlius.[168] (It is prodigious evidence of our community's bellicosity that the closure of

241, although a Roman magistrate may have been sent out to govern it only from ca. 227. M. Claudius Marcellus was consul five times (222, 215, 214, 210, 208, the year of his death).

[166] In 256, the year of M. Atilius Regulus' suffect consulship (cos. I 267).   [167] In 146 (1.12.5).

[168] In 235, when T. Manlius Torquatus was consul (cos. II 224).

143

VELLEIUS PATERCULUS

mel sub regibus, iterum hoc T. Manlio consule, tertio Augusto principe certae pacis argumentum[282] Ianus geminus clausus dedit.) in Hispaniam[283] primi omnium duxere exercitus Cn. et P. Scipiones initio secundi belli Punici abhinc annos CCL; inde varie possessa et saepe amissa partibus, universa ductu Augusti facta stipendiaria est. Macedoniam Paulus, Mummius Achaiam, Fulvius Nobilior subegit Aetoliam; Asiam L. Scipio, Africani frater, eripuit Antiocho, sed beneficio senatus populique Romani mox ab Attalis[284] possessam regibus M. Perpenna capto Aristonico fecit tributariam. Cyprus devicta nullius[285] adsignanda gloriae[286] est: quippe plebis scito,[287] ministerio Catonis, regis morte, quam ille conscientia acciverat, facta provincia est. Creta Metelli ductu longissimae libertatis fine multata est. Syria Pontusque Cn. Pompeii virtutis monumenta sunt.

---

[282] quod *et* certae pacis argumentum *secl. Cludius praeeunte Hudson*   [283] Hispaniam *Herel*: -as *PA*   [284] ab Attalis *Gelenius*: habita lis *PA*   [285] Cyprus . . . nullius *Laurent*: Cypro . . . nullis *PA*   [286] gloriae *Heinsius*: -ia *PA*
[287] plebis scito *Cuiacius*: senatus consulto *PA*

---

[169] The temple of Janus, in the northeastern corner of the forum, was a rectangular structure with double doors at two of its opposite ends; the god himself was often represented as having two faces, each looking in the opposite direction. The closing of the temple signified a state of peace across the Roman world, a practice allegedly started by Numa, Rome's second king. During Augustus' principate the temple doors were closed three times (29 and 25 BC, the third occasion being uncertain): see his *Res Gestae* 13.
[170] See 90.2–4.

144

BOOK 2.38

two-faced Janus only gave evidence of a lasting peace once under the kings, again in the consulship of this Manlius, and thirdly with Augustus as *princeps*.)[169] The first of all those who led armies into Spain were Gnaeus and Publius Scipio at the beginning of the Second Punic War, two hundred and fifty years ago; thereafter possession would change hands and often areas were lost, until the whole became taxable under the leadership of Augustus.[170] Macedonia was subdued by Paullus, Achaea by Mummius, Aetolia by Fulvius Nobilior;[171] Lucius Scipio, brother of Africanus, wrested Asia from Antiochus,[172] but thanks to the kindness of the senate and Roman people its possession later went to the Attalid kings, after which Marcus Perpenna made it liable for tribute after capturing Aristonicus.[173] The conquest of Cyprus is not to be assigned to anyone's glory: it became a province through a plebiscite, the services of Cato, and its king's death, which he had brought upon himself because of his guilty conscience.[174] Under Metellus' leadership Crete was punished by the termination of its lengthy liberty.[175] Syria and Pontus are monuments to the prowess of Pompey.

[171] L. Aemilius Paullus as consul in 168 defeated the king of Macedon at Pydna (1.9.4), though the province was not created until 146 after Metellus Macedonicus' defeat of Pseudophilippus (1.11.2n); L. Mummius Achaicus as consul in 146 sacked Corinth (1.13.1); Aetolia was defeated by M. Fulvius Nobilior as consul in 189.   [172] L. Cornelius Scipio Asiaticus as consul defeated Antiochus III the Great at Magnesia ad Sipylum in 190.

[173] See 2.4.1.   [174] See 45.4.

[175] In 67; Q. Caecilius Metellus Creticus had been consul in 69.

145

VELLEIUS PATERCULUS

39.Gallias primum ⟨a⟩[288] Domitio Fabio⟨que⟩[289] (nepote Pauli, qui Allobrogicus vocatus est) intratas cum exercitu, magna mox clade nostra, saepe et adfectavimus et omisimus;[290] sed fulgentissimum C. Caesaris opus in iis conspicitur: quippe eius ductu auspiciisque infractae paene idem quod totus terrarum orbis in annuum[291] con-

2 ferunt stipendium. ab eodem facta ***[292] Numidicus. Ciliciam perdomuit Isauricus et[293] post bellum Antiochinum Vulso Manlius Gallograeciam. Bithynia (ut praediximus) testamento Nicomedis relicta hereditaria. divus Augustus, praeter Hispanias aliasque gentes quarum titulis forum eius praenitet, paene idem facta Aegypto stipendiaria quantum pater eius Galliis[294] in aerarium reditus[295] con-

3 tulit. at[296] Ti. Caesar quam certam Hispanis parendi confessionem extorserat parens,[297] Illyriis Dalmatisque extorsit.[298] Raetiam autem et Vindelicos ac Noricos Pan-

---

288 *suppl. Rhenanus*   289 Fabio⟨que⟩ *Ursinus*
290 omisimus *Heinsius*: a- *PA*   291 in annuum *Woodman*
(in annum *iam Heinsius*): ignavum *PA*: in aerarium *Aldus*
292 *lacunam statuunt edd.*
293 Isauricus et *Sigonius*: visa vicisset *PA*
294 Galliis *Halm*: Galli *BPA*
295 reditus *P*: redditus *BA*
296 at *PA*: ad *B*
297 parens *Lipsius*: parem *BPA*
298 extorsit *BA, om. P*

---

176 For Domitius and Fabius see 2.10.2; the "disastrous cost" seems to be a reference to successive defeats by the Cimbri and Teutoni (2.8.3, 12.2).

177 See 46–47, below.

BOOK 2.39

39. As for the Gauls, which were first entered with an army by Domitius and Fabius (Paullus' grandson, who was called Allobrogicus) and later at very disastrous cost to us,[176] often did we lay claim to them and often forgo them; but in their case Caesar's most brilliant achievement is to be seen:[177] for, having been broken under his leadership and auspices, they bring in as an annual tax almost the same as the whole world. He likewise made *** Numidicus.[178] Cilicia was tamed by Isauricus and, after the war with Antiochus, Gallograecia by Vulso Manlius.[179] Bithynia (as we mentioned earlier)[180] was left as an inheritance in Nicomedes' will. Apart from the Spains and the other peoples with whose inscriptions his forum shines,[181] the Divine Augustus conveyed into the treasury almost the same amount of returns by making Egypt taxable as did his father with the Gauls.[182] Tiberius Caesar extracted from the Illyrians and Dalmatians the same lasting acknowledgment of obedience as had his father from the Spaniards; he added Raetia, the Vindelici, the Norici, Pan-

[178] The lacuna will have contained references to Julius Caesar's establishment of Africa Nova as a province in 46 and to the earlier achievements there of Metellus Numidicus (2.11.2).

[179] As proconsul in Cilicia, P. Servilius Vatia Isauricus (cos. 79) won a series of victories there in the first half of the 70s; as consul in 189, C. Manlius Vulso won a victory in Galatia ("Gallograecia").

[180] See 2.4.1.

[181] The forum of Augustus housed his temple to Mars Ultor ("Mars the Avenger"), dedicated in 2 BC (100.2), and colonnades adorned with statues of great men of the Roman past. No other source mentions these inscriptions, which were presumably of bronze, although Carrara marble is also a possibility.

[182] 30 BC.

147

VELLEIUS PATERCULUS

noniamque et Scordiscos[299] novas imperio nostro sub-
iunxit provincias. ut has armis, ita auctoritate Cappado-
ciam populo Romano fecit stipendiariam. sed revertamur
ad ordinem.

40. Secuta deinde Cn. Pompeii militia, gloriae labo-
risne maioris incertum est. penetratae cum victoria Media, Albania, Hiberia; deinde flexum agmen ad eas nationes quae dextra atque intima Ponti incolunt, Colchos
Heniochosque et Achaeos, et oppressus auspiciis Pompeii,
insidiis filii Pharnacis[300] Mithridates, ultimus omnium iu-
2 ris sui regum praeter Parthicos. tum victor omnium quas
adierat gentium Pompeius suoque et civium voto maior et
per omnia fortunam hominis egressus revertit[301] in Italiam. cuius reditum favorabilem opinio fecerat: quippe
plerique non sine exercitu venturum in urbem adfirma-
bant[302] et libertati publicae statuturum arbitrio suo mo-
3 dum. quo magis hoc homines timuerant, eo gratior civilis
tanti imperatoris reditus fuit: omni quippe Brundisii di-
misso exercitu nihil praeter nomen imperatoris retinens

299 Scordiscos *Gelenius*: Cordiscos *PA*
300 Pharnacis *A*: -es *P*
301 revertitur *A*   302 adfirmarant *Mommsen*

---

183 The Raeti, Vindelici, and Norici, who dwelt in and beyond
the Alps, were conquered by Tiberius and his brother Drusus in
15 BC. Tiberius campaigned in Dalmatia and Pannonia in 12–9
BC, extending Roman rule to the Danube, and crushed a major
rebellion there in AD 6–9 (see 90.1, 95.2, 96.2–3, 115.4).

184 The client kingdom of Cappadocia was annexed as a province in AD 17.

185 The following events belong to 66–63 BC.

BOOK 2.39–40

nonia, and the Scordisci to our empire as new provinces:[183] in these cases it was by warfare, but it was by his authority that he made Cappadocia taxable for the Roman people.[184] But we should return to the main narrative.

40. There next followed a period of campaigning by Pompey, but whether its glory or its trouble was the greater is uncertain.[185] The penetration of Media, Albania, and Iberia was accompanied by victory; next he wheeled his column to the nations that live in the hinterland on the right of Pontus, namely the Colchi, Heniochi, and Achaei;[186] under Pompey's auspices Mithridates was overwhelmed by the treachery of his son Pharnaces and was the last of all the independent kings except the Parthian.[187] Then Pompey—victorious over all the peoples against whom he had moved, greater than he or the citizens had ever hoped, and in every respect having transcended the fortune of a man—went back to Italy. The popularity of his return had been ensured by the expectation of it, since many had been affirming that he would not enter the City without his army and would establish a limit on public liberty at his own discretion. The more this had been men's fear, the more welcome was the citizen-like return of so great a commander: for, dismissing his entire army at Brundisium, and retaining nothing of the commander apart

[186] The peoples listed here dwelt between the Caspian and Black Seas. At 38.6 "Pontus" designates Mithridates' ancestral kingdom on the southern shore of the Black Sea, but here V. uses it to mean the Black Sea itself.

[187] Mithridates had retreated to his Bosporan kingdom at the approaches to the Sea of Azov in 65, and Pharnaces had him killed there in 63.

149

VELLEIUS PATERCULUS

cum privato comitatu, quem semper illum sectari[303] moris
fuit, in urbem rediit magnificentissimumque de tot regibus per biduum egit triumphum longeque maiorem omni
ante se inlata pecunia in aerarium, praeterquam a Paulo,
ex manubiis intulit.

4 Absente Cn. Pompeio T. Ampius et T. Labienus tribuni
plebis legem tulerant ut is ludis circensibus corona aurea
et omni cultu triumphantium uteretur, scaenicis autem
praetexta coronaque laurea;[304] id ille non plus quam semel
(et hoc sane nimium fuit) usurpare sustinuit. huius viri
fastigium tantis auctibus Fortuna extulit ut primum[305] ex
Africa, iterum ex Europa, tertio ex Asia triumpharet et,
quot partes terrarum orbis sunt, totidem faceret monu-
5 menta victoriae suae. numquam tamen[306] eminentia invidia carent. itaque et Lucullus memor acceptae iniuriae
et Metellus Creticus non iniuste querens (quippe ornamentum triumphi eius captivos duces[307] Pompeius subduxerat) et cum iis pars optimatium refragabatur ne aut
promissa civitatibus a Pompeio aut bene meritis praemia
ad arbitrium eius persolverentur.

41. Secutus deinde est consulatus C. Caesaris, qui
scribenti manum iniicit et quamlibet festinantem in se

---

303 illum sectari *Burman*: illa fatare *P (*illa fata remoris *A*): *alii
alia*

304 laurea *Lipsius*: aurea *PA*

305 primum *schol. ad Luc. 9.178*: primus *PA*

306 tamen, *post* memor *traditum, huc transpos. Castiglioni*

307 duces *Rhenanus, A*ᶜ: ducus *P*: duos *A*

BOOK 2.40–41

from the name, he returned to the City with only the personal escort by which it was always his custom to be accompanied; and for a two-day period he held a most magnificent triumph over a great number of kings,[188] and the money he paid into the treasury from his spoils was far greater than any paid in before him except by Paullus.[189]

During Pompey's absence, Titus Ampius and Titus Labienus, tribunes of the plebs, carried a law that at the circus games he should wear a golden crown and all the apparel of a triumpher, and at the theatrical shows a praetexta and laurel crown:[190] he could not bear to assert this right more than once. (And that was of course too much.) Fortune raised this man's pinnacle by such additions that he triumphed first over Africa, then over Europe, and thirdly over Asia, and he turned the three continents of the world into as many monuments of his victory. Yet eminence never wants for envy: Lucullus, mindful of the injustice he had suffered,[191] and Metellus Creticus, with his by no means unjust complaint (Pompey had stolen the captive leaders who were to have adorned the man's triumph), joined with a section of the optimates in opposing him, to prevent the implementation both of the promises made by Pompey to communities and of his intended rewards for the men who had served him well.

41. There next followed the consulship of Gaius Caesar,[192] who makes claims on a writer and compels even the

---

[188] On 28–29 September 61.   [189] See 1.9.6.

[190] See S. Weinstock, *Divus Julius* (Oxford, 1971), 108. For circus games see 27.6n; for the praetexta see 1.10.3n.

[191] See 33.1–2.   [192] In 59, to which V. returns at 44.1; the intervening narrative is a form of flashback.

151

VELLEIUS PATERCULUS

morari cogit. hic nobilissima Iuliorum genitus familia et (quod inter omnes antiquissimos constabat[308]) ab Anchise ac Venere deducens genus, forma omnium civium excellentissimus, vigore animi acerrimus, munificentia effusissimus, animo super humanam et naturam et fidem evectus, magnitudine cogitationum, celeritate bellandi, patientia periculorum Magno illi Alexandro (sed sobrio

2 neque iracundo) simillimus, qui denique semper et somno et cibo in vitam non in voluptatem uteretur, cum fuisset C. Mario sanguine coniunctissimus atque idem Cinnae gener (cuius filiam ut repudiaret nullo metu compelli potuit, cum M. Piso consularis Anniam, quae Cinnae uxor fuerat, in Sullae dimisisset gratiam) habuissetque fere XVIII annos eo tempore quo Sulla rerum potitus est, magis ministris Sullae adiutoribusque partium quam ipso conquirentibus eum ad necem mutata veste dissimilemque fortunae suae indutus habitum nocte urbe elapsus est.

3 Idem postea admodum iuvenis, cum a piratis captus esset, ita se per omne spatium quo ab iis retentus est apud eos gessit ut pariter iis terrori venerationique esset neque umquam aut nocte aut die (cur enim quod vel maximum est, si narrari verbis speciosis non potest, omittatur?) aut excalcearetur aut discingeretur, in hoc scilicet ne, si quando aliquid ex solito variaret, suspectus iis qui oculis

[308] antiquissimos constabat *PA*: constat, antiquissima *Acidalius*: antiquitatis studiosos constabat *Halm*: alii alia

---

[193] On 12 July 100. [194] Caesar's aunt was married to Marius. [195] M. Pupius Piso Frugi Calpurnianus was not consul until 61: "ex-consul" is anachronistic. [196] See 28.2.

BOOK 2.41

most hasty to dwell on him. Born into the most noble family of the Julii[193] and (as was agreed by all those of the greatest antiquity) deriving his lineage from Anchises and Venus, he was the most outstanding of all citizens in appearance, the keenest in intellectual energy, the most effusive in generosity, and elevated in spirit beyond human nature and credibility; in the magnitude of his conceptions, his speed of waging war, and his endurance of danger he was very like the famous Alexander the Great (but sober and not irascible); in short, the kind of man who always slept and ate for the purposes of survival, not pleasure. Closely related to Gaius Marius by blood,[194] he was likewise the son-in-law of Cinna (whose daughter no fear could compel him to divorce, although the ex-consul Marcus Piso[195] had given up Annia, who had been Cinna's wife, to please Sulla), and, though he was only about eighteen years old at the time when Sulla took charge of affairs,[196] Sulla's associates and party helpers—rather than the man himself—were searching for him with a view to killing him. With a change of clothing, and dressed very differently from his station in life, he slipped out of the City by night.

Afterward, when still just a young man, he was captured by pirates, and during the whole period that he was held he so conducted himself in their presence that he was an equal source of terror and respect to them and neither by night nor by day did he ever remove his shoes or his belt (why should a most important matter be omitted simply because it cannot be described in fine words?), evidently lest any change in his routine would arouse the suspicion of men whose guarding of him was merely

153

VELLEIUS PATERCULUS

tantummodo eum custodiebant foret. 42. longum est nar-
rare quid et quotiens ausus sit; quanto opere conata eius
qui obtinebat Asiam magistratus populi Romani impetu[309]
suo destituerit,[310] illud referatur, documentum tanti mox
2 evasuri viri. quae nox eam diem secuta est qua publica
civitatium pecunia redemptus est, ita tamen ut cogeret
ante obsides a piratis civitatibus dari, contracta classe et
privatus et tumultuaria ⟨manu⟩[311] invectus in eum locum
in quo ipsi praedones erant, partem classis fugavit, partem
3 mersit, aliquot naves multosque mortales cepit; laetusque
nocturnae expeditionis triumpho ad suos reversus est,
mandatisque custodiae quos ceperat, in Bithyniam per-
rexit ad proconsulem Iunium ⟨Iun⟩cum[312] (idem enim
Asiam eamque[313] obtinebat), petens ut auctor fieret
sumendi de captivis supplicii. quod cum ille se facturum
negasset venditurumque captivos dixisset (quippe seque-
batur invidia inertiam), incredibili celeritate revectus ad
mare, priusquam de ea re ulli proconsulis redderetur epis-
tula, omnes quos ceperat suffixit cruci.

43. Idem mox ad sacerdotium ineundum (quippe
absens pontifex factus erat in Cottae consularis locum,
⟨cum⟩[314] paene puer a Mario Cinnaque flamen Dialis

---

[309] impetu *Woodman*: motu *PA*   [310] destituerit *Rhenanus*:
-uere *PA*   [311] *suppl. Halm*   [312] ⟨Iun⟩cum *Nipperdey*
[313] eamque *Lipsius*: eam quam *PA*   [314] *suppl. Lipsius*

---

[197] The point seems to be that the pirates had not shackled
him: any unexpected movement on his part might be interpreted
as an attempt at escape, the prevention of which might lead to his
death.   [198] The ransom was evidently paid by Miletus (Plut.
Vit. Caes. 2.5; Polyaenus, *Strat.* 8.3.1).

[199] The archaizing and probably poetic phrase "many mor-

BOOK 2.41–43

visual.[197] 42. It would take too long to describe his many acts of daring, but, as illustration of the greatness to which he would shortly emerge, the following may be recorded, namely, how effectively on his own initiative he frustrated the designs of the man who was governing Asia as magistrate of the Roman people. On the night following the very day on which he was ransomed by the communities' public funds (but he compelled the pirates first to give hostages to the communities),[198] he assembled a fleet and, though a private individual with only an improvised unit, he sailed into the place where the brigands themselves were. Part of their fleet he put to flight, part he sank, and some ships he captured along with many mortals.[199] Delighted at the triumph of his nighttime expedition, he returned to his own people, and, entrusting his captives to custody, made straight for Bithynia and the proconsul Junius Juncus (who governed there too along with Asia), asking him to authorize the punishment of his captives. But, when the man refused to do so and said that he would sell the captives (his apathy was succeeded by envy), with incredible speed Caesar went back to sea and, before a letter from the proconsul about the matter could be sent to anyone, he crucified all those whom he had captured.

43. Later he was hurrying to Italy to enter upon his priesthood (in his absence he had been made a pontiff to replace the ex-consul Cotta: he had been created Flamen Dialis by Marius and Cinna almost in boyhood,[200] but he

---

tals," extremely common in Sallust and Livy, occurs only here in V. [200] Caesar was probably made Flamen Dialis (20.3n) in 84, when he was fifteen or sixteen; his new appointment as a pontiff probably dates to 73 on the recent death of C. Aurelius Cotta (cos. 75).

155

VELLEIUS PATERCULUS

creatus victoria Sullae, qui omnia ab iis acta fecerat irrita, amisisset id sacerdotium) festinans in Italiam, ne conspiceretur a praedonibus omnia tunc obtinentibus maria et merito iam[315] infestis sibi, quattuor scalmorum navem una cum duobus amicis decemque servis ingressus effusissi-

2 mum Adriatici maris traiecit sinum. quo quidem in cursu conspectis (ut putabat) piratarum navibus, cum exuisset vestem alligassetque pugionem ad femur alterutri se fortunae parans, mox intellexit frustratum esse visum suum arborumque ex longinquo ordinem antemnarum praebuisse imaginem.

3 Reliqua eius acta in urbe—nobilissimaque Dolabellae accusatio et maior civitatis in ea favor quam reis praestari solet; contentionesque civiles cum Q. Catulo atque aliis eminentissimis viris celeberrimae et ante praeturam victus ⟨in⟩[316] maximi pontificatus petitione Q. Catulus, om-

4 nium confessione senatus princeps; et restituta in aedilitate adversante quidem nobilitate monumenta C. Marii, simulque revocati ad ius dignitatis proscriptorum liberi; et praetura quaesturaque mirabili virtute atque industria obita in Hispania (cum esset quaestor sub Vetere Antistio,

---

[315] iam *Lipsius*: tam *PA*　　　　[316] suppl. *Halm*

---

[201] Presumably the alternatives were trying to swim to safety or fighting for his life.

[202] In 77 Caesar prosecuted Cn. Cornelius Dolabella (cos. 81) for extortion, a performance that brought him an oratorical reputation but did not secure Dolabella's conviction.

[203] In 63 (Caesar would be praetor in 62).　　　　[204] In 65.

[205] For the disabilities imposed on the children of the proscribed, see 28.4. They agitated in 63 for the restoration of their

BOOK 2.43

had lost that priesthood on the victory of Sulla, who had annulled all their enactments), and, to avoid being spotted by the brigands (who at the time were in control of every sea and now had good reason to be hostile to him), he boarded a ship of only four oars along with two friends and ten slaves and crossed the broad expanse of the Adriatic Sea. Spotting the pirates' ships (as he thought) in the course of his journey, he had stripped off his clothing and, strapping a dagger to his thigh, was preparing himself for one fate or the other[201] when he realized that his eyes had deceived him and that a row of trees in the distance had presented a semblance of sail yards.

As for his remaining activities in the City—the very notable prosecution of Dolabella and the community's greater goodwill in the matter than is usually shown to defendants;[202] the very celebrated civil conflicts with Quintus Catulus and other outstanding men and in particular his defeat, before his praetorship, of Catulus, by universal agreement the principal figure in the senate, when both of them were candidates for the office of Chief Pontiff;[203] and his restoration of Gaius Marius' monuments in his aedileship, despite opposition from the nobility,[204] and at the same time the recall of the children of the proscribed to their due rank;[205] and his praetorship[206] and quaestorship, discharged with remarkable prowess and industriousness in Spain (when he was quaestor under Vetus An-

right to stand for office; Caesar may have supported them, and, if so, it may be to this that V. refers. As dictator in 49 he restored their right.

206 V. is using "praetorship" to refer to Caesar's promagistracy in Further Spain in 61/60.

157

VELLEIUS PATERCULUS

avo huius Veteris consularis atque pontificis, duorum con-
sularium et sacerdotum patris, viri in tantum boni in quantum humana simplicitas intellegi potest)—quo notiora
sunt, minus egent stilo.

44. Hoc igitur consule inter eum et Cn. Pompeium et
M. Crassum inita potentiae societas quae urbi orbique
terrarum nec minus diverso cuique[317] tempore ipsis ex-
2 itiabilis fuit. hoc consilium sequendi Pompeius causam
habuerat ut tandem acta in transmarinis provinciis, quibus
(ut praediximus) multi obtrectabant, per Caesarem confir-
marentur consulem; Caesar autem quod animadvertebat
se cedendo Pompei gloriae aucturum suam et invidia
communis potentiae in illum relegata confirmaturum vires
suas; Crassus ut, quem principatum solus adsequi non pot-
3 erat, auctoritate Pompeii, viribus teneret Caesaris. adfinitas etiam inter Caesarem Pompeiumque contracta nuptiis:
4 quippe filiam[318] C. Caesaris Cn. Magnus duxit uxorem. in
hoc consulatu Caesar legem tulit ut ager Campanus plebei
divideretur, suasore legis Pompeio. ita circiter XX ⟨milia⟩
civium eo deducta et ius ab his[319] restitutum post annos
circiter CLII quam bello Punico ab Romanis Capua in
5 formam praefecturae redacta erat. Bibulus, collega Cae-

---

317 cuique *Laurent* (quoique *iam Acidalius*): quoque *PA*
318 ⟨Iuliam⟩ filiam *Orelli*   319 [ab] his *Lipsius: alii alia*

---

207 Antistius Vetus (pr. 70) was propraetor in Further Spain in
69.   208 C. Antistius Vetus (cos. 6 BC) was father of Gaius
(cos. AD 23) and Lucius (cos. suff. AD 28).   209 At 40.5.

210 The Campanian Territory was the former land of Capua,
confiscated after the crushing of its rebellion in 211 (cf. 1.7.3).
This measure, passed in May 59, was Caesar's second land-

158

BOOK 2.43–44

tistius,[207] grandfather of the present Vetus, who as ex-consul and pontiff, and father of two ex-consuls and priests,[208] is a man whose goodness reaches the furthest level that human straightforwardness can be understood to reach)—their need of my pen is less, in proportion to their greater renown.

44. When he was consul, an alliance of power was entered into between him, Pompey, and Marcus Crassus that was fatal for the City and the world and no less for themselves, though at a different time in each case. In following this course of action Pompey's motivation had been that at last his enactments in the overseas provinces, to which (as we mentioned earlier)[209] many were objecting, should be confirmed by Caesar as consul; Caesar's had been his estimation that by making a concession to Pompey's glory he would increase his own and that, with the resentment at their power-sharing deflected onto Pompey, his own strength would be confirmed; Crassus' had been that, thanks to Pompey's influence and Caesar's strength, he would occupy a position as a principal figure that he was not able to achieve on his own. A relationship between Caesar and Pompey was also agreed by means of a marriage: Pompey took Caesar's daughter as his wife. It was in his consulship that Caesar carried a law that the Campanian Territory be divided for the plebs (Pompey was a supporter of the law): thus around twenty thousand citizens were settled there and they reestablished its rights 152 years after Capua in the Punic War had been reduced by the Romans to the status of a prefecture.[210] Bibulus,

distribution law. His first, providing mainly for the distribution of purchased land, had been carried with violence early in the year.

159

VELLEIUS PATERCULUS

saris, cum actiones eius magis vellet impedire quam posset, maiore parte anni domi se tenuit; quo facto dum augere vult invidiam collegae, auxit potentiam. tum Caesari decretae in quinquennium Galliae.

45. Per idem tempus P. Clodius, homo nobilis, disertus, audax, qui ⟨ne⟩que[320] dicendi neque faciendi ullum nisi quem vellet nosset modum, malorum propositorum executor acerrimus, infamis etiam sororis stupro et actus incesti reus ob initum inter religiosissima populi Romani sacra adulterium, cum graves inimicitias cum M. Cicerone exerceret (quid enim inter tam dissimiles amicum esse poterat?) et a patribus ad plebem transisset, legem in tribunatu tulit ⟨ut⟩,[321] qui civem Romanum ⟨in⟩demnatum[322] interemisset, ei aqua et igni interdiceretur: cuius verbis 2 etsi non nominabatur, Cicero tamen solus petebatur. ita vir optime meritus de re publica conservatae patriae pretium calamitatem exilii tulit. non caruerunt suspicione oppressi Ciceronis Caesar et Pompeius; hoc sibi contraxisse videbatur Cicero quod inter XX viros dividendo 3 agro Campano esse noluisset. idem intra biennium sera

[320] ⟨ne⟩que *Vascosanus*
[321] *suppl. Novák*
[322] ⟨in⟩demnatum *Vascosanus*

---

[211] M. Calpurnius Bibulus retired to his house on the grounds that he was watching for omens, thereby rendering Caesar's legislation technically invalid.   [212] In 62 P. Clodius Pulcher (curule aedile 56) tricked his way into the Bona Dea festival (restricted to women) in a failed attempt at adultery with Caesar's wife; he was brought to trial the following year but, having bribed members of the jury, avoided conviction. That he had incestuous

BOOK 2.44–45

Caesar's colleague, whose desire to prevent his measures was greater than his ability to do so, kept himself in his house for the greater part of the year: by doing this he aimed to increase the resentment at his colleague, but he only increased his power.[211] Then the provinces of Gaul were decreed to Caesar for five years.

45. It was during the same period that Publius Clodius—a man of the nobility, articulate, revolutionary, the kind who knew no limit for his speech or actions except the one he wanted, the keenest perpetrator of wicked projects, notorious too for illicit sex with his sister, and defendant on a charge of profanation for embarking on adultery during some of the most solemn rituals of the Roman people,[212] and who was conducting serious hostilities with Cicero (for what friendship could there be between two so dissimilar?) and had transferred from the patricians to the plebs—carried a law during his tribunate that water and fire should be forbidden to anyone who had killed an uncondemned Roman citizen:[213] although not named in its wording, Cicero alone was the target. Thus a man who deserved the best of the commonwealth reaped the calamity of exile as his reward for saving his fatherland. Caesar and Pompey were not without suspicion in the matter of Cicero's overthrow, which Cicero seemed to have brought on himself because he had refused to be one of the Twenty for dividing up the Campanian Territory. But within two years—thanks to the belated but (as he

relations with his sister, the notorious Clodia, was a common allegation of the period.

213 The law was passed in 58. For "water and fire" see 24.2n.

161

VELLEIUS PATERCULUS

Cn. Pompeii cura verum (ut cupit[323]) intenta,[324] votisque Italiae ac[325] decretis senatus, virtute atque actione Annii Milonis tribuni plebis dignitati patriaeque restitutus est; neque post Numidici exilium ac reditum quisquam aut expulsus invidiosius aut receptus est laetius. cuius domus quam infeste a Clodio disiecta erat, tam speciose a senatu restituta est.

4 Idem P. Clodius in senatu[326] sub honorificentissimo ministerii titulo M. Catonem a re publica relegavit: quippe legem tulit ut is quaestor cum[327] iure praetorio, adiecto etiam quaestore, mitteretur in insulam Cyprum ad spoliandum regno Ptolemaeum, omnibus morum vitiis eam 5 contumeliam meritum. sed ille sub adventum Catonis vitae suae vim intulit: unde pecuniam longe sperata maiorem Cato Romam rettulit. cuius integritatem laudari nefas est, insolentia paene argui potest, quod una cum consulibus ac senatu effusa civitate obviam cum per Tiberim subiret, navibus non ante is egressus est quam ad eum locum pervenit ubi erat exponenda pecunia.

46. Cum deinde immanes res vix multis voluminibus explicandas C. Caesar in Gallia gereret nec contentus plu-

---

[323] ut cupit *Seebode*: et cupit *PA* [324] intenta *A (ut vid.)*, *Wopkens*: interita *PA^c* [325] ac *Ellis*: aut *PA* [326] in senatu *PA, secl. Cuiacius*: in tribunatu *Heinsius* [327] quaestor cum *PA*: quaestorius *Watt*: quaestor⟨ius⟩ cum *Lipsius*

---

[214] Cicero returned to Italy on 5 August 57. For Milo see 47.4n. [215] See 2.15.3–4. [216] King Ptolemy was brother of Ptolemy XII Auletes and son of Ptolemy IX; the date was 58.

[217] Cato was so famous for his integrity (e.g., Cic. *Sest.* 60; Sall. *Cat.* 54.2) that V. claims it would be sacrilege to presume to praise him for it.

BOOK 2.45–46

desired) attentive concern of Pompey, the prayers of Italy, and decrees of the senate, and the courageous action of Annius Milo, tribune of the plebs—Cicero was restored to his rank and his fatherland;[214] and, after the exile and return of Numidicus,[215] no one was banished with more resentment or welcomed back with more delight. His house was rebuilt by the senate, the degree of its impressiveness matching that of the hatred with which Clodius had torn it down.

Publius Clodius likewise effected in the senate the banishment of Marcus Cato from the commonwealth, under the very honorific title of a commission: he carried a law that as quaestor with praetorian power, and the extra assistance of a quaestor, Cato should be sent to the island of Cyprus to deprive Ptolemy of his kingdom, a humiliation that all his flaws of character deserved.[216] But in response to Cato's arrival he committed suicide: hence Cato brought back to Rome a far greater amount of money than expected. While it is sacrilege to praise his integrity,[217] he can almost be accused of insolence, since, when he was sailing up the Tiber and the whole community along with the consuls and senate had poured out to meet him, he did not disembark from his ships until he reached the place where the money was to be unloaded.

46. When Caesar in Gaul was subsequently performing prodigious exploits that are scarcely to be described in a multitude of volumes,[218] not content with his very numer-

[218] Caesar published his own "commentaries" on the Gallic war in seven volumes, an eighth being added by A. Hirtius (57.1n). A chronological table for his wars in the years 58 to 45 has been proposed by J. T. Ramsey and K. A. Raaflaub, *Histos* 11 (2017): 162–217.

163

VELLEIUS PATERCULUS

rimis ac felicissimis victoriis innumerabilibusque caesis et captis hostium milibus etiam in Britanniam traiecisset exercitum, alterum paene imperio nostro ac suo quaerens orbem, vetus par[328] consulum, Cn. Pompeius et M. Crassus, alterum iniere consulatum, qui neque petitus honeste 2 ab iis neque probabiliter gestus est. Caesari lege, quam Pompeius ad populum tulit, prorogatae in idem spatium temporis provinciae, Crasso bellum Parthicum in animo[329] molienti Syria decreta; qui, vir cetera sanctissimus immunisque voluptatibus neque in pecunia neque in gloria concupiscenda aut modum norat aut capiebat terminum. 3 hunc proficiscentem in Syriam diris cum[330] ominibus tribuni plebis frustra retinere conati; quorum execrationes si in ipsum tantummodo valuissent, vile[331] imperatoris dam- 4 num salvo exercitu fuisset rei publicae. transgressum Euphraten Crassum petentemque Seleuciam circumfusis immanibus copiis equitum rex Orodes una cum parte mai- 5 ore Romani exercitus interemit. reliquias legionum C. Cassius, atrocissimi mox auctor facinoris, tum quaestor, conservavit, Syriamque adeo in populi Romani potestate retinuit ut transgressos in eam Parthos felici rerum eventu fugaret ac funderet.

---

[328] vetus par *Ursinus*: victus pars *PA*: *alii alia*
[329] in animo *PA (in secl. Cludius)*: iam a- *Heinsius*
[330] cum *secl. Krause*
[331] vile *Puteanus*: utile *PA*

---

[219] In 55; there would be a second expedition in 54 (47.1).
[220] In 55; they had previously been consular colleagues in 70.
[221] That is, a second five-year period. The law was in fact carried by Pompey and Crassus together.

BOOK 2.46

ous and very prosperous victories (countless thousands of the enemy slain and captured), he also transported his army into Britain, seeking, as it were, a second world for our empire (and his own).[219] It was then that Pompey and Crassus, an old pair of consuls, entered upon a second consulship,[220] which they neither campaigned for honorably nor conducted commendably. By a law that Pompey carried before the people, Caesar's provinces were continued for the same period of time;[221] as for Crassus, whose mind was set on a Parthian War, Syria was decreed to him—a man who was otherwise completely scrupulous and impervious to pleasure but knew no limit and brooked no boundary in the matter of coveting money and glory. When he was setting off for Syria with dire omens, the tribunes of the plebs tried in vain to restrain him; if their imprecations had been effective only against himself, the loss of a commander, provided the army was safe, would have been cheap for the commonwealth. But, when Crassus had crossed the Euphrates and was making for Seleucia, King Orodes surrounded him with prodigious forces of cavalry and killed him, along with the greater part of the Roman army.[222] Remnants of the legions were preserved by Gaius Cassius, quaestor at the time but later the instigator of a most terrible crime,[223] and so successful was he at keeping Syria within the power of the Roman people that, in a happy outcome for events, he put to flight and routed the Parthians who had crossed into it.

[222] The battle of Carrhae (53) was one of the worst defeats in Roman history. Orodes himself was in fact elsewhere, and the battle was won by his commander in chief.

[223] The murder of Julius Caesar in 44.

165

VELLEIUS PATERCULUS

47. Per haec insequentiaque et quae praediximus tempora amplius CCCC milia hostium a C. Caesare caesa sunt, plura capta; pugnatum saepe derecta acie, saepe in agminibus, saepe eruptionibus; bis penetrata Britannia; ‹e›[332] novem denique aestatibus vix ulla non iustissimus triumphus emeritus, circa Alesiam vero tantae res gestae quantas audere vix hominis, perficere paene nullius nisi dei fuerit. quinto[333] ferme anno Caesar morabatur in Galliis cum medium iam ex invidia po‹te›ntiae ta‹m› male[334] cohaerentis inter Cn. Pompeium et C. Caesarem concordiae pignus Iulia, uxor Magni, decessit; atque omnia inter destinatos tanto discrimini duces dirimente Fortuna filius quoque parvus Pompeii, Iulia natus, intra breve spatium obiit.

Tum in gladios caedesque civium furente ambitu, cuius neque finis reperiebatur nec modus, tertius consulatus soli Cn. Pompeio etiam adversantium antea dignitati eius iudicio delatus est, cuius ille honoris gloria veluti reconciliatis sibi optimatibus maxime a C. Caesare alienatus est; sed eius consulatus omnem vim in coercitionem ambitus exercuit. quo tempore P. Clodius a Milone candidato consulatus exemplo inutili[ter],[335] facto salutari rei publicae

---

[332] *suppl. Krause*

[333] quinto *Krause*: septimo *PA*: quarto *Laurent*

[334] po‹te›ntiae *Lipsius,* ta‹m› *Woodman,* male *Rhenanus*: Ponti ac (et *A*) Camiliae *PA*   [335] inutili[ter] *Gelenius*

---

[224] At 46.1.

[225] That is, from 58 to 50.

[226] See Caes. *BGall.* 7.68–89 (52 BC).

[227] The reference is to electoral campaigning.

166

BOOK 2.47

47. During these and the following times, as well as those that we mentioned earlier,[224] more than four hundred thousand of the enemy were slain by Caesar, and more captured; the fighting often took place in battle line formation, often in the column, and often in breakouts; Britain was penetrated twice; in short, of the nine summer seasons,[225] there was scarcely one for which the fullest of triumphs was not deserved; and, as for his achievements in the vicinity of Alesia,[226] they were of such a magnitude that a mere man would scarcely have ventured upon them, and concluding them would have been beyond almost anyone except a god. It was about the fifth year of Caesar's stay in the Gauls that there occurred the death of Julia, Pompey's wife, the shared pledge of a harmony between him and Caesar that was now holding together very badly on account of their resentment of each other's power; and, as Fortune was sundering all links between leaders destined for a great crisis, Pompey's little son, Julia's boy, also died within a brief period.

Then, as the raging corruption[227] progressed to swords and the slaughter of citizens, to which neither end nor limit could be found, a third consulship was conferred on Pompey alone, that being the decision even of those who previously opposed his rank. Although the glory of the honor seemed to have reconciled the optimates to him, its main effect was to alienate him from Caesar; but he applied all the influence of his consulship to curbing corruption. This was the time when—in an act salutary for the commonwealth but useless as a precedent—Publius Clodius was slaughtered by the consular candidate Milo

167

VELLEIUS PATERCULUS

circa Bovillas contracta ex occursu rixa iugulatus est. Milonem reum non magis invidia facti quam Pompeii dam-
5 navit voluntas; quem quidem M. Cato palam lata absolvit sententia, qui si maturius tulisset, non defuissent qui sequerentur exemplum probarentque eum civem occisum quo nemo perniciosior rei publicae neque bonis inimicior vixerat.

48. Intra breve deinde spatium belli civilis exarserunt initia, cum iustissimus quisque et a Caesare et a Pompeio vellet dimitti exercitus. quippe Pompeius in secundo consulatu Hispanias sibi decerni voluerat easque per triennium absens ipse ac praesidens urbi per Afranium et Petreium, consularem ac praetorium, legatos suos, administrabat, et iis qui a Caesare dimittendos exercitus contendebant adsentabatur, iis qui ab ipso quoque adver-
2 sabatur. qui si ante biennium quam ad arma itum est, perfectis muneribus theatri et aliorum operum quae ei circumdedit, gravissima temptatus valetudine decessisset in Campania (quo quidem tempore universa Italia vota pro salute eius primi[336] omnium civium suscepit), defuisset

---

[336] primi *Vascosanus*: -o *PA*

---

[228] On 18 January 52. Pompey was elected sole consul fifty-eight days later to deal with the continuing anarchy after Clodius' murder.

[229] For "good men" see 2.2.2n.

[230] L. Afranius had been consul in 60, M. Petreius praetor in ?64. Pompey had received command of Nearer and Further Spain for five years in 55, the year of his second consulship, under the same law by which Crassus had been appointed to Syria (46.2), and his term was extended during his third consulship in 52.

168

BOOK 2.47–48

during a quarrel that had arisen when they met near Bovillae.[228] At his trial Milo was condemned not so much out of resentment at his act as by Pompey's wish; yet Marcus Cato, in an opinion openly delivered, acquitted him, and, if he had delivered it sooner, there would have been no lack of those to follow his example and approve the slaying of a citizen whose life had been more harmful to the commonwealth, and to good men more hostile,[229] than that of anyone else.

48. Then, within a short space of time, the beginnings of civil war flared up, although all the most right-minded wanted both Caesar and Pompey to dismiss their armies. For in his second consulship Pompey had wanted the Spains to be decreed to him, and, being absent from there while presiding over the City, he had been administering them for three years through Afranius and Petreius, respectively ex-consul and ex-praetor, his legates,[230] and he agreed with those who maintained that Caesar should dismiss his armies but opposed those who maintained that he himself should do so too. If, after completing his theater and the other public buildings with which he surrounded it, he had passed away two years previously, before the resort to arms and when he was afflicted by a very severe illness in Campania (the time when he was the first citizen of all to have the whole of Italy offer prayers for his health),[231]

231 Pompey's famous theater and its surrounding portico were dedicated in August 55; he fell ill at Naples in mid-50. The Latin may be describing Pompey as "the principal citizen" rather than the first citizen for whom prayers were offered.

169

VELLEIUS PATERCULUS

Fortunae destruendi eius locus et, quam apud superos habuerat magnitutudinem, inlibatam detulisset ad inferos.

3 Bello autem civili et tot quae deinde per continuos viginti annos consecuta sunt malis non alius maiorem flagrantioremque quam C. Curio tribunus plebis subiecit facem, vir nobilis, eloquens, audax, suae alienaeque et fortunae et pudicitiae prodigus, homo ingeniosissime ne-

4 quam et facundus malo publico, cuius animo ‹dedito›[337] voluptatibus vel libidinibus neque opes ullae neque facultates[338] sufficere possent. hic primo pro Pompeii partibus (id est, ut tunc habebatur, pro re publica), mox simulatione contra Pompeium et Caesarem sed animo pro Caesare stetit.[339] (id gratis an accepto centies HS fecerit, ut acce-

5 pimus, in medio relinquemus.) ad ultimum saluberrimas [et] coalescentis condiciones pacis, quas et Caesar iustissimo animo postulabat et Pompeius aequo recipiebat, discussit ac rupit, unice cavente Cicerone concordiae publicae.

Harum praeteritarumque rerum ordo cum iustis aliorum voluminibus promatur, tum (uti spero) nostris expli-

6 cabitur; nunc proposito operi sua forma reddatur si prius gratulatus ero Q. Catulo, duobus Lucullis Metelloque et Hortensio, qui, cum sine invidia in re publica floruissent eminuissentque sine periculo[340] quieta aut certe non prae-

[337] *suppl. Woodman* (animo *secl. Krause*: animi *Lipsius*)
[338] facultates *Woodman*: cupiditates *PA*: dignitates *Watt*
[339] stetit *Gelenius*: restitit *PA*
[340] *post* periculo *interpunxerunt alii*

170

BOOK 2.48

Fortune would have lacked the opportunity of destroying him and he would have taken undiminished to the inhabitants of the Underworld the Greatness that he had had among those of the Upper.

No bigger or more flaming firebrand was put to the civil war, and to the troubles which then ensued for twenty unbroken years, than that by Gaius Curio, tribune of the plebs, a man of the nobility, eloquent, revolutionary, prodigal of his own and others' fortune and chastity, a person of the most talented immorality, fluent to the public detriment, whose mind, dedicated to pleasure and lust, neither wealth nor means could satisfy at all. At first his stance was to support Pompey's party (that is, as was then thought, the commonwealth), then he pretended it was against Pompey as well as Caesar; but in his heart it was for Caesar. (Whether he did that for nothing or after receiving ten million sesterces, as we have been told, we shall leave undecided.) In the end, when salutary terms for a cohering peace were being demanded by Caesar in a spirit of fairness and accepted by Pompey in one of calmness, he shattered and ruptured them, despite Cicero's unique concern for public concord.

Details of these and previous events are published in the properly sized volumes of others but will also (as I hope) be described in ours; as it is, the present work may preserve its particular form when I have first congratulated Quintus Catulus, the two Luculli, Metellus, and Hortensius, who, after they had flourished without resentment and had been outstanding without danger in a commonwealth that was peaceful or at least not collapsing head-

VELLEIUS PATERCULUS

cipitata,[341] fatali[342] ante initium bellorum civilium morte
functi sunt.

49. Lentulo et Marcello consulibus post urbem conditam annis DCCIII, ante annos[343] LXXVIII quam tu, M.
Vinici, consulatum inires, bellum civile exarsit. alterius
2 ducis causa melior videbatur, alterius erat firmior; hic omnia speciosa, illic valentia; Pompeium senatus auctoritas,
Caesarem militum armavit fiducia. consules senatusque
3 causae non[344] Pompeio summam imperii detulerunt. nihil
relictum a Caesare quod servandae pacis causa temptari
posset, nihil receptum a Pompeianis, cum alter consul
iusto esset ferocior, Lentulus vero salva re publica salvus
esse non posset, M. autem Cato' moriendum antequam
ullam condicionem civis[345] accipiendam rei publicae con-
tenderet. vir antiquus et gravis Pompeii partes laudaret
magis, prudens sequeretur Caesaris, et illa gloriosa,[346]
haec terribiliora duceret.

4 Ut deinde spretis omnibus quae Caesar postulaverat,
tantummodo contentus cum una legione titulum retinere
provinciae, privatus ut[347] in urbem veniret et se in peti-

341 praecipitata ⟨civitate⟩ *Ruhnken*   342 fatali *secl. Arnoldt*
343 ante annos *Halm*: & annos *BA*: & *P*: et ⟨ante⟩ annos *Orelli*
344 non *obelis not. Watt*   345 civis *PA*: cuiusvis *Ruhnken*
346 glorios⟨ior⟩a *Cuper*
347 privatus ut *Mommsen*: privatusque *PA*

232 Q. Lutatius Catulus (32.1n) died late in 61 or early in 62;
L. Licinius Lucullus Ponticus (33.1n) died late in 57 or early in
56, shortly followed by his brother, M. Terentius Varro Lucullus
(28.1n); Q. Caecilius Metellus Creticus (34.1n) is last heard of in
54; Q. Hortensius Hortalus (2.16.3n) died in 49.

BOOK 2.48–49

long, died a natural death before the beginning of the civil wars.[232]

49. In the consulship of Lentulus and Marcellus,[233] 703 years after the founding of the City, seventy-eight years before you entered upon your consulship, Marcus Vinicius, civil war flared up. One leader's cause seemed the better, the other's the stronger; all was impressiveness on one side, effectiveness on the other; Pompey was armed with the authority of the senate, Caesar with confidence in his soldiers. The consuls and senate conferred supreme power not on Pompey but on his cause. Nothing was left untried by Caesar for the sake of preserving peace, nothing accepted by the Pompeians; the one consul was more defiant than was proper, Lentulus could not survive if the commonwealth survived,[234] and Marcus Cato maintained that there was an obligation to die before the commonwealth should accept any terms from a citizen. A man of old-fashioned seriousness would have praised Pompey's party more, but the prudent would have followed Caesar's, regarding the former as glorious but the latter as more terrifying.

Having rejected everything that had been demanded by Caesar, who was content only to retain a titular province with one legion, the senate had decreed that he should enter the City as a private individual and in a cam-

[233] L. Cornelius Lentulus Crus and C. Claudius Marcellus (49).

[234] According to Caesar (*BCiv.* 1.4.2), Lentulus was heavily in debt.

173

VELLEIUS PATERCULUS

tione consulatus suffragiis populi Romani committeret[348] decreverat[349] ⟨senatus⟩,[350] ratus bellandum Caesar cum exercitu Rubiconem transiit. Cn. Pompeius consulesque et maior pars senatus relicta urbe ac deinde Italia transmisere Dyrrachium. 50. at Caesar Domitio legionibusque Corfinii quae una cum eo fuerant potitus, duce aliisque qui voluerant[351] abire ad Pompeium sine dilatione dimissis, persecutus Brundisium ita ut appareret malle integris rebus et[352] condicionibus finire bellum quam opprimere

2 fugientes, cum[353] transgressos reperisset consules, in urbem revertit redditaque ratione consiliorum suorum in senatu et in contione ac miserrimae necessitudinis, cum alienis armis ad arma compulsus esset, Hispanias petere

3 decrevit. festinationem itineris eius aliquamdiu morata Massilia est, fide melior quam consilio prudentior, intempestive principalium armorum arbitria captans, quibus hi se debent interponere qui non parentem coercere pos-

4 sunt. exercitus deinde qui sub Afranio consulari ac Petreio praetorio fuerat ipsius adventus[354] vigore ac fulgore occupatus se Caesari tradidit; uterque legatorum et quisquis cuiusque ordinis sequi eos voluerat remissi ad Pompeium.

---

[348] veniret . . . committeret *Gelenius*: -ire . . . -ere *PA*
[349] decreverat *Burer*: decrevere *PA* (decreverit *P^m*)
[350] *suppl. Woodman*
[351] voluerant *Gelenius*: venerant *PA*
[352] et *secl. Nagel*
[353] cum *PA*: quod *Castiglioni*
[354] adventus *Gelenius*: -tu *PA*

---

[235] The night of 10–11 January 49. The text and interpretation of this sentence have been much disputed.

174

BOOK 2.49–50

paign for the consulship should submit himself to the votes of the Roman people; but, seeing no alternative to war, Caesar crossed the Rubicon with his army.[235] Pompey, the consuls, and the majority of the senate, abandoning the City and then Italy, crossed over to Dyrrachium. 50. But Caesar, having captured Domitius[236] and the legions at Corfinium that had been with him, dismissed the leader without delay, as well as any others who wanted to go off to Pompey, following on to Brundisium himself in such a way that it was clear he preferred to conclude the war while everything remained unaltered, including his terms, rather than to overwhelm the fugitives; but, when he discovered that the consuls had shipped across, he returned to the City, and, having rendered in the senate and at a public meeting an account of his plans and of the wretched constraint by which he had been forced to take up arms by the arms of another, he decided to make for the Spains. The speed of his journey was delayed for a while by Massilia,[237] which, better in loyalty than prudent in policy, assumed an untimely arbitration between the armed principals—the kind of intervention that is only for those who have the power to coerce the noncompliant. Then the army that had been under Afranius and Petreius, respectively ex-consul and ex-praetor, surprised by the lightning energy of the man's arrival, handed itself over to Caesar; the two legates and whoever of each order[238] wanted to follow them were sent back to Pompey.

[236] L. Domitius Ahenobarbus (cos. 54).
[237] Caesar arrived there in the spring of 49.
[238] That is, equestrian and senatorial (2.3.2n).

175

VELLEIUS PATERCULUS

51. Proximo anno, dum[355] Dyrrachium ac vicina ei urbi regio castris Pompeii retinetur, qui accitis ex omnibus transmarinis provinciis legionibus, equitum ac peditum auxiliis, regumque ⟨et⟩[356] tetrarcharum simulque dynastarum copiis immanem exercitum confecerat et mare praesidiis classium (ut rebatur) saepserat quominus Cae-
2 sar legiones posset transmittere, sua et celeritate et fortuna C. Caesar usus nihil in mora habuit quominus et cum[357] vellet ipse exercitusque classibus perveniret et primo paene castris Pompeii sua iungeret, mox etiam obsidione munimentisque eum complecteretur. sed in-
3 opia obsidentibus quam obsessis erat gravior. tum Balbus Cornelius excedente humanam fidem temeritate ingressus castra hostium saepiusque cum Lentulo conlocutus consulari[358] dubitante quanti se venderet, illis incrementis fecit viam quibus non Hispaniensis[359] natus sed Hispanus in triumphum et pontificatum adsurgeret fieretque ex privato consularis. variatum deinde proeliis, sed un⟨um e⟩o[360] longe magis Pompeianis prosperum quo[361] graviter impulsi sunt Caesaris milites.

---

[355] dum *Ellis*: cum *PA* (*unde mox* obtineretur *Heinsius*)
[356] *suppl. Gelenius*   [357] et cum *PA*: et quo *Acidalius*: eo cum *Vossius*: et cum ⟨vellet et quo⟩ *Ruhnken*
[358] consulari *Goodyear*: COS. *P*: consule *A*
[359] Hispaniensis *Lipsius*: Hispaniae Asiae *PA*
[360] un⟨um e⟩o . . . prosperum *Woodman*: uno . . . prospero *PA*
[361] quo *secl. Fröhlich*

---

[239] That is, 48.
[240] Eastern princes.
[241] The younger L. Cornelius Balbus became a pontiff probably no later than 39 and celebrated a triumph in 19 for exploits

176

BOOK 2.51

51. Next year[239] Dyrrachium and the region in the vicinity of the city were being held by the camp of Pompey, who—having summoned from all the overseas provinces legions, auxiliaries of cavalry and of infantry, and forces from kings and tetrarchs as well as dynasts[240]—had assembled a prodigious army and had closed the sea (as he thought) with naval patrols to prevent Caesar from being able to transport his legions. But Caesar, relying on his characteristic speed and good fortune, allowed nothing to delay him and his army from arriving by fleet (and when he wanted), and, having first almost joined his camp to Pompey's, he then encircled him also with siege works in a blockade; but the shortage of supplies was more serious for the blockaders than the blockaded. Then Balbus Cornelius, with a rashness exceeding human belief, entered the enemy camp and held frequent talks with Lentulus the ex-consul (who was wondering for how much to sell himself), and it was by stages such as this that he made his way, with the result that, though not simply born in Spain but a Spaniard, he rose to a triumph and pontificate and, from being a private individual, became a consular.[241] The subsequent battles fluctuated, but one was much the more favorable for the Pompeians, given the severity with which Caesar's soldiers were driven back.

in Africa; he was never consul but seems to have been adlected "among the consulars" by Augustus. Although V.'s metaphor for the man's career ("made his way") is conventional enough, it reads elliptically in its context: since we know from a letter of Pollio to Cicero that Balbus had written a play "about his journey to solicit Lentulus the proconsul" (Cic. *Fam.*10.32.3), V.'s choice of wording is perhaps an allusion to the play, which may have had the word "journey" in, or as, its title.

177

VELLEIUS PATERCULUS

52. Tum Caesar cum exercitu fatalem victoriae suae
2 Thessaliam petiit. Pompeius, longe diversa aliis suadentibus (quorum plerique hortabantur ut in Italiam transmit-
teret—neque, hercules, quidquam partibus illis salubrius
fuit!—alii ut bellum traheret quod dignatione partium in
dies ipsis magis prosperum fieret[362]), usus impetu suo hos-
3 tem secutus est. aciem Pharsalicam et illum cruentis-
simum Romano nomini diem tantumque utriusque exercitus profusum sanguinis et conlisa[363] inter se duo rei
publicae capita effossumque alterum Romani imperii lumen, tot talesque Pompeianarum partium caesos viros
4 non recipit enarranda hic scripturae modus. illud notandum est: ut primum C. Caesar inclinatam vidit Pompeia-
norum aciem, neque prius neque antiquius quidquam
habuit quam <ut>[364] in omnes partes (ut militari et verbo[365]
5 et consuetudine[366] utar) dimitteret ***.[367] pro dii immortales, quod huius voluntatis erga Brutum suae[368] postea
6 vir tam mitis pretium tulit! nihil illa victoria mirabilius,
magnificentius, clarius fuit, quando[369] neminem nisi acie
consumptum civem patria desideravit; sed munus miseri-
cordiae corrupit pertinacia, cum libentius vitam victor[iam][370] daret quam victi acciperent.

362 fieret *PA*: foret *Cludius*
363 conlisa *Gelenius*: consilio *PA*
364 *suppl. Vascosanus*
365 et verbo *P*: verbo *A*
366 et consuetudine *PA*: ex c- *Lipsius*
367 *lacunam post* dimitteret *vel alicubi statuunt edd.*
368 suum *Cludius*
369 illa . . . quando *PA*: <in> illa . . . quam quod *Haase*
370 victor[iam] *Gelenius*: victor iam *Burer*

178

BOOK 2.52

52. Then Caesar and his army made for Thessaly and a victorious destiny. As for Pompey, although some were advocating far different courses (the majority urged a crossing to Italy—as Hercules is my witness, nothing would have been more salutary for his party!—but others that he should prolong a war that, because of their party's esteem, was daily becoming more favorable for them), he relied on his own initiative and followed the enemy. The battle at Pharsalus, that goriest of days for the Roman race, so much blood shed by both armies, the clash of the commonwealth's two heads, the gouging out of one of the Roman Empire's eyes, so many fine men of the Pompeian party slain—all this the limitation on my present text has not the scope to describe in full. But the following is to be noted: as soon as Caesar saw that the Pompeians' battle line had given way, his immediate reaction was to dispatch to all quarters *** (if I may resort to a military term and custom).[242] By the immortal gods, to think of the reward that so mild a man reaped afterward for his goodwill toward Brutus! Nothing was more marvelous, more magnificent or more brilliant than that victory, because the fatherland lost no citizen except those killed in the battle line;[243] but the kindness of his compassion was spoiled by stubbornness, since the victor was giving life more gladly than the vanquished accepted it.

[242] The "military term and custom" seems to have been in the part of the sentence that is missing and perhaps also referred to Caesar's famous order that citizens should be spared (e.g., Suet. *Iul.* 75.2). The date of the battle was 9 August 48.

[243] That is, Caesar did not massacre the Pompeian survivors.

179

VELLEIUS PATERCULUS

53. Pompeius profugiens cum duobus Lentulis consularibus Sextoque filio et Favonio praetorio, quos comites ei Fortuna adgregaverat, aliis ut Parthos, aliis ut Africam peteret, in qua fidelissimum partium suarum haberet regem Iubam, suadentibus, Aegyptum petere proposuit, memor beneficiorum quae in patrem eius Ptolemaei, qui tum puero quam iuveni propior regnabat Alexandriae,

2 contulerat. sed quis in adversis beneficiorum servat memoriam? aut quis ullam calamitosis deberi putat gratiam? aut quando Fortuna non mutat fidem? missi itaque ab rege qui venientem Cn. Pompeium (is iam a Mytilenis Corneliam uxorem receptam in navem fugae comitem habere coeperat) consilio Theodoti et Achillae exciperent hortarenturque ut ex oneraria in eam navem quae obviam processerat transcenderet; quod cum fecisset, princeps Romani nominis imperio arbitrioque Aegyptii mancipii, C. Caesare P. Servilio consulibus, iugulatus est.

3 Hic post tres consulatus et totidem triumphos domitumque terrarum orbem sanctissimi atque praestantissimi viri in id evecti super quod ascendi non potest, duodesexagesimum annum agentis, pridie natalem ipsius, vitae fuit exitus, in tantum in illo viro a se discordante Fortuna ut, cui modo ad victoriam terra defuerat, deesset ad sepultu-

4 ram. quid aliud quam nimium occupatos dixerim quos in aetate et tanti et paene nostri saeculi viri fefellit quin-

---

[244] The consul of 49 (49.1n) and P. Cornelius Lentulus Spinther (cos. 57).   [245] M. Favonius had been praetor in 49.

[246] Juba I of Numidia (adjacent to the Roman province of Africa).   [247] Ptolemy XIII, born in 61, was the son of Ptolemy XII Auletes, whom Pompey had supported in the 50s.

[248] 28 September 48.

180

BOOK 2.53

53. Fleeing with the two consular Lentuli,[244] his son Sextus, and Favonius, an ex-praetor,[245] the companions whom Fortune had assembled for him, Pompey proposed—although some were advocating that he should make for the Parthians, others for Africa, where he had his party's most loyal supporter, King Juba[246]—to make for Egypt, remembering the good deeds that he had done for the father of the Ptolemy who, more a boy than a young man, was then ruling in Alexandria.[247] But in adversity who preserves a memory of good deeds? Who thinks that any favor is owed to the wretched? When does Fortune not change her loyalties? And so, on the advice of Theodotus and Achillas, a welcoming party was dispatched by the king for Pompey's arrival (Mytilene was where he started to have his wife Cornelia on board ship to keep him company in his flight) and urged him to transfer from his cargo vessel to the ship that had come out to meet him. When he had done so, the principal figure of the Roman race, on the command and authority of an Egyptian vassal, in the consulship of Gaius Caesar and Publius Servilius, was slaughtered.[248]

After three consulships, as many triumphs, and the taming of the world, this was the life's end of an entirely scrupulous and outstanding man, raised to a height beyond which ascent is impossible, in his fifty-eighth year, on the day before his own birthday—Fortune being so contrary in his case that there was no land to bury the man for whom so recently there was no land to conquer. As for those who have made a mistake of five years in the age of so great a man, who was almost of our own era, I would only say that they were too distracted, since the computa-

181

VELLEIUS PATERCULUS

quennium, cum a C. Atilio et Q. Servilio consulibus tam facilis[371] esset annorum digestio? quod adieci non ut arguerem sed ne arguerer.

54. Non fuit maior in Caesarem quam in Pompeium fuerat regis eorumque quorum is auctoritate regebatur fides. quippe cum venientem eum temptassent insidiis ac deinde bello lacessere auderent, utrique summo[372] imperatorum, alteri ‹mortuo, alteri›[373] superstiti meritas poenas luere suppliciis.

2 Nusquam erat Pompeius corpore, adhuc ubique vivebat[374] nomine. quippe ingens partium eius favor bellum excitaverat Africum, quod ciebat rex Iuba et Scipio (vir consularis, ante biennium[375] quam extingueretur Pompeius, lectus ab eo socer), eorumque copias auxerat M. 3 Cato, ingenti cum difficultate itinerum locorumque inopia perductis ad eos legionibus; qui vir, cum summum ei a militibus deferretur imperium, honoratiori parere maluit. 55. admonet promissae brevitatis fides quanto omnia transcursu dicenda sint. sequens fortunam suam Caesar pervectus in Africam est, quam occiso C. Curione, Iulianarum duce partium, Pompeiani obtinebant exercitus. ibi primo varia fortuna, mox pugnavit sua,[376] inclinataeque

371 facilis *Gelenius*: felix *PA*   372 summo‹rum› *Mommsen*
373 *suppl. Lipsius*   374 vivebat *Lipsius*: Iubae *P et (sed suprascr.* vivo) *A*   375 triennium *Lipsius*   376 fortuna, mox pugnavit sua *Acidalius*: fortunam expugnavit via *PA*

---

249 C. Atilius Serranus and Q. Servilius Caepio were consuls in 106, the more usual date given for Pompey's birth.

250 Caesar arrived in Egypt at the very beginning of Octo-

182

BOOK 2.53–55

tion of years from the consulship of Gaius Atilius and Quintus Servilius is so easy.[249] I have added this not to criticize but to avoid being criticized.

54. The loyalty of the king and of those by whose influence he was ruled was no greater toward Caesar than it had been toward Pompey: after attempts on him by intrigue when he arrived, they dared to challenge him in war, but by their punishments they paid to the two supreme commanders, one dead, one surviving, the penalty that they deserved.[250]

Although Pompey was nowhere in body, he still lived on everywhere through his name. The mighty goodwill enjoyed by his party had stirred up a war in Africa that was kept going by King Juba and Scipio (an ex-consul chosen as his father-in-law by Pompey two years before his life was snuffed out),[251] and their forces had been increased by Marcus Cato, who had led legions through to them despite the mighty difficulties of the journey and the barrenness of the localities: this was a man who, when the supreme command was being conferred on him by his soldiers, preferred to obey a higher rank.[252] 55. Fidelity to .my promise of brevity reminds me how much of a sketch is required for my accounts of everything. Caesar, following his characteristic fortune, traveled to Africa, which the Pompeian armies held after the slaying of Curio, leader of

ber 48. His war against Ptolemy was ended by the latter's death in late March 47.   [251] In 52, four years before his death, Pompey had married Cornelia (53.2), daughter of Q. Caecilius Metellus Pius Scipio Nasica, whom he had then taken as his consular colleague; Scipio was presently proconsul in Africa.   [252] That is, the proconsul Scipio, whereas Cato was only a propraetor.

183

VELLEIUS PATERCULUS

2 hostium copiae; nec dissimilis ibi adversus victos quam in priores clementia Caesaris fuit.

Victorem Africani belli Caesarem gravius excepit Hispaniense (nam victus ab eo Pharnaces vix quidquam gloriae eius adstruxit), quod Cn. Pompeius, Magni filius, adulescens impetus ad bella maximi, ingens ac terribile conflaverat, undique ad eum adhuc paterni nominis magnitudinem sequentium ex toto orbe terrarum auxiliis con-

3 fluentibus. sua Caesarem in Hispaniam comitata fortuna est, sed nullum umquam atrocius periculosiusque ab eo initum proelium, adeo ut plus quam dubio Marte descenderet equo consistensque ante recedentem suorum aciem, increpata prius Fortuna quod se in eum servasset exitum, denuntiaret militibus vestigio se non recessurum: proinde viderent quem et quo loco imperatorem deserturi

4 forent! verecundia magis quam virtute acies restituta, et a[377] duce quam a milite fortius. Cn. Pompeius gravis vulnere inventus inter solitudines avias interemptus est; Labienum Varumque acies abstulit.

56. Caesar omnium victor regressus in urbem, quod humanam excedat fidem, omnibus qui contra se arma tu-

---

[377] restituta *Heinsius,* et a *Ruhnken*: restitutae C.A. *B*: restitutae sunt a *PA*

---

[253] Curio (48.3) was killed in the summer of 49.

[254] The battle of Thapsus (6 April 46).

[255] Pharnaces II, king of Pontus, had been defeated at the battle of Zela in Asia Minor (2 August 47).

[256] The battle of Munda (17 March 45).

[257] Both P. Attius Varus and T. Labienus had fled from Africa to Spain. Attius, an ex-praetor, had held the province of Africa for the Pompeians until superseded by Scipio (54.3). After a tribu-

BOOK 2.55–56

the Julian party.[253] There he fought at first with variable fortune, then with that which was characteristic of him, and the enemy forces gave way;[254] and Caesar's clemency toward the vanquished was no different from that to others previously.

Victor in the African War, Caesar was confronted by the more serious Spanish (his victory over Pharnaces scarcely added anything to his glory):[255] mighty and terrifying, it had been kindled by Gnaeus Pompeius (Magnus' son, a young man whose greatest impulse was for war), with supporting forces flowing in from everywhere across the whole globe from those still following the greatness of his father's name. Caesar's characteristic fortune accompanied him to Spain, but no battle that he ever embarked on was more atrocious or dangerous,[256] to such a degree that, with its fate worse than in the balance, he dismounted from his horse and, taking his stand in front of his men's retreating battle line, he first upbraided Fortune because she had kept him for such an end, and then he announced to his soldiers that he would not retreat from where he had planted his foot: so let them see what kind of a commander they would be deserting, and in what circumstance! The battle line was restored more by shame than by courage, and more bravely by the leader than by his soldiery. Gnaeus Pompeius, severely wounded, was found amid trackless wastes and killed; Labienus and Varus were dispatched in the battle line.[257]

56. Victorious over everyone, Caesar returned to the City and (something to exceed human belief) pardoned all

nate (40.4) and praetorship, Labienus had served as Caesar's principal legate in Gaul, but joined the Pompeian side in 49.

185

VELLEIUS PATERCULUS

lerant ignovit; magnificentissimisque gladiatorii muneris, naumachiae et equitum peditumque simul elephantorum certaminis spectaculis epulique per multos dies dati cele-
2 bratione replevit eam. quinque egit triumphos: Gallici apparatus ex citro, Pontici ex acantho, Alexandrini testudine, Africi ebore, Hispaniensis argento rasili constitit. pecunia ex manubiis lata paulo amplius sexies milies sestertium.
3 Neque illi tanto viro et tam clementer omnibus victoriis suis[378] uso plus quinque mensium principalis quies contigit. quippe cum mense Octobri in urbem revertisset, idibus Martiis, coniurationis auctoribus Bruto et Cassio (quorum alterum promittendo consulatum non obligaverat, contra differendo Cassium offenderat), adiectis etiam consiliariis caedis familiarissimis omnium et fortuna partium eius in summum evectis fastigium, D. Bruto et C. Trebonio aliisque clari nominis viris, interemptus est.
4 cui magnam invidiam conciliarat M. Antonius, omnibus audendis paratissimus, consulatus collega, imponendo capiti eius Lupercalibus sedentis pro rostris insigne regium, quod ab eo ita[379] repulsum erat ut non offensus[380] videretur.

[378] victoribus suis *B, corr. Gelenius, om. PA*
[379] ita *Rhenanus*: id *PA*   [380] offensus *Rhenanus*: -um *PBA*

---

[258] The first four were held in September 46, that for Spain in early October 45.

[259] The references are to the models (e.g., of towns) that, like the pictures or tableaux (1.9.6n), would be carried on floats to symbolize the general's victories (Beard, 179).

[260] 15 March 44.   [261] D. Iunius Brutus Albinus was consul designate for 42; C. Trebonius had been suffect consul in 45.

186

BOOK 2.56

who had taken up arms against him; and he filled it with the most magnificent spectacles—a gladiatorial show, a naval battle, a contest of cavalry and infantry as well as elephants—and with a celebratory public feast given over many days. He held five triumphs:[258] the trappings in the Gallic consisted of citrus, in the Pontic of acanthus, in the Alexandrian of tortoiseshell, in the African of ivory, and in the Spanish of polished silver.[259] The money raised from the spoils was a little more than six hundred million sesterces.

Although he was such a great man and had shown such clemency after all his victories, no more than five months' rest fell to him as *princeps*. He had returned to the City in the month of October, but on the Ides of March[260] he was killed, a conspiracy having been instigated by Brutus and Cassius (the former he had failed to indebt despite promising him a consulship, whereas he had offended Cassius by deferring his), to whom were added, as associates in the assassination, the most familiar of all his friends, raised to the highest peak by the success of his party— Decimus Brutus, Gaius Trebonius, and other men of distinguished name.[261] He had become the object of great resentment thanks to Antony, his colleague in the consulship[262] and always ready for any venture, who placed upon his head, as he was sitting on the rostra at the Lupercalia, a royal diadem, which he brushed aside in such a way that he did not seem offended.[263]

[262] Of 44.

[263] The diadem was a headband worn as a mark of kingship in the contemporary Greek world. The Lupercalia festival was held on 15 February 44, only a month before the assassination.

VELLEIUS PATERCULUS

57. Laudandum experientia consilium est Pansae atque Hirtii, qui semper praedixerant Caesari ut principatum armis quaesitum armis teneret; ille, dictitans mori se quam timere[381] malle, dum clementiam quam praestiterat expectat, incautus ab ingratis occupatus est, cum quidem plurima ei praesagia atque indicia dii immortales futuri
2 obtulissent periculi. nam et haruspices praemonuerant ut diligentissime iduum Martiarum caveret diem, et uxor Calpurnia, territa nocturno visu, ut ea die domi subsisteret orabat, et libelli coniurationem nuntiantes dati neque pro-
3 tinus ab eo[382] lecti erant. sed profecto ineluctabilis Fatorum vis, cuiuscum⟨que⟩[383] fortunam mutare constituit, consilia corrumpit.

58. Quo anno id patravere facinus, Brutus[384] et [C.][385] Cassius praetores erant, D. Brutus consul designatus.
2 hi una cum coniurationis globo, stipati gladiatorum D. Bruti manu, Capitolium occupavere. tum[386] consul Antonius—quem cum simul interimendum censuisset Cassius testamentumque Caesaris abolendum, Brutus[387] repugnaverat dictitans nihil amplius civibus praeter tyranni (ita enim appellari Caesarem facto eius expediebat) peten-
3 dum esse sanguinem—convocato senatu, cum iam Dolabella (quem substituturus sibi Caesar designaverat con-

---

381 timere *(sed mut. in* timeri*)* A: timeri P
382 neque protinus ab eo A: ab eo n- p- P
383 cuiuscum⟨que⟩ *Gelenius*
384 ⟨M.⟩ Brutus *Heinsius*   385 C. PA, *secl. Stanger*
386 tum *Haase:* cum PA   387 ⟨M.⟩ Brutus *Ruhnken*

---

264 C. Vibius Pansa Caetronianus and A. Hirtius would be consuls in 43.

BOOK 2.57–58

57. In the light of experience there has to be praise for the advice of Pansa and Hirtius,[264] whose prescription for Caesar had always been that he should hold by armed force a position as *princeps* that had been won by armed force; but he insisted that he would rather die than live in fear. And, while he was hoping for the clemency that he himself had shown, he was caught unawares by the ungrateful, although in fact the immortal gods had offered him numerous indications foreboding future danger. The soothsayers had forewarned that he should carefully beware the day of the Ides of March; his wife Calpurnia, terrified by a dream in the night, kept begging him to stay at home that day; and, though notes reporting the conspiracy had been handed to him, he had not read them at once. But of course the inescapable power of the Fates destroys the discernment of anyone whose fortune it has decided to change.

58. The year that they perpetrated their crime, Brutus and Cassius were praetors, Decimus Brutus consul designate. Together with the group of conspirators, and flanked closely by a unit of Decimus Brutus' gladiators, they took possession of the Capitol. Then Antony as consul—who Cassius had opined should be killed at the same time and Caesar's will suppressed, but Brutus had objected, insisting that only the blood of a tyrant (it suited his deed that Caesar be so called) should be the target of citizens— convened the senate and, after Dolabella (whom Caesar had designated consul as his replacement)[265] had already

---

[265] Cn. Cornelius Dolabella was due to take over as consul when Caesar departed on campaign (59.4n).

189

VELLEIUS PATERCULUS

sulem) fasces atque insignia corripuisset consulis, velut
pacis auctor liberos suos obsides in Capitolium misit fi-
demque descendendi tuto interfectoribus Caesaris dedit;
4 et illud decreti Atheniensium celeberrimi exemplum, re-
latum a Cicerone, oblivionis praeteritarum rerum decreto
patrum comprobatum est. 59. Caesaris deinde testamen-
tum apertum est, quo C. Octavium, nepotem sororis suae
Iuliae, adoptabat; de cuius origine, etiam si praevenit
haec,[388] pauca dicenda sunt.
2 Fuit C. Octavius ⟨pater⟩,[389] ut non patricia, ita admodum speciosa equestri genitus familia, gravis, sanctus,
innocens, dives. hic praetor inter nobilissimos viros creatus primo loco, cum ei dignatio Iulia genitam Atiam
⟨iam⟩[390] conciliasset uxorem, ex eo honore sortitus Macedoniam appellatusque in ea imperator, decedens ad peti-
3 tionem consulatus obiit praetextato relicto filio. quem C.
Caesar, maior eius avunculus, educatum apud Philippum
vitricum dilexit ut suum, natumque annos XVIII Hispaniensis militiae adsecutum se postea comitem habuit,
numquam aut alio usum hospitio quam suo aut alio vec-
tum vehiculo, pontificatusque sacerdotio puerum honora-
4 vit; et patratis bellis civilibus ad erudiendam liberalibus

---

[388] haec *Woodman*: et *PA* (praeveniet *Ellis*: praenitet *Heinsius*: per se nitet *Burman*: properanti hic *Acidalius*: alii alia)
[389] *suppl. Cludius*   [390] *suppl. Woodman*

---

[266] On 17 March, when proposing an amnesty, Cicero had
recalled the famous amnesty agreed by the Athenians in 403 after
the rule of the Thirty Tyrants (*Phil.* 1.1).   [267] The elder Octavius had married Atia some years before his praetorship in 61;

BOOK 2.58–59

seized the consular fasces and insignia, he acted as the instigator of peace, sending his own son as hostage to the Capitol and guaranteeing a safe descent for Caesar's killers; and the famous precedent of the Athenians' celebrated decree, recalled in Cicero's proposal, was approved by a senatorial decree of amnesty for past actions.[266] 59. Then Caesar's will was opened, in which he was adopting Gaius Octavius, the grandson of his sister, Julia; and a little must be said about his origin, even if it precedes these events.

The elder Gaius Octavius, born into a rather impressive equestrian family, albeit not patrician, was serious, scrupulous, blameless, and rich. Created praetor in first place among men of the highest nobility (his rank had already won him Atia, Julia's daughter, as his wife), he was allotted Macedonia after his term of office and was hailed "commander" there;[267] but, on his departure to seek the consulship, he died, leaving a son still in the praetexta.[268] The latter was brought up in the home of Philippus, his stepfather,[269] but Caesar, his great-uncle, loved him as his own: he had the eighteen-year-old follow him to Spain, and on campaign there afterward kept him as his companion, never allowing him to enjoy anyone else's hospitality but his, nor to travel in anyone else's carriage. Caesar honored him, while he was still a boy, with the priestly office of pontiff, and after the conclusion of the civil wars, in order to educate the remarkable young man's character in

in 60–58 he was proconsul in Macedonia, where he conquered the Bessi (for "commander" see 24.1n).

[268] For the praetexta see 1.10.3n.   [269] L. Marcius Philippus (cos. 56) married Atia after the death of Octavius in 58.

191

VELLEIUS PATERCULUS

disciplinis singularis indolem iuvenis[391] Apolloniam eum
in studia miserat, mox belli Getici ac deinde Parthici habi-
turus commilitonem.

5 Cui ut est nuntiatum de caede avunculi, cum protinus
ex vicinis legionibus centuriones suam suorumque militum operam ei pollicerentur neque eam spernendam Salvidienus et Agrippa dicerent, ille festinans pervenire in
urbem omnem ordinem[392] et necis et testamenti Brundisii
6 comperit. cui adventanti Romam immanis amicorum oc-
currit frequentia, et, cum intraret urbem, solis orbis super
caput eius curvatus aequaliter rotundatusque in color⟨a-
t⟩um arcum[393] velut coronam tanti mox viri capiti impo-
nens conspectus est.

60. Non placebat Atiae matri Philippoque vitrico adiri
nomen invidiosae fortunae Caesaris, sed adserebant salu-
taria rei publicae terrarumque orbis[394] Fata conditorem
2 conservatoremque Romani nominis. sprevit itaque caeles-
tis animus humana consilia et cum periculo potius summa
quam tuto humilia proposuit sequi maluitque avunculo et
Caesari de se quam vitrico credere,[395] dictitans nefas esse,
quo nomine Caesari dignus esset visus, semet[396] ipsum
videri indignum.

---

391 indolis iuvenem *Vascosanus*   392 ordinem *Gelenius*:
ordinationem *PA*: ordine rationem *Heinsius*: ordinem ac rationem *Munker*   393 in color⟨at⟩um arcum *Woodman*: in
colorem arcus *PA*: ⟨om⟩ni colore arcus *Watt*: *alii alia*
394 orbi *Burman*   395 credere *Gelenius*: cedere *PA*
396 sibimet *Ursinus*

---

270 Caesar was due to depart on 18 March for great campaigns
against the Dacians (here referred to as Getae) on the lower

BOOK 2.59–60

liberal branches of learning, he had sent him to study in Apollonia, intending soon to have him as his fellow soldier in the Getic and then the Parthian War.[270]

When he was told of the slaughter of his uncle (at this, centurions from the nearby legions promptly promised him their own and their soldiers' support, which Salvidienus and Agrippa said was not to be spurned),[271] he hastened to reach the City and at Brundisium discovered all the details of both the assassination and the will. As he was approaching Rome, he was met by a prodigious crowd of friends, and, when he entered the City, over his head was seen the orb of the sun, encircling it perfectly and rounded into a colored halo,[272] as if placing a crown on the head of the man soon destined for greatness.

60. His mother Atia and stepfather Philippus were not in favor of his inheriting the name of Caesar, to which so much resentment was attached, but the salutary Fates of the commonwealth and of the world laid claim to the founder and defender of the Roman race. So his heavenly mind spurned human advice and he determined to aim for the heights with all their danger rather than a humble objective in safety, and he preferred what was believed about himself by an uncle—and a Caesar—rather than by his stepfather, insisting it was wrong that he should seem unworthy of the name of which he seemed worthy to Caesar.

Danube and against the Parthians (see also Suet. *Iul.* 44.3, *Aug.* 8.2; App. *B Civ.* 2.110.459).
[271] For Q. Salvidienus Rufus (cos. des. 39) see 76.4; M. Vipsanius Agrippa, Augustus' great minister, will feature increasingly from now on.   [272] The text and meaning are disputed.

193

VELLEIUS PATERCULUS

3   Hunc protinus Antonius consul superbe excepit[397] (neque is erat contemptus sed metus) vixque admisso in Pompeianos hortos loquendi secum tempus dedit, mox etiam velut insidiis eius petitus sceleste insimulare coepit, in quo
4 turpiter deprehensa eius vanitas est. aperte deinde Antonii ac Dolabellae consulum ad nefandam dominationem erupit furor. HS septies milies, depositum a C. Caesare ad aedem Opis, occupatum ad Antonio; actorum eiusdem insertis falsis ‹immunitatibus›[398] civitatibusque corrupti commentarii[399] atque omnia pretio temperata, vendente
5 rem publicam consule. idem provinciam D. Bruto designato consuli decretam Galliam occupare statuit, Dolabella transmarinas decrevit sibi; interque naturaliter dissimillimos ac diversa volentes crescebat odium, eoque C. Caesar iuvenis cotidianis Antonii petebatur insidiis.

    61. Torpebat oppressa dominatione Antonii civitas. indignatio et dolor omnibus, vis ad resistendum nulli aderat cum C. Caesar XVIIII[400] annum egressus,[401] mira ausus ac summa consecutus privato consilio maiorem senatu pro re
2 publica animum habuit primumque a Calatia, mox a Casilino veteranos excivit paternos; quorum exemplum secuti

---

[397] excepit *Cludius*: excipit *PA*   [398] *suppl. Perizonius*
[399] corrupti commentarii *Ruhnken*: -is -is *PA*
[400] XVIIII *PA*: XX vix *Watt (retento* ingressus*)*
[401] egressus *Chishull*: in- *PA*

---

[273] The temple was on the Capitoline Hill (2.1.2n).

[274] D. Brutus had been assigned Cisalpine Gaul; in the summer of 44 Antony arranged to exchange his assigned province, Macedonia, for both Cisalpine and Transalpine Gaul. Dolabella was assigned Syria.

BOOK 2.60–61

At the start the consul Antony received him haughtily (and that was not contempt but dread) and, on admitting him to the Gardens of Pompey, scarcely gave him time to speak with him; later (a matter in which his insincerity was shamefully detected) Antony also began the wicked charge that he had been the target of the young man's intrigues. Then the rage of the consuls Antony and Dolabella erupted openly into an unspeakable despotism. Seven hundred million sesterces deposited by Caesar at the temple of Ops were seized by Antony;[273] the records of Caesar's enactments were falsified by the insertion of spurious immunities and grants of citizenship; everything was regulated by its price, the commonwealth put up for sale by its consul. Likewise he decided to seize Gaul, the province decreed to Decimus Brutus, consul designate, while Dolabella decreed overseas ones to himself;[274] and between the two of them, naturally dissimilar and differently inclined, a hatred developed, on which account the young Caesar[275] became the target of Antony's daily intrigues.

61. The community was paralyzed under the weight of Antony's despotism. Everyone was feeling indignation and pain but no one had the power to resist, until Caesar, after emerging from his nineteenth year, aiming for the heights with remarkable daring, on his personal initiative showed a greater courage than the senate on behalf of the commonwealth and roused his father's veterans first from Calatia and then from Casilinum;[276] others followed their

[275] Modern writers conventionally refer to the young Caesar as Octavian until he acquired the name Augustus on 16 January 27 (91.1).   [276] October 44; Octavian had turned nineteen on 23 September.

195

VELLEIUS PATERCULUS

alii brevi[402] in formam iusti coiere exercitus. mox, cum Antonius occurrisset exercitui quem ex transmarinis provinciis Brundisium venire iusserat, legio Martia et quarta, cognita et senatus voluntate et tanti iuvenis indole, sublatis
3 signis ad Caesarem se contulerunt. eum senatus honoratum equestri statua, quae hodieque in rostris posita aetatem eius scriptura indicat (qui honor non alii per CCC annos quam L. Sullae et Cn. Pompeio et C. Caesari contigerat), pro praetore una cum consulibus designatis Hirtio
4 et Pansa bellum cum Antonio gerere iussit; ⟨id⟩[403] ab eo annum agente vicesimum fortissime circa Mutinam administratum est, et D. Brutus obsidione liberatus. Antonius turpi ac nuda fuga coactus deserere Italiam; consulum autem alter in acie, alter post paucos dies ex vulnere mortem obiit.

62. Omnia antequam fugaretur Antonius honorifice a senatu in Caesarem exercitumque eius decreta sunt maxime auctore Cicerone; sed, ut recessit metus, erupit volun-
2 tas protinusque Pompeianis partibus rediit animus. Bruto Cassioque provinciae, quas iam ipsi sine ullo senatus consulto occupaverant, decretae; laudati quicumque se iis exercitus tradidissent; omnia transmarina imperia eorum
3 commissa arbitrio. quippe M. Brutus et C. Cassius, nunc metuentes arma Antonii, nunc ad augendam eius invidiam simulantes se metuere, testati edictis libenter se vel in perpetuo exilio victuros, dum res publica constaret con-

---

402 brevi *BA*: in b- *P*   403 *suppl. Gelenius*

---

277 The decree was passed on 4 January 43, when Hirtius and Pansa were already consuls.   278 In April 43.

279 Respectively, Macedonia and Syria.

196

BOOK 2.61–62

example, and in a short time they assembled to form a properly sized army. Later, after Antony had met the army that he had ordered to come to Brundisium from the overseas provinces, the Martian Legion and the Fourth got to know both the senate's intentions and the character of the very great young man, and, taking up their standards, they betook themselves to Caesar. The senate honored him with an equestrian statue, which is still in place on the rostra and indicates his age in its text (this is an honor that in three hundred years had not fallen to anyone except Sulla, Pompey, and Caesar), and ordered him as propraetor, along with the consuls designate Hirtius and Pansa, to wage war on Antony.[277] It was conducted by the nineteen-year-old with the greatest bravery around Mutina, and Decimus Brutus was freed from its blockade.[278] Antony was forced to abandon Italy in flight, shamefully and unarmed; but one of the consuls met his death in the battle line, the other a few days later from a wound.

62. Before Antony was put to flight, every honor was decreed by the senate for Caesar and his army, mainly on the proposal of Cicero; but, as dread receded, their sympathies emerged, and spirit immediately returned to the Pompeian party. To Brutus and Cassius were decreed the provinces that they themselves had already seized without any senate's decision;[279] praise was given to whichever armies had handed themselves over to them; and all the overseas commands were entrusted to their adjudication: for Brutus and Cassius—at one moment dreading the armed forces of Antony, at another simulating dread in order to increase the resentment at him—had testified in edicts that they would gladly live even in perpetual exile, as long as the commonwealth held together in harmony;

197

VELLEIUS PATERCULUS

cordia, nec ullam belli civilis praebituros materiam, plurimum sibi honoris esse in conscientia facti sui, profecti
urbe atque Italia, intento ac pari animo sine auctoritate
publica provincias exercitusque occupaverant et, ubicumque ipsi essent, praetexentes esse rem publicam, pecunias
etiam quae ex transmarinis provinciis Romam ab quaesto-
4 ribus deportabantur a volentibus acceperant. quae omnia
senatus decretis comprensa et comprobata sunt, et D.
Bruto, cum[404] alieno beneficio viveret, decretus triumphus; Pansae atque Hirtii corpora publica sepultura hono-
5 rata; Caesaris adeo nulla habita mentio ut legati qui ad
exercitum eius missi erant iuberentur summoto eo milites
adloqui. non fuit tam[405] ingratus exercitus quam fuerat
senatus: nam cum eam iniuriam dissimulando Caesar[406]
ferret, negavere milites sine imperatore suo ulla se au-
6 dituros mandata. hoc est illud tempus quo Cicero insito
amore Pompeianarum partium Caesarem laudandum
et tollendum censebat, cum aliud diceret, aliud intellegi
vellet.

63. Interim Antonius fuga transgressus Alpes, primo
per conloquia repulsus a M. Lepido (qui pontifex maximus
in C. Caesaris locum furto creatus decreta sibi Hispania
adhuc in Gallia morabatur), mox saepius in conspectum
veniens militum, cum et Lepido omnes imperatores forent

---

[404] cum *(immo* quom) *Acidalius*: quod *PA*
[405] *an* tam<en tam>?   [406] Caesar *Gelenius*: -ri *PA*

---

[280] The Latin *tollere*, whose basic meanings are "to lift, ele-
vate," can also mean "to extol, exalt" and "to eliminate, kill." The
ambiguity of Cicero's comment (for which see *Fam.* 11.20.1, written 24 May 43) here depends on the English expressions "to give
someone a/the push."   [281] M. Aemilius Lepidus (cos. 46,

198

BOOK 2.62–63

that they would not provide any fuel for civil war; and that their chief honor resided in their consciousness of their act. Having set off from the City and from Italy with a determined and matching intention, they had seized provinces and armies without official authority and, pretending that the commonwealth was wherever they were themselves, they had even taken from (albeit willing) quaestors the money that was being transported to Rome from the overseas provinces. All of these things were covered by senate's decrees and confirmed; though Decimus Brutus was alive thanks to someone else, a triumph was decreed for him; and the bodies of Pansa and Hirtius were honored with a public burial. Of Caesar no mention was made at all, so much so that the legates who had been sent to his army were ordered to address the soldiers only after he had withdrawn. But the army was not as ungrateful as the senate had been: although Caesar bore the insult by pretending it away, the soldiers refused to listen to any instructions without their commander. This was the time when Cicero, with his innate affection for the Pompeian party, opined that Caesar should be given the praise and push that were needed, saying one thing but wanting another to be understood.[280]

63. Meanwhile Antony, having fled across the Alps, was at first repulsed in exchanges with Marcus Lepidus (who, created Chief Pontiff by stealth in Caesar's place, was still delaying in Gaul despite having had Spain decreed to him);[281] later he came more often within sight of the soldiers and, since any commander was better than Lepidus,

---

42), the future triumvir, had been appointed Chief Pontiff in spring 44, having earlier been appointed proconsul of Narbonese Gaul and Nearer Spain by Julius Caesar.

VELLEIUS PATERCULUS

meliores et multis Antonius (dum erat sobrius), per aversa castrorum proruto[407] vallo militibus[408] receptus est; qui titulo imperii cedebat Lepido, cum summa virium penes eum foret. sub Antonii ingressum in castra Iuventius Laterensis, vir vita ac morte consentaneus, cum acerrime suasisset Lepido ne se cum Antonio hoste iudicato iungeret, irritus consilii gladio se ipse transfixit.

3   Plancus deinde dubia (id est sua) fide, diu quarum esset partium secum luctatus ac sibi difficile consentiens, et nunc adiutor D. Bruti designati consulis, collegae sui, senatuique se litteris venditans, mox eiusdem proditor, Asinius autem Pollio firmus proposito et Iulianis partibus fidus, Pompeianis adversus, uterque exercitus tradidere Antonio. 64. D. Brutus desertus primo a Planco, postea etiam insidiis eiusdem petitus, paulatim relinquente eum exercitu fugiens in hospitis cuiusdam nobilis viri (nomine Camelii[409]) domo ab iis quos miserat Antonius iugulatus est iustissimasque optime de se merito viro C. Caesari

2 poenas dedit, cuius cum primus[410] omnium amicorum fuisset, interfector fuit, et fortunae, ex qua fructum tulerat, invidiam in auctorem relegabat censebatque aequum

---

407 aversa . . . proruto *Gelenius*: -am . . . -ta *PA*
408 ⟨a⟩ militibus *Heinsius*
409 Camelii *Vossius*: -eli *PA*
410 primus *A*: -is *P*: ⟨in⟩ primis *Heinsius*

---

282 Antony had been declared a public enemy on 26 April 43.
283 D. Brutus and L. Munatius Plancus were proconsular colleagues in Gaul (the former in Cisalpine Gaul, the latter in Transalpine) and were both designated as consuls for 42.

BOOK 2.63–64

and Antony (when sober) better than many, he was welcomed by the soldiers at the rear of the camp after they had dismantled the fortifications: though he yielded to Lepidus in nominal command, the real power rested with him. In response to Antony's entry into the camp Juventius Laterensis, a man consistent in life and in death, who had strongly urged Lepidus not to ally himself with a declared enemy like Antony,[282] now, thwarted in his advice, ran himself through with his sword.

Then Antony was handed armies both by Plancus, with his doubtful—that is, characteristic—loyalty (he had long struggled with himself over what party he should belong to and, finding self-consistency difficult, was now helping Decimus Brutus, consul designate and his colleague,[283] and promoting himself to the senate in repeated letters, though he would soon betray him), and by Asinius Pollio, contrastingly firm of purpose, faithful to the Julian party, and hostile to the Pompeians.[284] 64. But Decimus Brutus, having been first deserted by Plancus and afterward the target of his intrigues too, was being gradually abandoned by his army and, now a fugitive, was slaughtered in the house of some noble who was his host (Camelius by name) by men whom Antony had sent: he thereby paid the justest of penalties to Caesar, whom, deserving only the best from one who had been the first of his friends, he killed, shifting onto the originator of his good fortune, whose profits he had enjoyed, the resentment it had caused, and judging it

[284] C. Asinius Pollio was currently governor of Further Spain and would be consul in 40.

VELLEIUS PATERCULUS

quae acceperat a Caesare retinere, Caesarem, qui[411] illa
dederat, perire.[412]

3 Haec sunt tempora quibus M. Tullius continuis actio-
nibus aeternas Antonii memoriae inussit notas, sed hic
fulgentissimo et caelesti ore, at tribunus Cannutius ca-
4 nina[413] rabie lacerabat Antonium. utrique vindicta libertatis morte stetit; sed tribuni sanguine commissa proscriptio, Ciceronis vel[414] satiato Antonio poena finita.

Lepidus deinde a senatu hostis iudicatus est, ut ante
fuerat Antonius. 65. tum inter eum Caesaremque et Antonium commercia epistularum et condicionum facta[415]
mentio, cum Antonius subinde Caesarem admoneret et[416]
quam inimicae ipsi Pompeianae partes forent et in quod
iam emersissent fastigium et quanto Ciceronis studio
Brutus Cassiusque attollerentur, denuntiaretque se cum
Bruto Cassioque, qui iam decem et septem legionum
potentes erant, iuncturum vires suas, si Caesar eius asper-
naretur concordiam, diceretque plus Caesarem patris
2 quam se amici ultioni[417] debere. ‹igi›tur[418] inita potentiae
societas, et hortantibus orantibusque exercitibus inter
Antonium etiam et Caesarem facta adfinitas, cum esset

411 qui *Gelenius*: quia *PA*
412 perire *vel* perisse *Rhenanus*: peris *P (per isthaec A)*
413 canina *Ruhnken*: continua *P*: continna *A*
414 vel‹ut› *Puteanus*
415 facta *Burer*: iacta *PA*
416 et, *quod post* Antonius *habent PA, post* admoneret *transpos. ed. Bipont.*
417 ultioni *Gelenius*: -e *PA*
418 ‹igi›tur *Rhenanus*: tur *P*: tūc *A*

BOOK 2.64–65

only fair to retain what he had received from Caesar, while Caesar, who had given it to him, should perish.

It was at this time that Cicero in a series of addresses burned everlasting brands into the memory of Antony, but, whereas his delivery was like flashes of lightning from heaven, the tribune Cannutius tore into Antony with a canine frenzy.[285] Each paid with his death the price of championing freedom; but it was the tribune's blood that began the proscription and Cicero's that ended it, a punishment with which even Antony was satisfied.[286]

Lepidus was next declared an enemy by the senate,[287] as Antony had been earlier. 65. Then between him, Caesar, and Antony there were exchanges of letters and mention was made of terms, since Antony repeatedly warned Caesar about the degree of the Pompeian party's hostility to him, about the peak to which it had already risen, and about the enthusiasm with which Brutus and Cassius were being elevated by Cicero; and he gave notice that he would join his forces with Brutus and Cassius (who were already in possession of seventeen legions) if Caesar spurned an agreement with him; and he said that Caesar's obligation to avenge his father was greater than his to avenge his friend. So an alliance of power was entered upon,[288] and, at the urging and pleading of the armies, a relationship was also made between Antony and Caesar, since Antony's

[285] Cicero's *Philippics* were delivered between 2 September 44 and 20 March 43; Ti. Cannutius' invective was 2 October 44.

[286] Cannutius is said by Cassius Dio (48.14.4) not to have died until 41. [287] On 30 June 43.

[288] The triumvirate was confirmed by the Lex Titia of 27 November 43.

203

VELLEIUS PATERCULUS

privigna Antonii desponsa Caesari; consulatumque iniit
Caesar pridie quam viginti annos impleret, X Kal. Oc-
tobres, cum collega Q. Pedio, post urbem conditam
[abhinc][419] annis DCCVIIII, ante LXXII quam tu, M.
3 Vinici, consulatum inires. vidit hic annus Ventidium, per
quam urbem inter captivos Picentium in triumpho ductus
erat, in ea consularem praetextam iungentem praetoria;
idem hic postea triumphavit.

66. Furente deinde Antonio simulque Lepido, quorum
uterque (ut praediximus) hostes iudicati erant, cum ambo
mallent sibi nuntiari[420] quid passi essent quam quid eme-
ruissent, repugnante Caesare (sed frustra adversus duos),
2 instauratum Sullani exempli malum, proscriptio. nihil tam
indignum illo tempore fuit quam quod aut Caesar aliquem
proscribere coactus est aut ab ullo Cicero proscriptus est;
abscisaque scelere Antonii vox publica est, cum eius salu-
tem nemo defendisset qui per tot annos et publicam civitatis et privatam civium defenderat.

3 Nihil tamen egisti, M. Antoni—cogit enim excedere
propositi formam operis erumpens animo ac pectore in-
dignatio—nihil, inquam, egisti mercedem caelestissimi
oris et clarissimi capitis abscisi numerando auctoramen-

---

[419] abhinc *secl. Gelenius*
[420] nuntiare *Haase*

---

[289] Claudia, daughter of Fulvia (74.3n) and Clodius (45.1n).
[290] In fact, the date was 19 August (Tac. *Ann.* 1.9.1; Cass. Dio
56.30.4). V. has passed over the fact that Octavian became consul
before reaching agreement with Antony and Lepidus.

BOOK 2.65–66

stepdaughter[289] was betrothed to Caesar. And, the day before the completion of his twentieth year, on 22 September,[290] Caesar entered upon the consulship with Quintus Pedius as his colleague, 709 years after the founding of the City and seventy-two years before you, Marcus Vinicius, entered upon the consulship. This was the year that saw Ventidius join the consular praetexta to the praetorian in the City where he had been led in triumph among the captives from Picenum; afterward it was he who triumphed.[291]

66. Then Antony and Lepidus—each of whom (as we mentioned earlier) had been declared an enemy—went on a simultaneous rampage and, since both of them preferred to be told what they had suffered rather than what they had deserved, over Caesar's objections (in vain against the two of them) there was reinstated that evil of Sullan precedent: proscription. Nothing at that time was so shocking as the fact that Caesar was compelled to proscribe someone or that Cicero was proscribed by anyone: it was owing to the crime of Antony that the nation's voice was cut off, since no one had defended the safety of him who for so many years had defended the collective safety of the community and the individual safety of its citizens.

Yet, Antony, you achieved nothing—the indignation bursting from my mind and heart compels me to exceed the form of the present work—you achieved nothing, I repeat, by paying a reward for cutting off that most heavenly voice and most distinguished head, and by inciting,

---

[291] P. Ventidius Bassus (pr. and cos. suff. 43), who had been a victim of the Social War in 89, would celebrate a triumph in 38 for exploits in Parthia (78.1).

205

VELLEIUS PATERCULUS

toque funebri ad conservatoris quondam rei publicae
4 tantique consulis incitando[421] necem. rapuisti tu M.[422]
Ciceroni lucem sollicitam et aetatem senilem et vitam
miseriorem te principe quam sub te triumviro mortem;
famam vero gloriamque factorum atque dictorum adeo
5 non abstulisti ut auxeris. vivit vivetque per omnem saeculorum memoriam, dumque hoc vel forte vel providentia
vel utcumque constitutum rerum naturae corpus—quod
ille paene solus Romanorum animo vidit, ingenio complexus est, eloquentia inluminavit—manebit incolume,
comitem aevi sui laudem Ciceronis trahet; omnisque
posteritas illius in te scripta mirabitur, tuum in eum factum execrabitur, citiusque [in][423] mundo genus hominum
quam ⟨M. Cicero⟩[424] cedet.

67. Huius totius temporis fortunam ne deflere quidem
quisquam satis digne potuit, adeo nemo exprimere verbis
2 potest. id tamen notandum est, fuisse in proscriptos uxo-
rum fidem summam, libertorum mediam, servorum ali-
quam, filiorum nullam: adeo difficilis est hominibus ut-
3 cumque conceptae spei mora. ne quid ulli[425] sanctum
relinqueretur, velut[426] documentum[427] invitamentumque
sceleris, Antonius L. Caesarem avunculum, Lepidus Paulum fratrem proscripserant; nec Planco gratia defuit ad
impetrandum ut frater eius Plancus Plotius proscribere-

---

[421] incitando *Woodman*: inritando *PA*
[422] tu M. *Gelenius*: tum *PA*
[423] in *P, secl. Kritz* (citius quem mundo *A*)
[424] *suppl. Kritz*: ⟨Ciceronis nomen⟩ *Laurent*: *alii alia*
[425] usquam *Cludius*
[426] velut *Gelenius*: vel in *PA*
[427] documentum *Woodman*: dotem *PA*

206

BOOK 2.66–67

for a deadly fee, the assassination of the great consul who was once the preserver of the commonwealth. You robbed Cicero of a troubled survival, of old age, and of a life more wretched under you as *princeps* than was death under you as triumvir; but, so far from taking away the fame and glory of his actions and words, you increased them. He lives and will live in the memory of every era, and, as long as the physical world—whether constituted by chance or by Providence or however, the world he almost alone of the Romans perceived in his mind, grasped with his intellect, and illuminated with his eloquence—remains undamaged, it will be accompanied for all of its existence by praise of Cicero. All posterity will wonder at his writings against you and will curse your action against him. The human race will leave the earth sooner than will Marcus Cicero.

67. No one has been sufficiently able even to bewail the fortunes of this whole period, still less can anyone express them fully in words. But this is to be noted: in the case of loyalty to the proscribed, wives showed the most, freedmen average, slaves some, sons none: so true is it that men find it difficult to defer their hopes, however conceived.[292] Lest anything sacred be left to anyone, and as an example and inducement for crime, Antony had proscribed his uncle Lucius Caesar, and Lepidus his brother Paullus; and Plancus did not lack the influence to demand successfully that his brother Plancus Plotius be

---

[292] The impatience of a son to inherit his father's wealth was proverbial.

207

VELLEIUS PATERCULUS

4 tur. eoque inter iocos militares,[428] qui currum Lepidi Plancique secuti erant inter execrationem civium,[429] usurpabant hunc versum: "De germanis non de Gallis duo triumphant consules."

68. Suo praeteritum loco referatur: neque enim persona umbram actae rei capit. dum in acie Pharsalica [Africaque][430] de summa rerum Caesar dimicat, M. Caelius, vir eloquio animoque Curioni simillimus sed in utroque perfectior nec minus ingeniose nequam, cum ne modica[431] quidem servare[432] posset (quippe peior illi res familiaris 2 quam mens erat), in praetura novarum tabularum auctor extitit nequiitque senatus et consulis auctoritate[433] deterreri. accito etiam Milone Annio, qui non impetrato reditu Iulianis partibus infestus erat, in urbe seditionem aut[434] in agris[435] occulte bellicum tumultum movens, primo summotus a re publica, mox consularibus armis auctore senatu 3 circa Thurios oppressus est. ⟨in⟩[436] incepto pari similis

[428] inter . . . militares *secl. Bothe*

[429] inter . . . civium *secl. Novák*

[430] Africaque *PA, secl. Krause, obelis notavit Ellis*: acriter *Haupt*

[431] ne modica *Aldus*: in modica *P*: immodica *A*: *alii alia*

[432] servare *Fröhlich*: -ri *PA*

[433] consulis *(iam Lipsius)* auctoritate *Cludius*: auctoritate COSS. *(consulū A) PA*

[434] aut *Rhenanus*: haud *PA*: at *Ruhnken*

[435] in agris *Lipsius*: magis *PA*

[436] *suppl. Madvig*

208

BOOK 2.67–68

proscribed.[293] It was for this reason that the soldiers following the chariot of Lepidus and Plancus against a background of citizens' cursing took up this verse among their jokes: "It is over brothers-german, not the Gauls, that these two consuls triumph!"[294]

68. A matter passed over in its proper place needs to be recalled, since the character does not tolerate the role he played being overshadowed. While Caesar was in the battle line at Pharsalus [and in Africa] and fighting for control of affairs, Marcus Caelius, a man very like Curio in speech and spirit but more accomplished in both and no less talentedly immoral, was unable to preserve even his modest estate (his patrimony was in a worse condition than his mind) and in his praetorship[295] he instigated the cancellation of debts and could not be deterred by the influence of senate or consul. He also sent for Milo Annius (who, since his request to return to Italy had failed, was hostile to the Julian party) and was stirring up mutiny in the City and warlike turmoil secretly in the countryside. He was first banished from politics, then later overcome near Thurii by a consular army on the authority of the senate. In his comparable project a similar fortune was experienced by Milo, who, struck by a stone while block-

293 L. Iulius Caesar (cos. 64) was the brother of Julia, Antony's mother; L. Aemilius Paullus had been consul in 50: unlike L. Plotius Plancus (pr. 43), neither was in fact killed.

294 The Latin word *germanus* means both "brother" and "German." On return from their provinces (63.1–3nn), Lepidus and Plancus triumphed, respectively, on 29 December and 31 December 43, before becoming consuls on 1 January 42.

295 In 48.

209

VELLEIUS PATERCULUS

fortuna Milonis fuit, qui Compsam in Hirpinis oppugnans ictusque lapide tum[437] P. Clodio, tum patriae, quam armis petebat, poenas dedit, vir inquies et ultra fortem[438] teme-
4 rarius. quatenus autem aliquid ex omissis peto,[439] notetur immodica et intempestiva libertate usos adversus C. Caesarem Marullum Epidium Flavumque Caesetium, tribunos plebis, dum arguunt in eo regni voluntatem, paene
5 vim dominationis expertos. in hoc tamen saepe lacessiti principis ira excessit ut censoria potius contentus nota quam animadversione dictatoria summoveret eos a re publica, testareturque esse sibi miserrimum quod aut natura sua ei excedendum foret aut minuenda dignitas. sed ad ordinem revertendum est.

69. Iam et Dolabella in Asia C. Trebonium consularem, cui succedebat, fraude deceptum Zmyrnae occiderat, virum adversus merita Caesaris ingratissimum participemque caedis eius a quo ipse in consulare provectus fastigium
2 fuerat; et C. Cassius acceptis a Staio Murco et Crispo Marcio, praetoriis viris imperatoribusque, praevalidis in Syria legionibus, inclusum Dolabellam, qui praeoccupata

---

437 cum *Orelli*
438 fortem *B*: sortem *PA*
439 ‹re›peto *Heinsius*

---

296 See 47.4.
297 In 44.
298 Early in 44 Caesar had been appointed both censor and *dictator perpetuus*.
299 In mid-January 43.
300 For Trebonius (cos. suff. 45) as one of Julius Caesar's killers, see 56.3.

210

BOOK 2.68–69

ading Compsa in the territory of the Hirpini, paid the penalty both to Publius Clodius[296] and to the fatherland that was the target of his arms—a restless man and rash beyond brave. And, as I am seeking to make good some omissions, it should be noted that Marullus Epidius and Flavus Caesetius, tribunes of the plebs,[297] resorted to an unrestrained and untimely impertinence against Caesar, accused him of aiming at kingship, and almost felt the power of a despot; but, despite the provocative nature of their repeated attacks, the *princeps'* anger only reached the point where he banished them from politics, content with branding them in his role as censor rather than punishing them as dictator,[298] and he testified to the wretchedness of being obliged either to go against his nature or to have his dignity impaired. But a return should be made to the main narrative.

69. Already Dolabella in Asia had deceived the exconsul Gaius Trebonius, whom he was attempting to succeed, by means of a trick at Smyrna and had slain him,[299] a man of the greatest ingratitude in the face of Caesar's services and a participant in the assassination of one by whom he himself had been elevated to the pinnacle of the consulship.[300] As for Cassius, having received the strong legions in Syria from Staius Murcus and Crispus Marcius, ex-praetors with the title "commander,"[301] he had trapped

---

[301] L. Staius Murcus (pr. ?45) as proconsul in Syria had been besieging the Pompeian officer Caecilius Bassus, assisted by Q. Marcius Crispus (pr. ?46), proconsul of Bithynia, and both had taken the title "commander" (24.1n) for successes against Bassus. When Cassius arrived in Syria in early 43, Murcus, Marcius, and Bassus all handed over their forces to him.

211

VELLEIUS PATERCULUS

Asia in Syriam pervenerat, Laodiceae[440] expugnata ea urbe ‹mori› coegerat[441] (ita tamen ut ad ictum[442] servi sui Dolabella non segniter cervicem daret) et decem legiones
3 in eo tractu sui iuris fecerat; et M. Brutus C. Antonio, fratri M. Antonii, in Macedonia Vatinioque circa Dyrrachium volentes[443] legiones extorserat (sed Antonium bello lacessierat, Vatinium[444] dignatione obruerat), cum et Brutus cuilibet ducum praeferendus videretur et Vatinius
4 nulli hominum[445] non esset postferendus, in quo deformitas corporis cum turpitudine certabat ingenii, adeo ut animus eius dignissimo domicilio inclusus videretur, eratque
5 septem legionibus validus. at[446] lege Pedia, quam consul Pedius collega Caesaris tulerat, omnibus qui Caesarem patrem interfecerant damnatis aqua ignique interdictum[447] erat. quo tempore Capito, patruus meus, vir ordinis
6 senatorii, Agrippae subscripsit in C. Cassium. dumque ea in Italia geruntur, acri atque prosperrimo bello Cassius Rhodum (rem immanis operis) ceperat, Brutus Lycios devicerat, et inde in Macedoniam exercitus traiecerant, cum per omnia repugnans naturae suae Cassius etiam

---

[440] Laodiceae *Vossius*: -ia *BA*: -eam *P*

[441] ‹mori› coegerat *Novák*: fecerat *PA*: confecerat *vel* interfecerat *Rhenanus*: *alii alia*

[442] ac ictum *Rhenanus*: adiectum *PA*

[443] volentis *BA*: volv- *P*   [444] Vatinium *Gelenius*: -ius *PA*

[445] hominum *Woodman*: nomini *P* (noi *A*), *secl. Aldus*: homini *Vascosanus*: *alii alia*   [446] at *Lipsius*: et *P*: ea *A*: sed *Kreyssig*

[447] damnatis interdictum *PA* (damnatis *ante* aqua *transpos. Gruner, secl. Delbenius*)

---

[302] Where C. Antonius (pr. 44) was proconsul.

BOOK 2.69

Dolabella (who had arrived in Syria after his preemptive seizure of Asia) in Laodicea and, after storming the city, had forced the man to die (which Dolabella nevertheless did in such a way that he offered his neck unhesitatingly to the blow from his slave); and he had assumed jurisdiction over the ten legions in that tract of territory. As for Brutus, he had wrested legions both from Gaius Antonius, Antony's brother, in Macedonia[302] and from Vatinius around Dyrrachium (Brutus had challenged Antonius to war but had overwhelmed Vatinius by the strength of his own reputation); the legions were willing enough, since Brutus seemed superior to any of the leaders and there was no one on earth to whom Vatinius was not inferior, his physical deformity competing with his disgusting character such that his mind seemed trapped within the most apt of abodes;[303] and Brutus was seven legions strong. But by the Lex Pedia, which Caesar's consular colleague Pedius had carried,[304] all those who had killed Caesar's father had been condemned and forbidden fire and water;[305] and it was at this time that Capito, my uncle, a man of the senatorial order,[306] countersigned Agrippa's charge sheet against Cassius. And, while these things were happening in Italy, Cassius in a fierce and highly successful war had taken Rhodes (a prodigious task) and Brutus had defeated the Lycians, and thereafter they had transferred their armies to Macedonia, where Cassius, completely rebelling

[303] P. Vatinius (cos. 47), currently proconsul in Illyricum, famously had a tumor on his neck. [304] In late August 43, immediately after their election to the consulship (65.2).

[305] For "fire and water" see 24.2n.

[306] Son of C. Velleius (76.1n).

213

VELLEIUS PATERCULUS

Bruti clementiam vinceret; neque reperias quos aut pronior Fortuna comitata sit aut veluti fatigata maturius destituerit quam Brutum et Cassium.

70. Tum Caesar et Antonius traiecerunt exercitus in Macedoniam et apud urbem Philippos cum M. Bruto Cassioque acie concurrerunt. cornu cui Brutus praeerat impulsis hostibus castra Caesaris cepit (nam ipse Caesar, etiamsi infirmissimus valetudine erat, obibat munia ducis, oratus etiam ab Artorio medico ne in castris remaneret, manifesta[448] denuntiatione quietis territo); id autem in quo Cassius fuerat fugatum ac male mulcatum[449] in altiora

2 ‹se›[450] receperat loca. tum Cassius ex sua fortuna eventum collegae aestimans, cum dimisisset evocatum iussissetque nuntiare sibi quae esset multitudo ac vis hominum quae ad se tenderet, tardius eo nuntiante, cum in vicino esset agmen cursu ad eum tendentium neque pulvere facies aut signa dinotari[451] possent, existimans hostes esse qui irruerent, lacerna caput circumdedit extentamque

3 cervicem interritus liberto praebuit. deciderat Cassii caput cum evocatus advenit nuntians Brutum esse victorem; qui cum imperatorem prostratum videret, "Sequar," inquit, "eum quem mea occidit tarditas," et ita in gladium

4 incubuit. post paucos deinde dies Brutus conflixit cum hostibus et victus acie cum in tumulum[452] nocte ex fuga se

---

[448] manifesta *Heinsius*: -te *PA*
[449] mulcatum *Puteanus*: mult- *PA*
[450] *suppl. Gelenius*   [451] dinotari *Woodman*: de- *PA*
[452] tumulum *Vascosanus*: -ultum *PA*

---

[307] The Latin term *evocatus* refers to a discharged veteran recalled to serve as an elite soldier.

BOOK 2.69–70

against his own nature, defeated even Brutus in clemency; and you would not find anyone whom Fortune accompanied more willingly or deserted more quickly, as if exhausted, than Brutus and Cassius.

70. Then Caesar and Antony transferred their armies to Macedonia and near the city of Philippi engaged with Brutus and Cassius in the battle line. The flank of which Brutus was in charge took Caesar's camp after driving back the enemy (Caesar himself was fulfilling his leadership responsibilities, despite being seriously weakened by ill-health and although his doctor Artorius too, terrified by a clear warning in a dream, had begged him not to remain in camp); but the flank where Cassius was had been put to flight and, badly mauled, had withdrawn to higher ground. Then Cassius, using his own fortunes to gauge the outcome of his colleague, dispatched his aide[307] with orders to report to him on the identity of the large force of men that was making for them; but his report was too slow in coming and, when the column of those making for him at a run was close and neither their faces nor their standards could be distinguished for the dust, Cassius thought it was the enemy who was charging and, covering his head with his cloak, he held out his neck and offered it unafraid to his freedman. The man had cut off Cassius' head when the aide arrived to report that Brutus was the victor; when the veteran saw his prostrated commander, he said "I shall follow him whom my slowness has slain," and so fell on his sword. Then, after a few days, Brutus engaged with the enemy[308] and, defeated in the battle line, fled by night and

[308] On 23 October 42.

215

VELLEIUS PATERCULUS

recepisset, impetravit a Stratone Aegeate, familiari suo, ut manum morituro commodaret sibi; reiectoque laevo super caput bracchio, cum mucronem gladii eius dextera tenens sinistrae admovisset mamillae ad eum ipsum locum qua cor emicat, impellens se in vulnus uno ictu transfixus expiravit prot<inus. 71. Corv>inus[453] Messalla, fulgentissimus iuvenis, proximus in illis castris Bruti Cassiique auctoritati (cum essent qui eum ducem poscerent), servari beneficio Caesaris maluit quam dubiam spem armorum temptare amplius; nec aut Caesari quidquam ex victoriis suis fuit laetius quam servasse Corvinum aut maius exemplum hominis grati ac pii quam Corvinus in Caesarem fuit.

Non aliud bellum cruentius caede clarissimorum virorum fuit. tum Catonis filius cecidit; eadem Lucullum Hortensiumque, eminentissimorum civium filios, Fortuna abstulit; nam Varro ad ludibrium moriturus Antonii digna illo ac vera de exitu eius magna cum libertate ominatus est. Drusus Livius, Iuliae Augustae pater, et Varus Quintilius ne temptata quidem hostis misericordia alter se ipse in tabernaculo interemit; Varus autem liberti, quem id facere coegerat, manu, cum se insignibus honorum velasset, iugulatus est.

---

[453] prot<inus. Corv>inus *Halm*

---

[309] M. Valerius Messalla Corvinus was consul in 31 (84.1), when he commanded part of Octavian's fleet at the battle of Actium.   [310] Lucullus was son of the famous Lucullus (33.1n); Q. Hortensius (pr. 45?), currently proconsul in Macedonia, was son of the famous Hortensius (2.16.3n).   [311] The reference is usually thought to be to M. Terentius Varro Gibba (trib. pleb. 43), but neither the man's identity nor the meaning of the sen-

216

BOOK 2.70–71

withdrew to a knoll, where he prevailed upon an intimate of his, Strato of Aegeae, to lend him a helping hand in dying. Throwing his left arm over his head, he held the point of the man's sword in his right hand and guided it to his left nipple at the very place where the heart beats, and, thrusting himself forward to be wounded, he was pierced by a single stab and expired immediately. 71. Corvinus Messalla, a most brilliant young man and next in influence to Brutus and Cassius in their camp (there were those who demanded him as leader), preferred to be saved by Caesar's kindness than to make a further test of war's doubtful hopes; and there was nothing more delightful for Caesar in his victories than having saved Corvinus, nor was there a greater example of someone's gratitude and devotion than Corvinus' to Caesar.[309]

No other war was gorier in its death toll of distinguished men. It was then that Cato's son fell; Fortune likewise took off Lucullus and Hortensius, sons of the most outstanding citizens;[310] as for Varro, when he was about to die in mockery of Antony he delivered with great impertinence a prophecy that was both appropriate to the man and true concerning his end.[311] Drusus Livius, Julia Augusta's father, and Varus Quintilius did not even put their enemy's mercy to the test, but the former killed himself in his tent, while Varus, after covering himself with the insignia of his offices, was slaughtered by the hand of his freedman, whom he had forced to do it.[312]

tence as a whole is quite certain. [312] M. Livius Drusus Claudianus, father of Augustus' future wife (75.3), may have been praetor in 50; Sex. Quin(c)tilius Varus (quaestor 49) was the father of the ill-fated general (117.2).

217

VELLEIUS PATERCULUS

72. Hunc exitum M. Bruti partium XXXXII[454] annum agentis Fortuna esse voluit, ⟨in⟩corrupto[455] animo eius in diem quae illi omnes virtutes unius temeritate facti[456] abstulit. fuit autem dux Cassius melior quanto vir Brutus; e quibus Brutum amicum habere malles, inimicum magis timeres Cassium; in altero maior vis, in altero virtus; qui si vicissent, quantum rei publicae interfuit Caesarem potius habere quam Antonium principem, tantum retulisset habere Brutum quam Cassium.

Cn. Domitius, pater L. Domitii nuper a nobis visi, eminentissimae ac nobilissimae simplicitatis viri, avus huius Cn. Domitii, clarissimi iuvenis, occupatis navibus cum magno sequentium consilia sua comitatu fugae fortunaeque se commisit, semet ipso contentus duce partium. Staius Murcus, qui classi et custodiae maris praefuerat, cum omni commissa sibi parte exercitus naviumque Sex. Pompeium, Cn. Magni filium, qui ex Hispania revertens Siciliam armis occupaverat, petit. ad quem et e Brutianis castris et ex Italia aliisque terrarum partibus, quos praesenti periculo Fortuna subduxerat, proscripti confluebant. (quippe nullum habentibus statum quilibet dux erat idoneus, cum Fortuna non electionem daret, perfugium[457] ostenderet, exitialemque tempestatem fugientibus statio

---

[454] XXXXII *J.J. Paterson*: septimum & XXX *P*: & XXX[VII] *A*: III et XXXX *Cornelissen* [455] ⟨in⟩corrupto *Tollius*
[456] facti *Rhenanus*: fecit *PA* [457] ⟨sed⟩ perfugium *Gelenius*

---

[313] The three generations are: (1) Cn. Domitius Ahenobarbus (cos. 32 BC), a colleague of Staius Murcus in patrolling the Mediterranean; (2) L. Domitius Ahenobarbus (cos. 16 BC), who married Octavian's niece Octavia, was grandfather of the emperor

BOOK 2.72 ·

72. This was the end that Fortune wanted for the party of Brutus, then in his forty-second year, whose mind had remained untainted until the day that, thanks to one rash deed, robbed him of all his virtues. Cassius was as much a better leader as Brutus was a man; you would have found Brutus preferable as a friend, Cassius more terrifying as a foe; in the one was greater violence, in the other, virtue. And if they had won? Just as it mattered to the commonwealth to have Caesar as its *princeps* rather than Antony, so it would have been equally important to have Brutus, not Cassius.

Gnaeus Domitius, father of the Lucius Domitius whom we saw but recently (a man of the most outstanding and noblest straightforwardness) and grandfather of the present Gnaeus Domitius (a most distinguished young man),[313] seized some ships and, along with a great company of those following his plans, entrusted himself to flight and to fortune, content with himself as party leader. Staius Murcus, who had been in charge of the fleet guarding the sea, took the entire part of the army and ships that was entrusted to him and made for Sextus Pompeius, Pompey the Great's son, who on returning from Spain had seized Sicily by force: to him were flowing the proscribed whom Fortune had rescued from immediate danger, both those from Brutus' camp and those from Italy and other parts of the world. (To persons having no standing any leader was suitable, since Fortune was offering them no choice but was showing them a refuge, and to those fleeing a deadly

Nero, and died in AD 25; (3) Cn. Domitius Ahenobarbus (cos. AD 32, two years after V.'s dedicatee). See also 2.10.2n.

219

VELLEIUS PATERCULUS

pro portu foret.) 73. hic adulescens erat studiis rudis, sermone barbarus, impetu strenuus, manu promptus, cogitatione[458] celer, fide patri dissimillimus, libertorum suorum libertus servorumque servus, speciosis invidens ut pareret
2 humillimis; quem senatus paene totus adhuc e Pompeianis constans partibus post Antonii a Mutina[459] fugam, eodem illo tempore quo Bruto Cassioque transmarinas provincias decreverat, revocatum ex Hispania, ubi adversus eum clarissimum bellum Pollio Asinius praetorius gesserat, in
3 paterna bona restituerat et orae maritimae praefecerat. is tum (ut praediximus) occupata Sicilia servitia fugitivosque in numerum exercitus sui recipiens magnum modum legionum effecerat; perque Menam et Menecraten, paternos libertos, praefectos classium, latrociniis ac praedationibus infestato mari ad se exercitumque tuendum rapto utebatur, cum eum non depuderet[460] vindicatum armis ac ductu patris sui mare infestare piraticis sceleribus.

74. Fractis Brutianis Cassianisque partibus Antonius transmarinas obiturus provincias substitit; Caesar in Italiam se recepit eamque longe quam speraverat tumultuo-
2 siorem repperit. quippe L. Antonius consul, vitiorum fratris sui consors sed virtutum quae interdum in illo erant expers, modo apud veteranos criminatus Caesarem, modo eos qui instante[461] divisione praediorum nominatisque

---

[458] cogitatione *Rhenanus*: cogitator *PA*: cogitatu *Scheffer*

[459] Antonii a Mutina *Burer*: Antonii a Mutinam *B*: Antonianam *PA*

[460] dispuderet *Kenney*

[461] instante *E. Thomas, Goodyear*: iuste *PA*: iusta *Vascosanus*: instituta *Ruhnken*: *alii alia*

220

BOOK 2.72–74

storm an anchorage was as good as a harbor.) 73. The young Pompeius was intellectually unrefined, barbarian in speech, impulsively energetic, ready with his muscle, a quick thinker, quite unlike his father in loyalty, the freedman of his own freedmen and slave of his own slaves, envying the impressive but obedient to the lowest. The senate still consisted almost entirely of the Pompeian party and, in the period after Antony's flight from Mutina and at the same time as it had decreed the overseas provinces to Brutus and Cassius, it had recalled him from Spain (where the ex-praetor Pollio Asinius had waged a most distinguished war against him), had restored him to his father's property, and had placed him in charge of the sea coast. He had then seized Sicily (as we just mentioned) and, welcoming slaves and fugitives into the ranks of his army, had produced a large number of legions; and, infesting the sea by banditry and brigandage through the agency of Menas and Menecrates, his father's freedmen who were now prefects of his fleets, he resorted to raiding to sustain himself and his army, since he had no shame in infesting by criminal piracy the sea that had been reclaimed by the arms and leadership of his father.

74. With Brutus' and Cassius' party broken, Antony stayed on, intending to visit the overseas provinces; Caesar took himself to Italy, which he found in a far greater turmoil than he had expected. The consul Lucius Antonius, sharing his brother's vices but lacking the virtues that sometimes were in him, at one moment was accusing Caesar in front of the veterans, at another was rousing to arms those who (now that the colonies had been named) had

221

VELLEIUS PATERCULUS

coloniis[462] agros amiserant ad arma conciens magnum
3 exercitum conflaverat. ex altera parte uxor Antonii Fulvia,
nihil muliebre praeter corpus gerens, omnia armis tumul-
tuque miscebat. haec belli sedem Praeneste ceperat;
Antonius pulsus undique viribus Caesaris Perusiam se
contulerat; Plancus, Antonianarum adiutor partium, spem
4 magis ostenderat auxilii quam opem ferebat Antonio. usus
Caesar virtute et fortuna sua Perusiam expugnavit. Antonium inviolatum dimisit; in Perusinos magis ira militum
quam voluntate saevitum ducis; urbs incensa, cuius initium incendii princeps eius loci fecit Macedonicus, qui
subiecto rebus ac penatibus suis igni transfixum se gladio
flammae intulit.

75. Per eadem tempora exarserat in Campania bellum,
quod professus eorum qui perdiderant agros patrocinium
ciebat Ti. Claudius Nero, praetorius et pontifex, Ti. Caesaris pater, magni vir animi doctissimique[463] ingenii. id
quoque adventu Caesaris sepultum atque discussum est.
2 quis Fortunae mutationes, quis dubios rerum humanarum
casus satis mirari queat? quis non diversa praesentibus
3 contrariaque expectatis aut speret aut timeat? Livia, nobilissimi et fortissimi viri Drusi Claudiani[464] filia, genere,

---

[462] coloniis *Heinsius*: -nis *PA*
[463] clarissimique *Bothe*
[464] Claudiani *Burer*: Calidiani *PBA*

---

[314] The triumvirs had promised in 43 that after the war with
Brutus and Cassius veterans would be discharged and settled in
colonies to be founded on land taken from Italian cities. Octavian
was now responsible for carrying this out.

[315] Wife of *Mark* Antony.   [316] In 41–40.

222

BOOK 2.74–75

lost land in the imminent division of estates,[314] and he had gathered together a large army. Elsewhere Antony's wife Fulvia,[315] whose body was her sole womanly attribute, was causing general turmoil by armed force. She had taken Praeneste as her war base; Antonius, beaten on all fronts by Caesar's forces, had fallen back to Perusia; Plancus, an aider of the Antonian party, had held out the hope of assistance to Antonius rather than was bringing him actual help. Caesar, relying on his characteristic prowess and fortune, stormed Perusia.[316] He dismissed Antonius unharmed; the savagery directed against the Perusines was due more to the soldiers' anger than to their leader's intention; the city was burned down, the burning started by the principal figure of the place, Macedonicus, who set fire to his property and home and then, having run himself through with his sword, consigned himself to the flames.

75. During the same time war in Campania had flared up, which was being stirred by Tiberius Claudius Nero (an ex-praetor and pontiff, the father of Tiberius Caesar,[317] a man of great heart and the most learned mind), who had undertaken the patronage of those who had lost land. That war too was smothered and dispersed[318] by the arrival of Caesar. Who could wonder sufficiently at Fortune's changes and at the uncertainty of chance in human affairs? Who would not have hopes or fears for the opposite of present circumstances and for the contrary of those expected? Livia—daughter of Drusus Claudianus (the no-

[317] That is, the emperor Tiberius, whose father had been praetor in 42 and co-opted as pontiff in 46.   [318] The war, described as a fire being stoked in the previous sentence, is seemingly now put out and "its embers scattered" (Shipley).

223

VELLEIUS PATERCULUS

probitate, forma Romanarum eminentissima, quam postea coniugem Augusti vidimus, quam transgressi ad deos sacerdotem ac filiam, tum fugiens mox futuri sui Caesaris arma, <mi>nus[465] bimum hunc Tiberium Caesarem, vindicem Romani imperii futurumque eiusdem[466] Caesaris filium, gestans sinu, per avia itinerum vitatis militum gladiis uno comitante, quo facilius occultaretur fuga, pervenit ad mare et cum viro Nerone pervecta in Siciliam est.

76. Quod alieno testimonium redderem, [in] eo[467] non fraudabo avum meum. quippe C. Velleius, honoratissimo inter illos CCCLX iudices loco a Cn. Pompeio lectus, eiusdem Marcique Bruti ac Ti. Neronis[468] praefectus fabrum, vir nulli secundus in Campania, digressu Neronis a Neapoli, cuius ob singularem cum eo amicitiam partium adiutor fuerat, gravis iam aetate et corpore cum comes[469] esse non posset, gladio se ipse transfixit.

2 Inviolatam excedere Italia Caesar passus[470] Fulviam Plancumque, muliebris fugae comitem; nam Pollio Asinius cum septem legionibus, diu retenta in potestate Antonii Venetia, magnis speciosisque rebus circa Altinum aliasque eius regionis urbes editis, Antonium petens, vagum

465 <mi>nus *Vossius*: nus *P, om. A*
466 futurum eiusdemque *Acidalius*
467 in eo *P* (in *secl. Gelenius*): meo *A*
468 Ti. Neronis *Aldus*: Tyronis *P*: Ti- *A*
469 cum comes *Aldus*: cum *PA*: comes *B*
470 passus <est> *Cludius*

---

319 Livia married Octavian in 38 BC (79.2); after his death in AD 14 she was adopted in his will as Julia Augusta (the name used at 71.3, above) and entitled "priest of the divine Augustus."

BOOK 2.75–76

blest and bravest of men), outstanding among Roman women on account of her lineage, probity and appearance, whom afterward we saw as Augustus' spouse and, on his translation to the gods, as his priest and daughter[319]—was at that time fleeing the armed forces of the Caesar who would later be hers, carrying at her breast a child less than two years old, the present Tiberius Caesar, champion of the Roman Empire, and future son of that same Caesar.[320] Traveling across trackless territory, avoiding the swords of the soldiers, and with only one companion, the more easily to conceal her flight, she reached the sea and sailed to Sicily with Nero, her husband.

76. I will not cheat my grandfather of testimony that I would render to a stranger. C. Velleius—who had been chosen by Pompey in a most honorable place among his 360 judges[321] and was his and Brutus' and Tiberius Nero's Prefect of Engineers,[322] a man second to none in Campania—was unable to accompany Nero (whose party he had aided on account of his singular friendship with him) on his departure from Neapolis since his age and his body now weighed him down, and so he ran himself through with a sword.

Caesar allowed Fulvia to leave Italy unharmed, and Plancus too, to accompany the fugitive woman; as for Pollio Asinius with his seven legions, having kept Venetia in Antony's power for a long time and having done impressively great things around Altinum and other cities in that

[320] Augustus adopted Tiberius in AD 4 (103.3).
[321] A jury panel personally selected by Pompey in his third consulship in 52 (47.3–5) to try cases of violence and electoral corruption.   [322] The rank denotes a kind of senior staff officer.

225

VELLEIUS PATERCULUS

adhuc Domitium, quem digressum e Brutianis castris post
caedem eius praediximus et propriae classis factum ducem, consiliis suis defectum[471] [ac][472] fide data iunxit An-
3 tonio. quo facto quisquis aequum se praestiterit sciat non
minus a Pollione in Antonium quam ab Antonio in Pollionem esse conlatum.

Adventus deinde in Italiam Antonii praeparatusque
contra eum Caesaris[473] habuit belli metum, sed pax circa
4 Brundisium composita. per quae tempora Rufi Salvidieni
scelesta consilia patefacta sunt, qui natus obscurissimis
initiis parum habebat summa accepisse et proximus[474] a
Cn. Pompeio ipsoque Caesare ex equestri ordine[475] consul
creatus esse, nisi in id[476] ascendisset e quo infra se et Caesarem videret et rem publicam.

77. Tum expostulante consensu populi, quem gravis
urebat infesto mari annona, cum Pompeio quoque circa
Misenum pax inita, qui haud absurde, cum in navi Caesaremque et Antonium cena exciperet, dixit in Carinis suis
se cenam dare, referens hoc dictum ad loci nomen in quo
2 paterna domus ab Antonio possidebatur. in hoc pacis foe-

---

[471] defectum *Woodman*: electum *PA*: illectum *Gelenius*: eiec-
tum *Damsté*   [472] secl. *Cludius*

[473] contra eum Caesaris *BA*: C- c- e- *P*

[474] proximum . . . consulem creatum *Novák*

[475] ex equestri ordine *Gelenius*: ex equestri (sequestri *A*:
equestris *P*) ordinis *PBA*

[476] nisi in id *Puteanus*: nisi in is *BA*: ni simul *P*

---

[323] At 72.3.

[324] In the autumn of 40.

[325] Q. Salvidienus Rufus, currently holding a command in

BOOK 2.76–77

region, he made for Antony. Domitius was still at large (we mentioned earlier[323] his departure from Brutus' camp after the latter's death and his leadership of his own fleet) but was failing in his plans, so Pollio allied him to Antony after the giving of a pledge. Whoever is inclined to think of himself as fair-minded should know that by this action no less a service was done by Pollio for Antony than by Antony for Pollio.

Then Antony's arrival in Italy and Caesar's preparations against him prompted a dread of war, but peace between them was agreed near Brundisium.[324] This was the time when the criminal plans of Rufus Salvidienus were revealed, who, born in the utmost obscurity, regarded it as quite insufficient to have received the highest honors and to have been the first after Pompey and Caesar himself to be created consul from the equestrian order,[325] and he would have climbed to a point from which he could see both Caesar and the commonwealth beneath him.

77. Next, to meet the unanimous demands of the people (who were chafing at the heavy price of grain, caused by the hostilities at sea), peace with Pompeius too was entered upon near Misenum.[326] (When he was welcoming both Caesar and Antony to dinner on board ship, he remarked not inappropriately that he was giving the dinner "in his Keels," the remark referring to the name of the place where his father's house was now in the possession of Antony.[327]) In this peace treaty it was decided to grant

Gaul, was designated consul for 39 but committed suicide when Octavian was informed of his disloyalty.   [326] In 39.

[327] The Keels ("Carinae") was an exclusive area of Rome on the Esquiline Hill.

227

VELLEIUS PATERCULUS

dere placuit Siciliam Achaiamque Pompeio concedere, in quo tamen animus inquies manere non potuit; id unum tantummodo salutare adventu suo patriae attulit, quod omnibus proscriptis aliisque qui ad eum ex diversis causis

3 fugerant reditum salutemque pactus est. quae res et alios clarissimos viros et Neronem Claudium et M. Silanum Sentiumque Saturninum et Arruntium[477] ac Titium restituit rei publicae; Staium autem Murcum, qui adventu suo classisque celeberrimae vires eius duplicaverat, insimulatum falsis criminationibus, quia talem virum collegam officii Mena et Menecrates[478] fastidierant, Pompeius in Sicilia interfecerat.

78. Hoc tractu temporum Octaviam, sororem Caesaris, M. Antonius duxit uxorem. redierat Pompeius in Siciliam, Antonius in transmarinas provincias, quas magnis motibus[479] Labienus, ex Brutianis castris profectus ad Parthos, perducto[480] eorum exercitu in Syriam interfectoque legato Antonii concusserat; qui virtute et ductu Ventidii una cum Parthorum copiis celeberrimoque iuvenum Pacoro,

[477] Aruntium *Gelenius*: Atruntium *(vel sim.)* PBA
[478] Menocres *P, corr. Rhenanus* (Mencrates): Menotrades *B*: Menocrates *A*
[479] motibus *Krause*: momentis *PA*
[480] perducto *Arntzen*: pro- *PA*

---

[328] That is, at the peace conference.
[329] M. Iunius Silanus (cos. 25) had served under Antonius and Lepidus in 43; C. Sentius Saturninus (cos. 19) will feature quite frequently in V.'s later narrative; L. Arruntius (cos. 22) would achieve prominence as both politician and historian; M. Titius (cos. suff. 31) would later kill his present benefactor (79.5–6).

BOOK 2.77–78

Sicily and Achaea to Pompeius, but his restless temperament was unable to abide by it; the one salutary factor that he brought to his fatherland by turning up[328] was that he stipulated for the safe return of all the proscribed and of others who had fled to him for various reasons. This restored to the commonwealth some very distinguished men, including Nero Claudius, Marcus Silanus, Sentius Saturninus, Arruntius and Titius;[329] but Staius Murcus, who had doubled the man's forces when he arrived with his celebrated fleet, had been accused on false charges and, because Menas and Menecrates had looked down on such a man as their official colleague, had been killed by Pompeius in Sicily.

78. It was during this tract of time that Antony took Octavia, Caesar's sister, as his wife.[330] Pompeius had returned to Sicily, Antony to the overseas provinces, which had been shaken by great tremors when Labienus, having set off for the Parthians from Brutus' camp, led the Parthian army right into Syria and killed Antony's legate;[331] Labienus, together with the Parthian forces and Pacorus, who was the king's son[332] and the most celebrated of their young men, was destroyed by the courageous leadership

330 Late 40, as a result of the peace agreement reached at Brundisium (76.3); Fulvia had died in Greece earlier in the year (Plut. *Vit. Ant.* 30.5).

331 Q. Labienus, son of T. Labienus (40.4, 55.4), had been sent by Brutus and Cassius to seek military aid from Parthia, but after their defeat at Philippi he led the Parthians to invade Syria, subsequently killing the legate L. Decidius Saxa in Cilicia early in 40.

332 The king was Orodes II (46.4).

229

VELLEIUS PATERCULUS

2 regis filio, extinctus est. interim Caesar per haec tempora, ne res disciplinae inimicissima, otium, corrumperet militem, crebris in Illyrico Dalmatiaque expeditionibus patientia periculorum bellique experientia durabat exercitum.
3 eadem tempestate Calvinus Domitius, cum ex consulatu obtineret Hispaniam, gravissimi comparandique antiquis exempli auctor fuit: quippe primi pili centurionem (nomine Vibillium[481]) ob turpem ex acie fugam fusti percussit.

79. Crescente in dies et classe et fama Pompeii Caesar molem belli eius suscipere statuit. aedificandis navibus contrahendoque militem ac remigem[482] navalibusque adsuescendo certaminibus [atque exercitationibus][483] praefectus est M. Agrippa, ⟨vir⟩[484] virtutis nobilissimae, labore, vigilia, periculo invictus parendique (sed uni) scientissimus, aliis sane imperandi cupidus, et per omnia extra dilationes positus consultisque facta coniungens.
2 hic in Averno ac Lucrino lacu speciosissima classe fabricata cotidianis exercitationibus militem remigemque ad summam et militaris et maritimae rei perduxit scientiam. hac classi Caesar, cum prius despondente ei Nerone (cui ante nupta fuerat) Liviam auspicatis rei publicae ominibus

---

481 Vibillium *BA*: Iubillium *P*
482 militem . . . remigem *Ellis*: -e . . . -e *PA*: -i . . . -i *Gelenius*
483 *secl. Bothe*   484 ⟨vir⟩ *Ruhnken*

---

333 In 39–38.
334 V. seems to refer to Asinius Pollio's campaign in Illyricum in 39 rather than to Octavian's personal campaigning there in 35–33.
335 Cn. Domitius Calvinus (cos. 53, 40) was proconsul in Spain from 39 to 36.

BOOK 2.78–79

of Ventidius.[333] Meanwhile Caesar during this period,[334] to prevent his soldiery from being corrupted by inactivity, a condition extremely hostile to discipline, toughened his army by the endurance of danger and the experience of war in frequent campaigns in Illyricum and Dalmatia. In the same season Calvinus Domitius, when holding Spain after his consulship,[335] was responsible for the severest of precedents, comparable with the ancients: he had a first-rank centurion (Vibillius by name) clubbed to death with a cudgel on account of his shameful flight from the battle line.[336]

79. With Pompeius' fleet and reputation growing from day to day, Caesar decided to undertake the burdensome responsibility of war against him. In charge of building the ships, assembling the soldiery and rowers, and accustoming them to naval encounters, he placed Marcus Agrippa, a man of the noblest prowess, unconquerable by toil or wakefulness or danger, an expert in being compliant (but only with one man) yet assuredly desirous of commanding others, and in every respect a stranger to delay who coupled deeds to decisions. Having constructed an impressive fleet, he brought the soldiery and rowers up to the highest standard of military and naval expertise by means of daily exercises in Lake Avernus and Lucrinus.[337] This was the fleet with which Caesar—after first, with auspicious omens for the commonwealth, taking Livia as his wife,[338] who was betrothed to him by Nero (to whom she had been married

336 Such executions were a traditional form of punishment.

337 In 37 Agrippa joined the two lakes together by building a canal.

338 On 17 January 38.

231

VELLEIUS PATERCULUS

duxisset eam[485] uxorem, Pompeio Siciliaeque bellum intu-
3 lit. sed virum humana ope invictum graviter eo tempore
Fortuna concussit: quippe longe maiorem partem classis
circa Veliam Palinurique promontorium adorta vis Africi
laceravit ac distulit. ea patrando bello mora fuit, quod
4 postea dubia et interdum ancipiti fortuna gestum est. nam
et classis eodem loco vexata est tempestate et, ut navali
primo proelio apud Mylas ductu Agrippae pugnatum prospere, ita inopinato classis ⟨hostilis⟩[486] adventu gravis sub
ipsius Caesaris oculis circa Tauromenium accepta clades;
neque ab ipso periculum abfuit. legiones quae cum Cor-
nificio erant, legato Caesaris, expositae in terra[487] paene a
5 Pompeio oppressae sunt. sed ancipitis fortuna temporis
matura virtute correcta: explicatis quippe utriusque partis
classibus paene omnibus exutus navibus Pompeius Asiam
fuga petivit, iussuque M. Antonii, cuius opem petierat,
dum inter ducem et supplicem tumultuatur[488] et nunc
dignitatem retinet, nunc vitam precatur, a Titio iugulatus
6 est. cui in tantum duravit hoc facinore contractum odium
ut mox ludos in theatro Pompei faciens execratione populi
spectaculo quod praebebat pelleretur.

80. Acciverat gerens contra Pompeium bellum ex
Africa Caesar Lepidum cum XII semiplenis legionibus.
hic vir omnium vanissimus neque ulla virtute tam longam

---

[485] eam *secl. Heinsius*
[486] *suppl. Graevius*
[487] terram *Haase*
[488] tumultuatur *PA*: fluctuatur *Cornelissen*

---

[339] In the spring or summer of 36.
[340] He would become consul in 35.

232

BOOK 2.79–80

previously)—carried the war to Pompeius in Sicily;[339] but at that moment the man unconquerable by human efforts was struck heavily by Fortune: a strong southwesterly sprang up, mauling and scattering much the greater part of the fleet close to Velia and the promontory of Palinurus. That caused a delay in completing the war, which afterward was waged with uncertain and sometimes critical fortune: not only was the fleet damaged by a storm in the same area but, although the first naval battle off Mylae was fought successfully under the leadership of Agrippa, after the unexpected arrival of the enemy fleet a serious defeat was suffered close to Tauromenium under the eyes of Caesar himself, who was in some personal danger. The legions that were with Cornificius, Caesar's legate,[340] disembarked and were almost overwhelmed by Pompeius on land. But a situation of critical moment was rectified by timely courage: when the fleets of each side had been deployed,[341] Pompeius was deprived of almost all his ships and fled to Asia, where he sought the help of Antony. While he was swinging between leader and suppliant, at one moment maintaining his dignity, at another begging for his life, he was slaughtered by Titius on Antony's order. The hatred that Titius incurred for this act was so enduring that later, when he was putting on games in Pompey's theater, the people's curses drove him from the spectacle that he was presenting.

80. When waging war against Pompeius, Caesar had summoned Lepidus along with twelve half-strength legions from Africa. This man, vainer than anyone and quite without any virtue to justify Fortune's lengthy indulgence,

[341] The battle of Naulochus took place on 3 September 36.

233

VELLEIUS PATERCULUS

Fortunae indulgentiam meritus exercitum Pompeii, quia propior fuerat, sequentem non ipsius sed Caesaris aucto-
2 ritatem ac fidem, sibi iunxerat; inflatusque amplius XX legionum numero in id furoris processerat ut inutilis alienae victoriae comes (quam diu moratus erat dissidendo in consiliis Caesari[489] et semper diversa iis quae aliis placebant dicendo) totam[490] victoriam ut suam interpretaretur,[491] audebatque[492] denuntiare Caesari, excederet Sici-
3 lia. non ab Scipionibus aliisque veteribus Romanorum ducum quidquam ausum patratumque fortius quam tunc a Caesare. quippe cum inermis et lacernatus esset, praeter nomen nihil trahens, ingressus castra Lepidi, evitatis[493] quae iussu hominis pravissimi tela in eum acta[494] erant, cum lacerna eius perforata esset lancea, aquilam legionis
4 rapere ausus est. scires quid interesset inter duces: armati inermem secuti sunt, decimoque anno quam [ad][495] in dissimillimam vitae suae[496] potentiam pervenerat, Lepidus et a militibus et a Fortuna desertus pulloque velatus amiculo inter ultimam confluentium ad Caesarem turbam latens genibus eius advolutus est. vita rerumque suarum dominium concessa ei sunt, spoliata, quam tueri[497] non poterat, dignitas.

[489] Caesari *Acidalius*: -is *PA*
[490] totam *BA*: tutam *P*
[491] interpretaretur *Gelenius*: -batur *PA*
[492] auderetque *Ruhnken*
[493] evitatis ⟨telis⟩ *Orelli*
[494] iacta *Gelenius*
[495] secl. *Bothe*
[496] vitae suae *Rhenanus*: -a -a *PA* (ad indignissimam vita sua *Ruhnken*)   [497] tueri *P*: intueri *BA*: vi tueri *Acidalius*

234

BOOK 2.80

had attached Pompeius' army to himself because he had been the nearer,[342] though its loyalty lay in following not his but Caesar's authority; and, swollen by a total of more than twenty legions, he had reached such a degree of madness that, despite being the useless associate of another's victory (which he had held up for a long time by disagreeing with Caesar's plans and by always saying the opposite of what others favored), he interpreted the entire victory as his own and ventured to order Caesar to leave Sicily. Neither the Scipios nor any of the other old Roman leaders ventured and accomplished a braver deed than did Caesar at that moment. Although he was unarmed and wearing only his cloak, he entered Lepidus' camp bearing nothing but his name, and, avoiding the weapons that had been aimed at him on the order of this most perverted of men, he ventured to seize a legion's eagle, although his cloak had been pierced by a lance. You would have known what the difference was between the leaders: it was the unarmed whom the armed men followed, and Lepidus, in the tenth year after he had reached a power so different from his manner of life,[343] deserted both by his soldiers and by Fortune and covered in a dark mantle, lurked at the back of the crowd pouring up to Caesar and groveled at his knees. His life and ownership of his possessions were granted to him; it was his rank, which he could not protect, of which he was despoiled.[344]

[342] That is, Pompeius' army was nearer to Lepidus than to Octavian.

[343] The "power" is Lepidus' membership of the triumvirate, formed in 43.

[344] Octavian unilaterally expelled him from the triumvirate.

235

VELLEIUS PATERCULUS

81. Subita deinde exercitus seditio (qui plerumque contemplatus frequentiam suam a disciplina desciscit et, quod cogere se putat posse, rogare non sustinet) partim severitate, partim liberalitate discussa principis; speciosumque per idem tempus adiectum supplementum Campanae coloniae, cuius ⟨agri⟩[498] relicti erant publici: pro his longe uberiores reditus duodecies HS in Creta insula redditi et aqua promissa, quae hodieque singulare et salubritatis instrumentum[499] et amoenitatis ornamentum est. insigne coronae classicae, quo nemo umquam Romanorum donatus erat, hoc bello Agrippa singulari virtute meruit. victor deinde Caesar reversus in urbem contractas emptionibus complures domos per procuratores, quo laxior fieret ipsius, publicis se usibus destinare professus est, templumque Apollinis et circa porticus facturum promisit, quod ab eo singulari exstructum munificentia est.

82. Qua aestate Caesar tam prospere †Libium in Sicilia bene†[500] Fortuna in Caesare et in re publica titubavit[501] ad Orientem. quippe Antonius cum XIII[502] legionibus ingressus[503] Armeniam ac deinde Mediam et per eas regiones Parthos petens habuit regem eorum obvium.

---

[498] cuius ⟨agri⟩ *Woodman*: eius *PA* (⟨agri⟩ eius *Ruhnken*: *alii maiorem ante* eius *lacunam statuerunt*)

[499] instrumentum *Cludius*: instar *PA*

[500] Libium . . . bene (Bń A) *PA*, *obelis not. Woodman*: sepelivit . . . bellum *Ruhnken*: *alii alia*

[501] titubavit *Goodyear*: militavit *PA*: mutavit *Ruhnken*: *alii alia*

[502] XVI *Freinsheim*

[503] ingressus *Gelenius*: e- *PA*

BOOK 2.81–82

81. Then a sudden mutiny in the army (which often departs from discipline when it contemplates its own numbers, not stopping to ask for what it thinks it can compel) was broken up partly by the *princeps'* severity and partly by his generosity; and during this time an impressive reinforcement was attached to the Campanian colony[345] whose public land had been abandoned: in exchange it received far richer returns of 1.2 million sesterces on the island of Crete, and an aqueduct was promised, which still today is a singular source of health and a picturesque adornment. For his singular prowess in this war Agrippa won the distinction of a naval crown, with which no Roman had ever been presented. Then Caesar returned victorious to the City,[346] and, having contracted to buy through agents several houses to increase the area of his own, he announced that he was designating it for public use and he promised to build a temple of Apollo with porticoes all round, which he constructed with singular munificence.[347]

82. In the summer season that Caesar so successfully †. . .†,[348] in the East there was a faltering of Fortune in the case of Caesar and the commonwealth. Antony, having entered Armenia and subsequently Media with thirteen legions, was making his way through these regions to the Parthians when he was confronted by their king; and first

[345] That is, Capua (44.4n). The mutiny was resolved by discharging veterans with grants of land, some of it provided from public land held by Capua.   [346] On 13 November 36.

[347] The temple of Apollo Palatinus, dedicated in 28.

[348] The words athetized in the Latin make no sense, and no convincing emendation has been proposed.

237

VELLEIUS PATERCULUS

2 primoque duas legiones cum omnibus impedimentis tormentisque et Statiano legato amisit, mox saepius ipse cum summo totius exercitus discrimine ea adiit pericula <a>[504] quibus servari se posse desperaret;[505] amissaque non minus quarta parte militum captivi cuiusdam (sed Romani) consilio ac fide servatus,[506] qui clade Crassiani exercitus captus, cum fortuna[507] non animum mutasset, accessit nocte ad stationem Romanam praedixitque ne destinatum

3 iter peterent sed diverso silvestrique pervaderent. hoc M. Antonio ac tot illis legionibus saluti fuit; de quibus tamen totoque exercitu haud minus pars quarta (ut praediximus) militum, calonum servitiique desiderata tertia est; impedimentorum vix ulla superfuit. hanc tamen Antonius fugam suam, quia vivus exierat, victoriam vocabat; qui tertia aestate reversus in Armeniam regem eius Artavasden fraude deceptum catenis (sed, ne quid honori deesset,

4 aureis) vinxit. crescente deinde et amoris in Cleopatram incendio et vitiorum (quae semper facultatibus licentiaque et adsentationibus aluntur) magnitudine, bellum patriae inferre constituit, cum ante Novum se Liberum Patrem appellari iussisset, cum redimitus hederis coronaque velatus aurea et thyrsum tenens cothurnisque succinctus curru velut Liber Pater vectus esset Alexandriae.

83. Inter hunc apparatum belli Plancus, non iudicio recta legendi neque amore rei publicae aut Caesaris

[504] *suppl. Kreyssig*
[505] desperaret *Haupt*: -averat *PA*
[506] est *suppl. post* fide *Gelenius, post* servatus *Orelli*
[507] fortuna *BA*: -am *P*

BOOK 2.82–83

he lost two legions with all their equipment and catapults and his legate, Statianus; later, at the greatest risk to his entire army, he himself courted too often dangers from which he despaired of being able to be rescued. Having lost no less than a quarter of his soldiers, he was rescued by the loyalty and advice of a captive (but a Roman one), who had been captured in the disaster to Crassus' army[349] and, since his circumstance had not changed his feelings, approached the Roman position by night, warning them not to take their intended route but to make their way through the woods in the opposite direction. This was the salvation of Antony and all those legions; nevertheless, of them and the entire army, no less than a quarter of the soldiers (as we just mentioned) and a third of the attendants and slaves were lost; almost none of the equipment survived. Nevertheless, because he had emerged alive, Antony would call this flight of his a victory; and, returning to Armenia in the third summer season,[350] he deceived its king Artavasdes by a trick and shackled him with chains (but golden ones, lest there be any lack of respect). Then, as the fire of his love for Cleopatra and the magnitude of his vices (which are always nourished by means, license, and flattery) both grew, he decided to make war on his fatherland. (He had previously ordered that he be called "New Father Liber" and—wreathed in ivy, wearing a golden crown, holding a wand, and dressed in boots—he had been carried round Alexandria in a chariot like Father Liber.)[351]

83. Amid the preparations for this war, Plancus, not through any good judgment in choosing the right course

[349] See 46.3–4.   [350] That is, 34.
[351] Liber is an alternative name for Bacchus.

239

VELLEIUS PATERCULUS

(quippe haec semper impugnabat) sed morbo proditor, cum fuisset humillimus adsentator reginae et infra servos cliens, cum Antonii librarius, cum obscenissimarum rerum et auctor et minister, cum in omnia et [in][508] omnibus venalis, cum caeruleatus et nudus caputque redimitus arundine et caudam trahens genibus innixus Glaucum saltasset in convivio, refrigeratus ab Antonio ob manifestarum rapinarum indicia transfugit ad Caesarem. (et idem postea clementiam victoris pro sua virtute interpretabatur, dictitans id probatum a Caesare cui ille ignoverat. mox autem hunc avunculum Titius imitatus est.) haud absurde Coponius, vir e praetoriis[509] gravissimus, P.[510] Silii socer, cum recens transfuga multa ac nefanda Plancus absenti Antonio in senatu obiceret, "multa," inquit, "mehercules fecit Antonius pridie quam tu illum relinqueres!"

84. Caesare deinde et Messala Corvino consulibus debellatum apud Actium, ubi longe ante quam dimicaretur exploratissima Iulianarum partium fuit victoria. vigebat in hac parte miles atque imperator, ⟨in⟩[511] illa marcebant omnia; hinc remiges[512] firmissimi, illinc inopia adfectissimi; navium haec magnitudo modica nec celeritati[513] adversa, illa specie [et][514] terribilior; hinc ad Anto-

508 secl. Gelenius
509 e praetoriis Schegk: E. (om. P) praetorius BPA
510 P. Gelenius: pater PA
511 suppl. Vascosanus
512 remiges Lipsius: reges PA
513 nec celeritati Heinsius: ne (ve P) celeritate PBA
514 secl. Rhenanus

240

BOOK 2.83–84

nor through any love for the commonwealth or for Caesar—he was always attacking them—but a pathological traitor (having been not only the lowest flatterer of the queen and a client inferior to her slaves but also Antony's secretary, the instigator and administrator of his obscenest activities, venal with everyone and in every respect, who had danced as Glaucus at a party, painted blue, naked, his head wreathed with reed, trailing a tail and resting on his knees)[352] deserted to Caesar when Antony cold-shouldered him on account of the evidence of his flagrant pillaging. (This was the same man who afterward interpreted the victor's clemency in terms of his own virtue, insisting that Caesar had approved what he had only forgiven. Later Titius imitated this uncle of his.) When after his recent desertion Plancus was charging the absent Antony in the senate with many unspeakable acts, Coponius, a very serious member of the ex-praetors and father-in-law of Publius Silius, said, not inappropriately, "As Hercules is my witness, Antony did a lot on the day before you left him!"[353]

84. Then, in the consulship of Caesar and Messalla Corvinus, the war was fought to its conclusion at Actium, where, long before the contest, the victory of the Julian party was assured. On the one side was the energy of soldiery and commander, on the other it was all apathy; here the rowers were at their fittest, there they were afflicted by shortages; the size of one set of ships was modest and no hindrance to speed, that of the other was more frightening only in impression; no one from this side deserted

[352] Glaucus was a marine deity in the form of a merman.
[353] C. Coponius had been praetor in 49; P. Silius Nerva (cos. 20 BC) was father of V.'s commanding officer (101.3n).

241

VELLEIUS PATERCULUS

nium nemo, illinc ad Caesarem cotidie aliquis transfugiebat. denique in ore atque oculis Antonianae classis per
M. Agrippam Leucas expugnata, Patrae captae, Corinthus
occupata; bis ante ultimum discrimen classis hostium su-
2 perata. rex Amyntas meliora et utiliora secutus; nam Dellius,[515] exempli sui tenax, ut a[516] Dolabella ad ‹Cassium,
ita ab Antonio transiit ad›[517] Caesarem; virque clarissimus
Cn. Domitius, qui solus Antonianarum partium numquam
reginam nisi nomine salutavit, maximo et praecipiti periculo transmisit ad Caesarem.[518]

85. Advenit deinde maximi discriminis dies, quo Caesar Antoniusque productis classibus pro salute alter, in
2 ruinam alter terrarum orbis dimicavere. dextrum navium
Iulianarum cornu M. Lurio[519] commissum, laevum Arrun-
tio, Agrippae omne classici certaminis arbitrium; Caesar,
ei parti destinatus in quam a Fortuna vocaretur, ubique
aderat. classis Antonii regimen Publicolae Sosioque commissum. at in terra locatum exercitum Taurus Caesaris,
3 Antonii regebat Canidius. ubi initum certamen est, omnia
in altera parte fuere, dux, remiges, milites, in altera nihil
praeter milites. prima occupat fugam Cleopatra; Antonius
fugientis reginae quam pugnantis militis sui comes esse

515 Dellius *Lipsius*: de illius *PA*
516 exempli sui tenax ut a *Lipsius*: exemplis vitae naxuta *PA*
517 *suppl. Woodman: alii alia*
518 rex Amyntas . . . transmisit ad Caesarem *post* transfugiebat
transpos. Haase
519 Lurio *Ursinus*: Lario *PA*

BOOK 2.84–85

to Antony, but every day someone would desert from him to Caesar. Finally, within sight of the Antonian fleet, Leucas was stormed by Agrippa, Patrae captured, Corinth seized. Twice before the ultimate decider the enemy's fleet was overwhelmed. King Amyntas followed the better and more profitable course; as for Dellius, holding to his own precedent, he crossed from Antony to Caesar as he had from Dolabella to Cassius; and Gnaeus Domitius, the very distinguished man who alone on the Antonian side never greeted the queen except by her name,[354] went over to Caesar at very great imminent risk to himself.

85. Then there arrived the day of the great decider,[355] when Caesar and Antony deployed their fleets and competed, one for the salvation of the world, the other for its ruin. The right flank of the Julian ships was entrusted to Marcus Lurius, the left to Arruntius, jurisdiction over the whole of the naval engagement to Agrippa; Caesar, destined for any area to which he would be summoned by Fortune, was everywhere. Direction of Antony's fleet was entrusted to Publicola and Sosius.[356] As for the armies based on land, Caesar's was under the direction of Taurus, Antony's under that of Canidius.[357] When the engagement began, everything was on one side—leader, rowers, soldiers; on the other there was nothing except the soldiers. Cleopatra was the first to take flight, and Antony preferred to accompany his fleeing queen than his own fighting sol-

[354] That is, he did not use any of her titles.

[355] 2 September 31.   [356] L. Gellius Publicola had been consul in 36, C. Sosius in 32.   [357] T. Statilius Taurus (see also 127.1) had been suffect consul in 37 and would be consul again in 26; P. Canidius Crassus had been suffect in 40.

243

VELLEIUS PATERCULUS

maluit, et imperator qui in desertores saevire debuerat
4 desertor exercitus sui factus est. illis etiam detracto[520]
capite in longum fortissime pugnandi duravit constantia et
desperata victoria in mortem dimicabatur. Caesar, quos
ferro poterat interimere, verbis mulcere cupiens clami-
tansque et ostendens fugisse Antonium, quaerebat pro
5 quo et cum quo pugnarent. at illi cum diu pro absente
dimicassent duce, aegre summissis armis cessere victoriam, citiusque vitam veniamque Caesar promisit quam
illis ut ea precarentur persuasum est. fuitque in confesso
milites optimi imperatoris, imperatorem fugacissimi mili-
6 tis functum officio, ut dubites suo[521] an Cleopatrae arbitrio
victoriam temperaturus fuerit, qui ad eius arbitrium derexerit[522] fugam. idem locatus in terra fecit exercitus, cum
se Canidius praecipiti fuga rapuisset ad Antonium.

86. Quid ille dies terrarum orbi praestiterit, ex quo in
quem statum pervenerit fortuna publica, quis in hoc trans-
2 cursu tam artati operis exprimere audeat?[523] victoria vero
fuit clementissima, nec quisquam interemptus est ‹nisi›[524]
paucissimi et ii qui ‹ne› deprecari quidem pro se [non][525]
sustinerent; ex qua lenitate ducis colligi potuit quem ‹finem›[526] aut initio triumviratus sui aut in campis Philippiis,
si sic licuisset, victoriae suae facturus fuerit.[527] at Sosium

---

[520] detracto *Vascosanus*: detractato *PA*   [521] ut dubites
suone (-ne *om. Vossius*) *Burer*: videbit e suo *P*: videbitis ne *A*
[522] derexerit *Woodman* (direxerit *Halm*): -xit *PA*
[523] valeat *Cornelissen*
[524] *suppl. Heinsius*
[525] ‹ne›. . .[non] *Heinsius*
[526] *suppl. Goodyear*
[527] fuerit ‹modum› *Rhenanus*

BOOK 2.85–86

diery, and the commander who should have been savage with deserters became the deserter of his own army. Even with the removal of their head, their resolve to fight with the utmost bravery lasted a long time and, despite victory being hopeless, they battled to the death. Caesar, whose desire was to soothe with words those whom he could have killed with the sword, repeatedly shouted and indicated that Antony had fled, asking them for whom and with whom they were fighting. But, since they had battled a long time for their absent leader, it was only reluctantly that they laid down their weapons and conceded victory, and Caesar was quicker to promise them their life and their pardon than they were persuaded to plead for them. It was generally admitted that the soldiers had performed the function of the best of commanders, the commander that of the flightiest soldier, such that you would doubt whether the man whose flight was directed at the discretion of Cleopatra would have tempered his victory at his own discretion or hers. The army based on land did the same, after Canidius had taken himself off to Antony in headlong flight.

86. In a sketch such as is constituted by a very abridged work like this, who would venture to explain fully what that day gave to the world and what kind of transition was made by the public fortunes from one condition to another? The victory was one of the greatest clemency: only a very few were killed, and they were those who could not bear even to beg on their own behalf; from this mildness on the part of the leader one could have gathered the kind of limit he would have placed on victory at the beginning of his triumvirate or on the plains of Philippi, if he had been allowed to do so. As for Sosius, he was preserved

245

VELLEIUS PATERCULUS

L. Arruntii[528] prisca gravitate celeberrimi fides, mox diu
⟨cum⟩[529] clementia luctatus sua Caesar servavit incolu-
3 mem. non praetereatur Asinii Pollionis factum et dictum
memorabile. namque[530] cum se post Brundisinam pacem
continuisset in Italia neque aut vidisset umquam reginam
aut post enervatum amore eius Antonii animum partibus
eius se miscuisset,[531] rogante Caesare ut secum ad bellum
proficeretur Actiacum, "mea," inquit, "in Antonium maiora merita sunt, illius in me beneficia notiora: itaque discrimini[532] vestro me subtraham et ero praeda victoris."

87. Proximo deinde[533] anno persecutus reginam Anto-
niumque Alexandriam, ultimam bellis civilibus imposuit
manum. Antonius se ipse non segniter interemit, adeo ut
multa desidiae crimina morte redimeret;[534] at Cleopatra
frustratis custodibus inlata aspide, in[535] morsu sane eius
2 expers muliebris metus, spiritum reddidit. fuitque et fortuna et clementia Caesaris dignum quod nemo ex iis qui
contra eum arma tulerant ab eo iussuve eius interemptus:
D. Brutum Antonii interemit crudelitas; Sextum Pompeium ab eo devictum[536] idem Antonius, cum dignitatis
quoque servandae dedisset fidem, etiam spiritu privavit;
3 Brutus et Cassius, antequam victorum experirentur animum, voluntaria morte obierunt; Antonii Cleopatraeque
quis fuisset[537] exitus narravimus. Canidius timidius deces-

---

528 at Sosium L. Arruntii *Puteanus*: ad solium (folium *P*) ala-
runt in *PA*   529 *suppl. Lipsius*   530 namque *BA*: nam *P*
531 miscuisset *BA*: imm- *P*   532 discrimini *Acidalius*: -e *PA*
533 deinde *BA, om. P*   534 redemerit *Halm*
535 aspide in *B*: aspidem *A*: aspide *P*
536 ab eo devictum *Acidalius*: ab (ob *P*) eodem victum *BPA*
537 fuisset *PA^c*: fuerit *A, Krause*

246

BOOK 2.86–87

unharmed on the guarantee of Arruntius, who was celebrated for his old-fashioned earnestness, and later by Caesar, after a struggle with his characteristic clemency. A
memorable deed and saying of Asinius Pollio should not
be passed over. After the peace of Brundisium he had
confined himself to Italy and had never seen the queen or
mixed with Antony's party after the latter's emotions had
been crippled by his love for her, but, when Caesar asked
him to set off with him for the war at Actium, he said: "My
services to Antony are too great, and his kindnesses to me
too well known: so I shall remove myself from your decider and be the prize of the victor."

87. Then, in the next year, Caesar pursued the queen
and Antony to Alexandria, where he put the final touch on
the civil wars. Antony was not slow to kill himself,[358] such
that by his death he atoned for many charges of indolence;
as for Cleopatra, having tricked her guards and smuggled
in a snake, she discharged her life's breath quite devoid of
any womanly dread at its bite. It was in keeping with Caesar's fortune and clemency that none of those who had
borne arms against him was killed by him or on his order:
Decimus Brutus was killed by the cruelty of Antony; as for
Sextus Pompeius, though he was defeated by Caesar, it
was again Antony who, although he had given a guarantee
that he would preserve his rank as well, deprived him of
his life's breath too; Brutus and Cassius met a voluntary
death before they could experience the attitude of the
victors; Antony's and Cleopatra's end we have described.
Canidius perished more cravenly than comported with the

[358] On 1 August 30.

247

VELLEIUS PATERCULUS

sit quam professioni ei[538] qua semper usus erat congrue-
bat. ultimus autem ex interfectoribus Caesaris Parmensis
Cassius morte poenas dedit, ut dederat Trebonius ⟨pri-
mus⟩.[539]

88. Dum ultimam bello Actiaco Alexandrinoque Caesar imponit manum, M. Lepidus, iuvenis forma quam
mente melior, Lepidi eius qui triumvir fuerat rei publicae
constituendae filius, Iunia Bruti sorore natus, interfici-
endi, simul in urbem revertisset, Caesaris consilia inierat.
2 ⟨erat⟩[540] tunc urbis custodiis praepositus C. Maecenas,
equestri sed[541] splendido genere natus, vir, ubi res vigiliam
exigeret, sane exsomnis, providens atque agendi sciens,
simul vero aliquid ex negotio remitti posset, otio ac mollitiis paene ultra feminam fluens, non minus Agrippa Caesari carus sed minus honoratus (quippe vixit angusti clavi
purpura[542] contentus), nec minora consequi potuit sed
3 non tam concupivit. hic speculatus est per summam quie-
tem ac dissimulationem praecipitis consilia iuvenis et mira
celeritate nullaque cum perturbatione aut rerum aut hominum oppresso Lepido immane novi ac resurrecturi belli
civilis restinxit initium. et ille quidem male consultorum
poenas exsolvit; aequetur praedictae iam Antistii[543] Servi-

538 ei *Wopkens*: eius *PA*
539 primus *suppl. post* Trebonius *Halm, post* dederat *Aldus*
540 *suppl. Madvig*
541 equestri sed *Vascosanus*: equestris et *PA*
542 purpura *Laurent*: pene *P* (paene *A*), *obelis not. plerique*:
iure *P. Thomas* (angusto clavo [*iam Gelenius*] bene *Lipsius*): *alii
alia*
543 Antistii *Vossius*: -iae *PA*

BOOK 2.87–88

declaration that he had always made;[359] and the last of Caesar's killers to pay the penalty by dying was Parmensis Cassius,[360] as Trebonius had been the first.

88. While Caesar was putting the final touch on the Actian and Alexandrian War, Marcus Lepidus—a young man whose appearance was better than his disposition, son of the Lepidus who had been triumvir for the constitution of the commonwealth and of Brutus' sister Junia— had embarked on a plot to kill Caesar as soon as he returned to the City. Placed in charge of the City's guards at that time was Gaius Maecenas, born into an (albeit resplendent) equestrian family, a man quite sleepless whenever watchfulness was required, provident and an expert operator, but, as soon as there could be some relaxation from being active, he exuded the softness of inactivity almost more than a female; no less dear than Agrippa to Caesar, but less honored (he lived content with the narrow purple stripe),[361] he had the ability to achieve no less[362] but did not have an equivalent desire. With the utmost composure and dissembling he spied on the plans of the headstrong young man and, having snuffed out Lepidus with amazing speed and no disruption at all to affairs or persons, he extinguished the monstrous beginning of a new and resurgent civil war. The man for his part paid the penalty for his wicked designs; but Lepidus' wife, Servilia, can be compared with Antistius', mentioned earlier:[363]

[359] The nature of the "declaration" is unknown.

[360] C. Cassius Parmensis had been quaestor in 43.

[361] A narrow purple stripe on the tunic was a symbol of the equestrian order.

[362] That is, than Agrippa.   [363] At 26.3.

249

VELLEIUS PATERCULUS

lia Lepidi uxor, quae viro[544] igni devorato praematura morte[545] immortalem nominis sui pensavit memoriam.[546]

89. Caesar autem reversus in Italiam atque urbem ⟨qu⟩o concursu,[547] quo favore hominum omnium[548] aetatium, ordinum exceptus sit, quae magnificentia triumphorum eius, quae fuerit munerum, ne in operis quidem[549] iusti materia, nedum huius tam recisi digne exprimi pot-

2 est. nihil deinde optare a diis homines, nihil dii hominibus praestare possunt, nihil voto concipi, nihil felicitate consummari, quod non Augustus post reditum in urbem rei publicae populoque Romano terrarumque orbi repraesen-

3 taverit. finita vicesimo anno bella civilia, sepulta externa, revocata pax, sopitus ubique armorum furor; restituta vis legibus, iudiciis auctoritas, senatui maiestas; imperium magistratuum ad pristinum redactum modum: tantum-

4 modo octo praetoribus adiecti[550] duo. prisca illa et antiqua reipublicae forma revocata. rediit cultus agris, sacris honos, securitas hominibus, certa cuique rerum suarum possessio. leges emendatae utiliter, latae salubriter; senatus sine asperitate nec sine severitate lectus; principes viri triumphisque et amplissimis honoribus functi hortatu

5 principis ad ornandam urbem inlecti sunt. consulatus tan-

---

[544] viro A (*et van Herwerden*): vivo PA*c*

[545] praematura morte *Burer*: -am -em PA

[546] immortalem . . . memoriam A: -i . . . -a P

[547] ⟨qu⟩o concursu *Vascosanus*: occursus PA: ⟨quo⟩ occursu *Lipsius: alii alia*

[548] omnium hominum PA, *transpos. Woodman (praeeunte Halm)*

[549] ne . . . quidem *Gelenius*: nedum . . . siquidem PA

[550] adiecti *Halm*: allecti P: allectio A (ellectio A*c*)

250

BOOK 2.88–89

after her husband had been devoured by the fire,[364] she purchased by her premature death a deathless memory for her name.

89. The approving crowds of people of all ages and ranks by which Caesar was welcomed on his return to Italy and the City, the magnificence of his triumphs and games,[365] cannot be expressed fully even in the scope of a properly sized work, still less one as pared down as this. Thereafter there was nothing that man can desire from the gods or the gods present to man, nothing that can be conceived of in prayer or realized in happiness, that Augustus after his return to the City did not reinstate for the commonwealth, for the Roman people and for the world. The civil wars were ended in their twentieth year, external ones laid to rest; peace was recalled, raging armed conflict everywhere quelled. Force was restored to the laws, authority to the courts, sovereignty to the senate; the power of magistrates was returned to its former limits: to the eight praetors only two were added; that old-fashioned and ancient form of the commonwealth was recalled. Cultivation returned to the land, honor to sacred rituals, security to mankind, to each person the certainty of possessing his own goods. Laws were amended usefully, carried salutarily; the senate was chosen without harshness and yet not without strictness; the principal figures, having enjoyed triumphs and the highest offices, were enticed to the adornment of the City at the *princeps'* urging. The request

[364] It is uncertain what the Latin (if correct) means.

[365] There were three days of triumphs (13–15 August 29), respectively, for his victories in Illyricum, at Actium, and at Alexandria.

251

VELLEIUS PATERCULUS

tummodo usque ad undecimum ut[551] continuaret Caesar, cum saepe obnitens repugna‹turus e›sset,[552] impetrari[553] potuit: nam dictaturam quam pertinaciter ei deferebat
6 populus, tam constanter repulit. bella sub imperatore gesta pacatusque victoriis terrarum orbis et tot extra Italiam domique opera omne aevi sui spatium impensurum in id solum opus scriptorem fatigent;[554] nos memores professionis universam imaginem principatus eius oculis animisque subiecimus.

90. Sepultis (ut praediximus) bellis civilibus coalescentibusque reipublicae membris, †et coram aliero†[555] quae tam longa armorum series laceraverat. Dalmatia, XX et CC ‹annos›[556] rebellis, ad certam confessionem parata[557] est imperii; Alpes feris incultisque[558] nationibus celebres perdomitae; Hispaniae nunc ipsius praesentia, nunc Agrippae (quem usque in tertium consulatum et mox collegium tribuniciae potestatis amicitia principis evexerat) multo varioque Marte pacatae.

551 ut *Gelenius*: quem *PA*   552 *sic Woodman*
553 impetrari *Gelenius*: -e *P (prius* imperare *A) A*
554 fatigent *Acidalius*: -ant *PA*   555 et coram aliero *PA, obelis not. Woodman, secl. Gelenius*: et (etiam *Halm*) coaluere *Rhenanus: alii alia*   556 annos *suppl. hic Lipsius (per annos Novák), ante* XX *Orelli*   557 parata *Bothe*: pacata *PA*
558 incultisque *Heinsius*: multisque *PA*

---

366 His eleventh consulship was in 23.

367 The words athetized in the Latin evidently hide the main verb of the sentence and make no sense, but the following sentences suggest that V. may have made a reference to foreign parts.

368 From the First Illyrian War in 229 to Tiberius' conquest in 9 BC (96.2–3). The "lasting acknowledgment" of Roman rule came only with the crushing of the revolt in AD 6–9 (110–16).

252

BOOK 2.89–90

that Caesar should hold the consulship continuously was successful only up to the eleventh,[366] since he was about to refuse it strenuously and often; as for the dictatorship, he rejected it as resolutely as the people stubbornly offered it. The wars waged under his command, the world made peaceful by his victories, his very many achievements outside Italy and at home—these would exhaust a writer intending to spend the entire period of his life on this single task; remembering our assurance, we have placed before the mind's eye a comprehensive picture of his principate.

90. With the civil wars laid to rest (as we just mentioned) and the limbs of the commonwealth combining, †. . .† which had been torn by so long a series of armed conflicts.[367] Dalmatia, rebellious for 220 years,[368] was readied for its lasting acknowledgment of our empire; the Alps, well known for their wild and uncouth nations, were completely tamed;[369] the Spains, after much variable fighting, were pacified first by his own presence, then by that of Agrippa (who had been elevated by the *princeps'* friendship to a third consulship and later to partnership in the tribunician power).[370]

---

[369] The Alpine regions were subdued in successive campaigns (e.g., 95.2), and more than forty conquered Alpine tribes are listed on the massive monument set up in 7/6 BC at La Turbie in southern Gaul (cf. *CIL* 5.7817; Plin. *HN* 3.136–37).

[370] Augustus' campaign in northwestern Spain in 26–25 (see 38.4, 39.3), the last in which he participated personally, was followed by revolts, and control of the region was finally established by Agrippa in 19. Agrippa's third consulship was in 27; in 18 and 13 he received five-year grants of the tribunician power, which Augustus himself had been given for life in 23.

253

VELLEIUS PATERCULUS

2   In quas provincias cum initio Scipione[559] et Sempronio
Longo consulibus, primo anno secundi ⟨belli⟩[560] Punici,
abhinc annos CCL, Romani exercitus missi essent duce
Cn. Scipione, Africani patruo, per annos CC in iis multo
mutuoque ita certatum est sanguine ut amissis populi
Romani[561] imperatoribus exercitibusque saepe contume-
lia, nonnumquam etiam periculum Romano inferretur
3 imperio. illae enim provinciae Scipiones consumpserunt;
illae contumelioso XV[562] annorum bello sub duce Viriatho
maiores nostros exercuerunt; illae terrore Numantini belli
populum Romanum concusserunt; in illis turpe Q. Pompeii foedus turpiusque Mancini senatus cum ignominia
dediti imperatoris rescidit; illa⟨rum iuventus⟩[563] tot consulares, tot praetorios absumpsit duces, patrumque aetate
in tantum Sertorium armis extulit ut per quinquennium
diiudicari non potuerit, Hispanis Romanisne in armis plus
4 esset roboris et uter populus alteri pariturus foret. has
igitur provincias tam diffusas, tam frequentes, tam feras
ad eam pacem abhinc annos ferme L perduxit Caesar
Augustus ut, quae maximis bellis numquam vacaverant,

    559 ⟨P.⟩ Scipione *Goodyear*
    560 *suppl. Heinsius*
    561 populi Romani *Gelenius*: Praetor *PA*
    562 XV *Vossius*: XX *PA*
    563 *sic Woodman (cf. 2.1.4)*: illa ⟨natio⟩ *Goodyear*: illa ⟨terra⟩
Watt

---

    371 Cn. Cornelius Scipio Calvus (cos. 222); the year was 218.
    372 The brothers Cn. Cornelius Scipio Calvus (cos. 222) and
P. Cornelius Scipio (cos. 218), both of whom V. has just mentioned, were killed in 211.

254

BOOK 2.90

These last were the provinces into which—in the consulship of Scipio and Sempronius Longus, in the first year of the Second Punic War, two hundred and fifty years ago—Roman armies were initially sent under the leadership of Gnaeus Scipio (Africanus' uncle),[371] and for two hundred years the struggle there was conducted with so much mutual bloodshed that the loss of the Roman people's commanders and armies often inflicted humiliation and frequently also danger on the Roman Empire. Those provinces destroyed the Scipios;[372] they tested our ancestors in a humiliating war of fifteen years under the leadership of Viriathus;[373] they shook the Roman people in the terrifying Numantine War; they were the scene of the shameful treaty of Quintus Pompeius and the more shameful one of Mancinus, both of which the senate revoked, with the ignominious handing over of the latter commander;[374] their young men took off so many consular and so many praetorian leaders and in our forefathers' time exalted Sertorius so much by fighting that for five years[375] it could not be decided whether there was more strength in the Spanish or Roman armies or which people would obey the other. These, then, were the provinces— so vast, so populous, so wild—that Caesar Augustus brought to such a state of peace roughly fifty years ago that, having never been free of very great wars, under the

[373] If "fifteen years" is what V. wrote, it refers to the total period of heavy fighting in Further Spain from ca. 154 to 139, in which Viriathus was the enemy leader from ca. 146 (see 2.1.3n).

[374] For these various episodes see 2.1.3–2.1.

[375] Seemingly, from 80 to 75.

255

VELLEIUS PATERCULUS

eae sub C. Antistio[564] ac deinde P. Silio legato ceterisque
postea etiam latrociniis vacarent.

91. Dum pacatur Occidens, ab Oriente ac rege Parthorum signa Romana quae Crasso ⟨op⟩presso[565] Orodes,
quae Antonio pulso filius eius Phraates ceperant, Augusto
remissa sunt; quod cognomen illi viro[566] Planci sententia
consensus universi senatus populique Romani indidit.

2   Erant tamen qui hunc felicissimum statum odissent.
quippe L. Murena et Fannius Caepio, diversis moribus
(nam Murena sine hoc facinore potuit videri bonus, Caepio et ante hoc erat pessimus), cum iniissent occidendi
Caesaris consilia, oppressi auctoritate publica, quod vi fac-
3 ere voluerant, iure passi sunt. neque multo post Rufus
Egnatius, per omnia gladiatori quam senatori propior,
collecto in aedilitate favore populi, quem extinguendis
privata familia incendiis in dies auxerat, in tantum quidem
ut ei praeturam continuaret, mox etiam consulatum petere
ausus, cum esset omni flagitiorum scelerumque conscientia mersus[567] nec melior illi res familiaris quam mens foret,
adgregatis simillimis sibi interimere Caesarem statuit, ut,
quo salvo salvus esse non poterat, eo sublato moreretur.

---

564 Antistio *Gelenius*: Aristio *PA*   565 *sic Gelenius*
566 viro *PA*: viro ⟨divino⟩ *Watt*: vivo *Burman*
567 ceu sentina mersus *Heinsius*

---

376 C. Antistius Vetus (cos. suff. 30) was legate in 25; P. Silius
Nerva (cos. 20) was legate from 19. V.'s reference to freedom from
banditry is optimistic.

377 Octavian was given the name Augustus, deemed to have
some superhuman connotation, on 16 January 27, in response to
the constitutional settlement three days earlier, by which he

256

BOOK 2.90–91

legates Gaius Antistius and then Publius Silius and the others afterward they were free even from banditry.[376]

91. While the West was being pacified, in the East the Roman standards that had been taken by Orodes in the defeat of Crassus, as well as those by his son Phraates in the trouncing of Antony, were sent back by the Parthian king to Augustus (this cognomen had been bestowed on him, a *man*, at Plancus' proposal by a consensus of the entire senate and Roman people).[377]

Yet there were some who rejected this happiest of states. Lucius Murena and Fannius Caepio, men of differing morals (without this crime Murena could have seemed a good man, while Caepio was utterly wicked even before it), embarked on plans to slay Caesar,[378] but then felt the weight of public authority, suffering by law what they had aimed to perpetrate by violence. And not long afterward Rufus Egnatius, in every respect more like a gladiator than a senator, was so successful during his aedileship in amassing popular goodwill—which he had increased on a daily basis by using his personal gang of slaves to extinguish fires—that he joined on to it a praetorship, later daring to seek a consulship as well. But, since he was overwhelmed by an awareness of all his outrages and crimes, and his patrimony was in no better condition than his mind, he assembled persons similar to himself and decided to kill Caesar in order that he could die after removing the man by whose survival he was prevented from surviving. For it

claimed to have "transferred the commonwealth from my power to the control of the Roman senate and people" (*Res Gestae* 34.1). The standards were returned in 20.

[378] Almost certainly in 22, though the date is controversial.

257

VELLEIUS PATERCULUS

4 quippe ita se mores habent, ⟨ut⟩[568] publica quisque ruina malit occidere quam sua proteri et idem passurus minus conspici. neque hic prioribus in occultando felicior fuit, abditusque carcere cum consciis facinoris mortem dignissimam vita sua obiit.

92. Praeclarum excellentis viri factum C. Sentii Saturnini (circa ea tempora consulis) ne fraudetur memoria.
2 aberat in[569] ordinandis Asiae Orientisque rebus Caesar, circumferens terrarum orbi praesentia sua pacis suae bona. tum Sentius, forte et solus et absente Caesare consul, cum alia prisca severitate summaque constantia, vetere[570] consulum more ac gravitate[571] gessisset, protraxisset publicanorum fraudes, punisset avaritiam, redegisset[572] in aerarium pecunias publicas, tum in comitiis habendis
3 praecipuum egit consulem: nam et quaesturam petentes, quos indignos iudicavit, profiteri vetuit, et, cum id facturos se perseverarent, consularem, si in Campum de-
4 scendissent, vindictam minatus est; et Egnatium florentem favore publico sperantemque, ut praeturam aedilitati, ita consulatum praeturae se iuncturum, profiteri vetuit, et, cum id non obtinuisset, iuravit, etiam si factus esset consul suffragiis populi, tamen se eum non renuntiaturum. quod
5 ego factum cuilibet veterum consulum gloriae comparan-

---

[568] suppl. Burer
[569] in secl. Heinsius
[570] veterum Ruhnken
[571] ac gravitate Wopkens: ac severitate PA, secl. Ruhnken
[572] redegisset Stanger: regessisset PA

---

[379] In 19.
[380] That is, of candidacy.

258

BOOK 2.91–92

is a common pattern of behavior that each person prefers to fall in a general catastrophe than to be crushed by his own, and to be less conspicuous when about to suffer the same fate. Yet this man was no more successful than his predecessors in his concealment, and, hidden away in prison along with his accomplices in crime, he met a death in keeping with his life.

92. The distinguished action of the outstanding Gaius Sentius Saturninus (consul during that period) should not be cheated of its memorial. Caesar was absent, organizing the affairs of Asia and the East and distributing to the world by his very presence the benefits of his own peace. That was when Sentius, by chance sole consul,[379] and with Caesar absent, not only behaved in general with an old-fashioned severity and with the utmost resolution according to the grave manner of the consuls of old (exposing the cheating of tax collectors, punishing greed, and paying public money into the treasury) but especially acted the role of consul in the holding of the elections: he forbade declarations[380] by quaestorial candidates whom he judged unworthy, and, when they insisted they would do it, threatened them with consular retribution if they came down to the Campus;[381] and he forbade the declaration by Egnatius, who was thriving on the public's goodwill and hoping to join a consulship to his praetorship as he had a praetorship to his aedileship, and, when the ban failed to have any effect, he swore that, even if Egnatius were made consul by popular vote, he would still not return his name.[382] I deem this action comparable to any glorious deed of the

[381] That is, to participate in the elections, which were held in the Campus Martius.   [382] That is, as the winning candidate.

259

VELLEIUS PATERCULUS

dum reor—nisi quod naturaliter audita visis laudamus libentius et praesentia invidia, praeterita veneratione prosequimur et his nos obrui, illis instrui credimus.

93. Ante triennium fere quam Egnatianum scelus erumperet, circa Murenae Caepionisque coniurationis tempus, abhinc annos LII,[573] M. Marcellus, sororis Augusti Octaviae filius, quem homines ita, si quid accidisset Caesari, successorem potentiae eius arbitrabantur futurum ut tamen id per M. Agrippam securo[574] ei posse contingere non existimarent, magnificentissimo munere aedilitatis edito decessit admodum iuvenis, sane (ut aiunt) ingenuarum[575] virtutum laetusque animi et ingenii fortunaeque in quam alebatur capax. post cuius obitum Agrippa, qui sub specie ministeriorum principalium profectus in Asiam (ut fama loquitur) ob tacitas cum Marcello offensiones praesenti se subduxerat tempori, reversus inde filiam Caesaris Iuliam, quam in matrimonio Marcellus habuerat, duxit uxorem, feminam neque sibi neque rei publicae felicis uteri.

94. Hoc tractu temporum Ti. Claudius Nero—quo trimo[576] (ut praediximus) Livia, Drusi Claudiani filia, despondente[577] Ti.[578] Nerone (cui ante nupta fuerat), Caesari

[573] LII *Woodman*: L *PA*: LI *Krause*
[574] securo *Gelenius*: -os *PA*: -e *Rhenanus*
[575] ut aiunt ingenuarum *BA*: in- ut aiunt *P*
[576] trimo *Aldus*: primo *PA*
[577] despondente *Gelenius*: resp- *PBA*
[578] Ti. *A (s.l.), om. P*: ei *B*

260

BOOK 2.92–94

old consuls—although we are naturally more pleased to praise that of which we have been apprised than that which we have witnessed, and we regard the present with envy, the past with reverence, and believe that we are obscured by the former but instructed by the latter.

93. Roughly three years before Egnatius' crime erupted, around the time of the conspiracy of Murena and Caepio, fifty-two years ago, Marcus Marcellus, son of Octavia, Augustus' sister—who it was thought would succeed to Caesar's power in the event of something happening to him, but at the same time men supposed that, should he find himself in that situation, he would need to be concerned about Agrippa—passed away after putting on a most magnificent show as aedile;[383] he was just a young man, most decidedly (as they say) of genuine virtues, happy in spirit and disposition, and capable of the fortune for which he was being nurtured. After his death, Agrippa, who had departed into Asia under the pretext of services for the *princeps* but (as rumor has it) had removed himself from the present moment on account of his unspoken resentment at Marcellus, returned from there and took as his wife Caesar's daughter Julia, whom Marcellus had had in marriage, a woman whose womb brought good luck neither to herself nor to the commonwealth.[384]

94. It was during this tract of time that Tiberius Claudius Nero—who was three years old when, as we mentioned earlier,[385] Livia, the daughter of Drusus Claudianus,[386] married Caesar (having been betrothed to him by Tiberius Nero, to whom she had been married

383 In the latter half of 23.   384 Agrippa married Julia in 21.
385 At 79.2.   386 For him see 71.3n.

261

VELLEIUS PATERCULUS

2 nupserat—innutritus caelestium praeceptorum disciplinis, insignis[579] genere, forma, celsitudine corporis, optimis
studiis maximoque ingenio instructissimus, qui protinus
quantus est sperari potuerat visuque praetulerat[580] princi-
3 pem, quaestor undevicesimum annum agens capessere
coepit rem publicam, maximamque difficultatem annonae
ac rei frumentariae inopiam ita Ostiae atque[581] in urbe
mandato vitrici moderatus est ut per id quod agebat quantus evasurus esset eluceret.
4 Nec multo post missus ab eodem vitrico cum exercitu
ad visendas ordinandasque quae sub Oriente sunt provincias, praecipuis omnium virtutum experimentis in eo
tractu[582] editis, cum legionibus ingressus Armeniam, redacta ea in potestatem populi Romani regnum eius ⟨Ti-
grani, filio⟩ Artavasdis,[583] dedit, cuius ***.[584] rex quoque
Parthorum tanti nominis fama territus liberos suos ad
Caesarem misit obsides.

95. Reversum inde Neronem Caesar haud mediocris
belli mole[585] experiri statuit, adiutore operis dato fratre
ipsius Druso Claudio, quem intra Caesaris penates enixa
2 erat Livia. quippe uterque divisis partibus Raetos Vinde-

---

[579] insignis *S. J. Harrison*: iuvenis *PA*   [580] visuque praetulerat *Ursinus*: visusque -erit *PA*   [581] Ostiae atque *Rhenanus*:
ostia eratque *PA*   [582] tractu *Gelenius*: tractatu *PA*

[583] ⟨Tigrani, filio⟩ Artavasdis *Woodman*: Artavasdi *P*: Artauzdi
BA   [584] *post* cuius *(PA) lacunam stat. nonnulli*: cum *Lipsius*:
quin *Ruhnken*   [585] mole *Heinsius*: -em *P*: morem *A*

---

[387] The reference is to Tiberius' height: he was "of a stature
that exceeded the norm" (Suet. *Tib.* 68.1).

[388] In 23. (V. nowhere refers to Tiberius' praetorship in 16.)

BOOK 2.94–95

previously); who was educated by the teaching of heavenly precepts, was signal in lineage, appearance, and bodily build,[387] and was equipped with the best studies and the greatest talent; and who from the start had had the ability to raise expectations of his present greatness, and in his mien had prefigured a *princeps*—embarked on his political career as quaestor in his nineteenth year,[388] and at Ostia and in the City, on the order of his stepfather, he moderated the very troublesome price of corn and the shortage of grain in such a way that, through what he did, the greatness to which he would emerge shone out.

Not long afterward, accompanied by an army, he was sent, likewise by his stepfather, to inspect and organize the provinces in the East; and having provided outstanding proof of every quality in that tract of territory, he entered Armenia with his legions and, bringing it under the power of the Roman people, gave its kingship to Tigranes, son of ·Artavasdes, whose ***; the king of the Parthians too, terrified by the reputation of so great a name, sent his sons to Caesar as hostages.[389]

95. On Nero's return from there Caesar determined to prove him by the burdensome responsibility of a considerable war, giving him as his helper in the task his own brother, Drusus Claudius, to whom Livia had given birth in the household of Caesar.[390] Dividing their roles, each attacked the Raeti and Vindelici;[391] and after successful

[389] Phraates IV sent four sons to Rome ca. 10.

[390] Notoriously, Livia was pregnant with Claudius Drusus when in 38 she divorced Ti. Claudius Nero (75.1) and married Octavian (79.2, 94.1).   [391] In 15.

263

VELLEIUS PATERCULUS

licosque adgressi, multis urbium et castellorum oppug-
nationibus nec non derecta quoque acie feliciter functi
gentes locis tutissimas, aditu difficillimas, numero frequentes, feritate truces maiore cum periculo quam damno
Romani exercitus plurimo cum earum sanguine perdo-
muerunt.

3   Ante quae tempora censura Planci et Pauli acta inter
discordiam neque ipsis[586] honori neque rei publicae usui
fuerat,[587] cum[588] alteri vis censoria, alteri vita deesset,
Paulus vix posset implere censorem, Plancus timere deberet, nec[589] quicquam obiicere posset adulescentibus aut
obiicientes audire quod non agnosceret senex.[590]

    96. Mors deinde Agrippae, qui novitatem suam multis
rebus nobilitaverat atque in hoc perduxerat ut et Neronis
esset socer, cuiusque liberos nepotes suos divus Augustus
praepositis Gaii ac Lucii nominibus adoptaverat, admovit
propius Neronem Caesari: quippe filia eius, Iulia,[591] quae
fuerat Agrippae nupta, Neroni nupsit.

2   Subinde bellum Pannonicum, quod inchoatum ⟨ab⟩[592]
Agrippa Marcoque Vinicio, avo tuo, consul,[593] magnum

---

586 ipsis *Gelenius*: ipsi *PA*   587 fuerat *Orelli*: foret *PA*
588 cum . . . deberet *om. A*   589 nec *A*: ne *P*
590 ⟨in se⟩ senex *Heinsius*   591 filia eius Iulia *Gelenius*:
filia Iulia eius *PA*   592 *suppl. Lipsius*
593 consul (*vocat.*) *Woodman*: cos *A*: coss. *P*: consulari *Kritz*

---

392 In 22. For Plancus see 63.3n; Paullus Aemilius Lepidus
had been suffect consul in 34.   393 Agrippa, whose marriage
to Julia had produced Gaius Caesar (b. 20 BC, cos. AD 1) and
Lucius Caesar (b. 17 BC, the year in which both children were
adopted by Augustus), died early in 12 BC, whereupon Tiberius

264

BOOK 2.95–96

performances in many sieges, both of cities and of forts, as well as in battle-line formation, they tamed peoples who were protected by their location, difficult to approach, multiple in number, and of a ferocious wildness—with more danger than loss to the Roman army and a great deal of bloodshed on the other side.

Before this time the censorship of Plancus and Paullus had been conducted in mutual disharmony,[392] bringing neither honor to themselves nor benefit to the commonwealth, since the one lacked censorial power, the other a censorial lifestyle: Paullus was scarcely able to fulfill the office of censor, while Plancus ought to have feared it: he could not bring against young men, or hear others bringing against them, any charge that, despite his old age, he did not recognize as applicable to himself.

96. Next the death of Agrippa—who had ennobled his newness by many achievements and brought it to the point where he was even father-in-law of Nero, and whose children the Divine Augustus had adopted as his grandchildren, with the forenames Gaius and Lucius—moved Nero closer to Caesar: for Julia, the latter's daughter, who had been married to Agrippa, married Nero.[393]

Subsequently Nero waged the Pannonian War, which had been begun by Agrippa and Marcus Vinicius (your grandfather, consul[394]) and, on account of its magnitude,

was compelled to divorce Vipsania (Agrippa's daughter by his first wife, Caecilia Attica) and marry Julia. For "ennobled newness" see 34.3n.   [394] With "consul" (vocative case in the Latin), V. is addressing his dedicatee, the younger M. Vinicius, consul in AD 30 and grandson of the Marcus Vinicius named here. The war in question began in 13 BC.

265

VELLEIUS PATERCULUS

atroxque et perquam vicinum imminebat Italiae, per Ne-
3 ronem gestum est. gentes Pannoniorum Dalmatarumque
nationes situmque regionum ac fluminum numerumque
et modum virium excelsissimasque et multiplices eo bello
victorias tanti imperatoris alio loco explicabimus; hoc opus
servet formam suam. huius victoriae compos Nero ovans
triumphavit.

97. Sed dum in hac parte imperii omnia geruntur pros-
perrime, accepta in Germania clades sub legato M. Lollio,
homine in omnia pecuniae quam recte faciendi cupidiore
et inter summam vitiorum dissimulationem vitiosissimo,
amissaque legionis quintae aquila vocavit ab urbe in Gal-
2 lias Caesarem. cura deinde atque onus Germanici belli
delegata Druso Claudio, fratri Neronis, adulescenti tot
tantarumque virtutum quot et quantas natura mortalis
recipit vel industria perficit.[594] cuius ingenium utrum bel-
licis magis operibus an civilibus suffecerit artibus in in-
3 certo est: morum certe dulcedo ac suavitas et adversus
amicos aequa ac par sui[595] aestimatio inimitabilis fuisse
dicitur (nam pulchritudo corporis proxima fraternae fuit);
sed illum magna ex parte domitorem Germaniae, plurimo
eius gentis variis in locis profuso sanguine, Fatorum
iniquitas consulem agentem annum tricesimum rapuit.
4 moles deinde eius belli translata in Neronem est, quod is
sua et virtute et fortuna administravit; peragratusque[596]

---

[594] perficit *Lipsius*: percipit *PA*   [595] sibi *Heinsius*
[596] pervagatusque *Ruhnken*

---

[395] In 9 BC; an ovation was a lesser form of triumph (30.2n).
[396] Augustus went to Gaul in 16 BC, the year of the disaster
suffered by M. Lollius (cos. 21 BC).   [397] In 9 BC.

266

BOOK 2.96–97

terror, and extreme proximity, was threatening Italy. We shall describe elsewhere the Pannonian peoples and Dalmatian nations, the settings of regions and rivers, the number and type of forces, and the exalted and numerous victories of the great general in that war; the present work must preserve its particular form. Having achieved his victory, Nero triumphed with an ovation.[395]

97. But, while everything was being waged successfully in this part of the empire, a disaster suffered in Germany under the legate Marcus Lollius (a man altogether more desirous of money than of doing right, and highly depraved despite the utmost dissembling of his depravity) and the loss of the Fifth Legion's eagle summoned Caesar from the City to the provinces of Gaul.[396] The onerous management of the German War was then delegated to Drusus Claudius, Nero's brother, a young man of as many great virtues as mortal nature allows or as industriousness brings to perfection. Whether his talent was more suited to warlike operations or to civilian arts is uncertain: certainly the sweetness and charm of his character, just like his faculty of judgment (which was fair toward his friends and balanced in his own case), are said to have been inimitable (his physical beauty was very close to his brother's); but, having for the most part tamed Germany, much of that people's blood having been spilled in a number of different places, he was snatched away by the iniquity of the Fates when he was consul in his thirtieth year.[397] The burdensome responsibility of the war was then transferred to Nero, and he managed it with his usual courage and fortune: in a victorious sweep through all parts of

267

VELLEIUS PATERCULUS

victor omnes partes Germaniae sine ullo detrimento commissi exercitus, quod praecipue huic duci semper curae fuit, sic perdomuit eam ut in formam paene stipendiariae redigeret provinciae. tum alter triumphus cum altero consulatu ei oblatus est.

98. Dum ea quae praediximus in Pannonia Germaniaque geruntur, atrox in Thracia bellum ortum, omnibus eius gentis nationibus in arma accensis, L. Pisonis, quem hodieque diligentissimum atque eundem lenissimum securitatis urbanae custodem habemus, virtus compressit: 2 quippe legatus Caesaris triennio cum iis[597] bellavit gentesque ferocissimas plurimo cum earum excidio nunc acie, nunc expugnationibus in pristinum pacis redegit modum; eiusque patratione Asiae securitatem, Macedoniae pacem 3 reddidit. de quo viro hoc omnibus sentiendum ac praedicandum est, esse mores eius vigore ac lenitate mixtissimos[598] et vix quemquam reperiri posse qui aut otium validius diligat aut facilius sufficiat negotio et magis quae agenda sunt curet sine ulla ostentatione agendi.

99. Brevi interiecto spatio Ti. Nero, duobus consulatibus totidemque triumphis actis, tribuniciae potestatis consortione aequatus Augusto, civium post unum (et hoc quia volebat) eminentissimus, ducum maximus, fama fortunaque celeberrimus et vere alterum rei publi-

---

[597] iis *Orelli*: his *PA*
[598] mixtissimos *PA*: mixtis ‹iustis›simos *Heinsius*

---

[398] Tiberius was consul for the second time in 7 BC, celebrating his second (and first full) triumph on 1 January of that year.
[399] The war in Thrace was from 13 to 11 BC. L. Calpurnius

BOOK 2.97–99

Germany, without any loss of the army entrusted to him (which was always a special concern to this leader), he tamed it so thoroughly that he almost reduced it to the status of a taxable province. Then a second triumph along with a second consulship was offered to him.[398]

98. While the events that we just mentioned were happening in Pannonia and Germany, a terrible war arose in Thrace, with all the nations of that people fired up to fight, but it was suppressed by the prowess of Lucius Piso (whom we still have today as an extremely diligent—and at the same time very mild—guardian of security in the City):[399] as legate of Caesar, he waged war against them for three years and, partly in the battle line and partly by storming tactics, he reduced peoples of the greatest defiance to their previous way of peace, destroying very many of them in the process. With that achievement he restored security to Asia and peace to Macedonia. On the subject of this man, everyone should think and proclaim that his personality is a blend of energy and mildness and that scarcely anyone can be found with a stronger love of inactivity and an easier capacity for action, or who takes greater care of what needs to be done without any display of doing it.

99. After a brief interval Tiberius Nero—who had two consulships behind him and the same number of triumphs and was made equal with Augustus by his partnership in the tribunician power,[400] the second most outstanding of citizens (and that because it was his wish), the greatest of generals, celebrated in fame and fortune, and truly the

Piso the Chief Pontiff (cos. 15 BC), a heavy drinker, was later Prefect of the City (AD 13–32).

[400] Tribunician power granted for five years in 6 BC.

269

VELLEIUS PATERCULUS

2 cae lumen et caput, mira quadam et incredibili atque inenarrabili pietate (cuius causae mox detectae sunt cum Gaius Caesar sumpisset iam virilem togam, Lucius item maturus esset virili,[599] ne fulgor suus orientium iuvenum obstaret initiis), dissimulata causa consilii sui commeatum ab socero atque eodem vitrico adquiescendi a continu-

3 atione laborum petiit. quis fuerit eo tempore civitatis habitus, qui singulorum animi, quae digredientium a tanto viro omnium lacrimae, quam paene ei patria manum ini-

4 ecerit, iusto servemus operi; illud etiam in hoc transcursu dicendum est, ita septem annos Rhodi moratum[600] ut omnes qui pro consulibus legatique in transmarinas profecti provincias visendi eius gratia adpulerunt eum[601] convenientes semper privato (si[602] illa maiestas privata umquam[603] fuit) fasces suos summiserint fassique sint otium eius honoratius imperio suo. 100. sensit terrarum orbis digressum a custodia Neronem urbis: nam et Parthus desciscens a societate Romana adiecit Armeniae manum et Germania aversis domitoris sui oculis rebellavit.

2 At in urbe eo ipso anno quo magnificentissimis[604] gladiatorii muneris naumachiaeque spectaculis divus Augustus abhinc annos XXXI,[605] se et Gallo Caninio consulibus,

---

[599] virili *Withof*: viris *PA*: viribus *ed. Bipont.*
[600] moratum *BA*: moratum est *P*
[601] adpulerunt eum *Woodman*: ad quem *PA*: *alii alia*
[602] privato si *Lipsius*: privatos *PA*
[603] umquam *Aldus, Lipsius*: numquam *PA*
[604] magnificentissimis *Cuper*: -imi *PA*
[605] XXXI *Woodman*: XXX *PA*

270

BOOK 2.99–100

commonwealth's second eye and head—in a remarkable, incredible and indescribable form of devotion (the reasons for which were soon revealed when Gaius Caesar had now assumed the toga of manhood and Lucius was likewise ready for it, namely, that his own brilliance should not block the initial stages of the young men's rise) asked his father-in-law and stepfather, while concealing the motive behind his plan, for leave of absence from his ongoing labors. The community's demeanor at that time, the feelings of individuals, the tears of all those parting from the great man, and the closeness his fatherland came to claiming him—all this let us keep for our properly sized work; but even in this sketch the following must be said: his seven-year stay on Rhodes[401] was such that all the proconsuls and legates who had set off for overseas provinces, and put in for the purpose of visiting, always lowered their fasces on meeting him despite his private status (if such sovereignty was ever private) and acknowledged that his furlough was a source of greater honor than their own power of command. 100. Nero's departure from his guardianship of the City was felt worldwide: the Parthians abandoned their Roman alliance and laid hands on Armenia, and Germany rebelled when the eyes of its tamer were turned away.

In the City, in the very year that the Divine Augustus had dedicated the temple of Mars[402] and filled the hearts and eyes of the Roman people with the most magnificent spectacles of a gladiatorial show and naval battle—thirty-one years ago, when he and Gallus Caninius were con-

[401] 6 BC–AD 2.   [402] The famous temple of Mars Ultor, "Mars the Avenger" (2 BC).

271

VELLEIUS PATERCULUS

dedicato Martis templo animos oculosque populi Romani
repleverat, foeda dictu memoriaque horrenda in ipsius
3 domo tempestas erupit. quippe filia eius Iulia, per omnia
tanti parentis ac viri immemor, nihil quod facere aut pati
turpiter posset femina luxuria ⟨ac⟩[606] libidine infectum
reliquit, magnitudinemque fortunae suae peccandi licen-
4 tia metiebatur, quidquid liberet pro licito vindicans. tum
Iullus[607] Antonius, singulare exemplum clementiae Caesaris, violator eius domus, ipse sceleris a se commissi ultor
fuit (quem victo eius patre non tantum incolumitate dona-
verat sed sacerdotio, praetura, consulatu, provinciis honoratum, etiam matrimonio sororis suae filiae in artissimam
5 adfinitatem receperat); Quintiusque Crispinus, singularem nequitiam supercilio truci protegens, et Appius Claudius et Sempronius Gracchus ac Scipio aliique minoris
nominis utriusque ordinis viri, quas in[608] cuiuslibet uxore
violata poenas pependissent,[609] pependere cum Caesaris
filiam et Neronis violassent coniugem. Iulia relegata in
insulam patriaeque et parentum subducta oculis, quam
tamen comitata mater Scribonia voluntaria[610] exilii per-
mansit comes.

[606] suppl. Orelli   [607] Iullus Hülsen: Iulius PA
[608] quas in Purser: quasi PA
[609] pependissent A, om. P
[610] voluntaria Lipsius: -ii PA

---

[403] Iullus Antonius, son of Antony and Fulvia, married the
elder Marcella—daughter of Octavia, Augustus' sister—in 21 BC,
was praetor in 13, consul in 10, and subsequently governor of Asia
(7/6 BC); his priesthood was probably an augurate. Whether his
death (in 2 BC) was in fact suicide is disputed.

272

BOOK 2.100

suls—there erupted in his own house a storm that is foul to mention and makes one shudder to recall. His daughter Julia, completely unmindful of her great parent and husband, through her luxury and lust left undone nothing that a woman could do or experience in terms of shame, and she measured the greatness of her station by her license to sin, claiming as legitimate whatever she liked. Thereupon Iullus Antonius, a singular example of Caesar's clemency but a violator of his house, himself avenged the crime he had committed. (After the defeat of his father he had not only been presented with his survival but—honored with a priesthood, praetorship, consulship, and provinces—he had even been received into the closest relationship through marriage to the daughter of Caesar's own sister.)[403] And Quintius Crispinus, disguising his singular profligacy with a pitiless frown, and Appius Claudius and Sempronius Gracchus and Scipio, and other men of lesser name from both orders, paid the same penalty for violating Caesar's daughter and Nero's spouse that they would have paid for violating anyone's wife.[404] Relegated to an island, Julia was removed from the sight of her fatherland and parents,[405] although her mother Scribonia accompanied her and stayed as a voluntary companion of her exile.

[404] That is, exile. The four men named were all of noble families: T. Quinctius Crispinus Sulpicianus (cos. 9 BC), the younger Appius Claudius Pulcher, Sempronius Gracchus (a tragic poet), and Cornelius Scipio. See Syme (1986, 91).

[405] Relegation was the less severe of the two forms of banishment; by "parents" V. presumably means Augustus and Livia.

273

VELLEIUS PATERCULUS

101. Breve ab hoc intercesserat spatium cum C. Caesar, ante aliis provinciis ad discendum[611] obitis, in Syriam missus, convento prius Ti. Nerone (qui[612] omnem honorem ut superiori habuit) tam varie se ibi gessit ut nec laudaturum magna nec vituperaturum mediocris materia deficiat. cum rege Parthorum, iuvene excelsissimo, in insula[613] quam amnis Euphrates ambiebat, aequato utrius-
2 que partis numero coiit. quod spectaculum stantis ex diverso hinc Romani, illinc Parthorum exercitus, cum duo inter se eminentissima imperiorum et hominum coirent capita, perquam clarum et memorabile sub initia stipendiorum meorum tribuno militum mihi visere contigit.
3 (quem militiae gradum ante sub patre tuo, M. Vinici, et P. Silio auspicatus in Thracia Macedoniaque, mox Achaia Asiaque et omnibus ad Orientem visis prouinciis et ore atque utroque maris Pontici latere, haud iniucunda tot rerum, locorum, gentium, urbium recordatione perfruor.) prior Parthus apud Gaium in nostra ripa, posterior hic apud regem in hostili epulatus est. 102. quo tempore M. Lollii, quem veluti moderatorem iuuentae filii sui Augustus esse voluerat, perfida et plena subdoli ac versuti animi consilia per Parthum indicata Caesari fama vulgavit.[614]

---

[611] ad discendum *Purser (cf. Cass. Dio 55.10.17, ἐπῄει . . . ἐμάνθανεν)*: adsidendum *BA*: ad sedandum *P*: ad visendum *Lipsius*   [612] qui *Lipsius*: cui *PA*

[613] excelsissimo in insula *Gelenius*: excelsissimae insulae (-e -e *A*) *P*: *alii alia*

[614] Caesari fama vulgavit *Lipsius*: Caesaris iam avulgavit *PA*

---

[406] Phraataces (Phraates V); the date of the meeting is thought to have been AD 2.

BOOK 2.101–2

101. Only a brief period had intervened after this when Gaius Caesar, having previously gone to other provinces in order to learn, was sent to Syria and, having met beforehand with Tiberius Nero (who showed him, as his superior, every honor), he conducted himself so inconsistently there that there is no lack of major material for a eulogist nor of moderate material for a critic. On an island encircled by the River Euphrates he held a meeting with the king of the Parthians, a most exalted young man,[406] with an equal number of retinue on each side. The spectacle of the Roman and Parthian armies at attention, facing each other from their different positions, while the two outstanding heads of empires and peoples came together to meet, was exceptionally vivid and memorable, and it fell to me to witness it as military tribune in the early stages of my service. (This military rank I had entered upon previously, Marcus Vinicius, under your father and Publius Silius in Thrace and Macedonia,[407] and, having subsequently visited Achaea and Asia and all the eastern provinces and the mouth and both shores of the sea of Pontus, I enjoy a very pleasant memory of so many events, places, peoples, and cities.) The Parthian was the first to dine with Gaius on our bank, then the latter dined with the king on the enemy's. 102. It was at that moment that there were revealed to Caesar by the Parthian the treacherous intentions—full of the man's wily and shifty thoughts—of Marcus Lollius, whom Augustus had wanted to be a mentor for his young son; and rumor gave them publicity. Whether

[407] P. Vinicius (cos. AD 2) and P. Silius (cos. suff. AD 3) governed in Thrace and Macedonia in the very last years of the pre-Christian era (the exact dates are uncertain).

275

VELLEIUS PATERCULUS

cuius mors intra paucos dies fortuita an voluntaria fuerit
ignoro; sed quam hunc decessisse laetati homines, tam
paulo post obiisse Censorinum in iisdem provinciis graviter tulit ciuitas, virum demerendis hominibus genitum.

2   Armeniam deinde ‹Gaius›[615] ingressus prima parte
introitus prospere ‹rem›[616] gessit; mox in conloquio,[617]
cui se temere crediderat, circa Artageram graviter a quo-
dam (nomine Adduo) vulneratus, ex eo ut corpus minus
habile, ita animum minus utilem rei publicae habere coe-
3 pit. nec defuit conversatio hominum vitia eius adsentatione alentium (etenim semper magnae fortunae comes
adest adulatio), per quae eo ductus erat ut in ultimo ac
remotissimo terrarum orbis angulo consenescere quam
Romam regredi mallet. deinde reluctatus[618] invitusque
revertens in Italiam in urbe Lyciae (Limyra nominant)
morbo obiit, cum ante annum ferme L.[619] Caesar frater
eius Hispanias petens Massiliae[620] decessisset.

103. Sed Fortuna, quae subduxerat spem magni nominis, iam tum rei publicae sua praesidia reddiderat: quippe
ante utriusque horum obitum patre tuo P. Vinicio consule
Ti. Nero reversus Rhodo incredibili laetitia patriam reple-
2 verat. non est diu cunctatus Caesar Augustus: neque enim
quaerendus erat quem legeret[621] sed legendus qui emine-

---

615 *suppl. Krause*   616 *suppl. Heinsius*
617 conloquio *Gelenius*: -ium *PA*
618 se‹cum› luctatus *Purser (cf. 63.3)*
619 L. *Gelenius*: quinquagesimum *PA*
620 Massiliae *BA*: -ia *P*   621 legeret *P*: legerat *BA*

---

408 C. Marcius Censorinus (cos. 8 BC) died while proconsul
of Asia.

276

BOOK 2.102–3

his death within a few days was fortuitous or voluntary I do not know; but the general joy at his decease was matched by the community's heavy heart at the passing of Censorinus shortly after in the same provinces, a man born to endear himself to others.[408]

Then Gaius entered Armenia, and on the first part of his inward journey he conducted business successfully; but later, in a dialogue near Artagera to which he had rashly entrusted himself, he was seriously wounded by someone called Adduus, and as a result his body began to be less serviceable and his mind less useful for the commonwealth; nor did he lack the company of men feeding his flaws by their flattery (sycophancy is always the companion of great fortune), and all of this had brought him to the point where he preferred to grow old in the furthest and remotest corner of the globe than to go back to Rome. Then, while returning (after resistance on his part) unwillingly to Italy, he died of disease in a city of Lycia (it is called Limyra), his brother Lucius Caesar having passed away roughly a year before at Massilia while on his way to the Spains.[409]

103. But Fortune, which had withdrawn the expectation of a great name,[410] had already restored to the commonwealth its means of protection: for before the passing of this pair, in the consulship of Publius Vinicius,[411] your father, Tiberius Nero's return from Rhodes had filled the fatherland with incredible delight. Caesar Augustus did not delay for long: the need was not to search for someone

---

[409] L. Caesar died on 20 August, AD 2, his brother Gaius on 21 February, AD 4.

[410] Gaius and Lucius *Caesar*.   [411] AD 2.

277

VELLEIUS PATERCULUS

3 bat. itaque quod post Lucii mortem adhuc Gaio vivo facere voluerat eoque[622] vehementer repugnante Nerone
erat inhibitus, post utriusque adulescentium obitum facere perseveravit, ut et tribuniciae potestatis consortionem
Neroni constitueret (multum quidem eo cum domi tum in
senatu recusante) et eum Aelio Cato ‹Gaio›[623] Sentio
consulibus VI[624] Kal. Iulias, post urbem conditam annis
DCCLV,[625] abhinc annos XXVI[626] adoptaret.

4   Laetitiam illius diei concursumque ciuitatis et vota
paene inserentium caelo manus spemque conceptam[627]
perpetuae securitatis aeternitatisque Romani imperii vix
in illo iusto opere abunde persequi poterimus, nedum
hic[628] implere temptemus, ‹ausi›[629] id unum dixisse,

5 quam ille omnibus faverit:[630] tum refulsit certa spes libe-
rorum parentibus, viris matrimoniorum, dominis patrimo-
nii, omnibus hominibus salutis, quietis, pacis, tranquillita-
tis, adeo ut nec plus sperari potuerit nec spei responderi
felicius.

104. Adoptatus eadem die etiam M. Agrippa, quem
post mortem Agrippae Iulia enixa erat, sed in Neronis
adoptione illud adiectum his ipsis Caesaris verbis: "hoc,"
inquit, "rei publicae causa facio."

---

622 eoque *(uel* eo quod*) B*: atque *P*: quae eo *A*
623 ‹Gaio› *Woodman* (‹*C.*› *iam Aldus*)
624 VI *Rau*: V *PA*   625 DCCLV *Woodman*: D·CCLIIII *P*:
A·CC·L·IIII *B*: aCCLIIII *A*   626 XXVI *Aldus*: XXVII *PA*
627 conceptam *Boeclerus*: -ae *PA*   628 hic *Gelenius*: hinc *PA*
629 *suppl.Woodman*: ‹contenti› *post* dixisse *Rhenanus*: *alii
alia*   630 faverit *Madvig*: fuerit *PA*

---

412 This perhaps refers to the *contio*, or public meeting, at

BOOK 2.103–4

to choose; it was to choose the one who stood out. And so, after the passing of each of the young men, he persisted in doing what he had wanted to do after Lucius' death while Gaius was still alive but had been prevented by Nero's vehement opposition: he established for Nero a partnership in the tribunician power (despite the latter's strong protests both domestically and in the senate), and, in the consulship of Aelius Catus and Gaius Sentius, on 26 June, 755 years after the foundation of the City, twenty-six years ago, he adopted him.

The delight of that day, the congregating of the community,[412] the prayers of those stretching their hands almost to heaven, and the hope they conceived for everlasting security and for the eternity of the Roman Empire—all this we shall scarcely be able to pursue thoroughly in that properly sized work of ours, still less try to fill out here, venturing to say only this, how everyone was blessed by that day: it was then that an assured hope once again shone out to parents for their children, to husbands for their marriages, to owners for their estates, and to everyone for safety, calm, peace, and tranquility, so much so that there could be nothing further to be hoped for nor a happier response to that hope.

104. Adopted on the same day also was Marcus Agrippa, to whom Julia had given birth after the death of Agrippa;[413] but in the case of Nero's adoption there was the following addition in Caesar's actual words: "This," he said, "I do for the sake of the commonwealth."

which Augustus evidently spoke the words reported at 104.1 (Suet. *Tib.* 21.3).

[413] M. Vipsanius Agrippa Postumus was born in 12 BC.

VELLEIUS PATERCULUS

2   Non diu vindicem custodemque imperii sui morata in urbe patria protinus in Germaniam misit, ubi ante triennium sub M. Vinicio, avo tuo, clarissimo viro, immensum exarserat bellum. erat id[631] ab eo quibusdam in locis gestum, quibusdam sustentatum feliciter, eoque nomine decreta ei cum speciosissima inscriptione operum orna-

3 menta triumphalia. hoc tempus me, functum ante tribunatu, castrorum Ti. Caesaris militem fecit: quippe protinus ab adoptione missus cum eo praefectus equitum in Germaniam, successor officii patris mei, caelestissimorum eius operum per annos continuos VIIII praefectus aut legatus spectator, tum[632] pro captu mediocritatis meae adiutor fui. neque illi spectaculo quo fructus[633] sum simile condicio mortalis recipere videtur mihi, cum per celeberrimam Italiae partem ‹et›[634] tractum omnem Galliae provinciarum veterem imperatorem et ante meritis ac virtutibus[635] quam nomine Caesarem revisentes sibi quisque

4 quam illi gratularentur plenius. at vero militum conspectu eius elicitae gaudio lacrimae alacritasque et salutationis nova quaedam exultatio et contingendi manum cupiditas non continentium protinus quin adiicerent, "videmus te, imperator?" "salvum recepimus?" ac deinde "ego tecum, imperator, in Armenia, ego in Raetia fui," "ego a te in Vindelicis, ego in Pannonia, ego in Germania donatus

---

631 id *Lipsius*: & *PA*
632 spectator *Gelenius,* tum *Orelli*: spectatum *A*: spectatus *P*
633 fructus *B*: fruitus *P*: functus *A*
634 *suppl. Lallemand*   635 virtutibus *Lipsius*: viribus *PA*

---

414 The last general to hold a triumph had been L. Cornelius Balbus in 19 BC (51.3n): after this date triumphs were restricted

BOOK 2.104

The fatherland did not detain in the City for long the champion and guardian of its empire but sent him forthwith into Germany, where, three years before, an interminable war had flared up under Marcus Vinicius, your grandfather, a man of the utmost distinction: in some places he had been successful in waging it, in others in checking it, and on that account he was decreed the triumphal insignia along with a most impressive inscription of his achievements.[414] This was the period that saw me as a soldier in Tiberius Caesar's camp, having completed my tribunate previously: for immediately after his adoption I was sent with him into Germany as prefect of cavalry, succeeding my father in that position, and for nine unbroken years as prefect or legate I was a spectator of his heavenly achievements and also, allowing for the ordinariness of my ability, his helper. A man's mortal nature does not seem to me to admit of a spectacle similar to the one that I enjoyed, when, across the most populous part of Italy and the whole tract of the provinces of Gaul, everyone on seeing again their old commander—a Caesar for his services and virtues, before he was in name—congratulated themselves more profusely than they did him. The tears of joy elicited from the soldiers at the sight of him, their eagerness and unprecedented elation as they greeted him, their desire to touch his hand, unable to stop themselves from adding "Is it really you, commander, that we are seeing?" "Have we got you back safely?" and then "I was with you in Armenia, commander," "I was in Raetia," "You decorated me among the Vindelici," "and me in Pannonia," "and me in Ger-

to members of the imperial family, and successful generals were awarded the triumphal insignia instead. For M. Vinicius see 96.2.

281

VELLEIUS PATERCULUS

sum"—neque verbis exprimi et fortasse vix mereri fidem potest.

105. Intrata protinus Germania, subacti Canninefates, Chattuarii, Bructeri,[636] recepti Cherusci (gentes utinam minus[637] mox nostra clade nobiles), transitus Visurgis, penetrata ulteriora, cum omnem partem asperrimi et periculosissimi belli Caesar vindicaret sibi,[638] iis quae minoris erant discriminis Sentium Saturninum (qui tum legatus

2 patris eius in Germania fuerat[639]) praefecisset, virum multiplicem [in][640] virtutibus, gnavum, agilem, providum militariumque officiorum patientem ac peritum pariter, sed eundem, ubi negotia fecissent locum otio, liberaliter lauteque eo abutentem, ita tamen ut eum splendidum atque hilarem[641] potius quam luxuriosum aut desidem diceres. de cuius viri claro ingenio celebrique consulatu[642] prae-

3 diximus. anni eius aestiva usque in mensem Decembrem perducta[643] immanis emolumentum fecere victoriae. pietas sua Caesarem paene exstructis[644] hieme Alpibus in urbem traxit, at tutela[645] imperii eum veris initio reduxit

---

[636] Caninifaci (*em. Rhenanus*), Chattuari (*em. Will, cf. Strabo 7.1.3*), Bruteri (*em. Rhenanus*) *P*: cam vi faciat Tuari Bruoteri *A*

[637] utinam minus *Vossius*: et inamminus *B*: & inamminus *A*: et inamninus *P*   [638] sibi *Cludius*: in *PA, secl. Herel*

[639] fuerat *PA*: erat *Ruhnken*

[640] in *secl. Raphelengius*

[641] atque hilarem *Orelli*: ac hilarem *P*: Athilam *A*: aut hilarem *Ruhnken*

[642] claroq. ingenio celebriq. ~~ingenio~~ consulatu *A*: claro celebrique consulatu *P, fort. recte*

[643] producta *Lipsius*

[644] obstructis *Gelenius*

[645] at tutela *Lipsius*: ad tutelam *PA*

282

BOOK 2.104–5

many"—none of this can be expressed in words and perhaps can scarcely merit belief.

105. The entry into Germany was immediate. The Canninefates, Chattuarii, and Bructeri were subdued, the Cherusci reconquered (peoples whom one could wish less famed for their later defeat of us),[415] the Visurgis crossed and its hinterland penetrated, Caesar claiming every role for himself in this harshest and most dangerous of wars, while placing Sentius Saturninus (who at the time was a legate of his father[416] in Germany) in charge of the less critical aspects. The latter was a man of varied prowess, assiduous, energetic, and provident, with equal stamina and skill in his military duties, but at the same time, when his activities made room for inactivity, he used it to the full, liberally and lavishly, yet in such a way that you would have said he was resplendent and cheerful rather than a voluptuary or idler. His distinguished nature and celebrated consulship we have mentioned earlier.[417] The extension of that year's campaigning season into the month of December produced the benefit of a prodigious victory. Caesar's devotion drew him to the City despite the Alps being almost built up[418] in winter, but at the beginning of spring his protection of the empire brought him back into

[415] A reference to the Varian disaster of AD 9 (117–20, below).

[416] That is, Augustus.

[417] At 92, above.

[418] That is, with snow, a conceit that "almost" is meant to soften. Cf. Flor. 1.38.11, 1.45.22.

283

VELLEIUS PATERCULUS

in Germaniam, in cuius mediis finibus ad caput Lupiae[646]
fluminis hiberna digrediens princeps locaverat.

106. Pro dii boni, quanti voluminis opera insequenti
aestate sub duce Tiberio Caesare gessimus! perlustrata
armis tota Germania est, victae gentes paene nominibus
incognitae, receptae Cauchorum nationes: omnis eorum
iuventus infinita numero, immensa corporibus, situ locorum tutissima, traditis armis una cum ducibus suis saepta
fulgenti armatoque militum nostrorum agmine ante im-
2   peratoris procubuit tribunal. fracti Langobardi,[647] gens
etiam Germana feritate ferocior. denique—quod numquam antea spe conceptum, nedum opere temptatum
erat—ad quadringentesimum miliarium a Rheno usque
ad flumen Albim, qui Se<m>nonum Hermund<ur>orum-
que[648] fines praeterfluit, Romanus cum signis perductus
3   exercitus, et eodem, mira felicitate et cura ducis, temporum quoque observantia, classis, quae Oceani circum-
navigaverat sinus, ab inaudito atque incognito ante mari
flumine Albi subvecta, <cum>[649] plurimarum gentium
victoria, cum abundantissima rerum omnium copia exercitui Caesarique se iunxit.

---

[646] Lupiae *Lipsius*: Iuliae *PA*   [647] Langobardi *B*: Longo-
PA   [648] *sic Rhenanus*
[649] <cum> *Ellis*: <a> *Acidalius*

---

[419] Instead of "he had been the first to station," the Latin may
mean "the *princeps* had stationed" (see 115.3n). Whether *Lupiae*
(referring to the modern R. Lippe) is the right correction of the
transmitted *Iuliae* (which makes no sense) is uncertain.

[420] AD 5.

[421] In some other texts (e.g., Tac. *Germ.* 35.1, 36.1) called the
Chauci, the form more commonly used today.

284

BOOK 2.105–6

Germany, where, in the middle of the country, at the head of the River Lupia, he had been the first to station[419] winter quarters on his departure.

106. Good god, how large a volume would be needed for our achievements in the following summer season[420] under the leadership of Tiberius Caesar! The whole of Germany was traversed by our armed forces, peoples whose names were almost unknown were defeated, the nations of the Cauchi[421] were reconquered: all their young men—indefinite in number, physically huge, and protected by the position of their locations—handed over their arms and, surrounded by a column of our soldiers gleaming with weaponry, joined their leaders in bowing down in front of the commander's dais. The Langobardi were broken, a people more defiant even than the wildest of Germans. Finally (something that had never previously been hoped for in the imagination, still less attempted in practice)[422] a Roman army with its standards was led to the four hundredth milestone from the Rhine as far as the River Albis, which flows past the territory of the Semnones and Hermunduri—and, thanks to the remarkably successful care of our leader, as well as his observation of the conditions, the fleet, which had circumnavigated the Ocean inlets and sailed up the River Albis from a sea that was both unrecognized and unknown, joined up with Caesar and his army at the very same place, after victories over numerous peoples and with an abundant quantity of all types of goods.

[422] Since the R. Elbe had been reached by Drusus in 9 BC and by L. Domitius Ahenobarbus in AD 1, V. must be referring to the *joint* military and naval operation that he describes in the sentence as a whole.

285

VELLEIUS PATERCULUS

107. Non tempero mihi quin tantae rerum magnitudini
hoc, qualecumque est, inseram. cum citeriorem ripam
praedicti fluminis castris occupassemus et ulterior armata
hostium iuventute fulgeret sub omnem motum[650] nostra-
rum navium protinus refugientium, unus e barbaris aetate
senior, corpore excellens, dignitate (quantum ostendebat
cultus) eminens, cavatum (ut illis mos est) ex materia con-
scendit alveum solusque id navigii genus temperans ad
medium processit fluminis et petiit, liceret sibi sine periculo in eam quam armis tenebamus[651] egredi ripam ac
2 videre Caesarem. data[652] petenti facultas. tum adpulso
lintre et[653] diu tacitus contemplatus Caesarem, "nostra
quidem," inquit, "furit iuventus, quae, cum vestrum nu-
men absentium colat,[654] praesentium potius arma metuit
quam sequitur fidem. sed ego beneficio ac permissu tuo,
Caesar, quos ante audiebam, hodie vidi deos, nec feli-
ciorem ullum vitae meae aut optavi aut sensi diem." impetratoque[655] ut manum contingeret, reversus in naviculam,
sine fine respectans Caesarem ripae suorum adpulsus est.
3 Victor omnium gentium locorumque quos adierat,
Caesar incolumi inviolatoque et semel tantummodo
magna cum clade hostium fraude eorum temptato exercitu, in hiberna legiones reduxit, eadem qua priore anno
festinatione urbem petens.
108. Nihil erat iam in Germania quod vinci posset
praeter gentem Marcomannorum, quae Maroboduo duce

---

[650] motum *P*: metumque *B*: motūq. qi *A*: motum ‹sonitum›que
Watt: alii alia   [651] tenebamus *P*: tendebamus *BA*
[652] data *BA*: data a Caesare *P*   [653] [et] *Vascosanus*
[654] ‹non› colat *Madvig*
[655] impetratoque *P*: imperatoque *BA*

286

BOOK 2.107–8

107. I cannot refrain from inserting into these great events the following, such as it is. After we had taken possession of the nearer bank of the aforementioned river with our camp, and the farther one was gleaming with the armed youth of the enemy (who would immediately shrink back at every movement from our ships), one of the barbarians—older in age, outstanding in physique, and (as his dress showed) eminent in rank—climbed aboard a wooden dugout vessel (which is their usual type) and, guiding the bizarre craft on his own, advanced to the middle of the river and asked if he was allowed to get out safely on the bank that we held with our armed forces and to see Caesar. His request was granted. Then, having moored his boat and gazed at Caesar for a long time in silence, he said "Our young men are mad: they worship that godhead of yours when you are absent, yet, when you are present, they fear your armed forces rather than rely on your good faith. But not me: thanks to your kind permission, Caesar, today I have seen the gods of which previously I had only heard, and I have not desired or experienced a more fortunate day in my life." And having asked successfully to touch his hand, he returned to his bark and, without ceasing to look back at Caesar, landed on the bank of his own side.

Conqueror of all the peoples and places he had approached, Caesar, accompanied by an army that was unharmed, undamaged, and tested only once (by a treacherous enemy who was roundly defeated), led his legions back to winter quarters, making for the City with the same haste as in the previous year.

108. Nothing was now left in Germany that could be conquered apart from the Marcomanni, a people who had

287

VELLEIUS PATERCULUS

excita sedibus suis atque in interiora[656] refugiens incinctos
2 Hercynia silva[657] campos incolebat. nulla festinatio huius
viri mentionem transgredi debet. Maroboduus, genere
nobilis, corpore praevalens, animo ferox, natione magis
quam ratione barbarus, non tumultuarium neque fortui-
tum neque mobilem et ex[658] voluntate parentium[659] con-
stantem inter suos occupavit principatum, sed certum
imperium vimque regiam complexus animo statuit avocata
procul a Romanis gente sua eo progredi ubi, cum propter
potentiora arma refugisset, sua faceret potentissima.

Occupatis igitur quos[660] praediximus locis finitimos
omnes aut bello domuit aut condicionibus iuris sui fecit.
109. corpus suum custodientium[661] imperium, perpetuis
exercitiis paene ad Romanae disciplinae formam redactum, brevi in eminens et nostro quoque imperio timen-
dum perduxit fastigium; gerebatque se ita adversus Romanos ut neque bello nos ⟨lacesseret at, si⟩[662] lacesseretur,
superesse sibi vim ac voluntatem resistendi ⟨ostenderet⟩.[663]
2 legati quos mittebat ad Caesares interdum ut supplicem
commendabant, interdum ut pro pari loquebantur. gentibus hominibusque a nobis desciscentibus erat apud eum
perfugium, totumque ex male dissimulato agebat aemu-
lum; exercitumque (quem LX milium peditum, quattuor
equitum fecerat) adsiduis adversus finitimos bellis exer-
3 cendo maiori quam quod habebat operi praeparabat; erat-

[656] interiora *Rhenanus*: inf- *PA*   [657] Hercynia silva *Heinsius*: -ae -ae *PA*   [658] sed ex *Heinsius*
[659] parentium *BA*: -tum *P*   [660] quos *PA*: quis *BA^c*
[661] custodientium *Madvig*: custodia tum *PA*: *alii alia*
[662] *suppl. Rhenanus*
[663] *suppl. Burman*

288

BOOK 2.108–9

been forced from their homes under the leadership of Maroboduus and, retreating into the interior, were inhabiting the plains enclosed by the Hercynian Forest. No haste ought to pass over the mention of this man. Maroboduus—noble in lineage, physically very strong, defiant of spirit, a barbarian in kind rather than in mind—occupied among his fellows a principal position that resulted from neither emergency nor accident and was not precarious or dependent on the will of his subjects; but in his imagination he held a stable empire and royal power, and, having moved his people far from the Romans, he decided to push on to a place where, although he had retreated because of more powerful armed forces, he could make his the most powerful of all.

Having therefore taken possession of the places we just mentioned, he either tamed all his neighbors by war or placed them under his jurisdiction by treaties. 109. In a short while he brought the body of those guarding his empire, who had been converted almost to a Roman standard of discipline by perpetual training exercises, to a peak of preeminence that was to be feared even by our empire; and he so conducted himself toward the Romans that he did not challenge us in war but, if he was challenged himself, showed that he had the power and will to resist. The envoys whom he would send to the Caesars sometimes pressed his case as a suppliant, sometimes spoke as if for an equal. Peoples and individuals defecting from us found a refuge with him, and, after hiding it badly, he acted the complete rival. He trained his army (which he had made to total sixty thousand infantry and four thousand cavalry) by frequent wars against his neighbors, preparing it for a greater task than the one he had in hand; and he was also

289

VELLEIUS PATERCULUS

que etiam eo timendus quod, cum Germaniam ad laevam et in fronte, Pannoniam ad dextram, a tergo sedium suarum haberet Noricos, tamquam in omnes semper venturus ab omnibus timebatur. nec securam incrementi sui patiebatur esse Italiam, quippe cum a summis Alpium iugis, quae finem Italiae terminant, initium eius[664] finium haud multo plus CC milibus passuum abesset.

4

5 Hunc virum et hanc regionem proximo anno diversis e partibus Ti. Caesar adgredi statuit. Sentio Saturnino mandatum ut per Chattos excisis continentibus Hercyniae silvis legiones[665] *** Boiohaemum (id regioni quam incolebat Maroboduus nomen est); ipse a Carnunto (qui locus Norici regni proximus ab hac parte erat) exercitum qui in Illyrico merebat ducere in Marcomannos orsus est.

110. Rumpit interdum, ‹modo›[666] moratur proposita hominum Fortuna. praeparaverat iam hiberna Caesar ad Danubium, admotoque exercitu non plus quam quinque dierum iter a primis hostium, Saturninum[667] *** admoveri placuerat: paene aequali divisae intervallo ab hoste, intra paucos dies in praedicto loco cum Caesare ‹se›[668] iunctu-

2

---

[664] eius *P*: cuius *BA*: huius *Heinsius*

[665] *post* legiones *lacunam stat. Woodman*: ‹adduceret› *ante* legiones *Watt*: ‹duceret› *post* est *Lipsius*

[666] ‹modo› *Woodman*: ‹interdum› *Heinsius*

[667] *lacunam post* Saturninum *stat. Woodman*

[668] *suppl. Krause*

---

[423] The orientation is given as from Rome: Noricum was south of Maroboduus; see, e.g., *The Cambridge Ancient History*, vol. 10, 2nd ed. (Cambridge, 1996), Map 1, on pp. xvi–xvii.

[424] That is, AD 6.

BOOK 2.109–10

to be feared because—since he had Germany to the left and in front of his base, Pannonia to the right and the Norici at the rear[423]—he was feared by all of them as being likely to move against them all at any moment. Nor did he allow Italy to be safe from his expansionism, since, from the topmost ridges of the Alps, which mark the boundary of Italy, the beginning of his boundaries was not much more than two hundred miles distant.

This was the man and this the region that Tiberius Caesar decided to attack from different directions in the following year.[424] Sentius Saturninus' instructions were that, having cut down the forests adjoining the Hercynian, *** his legions through the Chatti to Boiohaemum (that is the name of the region that Maroboduus was inhabiting); from Carnuntum (the closest place in the kingdom of Noricum from this direction) he himself undertook to lead against the Marcomanni the army that was serving in Illyricum.

110. Fortune sometimes disrupts and at other times only delays the projects of man.[425] Caesar had already made advance preparations for his winter quarters by the Danube, and, after he had moved forward his army no more than five days' march from the nearest of the enemy, it had been decided that Saturninus should move forward ***:[426] separated from the enemy by an almost identical distance, within a few days they were about to link up

[425] V. here looks ahead a dozen years to the downfall of Maroboduus in AD 18 (129.3).   [426] Since the subject of the next sentence is feminine and plural ("they"), it is generally agreed that some form of the words *copiae* (forces) or *legiones* (legions) must have appeared in the lacuna.

291

VELLEIUS PATERCULUS

rae erant, cum[669] universa Pannonia, insolens longae pacis bonis et adulta viribus, Dalmatia omnibusque tractus eius gentibus in societatem adductis consilii,[670] arma corripuit.
3 tum necessaria gloriosis praeposita neque tutum visum abdito[671] in interiora exercitu vacuam tam vicino hosti relinquere Italiam.

Gentium nationumque quae rebellaverant omnis numerus amplius DCCC milibus explebat; CC fere peditum
4 colligebantur armis habilia, equitum VIIII. cuius immensae multitudinis, parentis[672] acerrimis ac peritissimis ducibus, pars petere[673] Italiam decreverat iunctam sibi Nauporti ac Tergestis confinio, pars ⟨se⟩ in Macedoniam effuderat,[674] pars suis sedibus praesidium esse destinaverat. maxima[675] duobus Batonibus ac Pinneti ducibus
5 auctoritas erat; in omnibus autem Pannoniis non disciplinae tantummodo sed linguae quoque notitia Romanae; plerisque etiam litterarum usus et familiaris animorum[676] erat exercitatio. itaque, hercules, nulla umquam natio tam mature consilio belli bellum iunxit ac decreta patrauit.
6 oppressi cives Romani, trucidati negotiatores, magnus vexillariorum numerus ad internecionem ea in regione quae plurimum ab imperatore aberat caesus, occupata armis Macedonia, omnia et in omnibus locis igni ferroque vastata.

Quin[677] etiam tantus huius belli metus fuit ut stabilem

---

669 cum *P*: tum *BA*   670 consilii *Fröhlich*: constitit *PA*
671 abdito *A*: addito *P*   672 parentis *BA*: pars *P*
673 pars petere *BA*: properare in *P*   674 ⟨se⟩ . . . effuderat
Ursinus, Lipsius: effug- *PA*   675 porro maxima (porro *om.
Kritz*) *Heinsius*: proxima *PA*   676 animorum *PA*: armorum
Bothe   677 quin *Vascosanus*: quia *PA*

292

BOOK 2.110

with Caesar at the appointed place when the whole of Pannonia—overweening from the benefits of a long peace and at the acme of its strength, and with Dalmatia and all the peoples of that tract of territory brought into partnership on the plan—took up arms. Necessity was then given precedence over glory: it did not seem safe to have the army ensconced in the interior and to leave Italy open to so close an enemy.

The total number of peoples and nations that had rebelled was more than eight hundred thousand: almost two hundred thousand infantry were assembled, proficient with weaponry, and nine thousand cavalry. Of this immense multitude, obeying the keenest and most skillful of leaders, some had decided to make for Italy, joined to them as it was by the frontier area of Nauportus and Tergeste, some had poured out into Macedonia, and some had determined to act as garrison for their homeland. The greatest authority rested with the two Batones and with Pinnes, the leaders; but in all the Pannonians there was a knowledge not only of Roman discipline but also of the language; many were even literate and familiar with exercising their intellects: the result, as Hercules is my witness, was that no nation was ever as quick in linking war with war plans or in putting its decisions into effect. Roman citizens were overwhelmed, businessmen butchered, a large number of specialist troops slain to the point of annihilation in the region furthest from the commander, Macedonia occupied by armed forces, everything in every location laid waste by fire and sword.

Moreover, so great was the dread of this war that it

293

VELLEIUS PATERCULUS

illum et formatum[678] tantorum bellorum experientia Caesaris Augusti animum quateret atque terreret. 111. habiti itaque dilectus, revocati[679] undique et omnes veterani, viri feminaeque ex censu libertinum coactae dare militem.[680] audita[681] in senatu vox principis, decimo die, ni caveretur, posse hostem in urbis Romae venire conspectum. senatorum equitumque Romanorum exactae ad id bellum ope-
2 rae; pollicitati. omnia haec frustra praeparassemus, nisi qui illa regeret fuisset. itaque ut praesidium limitum[682] res publica ab Augusto ducem in bellum poposcit Tiberium.
3 Habuit in hoc quoque bello mediocritas nostra speciosi ministerii[683] locum. finita equestri militia designatus quaestor necdum senator aequatus senatoribus, etiam designatis tribunis plebei, partem exercitus ab urbe traditi
4 ab Augusto perduxi[684] ad filium eius. in quaestura deinde remissa sorte provinciae legatus eiusdem ad eundem missus.[685]

Quas nos primo anno acies hostium vidimus! quantis prudentia ducis opportunitatibus furentes eorum[686] vires universas evasimus,[687] ⟨exhausimus⟩[688] partibus! quanto cum temperamento simul ***[689] utilitatis res auctoritate

[678] formatum *BA*: fortunatum *P*: firmatum *Burer*
[679] revocati *Gelenius*: -us *PA*
[680] militem *Rhenanus*: -um *PA*
[681] audita . . . pollicitati *post* terreret *(110.6) transpos. Haase*
[682] limitum *Purser*: militum *PA*: ultimum *Lipsius*
[683] ministerii *Lipsius*: ministri *PA*   [684] perduxi *Rhenanus*: -it *PA*   [685] missus ⟨sum⟩ *Halm*: missus *P*: missum *A*
[686] eorum *BA*: in eum *P*
[687] evasimus *PBA* (eius imus *A s.l.*): exhausimus *Gruter*
[688] *suppl. Woodman*   [689] *lacunam statuit Krause*

294

BOOK 2.110–11

shook and terrified the famous nerve of Caesar Augustus, so solid and molded by his experience of great wars. 111. Levies were therefore held, all veterans everywhere recalled, men and women compelled to provide freedmen as soldiers in proportion to their means. The voice of the *princeps* was heard in the senate: in ten days, unless measures were taken, the enemy could be coming within sight of the City of Rome. Senators and Roman equestrians were required to provide services for the war, and they promised them. All of these preparations we would have made in vain, had there not been the man to take control of them: so the commonwealth demanded of Augustus, as protection for its borders, Tiberius as war leader.

In this war too my ordinary abilities had the opportunity for some impressive service. My equestrian soldiering having ended, as quaestor designate (though not yet a senator, put on the same level as senators and even as tribunes designate of the plebs) I led from the City a part of the army that had been handed over by Augustus and took it to his son. Then, in my quaestorship, having forgone the allocation of a province, I was sent to the latter as the former's legate.

What enemy battle lines did we see in that first year![427] To think of the opportune places where, thanks to the leader's foresight, we eluded the rage of their massed forces but wore them out piecemeal! To think of the combination of both *** practicality with which we saw affairs

[427] AD 6. The reference in the preceding sentence to V.'s quaestorship in AD 7 is proleptic.

295

VELLEIUS PATERCULUS

imperatoris agi vidimus! qua prudentia hiberna disposita sunt! quanto opere inclusus custodiis exercitus nostri ‹hostis›,[690] ne qua posset erumpere inopsque copiarum et intra se furens viribus [hostis][691] elanguesceret!

112. Felix eventu, forte conatu prima aestate belli Mes-
2 salini opus mandandum est memoriae. qui vir animo etiam quam gente nobilior, dignissimus qui et patrem Corvinum habuisset et cognomen suum Cottae fratri relinqueret, praepositus Illyrico subita rebellione cum semiplena legione vicesima circumdatus hostili exercitu amplius XX ‹milia›[692] hostium fudit fugavitque et ob id ornamentis triumphalibus honoratus est.

3 Ita placebat barbaris numerus suus, ita fiducia virium, ut, ubicumque Caesar esset, nihil in se reponerent. pars exercitus eorum, proposita[693] ipsi duci et ad arbitrium utilitatemque nostram macerata perductaque ad exitiabilem famem, neque instantem[694] sustinere neque cum[695] facientibus copiam pugnandi derigentibusque aciem[696] ausa congredi, occupato monte Claudio munitione se defendit.

4 at ea[697] pars quae obviam se effuderat exercitui quem A.

---

[690] *suppl. Ruhnken*	[691] *secl. Kritz*	[692] milia *vulgo*
[693] opposita *Lipsius*	[694] instantes *Acidalius*	
[695] cum *Ruhnken*: ut *PA*	[696] aciem *B et (sed* aciam *s.l.)*	
A: etiam *P*	[697] at ea *B*: antea *P*: altera *A*	

---

[428] Words such as "concern and" (*curae atque*) have perhaps fallen out, "concern" being illustrated by the stationing of winter quarters, "practicality" by the hemming in of the enemy; but it is impossible to know for sure.

[429] M. Valerius Messalla Messalinus (cos. 3 BC) was son of the famous M. Valerius Messalla Corvinus (71.1n) and half brother

296

BOOK 2.111–12

being managed on the commander's authority![428] With what foresight winter quarters were stationed! How well our army kept the enemy under guard, hemming him in both to prevent a possible breakout anywhere and so that, low on supplies and directing inwardly his forces' rage, he might weaken!

112. The exploit of Messalinus in the first summer season of the war—blessed in outcome and brave in endeavor—needs to be placed on record. This man—even more notable for his courage than for his family, fully worthy both of having had Corvinus as his father and of leaving his cognomen to Cotta, his brother—was in charge of Illyricum:[429] along with the half-strength Twentieth Legion he was surrounded by an opposing army in a sudden rebellion but he routed and put to flight more than twenty thousand of the enemy and for that was honored with the triumphal insignia.

The barbarians were so displeased with their numbers, so unconfident in their forces, that, wherever Caesar was, they placed no trust in themselves.[430] The part of their army opposite the leader himself was softened up at will to our great advantage and reduced to terminal starvation; and, daring neither to sustain his attack nor to engage with his troops when they offered battle and formed their battle line, it seized Mount Claudius and defended itself behind fortifications. But, as for the part that had poured out to face the army that the ex-consuls Aulus

of the much younger M. Aurelius Cotta Maximus Messalinus (cos. AD 20), who had been adopted into his mother's family, the Aurelii Cottae. See Syme (1986, 230–39 and Table IX).

[430] V. seems now to be dealing with AD 7.

297

VELLEIUS PATERCULUS

Caecina et Silvanus Plautius consulares ex transmarinis adducebant provinciis, circumfusa quinque legionibus nostris auxiliaribusque et equitatui regio (quippe magnam Thracum manum iunctus[698] praedictis ducibus Rhoemetalces,[699] Thraciae rex, in adiutorium eius belli secum tra-
5 hebat) paene exitiabilem omnibus cladem intulit. fusa[700] regiorum equestris acies, fugatae alae, conversae cohortes sunt; apud signa quoque legionum trepidatum. sed Romani virtus militis plus eo tempore vindicavit[701] gloriae quam ducibus reliquit, qui multum a more imperatoris sui discrepantes[702] ante in hostem inciderunt quam per explo-
6 ratores ubi hostis esset cognoscerent. iam igitur in dubiis rebus semet ipsae legiones adhortatae, iugulatis ab hoste quibusdam tribunis militum, interempto praefecto castrorum praefectisque cohortium, non incruentis centurionibus, <e>[703] quibus[704] etiam primi ordines cecidere, invasere hostes nec sustinuisse contenti perrupta eorum acie ex insperato victoriam vindicaverunt.
7 Hoc fere tempore Agrippa, qui eodem die quo Tiberius adoptatus ab avo suo naturali erat et iam ante biennium qualis esset apparere coeperat, mira pravitate animi atque ingenii in praecipitia conversus, patris atque eius-

---

[698] magnam . . . manum iunctus *Rhenanus*: magna . . . manu vinctus *P*: magnam . . . manu i̶u̶n̶c̶t̶i̶s̶ iunctus *A*: iunctum *B*
[699] Rhoemetalces *Rhenanus*: Rhomo et Alces *PA*
[700] fusa *Vossius*: fuga *BA*: fugata *P*
[701] vindicavit *Puteanus*: -atum *PA*
[702] a more . . . discrepantes *Pontanus*: amore . . . crepantes *PA*
[703] *suppl. Boeclerus*
[704] quibus *BA*: qui *P*

BOOK 2.112

Caecina and Silvanus Plautius were bringing up from the overseas provinces, it surrounded five of our legions and auxiliaries and royal cavalry (Rhoemetalces, the king of Thrace, in concert with the leaders mentioned earlier, had brought with him a large unit of Thracians to help in the war) and almost inflicted a terminal disaster on all of them.[431] The king's cavalry line was routed, the wings put to flight, the cohorts forced to retreat; there was even trepidation among the legionary standards. But the prowess of the Roman soldier claimed more glory on that occasion than it left for its leaders, who, very different from the custom of their commander, encountered the enemy before they could know from scouts where the enemy was. In the uncertain circumstances, therefore, the legions now encouraged themselves, and—with some military tribunes slaughtered by the enemy, a camp prefect and some prefects of cohorts killed, and casualties among the centurions, of whom even some first ranks fell—they attacked the enemy and, not content at merely withstanding them, burst through their battle line and wrested from the hopeless situation a victorious result.

This was about the time that Agrippa, who had been adopted by his natural grandfather on the same day as Tiberius[432] and who already, two years beforehand, had begun to show what he was like, took a headlong turn for the worse on account of a remarkable perversion of mind and temperament: he alienated the feelings of his father

431 A. Caecina Severus (cos. suff. 1 BC) was governor of Moesia; M. Plautius Silvanus (cos. 2 BC) had been operating in Galatia. Rhoemetalces was brother of Rhascupolis (129.1n).

432 See 104.1.

299

VELLEIUS PATERCULUS

dem avi sui animum alienavit sibi, moxque crescentibus in dies vitiis dignum furore suo habuit exitum.

113. Accipe nunc, M. Vinici, tantum in bello ducem quantum in pace vides principem.[705] iunctis exercitibus, quique sub Caesare fuerant quique ad eum venerant, contractisque in una castra decem legionibus, LXX amplius cohortibus, †XIIII sed†[706] pluribus quam decem veteranorum milibus, ad hoc magno voluntariorum numero frequentique equite regio, tanto denique exercitu quantus nullo umquam loco post bella fuerat civilia, omnes eo ipso laeti erant maximamque fiduciam victoriae in numero 2 reponebant. at imperator, optimus eorum quae agebat iudex et utilia speciosis praeferens, quodque semper eum facientem vidi in omnibus bellis, quae probanda essent, non quae utique probarentur sequens, paucis diebus exercitum qui venerat ad refovendas ex itinere eius vires moratus, cum eum maiorem quam ut temperari posset neque 3 habilem gubernaculo cerneret, dimittere statuit; prosecutusque longo et perquam laborioso itinere (cuius difficultas narrari vix potest) ut neque universos quisquam auderet adgredi et partem digredientium, suorum quisque metu finium, universi temptare non possent, remisit eo unde venerant; et ipse asperrimae hiemis initio regres-

---

[705] vides principem *BA*: vides. principes *P*

[706] XIIII sed *PA^c* (XIIII set *A*), *obelis not. Woodman*: XIIII ⟨ali⟩s et *Lipsius*: X alis et *Laurent*

---

[433] Agrippa Postumus was banished to the island of Planasia in AD 7, the current narrative year, although many scholars think that V. is referring ahead to his murder in AD 14.

BOOK 2.112–13

(who was also his grandfather) and subsequently, as his flaws increased from day to day, he ended up as his madness deserved.[433]

113. Attend now, Marcus Vinicius, to as great a leader in war as you see in peace as *princeps*. The armies had linked up, both that which had been under Caesar and that which had come to him, and assembled into a single camp were ten legions, more than seventy cohorts †. . .† more than ten thousand veterans;[434] in addition there was a large number of volunteers and a full complement of royal cavalry—in short, a greater army than had ever been in one place since the civil wars, and all of them were delighted at the fact, their confidence in victory reposing mostly in their numbers. But the commander—the best judge of what he was doing, preferring the practical to the impressive, and (as I have always seen him doing in every war) following a course that demanded approval rather than one that would meet with approval regardless— waited a few days to allow the incoming army to recover its strength after its journey, and then, since he realized that it was too large to be maneuvered and would be unresponsive to the helm, he decided to send it back; and, having escorted it on its long and extremely laborious journey (whose difficulty can scarcely be described) in such a way that no one dared to attack its united front but neither were the enemy (each of them afraid for his own territory) able to make a united attempt on a division of those departing, Caesar returned the army to where it had come from. He himself went back to Siscia at the beginning of

[434] Some think that the corrupt passage contained a reference to cavalry wings.

301

VELLEIUS PATERCULUS

sus Sisciam[707] legatos, inter quos ipsi fuimus, partitis prae-
fecit hibernis.

114. O rem dictu non eminentem, sed solida veraque
virtute atque utilitate maximam, experientia suavissimam,
humanitate singularem! per omne belli Germanici Panno-
nicique tempus nemo e nobis gradumve nostrum aut prae-
cedentibus aut sequentibus imbecillus fuit cuius salus ac
valetudo non ita sustentaretur Caesaris cura tamquam
districtissimus[708] ille tantorum onerum mole huic uni
2   negotio[709] vacaret animus. erat desiderantibus paratum
iunctum vehiculum, lectica eius publicata, cuius ‹usum›[710]
cum alii tum ego sensi; iam medici, iam apparatus cibi, iam
‹tamquam›[711] in hoc solum portatum instrumentum bali-
nei nullius non succurrit valetudini: domus tantum ac
domestici deerant, ceterum nihil quod ab illis aut praestari
3   aut desiderari posset. adiiciam illud quod quisquis illis
temporibus interfuit, ut alia quae rettuli, agnoscet protinus: solus semper equo vectus est, solus cum iis quos
invitaverat maiore parte aestivarum expeditionum cenavit
sedens. non sequentibus disciplinam, quatenus exemplo
non nocebatur, ignovit: admonitio frequens, interdum[712]
castigatio, vindicta rarissima, agebatque medium plurima
dissimulantis, aliqua inhibentis.

[707] Sisciam *B*: Sistiam *P*: Sisci iam *A*
[708] districtissimus *Bentley*: distraximus *PA*
[709] uni negotio *Gelenius*: uni genitio *B*: unigenito *A*: uni *P*
[710] *suppl. Lipsius*
[711] *suppl. Woodman*
[712] interdum *nescioquis anno 1779*: inerat *PA*: infrequens
Watt

302

BOOK 2.113–14

a very harsh winter, after subdividing the winter quarters and putting legates (of whom I was one) in charge of them.

114. Now for something that is not outstanding to relate but is of the greatest importance for its solid and real excellence and practicality, sweet to experience and singular in its humanity. During the whole period of the German and Pannonian War, not one of us—nor any of those above or below us in rank—was ill without his well-being and health receiving the support of a concerned Caesar, as if that mind of his, though preoccupied with the burdensome responsibility of great tasks, had time for this one matter alone. His two-horse carriage was readied for those in need, his litter made available (the use of which I experienced, as did others); now it was his doctors, now his field kitchen, now his bathing equipment (carried as if for this very purpose) that came to the aid of everyone's health: only one's house and household were missing, but nothing else that they could provide or need. I shall add something that, like the other things I record, will be recognized immediately by anyone who was there at the time: he alone always rode on horseback, he alone dined sitting, along with those he had invited, for the greater part of the summer campaigns.[435] He pardoned those who did not follow discipline, as long as no harmful precedent was set; warnings were frequent, occasionally a reprimand, punishment very rare; and he drove a middle course of disregarding most things while preventing some others.

[435] Unlike other generals, he neither relied on a carriage nor reclined at meals; sitting was regarded as old-fashioned (Isid. *Orig.* 20.11.9) and thus morally superior.

303

VELLEIUS PATERCULUS

4   Hiems emolumentum patrati belli contulit,[713] et[714] insequenti aestate omnis Pannonia reliquiis totius belli in Dalmatia manentibus pacem petiit. ferocem illam tot milium iuventutem, paulo ante servitutem minatam Italiae, conferentem arma quibus usa erat apud flumen nomine Bathinum prosternentemque se universam genibus imperatoris, Batonemque et Pinnetem excelsissimos duces, captum alterum, ⟨alterum⟩[715] a se deditum iustis voluminibus ordine narrabimus, ut spero.

5   Autumni ⟨initio⟩[716] victor in hiberna reducitur exercitus, cuius omnibus copiis ⟨a⟩[717] Caesare M.[718] Lepidus praefectus est, vir nomini ac fortunae Caesarum[719] proximus, quem in quantum quisque aut cognoscere aut intellegere potuit, in tantum miratur ac diligit, tantorumque nominum quibus ortus est ornamentum iudicat. 115. Caesar ad alteram belli Dalmatici molem animum atque arma contulit; in qua regione quali adiutore legatoque fratre meo Magio Celere Velleiano[720] usus sit, ipsius patrisque eius praedicatione testatum est et amplissimorum hono-

713 contulit *PA*: non tulit *Friebel*: distulit *Watt*
714 et *Lipsius*: sed *PA*
715 *suppl. Rhenanus*
716 *suppl. Ellis*
717 *suppl. Rhenanus*
718 Caesare *Rhenanus,* M. *Burer*: Caesarem *PA*
719 Caesarum *Scheffer*: eorum *PA*
720 Velleiano *Gelenius*: ulli flano *P*: ulliflano *A*

---

436 If the transmitted text is right, V.'s statement leaves it unclear how the winter contributed to the conclusion of the war, since no campaigning is mentioned (contrast AD 4 at 105.3);

BOOK 2.114–15

The winter conferred the benefit of the war's conclusion,[436] and in the following summer season, although in Dalmatia there remained remnants of the war as a whole, all Pannonia sued for peace. In my properly sized volumes I shall, I hope, describe in detail the thousands of defiant young men (who only a little before had threatened Italy with slavery) at the river called the Bathinus piling up the weapons they had used, and all of them prostrating themselves at the commander's knees, and also Bato and Pinnes, most exalted of leaders, the one a captive, the other having surrendered.

At the beginning of autumn the victorious army was led back to its winter quarters. In charge of all its forces Caesar placed Marcus Lepidus, a man very close to the name and fortune of the Caesars and one for whom people have admiration and affection to the same degree that they have been able to get to know and understand him, judging him an adornment of the great names from which he is sprung.[437] 115. Caesar transferred his attention and armed forces to his other burdensome responsibility, the Dalmatian War. The kind of help he had in that region from my brother Magius Celer Velleianus, his legate, has been attested in the commendation from himself and his father

perhaps the Pannonians' morale collapsed after Tiberius' skillful show of force on the march back (113.3).

[437] M. Aemilius Lepidus (cos. AD 6) was the son of Paullus Aemilius Lepidus (95.3n). His brother, L. Aemilius Paullus (cos. AD 1), was married to Augustus' grand-daughter Julia and shared in her disgrace. Lepidus' son and daughter both married children of Germanicus. On Lepidus and his family, see Syme (1986, 104–40 and Table IV).

305

VELLEIUS PATERCULUS

rum quibus triumphans eum Caesar donavit signat memoria.

2 Initio aestatis Lepidus educto hibernis exercitu per gentes integras immunesque adhuc clade belli et eo feroces ac truces tendens ad Tiberium imperatorem et cum difficultate locorum et cum vi hostium luctatus, magna cum clade obsistentium excisis agris, exustis aedificiis, caesis viris, laetus victoria praedaque onustus pervenit ad

3 Caesarem, et ob ea, quae si propriis gessisset auspiciis, triumphare debuerat, ornamentis triumphalibus consentiente cum iudicio principum voluntate senatus ‹donatus›[721] est.

4 Illa aestas maximi belli consummauit effectus:[722] quippe Perustae, Daesitiates,[723] Dalmatae situ locorum ac montium, ingeniorum ferocia, mira etiam pugnandi scientia et praecipue angustiis saltuum paene inexpugnabiles, non iam ductu sed manibus atque armis ipsius Caesaris tum demum pacati sunt, cum paene funditus eversi forent.

5 Nihil in hoc tanto bello, nihil in Germania aut videre maius aut mirari magis potui quam quod imperatori numquam adeo ulla opportuna visa est victoriae occasio quam

[721] *suppl. Rhenanus*
[722] effectum *Watt*
[723] Perustae ac *Vossius* (ac *om. P. M. Swan*), Desitiates *Gelenius*: Perusia aede siciales *P*: perusia aedesitiales *A*

---

[438] Tiberius' triumph for his exploits in Illyricum was delayed until (probably) AD 12 (121.2n).
[439] In AD 9.

306

BOOK 2.115

and is stamped in the record of the very full honors with which Caesar presented him at his triumph.[438]

At the beginning of the summer season[439] Lepidus led out his army from its winter quarters to make his way to Tiberius, his commander, through peoples still untouched and unscathed by the disaster of war and hence defiant and brutal; and, contending with difficult localities and violent enemies, he effected considerable destruction of those standing in his way—laying waste the land, burning buildings, and slaying men—and, happy with his victory and laden with plunder, he reached Caesar. For these exploits (for which, if he had carried them out under his own auspices, he ought to have triumphed) he was presented with the triumphal insignia, the will of the senate coinciding with the judgment of each *princeps*.[440]

That summer season concluded the execution of this greatest of wars. It was only after the Perustae, Daesitiates, and Dalmatians—almost unassailable thanks to the siting of their mountain locations, their defiance of character, as well as their remarkable knowledge of fighting and especially the narrowness of their defiles—had been overthrown almost completely that they were pacified at last, no longer simply under Caesar's leadership but with the active and armed participation of the man himself.

There was nothing more important in this great war, nothing in Germany, that I could see or admire more than the fact that no opportunity of victory ever seemed at all favorable to the commander if the cost was the loss of his

440 That is, Tiberius as well as Augustus: *princeps* can be used of other leading members of the imperial family besides the emperor.

307

VELLEIUS PATERCULUS

damno amissi pensaret militis, semperque visum est glo-
riosum quod esset tutissimum, et ante conscientiae quam
famae consultum nec umquam[724] consilia ducis iudicio
exercitus, sed exercitus providentia ducis rectus est.

116. Magna in bello Dalmatico experimenta virtutis in
multos ac difficiles locos praemissus Germanicus dedit;
2 celebri etiam opera diligentique Vibius Postumus,[725] vir
consularis, praepositus Dalmatiae, ornamenta meruit triumphalia. (quem honorem ante paucos annos Passienus
et Cossus, viri quibusdam[726] diversi,[727] virtutibus celebres,
in Africa meruerant; sed Cossus victoriae testimonium
etiam in cognomen filii contulit, adulescentis in omnium
3 virtutum exempla geniti.) at Postumi operum L. Apronius
particeps illa quoque militia eos quos mox consecutus est
honores excellenti virtute meruit.

Utinam non maioribus experimentis testatum esset
quantum in omni re Fortuna posset, sed in hoc[728] quoque
genere abunde agnosci vis eius potest. nam et Aelius La-

[724] nec umquam *P*: ne cum quod *B*: necum quod *A*
[725] diligentique *Vossius,* Vibius Postumus *Pighi*: diligenti
quib. ius postumus *A*: diligenti quibus Iulius Posthumius *P*: Iul.
Postumus *B*
[726] quibusdam *PA*: quamvis *Bothe*: *alii alia*
[727] diversi *Walter*: -is *PA*   [728] hoc *Gelenius*: loco *PA*

---

[441] The latter seems a statement of the obvious, but perhaps
V. had in mind the recent case of the treasonous Piso (130.3n),
"who had corrupted military discipline . . . by indulging the soldiers so that they would not obey their superiors" (*SCPP*, 52–54).

[442] C. Vibius Postumus (cos. suff. AD 5), first governor of
Dalmatia, was later proconsul of Asia (12–15).

308

BOOK 2.115–16

soldiers, and that he considered the glorious course to be that which was safest. His conscience took precedence over his reputation, and the plans of the leader were never guided by the judgment of the army but the army by the foresight of the leader.[441]

116. In the Dalmatian War Germanicus was sent ahead into many difficult places and gave great proof of his prowess. Also Vibius Postumus, the ex-consul in charge of Dalmatia, earned the triumphal insignia for his celebrated and diligent efforts.[442] (This honor had been earned in Africa a few years before by Passienus and Cossus, men as different in some respects as celebrated in prowess; but Cossus by means of his cognomen also conferred the evidence of his victory on his son, a young man born to exemplify every virtue.)[443] Lucius Apronius, a participant in Postumus' exploits, deserved for his outstanding prowess in that campaign too the honors he won later.[444]

Would that lesser proofs had demonstrated the extent of Fortune's influence in every respect, but in this area too her power can be amply identified. Aelius Lamia, a man

[443] L. Passienus Rufus (cos. 4 BC) was proconsul of Africa in AD 3 to 5 and was succeeded by Cossus Cornelius Lentulus (cos. 1 BC), who celebrated a victory over the Gaetulians in AD 6; the resulting cognomen "Gaetulicus" was acquired by his younger son, Cn. Cornelius Lentulus Gaetulicus (cos. AD 26), whereas Passienus' son (cos. suff. AD 27) had acquired his current name (C. Sallustius Crispus Passienus) through adoption by Augustus' minister Sallustius Crispus: this explains V.'s contrast between the two men ("but Cossus . . .").

[444] L. Apronius (cos. suff. AD 8) was proconsul of Africa from AD 18 to 20, when he won the triumphal insignia for fighting Tacfarinas.

309

VELLEIUS PATERCULUS

mia,[729] vir antiquissimi moris et priscam gravitatem semper humanitate temperans, in Germania Illyricoque et mox in Africa splendidissimis functus ministeriis, non merito sed materia adipiscendi triumphalia defectus est; 4 et A. Licinius Nerva Silianus, P. Silii filius, quem virum ne qui intellexit quidem abunde miratus est, [ne][730] nihil ⟨quod⟩ non[731] optimo civi,[732] simplicissimo duci par esset[733] praeferens, immatura ⟨morte⟩[734] et fructu amplissimae principis amicitiae et consummatione evectae in altissimum paternumque fastigium imaginis defectus est. 5 horum[735] virorum mentioni si quis quaesisse me dicet locum, fatentem arguet: neque enim iustus sine mendacio candor apud bonos crimini est.

117. Tantum quod ultimam imposuerat Pannonico ac Dalmatico bello Caesar manum, cum intra quinque consummati tanti operis dies funestae ex Germania epistulae caesi Vari trucidatarumque legionum trium totidemque alarum et sex cohortium ***,[736] velut in hoc saltem tantummodo indulgente nobis Fortuna, ne occupato duce[737] *** et causa ⟨et⟩[738] persona moram exigit.

---

[729] Aelius Lamia *Ruhnken*: etiam *PA*   [730] ne *PB, secl. Cludius*: me *A*   [731] nihil non *BA*: nihil *P* (quod *post* nihil *suppl. Woodman, post* non *Halm*)   [732] optimo civi *PB*: optimos civis *A*   [733] par esset *Woodman*: perisset *PBA*: superesset *P. Thomas*: superesse *Ellis*: alii alia   [734] *suppl. Orelli*   [735] horum *Burer*: honorum *BA*: quorum *P stat. edd.*   [736] *lac. hic et mox*   [737] duce *Gelenius*: -em *PA*   [738] *suppl. Lipsius*

---

[445] L. Aelius Lamia (cos. AD 3) was governor of Africa AD 15/16 or 16/17; his activities in Germany and Illyricum are unknown.

310

BOOK 2.116–17

of antique habits yet always moderating his old-fashioned gravity with humanity, performed shining service in Germany and Illyricum and later in Africa, but despite his deserts he was deprived of the opportunity for acquiring the insignia.[445] And Aulus Licinius Nerva Silianus, Publius Silius' son—a man not adequately admired even by anyone that understood him, and who displayed nothing that did not match up to the very good citizen and very straightforward leader that he was—was deprived by his premature death both of the fruits of the *princeps'* unreserved friendship and of completing an image as elevated as the very high level set by his father.[446] If anyone says that I have sought out an opportunity to mention these men, his accusation will be met by my admission: among good people, justified kindness without falsehood is no crime.

117. Caesar had only just put the final touch on the Pannonian and Dalmatian War when, within five days of his completing this substantial task, doom-laden letters from Germany *** about the slaying of Varus and the butchery of three legions, as many wings, and six cohorts—Fortune seeming to indulge us at least in one respect, that it was not when the leader was preoccupied that ***.[447] Dwelling on the character responsible is called for.

[446] Nerva Silianus (cos. suff. AD 7) was the son of P. Silius Nerva (101.3n).

[447] The first lacuna could be filled by, e.g., "brought news," the second by, e.g., "the disaster was learned of." The disaster, one of the worst in Roman history, took place in AD 9; its location is now generally thought to have been Kalkriese, just north of Osnabrück in the northwest of Germany (*BA* 10: E4).

311

VELLEIUS PATERCULUS

2   Varus Quintilius, inlustri magis quam nobili[739] ortus
familia, vir ingenio mitis, moribus quietus, ut corpore et[740]
animo immobilior, otio magis castrorum quam bellicae
adsuetus militiae, pecuniae vero quam non contemptor
Syria (cui praefuerat) declaravit, quam pauper divitem
3 ingressus dives pauperem reliquit,—is cum exercitui qui
erat in Germania praeesset, concepit esse homines qui
nihil praeter vocem membraque habent[741] hominum, qui-
4 que gladiis domari non poterant posse iure mulceri. quo
proposito mediam ingressus Germaniam, velut inter viros
pacis gaudentes dulcedine iurisdictionibus agendoque pro
tribunali ordine trahebat aestiua. 118. at illi (quod nisi
expertus vix credat[742]) in summa feritate versutissimi natumque mendacio genus, simulantes fictas litium series
et nunc provocantes[743] alter alterum in iurgia,[744] nunc
agentes gratias quod ea Romana iustitia finiret feritasque
sua novitate incognitae disciplinae mitesceret[745] et solita
armis decerni[746] iure terminarentur, in summam socor-
diam perduxere Quintilium, usque eo ut se praetorem

    [739] nobili . . . inlustri *Ruhnken*
    [740] ut . . . et *PA*: et . . . et *Rhenanus*: ut . . . ita *Bucretius*
    [741] habent *Cludius*: -erent *PA*: -ebant *Cornelissen*
    [742] credat *Lipsius*: credebat *PA*
    [743] provocantes *Rhenanus et sub litura A*: "procaces in exem-
plari" A^{mg}: procaces *P*: procataes *B*
    [744] in iurgia *Madvig*: iniuria *PA*
    [745] mitesceret PA^c: mut- *BA*
    [746] decerni *Gelenius*: dis- *PA*

---

    [448] P. Quin(c)tilius Varus had been consul with Tiberius in 13
BC, proconsul of Africa ca. 8/7 BC, and legate of Syria from 7 to

BOOK 2.117–18

Varus Quintilius, sprung from an illustrious rather than a noble family, was of mild disposition and quiet habits, rather passive both physically and mentally, and more suited to the inactivity of camp than to warlike campaigning.[448] The degree to which he lacked any contempt for money was made clear in Syria, where he had been in charge: he entered the rich province a poor man, but on leaving he was rich and the province poor. When he was in charge of the army in Germany, he conceived the notion that those who have nothing human about them, save voice and limbs, were human, and that those who could not be tamed by the sword could be made mild by the law. It was with the latter intention that he entered central Germany, and he whiled away the campaigning season with a succession of assizes and official cases, as if among men who rejoiced in the sweetness of peace. 118. But—and this is scarcely credible unless one has experienced it—they are highly cunning despite their extreme wildness, a race of born liars, and, feigning a series of fictitious disputes (now challenging each other to quarrels, now giving thanks that Roman justice was settling them, that their normal wildness was softening under the novelty of an unfamiliar discipline, and that matters customarily decided with weapons were being concluded by law), they brought Quintilius to such a point of inattention that he

4 BC. He became consular legate in Germany in AD 6 or 7. The Quin(c)tilii were patricians and had achieved consular positions in the fifth century BC, but subsequently had not risen above the praetorship: there are thus arguments in favor of both the transmitted text and Ruhnken's transposition.

313

VELLEIUS PATERCULUS

urbanum in foro ius dicere, non in mediis Germaniae finibus exercitui praeesse crederet.

2 Tum iuvenis genere nobilis, manu fortis, sensu celer, ultra barbarum promptus ingenio, nomine Arminius, Sigimeri principis gentis eius filius, ardorem animi vultu oculisque praeferens, adsiduus militiae nostrae prioris comes, iure[747] etiam civitatis Romanae ius[748] equestris consequens[749] gradus, segnitia ducis in occasionem sceleris usus est, haud imprudenter speculatus ***[750] neminem celerius opprimi quam qui nihil timeret, et frequentissimum initium esse calamitatis securitatem.

3 Primo igitur paucos, mox plures in societatem consilii recepit;[751] opprimi posse Romanos et dicit et persuadet,
4 decretis facta iungit, tempus insidiarum constituit. id Varo per virum eius gentis fidelem clarique nominis, Segesten, indicatur; postulabat etiam **[752] Fata consiliis omnemque animi eius aciem praestrinxerant:[753] quippe ita se res habet ut plerumque cuius[754] fortunam mutaturus ⟨est⟩[755]

747 ⟨cum⟩ iure *Heinsius*
748 Romanae ius *Burer*: Romae ius *P*: Roma eius *A*
749 consecutus *Gelenius*
750 *lacunam stat. Woodman*
751 societatem . . . recepit *Rhenanus*: -e . . . praecepit *PA*
752 *lacunam stat. Ellis*
753 praestrinxerant *Gelenius*: -struxerat *PA*
754 cuius *ed. Bipont.*: qui *PA*: cui *Vossius*
755 *suppl. ed. Bipont.*

449 Arminius is commemorated by the famous Hermannsdenkmal (Hermann Monument), erected in the nineteenth century in North Rhine-Westphalia in Germany.

314

BOOK 2.118

believed he was in the forum administering justice as urban praetor, not in the middle of German territory in charge of an army.

There was at the time a young man of noble lineage, physically brave and intellectually alert, and more energetic in temperament than the usual barbarian—Arminius by name, son of the principal figure of that people, Sigimerus.[449] Exhibiting hotheadedness in his eyes and look, he had been a constant companion of ours in our earlier campaigning and had acquired the prerogative of equestrian rank by virtue of Roman citizenship. He now turned the leader's negligence into a criminal opportunity, very prudently looking out for ***[450] that no one was more quickly taken by surprise than the man who feared nothing, and that a sense of security was the most frequent starting point for disaster.

He therefore admitted others—at first only a few, and then more later—to partnership in his plan. No sooner had he spoken to them than they were persuaded that the Romans could be taken by surprise; he matched his decisions with action; and he set a time for the ambush. Varus was informed of all this by a loyalist from their people, a man of distinguished name—Segestes. He also demanded ***[451] judgment from the Fates, who had blunted all his mental sharpness: for it is the case that a god generally spoils the judgment of one whose fortune he is about

[450] The lacuna perhaps contained words to the effect "the right moment and declaring."

[451] The lacuna may be filled from Tac. *Ann.* 1.55.2 and 58.2 with some such words as these: "of Varus that the accessories be shackled, but there was interference with the latter's."

315

VELLEIUS PATERCULUS

deus, consilia corrumpat, efficiatque (quod miserrimum
est) ut quod accidit ei etiam[756] merito accidisse videatur,
et casus in culpam[757] transeat. negat itaque se credere
speciemque[758] in se benevolentiae ex merito aestimare
profitetur. nec diutius post primum indicem secundo re-
lictus locus.

119. Ordinem atrocissimae calamitatis, qua[759] nulla
post Crassi[760] in Parthis damnum in externis gentibus gravior Romanis fuit, iustis voluminibus ut alii ita nos cona-
2 bimur exponere; nunc summa deflenda est. exercitus
omnium fortissimus, disciplina, manu experientiaque bellorum inter Romanos milites princeps, marcore ducis,
perfidia hostis, iniquitate Fortunae circumventus, cum ne
pugnandi quidem egrediendive occasio iis,[761] in quantum
voluerant,[762] data esset immunis,[763] castigatis etiam quibusdam gravi poena quia Romanis et armis et animis usi
fuissent, inclusus silvis, paludibus,[764] insidiis ab eo hoste
ad internecionem trucidatus est quem ita semper more
pecudum trucidaverat ut vitam aut mortem eius nunc ira
3 nunc venia temperaret. duci plus ad moriendum quam ad
pugnandum animi fuit: quippe paterni avitique[765] succes-
4 sor exempli se ipse transfixit. at e praefectis castrorum

---

[756] ei etiam *Kritz*: et etiam *BA*: etiam *P*

[757] culpam *P*: -a *BA*

[758] speciemque *Burman*: spemque *PA*

[759] qua *PB*: quae *A*   [760] Crassi *P*: Cassi *BA*

[761] egrediendive occasio iis *Vossius*: egregie *(sed prius* egre-
die *A*: egrediē *B)* aut occasionis *PA*   [762] in quantum voluerant *secl. Gruter*   [763] immunis *plerisque suspectum*

[764] paludibus *Gelenius*: -dis *PA*

[765] avitique *P*: avique *BA*

316

BOOK 2.118–19

to change, and ensures (and this is the most wretched thing) that what happens to him seems actually to have happened deservedly, and contingency is transformed into culpability. So Varus refused to believe it, and declared that he deserved to take at face value the goodwill toward himself. And after this first informant no further opening was left for a second.

119. Details of this most fearful disaster—which among foreign peoples was more serious to the Romans than any other after the loss of Crassus in Parthia[452]—we, like others, shall try to set out in properly sized volumes; now it is the sum total that must be lamented. An army that was the bravest of all, the first among Roman soldiers for its discipline, muscle, and warlike experience, was surrounded, thanks to the apathy of its leader, the treachery of the enemy, and the iniquity of Fortune. They had no free opportunity, to the extent that they would have wished, even to fight or move out (some too were punished with a heavy penalty because they had relied on the weaponry and spirit of true Romans),[453] but, hemmed in by woods, marshes, and the ambush, the army was butchered to the point of annihilation by an enemy whom it had always butchered like sheep and whose life or death would depend on the anger or forgiveness of the moment. The leader had more spirit for dying than for fighting: following the example of his father and grandfather,[454] he ran himself through. As for the two camp prefects, the distin-

[452] See 46.3–4, above.

[453] The text here is uncertain and the meaning obscure.

[454] For his father see 71.3, above; nothing is known of his grandfather's suicide.

317

VELLEIUS PATERCULUS

duobus quam clarum exemplum L. Eggius,[766] tam turpe
Ceionius prodidit, qui, cum longe maximam partem ab-
sumpsisset acies, auctor deditionis supplicio quam proelio
mori maluit. at Vala Numonius,[767] legatus Vari, cetera
quietus ac probus, diri auctor exempli, spoliatum equite[768]
peditem relinquens fuga cum alis[769] Rhenum petere ingressus est; quod factum eius Fortuna ulta est: non enim
5 desertis superfuit sed desertor occidit.[770] Vari corpus se-
miustum hostium[771] laceraverat feritas; caput eius abscisum latumque ad Maroboduum et ab eo missum ad Caesarem gentilicii tamen[772] tumuli sepultura honoratum est.

120. His auditis[773] revolat ad patrem Caesar: perpetuus
patronus Romani imperii adsuetam sibi causam suscipit.
mittitur ad Germaniam, Gallias confirmat, disponit exercitus, praesidia munit, se magnitudine sua non fiducia hostium metiens qui Cimbricam Teutonicamque militiam
Italiae minabantur.[774] ultro[775] Rhenum cum exercitu
2 transgreditur ⟨et⟩[776] arma infert[777] quae arcuisse[778] pater
et patria contenti erant: penetrat interius, aperit limites,
vastat agros, urit domos, fundit obvios,[779] maximaque cum
gloria, incolumi omnium quos transduxerat numero, in
hiberna revertitur.

[766] *post* Eggius *lacunam tent. Delz*   [767] Vala Numonius
Ursinus: Valnumonius *PA*   [768] equite *Gelenius*: -em *PA*

[769] alis *Gelenius*: aliis *PBA*   [770] *post* occidit *transposuit*
Reddatur . . . exspiraret *(120.3–6) Delz*   [771] hostium *P*: -ti *BA*

[772] tandem *Gelenius*   [773] His auditis . . . revertitur *post*
expiraret *(120.6) transposuit Haase*   [774] minabantur *P*: -batur
BA   [775] ultra *P*   [776] *suppl. Woodman*

[777] infert *Lipsius*: interfecti *PA* (infert hosti quem arcuisse
Vossius)   [778] arcuisse *Lipsius*: arg- *PA*   [779] obvios *P*:
obulos *BA*

318

BOOK 2.119–20

guished example shown by Lucius Eggius was matched by the disgraceful one of Ceionius, who, after by far the greatest part of the army had been taken off in the battle line, instigated a surrender, preferring to die by torture than fighting. As for Vala Numonius, the otherwise quiet and upright legate of Varus, he instigated a terrible example: leaving the infantry denuded of cavalry, he started to make for the Rhine, fleeing at the head of the wings.[455] But Fortune avenged his action, because he did not survive those whom he had deserted but died a deserter himself. Varus' half-burned body was mauled by the enemy, wild as ever: his head was cut off and carried to Maroboduus and sent on by him to Caesar; it was nevertheless honored with burial in the family tomb.

120. On hearing of these events, Caesar flew back to his father, and the perennial patron of the Roman Empire took up the cause to which he was accustomed. He was sent to Germany, consolidated the provinces of Gaul, deployed armies, and fortified strongholds, measuring himself by his own greatness and not by trust in an enemy who was threatening Italy with a campaign like that of the Cimbri and Teutoni.[456] He took the initiative in crossing the Rhine with his army and in going on the offensive in a war that his father and fatherland had been content merely to have fended off. He penetrated into the interior, opened up trackways, laid waste territory, burned homes, routed opposition, and, given that the entire number of those whom he had transported[457] was unscathed, returned to winter quarters in the greatest glory.

[455] A "wing" (*ala*) was a unit of cavalry.
[456] See 2.8.3, 12.2, 12.4, above.
[457] That is, across the Rhine.

319

VELLEIUS PATERCULUS

3   Reddatur verum L. Asprenati testimonium, qui legatus sub avunculo suo Varo militans gnava virilique opera duarum legionum quibus praeerat exercitum immunem tanta calamitate servavit, matureque ad inferiora hiberna descendendo vacillantium etiam cis Rhenum[780] sitarum gentium animos confirmavit. sunt tamen qui, ut vivos ab eo vindicatos, ita iugulatorum sub Varo occupata crediderint patrimonia hereditatemque occisi exercitus, in quantum 4 voluerit,[781] ab eo aditam. L. etiam Caedicii praefecti castrorum eorumque qui una circumdati Alisone immensis Germanorum copiis obsidebantur laudanda virtus est, qui omnibus difficultatibus superatis quas inopia rerum intolerabiles, vis hostium faciebat inexsuperabiles, nec temerario consilio nec segni providentia[782] victi,[783] speculatique opportunitatem, ferro sibi ad suos peperere reditum. 5 ex quo apparet Varum, sane gravem et bonae voluntatis virum, magis imperatoris defectum consilio quam virtute destitutum militum se magnificentissimumque perdidisse 6 exercitum. cum in captivos saeviretur a Germanis, praeclari facinoris auctor fuit Caldus Coelius,[784] ad[785] vetustatem[786] familiae suae dignissimus, qui complexus catenarum quibus vinctus erat seriem ita illas inlisit capiti suo ut protinus pariter sanguinis cerebrique effluvio[787] expiraret.

---

    [780] Rhenum *Gelenius*: -o *PA*   [781] valuerit *Lipsius*
    [782] providentia *BP*: prud- *A*   [783] victi *E. Thomas*: viti *B*: usi *P*: niti *A*   [784] Coelius *A*: Caelius *P*
    [785] ad *PA*: ad⟨ulescens⟩ *Ruhnken*   [786] vetustate *Gelenius*
    [787] effluvio *Lipsius*: influvio *P*: in fluvio *A*

---

    [458] L. Nonius Asprenas had been suffect consul in AD 6. See also Syme (1986, Table XXVI).

BOOK 2.120

Proper testimony must be rendered to Lucius Aspre-nas, who, campaigning as legate under Varus, his uncle, by assiduous and virile effort kept the army of two legions of which he was in charge safe from the great disaster; and, by traveling down quickly to the lower winter quarters, he bolstered the spirits even of the peoples situated on this side of the Rhine, who were wavering.[458] There are nevertheless those who believed that, although he protected the living, he appropriated the patrimonies of those slaughtered under Varus and came into as many inheritances from the slain army as he wished. Also to be praised is the courage of Lucius Caedicius, camp prefect, and of those surrounded with him at Aliso who were being besieged by huge forces of Germans: having overcome all the difficulties that the shortage of provisions made intolerable and that the strength of the enemy made insuperable, defeated neither by rash planning nor by a cowardly prudence, they looked out for their chance and by means of the sword procured for themselves a return to their own side. From this it is clear that Varus, albeit a serious and well-intentioned man, was failed by his judgment as a commander rather than forsaken by the courage of his soldiers, destroying himself and his magnificent army. When the Germans were practicing their savagery on their captives, an outstanding deed was performed by Caldus Coelius, who was thoroughly worthy of his ancient family: gripping the linked chains with which he had been bound, he dashed them against his head with such force that he expired immediately from the simultaneous emission of blood and brain.

321

VELLEIUS PATERCULUS

121. Eadem et virtus et fortuna subsequenti tempore ingressi Germaniam[788] imperatoris Tiberii fuit quae initio fuerat. qui, concussis hostium viribus classicis peditumque expeditionibus, cum res Galliarum maximae molis accensaque plebe[789] Viennensium dissensiones coercitione magis quam poena mollisset, senatus populusque Romanus postulante patre eius ut aequum ei ius[790] in omnibus provinciis exercitibusque esset quam erat ipsi decreto complexus est.[791] etenim absurdum erat non esse sub illo quae

2 ab illo vindicabantur, et qui ad opem ferendam primus erat ad vindicandum honorem non iudicari parem.

In urbem reversus iam pridem debitum, sed continuatione bellorum dilatum, ex Pannoniis Dalmatisque egit triumphum. cuius magnificentiam quis miretur in Caesare? Fortunae vero quis non miretur indulgentiam?

3 quippe omnes eminentissimos hostium duces non occisos fama narravit sed vinctos triumphus ostendit (quem mihi[792] fratrique meo inter praecipuos praecipuisque donis adornatos viros comitari contigit). 122. quis non inter reliqua quibus singularis moderatio Ti. Caesaris elucet atque eminet, hoc quoque miretur quod, cum sine ulla dubitatione septem triumphos meruerit, tribus contentus

---

[788] ingressi Germaniam *Bardili*: ingressa animam (-um *P*) *PBA*

[789] accensaque plebe *A*: accensaque plebis *B*: accensasque plebis *P*: accensaeque plebis *Vossius*

[790] aequum ei ius *Rhenanus*: equum eius *PA*

[791] est *Ellis*: esset *PA*

[792] mihi *Burer*: militi *PA*

BOOK 2.121–22

121. Tiberius' courage and fortune when subsequently he entered Germany as commander were the same as at the beginning: he shattered the enemy forces in naval and infantry operations, and then, by measures aimed at restraint rather than punishment, he calmed a situation of the greatest difficulty in the Gauls and dissension among the Viennenses, whose plebs were ablaze. At his father's request, the senate and Roman people effected by decree that in all provinces and armies his jurisdiction should be equal to that of himself:[459] for it would have been absurd if he did not have under him everything that he had championed, and if the first in bringing help were not judged to be comparable in claiming honor.[460]

On his return to the City he celebrated a triumph—owed to him long since but delayed by the continuing warfare—for his Pannonian and Dalmatian exploits.[461] No one would marvel at its magnificence in the case of Caesar, but who would not marvel at Fortune's indulgence of him? So far from all the most outstanding enemy leaders being reported by rumor as slain, they were displayed shackled in his triumph. (And it fell to me and my brother to be participants, among the notables and the men decorated with notable awards.) 122. And among the other areas in which Tiberius' unique moderation stands out so conspicuously, who would not marvel at this too, that, although without any doubt he deserved seven triumphs, he was

[459] That is, equal to that of Augustus. The date of the decree is uncertain, probably AD 13.

[460] The term "comparable" is not simply a synonym for "first" but implies parity with Augustus (contrast 99.1).

[461] The year was probably AD 12 (23 October).

323

VELLEIUS PATERCULUS

fuit?[793] quis enim dubitare potest quin ex Armenia recepta
et ex rege ⟨ei⟩ praeposito,[794] cuius capiti insigne regium
sua manu imposuerat, ordinatisque rebus Orientis ovans
triumphare debuerit, et Vindelicorum Raetorumque victor curru urbem ingredi? fractis deinde post adoptionem
continua triennii militia Germaniae viribus idem illi honor
et deferendus et recipiendus fuerit? et post cladem sub
Varo acceptam, totius[795] *** prosperrimo rerum eventu
eadem excisa Germania triumphus[796] summi ducis adornari[797] debuerit? sed in hoc viro nescias utrum magis mi-
reris quod laborum periculorumque semper excessit modum an quod honorum temperavit.

123. Venitur ad tempus in quo fuit plurimum metus.
quippe Caesar Augustus cum Germanicum nepotem
suum reliqua belli patraturum misisset in Germaniam,
Tiberium autem filium missurus esset in Illyricum ad firmanda[798] pace quae bello subegerat, prosequens eum simulque interfuturus athletarum certamini[799] ludicro quod
eius honori sacratum a Neapolitanis est, processit in Campaniam. quamquam iam motus imbecillitatis inclinataeque in deterius principia valetudinis senserat, tamen ob-
nitente vi animi prosecutus filium digressusque ab eo
Beneventi ipse Nolam petiit; et ingravescente in dies vale-

793 fuit *Haase*: fuerit *PA*
794 ⟨ei⟩ praeposito *Rhenanus*: praepositi *BA*: propositi *P*
795 totius *BA, post quod lacunam statuit Woodman (e.g.* ⟨mili-
tiae eius⟩): ocyus *P*: tertius *Scriner*
796 triumphus *Heinsius*: -um *PA*
797 adornari *BA*: -re *P*
798 firmanda *Burer*: formanda *PBA*
799 certamini *Cellarius*: -is *PA*

324

BOOK 2.122–23

content with three? For who can doubt that he ought to have triumphed with an ovation for the recovery of Armenia, for the installation of its king (on whose head he placed the royal diadem with his own hand), and for organizing affairs in the East? And to have entered the City by chariot as conqueror of the Vindelici and Raeti?[462] That the same honor should have been conferred on him and accepted when later, after his adoption, the forces of Germany were broken in a continuous three-year campaign? And that after the disaster suffered under Varus, when in the most successful outcome of his whole ***[463] the very same Germany was devastated, a triumph should have been laid on for the ultimate leader? But in the case of this man one does not know whether to marvel more that he has always exceeded the due limit of perilous tasks or has regulated the due number of honors.

123. We are coming to a time in which there was a great deal of dread. Caesar Augustus had sent his grandson Germanicus to Germany to finish off the remnants of the war, and he intended to send his son Tiberius to Illyricum to confirm in peace what he had subjugated in war; going with him as his escort, and with the simultaneous intention of attending the athletic competition that was consecrated to his honor by the Neapolitans, he advanced into Campania. Although he had already felt symptoms of weakness and the beginnings of a deterioration in his health, his strength of mind resisted them and, after escorting his son and leaving him at Beneventum, he made for Nola by

---

[462] The chariot symbolizes the triumph and distinguishes it from the ovation (30.2n).

[463] Perhaps supply, e.g., "military career."

325

VELLEIUS PATERCULUS

tudine, cum sciret quis volenti omnia post se salva rema-
nere accersendus foret, festinanter revocavit filium; ille ad
2 patrem [patriae][800] expectato revolavit maturius. tum se-
curum se Augustus praedicans circumfususque amplexi-
bus Tiberii sui, commendans illi sua atque ipsius opera nec
quidquam iam de fine, si Fata poscerent, recusans, subre-
fectus primo conspectu alloquioque carissimi sibi spiritus,
mox, cum omnem curam Fata vincerent, in sua resolutus
initia Pompeio Apuleioque consulibus septuagesimo et
sexto anno animam caelestem caelo[801] reddidit.

124. Quid tunc homines timuerint, quae senatus trepi-
datio, quae populi confusio, quis orbis[802] metus, in quam
arto salutis exitiique fuerimus confinio, neque mihi tam
festinanti exprimere vacat neque cui vacat potest. id solum
voce publica dixisse habeo:[803] cuius orbis ruinam timuera-
mus, eum ne commotum quidem sensimus, tantaque
unius viri maiestas fuit ut nec bonis ***[804] neque[805] contra
2 malos opus armis foret. una tamen veluti luctatio civitatis
fuit, pugnantis cum Caesare senatus populique Romani ut
stationi paternae succederet, illius ut potius aequalem civem quam eminentem liceret agere principem. tandem
magis ratione[806] quam honore victus est, cum quidquid

800 patriae *secl. Acidalius*
801 caelo *P*: deo *A*
802 orbis *P*: urbis *A*
803 ⟨satis⟩ habeo *Ruhnken*
804 *lacunam statuit Woodman*
805 neque *secl. Orelli*   806 magis ratione *BA*: r- m- *P*

---

464 Augustus died on 19 August AD 14. V. refers to his death
in terms of the Four Element Theory (see too Cass. Dio 56.41.9).

BOOK 2.123–24

himself. His health worsened from one day to the next, and, knowing whom he should summon if he wanted everything to remain sound after him, he hurriedly recalled his son; and he for his part flew back to his father more quickly than expected. Only then did Augustus pronounce himself free of care, and, clasped in the embraces of his only Tiberius, he commended to him their joint achievements and no longer raised any objection to the end, if the Fates so demanded. Though somewhat revived by the first sight and conversation of a soul so dear to him, later, when the Fates were overcoming his every concern, he was resolved into his elements and, in the consulship of Pompeius and Apuleius, in his seventy-sixth year, he rendered to heaven his heavenly spirit.[464]

124. The fears of individuals at that moment, the trepidation of the senate, the consternation of the people, the dread of the world, the very narrow margin between safety and destruction in which we found ourselves—all this, in my haste, I have no time to express, and no one who has the time has the power. With the nation's voice I have only this to say: we had feared the collapse of the world, but we felt not even a tremor, and such was one man's majesty that arms were needed neither for *** the good nor against the bad.[465] There was nevertheless one tussle (so to speak) in the community, the senate and Roman people fighting with Caesar that he should succeed to his father's post, he with them that he should be allowed the role of an equal citizen rather than that of transcendent *princeps*. At length he was defeated by reason rather than by the honor,

[465] Both text and meaning are unsure: sense would be achieved by some such insertion as "protection of."

327

VELLEIUS PATERCULUS

tuendum non suscepisset periturum videret, solique huic
contigit paene diutius recusare principatum quam, ut oc-
cuparent eum, alii armis pugnaverant.

3 Post redditum caelo patrem et corpus eius humanis
honoribus, nomen divinis honoratum, primum principalium eius operum fuit ordinatio comitiorum, quam manu
4 sua scriptam divus Augustus reliquerat. quo tempore mihi
fratrique meo, candidatis Caesaris, proxime a nobilissimis
ac sacerdotalibus[807] viris destinari praetoribus contigit,
consecutis ut neque post nos quemquam divus Augustus
neque ante nos Caesar commendaret Tiberius.

125. Tulit protinus ut voti et[808] consilii sui pretium res
publica, neque diu latuit aut quid non impetrando passuri
fuissemus aut quid impetrando profecissemus. quippe exercitus qui in Germania militabat praesentisque Germanici imperio regebatur, simulque legiones quae in Illyrico
erant, rabie quadam et profunda confundendi omnia cupi-
ditate novum ducem, novum statum, novam quaerebant
rem publicam; quin etiam ausi sunt minari daturos sena-
2 tui, daturos principi leges; modum stipendii, finem militiae sibi ipsi constituere conati sunt. processum etiam in
arma, ferrumque strictum est, et paene in ultimam[809] ‹cla-

807 sacerdotalibus *Scheffer*: sacerdotibus *PA*
808 ut . . . et *PA*: et . . . et *Gelenius*: ut . . . ita *Burman*
809 ultimam *BA*: -um *P* (in ultima *Vossius*)

---

466 After Augustus' body arrived in Rome from Nola, the senate arranged for his funeral, after which, at a further meeting on
17 September, they decreed him divine honors.

467 The elections of magistrates were transferred from the

328

BOOK 2.124–25

since he saw that whatever he did not undertake to protect would perish; and it fell to him alone to refuse the principate for almost longer than others had fought with weapons to seize it.

After the due rendering of his father to heaven and the honoring of his body and name with respectively human and divine honors,[466] the first of his tasks as *princeps* was the organization of the elections that the Divine Augustus had left written out in his own hand.[467] It was at this time that it fell to me and my brother, as candidates of Caesar, to be designated for the praetorship immediately after men of the most noble and priestly backgrounds, thereby achieving that the Divine Augustus commended no one after us and Tiberius Caesar no one before us.[468]

125. The commonwealth was at once rewarded for its prayer and advice, and it did not take us long to discover what we would have suffered by a failed request or what we had gained by a successful one. For, in a kind of madness and with a deep desire for general disruption, the army that was serving in Germany and was under the personal command of Germanicus, as well as the legions that were in Illyricum, began demanding a new leader, a new system, and a new commonwealth: they even threatened that they would "dictate laws to the senate, dictate them to the *princeps*"; and for themselves they tried to establish a limit on service and an end to campaigning. It got even

electoral assemblies to the control of the senate, although the details are controversial.

[468] An individual who was "commended" by the emperor became a "candidate of Caesar" and was "designated" for inevitable election.

329

VELLEIUS PATERCULUS

dem ⟩[810] gladiorum erupit impunitas, defuitque qui contra
3 rem publicam duceret, non qui sequerentur. sed haec omnia veteris imperatoris maturitas, multa inhibentis, aliqua
cum gravitate pollicentis, ⟨et⟩[811] inter severam praecipue
noxiorum[812] ultionem mitis aliorum castigatio brevi sopiit
4 ac sustulit. quo quidem tempore ut pleraque ignovit[813]
Germanicus, ita Drusus,[814] qui a patre in id ipsum plurimo
quidem igne emicans incendium militaris tumultus missus
erat, prisca antiquaque severitate usus ancipitia sibi
⟨sus⟩tinere[815] ⟨maluit⟩[816] quam exemplo perniciosa, et iis
ipsis militum gladiis quibus obsessus erat obsidentes coer-
5 cuit, singulari adiutore in eo negotio usus Iunio Blaeso,
viro nescias utiliore in castris an meliore in toga, qui post
paucos annos proconsul in Africa ornamenta triumphalia
cum appellatione imperatoria meruit.

†ad Hispanias exercitumque†[817] virtutibus celeberri-
maque in Illyrico militia praediximus, cum imperio obtineret, in summa pace ⟨et⟩[818] quiete continuit, cum ei

---

810 ⟨cladem⟩ *Woodman*   811 *suppl. Krause*
812 noxiorum *Gronovius*: nostrorum *PA*   813 ignovit *ed.
Bipont.*: ignave *PA*   814 Drusus *Gelenius*: Brutus *PA*
815 ⟨sus⟩tinere *Woodman*: timere *BA*: tam re *P*: tentare *Novák: alii alia*
816 maluit *hic suppl. Woodman, post* sibi *Madvig*
817 ad *(B*: ac *P*: At *A)* Hispanias exercitumque *locus corruptus
et lacunosus*   818 *suppl. Orelli*

---

469 Q. Iunius Blaesus (cos. suff. AD 10), uncle of Sejanus
(127.3), was proconsul of Africa from 21 to 23. This was the last
occasion on which the title of "commander" (24.1n) was permitted (Tac. *Ann.* 3.74.4).

330

BOOK 2.125

as far as weapons, blades were drawn, and the impunity provided by the sword almost erupted into the ultimate disaster: the only missing element was who would take the lead against the commonwealth, not who would follow him. But all this was calmed and crushed in a short while by the mature judgment of the veteran commander, imposing many restrictions and making some promises with dignity, and by his combination of severe reprisals for the particularly guilty with mild punishment for others. It was at this time that, while Germanicus was largely forgiving, Drusus—who had been sent by his father into the very conflagration of the military uprising despite the magnitude of the blazing fire—applied the old-fashioned severity of the ancients, preferring to tolerate personal danger rather than pernicious precedents, and he punished his besiegers with the very soldiers' swords with which he had been besieged. In that task he enjoyed the singular assistance of Junius Blaesus (though whether the man is more useful in camp or better in the toga one would not know), who a few years afterward as proconsul in Africa earned the triumphal insignia along with the title "commander."[469]

†to the Spains and the army† virtues and celebrated service in Illyricum we mentioned earlier,[470] he was holding with the power of command, he maintained it in the greatest peace and quiet, since he possessed in abundance

[470] This whole sentence is self-evidently corrupt and lacunose. Previous service in Illyricum has been mentioned apropos of M. Aemilius Lepidus (114.5–115.3) and L. Aelius Lamia (116.3), but neither is elsewhere recorded as having been in Spain; we simply do not know the identity of the person being discussed or the region ("it") to which V. is referring.

331

VELLEIUS PATERCULUS

⟨pro⟩prietas[819] rectissima sentiendi et auctoritas quae
sentiebat obtinendi superesset. cuius curam ac fidem
Dolabella quoque, vir simplicitatis generosissimae, in
maritima parte Illyrici per omnia imitatus est.

126. Horum XVI annorum opera quis, cum versata sint
in[820] oculis animisque omnium, [in][821] partibus eloquatur?
sacravit parentem suum Caesar non imperio sed religione,
2 non appellavit eum sed fecit deum. revocata in forum
fides, summota e foro seditio, ambitio campo, discordia
curia,[822] sepultaeque[823] ac situ obsitae[824] iustitia, aequitas,
industria civitati redditae; accessit magistratibus[825] auctoritas, senatui maiestas, iudiciis gravitas; compressa thea-
tralis seditio; recte faciendi omnibus aut incussa voluntas
3 aut imposita necessitas: honorantur recta, prava puniun-
tur; suspicit potentem humilis, non timet, antecedit, non
contemnit humiliorem potens. quando annona modera-
tior? quando pax laetior? diffusa in Orientis Occidentis-
que tractus et quidquid meridiano aut septentrione finitur
pax augusta per omnes terrarum orbis angulos ⟨nos⟩[826] a

819 ⟨pro⟩prietas *Woodman*: pietas *PA*: facultas *Watt*
820 versata sint in *Woodman (cf. Cic. Verr. 5.144)*: inserta sint
P: insera *BA*: inhaereant *Krause*: *alii alia*
821 [in] *Vossius*   822 curia *Gelenius*: -iae *PA*
823 sepultaeque *BA*: sepultae *P*
824 obsitae *Gelenius*: oppositae *PBA*
825 magistratibus *Gelenius*: militibus *PA*
826 *suppl. Heinsius*

471 P. Cornelius Dolabella (cos. AD 10) was in charge of Dalmatia until ca. 20; he was proconsul of Africa in 23/24.
472 AD 14 to 29, counting inclusively.

BOOK 2.125–26

the quality of thinking correctly and the authority to effect what he thought. It was his concern and loyalty that Dolabella too, a man of the most genteel straightforwardness, imitated in every respect in the coastal region of Illyricum.[471]

126. Since the achievements of the past sixteen years[472] have been in the eyes and hearts of all, who would describe them individually? Caesar sanctified his father not by virtue of his power of command but by religion, he did not call him a god but made him one. Credit has been restored to the forum. Rioting has been removed from the forum, canvassing from the Campus, discord from the Curia;[473] and justice, fairness and industriousness—each buried and covered with decay—have been returned to the community. Magistrates have acquired authority, the senate majesty, the courts gravity. Rioting in the theater has been suppressed; the wish to act correctly has been impressed on everyone, or the necessity imposed: rectitude is honored, crookedness punished. The humble look up to the powerful but do not fear them, the powerful take precedence over the humble but do not disdain them. When has the price of grain been more moderate? When has peace been happier? The Augustan Peace, spread into tracts of territory east and west and to every southern and northern border, keeps us safe from the fear of banditry

---

[473] The rioting, canvassing, and discord are references to the electoral reforms that Augustus had planned (124.3n): the election of lesser magistrates took place in the forum, that of consuls and praetors in the Campus Martius (cf. 92.3); the Curia was the meeting place of the senate.

VELLEIUS PATERCULUS

4 latrociniorum metu servat immunes. fortuita non civium tantummodo sed urbium damna principis munificentia vindicat: restitutae urbes Asiae, vindicatae ab iniuriis magistratuum provinciae; honor dignis paratissimus, poena in malos sera sed aliqua. superatur aequitate gratia, ambitio virtute: nam facere recte cives suos princeps optimus faciendo docet, cumque sit imperio maximus, exemplo maior est.

127. Raro eminentes viri non magnis adiutoribus ad gubernandam fortunam suam usi sunt, ut duo Scipiones duobus Laeliis, quos per omnia aequaverunt sibi, ut divus Augustus M. Agrippa et proxime[827] ab eo Statilio Tauro, quibus novitas familiae haud obstitit quominus ad multiplices consulatus triumphosque et complura eveheren-

2 tur[828] sacerdotia. etenim magna negotia magnis adiutoribus egent †neque in parva paucitas ministeria defecit†[829] interestque rei publicae quod usu necessarium est[830] dig-

3 nitate eminere utilitatemque auctoritate muniri. sub his exemplis Ti. Caesar Seianum Aelium, principe equestris

> [827] proxime *Scheffer*: maxime *PA*
> [828] eveherentur *Vascosanus*: enumerentur *B*: enumerarentur *P*: ~~nominentur~~ numerentur *A*
> [829] neque . . . defecit *obelis notavit Ellis, secl. Vossius*
> [830] est *Ruhnken*: et *P*: e *A*

---

[474] The Ara Pacis, or Altar of Augustan Peace, which survives today in a rebuilt form, was decreed in 13 BC and dedicated in 9 BC. The geographer Strabo, a contemporary of V., refers to a recently founded city called Augustan Peace in Spain (Strabo 3.2.15).

[475] After an earthquake in AD 17.

BOOK 2.126–27

in every corner of the globe.[474] Accidental losses, not only in the case of citizens but of cities, are compensated by the *princeps'* generosity: cities in Asia have been rebuilt,[475] the provinces have been rescued from magistrates' injustices. Honors are available for the worthy; punishment for the wicked is slow but sure. Fairness prevails over favoritism, prowess over self-aggrandizement. The best *princeps* teaches his citizens to act correctly by acting so himself, and, although in his power of command he is the greatest, as an example he is greater still.

127. It is rare for outstanding men not to make use of great helpers to administer their life's allotment, as the two Scipios did with the two Laelii, whom in every respect they treated as equal to themselves, and as the Divine Augustus did with Marcus Agrippa and, immediately after him, Statilius Taurus, the newness of whose families was no obstacle to their elevation to numerous consulships and triumphs and to several priesthoods.[476] Great activities need great helpers,[477] and it is in the interest of the commonwealth that what is necessary in terms of use should stand out in terms of rank and that usefulness is buttressed by authority. It was with these precedents in mind that, as his singular helper in every aspect of his tasks as *princeps*, Tiberius Caesar has had and still has Sejanus Aelius, whose

[476] The first references are to (1) Scipio Africanus (1.10.3n) and C. Laelius (cos. 190 BC) and (2) Scipio Aemilianus (1.12.3n) and C. Laelius Sapiens (1.17.3n). For Agrippa see 59.5n; for Statilius Taurus see 85.2n.

[477] This statement is followed in P and A by six nonsensical words that editors variously athetize, delete, or emend.

335

VELLEIUS PATERCULUS

ordinis patre natum, materno vero genere clarissimas veteresque et insignes honoribus complexum familias, habentem consulares fratres, consobrinos, avunculum, ipsum vero laboris ac fidei capacissimum, sufficiente etiam vigori animi compage corporis, singularem principalium 4 onerum adiutorem in omnia habuit atque habet, virum priscae severitatis, laetissimae hilaritatis,[831] actu otiosis simillimum, nihil sibi vindicantem eoque adsequentem omnia, semperque[832] infra aliorum aestimationes se metientem, vultu vitaque tranquillum, animo exsomnem.

128. In huius virtutum aestimatione[833] iam pridem iudicia civitatis cum iudiciis principis certant, neque novus hic mos senatus populique Romani est putandi quod optimum sit esse nobilissimum. nam et illi antiqui ⟨qui⟩ ante primum bellum[834] Punicum abhinc annos trecentos Ti. Coruncanium, hominem novum, cum aliis omnibus honoribus tum pontificatu etiam maximo ad principale extulere 2 fastigium; et ⟨qui⟩[835] equestri loco natum Sp. Carvilium et mox M. Catonem, novum etiam[836] Tusculo, urbis inquilinum, Mummiumque Achaicum in consulatus, censuras

---

[831] priscae severitatis, laetissimae hilaritatis *Bothe*: s- l-, h- p- *PA*

[832] semperque *BA*: semper *P*

[833] virtutum aestimatione *P*: -em -em *BA*

[834] illi antiqui ante primum bellum *P* (⟨qui⟩ *Halm*): illi primi ante bellum *A*   [835] *suppl. Fröhlich*

[836] etiam *PA*: item *Watt*: ex *ed. Bipont.*

---

[478] L. Aelius Sejanus, Prefect of the Praetorian Guard and an exact contemporary of V., is described by Dio under AD 20 as "adviser and helper in every respect" (Cass. Dio 57.19.7); accord-

336

BOOK 2.127–28

father was a principal figure in the equestrian order and who on his mother's side embraces families of the greatest distinction, ancient and noted for their honors.[478] Having consular brothers, cousins, and uncle, he himself has the greatest capacity for hard work and loyalty, his physical frame equal to his mental vigor, a man of old-fashioned severity and the most delightful cheerfulness, in action very like a man of leisure, making no claims for himself and therefore achieving everything, and always measuring himself below the estimation of others, tranquil in his looks and life, with a mind that never sleeps.

128. In the estimation of this man's virtues the judgment of the community has long since been competing with the judgment of the *princeps*, and it is no new custom of the senate and Roman people to think that what is best is most noble. The ancients before the First Punic War, three hundred years ago, who employed all other honors and even the office of Chief Pontiff to raise Tiberius Coruncanius, a new man, to his peak as a principal figure;[479] and those who advanced Spurius Carvilius, of equestrian birth, and subsequently Marcus Cato, a new man too, from Tusculum, and an immigrant to the City, and Mummius Achaicus as well, to consulships, censorships, and tri-

ing to Tacitus under AD 23 Tiberius referred to him as "partner in his labors," while Drusus, Tiberius' son, described him as "helper in command" (Tac. *Ann.* 4.2.3, 7.1). His father was Seius Strabo, who had been Prefect of Egypt, but the ramifications of his family are much disputed (see Syme 1986, 300–312 and Table XXIII). His uncle was the Iunius Blaesus of 125.5, above.

[479] Ti. Coruncanius (cos. 280 BC) was the first plebeian Chief Pontiff.

337

VELLEIUS PATERCULUS

3 et triumphos provexere; et qui C. Marium ignotae originis usque ad sextum consulatum sine dubitatione Romani nominis habuere principem; et qui M. Tullio[837] tantum tribuere ut paene adsentatione sua quibus vellet principatus conciliaret; quique nihil Asinio Pollioni negaverunt quod nobilissimis summo cum sudore consequendum foret—profecto hoc senserunt: in cuiuscumque animo virtus ines-

4 set, ei plurimum esse tribuendum. haec naturalis exempli imitatio ad experiendum Seianum Caesarem, ad iuvanda vero onera principis Seianum propulit,[838] senatumque et populum Romanum eo perduxit[839] ut, quod usu optimum intellegit, id in tutelam securitatis suae libenter advocet.

129. Sed proposita quasi universa principatus Ti. Caesaris ‹imagine›[840] singula recenseamus. qua ille prudentia Rhascupolim, interemptorem fratris sui filii Cotyis consortisque eiusdem imperii, Romam[841] evocavit, singulari in eo negotio usus opera Flacci Pomponii consularis, viri nati ad omnia quae recte facienda sunt, simplicique virtute

2 merentis semper quam[842] captantis gloriam! cum quanta gravitate ut senator et iudex, non ut princeps, *** et causas

---

[837] Tullio *Lipsius*: Fulvio *PA*
[838] propulit *Acidalius*: -tulit *PA*
[839] perduxit *P*: prod- *BA*   [840] ‹imagine› *Sinko*: ‹forma› *Rhenanus*   [841] Romam *Ursinus*: formam *PBA*
[842] ‹magis› quam *Vascosanus*: ‹num›quam *Orelli*

---

[480] Sp. Carvilius Maximus was twice consul (293, 272 BC) and a triumpher; for Cato the Elder see 1.7.3n, and for Mummius Achaicus see 1.12.1n.

[481] Rhascupolis (also known as Rhescuporis) shared the kingdom of Thrace with his nephew, Cotys, an arrangement set in

BOOK 2.128–29

umphs;[480] and those who had no doubt in regarding Gaius Marius, despite his ignoble origin, to be the principal figure in the Roman nation up to his sixth consulship; and those who granted so much to Cicero that it was almost on his say-so that he obtained principal roles for whomsoever he wished; and those who denied to Asinius Pollio nothing that had to be won with the utmost sweat by the noblest men—all of them assuredly thought that most should be granted to the man in whose heart virtue resided. It is imitation of this natural example that has propelled Caesar to test Sejanus and has propelled Sejanus to assist with the *princeps'* burdens, and that has brought the senate and Roman people to the point where, to protect their own security, they gladly summon whatever they consider best in terms of usefulness.

129. Having set forth a general picture (as it were) of Tiberius Caesar's principate, let us enumerate individual items. With what prudence he summoned Rhascupolis (the murderer of Cotys, his own brother's son and partner in his empire) to Rome, using in that task the singular support of the ex-consul Flaccus Pomponius, a man born for every form of correct activity and always deserving glory for his straightforward prowess rather than hunting for it![481] With what seriousness, as senator and judge, not

place by Augustus. After Cotys' murder, Rhascupolis was tricked into Roman custody and escorted to Rome, an operation managed by L. Pomponius Flaccus (cos. AD 17), governor of Moesia and one of Tiberius' drinking partners. After being tried and condemned, the king was taken to Alexandria, where he was killed. The story is told by Tacitus under AD 19 (*Ann.* 2.64.2–67.3).

339

VELLEIUS PATERCULUS

pressius audit! quam celeriter ingratum *** et nova molientem oppressit![843] quibus praeceptis instructum Germanicum suum imbutumque rudimentis militiae secum actae domitorem recepit Germaniae! quibus iuventam eius exaggeravit honoribus, respondente[844] cultu triumphi
3 rerum quas gesserat magnitudini! quotiens populum congiariis honoravit senatorumque censum, cum id senatu auctore facere potuit, quam libenter explevit, ut neque luxuriam invitaret neque honestam paupertatem pateretur dignitate destitui! quanto cum honore Germanicum suum in transmarinas misit provincias! qua vi consiliorum suorum,[845] ministro et adiutore usus Druso filio suo, Maroboduum inhaerentem occupati regni finibus (pace maiestatis eius dixerim) velut serpentem abstrusam terra[846] salubribus consiliorum suorum[847] medicamentis coegit

[843] *pleraque verba excidisse videntur*
[844] respondente *P*: -em *BA*
[845] consiliorum suorum *secl. Bothe*
[846] terra *Cludius*: -ae *PA*
[847] consiliorum suorum *secl. Ruhnken*

---

[482] The words "not as *princeps*" recur in the speech that Tacitus (*Ann.* 3.12.2, as emended by Lipsius) puts into the mouth of Tiberius at the trial of Cn. Calpurnius Piso in AD 20.

[483] These sentences exhibit various lacunae, of which the last has often been thought to conceal the name of Libo Drusus (130.3, below), accused of "building up to revolt" in AD 16 (Tac. *Ann.* 2.27.1; the wording is almost identical). Another possibility is Archelaus, king of Cappadocia, who was also supposed to be harboring revolutionary designs (Cass. Dio 57.17.4); he had cause to be grateful to Tiberius, who as a young man had achieved his acquittal in a court case (Suet. *Tib.* 8).

340

BOOK 2.129

as *princeps*,[482] *** and hears cases more attentively ***! How speedily he suppressed the ungrateful *** when he was building up to revolution![483] With what precepts had he equipped his own Germanicus, with what training had he instructed him when he was serving at his side, such that he welcomed him as the tamer of Germany! What honors did he heap upon the young man, the pageantry of his triumph corresponding to the magnitude of his achievements![484] How often has he honored the people with donatives,[485] and, when he could do so with the senate's support, how willingly did he make good the property qualification of senators, such that he neither encouraged luxury nor allowed the removal of rank for honest impoverishment![486] With what honor did he send his own Germanicus to the overseas provinces![487] With what effective personal strategy, and using his own son Drusus as his associate and helper, did he compel Maroboduus—who, like a serpent hiding in the ground (I speak with deference to his sovereignty), was clinging to the territory of the kingdom he had occupied—to move out, his personal

484 In AD 17 Tiberius designated himself as colleague of Germanicus for the consulship of 18, a great honor; the latter's German triumph on 26 May 17 is vividly described by Tacitus (*Ann.* 2.41.2–3).

485 See, e.g., Tac. *Ann.* 2.42.1 (evidently 26 May 17), 3.29.3 (7 June 20).

486 See, e.g., Tac. *Ann.* 1.75.3–4, 2.48.3; in the latter passage (AD 17), Tacitus uses the same phrase "honest impoverishment" (*honestam paupertatem*) as does V. here; its only other occurrence is at Amm. Marc. 24.3.5.

487 For Germanicus' mission, and the *imperium* that was granted to him, see Tac. *Ann.* 2.43.1 (AD 17).

341

VELLEIUS PATERCULUS

egredi! quam illum ut honorate ita[848] secure continet!
quantae molis bellum principe Galliarum ciente Sacroviro
Floroque Iulio[849] mira celeritate ac virtute compressit, ut
ante populus Romanus vicisse se quam bellare cognos-
ceret nuntiosque periculi victoriae praecederet nuntius!
4 magni etiam terroris bellum Africum et cotidiano auctu
maius auspiciis consiliisque eius brevi sepultum est.

130. Quanta suo[850] suorumque nomine exstruxit opera!
quam pia munificentia superque humanam evecta fidem
templum patri molitur! quam magnifico animi temperamento Cn. quoque Pompei munera absumpta igni restituit, qui, quicquid umquam[851] claritudine eminuit, id ve-

---

[848] ita *Novák*: nec *PA*: sic *Burman*
[849] Iuliis *Ruhnken*
[850] suo *Acidalius*: sua *PA*
[851] qui quicquid umquam *Rhenanus*: qui quidem quam *PA*

---

[488] The earlier conquests of Maroboduus, king of the Marcomanni, have been described at 108–9, above; but his increasing
age and internecine conflict among the Germans led to his
eclipse, and, in response to his appeal to Tiberius for help, Drusus
was dispatched and so managed affairs that the king was forced
to seek exile in Italy. See Tac. *Ann.* 2.44–46, 62.1–63.4 (AD 17,
19). V.'s double reference to Tiberius' "personal strategy" looks
odd, but exactly the same expression (*sua . . . consilia*) occurs in
exactly the same context at Tac. *Ann.* 2.63.3, where Tacitus implies that his source is an extant speech of the emperor's. See also
next note.

[489] Tiberius had promised the king a "a safe and honorable
home in Italy" (Tac. *Ann.* 2.63.2), wording very similar—and, in
the case of "honorable" (*honoratam*), identical—to that used by

342

BOOK 2.129–30

strategy acting as the salutary drug![488] How honorably, and yet how securely, he contains him![489] What a troublesome war was being stirred up by Sacrovir and Florus Julius (principal figures in their respective Gauls),[490] which he stifled with such remarkable speed and courage that the Roman people knew they had won before they knew they were fighting, and the report of victory preceded the reports of danger![491] The African War too, a source of great terror and increasingly worse every day, was laid to rest in a short while under his auspices and by his strategy.[492]

130. How great are the buildings he has erected in his own and his family's name![493] With what devoted munificence, exceeding human credibility, is he constructing a temple to his father! How magnificent the emotional self-control with which he is restoring Pompey's gutted edifice too, thinking that anything that has ever stood out for its

V. here (see also previous note). The king lived out the rest of his life at Ravenna.

[490] The former came from Gallia Lugdunensis, the latter from Gallia Belgica.

[491] Only when the war had been won (AD 21) did Tiberius provide the senate with the simultaneous report that "the war had broken out and been completed" (Tac. *Ann.* 3.47.1).

[492] War in Africa lasted eight years, from AD 17 to 24 (Tac. *Ann.* 2.52, 3.20–21, 3.72.4–74, 4.23–26).

[493] The two public buildings known to have been erected in the names of Tiberius and his brother Drusus are the temple of Castor and Pollux and the temple of Concord (Suet. *Tib.* 20; Cass. Dio 55.27.4), but their dedications (respectively, 27 January AD 6, and 16 January AD 10) precede his accession to the principate.

343

VELLEIUS PATERCULUS

2 luti cognatum censet tuendum! qua liberalitate cum alias tum proxime incenso monte Caelio omnis ordinis hominum iacturae patrimonio succurrit suo! quanta cum quiete hominum rem perpetui praecipuique timoris, supplementum, sine trepidatione dilectus providet!

3   Si aut natura patitur aut mediocritas recipit hominum, audeo cum deis[852] queri. quid hic meruit primum ut scelerata Drusus Libo iniret consilia, deinde ut Silium Pisonemque tam ***[853] alterius dignitatem constituit, auxit alterius? ut ad maiora transcendam (quamquam et haec ille duxit[854] maxima) quid ut iuvenes amitteret filios? quid

---

[852] audeo cum deis *Heinsius*: auro deo cum de his *PA*
[853] *lacunam statuit Rhenanus*
[854] duxit *Rhenanus*: dixit *PA*

---

[494] The temple to Augustus, whose construction was probably credited to Livia as well as to Tiberius (Cass. Dio 56.46.3), and Pompey's theater were the only two public buildings associated with Tiberius' reign, although neither was completed in his lifetime (Tac. *Ann.* 6.45.1; Suet. *Tib.* 47). The theater had burned down in AD 22, and Tacitus says that Tiberius' stated reason for his rebuilding of it was that no one of Pompey's own family was capable of doing so (Tac. *Ann.* 3.72.2): this explains V.'s otherwise strange phrase "as a matter of kinship."

[495] The fire was in AD 27 (Tac. *Ann.* 4.64; Suet. *Tib.* 48.1).

[496] The case of L. Scribonius Libo Drusus in AD 16, the year of his praetorship, is fully described at Tac. *Ann.* 2.27–32; he committed suicide. C. Silius A. Caecina Largus (cos. AD 13) was charged in 24 with treason and likewise committed suicide

BOOK 2.130

brilliance should be protected as a matter of kinship![494] With what generosity does he use his patrimony to aid the loss of men of all ranks, both on other occasions and then most recently after the fire on the Caelian Hill![495] To think how men are undisturbed when he sees to a matter of perpetual and particular fear—recruitment—without any of the terror of a levy!

If man's nature allows or his ordinariness permits, I dare to raise a complaint with the gods. Why did he deserve, first, that Drusus Libo should embark on criminal plotting, and, second, that Silius and Piso so *** he established the rank of the one and increased that of the other?[496] To pass to more important matters (although he regarded even the former as very important), why did he deserve to lose his sons as young men?[497] Or his grandson

(*Ann.* 4.18–19). Tacitus later (*Ann.* 4.21.1–2) juxtaposes this second case with that of L. Calpurnius Piso the Augur (cos. 1 BC), who died a natural death before he could be prosecuted, but it is perhaps more probable that V. is referring to Piso's brother, Cn. Calpurnius Piso (cos. 7 BC), whose notorious trial in AD 20 on various treasonable charges, including the poisoning of Germanicus, is recorded by Tacitus at length (*Ann.* 3.7–19) and is the subject of the *Senatus Consultum de Pisone Patre* (*SCPP*). How Tiberius could be said to have affected the men's rank is unclear.

[497] Germanicus, Tiberius' nephew and adopted son, died on 10 October, AD 19, at the age of thirty-three; Drusus, Tiberius' biological son, was buried on 14 September, AD 23, at the age of thirty-four or thirty-five.

345

VELLEIUS PATERCULUS

4 ut nepotem[855] ex Druso suo?[856] dolenda adhuc retulimus; veniendum ad erubescenda est.[857] quantis hoc triennium, M. Vinici, doloribus laceravit animum eius! quam diu abstruso (quod miserrimum est) pectus eius flagravit incendio, quod ex nuru, quod ex nepote dolere, indignari,
5 erubescere[858] coactus est! cuius temporis aegritudinem auxit amissa mater, eminentissima et per omnia deis quam hominibus similior femina, cuius potentiam nemo sensit nisi aut levatione periculi aut accessione dignitatis.

131. Voto finiendum volumen est.[859] Iuppiter Capitoline, et auctor ac stator[860] Romani nominis Gradive Mars, perpetuorumque custos Vesta ignium, et quicquid numinum hanc Romani[861] imperii molem in amplissimum ter-

---

[855] nepotes *Mallan*

[856] Druso suo *Burer*: Drusuo *B*: Druso *PA*

[857] est *BA, om. P*

[858] erubescere *BA, om. P*

[859] est *Orelli*: sit *PA*

[860] Capitoline et auctor ac (*B*: et *PA*) stator *PA*: Capitoline et stator, et auctor *Puteanus*: Capitoline, et auctor ac sator *Ursinus*

[861] numinum hanc Romani *P* (hanc Romani *A^{mg}*): nominum honor omni *BA*

---

[498] This is the little Germanicus, who died in AD 23 as a small child (Tac. *Ann.* 4.15.1); he was the twin of Tiberius Gemellus, but their exact date of birth is disputed (AD 19 or 21 are the two most favored years). According to Cass. Dio 57.14.6, Drusus had lost another little son in AD 15, and it has been suggested that V.'s text should be emended to read the plural "grandsons" here (C. T. Mallan, *RhM* 159 [2016]: 219–21).

[499] From AD 27 to 29, counting inclusively.

BOOK 2.130–31

by his own son Drusus?[498] Hitherto we have mentioned grievous matters, but we must come to the shameful. What griefs, Marcus Vinicius, have torn at his heart these past three years![499] To think how long was hidden (this is the most wretched aspect) the fire that blazed in his breast because of the grief, indignation, and shame to which he was compelled by his daughter-in-law and grandson![500] The malady of this period was intensified by the loss of his mother, an outstanding woman and in general more godlike than human, whose power no one felt except for the alleviation of their danger or the acquisition of rank.[501]

131. My volume must conclude with a prayer. Capitoline Jupiter, and Mars Gradivus, author and stayer of the name of Rome,[502] and Vesta, guardian of the perpetual fire, and whichever godhead has raised this weighty Roman Empire to the most powerful pinnacle of the globe,

---

[500] Respectively, Agrippina, widow of Germanicus, and their son, Nero Julius Caesar, who were publicly attacked by Tiberius in AD 29 (Tac. *Ann.* 5.3–5). He was banished to the island of Pontia and died very soon after; she was banished to the island of Pandateria, where she died on 18 October, AD 33.

[501] Livia died in AD 29. She had saved Cornelius Cinna Magnus from the wrath of Augustus (Sen. *Clem.* 1.9) and had used her influence to gain senatorial rank for M. Salvius Otho, grandfather of the emperor (Suet. *Otho* 1.1).

[502] Mars was the father of Romulus, and, although it is usually Jupiter who is given the title "stayer," in the Hymn of the Arval Brethren the refrain "Mars, stay" is repeated three times (ll. 7–9): see E. H. Warmington, *Remains of Old Latin, Volume 4* (LCL 359; Cambridge, MA, 1940), 250–53.

VELLEIUS PATERCULUS

rarum orbis fastigium extulit, vos publica voce obtestor atque precor: custodite, servate, protegite hunc statum, hanc pacem, ⟨hunc principem⟩,[862] eique functo longissima statione mortali destinate successores quam serissimos, sed eos quorum cervices tam fortiter sustinendo terrarum orbis imperio sufficiant quam huius suffecisse sensimus, consiliaque omnium civium aut pia ***[863]

[862] ⟨hunc principem⟩ *Lipsius*
[863] *post* pia *textus deficit*

BOOK 2.131

with the nation's voice I implore you and pray: guard, preserve, and protect this system, this peace, and this *princeps*, and, when he has completed the longest of mortal stations, designate for him the latest possible successors, but ones whose shoulders are equal to upholding command of the globe as courageously as we have perceived his to have done, and, as for the plans of every citizen, either the devoted ***[503]

[503] The text breaks off at this point: it is likely that V. continued his prayer by urging the gods to support the devoted, and to frustrate the disloyal, plans of the citizens.

DIRECTORY OF PEOPLES AND PLACES (EXCLUDING ROME)

In the translation I have usually used ancient rather than modern names but have not been absolutely consistent. The following list includes all the peoples and places that are mentioned by Velleius, excluding Rome and a few places that may be deemed self-explanatory; italics denote the modern name or nearest location as given in the *Barrington Atlas of the Greek and Roman World* (2000), to which references are given wherever possible (map number precedes grid reference in each case). For further details see the relevant entries in the *Oxford Classical Dictionary* or *Brill's New Pauly*.

Acerrani: inhabitants of Acerrae (*Acerra*), a town in Campania (44 F4).

Achaea (*Achaea*): originally a region in the northern Peloponnese (58 B1). By the early second century BC all the Peloponnese had been united in the Achaean League, which rebelled and was defeated by Metellus Macedonicus and Mummius in 146 (1.12.1, 38.5). V. subsequently (23.3, 77.2, 101.3) uses "Achaea" to refer to central and southern Greece, which was united under that name as a Roman province from 27 BC (100 L4). Achaea was also (cf. 40.1) the name of a region to the east of the Black Sea (84 E4, 87 E1).

Actium (*Aktion*): town on the Adriatic coast of Greece at the entrance to the Ambracian Gulf (54 C4).

Aeculanum (*Mirabella Eclano*): town in Campania (44 H3, 45 B2).

Aefula (*Monte S. Angelo*): town just south of Tibur, east of Rome (43 D2).

Aegeae (*Vergina*): town in Macedonia (49 E3, 50 B4).

Aenaria (*Ischia*): island just off the Gulf of Naples (44 E4).

351

DIRECTORY OF PEOPLES AND PLACES

Aeolians: name given to early inhabitants of Thessaly and/or parts of Asia Minor.

Aesernia (*Isernia*): Apennine town in Samnium (44 F2).

Aetolia: area of Greece that lies along the northern side of the Gulf of Corinth (55 A3).

Africa: the original province of Africa was constituted in 146 BC after the destruction of Carthage; Julius Caesar annexed part of Numidia to form a new province called Africa Nova (46 BC), and under Augustus the whole expanded area became known simply as the province of Africa.

Alba Fucens: ancient town near the foot of Monte Velino in central Italy (44 D1).

Alba Longa: possibly to be identified with *Castel Gandolfo* on the western shore of Lake Albano, about fifteen miles southeast of Rome (43 C3).

Albania: region on the western side of the Caspian Sea and not to be identified with the modern country of the same name (88 F3).

Albis (*Elbe*): river in Germany (10 F3–I4).

Alesia (*Alise-Sainte-Reine*): town in central Gaul (18 B2).

Alexandria: city on the Mediterranean coast of Egypt (74 B2).

Aliso: stronghold near the River Lippe, western Germany, perhaps to be identified with the excavated fort at Haltern; mentioned also by Tacitus (*Ann.* 2.7.3).

Allobroges: Gallic tribe occupying a large swath of territory on the eastern side of the Rhone valley, from south of Vienna (*Vienne*), their capital, northeastward to the southern shore of Lake Geneva (17 E3–H2).

Alps: the various Alpine provinces were not constituted until the mid-first century AD.

Alsium (*Palo*): coastal town almost due west of Rome (43 A2, 44 B2).

Altinum (*Quarto di Altino*): Italian town on the northern coast of the Adriatic (40 C1).

Andros: island in the central Aegean (57 C4).

Apollonia: city in southern Illyricum, near *Pojan* in modern Albania (49 B3).

Apulia (*Puglia*): southeastern region of Italy, just above the "heel" (45 C2).

Aquae Sextiae (*Aix-en-Provence*): town in Gallia Narbonensis (15 E2).

Aquileia (*Aquileia*): town at the very head of the Adriatic (19 F4).

352

DIRECTORY OF PEOPLES AND PLACES

Argos (*Argos*): town in the northeast Peloponnese (58 D2).

Aricini: inhabitants of Aricia (*Ariccia*), a town sixteen miles southeast of Rome on the Via Appia, and first stop for the poet Horace (*Sat.* 1.5.1) on his famous Journey to Brundisium (43 C3, 44 C2).

Ariminum (*Rimini*): town on the Adriatic coast of Italy (40 D4).

Armenia: mountainous kingdom in eastern Anatolia extending to the Caspian Sea (88 B4–E4, 89 C1–F1). Tigranes II greatly extended its territory, but, following Pompey's settlement in 66 BC, he and his successors were largely confined to their ancestral borders (37.5).

Artagera: fortified town of uncertain location in Armenia (see Swan on Dio 55.10ᵃ.6).

Arverni: Celtic tribe in the region of the modern *Auvergne* (17 B2), west of Lugdunum (*Lyon*).

Ascra (*Pyrgaki-Episkopi*): town in Boeotia (55 E4).

Asculum (*Ascoli*)/Asculani: town on the Adriatic coast of Italy (42 F3).

Asia: from 133 BC a Roman province in western and central Asia Minor, although its boundaries changed over time as the Roman empire expanded (1, 100 M4).

Assyrians: inhabitants of an ancient empire in the region of the upper Tigris in modern Iraq (3 C2–D3).

Attica: region around Athens (59).

Avernus (*Lago Averno*): lake just south of Cumae (44 F4). Agrippa joined it to the Lucrine Lake by means of a canal.

Auximum (*Osimo*): town due south of Ancona on Italy's Adriatic coast (42 E2).

Bagienni: tribe in northwestern Italy; their chief town was Augusta Bagiennorum (*Bene Vagienna*) on the River Tanaro.

Bathinus (*Bosna*): river in modern Bosnia (20 F5).

Beneventum (*Benevento*): town in Campania (44 G3).

Bessi: a people inhabiting a region in modern Bulgaria (22 B6).

Bithynia: region and kingdom in northwestern Asia Minor along the southern shore of the Sea of Marmara; bequeathed to Rome on the death of its king in 74 BC, it was joined with Pontus as a Roman province in 63 BC (52 E4–G3).

Boeotia: area of Greece immediately north of Attica (55 D3–E4).

Boiohaemum: area of Germany from which *Bohemia* gets its name, now in the Czech Republic/Czechia (12 G2–I2).

Bononia (*Bologna*): town in northeastern Italy (40 A3–4).

353

DIRECTORY OF PEOPLES AND PLACES

Bovillae (*Frattocchie*): town roughly ten miles southeast of Rome on the Via Appia (43 C2).

Britain: Having been invaded by Julius Caesar in 55 and 54 BC, Britain was gradually absorbed into the Roman Empire after Claudius' invasion in AD 43.

Bructeri: tribe in northern Germany, in modern North Rhine-Westphalia (10 D5).

Brundisium (*Brindisi*): Adriatic seaport in Calabria in the "heel" of Italy (45 G3).

Buxentum (*Policastro Bussentino*): town in southwestern Italy on the Gulf of Policastro (45 C4, 46 C1).

Byzantium (*Istanbul*): city on the southeastern shore of the Bosporus, later known as Constantinople (53 A2).

Calabria: roughly commensurate with the "heel" of Italy, the area now known as Salento (45 G3). Modern-day Calabria comprises the "toe" of Italy.

Calatia (*S. Giacomo delle Galazze*): town in Campania (44 F3).

Cales (*Calvi*): town in Campania (44 F3).

Callaeci: a people of northwestern Spain (24 C2–D1).

Campani/Campania/Campanus Ager: Campania is an area in southwestern Italy; the Campanus Ager (translated in this edition as the Campanian Territory) stretches from Capua, the region's chief city, southwest toward the coast (44 F3–4).

Cannae (*Canne*): town in Apulia (45 D2).

Canninefates: German tribe on the North Sea coast of the modern Netherlands.

Cappadocia: area of western Asia Minor that became a province in AD 17 (64 B2).

Capua (*S. Maria Capua Vetere*): chief town of Campania (44 F3).

Carnuntum (*Bad Deutsch-Altenburg*): legionary station in Pannonia, now in modern Austria (13 B4).

Carrhae (*Harran*): town in Mesopotamia (1 K3, 3 C2, 67 H3, 89 B4).

Carseoli (*Carsoli*): town roughly forty miles east-northeast of Rome on the Via Valeria (44 D1).

Carthage: town on the Gulf of Tunis, modern Tunisia (32 F3).

Casilinum (*Capua*): town in Campania at the junction of the Via Appia and the Via Latina (44 F3).

354

DIRECTORY OF PEOPLES AND PLACES

Castrum (*Giulianova*): town on the Adriatic coast of central Italy (42 F3).

Cauchi: tribe in northern Germany to the west of the River Elbe (10 D3); also known as the Chauci.

Caudini: people of Caudium, a town (near *Montesarchio*) in Campania on the Via Appia (44 G3).

Chalcis (*Chalkida*)/Chalcidians: chief town of the island of Euboea (55 B4).

Chatti: tribe in central Germany (11 I2, 12 B2).

Chattuarii: tribe in northern Germany (10 D4).

Cherusci: tribe in central Germany (10 F4).

Chios: Aegean island off the coast of Asia Minor (56 B5).

Cilicia: region of southeastern Asia Minor, a Roman province from the early first century BC (64 B3–4).

Cimbri: Germanic tribe, seemingly originating from modern Jutland.

Mount Claudius: perhaps a mountain in the Papuk range in modern Croatia.

Clazomenae: city (near *Urla* in modern Turkey) on the Ionian coast of Asia Minor (56 D5).

Clusium (*Chiusi*): town in Etruria, just south of Lake Trasimene (42 B2).

Colchi: a people on the eastern coast of the Black Sea (1 L2, 88 A2).

Colophon: city (near *Değirmendere* in mod. Turkey) on the Ionian coast of Asia Minor (56 E1).

Compsa (*Conza della Campania*): town in the Apennines on the eastern border of Campania (45 B3).

Contrebia: There were at least two towns of this name in central Spain, Contrebia Belaisca (*Botorrita*) and Contrebia Leucada (*Aguilar del Río Alhama*), roughly one hundred miles apart (25 D3–4). It is not clear to which V. refers (2.5.2).

Corfinium (*Corfinio*): town in central Italy (42 F4).

Corinth: town on the isthmus between central Greece and the Peloponnese (58 D2).

Cosa (*Ansedonia*): town on the west coast of central Italy (42 A4).

Cremona (*Cremona*): town in northern Italy (39 G3).

Crete: island that was combined with Cyrenaica and became a Roman province in 67 BC (60 A1–F2).

Cumae (*Cuma*): town in Campania (44 F4).

355

DIRECTORY OF PEOPLES AND PLACES

Cyme: coastal town (*Nemrut Limanı* in mod. Turkey) in western Asia Minor (56 D4).

Cynoscephalae: range of hills in Thessaly, west-central Greece (55 D2).

Cyprus: island that was a Ptolemaic possession, annexed for Rome in 58 BC (38.6, 45.4), returned to Ptolemaic rule by Caesar in 48, and finally became a Roman province under Augustus (72).

Cyzicus (*Belkiz Kale*): town on the southern shore of the Sea of Marmara (52 B4).

Daesitiates: Illyrian tribe in modern Bosnia along the River Bosna (Bathinus); their capital was possibly near the modern Breza (20 F5).

Dalmatia: region along the eastern shore of the Adriatic, a Roman province from AD 9 (20 C5–E6).

Delos: one of the Cyclades islands in the southern Aegean Sea (57 D4).

Delphi: town in southern-central Greece (55 C–D4).

Dertona (*Tortona*): town in northwestern Italy (39 D4).

Dyrrachium (*Durrës*): seaport on the eastern shore of the Adriatic in modern Albania (49 B2).

Ephesus (*Efes*): town on the west coast of Asia Minor (61 E2).

Ephyra (*Mesopotamon*): town in Epirus on the eastern coast of the Adriatic (54 C3).

Ephyre: alternative name for ancient Corinth.

Epirus: coastal region along the eastern shore of the Adriatic, now straddling modern Albania and Greece (54 B2–D3).

Eporedia (*Ivrea*): town in northwestern Italy (39 B3).

Eretria (*Eretria*): town on the southern shore of the island of Euboea (55 F4).

Erythrae (*Ildır*): Ionian town on the coast of southwestern Asia Minor (56 C5).

Etruscans: ancient inhabitants of Etruria, the region of Italy north of Rome that was very powerful in pre-Roman times (42 B1–3, 43 A1–B2).

Euboea: large Aegean island off the eastern coast of central Greece (55 E2–H4).

356

DIRECTORY OF PEOPLES AND PLACES

Fabrateria (*Falvaterra*): two identically named towns in Latium; V. refers (1.15.4) to Fabrateria Nova (44 E2).

Faventia (*Faenza*): town in northeastern Italy on the Via Aemilia (40 B4).

Fidentia (*Fidenza*): town in northern Italy on the Via Aemilia (39 G4).

Firmum (*Fermo*): town in Picenum near the Adriatic coast (42 F2).

Formiae (*Formia*): town on the Via Appia halfway between Rome and Naples (44 E3).

Fregellae: town (near *Ceprano*) in central Italy on the Via Latina (44 E2).

Fregenae: coastal town west of Rome, halfway between Alsium and Ostia (44 B2).

Fundi (*Fondi*): town on the Via Appia, northwest of Formiae (44 D3).

Gades (*Cadiz*): town in southwestern Spain (26 D5).

Galatia: region of central Asia Minor; it became a province in 25 BC (63 B1–D1, 100 N4–P4).

Gallograecia: alternative name for Galatia, an area in central Asia Minor that became a province in the mid-20s BC (63 B1).

Gaul(s): Until late-republican times, Cisalpine Gaul denoted the area of northern Italy along the valley of the River Po, while Transalpine Gaul comprised the whole of modern France together with territory as far east as the Rhine. By the late 40s BC, Cisalpine Gaul had been integrated within Italy; under Augustus Transalpine Gaul was divided into the four provinces of (anti-clockwise from northeast) Belgica, Lugdunensis, Aquitania, and Narbonensis.

Germans/Germany: The Roman name "Germania" describes a vast area of territory stretching from west of the Rhine eastward at least as far as the River Oder, and from the North Sea as far south as the Danube; within this area were many different peoples, such as the Chatti and Hermunduri. Although the provinces of Upper Germany (centered on mod. Mainz) and Lower Germany (centered on mod. Cologne) were not formally established until the late first century AD, their names were in use from Augustan times.

Getae: a people who inhabited the western hinterland of the Black Sea (22 C4–E5, 23 B3).

357

DIRECTORY OF PEOPLES AND PLACES

Granicus (*Biga*): river in northwestern Asia Minor that debouches into the Sea of Marmara (52 A4, 56 E1).

Gravisca (*Porto Clementino*): coastal town northwest of Rome (42 B4).

Heniochi: a people in the southeastern hinterland of the Black Sea (87 F4–G4, 88 A4).

Herculaneum: now-famous town southeast of Naples (44 F4).

Hercynian Forest: name for a vast area of west central Europe whose boundaries remain unclear; relics of the forest no doubt include the Ardennes and Black Forest, but these give no real idea of its original extent.

Hermunduri: a people of central Germany (12 C–D3, F1).

Hirpini: a people of southern Italy (45 A2–B2).

Iberia: area more or less equivalent to the modern country of Georgia and not to be identified with the peninsula of the same name in southwestern Europe (88 B2–D3).

Icarian Sea: name given to part of the eastern Aegean between the Cyclades and Asia Minor (61 C3–E3).

Ilium (*Hisarlik*): alternative name for Troy, in western Asia Minor (56 C2).

Illyria/Illyricum: names for the region east of the Adriatic, partly commensurate with the later province of Dalmatia and nowadays straddling Croatia, Albania, and Greece (49 B2–3).

Interamna: town on the River Liris in west-central Italy due north of Minturnae; called Interamna Lirenas to distinguish it from Interamna Nahars further north (44 E3).

Ionia: coastal region of Asia Minor (1 I3, 56 C4–E5).

Lacedaemonians: alternative name for Spartans.

Laconia: southeastern area of the Peloponnese (58 C3–-E4).

Langobardi: tribe of northern Germany (10 G3).

Laodicea: name of various towns in Syria and Asia Minor; at 69.2 V. mentions the one (*Latakia*) on the northwestern Syrian coast (68 A2).

Larissa: name of various towns in Greece and Asia Minor; V.'s adjacent references to Smyrna, Cyme, and Myrina (1.4.4) suggest that he

358

DIRECTORY OF PEOPLES AND PLACES

means the one in Asia Minor sometimes identified with *Buruncuk* (56 E4).

Laurentine Marshes: seemingly otherwise unattested but perhaps to be identified with the "swamps" and "Laurentian marsh" mentioned by Virgil (*Aen.* 7.150, 10.709); the low-lying "Laurentine" area lay between Ostia and Lavinium on the coast southwest of Rome (43 B3), although Pliny makes no mention of a marsh on the approach to his villa there (*Ep.* 2.17.2–3).

Lebedos (*Kisik*): town on the coast of Asia Minor (57 E3, 61 D1).

Lesbos: Aegean island (57 D–E2).

Leucas (*Leukada*): island in the Adriatic, just offshore from Actium (54 C4).

Limyra (*Finike*): town in southern Asia Minor (65 D5).

Luceria (*Lucera*): town in southeastern Italy (44 H2, 45 B1).

Lucrine Lake (*Lago Lucrino*): lake just south of Cumae (44 F4). Agrippa joined it to Lake Avernus by means of a canal.

Luna (*Luni*): town on the Via Aurelia in northwestern Italy (41 C1).

Lupia (*Lippe*): river in Germany (11 H1, 12 B1).

Lycia: region on the southern coast of Asia Minor (65 B4–C4).

Lydia: region in west-central Asia Minor (56 F4–G5).

Macedonia: region in northeastern Greece; a Roman province from 146 BC (49 D3–F3, 50 A2–D2).

Magnesia: name of towns in Asia Minor. V.'s reference (1.4.1) is probably to Magnesia-on-Meander (61 F2), modern *Tekin*; Magnesia ad Sipylum (56 E4), modern *Manisa*, was the site of Antiochus' defeat in 190 BC.

Marathon: town in northeastern Attica (55 F4).

Marcomanni: a people of central Germany (12 G2–I2).

Marica's Marsh: area near Minturnae (44 E3).

Marsi: a people of central Italy (44 E2).

Massilia: modern *Marseille* (15 E3).

Mauretania: region of northern Africa comprising the northern part of modern Morocco and Algeria. Not to be confused with modern Mauritania, on the northwestern coast of Africa, it became two provinces in AD 42 (31 B4–D3).

Media: area of Asia Minor (3 D3–F2). The Medes were an ancient

359

DIRECTORY OF PEOPLES AND PLACES

people whose empire was called after them; in classical literature they are often identified with the Persians.

Megara (*Megara*): town just north of the Isthmus of Corinth (58 E2).

Metapontum (*Metaponto*): town on the Gulf of Taranto in southern Italy (45 E4).

Miletus (*Balat*): town on the coast of Asia Minor (61 E2).

Minturnae (*Minturno*): town on the Via Appia overlooking the so-called Amynclan Bay (44 E3).

Misenum (*Miseno*): port at the northern end of the Bay of Naples and one of the bases of the Roman fleet (44 F4).

Moesia: area of the Balkans incorporating parts of modern Serbia, Macedonia, and Bulgaria; in the late first century AD it had become the provinces of Moesia Superior and Moesia Inferior (100 L3–M3).

Munda: town in southwestern Spain (26 E4).

Mutina (*Modena*): town in northern Italy (39 H4).

Mycenae: unidentified town on Crete. See 60 A1.

Mylae (*Milazzo*): town on the northeastern coast of Sicily (47 G2).

Myrina: town on the coast of Asia Minor, just north of Cyme (56 D4).

Mytilene (*Mytilene*): town on the island of Lesbos (56 D3).

Myus (*Afşar*): town on the River Meander in Asia Minor (61 E2).

Narbo Martius (*Narbonne*): Mediterranean town in the far south of France (25 H2).

Naulochus: town (near *Spadafora*) on the northeastern coast of Sicily (47 G2).

Nauportus (*Vrhnika*): town in Pannonia, modern Slovenia (20 B4).

Neapolis (*Naples*): city in Campania (44 F4).

Nepe (*Nepi*): town in Etruria (42 C4).

Nola (*Nola*): town in Campania (44 G4).

Noricum: region straddling what is now Austria and Slovenia; the kingdom of Noricum was incorporated into the Roman Empire in 16 BC (19 E3–F2, 100 J2–K2).

Numantia (*Numancia*): town in northern Spain (25 C4).

Olympia (*Archaia Olympia*): town in the western Peloponnese and site of the Olympic Games (58 B2).

Osca (*Huesca*): town in northeastern Spain (25 E3).

Ostia (*Ostia Antica*): port of Rome (43 B2).

360

DIRECTORY OF PEOPLES AND PLACES

Paestum (*Paestum*): town in southwestern Italy (45 A4).

Palinurus: promontory in southwestern Italy (45 B4).

Pandateria: modern island of *Ventotene*, off the western coast of central Italy (44 D4).

Pannonia: area of central Europe that is now covered by parts of Austria, Hungary, Serbia, and other countries; created a Roman province in AD 9 (20 C3–E4, 100 K2).

Paros (*Paros*): Aegean island (57 D4, 61 A3).

Parthia: the vast Parthian Empire stretched eastward from south of Armenia as far as the northwestern border of India (97 C1–E2).

Patrae (*Patras*): town on the northern coast of the Peloponnese (58 B1).

Pelasgians: general term for very early inhabitants of the Aegean lands.

Pergamum (*Bergama*): city in western Asia Minor (56 E3).

Pergamus (*Grimbiliana*): town on the northwestern coast of Crete (60 A1).

Perusia (*Perugia*): town in central Italy (42 C2).

Perustae: a Balkan people in eastern Dalmatia.

Pharsalus (*Pharsala*): town in central Greece (55 C2).

Philippi (*Filippoi*): town in northeastern Greece (51 C2).

Phocaea (*Foça*): town on the coast of Asia Minor (56 D4).

Picenum: region of east central Italy, now straddling the southern Marche and northern Abruzzo (42 E2–F3).

Piraeus: port of Athens (58 A2).

Pisaurum (*Pésaro*): town on the eastern coast of Italy (42 D1).

Placentia (*Piacenza*): town on the River Po in northern Italy (39 F3).

Planasia: modern island of *Pianosa*, off the western coast of central Italy (41 C4).

Pompeii: famous town in the shadow of Mount Vesuvius (44 F4).

Pontia: modern island of *Ponza*, off the western coast of central Italy (44 C4).

Pontus: region stretching along the southern shore of the Black Sea; the kingdom of Pontus was gradually incorporated into the Roman Empire from the mid-first century BC onward (87 B4–D4). The name can also denote the Black Sea itself, as apparently at 40.1 (cf. 101.3).

Potentia (*Porto Recanati*): town on the eastern coast of Italy (42 F2).

Praeneste (*Palestrina*): town just over twenty miles east-southeast of Rome (44 C2).

361

DIRECTORY OF PEOPLES AND PLACES

Priene (*Güllübahçe*): town in western Asia Minor (61 E2).

Puteoli (*Pozzuoli*): town on the northern Bay of Naples (44 F4).

Pydna: town (near *Makrigialos*) on the northwestern shore of the Thermaic Gulf (50 C4).

Raetia: region roughly equivalent to modern Switzerland; incorporated into the Roman Empire in 15 BC (19 B3–C2).

Raudian Plains: assumed to be in the vicinity of Vercellae (*Vercelli*) in northwestern Italy (39 C3).

Rubicon (*Pisciatello*): river in northeastern Italy that marked the boundary between Cisalpine Gaul and Italy proper (40 C4).

Sabines: a people of central Italy (42 D4–E3).

Sacriportus: town south of Praeneste, perhaps near the modern Piombinara.

Salamis: town on the east coast of Cyprus, north of Famagusta (72 D2).

Salernum (*Salerno*): coastal town in southwestern Italy on the Gulf of Salerno (44 G4).

Sallues: a people in the area of northwestern Italy/southeastern Cisalpine Gaul (cf. Plin. *HN* 3.47).

Samnites: a people of southern Italy (45 A2–B2).

Samos (*Samos*): island off the coast of Asia Minor (61 D2).

Samothrace (*Samothraki*): island in the northern Aegean (51 F4).

Sardinia: island on which Roman rule (48) is dated by V. (38.2) from 235 BC, the first of five years of campaigns; a praetor was sent out as governor from 227. Whether there was a Roman presence there in 230–228 is unknown.

Saticula (*S. Agata dei Goti*): town in Campania (44 G3).

Scolacium Minervia (*Roccelletta*): coastal town on the Gulf of Squillace near the southern tip of the "toe" of Italy (46 E4).

Scordisci: a Balkan people (21 B5–D5).

Seleucia (*Tall 'Umar*): famous city on the River Tigris in modern Iraq (91 F4).

Semnones: a people of eastern Germany (10 I4).

Setia (*Sezze*): town forty miles southeast of Rome (44 D2).

Sicily: From 227 BC the western end of the island (47) was a province under a praetor, which was extended to cover the whole of the

362

DIRECTORY OF PEOPLES AND PLACES

island in 211–210 following the capture of Syracuse. Rome had achieved effective control of all Sicily except for the Syracusan kingdom in the southeast at the end of the First Punic War in 241, but it is disputed whether this at first involved anything that could be called provincial administration.

Sinuessa (*Torre S. Limato*): coastal town in Campania just south of Minturnae (44 E3).

Siscia (*Sisak*): Pannonian town now in modern Croatia (20 D4).

Smyrna (*Izmir*): town on the coast of Asia Minor (56 E5).

Sora (*Sora*): town in central Italy (44 E2).

Spain: In the early second century BC parts of Spain were formed into the two provinces of Hispania Ulterior (Further Spain) in the south and Hispania Citerior (Nearer Spain) in the east; under the reorganization of Augustus, an area roughly equivalent to modern Portugal was called the province of Lusitania, Ulterior was renamed Baetica, and the remainder of the peninsula was called Tarraconensis.

Sparta (*Sparti*): city-state in the southern Peloponnese (58 C3).

Spoletium (*Spoleto*): town on the Via Flaminia in central Italy (42 D3).

Suessa Aurunca (*Sessa*): Campanian town just inland from Minturnae (44 E3).

Sutrium (*Sutri*): town on the Via Cassia roughly thirty miles north of Rome (42 C4).

Syracuse (*Siracusa*): a principal city of Sicily (47 G4).

Syria: formerly the heartland of the Seleucid Empire; the region was annexed by Pompey in 64 BC (37.5) and was thereafter a Roman province (100 P4–5).

Tarentum Neptunia (*Taranto*): town on the Gulf of Taranto in southern Italy (45 F4).

Tarracina (*Terracina*): coastal town in southern Latium on the Via Appia (44 D3).

Tauromenium (*Taormina*): town in northeastern Sicily (47 G3).

Tegea: unidentified town on Crete.

Tenos (*Tinos*): one of the Cyclades islands in the Aegean (60 B4).

Tergeste (*Trieste*): town in northeastern Italy on the Gulf of Trieste, close to the border with modern Slovenia (19 F4).

Thapsus (*Ras-Dimas*): town on the coast of modern Tunisia (33 H1).

363

DIRECTORY OF PEOPLES AND PLACES

Thebes (*Thivai*): a principal town of Boeotia (55 E4).

Thesprotia: area of Greece along the east coast of the Adriatic (54 B2–C3).

Thessaly: region in central Greece (55 B2–C2).

Thrace: largely mountainous area in northeastern Greece (51).

Thurii (*Sibari*): town in the "toe" of Italy (46 D2).

Mount Tifata (*Monti di Maddaloni*): mountain in Campania (44 F3).

Troia (*Hisarlik*): Troy, in western Asia Minor (56 C2).

Tusculum (*Tuscolo*): town just off the Via Latina about fifteen miles from Rome (43 C2).

Tyre (*Sur*): town on the eastern coast of the Mediterranean in modern Lebanon (69 B3).

Utica (*Henchir-bou-Chateur*): town on the northern African coast just north of Carthage (32 F2).

Valentia (*Valence*): town on the River Rhone, south of modern Vienne in France (17 D4).

Veii (*Veio*): town just north of Rome (43 B1).

Velia (*Castellamare di Velia*): town on the northwestern coast of the "toe" of Italy (46 B1).

Venetia: region of northeastern Italy (40 A1–C1).

Venusia (*Venosa*): town in Apulia, birthplace of the poet Horace (45 C3).

Vesuvius (*Monte Vesuvio*): famous volcano in Campania (44 F4).

Vienna (*Vienne*): town on the River Rhone, south of Lyon in modern France (17 D2).

Visurgis: River *Weser* in Germany (10 E3).

Zama (*Jama*): town in modern Tunisia (32 D4).

364

INDEX OF NAMES

References are to Velleius' text. All dates are BC unless stated otherwise.

Accius, 1.17.1, 2.9.3
Acerrani, 1.14.4
Achaea/Achaeans, 1.3.1, 1.11.2, 1.12.1, 23.3, 38.5, 77.2, 101.3
Achaei (a people east of the Black Sea), 40.1
Achillas (Egyptian royal adviser), 53.2
Achilles, 1.1.1, 1.1.3, 1.6.5
Actium, 84–86, 88.1
Adduus (assassin), 102.2
Adriatic Sea, 43.1
Aeculanum, 2.16.2
Aefula, 1.14.8
Aegeae, 70.4
Aegean Sea, 1.4.3
Aegisthus, 1.1.2–3
Aelius Catus, Sex. (cos. AD 4), 103.3
Aelius Lamia, L. (cos. AD 3), 116.3
Aelius Sejanus, L. (cos. AD 31), 127–28
Aemilius Lepidus, M. (cos. 46, 42; triumvir), 63.1–2, 64.4, 66.1, 67.3–4, 80.1–4, 88.1

Aemilius Lepidus, M. (son of above), 88
Aemilius Lepidus, M. (cos. AD 6), 114.5, 115.2
Aemilius Lepidus, Paul(l)us (cos. suff. 34), 95.3
Aemilius Lepidus Porcina, M. (cos. 137), 2.10.1
Aemilius Paul(l)us, L. (cos. 219, 216), 1.9.3
Aemilius Paul(l)us, L. (cos. 50), 67.3
Aemilius Paul(l)us Macedonicus, L. (cos. 182, 168), 1.9.3–6, 1.10.3, 1.12.3, 2.5.3, 2.10.2, 38.5, 39.1, 40.3
[Aemilius Sura (historical writer), 1.6.6]
Aenaria, 19.4
Aeolians, 1.4.4
Aeschylus, 1.16.3
Aesernia, 1.14.8
Aetolia, 38.5
Afranius, L. (writer of *fabulae togatae*), 1.17.1, 2.9.3
Afranius, L. (cos. 60), 48.1, 50.4

365

INDEX OF NAMES

Africa, 1.2.3, 1.12.4, 1.15.4,
 2.4.2, 2.11.2, 19.4, 38.2, 40.4,
 53.1, 54.2, 55.1–2, [68.1],
 80.1, 116.2–3, 125.5, 129.4
Africanus. *See* Cornelius Scipio
Agamemnon, 1.1.2
Agrippa. *See* Vipsanius Agrippa
Agrippina (the elder), 130.4
Alba Fucens, 1.11.1, 1.14.5
Albania, 40.1
Albis (river), 106.2–3
Alcmaeon, 1.8.3
Alcman, 1.18.3
Alesia, 47.1
Aletes, 1.3.3, 1.13.1
Alexander the Great, 1.6.5,
 1.11.4, 41.1
Alexandria, 1.10.1, 1.14.3, 53.1,
 56.2, 82.4, 87.1, 88.1
Aliso (stronghold), 120.4
Allobroges, 2.10.2
Alps, 2.6.2, 2.12.4–5, 63.1, 90.1,
 105.3, 109.4
Alsium, 1.14.8
Altinum, 76.2
Ampius Balbus, T. (pr. 58),
 40.4
Amyntas (king of Galatia), 84.2
Anchises, 41.1
Andros, 1.4.3
Anicius Gallus, L. (cos. 160),
 1.9.5–6
Annia (wife of Cinna), 41.2
Annius Milo, T. (pr. 55), 45.3,
 47.4, 68.2–3
Antiochus III the Great (Seleu-
 cid king), 1.6.[6], 38.5
Antiochus IV Epiphanes (Seleu-
 cid king), 1.10.1

Antistius, P. (trib. pleb. 88),
 26.2–3, 88.3
Antistius Vetus, ?C. (pr. 70),
 43.4
Antistius Vetus, C. (cos. suff.
 30), 90.4
Antistius Vetus, C. (cos. 6), 43.4
Antistius Vetus, C. (cos. AD 23),
 43.4
Antistius Vetus, L. (cos. suff.
 AD 28), 43.4
Antonius, C. (pr. 44; brother of
 the triumvir), 69.3
Antonius, Iullus (cos. 10; son of
 the triumvir), 100.4
Antonius, L. (cos. 41; brother of
 the triumvir), 74.2–4
Antonius, M. (cos. 99; orator),
 2.9.1, 22.3, 36.2
Antonius, M. (cos. 44, triumvir),
 56–87, 91.1
Antonius Creticus, M. (pr. 74),
 31.3–4
Apollo, temple of, 81.3
Apollonia, 59.4
Appius. *See* Claudius
Apronius, L. (cos. suff. AD 8),
 116.3
Apuleius, Sex. (cos. AD 14),
 123.3
Apuleius Saturninus, L. (trib.
 pleb. 103, 100), 2.12.6, 2.15.4
Apulia, 25.1
Aquae Sextiae, 1.15.4, 2.12.4
Aquileia, 1.15.2
Aquilius, M'. (cos. 129), 2.4.1,
 2.4.5
Aquilius, M'. (cos. 101), 2.18.3
Arbaces, 1.6.2

366

INDEX OF NAMES

(?) Archelaus (king of Cappadocia), 129.2
Archilochus, 1.5.2
Argos, 1.6.5, 1.18.2
Aricia, 1.14.2
Ariminum, 1.14.7
Aristodemus, 1.2.1
Aristonicus, 2.4.1, 38.5
Aristophanes, 1.16.3
Aristotle, 1.16.4
Armenia, 33.1, 37.2–5, 82.1–3, 94.4, 100.1, 102.2, 104.4, 122.1
Arminius, 118.2
Arruntius, L. (cos. 22), 77.3, 85.2, 86.2
Artagera, 102.2
Artavasdes II (king of Armenia), 94.4
Artorius (doctor), 70.1
Arverni, 2.10.2
Asculum, 21.1
Asia, 1.4.1, 1.4.3, 1.6.1, 2.4.1, 2.18.1, 2.18.3, 23.3, 23.6, 33.1, 38.5, 40.4, 42.1, 42.3, 69.1–2, 79.5, 92.2, 93.2, 98.2, 101.3, 126.4
Asinius Herius (leader of Italians), 2.16.1
Asinius Pollio, C. (cos. 40), 36.2, 63.3, 73.2, 76.2–3, 86.3, 128.3
Assyrians, 1.6.1, 1.6.[6]
Athens/Athenians, 1.2.1–2, 1.3.1, 1.4.1, 1.4.3, 1.8.3, 1.10.1, 1.18.1, 23.3–4, 58.4
Atia, 59.2, 60.1
Atilius Regulus, M. (cos. 267, suff. 256), 38.2

Atilius Serranus, C. (cos. 106), 53.4
Atreus, 1.8.2
Attalids, 38.5
Attalus II (king of Pergamum), 1.9.2
Attalus III (king of Pergamum), 2.4.1
Attica, 1.2.1–2, 1.4.1, 1.18.1
Attius Varus, P. (pr. ?53), 55.4
Augustus (Octavian), 36.1, 38.3–4, 39.2, 59–124, 126.1, 127.1
Aurelius Cotta, C. (cos. 75), 43.1
Aurelius Cotta, L. (cos. 65), 32.3
Aurelius Cotta Maximus Messalinus, M. (cos. AD 20), 112.2
Aurelius Scaurus, M. (cos. suff. 108), 2.9.1, 2.12.2
Auximum, 1.15.3
Aventine Hill, 2.6.6
Avernus (lake), 79.2

Babylon, 1.6.2
Bagienni, 1.15.5
Balbus. See Cornelius
Bathinus (river), 114.4
Bato(nes) (leader[s] of Pannonians), 110.4, 114.4
Beneventum, 1.14.7, 123.1
Bestia. See Calpurnius
Bithynia, 2.4.1, 39.2, 42.3
Bocchus (king of Mauretania), 2.12.1
Boeotia, 23.3
Boiohaemum, 109.5
Bononia, 1.15.2

367

INDEX OF NAMES

Bovillae, 47.4
Britain, 46.1, 47.1
Bructeri, 105.1
Brundisium, 1.14.8, 24.3, 40.3, 50.1, 59.5, 61.2, 76.3, 86.3
Brutus. *See* Junius
Buxentum, 1.15.3
Byzantium, 2.7.7

Caecilii, 2.11.3
Caecilius (comic poet), 1.17.1
Caecilius Metellus, M. (cos. 115), 1.11.7, 2.8.2
Caecilius Metellus Balearicus, Q. (cos. 123), 1.11.7
Caecilius Metellus Caprarius, C. (cos. 113), 1.11.7, 2.8.2
Caecilius Metellus Creticus, Q. (cos. 69), 34.1–2, 38.6, 40.5, 48.6
Caecilius Metellus Diadematus, L. (cos. 117), 1.11.7
Caecilius Metellus Macedonicus, Q. (cos. 143), 1.11.2–6, 1.12.1, 2.1.2, 2.5.2
Caecilius Metellus Numidicus, Q. (cos. 109), 2.8.2, 2.9.2, 2.11.1–2, 2.15.3–4, 39.2, 45.3
Caecilius Metellus Pius, Q. (cos. 80), 2.15.3, 28.1, 29.5, 30.2
Caecilius Metellus Pius Scipio, Q. (cos. 52), 54.2
Caecina Severus, A. (cos. suff. 1), 112.4
Caedicius, L. (camp prefect), 120.4
Caelian Hill, 130.2

Caelius Rufus, M. (pr. 48), 36.2, 68.1
Caepio. *See* Fannius; Servilius
Caesar. *See* Julius
Caesetius Flavus, L. (trib. pleb. 44), 68.4
Calabria, 25.1
Calatia, 61.2
Caldus. *See* Coelius
Cales, 1.14.3
Calidius, M. (pr. 57), 36.2
Calpurnia (wife of Antistius), 26.3, 88.3
Calpurnia (wife of Caesar), 57.2
Calpurnius Bestia, L. (cos. 111), 26.3
Calpurnius Bibulus, M. (cos. 59), 44.5
(?) Calpurnius Piso, Cn. (cos. 7), 130.3
Calpurnius Piso, L. (cos. 15), 98.1
(?) Calpurnius Piso, L. (cos. 1), 130.3
Calpurnius Piso Frugi, L. (cos. 133), 2.2.2
Camelius, 64.1
Campania, 20.3, 25.1, 44.4, 45.2, 48.2, 75.1, 76.1, 123.1
Campus Martius, 92.3, 126.2
Canidius Crassus, P. (cos. suff. 40), 85.2, 85.6, 87.3
Caninius Gallus, L. (cos. suff. 2), 100.2
Cannae, 1.9.3
Canninefates, 105.1
Cannutius, Ti. (trib. pleb. 44), 64.3

368

INDEX OF NAMES

Capitol, 2.1.2, 2.3.1–2, 58.2–3, 131.1
Cappadocia, 39.3
Capua, 1.7.2–4, 2.8.2, 25.2, 30.5, 44.4
Caranus, 1.6.5
Carbo. *See* Papirius
Carnuntum, 109.5
Carrhae, 46.4, 82.3, 91.1, 119.1
Carseoli, 1.14.5
Carthage, 1.6.4, 1.6.[6], 1.12.2, 1.12.4–7, 1.13.1, 1.15.4, 2.1.1, 2.4.2–3, 2.7.7–8, 19.4, 38.2
Carvilius Maximus, Sp. (cos. 293, 272), 128.2
Casilinum, 61.2
Cassius Longinus, C. (cos. 171), 1.15.3
C. Cassius Longinus, C. (cos. 124), 1.15.4
Cassius Longinus, C. (pr. 44), 46.5, 56.3, 58.1–2, 62.2–3, 65.1, 69.2–6, 70.1–3, 71.1, 72.2, 73.2, ?84.2, 87.3
Cassius Longinus, L. (cos. AD 30), 1.8.4
Cassius Longinus Ravilla, L. (cos. 127), 2.10.1
Cassius Parmensis, C. (qu. 43), 87.3
Castrum, 1.14.8
Catilina. *See* Sergius
Cato. *See* Insteius; Porcius
Catullus, 36.2
Catus. *See* Aelius
Cauchi, 106.1
Caudini, 2.1.5
Ceionius (camp prefect), 119.4
Censorinus. *See* Marcius

Ceres, rites of, 1.4.1
Cestius Macedonicus (Perusine leader), 74.4
Cethegus. *See* Cornelius
Chalcidians, 1.4.1
Charops, 1.2.2, 1.8.3
Chatti, 109.5
Chattuarii, 105.1
Cherusci, 105.1
Chios, 1.4.3
Cicero. *See* Tullius
Cilicia, 32.4, 39.2
Cimbri, 2.8.3, 2.12.2, 19.3, 22.4, 120.1
Cimon, 1.8.6
Cinna. *See* Cornelius
Claudia (daughter of Fulvia and Clodius), 65.2
Claudius (mountain), 112.3
Claudius Caecus, Ap. (cos. 307), 1.14.7
Claudius Canina, C. (cos. 273), 1.14.7
Claudius Caudex, Ap. (cos. 264), 1.12.6, 38.2
Claudius Drusus. *See* Nero
Claudius Marcellus, C. (cos. 49), 49.1, 49.3
Claudius Marcellus, M. (cos. 222, etc.), 38.2
Claudius Marcellus, M. (son of Octavia), 93.1–2
Claudius Nero, Ti. (pr. 42; father of Tiberius), 75.1, 75.3, 76.1, 77.3, 79.2, 94.1
Claudius Pulcher, Ap. (cos. 143), 2.2.3
Claudius Pulcher, Ap. (lover of Julia), 100.5

369

INDEX OF NAMES

Claudius Quadrigarius, Q. (historian), 2.9.6
Claudius Russus, Ap. (cos. 268), 1.14.7
Clazomenae, 1.4.3
Cleopatra, 82.4, 83.1, 84.2, 85.3, 85.6, 86.3, 87.1–3
Clodia, 45.1
Clodius Pulcher, P. (trib. pleb. 58), 45.1–4, 47.4, 68.3
Clusium, 28.1
Codrus, 1.2.1–2
Coelius Antipater, L., 2.9.6
Coelius Caldus, 120.6
Colchi, 40.1
Colline Gate, 27.1
Colophon, 1.4.3
Compsa, 2.16.2, 68.3
Contrebia, 2.5.2
Coponius, C. (pr. 49), 83.3
Corfinium, 2.16.4, 50.1
Corinth/Corinthians, 1.2.2, 1.3.3, 1.12.1, 1.13.1, 1.13.4, 2.7.7, 84.2
Cornelia (daughter of Cinna and wife of Caesar), 41.2
Cornelia (mother of the Gracchi), 2.7.1
Cornelia (wife of Pompey), 53.2
Cornelius Balbus, L., 51.3
Cornelius Cethegus, C., 34.3–4
Cornelius Cinna, L. (cos. 87–84), 20.2, 20.4, 21.1–6, 22.2–3, 23.1, 23.3, 24.5, 41.2, 43.1
Cornelius Dolabella, Cn. (cos. 81), 43.3
Cornelius Dolabella, P. (cos. suff. 44), 58.3, 60.4–5, 69.1–2, 84.2

Cornelius Dolabella, P. (cos. AD 10), 125.5
Cornelius Lentulus, Cn. (cos. 146), 1.12.5
Cornelius Lentulus, Cossus (cos. 1), 116.2
Cornelius Lentulus Crus, L. (cos. 49), 49.1, 49.3, 51.3, 53.1
Cornelius Lentulus Gaetulicus, Cn. (cos. AD 26), 116.2
Cornelius Lentulus Spinther, P. (cos. 57), 53.1
Cornelius Lentulus Sura, P. (cos. 71), 34.3–4, 35.3
Cornelius Merula, L. (cos. 87), 20.3, 22.2
Cornelius Rufinus, P. (cos. 290, 277), 1.14.6, 2.17.2
Cornelius Scipio (lover of Julia), 100.5
Cornelius Scipio, P. (cos. 218), 38.4, 90.2
Cornelius Scipio Aemilianus Africanus, P. (cos. 147, 134), 1.10.3, 1.12.3, 1.13.2–3, 1.17.3, 2.1.1, 2.4.2, 2.9.1, 2.9.4, 38.2, 127.1
Cornelius Scipio Africanus, P. (cos. 205, 194), 1.10.3, 1.12.3, 2.1.1, 2.2.1, 2.3.1, 2.7.1, 2.8.1, 38.5, 90.2, 127.1
Cornelius Scipio Asiaticus, L. (cos. 190), 38.5
Cornelius Scipio Asiaticus, L. (cos. 83), 25.2
Cornelius Scipio Calvus, Cn. (cos. 222), 2.3.1, 38.4, 90.2
Cornelius Scipio Nasica, P. (cos. 191), 2.3.1

370

INDEX OF NAMES

Cornelius Scipio Nasica Corculum, P. (cos. 162, 155), 2.1.2, 2.3.1

Cornelius Scipio Nasica Serapio, P. (cos. 138), 2.3.1

Cornelius Sisenna, L. (pr. 78; historian), 2.9.5–6

Cornelius Sulla Felix, L. (cos. 88, 80), 2.12.1, 2.15.3, 2.16.2–4, 2.17.1, 2.18.3, 2.18.6, 19.1–2, 20.1, 23–30, 32.3, 41.2, 43.1, 61.3

Cornificius, L. (cos. 35), 79.4

Coruncanius, Ti. (cos. 280), 128.1

Corvinus. *See* Valerius

Cosa, 1.14.7

Cotta. *See* Aurelius

Cotys (king of Thrace), 129.1

Crassus. *See* Licinius

Cratinus, 1.16.3

Cremona, 1.14.8

Creon, 1.8.3

Cresphontes, 1.2.1

Crete, 1.1.2, 34.1, 38.6, 81.2

Cumae, 1.4.1–2

Curia Hostilia, 2.12.6, 26.2

Curio. *See* Scribonius

Curius Dentatus, M'. (cos. 290), 1.14.6

Cyme, 1.4.4

Cyprus, 1.1.1, 38.6, 45.4

Cyzicus, 2.7.7, 33.1

Daesitiates, 115.4

Dalmatia/Dalmatians, 39.3, 78.2, 90.1, 96.3, 110.2, 114.4, 115.1, 115.4, 116.1–2, 117.1, 121.2

Damasippus. *See* Junius

Danube (river), 110.1

Decidius Saxa, L. (trib. pleb. 44), 78.1

Decius Mus, P. (cos. 312, etc.), 1.14.6

Dellius, Q., 84.2

Delos, 1.4.3

Delphi, 1.1.3

Dertona, 1.15.5

Diana (divinity), 25.4

Didius, T. (cos. 98), 2.16.2

Dido, 1.6.4

Diphilus, 1.16.3

Dolabella. *See* Cornelius

Domitii, 2.10.2, 2.12.3

Domitius Ahenobarbus, Cn. (cos. 122), 2.10.2, 39.1

Domitius Ahenobarbus, Cn. (cos. 96), 2.12.3

Domitius Ahenobarbus, Cn. (cos. 32), 72.3, 76.2, 84.2

Domitius Ahenobarbus, Cn. (cos. AD 32), 2.10.2, 72.3

Domitius Ahenobarbus, L. (cos. 94), 26.2

Domitius Ahenobarbus, L. (cos. 54), 50.1

Domitius Ahenobarbus, L. (cos. 16), 72.3

Domitius Calvinus, Cn. (cos. 53, 40), 78.3

Drusus. *See* Livius; Nero

Drusus Julius Caesar (cos. AD 15, 21; son of Tiberius), 125.4, 129.3, 130.3

Dyrrachium, 49.4, 51.1, 69.3

Eggius, L. (camp prefect), 119.4

371

INDEX OF NAMES

Egnatius, Marius (leader of Italians), 2.16.1
Egnatius Rufus, M. (pr. 21), 91.3, 92.4, 93.1
Egypt, 39.2, 53.1–2
Electra, 1.1.3
Elis, 1.8.1
Elissa (Dido), 1.6.4
(Epeus, 1.1.1)
Ephesus, 1.4.3
Ephyra (in Thesprotia), 1.1.1
Ephyre (Corinth), 1.3.3
Epidius Marullus, C. (trib. pleb. 44), 68.4
Epirus, 1.1.1
Eporedia, 1.15.5
Eretria, 1.4.1
Erythrae, 1.4.3
Eryxias, 1.8.3
Etruscans, 1.7.2–3, 1.8.5
Euboea, 1.4.1
Eumenes II (king of Pergamum), 1.9.2
Euphrates (river), 46.4, 101.1
Eupolis, 1.16.3
Euporus (slave of C. Gracchus), 2.6.6
Euripides, 1.16.3
Europe, 40.4

Fabius (?Dorso) Licinus, C. (cos. 273), 1.14.7
Fabius Maximus, Q. (pr. 181), 1.10.3
Fabius Maximus Aemilianus, Q. (cos. 145), 1.10.3, 2.5.3
Fabius Maximus Allobrogicus, Q. (cos. 121), 2.10.2, 39.1

Fabius Maximus Rullianus, Q. (cos. 295), 1.14.6
(?) Fabius Maximus Servilianus, Q. (cos. 142), 2.5.3
Fabrateria, 1.15.4
Fannius, C. (cos. 122), 1.17.3, 2.9.1
Fannius Caepio, 91.2, 93.1
Father Liber, 82.4
Faventia, 28.1
Favonius, M. (pr. 49), 53.1
Fidentia, 28.1
Firmum, 1.14.8, 29.1
Flavius Fimbria, C., 24.1
Floralia, 1.14.8
Fonteius (legate of Q. Servilius, pr. 91), 2.15.1
Formiae, 1.14.3
Fregellae, 2.6.4
Fregenae, 1.14.8
Fulvia (wife of Mark Antony), 74.3, 76.2
Fulvius Flaccus, ?Cn. (brother of Q. Fulvius Flaccus, cos. 179), 1.10.6
Fulvius Flaccus, M. (cos. 264), 1.12.6
Fulvius Flaccus, M. (cos. 125), 2.6.4–6, 2.7.2
Fulvius Flaccus, Q. (cos. 237, etc.), 2.8.2
Fulvius Flaccus, Q. (cos. 179), 1.10.6, 2.8.2
Fulvius Flaccus, Q. (son of the consul of 125), 2.7.2
Fulvius Nobilior, M. (cos. 189), 1.15.2, 38.5
Fundi, 1.14.3

372

INDEX OF NAMES

Gabinius, A. (cos. 58), 31.2

Gades, 1.2.3

Gallograecia, 39.2

Gaul/Gauls, 1.15.5, 2.12.2, 2.17.3, 39.1–2, 44.5, 46.1, 47.2, 60.5, 63.1, 97.1, 104.3, 120.6, 121.1, 129.3

Gellius Publicola, L. (cos. 36), 85.2

Gentius (king of Illyrians), 1.9.5

Germanicus Julius Caesar (cos. AD 12, 18; nephew and adopted son of Tiberius), 116.1, 123.1, 125.1, 125.4, 129.2–3, 130.3

Germanicus Julius Caesar, Ti. (grandson of Tiberius), 130.3

Germany/Germans, 97–98, 100.1, 104–9, 114.1, 115–18, 120–23, 125.1, 129.2

Getae, 59.4

Glaucus (divinity), 83.2

Gracchus. *See* Sempronius

Granicus (river), 1.11.4

Gravisca, 1.15.2

Greece/Greeks, 1.3.1, 1.4.3–4, 1.6.3, 1.9.1, 1.17.1, 1.18.1, 2.9.3

Hannibal, 1.14.8, 1.15.1, 2.18.1, 27.2, 28.2

Helen, 1.1.3

Heniochi, 40.1

Heraclidae, 1.2.1, 1.2.3

Herculaneum, 2.16.2

Hercules, 1.2.1, 1.3.2–3, 1.6.5, 1.8.2

Hercynian Forest, 108.1, 109.5

Hermione, 1.1.3

Hermunduri, 106.2

Hesiod, 1.7.1

Hippocles, 1.4.1

Hippotes, 1.3.3, 1.13.1

Hirpini, 2.16.2, 68.3

Hirtius, A. (cos. 43), 57.1, 61.3, 62.4

Homer, 1.3.3, 1.5.1–2, 1.7.1

Horatius Cocles, 2.6.6

Hortensius, Q. (pr. ?45), 71.2

Hortensius Hortalus, Q. (cos. 69; orator and historian), 2.16.3, 36.2, 48.6

Hostilius Mancinus, C. (cos. 137), 2.1.4–5, 2.2.1, 90.3

Iberia, 40.1

Icarian Sea, 1.4.3

Ilium, 1.3.3

Illyria/Illyricum/Illyrians, 1.9.5, 39.3, 78.2, 109.5, 112.2, 116.3, 123.1, 125.1, 125.5

Insteius Cato (leader of Italians), 2.16.1

Interamna, 1.14.4

Ion, 1.4.3

Ionia, 1.3.3, 1.4.3

Iphitus, 1.8.1

Isocrates, 1.16.5

Isthmus, 1.3.3

Italicum, 2.16.4

Janus, 38.3

Juba I (king of Numidia), 53.1, 54.2

Jugurtha, 2.9.4, 2.11.1–2, 2.12.1

373

INDEX OF NAMES

Julia (daughter of Augustus), 93.2, 96.1, 100.3, 100.5, 104.1
Julia (daughter of Julius Caesar), 44.3, 47.2
Julia (sister of Julius Caesar), 59.1–2
Julius Caesar, C. (cos. 59, etc.), 30.3, 36.2, 39.1, 41–64, 68.1, 68.4, 69.1, 69.5, 87.3
Julius Caesar, C. (cos. AD 1; grandson of Augustus), 96.1, 99.2, 101–3
Julius Caesar, L. (cos. 90), 2.15.1
Julius Caesar, L. (cos. 64), 67.3
Julius Caesar, L. (grandson of Augustus), 96.1, 99.2, 102–3
Julius Caesar Strabo, C. (orator), 2.9.2
Julius Florus (Gallic rebel), 129.3
Julius Sacrovir (Gallic rebel), 129.3
Junia (sister of Brutus), 88.1
Junius Blaesus, Q. (cos. suff. AD 10), 125.5
Junius Brutus, M. (pr. 44), 36.2, 52.5, 56.3, 58.1–2, 62.2–3, 65.1, 69–73, 76.1, 87.3, 88.1
Junius Brutus Albinus, D. (cos. des. 43), 56.3, 58.1–2, 60.5, 61.4, 62.4, 63.3, 64.1, 87.2
Junius Brutus Damasippus, L. (pr. 82), 26.2
Junius Brutus Gallaecus (Callaicus), D. (cos. 138), 2.5.1
Junius Juncus, M. (pr. 76), 42.3
Junius Silanus, M. (cos. 109), 2.12.2

Junius Silanus, M. (cos. 25), 77.3
Jupiter Capitolinus, 131.1
Juventius Laterensis, M. (pr. 51), 63.2

Labienus, Q. (son of next), 78.1
Labienus, T. (trib. pleb. 63), 40.4, 55.4
Lacedaemonians, 1.6.3, 1.18.2
Laconia/Laconians, 1.3.1, 1.18.3
Laelius, C. (cos. 190), 127.1
Laelius Sapiens, C. (cos. 140), 1.17.3, 2.9.1, 127.1
Laenas. *See* Popilius
Lamia. *See* Aelius
Langobardi, 106.2
Laodicea, 69.2
Larissa, 1.4.4
Lasthenes (Cretan leader), 34.1
Laurentine Marshes, 19.1
Lebedus, 1.4.3
Lentulus. *See* Cornelius
Lepidus. *See* Aemilius
Lesbos, 1.2.3, 1.4.4
Leucas, 84.2
Libo. *See* Scribonius
Licinius Calvus, C. (orator and poet), 36.2
Licinius Crassus, L. (cos. 95), 2.9.1, [36.2]
Licinius Crassus, M. (cos. 70, 55), 30.6, 44.1–2, 46.1–4, 91.1, 119.1
Licinius Crassus Dives Mucianus, P. (cos. 131), 1.17.3, 2.4.1
Licinius Lucullus, M. (son of next), 71.2

374

INDEX OF NAMES

Licinius Lucullus Ponticus, L. (cos. 74), 33.1–4, 34.2, 37.1–2, 40.5, 48.6

Licinius Nerva Silianus, A. (cos. AD 7), 116.4

Limyra, 102.3

Livia (wife of Augustus), 71.3, 75.3, 79.2, 94.1, 95.1, 130.5

(?) Livius Andronicus, 1.17.1

Livius Drusus, M. (trib. pleb. 91), 2.13–15

Livius Drusus Claudianus, M. (?pr. 50; father of Livia), 71.3, 75.3, 94.1

Livy, [1.17.2], 36.3

Lollius, M. (cos. 21), 97.1, 102.1

Luceria, 1.14.4

Lucilia (mother of Pompey), 29.2

Lucilius, C. (poet), 2.9.4

Lucilius, Sex. (trib. pleb. 87), 24.2

Lucretius, 36.2

Lucretius Ofella, Q., 27.6

Lucrinus (lake), 79.2

Lucullus. *See* Licinius

Luna, 1.15.2

Lupercal, 1.15.3

Lupercalia, 56.4

Lupia (river), 105.3

Lurius, M. (naval commander), 85.2

Lutatius Catulus, Q. (cos. 102), 2.12.5, 22.4

Lutatius Catulus, Q. (cos. 78), 32.1, 43.3, 48.6

Lycia/Lycians, 69.6, 102.3

Lycurgus, 1.6.3

Lydia, 1.1.4

Lydus, 1.1.4

Lysippus, 1.11.4

Macedonia, 1.6.5, 1.6.[6], 1.9.4, 1.11.1, 1.11.3, 2.8.1, 23.3, 38.5, 59.2, 69.3, 69.6, 70.1, 98.2, 101.3, 110.4, 110.6

Macedonicus. *See* Cestius

Maecenas, C., 88.2

Magius, Decius, 2.16.2

Magius, Minatius, 2.16.2

Magius Celer Velleianus (brother of Velleius), 115.1, 121.3, 124.4

Magnesia, 1.4.1

Mallius Maximus, Cn. (cos. 105), 2.12.2

Mancinus. *See* Hostilius

Manilius, C. (trib. pleb. 66), 33.1

Manilius, M. (cos. 149), 1.13.1

Manlius Acidinus, L. (pr. 210), 2.8.2

Manlius Acidinus Fulvianus, L. (cos. 179), 2.8.2

Manlius Torquatus, A. (cos. 244), 1.14.8

Manlius Torquatus, T. (cos. 235, 224), 38.2–3

Manlius Vulso, Cn. (cos. 189), 1.15.2, 39.2

Marcellus. *See* Claudius

Marcius Censorinus, C. (cos. 8), 102.1

Marcius Censorinus, L. (cos. 149), 1.13.1

Marcius Censorinus, L. (cos. 39), 2.14.3

375

INDEX OF NAMES

Marcius Crispus, Q. (pr. 46), 69.2
Marcius Philippus, L. (cos. 56), 59.3, 60.1
Marcius Rex, Q. (cos. 118), 1.15.5, 2.7.8
Marcomanni, 108.1, 109.5
Marica's Marsh, 19.2
Marius, C. (cos. 107, etc.), 1.15.5, 2.9.4, 2.11–12, 2.15–23, 26.1, 41.2, 43.1, 43.4, 128.3
Marius, C. (cos. 82), 19.1, 19.4, 20.5, 26–27
Maroboduus, 108–9, 120.5, 129.3
Mars, 1.8.4, 55.3, 90.1, 100.2, 131.1
Marsi, 2.15.1, 21.1, 29.1
Massilia, 2.7.7, 50.3, 102.3
Media/Medes, 1.6.1, 1.6.[6], 40.1, 82.1
Medon, 1.2.2
Medontidae, 1.2.2
Megara, 1.2.2
Megasthenes, 1.4.1
Melanthus, 1.2.1
Menander, 1.16.3
Menas (naval commander), 73.3, 77.3
Menecrates (naval commander), 73.3, 77.3
Menelaus, 1.1.3
Merula. See Cornelius
Messal(l)a and Messalinus. See Valerius
Metapontum, 1.1.1
Metellus. See Caecilius

Miletus, 1.4.3, 2.7.7
Milo. See Annius
Miltiades, 1.8.6
Minatius. See Magius
Minturnae, 1.14.6, 19.2
Minucius Rufus, M. (cos. 110), 2.8.3
Misenum, 77.1
Mithridates VI Eupator (king of Pontus), 2.18.1, 2.18.3, 23.3–6, 24.1, 33.1, 37.1, 40.1
Mucius Scaevola, P. (cos. 133), 2.2.2
Mucius Scaevola, Q. (cos. 95), 2.9.2, 26.2
Mummius Achaicus, L. (cos. 146), 1.12.1, 1.12.5, 1.13.1–4, 38.5, 128.2
Munatius Plancus, L. (cos. 42), 63.3, 64.1, 67.3–4, 74.3, 76.2, 83.1, 83.3, 91.1, 95.3
Murena, L., 91.2, 93.1
Mutina, 61.4, 73.2
Mycenae, 1.1.2
Mylae, 79.4
Myrina, 1.4.4
Myrmidons, 1.3.1
Mytilene, 1.4.4, 2.18.3, 53.2
Myus, 1.4.3

Narbo Martius, 1.15.5, 2.7.8
Nauportus, 110.4
Neapolis, 1.4.2, 76.1, 123.1
Nepe, 1.14.2
Nero Claudius Drusus (cos. 9; brother of Tiberius), 95.1–2, 97.2–3
Nero Julius Caesar (son of Ger-

376

INDEX OF NAMES

manicus and grandson of
Tiberius), 130.4
Nestor, 1.1.1
Nicomedes IV (king of
Bithynia), 2.4.1, 39.2
Ninus (?Tukulti-Ninurta I),
1.6.2, 1.6.[6]
Nola, 1.7.2–3, 2.17.1, 2.18.4,
20.4, 123.1
Nonius Asprenas, L. (cos. suff.
AD 6), 120.3
Norbanus, C. (cos. 83), 25.2,
25.4
Noricum, 39.3, 109.3, 109.5
Numantia, 2.1.3–4, 2.4.2–3,
2.5.1, 2.9.4, 90.3
Numidicus. *See* Caecilius
Numitor, 1.8.4
Numonius Vala, 119.4

Ocean, 1.2.3, 106.3
Octavia (sister of Augustus),
1.11.3, 78.1, 93.1
Octavian. *See* Augustus
Octavius, C. (pr. 61; father of
Augustus), 59.2
Octavius, Cn. (cos. 165), 1.9.4–
6, 2.1.2
Octavius, Cn. (cos. 87), 22.2
Octavius, M. (trib. pleb. 133),
2.2.3
Olympic Games, 1.8.1
Olympieum, 1.10.1
Opimius, L. (cos. 121), 2.6.4–6,
2.7.2–6
Oppius Statianus, 82.2
Ops, temple of, 60.4
Orestes, 1.1.3–4, 1.2.3

Orodes II (king of Parthians),
46.4, 91.1
Osca, 30.1
Ostia, 94.3
Ovid, 36.3

Pacorus I (son of Parthian
king), 78.1
Pacuvius, 2.9.3
Paestum, 1.14.7
Palatine Hill, 1.8.4, 1.15.3,
2.14.3, 81.3
Palinurus (promontory), 79.3
Panaetius, 1.13.3
Panares (Cretan leader), 34.1
Pannonia/Pannonians, 39.3,
96.2–3, 98.1, 104.4, 109.3,
110.2, 110.5, 114.1, 114.4,
117.1, 121.2
Pansa. *See* Vibius
Papirius Carbo, C. (cos. 120),
2.4.4, 2.9.1
Papirius Carbo, Cn. (cos. 113),
2.12.2
Papirius Carbo, Cn. (cos. 85,
etc.), 24.5, 26.1, 27.1
Papirius Carbo Arvina, C. (pr.
?83), 26.2
Papius Mutilus, C., 2.16.1
Parilia, 1.8.4
Paros, 1.4.3
Parthia/Parthians, 24.3, 40.1,
46.2, 46.5, 53.1, 59.4, 78.1,
82.1, 91.1, 94.4, 100.1, 101.1–
3, 102.1, 119.1
Passienus Rufus, L. (cos. 4),
116.2
Paulus. *See* Aemilius

377

INDEX OF NAMES

Pedius, Q. (cos. suff. 43), 65.2, 69.5

Pelasgians, 1.3.1

Peloponnese/Peloponnesians, 1.2.1–2, 1.3.3

Pelops, 1.2.1, 1.8.2

Penthilus, 1.1.4

Pergamus, 1.1.2

Perpenna, M. (cos. 130), 2.4.1, 38.5

Perpenna, M. (pr. 82), 30.1

Perseus (king of Macedon), (1.9.1), 1.9.4, 1.9.6, 1.11.1

Persians, 1.6.[6]

Perusia, 74.3–4

Perustae, 115.4

Petreius, M. (pr. ?64), 48.1, 50.4

Pharnaces II (son of Mithridates and king of Pontus), 40.1, 55.2

Pharsalus, 52.3, 68.1

Phidippus, 1.1.1

Philemon, 1.16.3

Philip V (king of Macedon), 1.6.[6], 1.11.1

Philippi, 86.2

Phocaea, 1.4.3, 2.7.7

Phraates IV (king of Parthia), 82.1, 91.1, 94.4

Phraates V (Phraataces; king of Parthia), 101.1–2

Picenum, 1.15.3, 21.1, 29.1, 65.3

Pindar, 1.18.3

Pinnes (leader of Pannonians), 110.4, 114.4

Piraeus, 23.3

Pisaurum, 1.15.2

Piso. *See* Calpurnius; Pupius

Pius. *See* Caecilius Metellus

Placentia, 1.14.8

Plato, 1.16.4

Plautius Silvanus, M. (cos. 2), 112.4

Plotius Plancus, L. (pr. 43), 67.3

Pollio. *See* Asinius

Polybius, 1.13.3

Pompeii, 2.16.2

Pompeius, Q. (cos. 141), 2.1.4–5, 21.5, 90.3

Pompeius, Sex. (cos. AD 14), 123.2

Pompeius Magnus, Cn. (cos. 70, etc.; Pompey the Great), 2.15.3, 2.18.3, 21.1, 29–55, 61.3, 72.4, 76.1, 76.4, 79.6, 130.1

Pompeius Magnus, Cn. (son of above), 55.2, 55.4

Pompeius Magnus Pius, Sex. (cos. des. 35; son of Pompey the Great), 53.1, 72.4, 77–80, 87.2

Pompeius Rufus, Q. (cos. 88), 2.17.1, 2.18.6, 20.1

Pompeius Strabo, Cn. (cos. 89), 2.15.3, 2.16.4, 20.1, 21.1, 21.4, 29.1, 29.5

Pomponius, L. (writer of Atellan farces), 2.9.6

Pomponius, M. (friend of C. Gracchus), 2.6.6

Pomponius Flaccus, L. (cos. AD 17), 129.1

Pontidius, C. (leader of Italians), 2.16.1

378

INDEX OF NAMES

Pontius Telesinus (leader of Italians), 2.16.1, 27.1–6

Pontus, 38.6, 40.1

Popaedius Silo, Q. (leader of Italians), 2.16.1

(Popilius Laenas, C. [cos. 172], 1.10.1)

Popilius Laenas, M. (cos. 173), 1.10.1

Popilius Laenas, P. (cos. 132), 2.7.4

Popilius Laenas, P. (trib. pleb. 86), 24.2

Popilius Laenas, P. (trib. pleb. 84), 99

Porcius Cato, C. (cos. 114), 2.8.1

Porcius Cato, L. (cos. 89), 2.16.4

Porcius Cato, M. (cos. 195; Cato the Censor), 1.7.3–4, 1.13.1, 1.17.2–3, 2.8.1, 35.2, [36.2], 128.2

Porcius Cato, M. (cos. 118), 1.15.5, 2.7.8

Porcius Cato, M. (pr. 54; great-grandson of the Censor), 35.1–4, 38.6, 45.4–5, 47.5, 49.3, 54.3, 71.2

Porcius Cato, M. (son of the above), 71.2

Postumius Albinus, A. (cos. 180), 1.10.6

Postumius Albinus, Sp. (cos. 334, 321), 1.14.3–4

Postumus. *See* Vibius; Vipsanius

Potentia, 1.15.2

Praeneste, 26.1, 27.3, 27.6, 74.3

Priene, 1.4.3

Pseudophilippus, 1.11.1

Ptolemy (king of Cyprus), 38.6, 45.4

Ptolemy VI Philometor (king of Egypt), 1.10.1

Ptolemy XII Auletes (king of Egypt), 53.1

Ptolemy XIII Theos Philopator (king of Egypt), 53.1, 54.1

Publilius Philo, Q. (cos. 339, etc.), 1.14.4

Punic Wars, 1.14.8, 2.18.4, 38.2, 38.4, 44.4, 90.2, 128.1

Pupius Piso Frugi Calpurnianus, M. (cos. 61), 41.2

Puteoli, 1.15.3

Pydna, 1.9.4

Pyrrhus (king of Epirus), 1.14.6, 2.17.2

Pyrrhus (son of Achilles), 1.1.1, 1.1.3

Quin(c)tilius Varus, P. (cos. 13), 117–19, 120.3, 120.5, 122.2

Quin(c)tilius Varus, Sex. (qu. 49), 71.3, 119.3

Quin(c)tius Crispinus Sulpicianus, T. (cos. 9; lover of Julia), 100.5

Rabirius (poet), 36.3

Raetia/Raeti, 39.3, 95.2, 104.4, 122.1

Raudian Plains, 2.12.5

Regulus. *See* Atilius

Rhascupolis (king of Thrace), 129.1

Rhine (river), 2.8.3, 106.2, 119.4, 120.1, 120.6

379

INDEX OF NAMES

Rhodes/Rhodians, 1.9.2, 2.18.3, 69.6, 99.4, 103.1

Rhoemetalces (king of Thrace), 112.4

Romulus, 1.8.4–5

Roscius Otho, L. (trib. pleb. 67), 32.3

Rubicon (river), 49.4

Rupilius, P. (cos. 132), 2.7.4

Rutilius Lupus, P. (cos. 90), 2.15.1, 2.16.4

Rutilius Rufus, P. (cos. 105), 2.9.6, 2.13.2

Sabines, 1.8.5, 1.8.[6], 1.14.6–7

Sacriportus, 26.1–2, 28.1

Salamis (town in Cyprus), 1.1.1

Salernum, 1.15.3

Sallues, 1.15.4

Sallust, 36.2–3

Salvidienus Rufus, Q. (cos. des. 39), 59.5, 76.4

Samnites, 1.14.3, 27.1, 27.6

Samos, 1.4.3

Samothrace, 1.9.4

Sardanapalus (Assurbanipal; king of Assyria), 1.6.2

Sardinia, 38.2

Saticula, 1.14.4

Saturninus. See Apuleius; Sentius

Scaevola. See Mucius

Scaurus. See Aurelius

Scipio. See Cornelius

Scolacium Minervia, 1.15.4

Scordisci, 2.8.3, 39.3

Scribonia (wife of Octavian and mother of Julia), 100.5

Scribonius Curio, C. (trib. pleb., suff. 50), 48.3, 55.1, 68.1

Scribonius Libo Drusus, M. (pr. AD 15), ?129.2, 130.3

Segestes (German leader), 118.4

Seius Strabo, L. (father of Sejanus), 127.3

Sejanus. See Aelius

Seleucia, 46.4

Semiramis, 1.6.2

Semnones, 106.2

Sempronius Blaesus, C. (cos. 253, 244), 1.14.8

Sempronius Gracchus, C. (trib. pleb. 123, 122), 1.17.3, 2.2.3, 2.6–7, 2.9.1, 32.3

Sempronius Gracchus, Ti. (cos. 177, 163; father of the Gracchi), 2.2.1, 2.7.1

Sempronius Gracchus, Ti. (lover of Julia), 100.5

Sempronius Gracchus, Ti. (trib. pleb. 133), 1.17.3, 2.2–4, 2.6–7, 2.9.1

Sempronius Longus, Ti. (cos. 218), 90.2

Sempronius Sophus, P. (cos. 268), 1.14.7

Sempronius Tuditanus, C. (cos. 129), 2.4.5

Sentius Saturninus, C. (cos. 19), 77.3, 92.1–2, 105.1, 109.5, 110.2

Sentius Saturninus, C. (cos. AD 4), 103.3

Sergius Catilina, L. (pr. 68), 34.3–4, 35.5

380

INDEX OF NAMES

Sertorius, Q. (pr. 83), 25.3, 29.5, 30.1, 30.5, 90.3

Servilia (wife of M. Lepidus), 88.3

Servilii (two Sullan leaders), 28.1

Servilius, Q. (pr. 91), 2.15.1

(?) Servilius Caepio (consul), 1.15.3

Servilius Caepio, Cn. (cos. 141), 2.10.1, 21.5

Servilius Caepio, Q. (cos. 140), 2.1.3

Servilius Caepio, Q. (cos. 106), 2.12.2, 53.4

Servilius Glaucia, C. (pr. 100), 2.12.6

Servilius Isauricus, P. (cos. 48, 41), 53.2

Servilius Vatia Isauricus, P. (cos. 79), ?28.1, 39.2

Setia, 1.14.2

Sextius Calvinus, C. (cos. 124), 1.15.4

Sicily, 38.2, 72.4, 73.3, 75.3, 77.2–3, 78.1, 79.2, 80.2, 82.1

Sigimerus (German chief), 118.2

Silanus. *See* Junius

Silius, P. (cos. suff. AD 3), 101.3

Silius A. Caecina Largus, C. (cos. AD 13), 130.3

Silius Nerva, P. (cos. 20), 83.3, 90.4, 116.4

Sinuessa, 1.14.6

Siscia, 113.3

Sisenna. *See* Cornelius

Sisenna Statilius Taurus, T. (cos. AD 16), 2.14.3

Smyrna, 1.4.4, 69.1

Socrates, 1.16.4

Sophocles, 1.16.3

Sora, 1.14.5

Sosius, C. (cos. 32), 85.2, 86.2

Spain, 1.2.3, 1.12.4, 2.1.3, 2.4.2, 2.5.1–3, 30.2, 30.5, 38.4, 39.2–3, 43.4, 48.1, 50.2, 55.3, 63.1, 72.4, 73.2, 78.3, 90.1–4, 102.3, 125.5

Sparta, 1.6.3

Spartacus, 30.5

Spoletium, 1.14.8

Staius Murcius, L. (pr. 45), 69.2, 72.4, 77.3

Statilius Taurus, T. (cos. suff. 37), 85.2, 127.1

Strato of Aegeae, 70.4

Suessa Aurunca, 1.14.4

Sulla. *See* Cornelius

Sulpicius Galba, Ser. (cos. 144), 1.17.3, 2.9.1

Sulpicius Rufus, P. (trib. pleb. 88), 2.9.2, 2.18.5, 19.1, 20.2, [36.2]

Sutrium, 1.14.2

Syracuse, 2.7.7, 38.2

Syria, 1.10.1, 37.5, 38.6, 46.2–5, 69.2, 78.1, 101.1, 117.2

Tarentum Neptunia, 1.15.4

Tarpeian Rock, 24.2

Tarracina, 1.14.4

Tauromenium, 79.4

Tegea, 1.1.2

Telamon, 1.1.1

381

INDEX OF NAMES

Temenus, 1.2.1

Tenos, 1.4.3

Terence (comic poet), 1.17.1

Terentius Varro Atacinus, P. (poet), 36.2

(?) Terentius Varro Gibba (trib. pleb. 43), 71.3

Terentius Varro Lucullus, M. (cos. 73), 28.1, 48.6

(?) Terentius Varro Reatinus, M. (pr. 68; polymath), 36.2

Tergeste, 110.4

Teucer, 1.1.1

Teutoni, 2.8.3, 2.12.2, 2.12.4, 120.1

Thebes, 1.18.3

Theodotus (Egyptian royal adviser), 53.2

Theophanes (historian of Pompey), 2.18.3

Thesprotia, 1.1.1

Thessalus (son of Hercules), 1.3.2

Thessalus (of Thesprotia), 1.3.1–2

Thessaly, 1.3.1–2, 52.1

Thrace/Thracians, 98.1, 101.3, 112.4

Thucydides, 36.2

Thurii, 68.2

Tiber (river), 2.6.7, 45.5

Tiberius (emperor), 39.3, 75.1, 75.3, 94–131

Tibullus, 36.3

Tifata (mountain), 25.4

Tigranes I (king of Armenia), 33.1, 37.2–3

Tigranes III (king of Armenia), ?94.4, 122.1

Tisamenus, 1.1.4

Titius, M. (cos. suff. 31), 77.3, 79.5, 83.2

Torquatus. See Manlius

Trebonius, C. (cos. suff. 45), 56.3, 69.1, 87.3

Trojan War, 1.5.3

Troy, 1.2.1, 1.8.4

Tullius Cicero, M. (cos. 63), 1.17.3, 2.14.3, 34.3, 35.4, 36.1–2, 45.1–2, 48.5, 58.4, 62.1, 62.6, 64.3–4, 65.1, 66.2–5, 128.3

Tusculum, 128.2

Tyre, 1.2.3, 1.6.4, 2.7.7

Tyrrhenus, 1.1.4

Utica, 1.2.3

Valentia, 1.14.8

Valerius Antias (historian), 2.9.6

Valerius Flaccus, L. (cos. 100), 1.15.5

Valerius Flaccus, L. (cos. suff. 86), 23.2, 24.1

Valerius Messalla Corvinus, M. (cos. suff. 31), 36.2, 71.1, 84.1, 112.2

Valerius Messalla Messalinus, M. (cos. 3), 112.1

Varro. See Terentius

Varus. See Attius; Quin(c)tilius

Vatinius, P. (cos. 47), 69.3

Veientines, 1.8.5

Velia, 79.3

Velleius, C. (grandfather of historian), 76.1

Velleius Capito (son of the above), 69.5

382

Bayangali Alimzhanov

A HUNDRED YEARS ON THE STEPPE

A Novel
&
a Collection of Stories

London 2020

Printed in United Kingdom
Hertfordshire Press Ltd © 2020
e-mail: publisher@hertfordshirepress.com
www.hertfordshirepress.com

On behalf of Eurasian Creative Guild, London

Bayangali Alimzhanov ©
A HUNDRED YEARS ON THE STEPPE
A Novel & a Collection of Stories

English

Translation by Jonathan Campion and Timur Akhmedjanov
Editing by Stephen M. Bland
Proofreading by Caroline Walton
Design by Alexandra Rey
Project manager by Angelina Krasnogir

All rights reserved. No part of this book may be reprinted or reproduced or utilised in any form or by any electronic, mechanical, or other means, now known or hereafter invented, including photocopying and recording, or in any information storage or retrieval system, without permission in writing from the publishers.

*British Library Catalogue in Publication Data
A catalogue record for this book is available from the British Library
Library of Congress in Publication Data
A catalogue record for this book has been requested*

ISBN: 978-1-913356-10-1

*We express our gratitude
to the sponsors of this publication:*

*Omarov Zhomart Zhaksylykuly
&
Tleubaev Bakhytzhan Namenovich.*

ABOUT BOOK

This book is a collection of stories originally written in Russian by the Kazakh poet and author, Bayangali Alimzhanov. *A Hundred Years on the Steppe* centres on the life of one-hundred-year-old Asanbai Bektemirov, an unassuming man of the Kazakh countryside. He has lived through a century of upheaval and suffering: the nationalist uprising of Kazakhs against tsarist rule, revolution and civil war, the famine of 1932 and the purges of 1937, the Second World War, capture by the Germans and Stalin's gulags, mayhem under Khrushchev and stagnation under Brezhnev, and the collapse of the USSR. Asanbai survives to witness a new era where the steppe is independent and tells his grandchildren and great-grandchildren about his life and what he has seen. This wise old *aksakal* (elder) shares closely-held secrets and thoughts that have arisen from his pain, about war and peace, and about feuds and friendships between people and nations. We are taken back to the defining moments of Asanbai's hundred years, which are inextricably linked to the history of the twentieth cetury.

The story "Let me live!" is a cry from the heart of a man wounded in the war. He writes to his General: 'My General, Sir! Let me live! I grant you permission!' Convinced that all of humanity's ills are caused by a lack of conscience and sense of fairness, he roams around in his unique wheelchair, the 'Yangalibus,' trying to awaken a sense of conscience and fairness in whoever is in power, whilst using fantastical powers of his own.

The epic story "Khan Ablai and His Horsemen" is based on legends and fables of the Kazakh people. It takes inspiration from folk tales, dramatic events in the life of Khan Ablai, staggering deeds by the heroes of the wars between the Kazakhs and the Dzungars, and the wisdom and kindness of the nomads of the steppe.

CONTENTS

A HUNDRED YEARS ON THE STEPPE   *9*

LET ME LIVE!   *265*

Great Legends of the Steppe
Khan Ablai and His Horsemen   *347*

Bayangali Alimzhanov

A HUNDRED YEARS ON THE STEPPE

A folk novel about war and friendship between Kazakhs, Russians and Germans

> *The history of war must teach us to live in peace.*
> *The history of hatred must teach us to be friends.*

Serfs of the White Tsar

My name is Asanbai Bektemirov, son of Amanzhol. I was born in 1900 in the steppe region of Kenashchi, which means 'expanse of rough soil.' They say I'm as old as the century. Many people even attach some sacred meaning to this and treat me with the greatest of respect. I'm certainly a rarity: a hundred-year-old man still moving on his own (with a little help from a walking stick) who is only slightly senile.

Once, I took my grandsons and great-grandsons to a museum. Among the many peculiar items on display, what caught our eye the most were the *balbal tas* - a type of stone statue. These strange and ancient sculptures greatly interested my grandsons and great-grandsons. They looked at them carefully.

'Grandad! *Ata!* one of them said; 'they look like you.'

I laughed at first, but then, looking closer, I was taken aback. The child's comparison shocked me. Eaten away by centuries of winds, baked under the hot sun, infused with the scent of sage and feather grass, tempered by time itself, the balbals symbolised the calm and tolerance of the steppe and kept eternal secrets inside them. And to the younger generations, my own face - broad, weather-beaten and wrinkled, marked by what it has been through: blood and sweat, rage and mercy, wind and fire - probably looked like something ancient too.

This is how I looked at seventy, and this is how I looked at ninety. It was as if time had stood still on my face. Now, I'm a hundred. In this tumultuous twentieth century there have been so many contradictory, unbelievable and jaw-dropping events that it is impossible to count them. I've wanted to tell people about what I have seen and lived through for a long time, but only the things that are meaningful. Yes, only the meaningful, because what you see and feel doesn't always mean anything to others. For a long time, I had to stay quiet; firstly, because in the age of the Iron Curtain we had something to hide, and secondly, because putting pen to paper is a complex undertaking which for many is overwhelming. But then one of my great-grandchildren gave me an idea, a simple but meaningful one.

'Tell your story to us, and we'll record you on a Dictaphone,' he said to me. 'Then we'll type it up onto a computer and edit it as we go along. We can save it all on a USB

A HUNDRED YEARS ON THE STEPPE

drive, print out a few copies, and there's your book.'

'You're as clever as your great-grandfather,' I replied.

Some people say that you get wiser as you get older. Others think old people lose more of their senses every day. They are probably both right. Why? Because with each day, old people forget more and more; they lose what they used to know. Their memory fails them, and little by little their intelligence recedes. On the other hand, polished over time their life story and experiences become like a real gem.

So, on long winter evenings after hearty dinners of horsemeat, I started to tell my stories, trying to talk about events in the right order. To begin with, I was afraid of the Dictaphone; I would cough, get in a muddle, and repeat myself. After a while, I became more comfortable, though, and as the stories flowed, my grandsons and great-grandsons listened to me, their mouths wide in amazement. I guess their old grandfather, who they probably thought of as a sort of Holy Ghost, seemed very different to them. I think it made them respect me even more.

'Grandad! Ata! How did you even stay alive? How did you live to be a hundred in such good health and sound mind?' my loved ones asked.

'I'm surprised myself,' I answered. 'Probably the Almighty wanted you all to be born, and he had to keep me alive to drag me through the fire and ice of the godless people.'

There were moments, though, when the young ones just didn't understand what I was talking about. Our history, so closely tied to the politics of people's lives, was something unknown and mysterious to them. I thought everything was obvious and understandable - after all, only a few decades have passed - but no, I learnt that for their generation this history is already forgotten, or rather, it has never been known. The children interrupted me with questions, but I didn't get angry with them. I appreciated that they took an interest in the events and the emotions of my life. So, as I spoke, we took little trips back in time, and I gave them my explanations about one event or another.

When the long winter came to an end and I had told my grandsons everything I had to say, they typed it all up on their computer. They wanted to embellish my stories, adding extra drama to them, but I forbade them.

'Your grandfather's true stories are better than something in a cinema,' I told them. 'The truth is beautiful in any form. Accept her the way she is, and anyone who doesn't like it doesn't have to read it. I won't take offence. I'll be very pleased if some people are interested in the story of my hundred years on the steppe and if it stays with my children.'

This made them even happier, and they printed my stories as I'd told them with just a few corrections. I was grateful for this and gave their work my blessing.

The age we are living in has been surprising and complicated. The twentieth century came, groaning with the sound of railway tracks, trampling on all of our gentle old ways. Aeroplanes made lines in the sky and ships left furrows in the ocean. Meanwhile, we nomads, kind children of nature, had no idea about this and lived in a similar way to our ancestors. We loved the freedom of the steppe more

A HUNDRED YEARS ON THE STEPPE

than anything. We thought of ourselves as independent and were very proud of this.

'Listen - the Kazakhs aren't free!' wailed our musicians in their songs. "We are serfs; subjects of the White Tsar.'

As they listened, the men of the steppe held their breath, then clucked their tongues and toyed with their beards. Some wiped away tears.

After Khan Kenesary and Nauryzbai Batyr, the disobedient soul of Kokbory, the grey wolf left us too, and the aksakals, the white-bearded elders shook their heads sorrowfully. We didn't even understand the word serf. We made fun of it, pronouncing it in different ways. How could our childlike consciousness have understood the concept?

Later on, as I grew up, I began to ask myself: why are we serfs and who makes us be them? How can one people be slaves to another? With time, I started to understand the awful essence of this; the political meaning of serfdom. To be the subject of the tsar of another land means not having your own country. It means being always dependent. The freedom we felt on the steppe was only an imaginary freedom. Our steppe had really become a colony of the Russian Empire.

This understanding hurt me like a bullet. It has been a deep wound for almost all of my hundred years. At the start of our lives, though, we children of nature didn't understand this, and this brought its own kind of happiness.

The Free Man of the Steppe

We come from the ancient Kazakh Aksary Kerey people. From our clan came Maral Ishan, a saint, faith-healer, Muslim religious figure and spiritual inspiration of the national liberation movement of Khan Kenesary and Nauryzbai Batyr. Nowadays, the mausoleum to Maral Ishan in Karmachki, in the desert of Syr-Darya, is a place of pilgrimage. People come here from all ends of the earth, spend the night here and pray to the Almighty for help. Here, the terminally ill miraculously find their health restored.

Another to come from the Aksary Kerey Clan is the saint and spiritual healer, Salyk Mullah. People say that violent madmen would suddenly be becalmed as soon as they crossed the threshold of the mullah's house. To this day, if anyone fails to offer a prayer when they pass his grave near Kokshetau, they will suffer misfortune. One such man passed by on a wagon, drunk and laughing and swearing loudly. When he got home, he found that his mouth was twisted and his tongue was paralysed. His mother quickly sacrificed a sheep and went to pray at the mullah's grave, and her son recovered.

Another of our people is Birzhan-sal, the great composer, poet and singer of the Kazakh steppe. His legend has it that one quiet, moonlit night, as Birzhan-sal sang on top of the hill at Berkut, Orlinaya, his voice was heard in the surrounding villages and carried fifteen miles to the peak of Namazgul Mountain. As he sang the highest notes with all the might of his heavenly voice, a bird flying high in the sky

A HUNDRED YEARS ON THE STEPPE

fell to the earth like a stone, and only just before she touched the ground could she open her wings again to fly upwards towards the enchanting melody.

There were seven of us: five brothers and two sisters. Our youngest brother died whilst he was still in the cradle. At the start of the twentieth century, an unknown epidemic cut through the villages of the Kazakh steppe. Some days they would bury several children from the same family. We got sick too, but, by a miracle, we lived. It was probably measles or ordinary rose-rash. What can you do when almost none of the medicine in Tsarist Russia reached the depths of the steppe and children had nothing to protect them from infections? In those times, our main saviour from illness was the purity of our blood and our natural hardiness from growing up on the steppe. We grew up in a wild environment, ate only natural food, and were always active. From a very young age, the calm grandeur of the steppe taught us to be patient, and this patience saved me from a violent turn of events on more than one occasion.

We, the children of the villages, loved the steppe. We spent entire days wandering the expanses and playing ancient games. Sometimes we would pretend to be grownups and hunt for marmots and badgers. In the summer, we lived in yurts on the *jailoo* - a summer pasture. In spring, we migrated together as a family or an entire village. After the snows and storms of winter, we children loved running around in the blossoming fields.

I remember how, outside our village, our mare grazed on the slope of a hill. She had a little red-haired foal who was devoted to her. My mother and father used to go and milk her. I would come with them; for me, aged six, this was a real journey. Summer was only just beginning, and the steppe was coming into bloom. Butterflies were fluttering, grasshoppers were jumping, and dragonflies were floating in the wind. I would run after them, and they would fly away in different directions. I still hear their song, the choir of the steppe in my ears. The scent was of wormwood and needlegrass. I inhaled the aroma of the steppe's wild herbs and was intoxicated with pleasure. Separated from its mother, the foal came to greet me and I put my arms around its neck. My father kept the mare, and my mother drew its milk into a wooden bucket. The smell of *saumal*, fresh mare's milk, tickled my nose and stirred up my blood. I felt as if I had the whole village in the palm of my hand. The sky was high and clear; a few white clouds quietly floated off to other places. The sun shone down and warmed us. My parents looked at me with love in their eyes, and I was immeasurably happy.

This picture is from my childhood long ago; a tiny fragment of a long life which now and again comes back from the depths of my memory to appear once more in front of my eyes, comforting my soul. Then my ancient eyes fill with tears. I don't know whether this is from happiness or from heartache; all of a sudden this irretrievable moment of my life comes back to me, and I feel once more the warmth of my carefree childhood. At the same time, though, I feel an exquisite regret in understanding that it has gone forever.

Out of curiosity, people sometimes ask me about my

A HUNDRED YEARS ON THE STEPPE

17

earliest memory. They are probably interested to know from what age a hundred-year-old man remembers his life. My reply often shocks them. I remember one thing from when I was two-and-a-half, though in truth my parents told me more about it later.

I was playing in front of the yurt whilst the elders sat on the grass listening to stories from our hero, Kurentai Batyr, a warrior who'd come to visit from the next village, when our big black ram walked up to us. He was very strong and would butt anything - even the elders were cautious around him - but I, running to play with him, caught my feet and fell right in front of him. Seeing a person on all fours, the ram took this as a challenge. And then came the miracle, the moment I remember. The black ram first smelled the crown of my head, and then took some steps back, getting ready to charge at me. I began to cry in front of him. The ram hesitated, and then came the screams of the grown-ups and my father and mother rushing towards me. This I remember perfectly. What happened after that my parents told me many times. Apparently, the ram sprang backwards, frightened by their desperate screams; but after a second he prepared to attack once more. Suddenly, between me and the ram appeared a figure, the old warrior Kurentai Batyr, who was already eighty-five-years-old. 'We had no idea how he got there so fast,' my parents told me. While my mother, shaking with tears, managed to grab me, old Kurentai calmly grabbed the ram by one of its horns and gave it a fierce shake. With one hard jerk he broke its neck, and my father prepared the sheep to eat. My parents didn't mind this; they were happy even. '*Kurbandyk* - a sacrifice!' they announced, and gave the ram's meat to all our neighbours. Everyone said that Allah had saved my life and gave thanks to Him: it was an omen that I would live a long life.

One of the clearest memories from my childhood is my friendship with foals. Almost every little boy on the steppe had his own foal, and when they were big enough, the older boys rode on yearlings called *tays*. Broken in and docile, these lovely creatures became true friends. It felt then as if our friendship would last forever. We loved riding our *tays* across the steppe and organising races. The wind whistled in our ears and it felt as if the earth was flying under our feet. Covering the steppe together, we bonded with our horses, becoming one animal, like centaurs.

Sometimes, we pretended to be grown-ups and organised a *kokpar* - a sport played on horses, where groups of horsemen fight over the carcass of a goat, trying to rip it from the arms of their opponents before galloping off with it. Instead of a carcass, though, we used a dried animal skin. Playing kokpar was more fun than I could ever describe. Sometimes, after we had grabbed hold of the prize and were desperate not to give it back to the other team, we lost sight of a bigger opponent in front of us and fell off our horses onto the grass. The steppe echoed with children's voices and laughter, announcing to the whole world that here lived the descendants of nomads - free-spirited children of the great steppe. It was the best time of our lives.

On the *takyr*, a flat pasture, we played *saka*. A *saka* is the knee-joint of a cow and is the main weapon in this ancient

A HUNDRED YEARS ON THE STEPPE

game. The knuckles from the feet of cows and horses, which you hit with the saka, are called *dyi*. The aim of the game is to throw your saka to hit the dyi the other players have collected. When you hit a dyi, you keep it. Each player must have his own saka and a few dyi. At the start of the game, the players take it in turns to throw their saka in the air; if it falls with the knee pointing at the sky, then its owner has the right to throw it at the dyi; but if it falls on one side, then he misses his turn. Once it's his turn to throw, a boy very carefully takes aim, and, artfully spinning the saka on its joint, throws it as hard as he can at the dyi. When the saka lands in the middle of dyi placed close together, several dyi fly off in different directions. The thrower paces out the distance between where his saka lands and each of the scattered dyi. If the dyi are less than three paces away - or five, depending on what the boys agree on beforehand - then the boy wins them. If they land further from the saka, then they stay on the ground. The game continues until there are no dyi left. The game is very active; you need sharpness, dexterity, speed and persistence. It's useful for helping children to develop and keeping them healthy. When we kids got carried away, we would argue with reason and without; we would shout until we lost our voices from the joy of victory or the pain of defeat. It's funny to think now, but at that age it really seemed that there was nothing more important in life than winning at saka. How naive and pure we were.

When we were tired of our games, we loved to sit in silence on top of the hill and muse about life. It was as if the waves of a great ocean rocked us, carrying our childish fantasies away to unknown pastures. The scent of wormwood tickled my nose. This aroma of the steppe has stayed with me throughout my life; it runs through my blood and my soul.

In those years, I had an incredibly strong longing for journeys and adventures. I felt this especially at sunset. Sunset on the steppe is unforgettable. Gazing at the reddening horizon, tentatively feeling the world's majesty and mystery, I would sigh, not understanding what it was that I was yearning for.

At night, we loved looking up at the stars which seemed to be beckoning us. I was fascinated most of all by the Milky Way - *Kus zholy*. Kazakhs call Ursa Major, *Zhetikarakshy* - the Seven Bandits. The North Star is *Temirkazyk* - the Iron Staff - and the two furthest stars at the very edge of Ursa Minor are *Ak boz at* - the White Horse, and *Kok boz at* - the Grey Horse. In nomad mythology, for centuries the seven bandits have tried to steal these horses from Temirkazyk, but have never succeeded because Temirkazyk rotates on its axis, preventing the bandits from getting too close. The bandits circle endlessly around Temirkazyk. The myth has it that if the seven bandits ever succeed in stealing the horses, there will be a catastrophe in the universe, but people believe that Temirkazyk will never allow it. Oh, how I longed to fly into the night sky and roam among the brightest stars; to hold Temirkazyk in my palms and to ride Ak boz at and Kok boz at.

Sometimes, our village was visited by *zhyrshy* - storytellers. In the evenings, we would gather to listen to them

A HUNDRED YEARS ON THE STEPPE

21

tell the epic tales of heroic warriors. Words of spellbinding ancient poetry flowed into our young souls, and we fell in love with the musical rhapsodies of the steppe, unchanged through the ages. We children literally attached ourselves to the storytellers, devouring every word, every note. I felt as if the zhyrshy were injecting into me the spirit of my ancestors.

All of our history passed from generation to generation by word of mouth: legends and fables, parables and myths, always told with such energy. They are the canon of our era, and with them our people have preserved their memories and protected their identity. At the time, we didn't think of it like this, but still, we felt something otherworldly and profound in the old tales and songs. It was from the tales of the aksakals and the storytelling zhyrshy that we learnt that the Kazakhs had not always been serfs of the White Tsar. We had our own glorious and heroic ancient history which stretched back for tens of centuries.

My father, Amanzhol wasn't a storyteller, but he knew many songs and legends by heart and performed them for us on some evenings. He read to us from books printed in Kazan in Arabic script that he kept in a wooden box. There were Kazakh songs about brave warriors and parables about prophets and Muslim saints. The yellowed pages of these thin little books carried the scent of something ancient and mysterious. It wasn't for us children to understand, but already it was close to our hearts.

Father told us about missionaries who translated the Bible into the Kazakh language. He explained that these missionaries, under the guise of teachers and ethnographers, set out with other aims entirely. They attempted to spread and nurture tales of Christianity among Kazakhs so it would be easier to convert them. The sharp and literate men of the steppe understood their motives straight away, though, and began to disseminate books promoting the spiritual values of Islam. The zhyrshy composed and performed *dastans* - epic poems about the Prophet Mohammed and Kazakh Muslim heroes. It was a protest against religious politics and a strong spiritual shield for our national consciousness.

Father told us how our great-great-grandfather, Bektemir from the Shorayak Clan was known as Bektemir Batyr the Lame. Once, in a battle against the Dzungars, he was wounded in the hip by an arrow. After the fierce battle, the warriors returned home. Bektemir Batyr's leg swelled up and filled with pus, probably from gangrene. He sharpened a sword and cut his own leg off so that he might live.

Our winter home was made from pine logs. This was a rarity for Kazakhs at that time, because most people lived in clay-walled huts. Very poor Kazakhs even dug trenches to sleep in. The roof of our comfortable home was lined with wooden beams. No one painted them, so the panels were completely decorated with natural patterns which were beautiful even in the places spoilt by knots. I would often stare at the ceiling of the hut I grew up in, and every time I found a new pattern among the grains. I thought I could see a fortress that I'd heard about in the tales of the zhyrshy, and our warriors capturing it; then a wild animal or a *samruk* bird; then a little girl walking to fetch water. Sometimes, the

A HUNDRED YEARS ON THE STEPPE

scene would suddenly turn into a *zhalmauiz*, a nightmare, and there was an old witch or a cruel shepherd chasing after some children. Our ceiling developed our imagination; it was our television, our internet, our virtual world.

The windows of our house were small. In the winter, when the bitter cold wreaked havoc, all of us loved to look outside. The frost created striking patterns on the windows, and we breathed holes in them to stare out at the snowy steppe. On days when the wind howled, no one could get us, especially my younger brother Salim and me, away from the window. I literally stuck myself to the glass and imagined that I was flying with the snowstorm to places faraway. This is how we grew up, looking at the great world through the little windows of our parents' home.

Our mother kept the fire going with birch branches, and we loved looking into the flames. The wood burnt, the flames grew stronger, and the hut became warmer. When the fire went out, Mother placed the big, red coals in even rows. On top of them she placed a *taba* - a round cast-iron pan - filled with flour. When the bread was ready, we noisily ate hot *taba naan* with butter. The bread was tasty and the feeling of biting into the crust brought joy like no other. We thanked our parents, and mother looked at us and murmured 'Shukr, Allah, tauba!' Father would stroke his beard and drink salted *ayran* yoghurt from a wooden mug.

Our mother, Batima was from a family of Argyns and Karauyls. Sometimes, when she was in a good mood, she would sing us her favourite old songs. The four walls of our house were like the four corners of the world. We played in every corner, and every time we played it was as if we entered another world.

I remember to this day how, when we were small, Salim and I would go to visit our elder sister, Mariyam. She lived with her husband and children in the village of Kudukagash on the edge of a pine forest by a mountain called Makpal. There were lots of sheep in the village. One of the elders would bring us from our village and leave us there for weeks on end. To us children, those forty-five kilometres seemed like an epic journey. In those days, there were no cars or buses, so we travelled the whole way in horse-drawn sleighs. Coming from the steppe, we were completely in awe of the wild nature of the forest.

We would often go into the forest with our nephews, arming ourselves with axes, spades or sticks. The pure white snow was like an open book, the footprints of birds and animals like sentences on the page. We tried to read them and track them down. Lost in the hunt, we walked to the edge of the forest, stopping among the tall pines and breathing the fresh, cold air into our lungs, savouring these moments of bliss. The pine forest filled us with health and a unique energy. Salim, restless and naughty, was always digging up heaps of snow in search of animals or climbing on the stumps of fallen trees. I would look up instead, to where the tops of the majestic pines seemed to touch the thick white clouds. In the silence, I could hear the blood pumping in my ears. I wanted so much to sail away with the clouds to faraway places, but I knew I couldn't. Instead, I quietly asked the clouds to pass on my messages to people living in distant

A HUNDRED YEARS ON THE STEPPE

25

countries. Sometimes, the *tuk-tuk-tuk* sound of a woodpecker's beak would break the silence. We listened. Sometimes, weakened from the cold, a tree branch would snap and fall to the ground with a crash.

We came home as the sun began to set, tired, but happy, and with faces red from the freezing air. Our sister, Mariyam fed us meat in a hot broth. When we couldn't eat any more, we cuddled up next to Altyn-apa, the mother of Mariyam's husband, and asked her to tell us stories. Altyn-apa was a kind, sincere woman. She wore a *zhaulyk* - a white scarf that covered her head, neck and shoulders. As she absorbed herself in telling us stories and legends, her eyes filled with a warm light. By the glow of a kerosene lamp, our silhouettes flickered, and it was as if the characters from the stories were moving in the corners of the hut. Altyn-apa told us tales from the steppe and from the East. I'm grateful to her to this day. Whenever I think of her, I remember how it felt to be ten years old. I sometimes think that those winter evenings filled with stories in my sister's hut were the happiest moments of my life.

One of Altyn-apa's parables stuck in my memory. Once upon a time, the Prophet Muhammad was visited by the warrior, Khazret Gali. The warrior said he felt so strong that he thought he could lift the Earth above his head and spin it like a ball if only the Almighty would give him a handle to hold it with. The Prophet gave Khazret Gali a knowing smile but didn't say anything. The warrior kept travelling on his horse, Duldul, until he reached the steppe and met a white-bearded elder. Gali greeted the aksakal, and the old man replied politely, placing his small bag upon the ground. After making a little small talk with Gali, the old man asked him to pass him his bag as it was painful for him to bend down. Without dismounting from his horse, Gali tried to pick up the bag with his whip, but he couldn't do it. Surprised, he bent down and tried to pick up the bag with his little finger, but again, he couldn't do it. Angrily, the warrior leapt from his horse, took the old man's bag in his huge hands and pulled, but the bag didn't move an inch. Gali's blood began to boil. Consumed by rage, with all his legendary strength he tried to lift the little bag, putting a foot in one of his stirrups for balance. He pulled with such force that Duldul's legs sank into the ground, but still, the bag didn't move. At this moment, the old man walked up to Gali, apologised for troubling him, picked up the bag with two fingers and walked away.

Dismayed, Khazret Gali went back to the Prophet and asked him to explain.

The Prophet smiled again, and this time he spoke.

'You were arrogant,' he replied. 'Did you really think you were strong enough to lift the Earth above your head? That was Allah letting you touch the handle you asked for so you could swallow your pride.'

Khazret Gali learnt his lesson.

This story and its meaning, I think, should be taught to every person on Earth. No one has the right to grab the world and play with it as they please; no one has the right to decide the fate of the planet. Only the Almighty can choose the fate of the Earth and the Universe. People must live in

A HUNDRED YEARS ON THE STEPPE

27

peace and understanding in this Ark of humanity, leaving only a furrow behind in the infinite ocean of the cosmos.

I have one more clear memory from my childhood: the Russian settlers. They say that to begin with our people gave them a hostile welcome. We thought they'd come to take our land, and so we treated them as outsiders, enemies. In despair, the braver Kazakhs hurt the Russians in any way they could. They would even kill them if given a chance. People told stories about how Kurentai Batyr fought long battles against these outsiders before coming to understand that it was impossible to stop the Russians from settling on our steppe and making peace with them.

With time, we became accustomed to our new neighbours. Gradually, we began to talk to them, swap things we had at home and learn from each other. To everyone's surprise, our father, who had strongly opposed this tsarist colonisation, became friends with a settler called Maidaikin. He came from a village by Zhokei-Dzhukei Lake. It's beautiful there, and the land is fertile. These fields used to belong to Kazakhs, but the tsarist rulers simply took them. In those years, Russian settlers and Cossacks took all the land that was fertile.

Maidaikin was a giant of a man. I remember how he used to walk with long, clumsy strides. He spoke loudly and bluntly. The Kazakh villagers called him *"Sary-orys"* - the Yellow Russian. It surprised me that almost all Russians were pale; you could call all of them yellow, but the name Sary-orys fit Maidaikin best of all. Not only was his skin golden, but his hair as well. He liked his nickname and even got

28 *Bayangali Alimzhanov*

angry if he heard a Kazakh say - as we did - that all Russians were yellow. He wanted everyone to know that he was the original Yellow Russian. Our Kazakhs called my father and Maidaikin *tamyrs*. Among our people, if a Kazakh became friends with a Russian they would call them a tamyr. The word has two meanings: a tamyr is the root of a tree and also a vein or an artery. I think that in this word you can feel the importance of friendship between Kazakhs and Russians. It's as if our roots have become knitted together or we have become blood-brothers. With our Maidaikin there was truth in this. Whatever else was said back then, our yellow Russian was a real tamyr.

Maidaikin spent a lot of time with us. Father also went to visit him, and each time he brought him something from our home. The men used to exchange gifts that the other thought was bizarre. One time, he took me and Salim with him. For us, it was like travelling to another world. We saw things we didn't know even existed. We were amazed by the tools made of iron. We tried to use his fantastic wooden plough: I was the horse in the harness and tried to pull the heavy plough, whilst Salim deftly steered me. Most of all, though, we were astounded by Maidaikin's gun.

Our tamyr let us touch the gun, and Salim and I fought to grab hold of it, but once we had it in our hands we didn't know what to do with it. I held the gun by its barrel and waved it like a sword. Salim took it by the butt and made a few stabbing motions as if he was spearing fish. Maidaikin laughed and showed us how to load the gun, aim and fire. We had no idea what guns were for, but touching the

A HUNDRED YEARS ON THE STEPPE 29

smooth, cold metal, we intuitively felt a frightening power. Salim was quicker to learn and started to pretend he was shooting without taking aim at anything, shouting 'pukh, pakh, pukh!' as he waved his hands around. Father was smitten with his agility, but Sary-orys picked at his beard and shook his head sorrowfully.

This was the first time that naive children from the steppe had touched a gun. Later, I came to understand why our tamyr had looked so distraught.

Invited to stay for dinner, Maidaikin's wife poured tea from a fat shiny samovar and fed us hot pies filled with fermented cabbage. We'd never eaten pies before and thought they were the most delicious thing we'd ever tasted. Father spoke with Maidaikin. We didn't understand what they were talking about, but I remember that sometimes they'd raise their voices and argue, and this scared us. Afterwards, on the way back to our village, our father told us what the conversation was about.

'He was saying: "listen to me, Amanzhol, and understand me once and for all: when a Russian leaves his home and arrives on your steppe, it isn't because he chose to. They were sent here. Guess who sent them all?" he asked, pointing a finger to the sky.'

'Who?' Salim and I enquired in unison.

'You know who... the White Tsar, their lord!'

Father gave a sad grunt.

Father taught us to read and write when we were young. I learnt quickly; Arabic characters lit up my world. I loved to decipher Arabic texts letter by letter, putting syllables together into whole words, then sentences, then trying to grasp their meaning. Later, I taught myself Cyrillic and learnt to read and write in Russian. This opened up a completely different world to me.

A People's Fury

In 1914, the First World War began. The Tsarist Empire fought against the Kaiser's Germany. No one in the village knew what was happening or what they were fighting about. We only heard rumours, which reached us as they were passed along the *uzunkulak* - the steppe grapevine. We had no idea who the Germans were, where they lived, or what they wanted.

I remember how people used to play with how similar this new word 'Germaniya' sounded to Kerey - the name of our clan. *Kermaniya, Kereymaniya!* Their explanation was that both prefixes 'ger' and 'ker' came from the word Kerey, and 'man' was the German word for 'person.' So, they were 'ger-people.' Everyone enjoyed these jokes. No one could have imagined how closely our fate was to be tied to that of Germany.

In June 1916, the whole of the steppe was stunned when the White Tsar ordered that all Kazakh men between the ages of nineteen and thirty be sent to do manual labour on the front lines. This decree was a tragedy for Kazakhs. Families didn't want to send their children to face certain death. The nation remembered the Tsar's promise that the Russian Empire would not conscript Kazakhs into the mil-

A HUNDRED YEARS ON THE STEPPE 31

itary. They even tried to remind the governor-general that the Tsar had signed the promise in his own hand and had put his imperial seal on the dogskin it was written on. But the dogskin was lost, the Tsar forgot his promise, and the Kazakhs revolted.

I read somewhere that during tsarist Russia's colonisation of the Kazakh steppe there were about three-hundred nationalist uprisings, both great and small. Some of the fiercest were during 1916, when many parts of the vast steppe went up in flames from the fire of the Kazakhs' war against the Tsar's imperialists. Some historians believe that the Tsar gave the order to conscript the Kazakhs to deliberately provoke them into violence, which would have cleared Russia's debts to its neighbour: 'It appears we are faced with disorder, a mutiny; and when such unfortunate political events happen in a country, all debts to that country are written off.'

I think there's some truth to that version of events, but wherever the truth lay, the fact was that the men of the steppe were fighting against Tsarist tyranny. Of course, the sides were far from equal. The Tsarist Empire, at war with the Kaiser's Germany and suffering terrible losses at the front, could still find the resources to cut down the revolts. Special forces armed with cannons, machine guns and the most sophisticated firearms of that era - guns with five chambers - shot without mercy at the cavalry of the defiant Kazakhs, who were armed with no more than swords, spears , bows and arrows, and often carrying only fighting sticks cut from birch branches. Many courageous young men died from bullet wounds inflicted by those death squads. Almost all of the uprisings were quickly stamped out, and their leaders shot or hung without trial. Anyone who was captured by those squads was tortured in prison or expelled to Siberia, and many of those who survived after taking part in the uprisings fled to China. The heads of some villages understood that standing in front of machine guns with birch sticks was a hopeless cause and left without fighting with their whole family in tow. Only now, decades later, are they returning to their homeland. It is a new country now, and the descendants of those who fled to foreign lands are now settling in the independent Republic of Kazakhstan. They call them *oralman*, those who have returned. Their ancestors were our brothers, and how they suffered.

The only Kazakh uprising that wasn't put down was the revolt by the people of the Torgai Region. Led by the warrior Amangeldy Batyr Imanov, his rebellious followers went on to join the ranks of first the February, and then the October revolutionaries. They played an active part in putting the steppe under Soviet rule, but as soon as they'd done so, these bloodthirsty fighters tricked and murdered Amangeldy. His death was shrouded in mystery. People said that the Reds had no use for a hero who was Kazakh, free and insubordinate, and the leader of an army of several thousand. Amangeldy Batyr is a national hero. His life and legend place him amongst the most cherished sons of the steppe.

This is history now, so we can talk about it calmly and attempt to justify the bloodshed. At the time, though, it wasn't so simple. My father, Amanzhol joined the revolt at

A HUNDRED YEARS ON THE STEPPE

the very beginning and fought for our cause.

Once, some Kazakh rebels attacked a small village of settlers. I joined them with my older brothers Alimzhan, who was twenty, and Meirambai, who was nineteen. Our part didn't amount to anything as we didn't even have any weapons. We joined the fight out of curiosity, and for the thrill of it. Now, I think our father only let us come because he wanted to toughen us up.

Their village was almost empty. Places like this had become dangerous, and many settlers had already left. Only one home had people inside. Our men found the family's horses and frightened them with shouts and swords held aloft until they galloped away. Then, they surrounded the hut. When they broke in and forced the inhabitants outside, they had a guest with them: Maidaikin. He'd probably come for dinner with his family.

Intoxicated with their bloodlust, our men decided to do away with all of the settlers. To them, they were the embodiment of the cruelties dished out by their tsar. Those on horses began to destroy the wooden fence around the hut and attack the hut with spears, smashing the windows and breaking the roof. Maidaikin spotted us, but before he could do anything our horsemen formed a circle around him and began to beat him with their whips. Father stood up for his friend and yelled at our men to stop hurting him, but not all of them listened. A few moved to throw a lasso around Sary-orys's neck and drag him behind one of the horses. Maidaikin fought them furiously, but one horseman came from behind and managed to throw the slipknot around his neck. Calling upon every ounce of his considerable strength, Maidaikin stopped himself from falling and tried with all his might to free himself from the heavy noose. No one can break a horsehair lasso, though, and soon he began to choke. Blood-soaked froth trickled from his mouth. His wife screamed hysterically, whilst his two adult children looked on in silence, agony burning in their eyes. As Maidaikin was about to fall unconscious, grunting and collapsing on the ground, there was a flash of light. My father's sword glinted as he cut the noose from our tamyr's neck. Father then shoved his sword against the neck of the boy on the horse.

'Leave my friend alone!' he bellowed. 'None of this is his fault! Either we all leave this place in peace, or I will kill you!'

Father was respected in our clan, and the rebels listened to him. He saved Maidaikin's family and the people whose home they were in. Sary-orys's wife and sons threw their arms around him. Maidaikin turned to my father, and, unable to speak, thanked him with a look. Father gave a mournful nod in reply, and we left the village.

The harsh reality cooled our passions. So this is what war looks like and how it feels to be victorious, we thought. To be the victor, you have to hurt others, if not kill them. The heroism glorified in epic tales and songs has a partner: tragedy. There can never be celebration and glory without the blood and agony of the defeated.

Soon, the war took over everything. Father decided to go with his clansmen to join Amangeldy Batyr's army on the Torgai Steppe. He ordered the rest of us to stay in the village

A HUNDRED YEARS ON THE STEPPE

and keep the family safe. A father's word was the law for Kazakhs, and we did as he said without hesitation.

Recently, I came across an article written at that time. It was about how the uprisings on the steppe and the methods used to quell them were scrutinised in the Tsar's court. Officials noted in horror that clashes between native clans and settlers and retaliations by tsarist forces had killed tens of thousands of Kazakhs and thousands of Russians. They explicitly blamed the tsarist regime. Issuing an unlawful decree and implementing it in such an inhumane way had caused the revolts and lawlessness on the steppe, which had led to mass bloodshed throughout the empire.

Of course, it's good that these officials saw the actions as inhumane, but I'm not sure this changed anything. The steppe's grapevine, the uzunkulak carried to every hamlet the words of the Tsar's governor when he told the representatives of the Kazakhs: 'You thought you could speak against us? We will destroy all of you. We won't leave anyone alive - not your women, not your children, and not your elders.'

The death squads did awful things on the steppe, killing innocent and peaceful souls. They hunted like packs of hungry wolves, searching for Kazakh villages. As they knew the steppe well, local Cossacks joined them and showed them where to look. They mercilessly attacked everyone who they suspected of supporting the uprisings.

My second oldest brother, Meirambai fell into their hands. It was the middle of autumn, and he was riding home after meeting the girl he was to marry. The wedding had been set for the following spring. On the way home,

Meirambai stopped at a lake to let his horse drink. As soon as he dismounted, a group of armed raiders leapt out from the bushes and surrounded him. One of them grabbed the reins and took his horse. The rest took it in turns to terrify the nineteen-year-old boy, threatening him with sabres, bayonets and guns. Backing away from their weapons, Meirambai found himself at the edge of the lake. The raiders kept closing in until he could do nothing but throw himself into the water. The lake was deep, and Meirambai dived in headfirst. Spluttering, he tried to climb back onto the bank, but the raiders kept attacking him with their sabres, forcing him underwater whilst laughing at their display of strength. My brother kept afloat as best he could and took his humiliation. Eventually, the raiders left, taking Meirambai's horse with them. As soon as they were out of sight, Meirambai climbed out of the water, rang out his clothes and ran home to the village. It was a long way, and the cold autumn wind froze him to the bone.

The Tsar's raiders were clever as well as cruel. They didn't use a single bullet or leave a single mark. They knew that the freezing water, the autumn chill, the wet clothes and the open steppe would do their damage for them.

Our brother made it home the next morning, blue from the cold and barely conscious. His body was burning by then, and he was delirious. Meirambai died a few days later from pneumonia. News of his death soon spread across the steppe. People shared our grief and tried to soothe the pain of our loss. I was sixteen then, and Salim was fifteen. We were so shaken by our brother's death that the pain re-

A HUNDRED YEARS ON THE STEPPE 37

mained in our hearts for the rest of our lives. It was the first time I'd lost someone in my family. Mother cried uncontrollably, and the sound of her sobbing broke my heart. Our mullah tirelessly recited the *salauat* – '*La ilaha ilallah*' - and this somehow comforted us and helped make peace with the fact that fate cannot be reversed. Even now, when I remember what happened so long ago, my ancient eyes fill with tears and I hear the sound of my mother, Batima crying.

The death of Meirambai hardened us and strengthened our hatred for the Tsar's rulers and colonisers, but it wasn't a fair fight, modern metal firearms against kind-hearted children of nature.

Our father never returned from Torgai. He was forty-five. His brigade was massacred in a bloody battle with a troop of raiders who were armed to the teeth. Rumours reached us that father had died in this battle. He will lie forevermore on the steppe next to the men he fought alongside. A year later, someone came to our village who'd witnessed the battle. He was a cripple by then. He confirmed to us that our father was gone. After reading a passage from the Quran, he told the story of how the men from the steppe had been slaughtered. In a hollow, crestfallen voice, he told me how our fighters, after they were ambushed, selflessly placed themselves in front of the cannons and machine guns.

'Do you need much intelligence or talent to shoot at horsemen armed with birch sticks or spears?' he mused, gazing into the distance. 'In a short space of time these fearless nomads, howling their battle cries, their horses' hooves making the ground beneath them shake, were annihilated.

Almost all of them ended up on the ground, to rest among the wormwood and feather grass of their beloved steppe. Only a few desperate, lucky fighters managed to reach their opponents and hammer a spear through their heads. I rode next to your father, and I saw how he brought his horse to a full gallop and thrust his spear into a gunman. But the gunman fired one last shot. Amanzhol's spear went through his throat, but he'd cut through your father like a blade of grass. I took a heavy blow to my hip, fell off my horse and lost consciousness. But I lived.'

These images have stayed with me. Throughout my life, I've imagined my father covered in blood and desperately charging at a Russian gunman with his spear held high.

'I am proud of my father,' Salim would say with pain in his eyes, 'but I would never throw myself in front of a machine gun, however heroic it may be. I'll be a smart, cunning fighter. I would dodge that bullet, come from behind and kill all the gunmen I'd fire at all of them with an even more powerful gun.'

Salim kept his word. He became a cunning, experienced and battle-hardened fighter.

After the uprisings on the steppe were put down, our elder brother, twenty-year-old Alimzhan was called up to the front. We received two letters from him before he stopped writing and disappeared without a trace. Russia was dealing with so many events that the authorities couldn't have cared less about our brother. We hoped, and hope to this day that he stayed alive, got caught up in the turmoil, and eventually found a new home in our land or someone else's. If only

A HUNDRED YEARS ON THE STEPPE

our beloved brother could have lived. At home, we read his letters over and over again and tried to understand from his beautiful Arabic handwriting what had happened to him. From these letters, it seemed that there was no purpose in his being at the front.

Alimzhan wrote that everyone was safe, alive and well, but they weren't being given the horses that were killed in battle. The Russian soldiers didn't eat horsemeat, and dead animals were buried or left out for the crows. It never occurred to anyone to give them to the Kazakh labourers. It would have solved the burden of feeding them, but it was beneath the officers to care about simple nomads.

A few years ago, I read an article about the lives of manual labourers on the front lines during the First World War. Apparently, they were treated in the same way as prisoners: led to work in a convoy and punished for the smallest mistakes. I remembered my loving brother, Alimzhan, who had disappeared without a trace, and my heart broke for him once more.

Anarchy Among the People

The year of 1917 began with a crack of thunder: the overthrow of Tsar Nicholas II. Excitement spread through the steppe; we thought that peace had returned. This was the February Revolution, after which an interim government was put in place. Later, we came to understand that this meant the country was under constitutional rule.

The February Revolution stopped the attacks on us by the Tsar's raiders. These squads, who had turned the steppe into a bloodbath and were ready to bring down every uprising and destroy every defenceless Kazakh village, no longer knew what to do. The vast empire had had its head cut off.

We'd only just begun to fathom what had happened when a second crack of thunder shook us: the October Revolution forced out the interim government and brought about the dictatorship of the proletariat. The steppe began to simmer again. The first signs filtered through of another disaster on the horizon and more big changes. This time the rumours were yelled hysterically: the time has come to blast the old world to smithereens and create a new, fairer world! We, the lowly Kazakhs, led by the Russians and the worldwide proletariat, commanded in turn by our great leader, Comrade Lenin, have a duty to banish and ruin the rich landowners and oppressors of the working people and take power into our own hands! In truth, before any real action was taken, the steppe was already divided into dozens of different dissenting groups.

Representatives of the national party of the Kazakhs, the Alash Orda tried to show the people what was best for us.

'We Kazakhs are one nation,' they argued. 'There are too few of us to divide us into rich and poor and tear each other apart. All Kazakhs are brothers: one family, one people.'

The Alash Orda were the first to fight to revive the Kazakh nation.

A HUNDRED YEARS ON THE STEPPE

Now, almost a hundred years later, we can analyse and try to make sense of the events of those frightening years. Whilst we were living through it, though, there was no understanding of what was happening to us. It was chaos, bedlam, turmoil; hunger, cold and death. The Russian Revolution burst onto our tranquil steppe, turning it into a battlefield in an internal war, covering all that was alive in blood and turning the lives of peaceful Kazakhs into a nightmare. The aggressors lurching through the steppe clearly wanted anarchy. Reckless and fearless, they attacked our villages with relish. The steppe shook from more bursts of gunfire, and more of our relatives were killed. The concept of good and evil lost its meaning. The fates of thousands, millions of people collided. We felt fear and disgust in the pits of our stomachs. Who is my friend? Who is trying to kill me? Where do I go? Who with? No one knew anymore. We tried to adapt to this new life, but we'd been brainwashed by chancers, anarchists and socialists. They all spread their propaganda with beautiful words about freedom, equality and brotherhood, promising a golden future where there were no tsars or landowners. We listened most intently, however, to our own people, the Kazakh nationalists who were calling for nationhood, freedom and autonomy.

Rulers on the steppe changed like a kaleidoscope. The tsarist regime was replaced by an interim government, then the Soviet of Deputies, then the Alash Orda, then the Whites, Kolchakists, Annenkovists, Reds… our people couldn't keep up with it. We didn't know who to believe or who to follow.

Salim was a committed supporter of the Alash Orda.

'Autonomy for every nation; that's brilliant,' he enthused. 'If Comrade Lenin is giving freedom to the oppressed peoples of the Russian Empire, then we must take this opportunity to form our own government.'

Many of us liked this idea. We hoped and believed, but were consumed with doubt. I often asked myself and spoke to the steppe, the sky, the wind - what are we to do? After agonising over the possible answers, I found the one that made the most sense to me: be with your people. Protect your brothers, and fight for their freedom and happiness.

But what if your brothers have already segregated into different groups? Some were with the Whites, others with the Reds, and others with the nationalists of the Alash Orda. Furthermore, this wasn't simply a difference of opinion, but an armed conflict. Our brothers were killing each other. How can you shoot a Kazakh to make another Kazakh happy? My head hurt and my soul felt sick, but I couldn't find an answer - not then, and not now. My mind refused to understand and my body couldn't accept it. For me, all Kazakhs were brothers and part of the same family. It was the hypocritical, deceitful politicians who didn't want to let us remain brothers. The only thing I could do personally was to promise myself I would never shoot at a Kazakh, whether he was White or Red, rich or poor.

At this time, the place we'd made our home was a remote village called Koitas. The area was also known as Ovtsekamen - 'the sheep stones' - after the boulders which covered this part of the steppe, half sunk into the earth but still as tall as a ram. Each handsome stone had a unique shape

A HUNDRED YEARS ON THE STEPPE   *43*

formed by nature and refined by the passage of time. Where they came from, whether they fell from the sky or grew out of the ground, no one has ever known.

We moved here to save ourselves from the raiders and then decided to stay. For nomads, the sheep stones were a kind of fortress; whole villages could hide there from the Whites or the Reds. And we really did need to hide from them. In these years, the steppe was lawless and violent. When you ran into a White or a Red, your life depended on what mood they were in. If a commander was in a bad mood, he could snap and set fire to or gun down a whole village. There were no trials or consequences, nor any guilt; these men did what they felt like. If they were in a good mood, they would just steal whatever they wanted and leave. This is how it was.

The elder of our village, our aksakal was Malai ata. He was a wise man of seventy years of age. He was our moral compass, the embodiment of our sacred history and the father of our clan. His beard, as thick and white as snow, reached down to his belt. Whenever he came to our yurt, it felt lighter, brighter inside, and we felt a powerful energy emanating from this special person. As he walked towards us, the steppe's gentle breeze, the *samal* would run through his beard, and we stood motionless in awe of him. We knew he was mortal, flesh and blood like us, but to us he was an *aruakh* - the spirit of our ancestors, the guardian of our clan. I can still see Malai ata wandering the steppe. His energy enters me and fills my lungs as it did all those years ago.

Malai ata was fair and intelligent, knew many legends,

understood politics and fought fiercely to preserve our clan.

'What difference does it make what colour an invader is?' he would say. 'White or Red, yellow or green, an invader is an invader. If the Whites come, we'll receive them in a white yurt. We'll feed them on a white tablecloth and give them whatever they want to drink; we'll give them everything we have. Even if they're idiots, they'll know we're not doing it out of kindness. If we don't give it to them they're going to take it anyway, and would probably shoot us afterwards. If the Reds come next, we'll do the same. They'll ask who we support, and we'll say, "you, of course." Do you think this is dishonest? Only a fool is honest with his enemy. And am I lying to gain something for myself? No, it's to save the village from another bloodbath and keep this clan alive. I'll do this even though there are enough idiots in this clan who went to fight a foreigners' war for them and forgot their own names when the foreigners told them to.'

I listened to him with my mouth open, devouring every word.

'Do you really think that the rulers in another land care about the Kazakhs more than our own aksakals? Tell me honestly: do you trust those mongrel Russians?'

I hung on my aksakal's every word and shook my head, no.

'Be honest and faithful only to the Almighty and your own people. With the so-called politicians and outsiders, be more careful. You don't need to be honest and genuine with those who aren't honest and genuine in return. You should always cheat your enemies if you want to stay alive in a time like this.'

Malai ata taught me how to live. His words made me look differently at the changes happening throughout the land.

'This isn't our fate. This isn't our war. Our people have been dragged onto a different path, thrown into someone else's war, and have begun killing each other. Now, we have to live under different laws. I'm afraid that life will become even harder for us, and there is more pain to come.'

Time proved the wise man right. Our villages and our families suffered in every way imaginable. We had no weapons apart from two rusty hunting rifles and a few rounds. Even if we were armed, how could we have gone to battle against the trained ranks of the White and Red armies?

My family's fate had left me as the oldest man in the house. I was eighteen-years-old and like all young men, I wanted to be at the centre of the action. I was ready to fight for a new, fairer world with a gun in my hand and the Alash Orda beside me. I had to follow my father's orders, though, to keep the village safe, look after my mother and protect our clan.

In the village there were twelve yurts and about seventy people, most of them women, children and a few elderly men. The rest had left to fight. The weight on my shoulders made me act responsibly, and as much as I could I stopped hot-headed Salim from doing anything dangerous. Although he was only one year younger than me, he thought that his older brother would always get him out of trouble. Ever reckless, he joined up with the Alash Orda. For a while,

I'd been able to keep him at home, but in 1918, when he'd just turned seventeen, he joined the ranks of those fighting for the same cause as us: Kazakh freedom and equality. Salim came home to visit us just under a year later. A few days after that, we received unexpected guests.

Two bands of troops bore down on the village from different sides: six Reds and six Whites. We greeted these guests with both happiness and fear, for, you see, we knew the leaders of each of these troops. Though we hadn't seen each other since we were small children, Akimzhan and Karimzhan were both our second cousins. Missing the steppe, they'd decided to visit their family in our village and to try, if they could, to get us on their side. Our grandfathers had been brothers. I took my great-grandfather's surname, Bektemirov, whilst they were Abzhanov and Abishev, after their grandfathers. But the cruel hand of fate had dictated that these two cousins would stand on opposite sides of the barricades. They would become mortal enemies.

I had to be as diplomatic as possible, to sit our guests who were armed and ready for war around the same table. Both of my relatives expected to sit at the head of the table, so I had to sit them next to each other in such a way that they would both feel they were the guest of honour. The other members of their troop sat across the table from each other. There were smiles between the young men, but the mood remained tense. Each of my cousins had their leader, their general beside them. The lower a man's rank, the higher his self-regard. Akimzhan and Karimzhan were serving another land's army. They were soldiers of low rank, always

A HUNDRED YEARS ON THE STEPPE

at the mercy of the generals above them; but here, in our village, they felt superior. They sat with straight backs, their noses in the air, not even trying to conceal their feelings of superiority over their hosts, their poor relatives.

We sat meekly, scared to make a sound. There was such tension in the yurt that I could hear my heart pulsating. The moment when we served the meat dish – *tabak* - made us feel even queasier, for we didn't know who should be given the head of the ram. The ancient custom among nomads is for the head to be placed upon the plate of the most impor- tant guest: the head of the family, the father of the daughter- in-law or the oldest person at the table. The person with the highest status in the yurt is the one who cuts up the head, but this is during peaceful times. What do you do in a yurt full of soldiers at war with each other and ready to open fire at the first sign of provocation? If I served the ram's head to the Red general, then everyone would think I want them to be victorious, and if I served it to the White general, then I automatically become an enemy of the Reds. Better to give everyone a ram's head; but Kazakh custom would never al- low for two heads to be served at one meal. Therein was my dilemma.

I made the only choice I could by offering the ram's head to Akimzhan, who was two years older than Karimzhan. Re- spect for your elders is an incontestable law of the steppe, and no one, at least out loud, could question Akimzhan's seniority. The faces of the White Kazakhs brightened; they looked upon this as a good omen and a sign of respect. The Reds furrowed their brows and gave each other knowing looks as if to suggest that the ram wouldn't be the only one to have his head split open that day.

With their guns slung over their shoulders, the twelve soldiers sat around the table and ate another dish of fatty mutton with smoke-dried horsemeat accompanied by *kumis* (fermented mare's milk). All were dressed in their military uniforms.

'Where is Salim? I haven't seen our little cousin yet,' Karimzhan suddenly enquired.

It was a natural question to ask, but it made me shudder. As one of the Alash Orda, Salim was passionately against all of our guests. Before they'd reached our village, I'd sent him as far away as possible so that his temper didn't cause an ugly scene.

'He's probably out hunting,' I replied. 'There are red foxes on this part of the steppe this time of year.'

I don't know what possessed me to mention foxes; even more so red ones. I should have said he'd gone to meet a girl, and then the conversation would have been over.

'How come everyone is hunting the reds?' Akimzhan tried to joke.

'Only they'll soon turn red themselves,' Karimzhan shot back.

'We know what you're like. We've lost count of how many Reds have turned White out here,' replied Akimzhan sharply, this time with real anger in his voice.

Everyone knew what the brothers were talking about. We'd heard about soldiers lying in pools of blood on the steppe and others left in shallow graves, their bones pale un-

A HUNDRED YEARS ON THE STEPPE 49

der the moonlit sky.

The hostility between the men had risen to the surface now, but the youngest of the Red soldiers helped to restore the peace. He must have been a new recruit because he still resembled an urchin from one of the steppe's backwaters. He looked uncomfortable in his Red Army uniform.

'Right, I'm ready; let's get started,' he yelled, showing everyone his *zhilik* - a large belt buckle made from a horse's shinbone.

For Northern Kazakhs, hitting your belt buckle is a challenge to a test of strength. Usually, they strike it with a cloth-strapped fist or the side of an axe, but real warriors love to heighten the sense of drama and punch it with their bare fist. In this way, they can judge where the bone's weak spot is from the sound it makes. It's more difficult this way, and sometimes the bone needs to be struck several times before it shatters.

At the sight of the zhilik, the Kazakhs in the yurt jumped to their feet, beat their chests and prepared to compete. One after the other, they rained measured punches on the shin bone, but the bone was solid and the soldiers weren't using all of their strength as they were afraid to break their fingers. Suddenly, one of the Russian Whites, a cross-eyed lad with blonde hair approached the group.

'Can we have a go?' he asked loudly. 'It looks like you need us to show you how to do it.'

'Go on!' the Kazakhs on both sides shouted having already forgotten they were enemies.

'Here, Kostya, show them!' another Russian yelled, sure

of his compatriot's strength.

The soldier was a brute of a man. He rolled up his sleeves, rubbed his palms together, pulled his enormous right fist back and struck violently at the bone. At first, we all thought he'd broken the zhilik, but a second later he grunted, swore, and hid his fist in his other hand. The zhilik was still in one piece, and the brute's hand was broken. He was so confident in his own strength that he hadn't bothered to look for a weak spot on the bone. All that we could do was wrap his hand in a cloth, give him a mug of vodka and tell him to wait for the pain to wear off.

Eventually, the Kazakh urchin cracked the bone with his first punch. The Reds celebrated, whilst the Whites looked distraught. I moved quickly to keep the peace, reminding the men that one side had eaten the ram's head, and the other had smashed the horse's shin. The Kazakhs appreciated this parity. With their equality established, the soldiers from both sides raised their mugs and gave toasts to friendship.

'May you all turn red!' laughed the Reds, meaning may your blood soak the steppe.

'May you all become white!' replied the Whites; that was to say may your bones be bleached in the sun.

In these times, these were our toasts, and this was our friendship.

Everyone laughed and drank, and I drank with them. Drinking always brought people together, somehow smoothing over the rough words exchanged between them. For us, giving our unexpected guests something to drink was of the

A HUNDRED YEARS ON THE STEPPE

utmost importance, for we hoped that Russians, White and Red alike, would not shoot people who they'd drunk with.

What came to pass next was what I'd been most afraid of. The door opened and there stood Salim.

Greeting our guests calmly, he sat next to me with his legs crossed in the Kazakh way. He was holding a *kamcha*, a horsewhip, in his hand. The kamcha was as long as his arm and had six leather tails, each the length of a palm. They used to say that a whip this size gave the most powerful blows. Salim, always so agile, could make an enemy howl from pain and writhe on the ground with one crack to his elbow or knee. He could also kill a man with one lash to his temple, crown, kidney or liver, but those who hadn't witnessed it could never have imagined that this wiry boy from the steppe could be so powerful.

It was common to bring a whip to a debate. When a man wanted to speak, he would raise his whip or throw it onto the table. Debates would often become aggressive, and the kamcha was a timeless part of steppe democracy and nomad etiquette. For Salim, it was also a deadly weapon.

After the cousins had exchanged small talk, Salim began the conversation that I was so afraid of and had tried my best to avoid.

'Tell me,' he asked coarsely and angrily, 'what are you fighting for?'

'We want to establish a monarchy and bring order to the Russian Empire and to the steppe,' replied the White, Akimzhan.

'We've come to free our proletarian brothers from oppression at the hands of rich landowners and governors,' said Karimzhan, the Red.

'You're both deluded! We've lived through a monarchy, and we aren't going to be slaves again,' hissed Salim. 'The Reds have nothing for us either. The Soviets won't give our people their independence, and that's what we Alash Orda want: freedom for the Kazakh nation.'

'Nonsense; that's just an empty fantasy,' snorted Akimzhan.

'The political situation won't allow the Kazakhs to live separately from Russia. Moscow won't allow you to form your own government,' said Karimzhan more respectfully.

'We're not asking for your permission,' snapped Salim. 'We'll get what we want through our own blood and sweat.'

'Are you strong enough, little brother? When did you get so cocky? Look around you; look at what's happening and see if you think it's worth it. Think carefully before you pick up a gun,' Akimzhan replied more calmly.

'All of our nation's suffering is because of people like you,' Salim railed relentlessly. 'If we all joined together, we would get our freedom.'

'No, little brother; please,' Karimzhan countered. 'Even if the whole steppe came together, all the Kazakhs, we still won't get our independence by going to war. The only way to a happy future is through socialism. We, the Kazakh poor, together with the working class in Russia, in unity with the peasantry and guided by the great leader of the worldwide proletariat, Comrade Lenin, must fight for our future.'

'Poor, you say? And how can I be a rich, respected Ka-

A HUNDRED YEARS ON THE STEPPE

zakh; or do you plan to bury them all?'

'If you're not with us, you're against us,' sneered Karimzhan.

'There is your mistake!' Salim shouted, pointing his whip at our cousins. 'You're dividing our people into rich and poor, and we're killing each other. We, the Alash Orda, are for national unity and brotherhood between all Kazakhs, no matter what clan or class.'

The debate was quickly descending into an argument, but then, Malai ata interrupted.

'Pipe down,' the aksakal said quietly. 'Thank the Almighty that you met here in your relatives' village, otherwise you would have murdered each other somewhere out on the steppe. Some cousins you are to each other. And what are you trying to achieve? Maybe you think you're doing the right thing, but in this awful tale that doesn't matter. The Empire needed to divide the nation; it needed to release a poison that turned brothers against each other. Then, the idea of a class war came to them. This isn't our path. It isn't our choice. It was forced upon us from above by selfishness, cunning and cruelty. We've ended up in this nightmare and we can't wake from it. At least remain as human beings as much as is possible, and never, not under any circumstances, shoot at your own brothers.'

The yurt fell silent as everyone lost himself in deep thought. The cruel circumstances were hurting us all, but the wise words touched each one of us.

At that time, I was burning with resentment and I took my anger out on my brothers. Now, I'm sitting next to them again in our clan's cemetery in the village of Bulakbasy: the start of life and the end of life. Now, my restless brothers lay peacefully with each other, but while they were alive, they could never live together because of the ideas brainwashed into them by the Tsar's and the Communists' rulers. Now, I don't dare judge them. Nowadays, everybody squabbles over the past and those with the loudest voices are the pretend historians and the populists, the biased and the hysterical. If you consider it, the story of the Kazakh people in the first half of the twentieth century, when everything came together in a bloody war, is extremely complex. My countrymen were just over twenty, sometimes thirtyyearsold, just young men whose bodies and minds had barely had time to develop. They didn't know what they wanted. You could have done anything to them.

The father of our second cousin Akimzhan was a wealthy man who supported the Tsar. Akimzhan fought on the side of the Whites, and in 1920 died in a battle close to his home. Our other cousin, Karimzhan was obsessed with the ideas of the Bolsheviks, of equality and brotherhood between peoples. He became an orphan when he was a small boy. His parents died from an epidemic the name of which no one in the village knew. Karimzhan spent his childhood in poverty, but the hardships he suffered did not break him; rather they gave him his strong character and made him a horseman with nerves of steel. The stamina and courage he developed in his youth, coupled with his quick mind and sharp tongue brought him to the highest rungs of revolutionary power, and he rose to every challenge that was put

A HUNDRED YEARS ON THE STEPPE

in front of him.

To Karimzhan's credit, he was no blind fanatic of communist ideology, unlike certain uneducated types. His actions were guided not only by Marxist-Leninist doctrines but also by lessons learnt from life on the steppe and nomadic wisdom. His people saw in him an honest and fair Communist Party member, and a worthy representative of the Soviet power that had brought about the new order. Many people came to him for advice and help and could speak with him openly about their problems in adapting to this new life. Karimzhan always tried to think things through to their logical conclusion, and nearly always came to the right decision. Unfortunately, in 1923 some 'class enemies' shot him in his home one night whilst he was writing a report. The chilling realities of that era didn't spare anyone.

On that day in our village, which would be the last time I would ever see them, the brothers argued until their heads ached but still couldn't see eye to eye. We understand now that everyone has a right to his opinion; but then, engulfed by revolutions and wars, people couldn't tolerate those who thought differently to them. Fanatics were prepared to kill or be killed for an idea.

On that evening, at least, no blood was spilt. The brothers parted, each in their own direction: Karimzhan to the Reds, Akimzhan to the Whites, and Salim to the Alash Orda. Obeying my father's orders to protect the village and take care of my mother, I stayed at home in the yurt, but as the three brothers went their separate ways, my heart split into three pieces and tears ran down my cheeks.

One day in about 1920, I was sitting on a hill close to the village and looking after the cattle. The sunset soothed me. I gazed at it for a long time, unable to take my eyes from the soft, warm glow of the huge sun, losing myself in comforting thoughts of past memories and the eternity ahead.

Suddenly, a cavalry appeared from behind a mound. It was the White officers of the Tsarist Army. In front, on a tall white horse rode a burly captain in a military tunic. The officers, all equally well-built, trailed behind him. With the light of the sunset shining on their red, blue and white dress-coats and their golden epaulettes and medals, they stood out handsomely against the dry steppe. Though their horses seemed exhausted from endless marches, they looked impressive too. The men carried sophisticated rifles and sabres in well-crafted sheaths. How beautiful were the uniforms and weapons of the Imperial Army, and how handsome the noble officers and their steeds. What a precious sight. How on Earth could anyone think to shoot at them? They say that beauty will save the world, but this beauty tore up the world and destroyed it.

Now, in my old age, I think it isn't beauty that will save the world, but the kindness of the Almighty and of people. Look how beautifully-made fighter planes are, how they fly over the ground and the ocean, but they bring death. Still, perhaps beauty can help to awaken people's sense of kindness. Maybe I'm getting carried away, asking questions as old as time itself, which is never wise if you want to live happily and peacefully. This lazy kind of wisdom squeezes the life out of a person. I prefer to tell myself that every day

A HUNDRED YEARS ON THE STEPPE

is a lesson. It's probably why I haven't gone mad.

Anyway, the line of handsome soldiers arrived in our village. There were only six of them, but for us, this was a real army. We gave our uninvited guests a polite welcome, but our hospitality didn't mean much to them. The Whites behaved calmly but with arrogance, as if our village belonged to them.

We quickly cut up our fattest ram and offered the uninvited guests much more besides. Giving me a wink, Malai ata presented them with a couple of bottles of moonshine. Under the supervision of my mother, Batima, the women brought a host of dishes to the table: hot wheat cakes, pancakes, sour cream, dried curd, salted yoghurt, fermented milk, kumis, butter. The hungry soldiers devoured the wheat cakes with sour cream, and, satisfied, thanked our women. We all breathed a sigh of relief.

When the officers were full and the bottles of moonshine were almost empty, the captain asked us to sing them a song from the steppe. A request from a guest is the law for our people - even more so if that visitor is carrying a rifle - but none of us could sing. After running his hand pensively through his long white beard, eventually, Malai ata came forward to sing "Elim-ai" ("Oh, my country"). This song comes from the time of the Dzungar invasions, a tragic era for our people when many Kazakhs perished at the hands of the hordes. Those who survived were forced to flee their homeland. Malai ata sang in a soft, touching voice, taking care over each word. He sang about cruelty, about lost happiness and peace. It felt as if the Russians appreciated the tragedy of the song, for when Malai ata finished they bowed their heads and exchanged glances with each other. Then, the captain began to sing. He began slowly, turning the lyrics into a mournful melody. I still remember that song about his birthplace and the comfort of his home. I remember all the aching pain in that song. Even though it belonged to an enemy, he had a wonderful voice.

We were touched by the foreign but beguiling song and its moving words. Up until that moment, I'd never thought that Russians could also suffer and could miss their homes and families. I'd just imagined they spent their lives ransacking other people's lands with their guns, humiliating and killing at will. *But then, why are they here?* I wondered. *Why are they wandering through our steppes, bringing fear and death? Did they really have to leave their homes and come here? What makes them do it and who sent them here?* These thoughts distracted me, and I only came to my senses when the captain finished his song.

The soldiers applauded and gave toasts to the health of their captain.

'Are there any girls in this village who can sing with us,' the captain asked me tipsily, 'or have you hidden them all away?'

I was afraid of disappointing him, so we had to call for Khalilya.

My younger sister, Khalilya was a beauty. Whenever she walked into a yurt, it immediately became lighter. She played the *dombra* - the steppe mandolin - perfectly, and sang like a nightingale. Her voice mesmerised those who listened, and her face reflected an ethereal light. When the mood took her, she could play the dombra with her toes.

On this ill-fated day, we asked Khalilya to sings some songs for our uninvited guests. We had no choice but to do as they asked, but we also wanted to show the White officers a little of our own culture. We hoped that our music would impress them, and they would think well of our village. So, Khalilya played some melodies from the steppe, and the soldiers were stunned by her. She sang several songs, and finished by performing the requiem, "Temirtas" from the time of our forefather, Birzhan-sal. I still remember her stunning face and voice.

The captain and Khalilya began to take it in turns, she performing a Kazakh song and he replying with one in Russian. The faces of the officers lit up as they joined in with the songs. For a while, everyone forgot about the painful times; about the fact that the men singing in our yurt were our enemies who at any moment could destroy our village. When Khalilya played on her dombra a Russian song that she'd only heard a few moments before, the soldiers cheered at the tops of their voices and drank to her health and her talent. The captain looked most enchanted of all, and I began to notice how he was looking at her.

A song cannot exist without love. Love gives birth to music, but music can also create love. Malai ata and I looked at each other and realised how stupid we had been. We should have hidden Khalilya from these armed men. That is what we'd done before, but this time something came over us. We'd wanted to show off in front of our foreign visitors, and we were punished for it.

The soldiers left early the next morning without saying goodbye. They took with them as much food as they could steal. They also took my sister.

The village was in shock. Mother wailed and clung to me. I was gritting my teeth and trying to comfort her when Salim appeared. Seeing him I became worried, and Mother wailed even more. When Malai ata told him what had happened, Salim turned wild. Malai ata didn't try to talk us out of searching for Khalilya. He only warned us not to get into a fight, and to try to negotiate her release.

'Don't take weapons with you; it's useless,' he told us. 'Talk to them. Shame them if you can. The only things you can hope will save her are the men's consciences and sense of fairness.'

On the way, Salim explained that he'd requested leave from his commanders to pay us a visit. From his words, I guessed that the Alash Orda didn't have much to do. Neither the Reds nor the Whites trusted them and would treat them as enemies, but the Alash Orda had little influence and suffered from a serious lack of weapons and ammunition. As Salim had given his rifle to a friend, he had no gun at all.

'Oh, if you could have seen that rifle,' he bragged. 'I killed a few Whites with it in, even an officer, a Kazakh.'

'How could you shoot at your own people?' I yelled at my brother.

Salim looked surprised.

'He's not one of us! He was a White Army officer!'

'What does it matter, Red or White? He was a Kazakh,

A HUNDRED YEARS ON THE STEPPE   *61*

our brother.'

'A brother to you, maybe, but to me, he was the enemy. He had a revolver in his hand and was firing at me. If I didn't kill him, he would have killed me. Would you have preferred that?'

I couldn't reply. This morbid philosophy had been forced upon us from the outside by the tyrannical White Army and the proletarian dictatorship. Foreign tactics and a foreign revolution had led Kazakhs to destroy each other.

'All Kazakhs are brothers,' I said. 'We have the same blood, and this is more important than the colour of a flag. It doesn't matter if you're White or Red, rich or poor, which clan or region you come from: a Kazakh is always your brother.'

Salim shut up and looked distressed.

Kazakhs rarely killed each other even when they fought amongst themselves. During feuds, they only used to use lances and tried not to hit their opponent's head. We would aim for knees, ankles or forearms. This was enough to make an opponent fall from his horse.

Salim was a true Kazakh and never contradicted his elder brother.

'I understand you,' I said, softening my voice. 'It's the times we're living in which make brothers turn their weapons on each other, but we can't blame everything on the times. There are so few of us; we can't just shoot at each other.'

'You're right, Asanbai,' replied Salim in a less confrontational tone, 'but not everything depends on us.'

This time I didn't say anything. I knew he was right too.

A man who never did anything by halves, Salim was devoted to the cause of the Alash Orda. He was a phenomenal marksman who could shoot the ear off a fox without even taking aim. He was lean, wiry and incredibly energetic. Despite being slightly smaller than average, he was extremely strong. Apart from his marksmanship, his most impressive quality was his agility. He could perform tricks on a galloping horse that impressed even his enemies. His attitude to war was remorseless but pragmatic.

'War is war,' he used to say. 'An enemy should be killed before he can kill you, so always be the first to shoot.'

Without fail he could find his way on the steppe using the sun by day and the stars by night.

'If you lose your bearings on the steppe at night, always trust your intuition and your horse,' he would say. 'Loosen your reins, let the horse make the decisions, and she will take you where you need to go. The Polar Star, Temirkazyk will always guide you north.'

A day later, we caught up with the White soldiers on the banks on the Sileti River, where the captain greeted us as if nothing had happened.

'Forgive us,' he said nonchalantly. 'These things happen.'

I tried to explain to him that they'd hurt us deeply and dishonoured our hospitality. Nowhere in the world is it acceptable to abuse hosts who have let you into their homes and shared their bread with you. The man was unrepentant, though.

A HUNDRED YEARS ON THE STEPPE

'Listen, we're not some band of thugs. We're officers of the White Army and we took from our subjects something we needed. So, let's part ways without any unpleasantness. Take some compensation for your sister. Isn't that what your people call a *kalym*?'

Only then, with every word he spoke feeling like a knife through my heart, did I realise how naive we'd been to think we could shame him into giving Khalilya back. The click of guns and the clanking of steel swords quickly brought me back to my senses.

'On second thoughts, let's do without a kalym,' he said coldly, placing a revolver to my forehead. It's dangerous on your steppe, and we don't have anything valuable with us.'

I felt the blood rushing to my head. Only the man's revolver stopped me from tearing him to pieces.

'So, your people can just take our sisters and hold them captive?' I hissed.

'I'm not holding her captive,' he replied. 'I like your sister a lot. In fact, I think I'm in love with her, and I think she loves me too.'

At this, I almost fainted, but Salim kept his composure, catching the captain's attention and casting his eyes towards the man's revolver. In broken Russian, he began to ask him about it. The captain was amused by Salim's naivety, and enthusiastically explained to him the advantages of using a gun with six chambers instead of five. Playing the impressionable youth, Salim pretended to hang on his every word. The other soldiers who had been watching us nervously became relaxed and laughed at the simple Kazakh boy who they surmised from his questions had never seen a gun before. When Salim asked how many enemies could be killed with a single bullet and if the number depended on whether the enemies were fat or thin, rich or poor, a heated debate began. All six White soldiers gathered around Salim and started to explain the complexities of marksmanship. Salim stared wide-eyed at each of their guns and held them upside down in his hands.

I asked the captain to let me see Khalilya. There was nothing else I could do. He waved his hand towards the river, where I found my sister sitting next to the water. I could barely recognise her; there was no trace of her beauty left.

Angrily, she refused to come back to the village.

'Leave me with him or kill me!' she cried. 'How can I show my face to people now?'

Covering her face with her hands, she burst into tears. I held her and tried to comfort her.

The sound of gunfire broke our embrace. Before I knew what was happening, the shots were following each other like bolts of lightning. When the shooting stopped and I could look up, I saw five of the White soldiers lying dead on the ground. Standing over them was Salim, with a revolver in each hand trained on the captain who stood motionless in front of him. Khalilya and I ran towards him. Salim had gone horribly pale. He was gnashing his teeth, his clothes covered in the officers' blood. Khalilya started wailing again.

'This isn't fair!' yelled the captain.

'And what do you think is fair?' Salim shouted back. 'That you came to our country, into our home with guns?

A HUNDRED YEARS ON THE STEPPE

That you murdered whole families, raped our women and torched our villages? Is that fair to you, you fucking dog?'

'In the Tsar's Russia, when men used words like that we used to fight for our honour in a duel,' the captain replied. 'But I'm sure you savages wouldn't understand what honour is.'

Salim pointed the revolvers at the captain's head once more. The captain grew even paler but stayed on his feet. I froze and waited for the gunshots, but Khalilya shrieked and threw herself at Salim.

'Stop, brother, please stop,' she cried, 'or kill me together with him.'

Her words paralysed me.

'What, the kisses of the Tsar's servants mean more to you than your own family?' Salim hissed.

'No! But I have no choice. Either I become his wife, or...'

'Shut up!' Salim screamed. 'How dare you talk like that? I'm not letting some foreign mongrel take you.'

Salim shook Khalilya off him, and she fell several metres away. Burying her face in the ground, she burst into tears again. I couldn't stop myself from starting to run to her, but Salim's next words froze me to the spot.

'So, Sir, you piece of scum, are you going to show me what a duel is?'

Salim gave the captain a look of utter contempt and threw him his revolver. The captain grabbed at it with numb fingers. Turning his back on the captain, Salim began to count the steps away from him.

'Why spill blood?' Khalilya implored him, springing from the ground. 'Why stand in front of a bullet, Salim? Can't you just let us go?'

Salim didn't turn round as he counted each pace loudly. Khalilya fell again and lay on the ground with her face in the grass. After counting out thirty paces, Salim stopped and turned around, but the captain was already ready with his gun raised.

'Not another word!' Salim shouted at me.

I wanted to say something, but I knew that nothing could have stopped my brother. Against my will, I had become the witness to the duel and stood between the two men. From his stance, it was clear that the captain had been in many duels before, whilst Salim had only heard stories about them.

The opponents faced one another.

Shaking, I lowered my arm to start the duel.

A shot was fired; only one.

I looked to my brother. He stood calmly on the spot, the revolver resting by his side. Across from him, the captain was lying on the ground. As we approached him, we saw that he had a bullet hole between his eyes.

Khalilya lay motionless. She had lost consciousness.

Hurriedly, we piled up the six corpses and threw some soil over them. We took their weapons: six rifles, seven revolvers with ammunition, swords and *kinzhal* knives, as well as their horses and camping equipment. With difficulty, we resuscitated Khalilya, placed her on a horse and headed for the village. She didn't put up a struggle, and once we set off,

A HUNDRED YEARS ON THE STEPPE

she quietly sang mournful songs.

It was soon dark, so we made camp for the night. After eating the rest of our food, we fell into a deep sleep. Suddenly, a deafening gunshot shattered the silence of the night, and we jumped up and scrambled to find the weapons. By the time I was on my feet, Salim already had a rifle in his hands and was ready to shoot; but there was no enemy. We breathed a little easier and went to look for Khalilya. When we found her, she was dead.

To this day I ask myself why she shot herself. Had the shock of her kidnapping broken her young, pure heart? Could she not live with the shame of what the captain had done to her? One idea frightens me most of all: had she really loved that Russian soldier, the enemy of our people? No, surely that can't be true. She knew that he'd killed her fellow Kazakhs. She couldn't have loved him. Or could she?

Everyone in our village mourned our little sister. Our mother suffered most of all. After Khalilya was buried, she couldn't speak for weeks. I can still hear the sound of her sobbing. Salim took half of the weapons we had collected for the men in his brigade, and we gave the rest to the men in the village.

These turbulent years forced Salim to play some cruel and dangerous games. My hot-headed and sharp-witted brother found himself in company that was at times heroic, and at others suspicious. He couldn't spend a week at home without becoming restless. The surrounding whirlpool of events sucked him in, and instead of striving to avoid them as I did, he was always seeking out his next fight. He was one of the best marksmen in the Alash Orda cavalry. As a proud descendant of nomads, he hated anyone having control over him. I spent my life scared for him, but whenever I tried to warn or protect him, he would only laugh and say: 'You look after yourself, big brother, and I'll look after myself.' He came to visit us less and less until one day he disappeared for good.

In the autumn of 1920, I lost Malai ata as well.

Once, I travelled into the steppe to bring our cattle closer to the village. When I returned the next day, every person in our clan was in mourning. In tears, the women told me what had happened. Another group of White soldiers had come into the village. Malai ata welcomed them, but they'd eaten and were already drunk, so refused his invitation into the yurt. Already behaving aggressively, they threatened Malai ata and the women that if they sympathised with the Reds or were sheltering any of them in the village, they would burn every home to the ground. Satisfied that there were no enemies in the village, they started to leave. But then a local Cossack captain, so drunk he was falling off his horse, made a bet with one of the tsarist officers to show him how skilled he was at throwing a lance.

He ordered Malai ata to run out of the village and into the steppe. If he couldn't split him in two with his first throw, then he'd leave the aksakal alone and ride out of the village, but if the old man refused, he'd kill everyone in the village on the spot. There was no way out, and the seventy-two-year-old Malai ata hobbled out onto the steppe as fast as he could with the Cossack soon catching up with him on

A HUNDRED YEARS ON THE STEPPE   *69*

his horse. When he got close enough to hear the old man's footsteps, he threw the sharp lance at his head with all his might. Mala ata had fought many battles on horseback in his youth, and as soon as he heard the spear flying towards him, he threw himself to the ground, and the lance whistled over his head. The White officers applauded the old man and began to make fun of the drunken Cossack. Everyone was relieved that the ordeal was over.

The troops were getting ready to leave the village when the Cossack, enraged, picked up his lance and drove it hard through Malai ata's temple. Blood poured from him and soaked his white beard. The old man fell dead without a sound. The officers looked at the Cossack in horror, and the Cossack, digging his spurs into his horse's belly, gave a demented cry and galloped away. The women threw themselves on the body of the man they loved so much and began to weep. We buried Malai ata in the ancient tradition of our ancestors. We were desperate to avenge his death, but we were powerless to do anything. We stayed in Koitas, among the sheep stones until the end of the civil war.

One day, I was on the steppe herding our village's horses, cows, sheep and goats, when a group of Red Army soldiers jumped out from behind some tall stones and pointed their rifles at me.

'Stop! Don't move!' they ordered. 'Put your hands up.'

I was stunned, and raised my hands. They relaxed a little when they saw how calm I was.

'Whose side are you on, Whites or Reds? What are you, rich or poor?'

70 *Bayangali Alimzhanov*

'Ha! What poor man has that many cattle?' commented one of them. 'He must be the lord around here.'

'I'm on the same side as you,' I tried to bluff.

'You piece of shit! We should kill you like an enemy of the people,' they laughed.

'What do you want; my blood or the cows?' I said, pointing to the animals, trying to bargain with them; but they weren't interested in negotiating.

'We'll let you choose your own fate.'

The elder of the two men took a copper five-kopeck coin out of his trouser pocket.

'I'm going to flip this coin,' he said. 'If it lands on the eagle, it means you're not on anyone's side; but you know that we can't let you go. There's a war on, after all; you might run off and join the Whites. We'll just tie you to that rock and let fate decide who comes for you, your clansmen or the wolves. If the coin falls on the side with the head, it means you're with the Whites, and we'll shoot you on the spot.'

It was pointless to explain anything, let alone argue. I felt calm; it didn't feel as if my time had come. I prayed to the Almighty and to my ancestors for help. The elder man threw the coin high in the air, and it shone in the sunlight as it spun before falling on the grass between us. The soldier and I ran to look at it. It had landed on the head.

'It isn't our fault - your own fate has spoken,' the soldier said emotionlessly.

They marched me to the centre of the sheep stones. I could barely feel my legs.

The Red Army soldiers giggled at each other's vulgar

jokes. These men, so sure they were creating a new, better life from the wreckage of the old world, didn't care at all that they were putting a man to death. Out of the corner of my eye then, I saw a group of horsemen coming towards us. *Could they be Kazakhs or Whites*, I thought, but a moment later, I realised they were Reds.

Two of the soldiers stayed where they were and two dragged me to one of the stones, trying to force me to my knees. I'd decided to die with honour, though, on my feet and looking at my killers. I forced myself from their grip, turned to face them and lifted my head. I prayed to Allah again: '*La ilaha ilallah*,' and waited for my death. I didn't want to die, though. Life had only just begun.

The other horsemen came at a gallop. *They're probably hurrying to shoot me*, I thought. My executioners glanced at one another, the look on their faces extinguishing my last hope of being spared. Shooting a man who is looking straight at you is a difficult thing to do, however, so they gestured angrily for me to turn around and sink to my knees, but I continued to stand and stare at them.

'Get ready!' the commander cried cruelly and coldly.

Three men picked up their guns and pointed them at me. Looking down their barrels, I said goodbye to this world; but then came another command.

'Guns down!'

The Red Army soldiers put their rifles to their sides and stood to attention. The tension was unbearable. It took all of my strength to stay on my feet.

The horseman who had barked this order was the first

to arrive at the stone. Looking me up and down, he shouted:

'Asan! You're Asanbai, Amanzhol's son!'

Leaping from his horse, he hugged me.

'What, you don't recognise your friend? I'm Timofei Maidaikin, the son of your tamyr!'

We embraced. I was saved.

Maidaikin turned to his men.

'This is no enemy!' he bellowed. 'He's with us, and you're to show him nothing but respect.'

This is how much my life had changed. Timofei Maidaikin, the son of my father's friend, had joined the Red Army, risen to the rank of commander and saved me. For the first time in my life, I had no other choice but to be thankful for Soviet rule.

With the decisiveness befitting a commander, Maidaikin ordered me to go and study.

'This fighting has gone on long enough,' he said sharply. 'It's time to accept that a new era has begun and to accept the new authorities. Otherwise...' He paused to think, and when he continued, his voice was calmer. 'The Soviet system needs teachers. So, go and study, learn, then teach your people about the justness of socialism.'

I thanked him from the bottom of my heart.

'And thank you to your father. We were very fond of him,' he said, smiling as he left. 'Teaching children is an honourable task. Remember that for the rest of your days. We will see each other again, and together we will build a new life.'

On Timofei's recommendation, I went to the nearest

A HUNDRED YEARS ON THE STEPPE   73

town to take a short training course in order to become a teacher. At that time, teaching was a very highly regarded profession. Children were encouraged by their elders to become teachers, as our people had a shortage. So it was that I found my calling.

Gradually, life became peaceful again. Old feuds were forgotten, and the new ways gained momentum. While I had no affection for the Soviets and their slogans, it was impossible to escape them. In these relatively tranquil years, people worked and raised a generation of Soviet children.

When I turned twenty-five, I got married; or rather, I was married off. My wife was called Khalima. She came from a clan of Argyns and Karauyls. Long before then, when I was only seven and my bride to be was still in her cradle, our parents had arranged the marriage and our fate was set. The law of the steppe was harsh but sensible. Our parents knew each other; they knew each other's families and their histories. They knew what they wanted for their children. Of course, they never asked what we thought about this. As a kalym for my future bride, my father gave forty-seven head of cattle, as was the nomadic custom.

I remember my first date with Khalima; it still feels like a wonderful dream. It was summer, and the steppe was in bloom. The scent of grasses and delicate flowers tickled my nose, filling my lungs with the powerful energy of the steppe's wild nature. Birds warbled and grasshoppers chirped. As our custom dictated, I came to my bride's village with several friends. In the evening, the young people in the village built an *altybakan* - a swing made from six poles - in our honour. Khalima and I sat on the ropes next to each other, and a boy and a girl began to push us harder and harder. We all sang songs about love, faithfulness and happiness. We rose so high in the swing that it felt as if we could touch the moon; we came back to earth so fast my head began to spin, either from the gravity or from joy. When it became completely dark, we played a game called *aksuyek*, which means 'the white bone.' To play aksuyek, the bride-to-be throws an animal bone as far as she can, and all the groom's friends run to look for it. They're only pretending to look, however; what they're really doing is giving the couple some time alone. Good friends take until midnight to find the bone.

Khalima and I waited a long time for the aksuyek to be found. This was our first date. Our wedding was a week later. It was 1925. We lived happily and peacefully in the town of Stepnyak.

The Path to Destruction

In the mid-1920s, Filipp Isayevich Goloshchyokin became First Secretary of the Kazakh Regional Committee of the Communist Party. The First Secretary practically owned the Republic. Rumours spread among our people that he was a Jew, and that his real name was Shaya Itskovich. People also used to gossip when they were sure no one was listening that it was this Goloshchyokin-Itskovich who'd shot Tsar Nicholas II. No one knew anything about him when

A HUNDRED YEARS ON THE STEPPE

he arrived or what orders he'd been given by the Central Committee, but as soon as power was in his hands, he did something monstrous.

On his first visit to Kazakhstan, Goloshchyokin was surprised by how life was on the steppe: people seemed to be living comfortably, and families often had a lot of cattle. It appeared to him that the revolution and the resulting chaos and famine hadn't touched these people. Local politicians patiently explained to him that Kazakhs are a nomadic people, and for centuries, cows had been their main source of food and transport, but Goloshchyokin had other ideas. He believed that in a Soviet country there could be no nomads, and everyone must have a registered address. Everyone must live as a Soviet citizen. A few dozen or even hundred head of cattle in one pasture was not the Russian way; not the revolutionary way. It was bourgeois.

The local Party members tried to explain that a hundred cattle was not a sign of wealth here, but the minimum needed to survive, to eat, exchange for other goods and maintain the population. On the steppe, cattle-herders were considered poor; only a few were able to live in comfort. The First Secretary would not listen. He said that by Soviet standards these people were bourgeois kulaks. If their wealth was confiscated and these rich herders and their cows put into kolkhozes (collective farms), then they would become a real working class. Think what potential they had and how wealthy we could be. All our targets would be met.

'But that would bring misery,' the Kazakhs argued, trying to make Goloshchyokin see sense. 'What will people eat? We need to consider the realities of their lives. If you take away their cattle, they'll starve.'

'How can that be true?' Goloshchyokin replied indignantly. 'Other people live perfectly happily without cows.'

They explained once more, in vain, that Kazakhs are a nomadic people who have herded cattle for millennia. Such a sudden change to their way of life could bring about a catastrophe. With a dismissive wave of his hand, Goloshchyokin told them not to worry.

'The Communist Party cares about the Kazakh people,' he said. 'I'm convinced that what Kazakhstan needs is another revolution; a second October, if you like. Continuing the class war is necessary in order to develop socialism. We took the decision to confiscate the property of the rich and banish them to hasten the process of collectivisation. I wrote a letter to Comrade Stalin about the need for a second, smaller October Revolution in Kazakhstan, and Comrade Stalin supported my idea. Furthermore, Comrade Stalin wrote in his own hand that this was the correct decision. Do you people understand, or are you saying I'm wrong? Do you think Comrade Stalin is wrong? Do you?'

At this, most people fell silent. Some heroes remained, though. They knew that the fate of the entire Kazakh nation was at stake and stood up for their people until the end. Whatever tragedy was about to happen, innocent people should not suffer. Goloshchyokin – who'd participated in the punishment and assassination of Tsar Nicholas II and his children - was unmoved.

'There are no revolutions without sacrifices. Of course,

A HUNDRED YEARS ON THE STEPPE   *77*

we shall try to ensure not too many die, but we can do without the weak. So, let us begin our next revolution - Little October!'

And that is how it happened. Goloshchyokin silenced his opponents with support from the Central Committee. He had the most vocal of them killed. There is still mystery surrounding the death of Smagul Sadvakasov, the politically shrewd, phenomenally gifted and truly brave Kazakh who was the fiercest opponent of Goloshchyokin's policies. All that's known is that he was invited to work in Moscow, and soon after arriving there he was poisoned. At the start of the 1930s, a wave of repression began. Many well-known, influential individuals were banished into exile, sent to prison, or simply shot without a trial.

In this way, having consolidated his position, Goloshchyokin got on with his bloodthirsty plan: a second socialist revolution on the steppe; the 'Little October' that would wipe out the majority of the Kazakh nation. Everywhere, so-called 'rich' Kazakhs had their property confiscated, the Republic's leadership making sure that the poor were involved in carrying out the raids. This was an awful thing to witness, that poorer Kazakhs had truly been made to believe that wealthy people were bad people who must be destroyed; that these people's destruction was important for the future of the Republic.

So, poor people got on their horses. Confiscation was in full swing in 1929. Even the more comfortable among the working class were not safe. Landowners and their families were exiled to Siberia. I once watched as the richest among my Kerey Clan, Kenesbai, was dispossessed. People loved to talk about his wealth. They told a story that one day, as Kenesbai was riding on the steppe he came across a group of men leading a herd of horses to Omsk to sell them at the livestock market.

'Isn't it a bit early to be going to the market? The horses haven't fattened up yet; the prices will be low,' he said, casting a nomad's eye over the drove.

'It's true, but we really need the money,' the men replied.

'Then sell them to me for the price you'd get in Omsk, and save yourself the trip,' Kenesbai offered.

The men were overjoyed as it was still hundreds of kilometres to Omsk and they'd be able to get home much sooner. Kenesbai took out a purse from under his saddle and paid the men, but they started to wonder, if he carries that much money under his saddle, how much must he have in his money box at home?

Every year, Kenesbai gave each of his clansmen a sogym - a horse to be slaughtered for its meat for the winter. You could say that everyone in his village worked for him: Kenesbai kept cattle, and his cattle kept them. Thanks to him, no one was ever hungry.

But this life was over now. The convoy guards came for Kenesbai and his wives. His children were terrified and hid under their mothers' skirts. The armed guards threw the family into a wagon and took them away in silence. The silence made everything even more painful, as no one had the chance to say goodbye to them. People who saw them in

A HUNDRED YEARS ON THE STEPPE

the wagon would quietly murmur: '*kosh bol*' – farewell - and Kenesbai would bow his head.

A large crowd gathered, and the head of the local Communist Party barked at them.

'So, you feel sorry for him? He's an oppressor, a leech. How much has he taken from you? Now, all of his cattle belong to you. You should be celebrating, fellow proletarians, that the Soviet leaders and Bolsheviks are freeing you from exploitation. He belongs in Siberia, and that's where he's going.'

Kenesbai's wagon screeched as it carried him and his family into the abyss. The Soviets took all of his livestock, thousands of heads of cattle and sheep, horses and goats. They said they were sending them to a meat processing factory to meet the needs of the people.

The steppe began to feel empty. No one could understand why these policies were being forced upon us. The dispossession and exile of our landlords, however, didn't always go to plan. The steppe grapevine, the uzunkulak brought awful news. There were stories of mortal combat between the heads of clans and the confiscators. In many parts of the steppe, there were more uprisings. Rumours reached us that Salim had joined one of the uprisings and was fighting against the Soviet authorities. This was very dangerous, and we lived in constant fear.

After the confiscations and the forced collectivisation, they brought in a tax on food - a tithe. And so it went on. In some places, they tried to follow the authorities' orders to the letter. Tax collectors would roam the steppe like hungry packs of wolves, entering peaceful villages and turning everything upside down. Each time, they would demand more and more. Sometimes, it would be a family's entire winter reserves down to the last grain of wheat and the last morsel of meat. When people got angry, they were told that if they handed over this tithe, the Soviets would give everyone everything they needed. Many people naively believed them, and whoever dared to protest was arrested and tried as an enemy of the workers and the peasants. Often, they were beaten to death.

The Kazakhs detested these tax collectors. Of course, they answered to the dictators in the Kremlin and their commissars in the provinces, but the simple people of the villages thought that the collectors had dreamt up this policy to ruin the Kazakh nation themselves. But no, these mindless people were just an effective tool in the hands of those who were really responsible for the anarchy and genocide; those who said: 'Look, the Kazakhs are crushing the enemies of their working class themselves and creating a new, fair world. It has nothing to do with us.'

Kazakhs who were strangled by the iron grip of these tax collectors told the most horrifying stories. They took literally everything. Some families tried to bury their bags of grain, but the collectors found them and took every last seed. They arrested one farmer for hiding his harvest; the poor man was sentenced to ten years in prison as a saboteur and an enemy of the people.

In the autumn of 1931, all the animals from the surrounding villages were driven to the town of Kazagorodok.

A HUNDRED YEARS ON THE STEPPE

It was assumed they would be slaughtered and sent to the meat processing plant, but the factory wasn't able to hold so many. Given this, people guessed that the meat would be sent to other parts of the country, but after a few days, the stench from the mountain of meat began to waft back to the villages. Those who were starving weren't given any of it. Armed guards threatened the hungry who approached as the meat sat there rotting.

As a result of policies like this, in the winter of 1932, a famine swept through the nation. For as long as people could remember, there had never been such a disaster. We heard stories of entire families scraping by on discarded animal skins which they would boil into a broth.

Finally, the authorities slowly began to send food to the starving steppe. Once, I was called up to distribute the rations. I visited the most remote villages with a compatriot, travelling on two sleighs stacked with supplies. It would be impossible to put into words everything we saw. On the tracks that ran through the steppe, we saw the corpses of countless people who had died of starvation. I can still see a horrific scene in my head of a dead man lying in a gully. His body was frozen solid and half-covered with snow. The man had fought until the very end and had fallen only two paces from salvation. He lay face down in the snow with his right hand outstretched. His eyes were wide open and staring dead ahead. When we saw what he was reaching for, our hearts broke. It was a dead marmot. The man had used his last ounce of strength trying to catch it and had fallen two paces short. If he'd eaten the marmot, perhaps he would have been able to reach the town.

Not far from there, we found a small village. The little mud huts seemed very cold, and there was no smoke coming from any of them. We were overcome by fear. There was a deathly silence in the village; there were no traces of life. The entrances to the huts were covered in snow. We hoped that the people who lived here had gone to the town. We tried to open the door to the first house, but it was locked. We knocked on the door for a long time and then began to shout: 'Is anyone there? We've brought you some food!'

Greeted by silence, with our hearts sick with worry we decided to break down the door. Slowly, we stepped inside. There was something frightening in that awful hush; we could feel the breath of death on our necks. There was no one in the living room, but three people were lying in the bed, a woman and two children. They were dead. Full of sorrow, I imagined them alive. I pictured the mother as their lives slipped away, holding her children in her arms and putting them to bed: 'Try to fall asleep and sleep deeply. When you wake up, people from the town will come with the food they promised.'

In pain, we left the dead village. The pure, frozen air gave us a little more strength, but we travelled in silence, too sad to talk, the only sound the crunching of snow under our horses' hooves. When we reached the next village, some people were still alive, but looking at them filled me with dread. Emaciated from hunger, they'd lost all hope of being saved. As soon as we arrived, they threw themselves at the bread. By handing out these meagre rations, we managed to

A HUNDRED YEARS ON THE STEPPE

save a few families.

With our spirits raised a little by this small success, we rested in the village for a day. Leaving more food with them, we promised to take some people to the town. From there, we set out to the most remote village in our part of the steppe. When we finally arrived, this place frightened us again with its silence. We couldn't find a single living soul; in every house we went to the people were dead. But then we heard something. The noise was faint and we couldn't tell what it was, but we knew it was coming from a living creature. We stepped towards the sound with trepidation. As we drew closer to the house, the sound became clearer; it was somewhere between the lowing of a cow and the barking of a dog. Scared, we opened the door and stepped inside. It was dark, and I carefully drew the curtains.

In the room, a little girl of about seven, half-naked and covered in dirt and blood, was holding in her hands the arm of her baby brother that she'd torn from his dead body. She was sitting with her back to us, making painful grunts as she tore at the flesh of the little boy's hand. Hearing our footsteps, she spun around to face us. It was a frightful scene: the girl's face was smeared in blood and her eyes shone with a manic fire. Baring her teeth, she howled at us. We lost control of ourselves and ran out of the house, out of the village without looking back.

I don't know how long we'd been travelling across the snow-covered tracks when I heard the sound of a person crying and looked around. The horses spooked, and my colleague looked at me fearfully. Only then did I realise that it was me who was crying. Jumping off the sleigh, I buried my head in the snow. I couldn't stop myself; my tears were choking me. At this moment, I wanted to go to Stalin and Goloshchyokin, burn them alive and throw their ashes to the bitter wind. When I couldn't cry any more, I turned to my colleague.

'Why has this happened? Why to us?' I screamed at the top of my voice. 'How could we, a whole nation, allow them to do something so monstrous to us? How could we, the sons and daughters of nomads who never knew what hunger was, let ourselves be annihilated like this? These psychopaths have sent our nation to its death. No fighting, no war – they've just destroyed us. How could they do something like this? Why? Do you understand what has happened? They did this on purpose. They deliberately massacred the Kazakhs to make our nation disappear. They emptied the steppe in order for their own people to take it!'

To begin with, my partner listened to me, but when the truth became too much for him, he looked away. He was about eight years younger than me, an ordinary Kazakh boy from a poor family. Sometimes, he would tell me proudly about how he'd taken part in the dispossession of the wealthy members of his clan. He literally prayed to Lenin and Stalin, believing they'd not only made him an equal of the landowners but had put him above them. Thanks to the Soviets, Kazakhstan now belonged to him.

He too was shocked by the consequences of the famine, but his sympathy was shallow. Of course, when a man sees another man die, he feels sorry; especially if that man was completely innocent. But this Kazakh boy didn't understand or didn't care about why our nation had turned into a tragedy.

I regained my composure, and with heavy hearts, we turned around and went back to the remote village. The little girl was very ill, and we couldn't leave her alone among the dead bodies. We had no idea what we should do; all we could think of was to take her with us to the town and find someone there who'd take her in.

With difficulty, we approached the settlement. The horses didn't want to go any further. Veering from side to side, they slowed and then stopped completely. We resorted to using our whips, but we couldn't be too strict with them as we knew how they felt.

Standing silently together, we stepped into the cursed hut once more. Our nerves were frayed, but we were prepared for whatever awaited us. The little girl who'd terrified us was lying motionless on the floor. We spoke to her, but she didn't move. I prodded her shoulder with the end of my whip, but still, she didn't move. The girl was dead. She had suffocated. A bone from her brother's arm had got stuck in her throat.

Numb from the shock, we stood over the girl for a while and prayed: '*La ilaha ilallah*,' and then we left. I imagined that in their desperation, the children's parents had tried to reach the town in search of food, and had left their daughter and infant son at home. The little boy must have passed away soon after, and his sister had gone mad and eaten him. I still often see her face.

The next year, 1933, Goloshchyokin was removed from his position and brought back to Moscow. A few years later, he was arrested and shot. He got what he deserved, but that was no comfort to those who had suffered and died from the evil he unleashed.

As the years and decades passed, we began to understand the scale and the senseless cruelty of the national and human tragedy those monsters had inflicted upon us. Some historians write that more than three million Kazakhs died in the year of the famine. Soviet records put the number as one and a half million. The most awful thing is that no one knows exactly how many human bones are lying on the steppe. Historians around the world pick numbers out of thin air: some say two million, others three. Not tens, hundreds or even thousands, but *millions*.

After the famine, I no longer believed in the Soviet life.

A Tyrannical Fire

As more of our blood and tears were spilt, we began to realise that our country was ruled by a tyrant. Of course, no one could say this out loud, though, so we swallowed our hatred, lived obediently and worked hard under these leaders.

I taught Kazakh language and literature at a school. Teaching children about the kindness in the world, educating the next generation felt like what I was born to do. My wife, Khalima was my soulmate, and our three children, two

A HUNDRED YEARS ON THE STEPPE   *87*

sons and a daughter went to the school. Stepnyak was a large town in those days, with tens of thousands of people from many clans and nationalities living there. During the year of the famine, if you made it to Stepnyak, you would survive.

People said that a few centuries ago they used to mine gold here, and the place was called Mynshukur - the thousand pits. Those pits, still intact in my time, were later used by Russian and British gold miners. In the years before the war, people often used to find gold dust in the river. Small boys would jump into the river, come across shiny sand, sieve it in a tin can and take it to one of the local shops. There the gold dust was weighed, and the boys were paid a bond for what it was worth. Bonds were a special kind of money, which were given only in exchange for gold, and which were only traded here.

Kazakhstan's communist leaders wrote glowing reports to their superiors in Moscow about the fantastical achievements of the gold miners. Newspapers wrote about the successes of Soviet production and agriculture. People all over the Union had heard of Stepnyak. In 1934, Sergei Mironovich Kirov, then the second most powerful man in the country after Stalin, paid a visit to the town. It was said that the leaders used to love boasting about the twenty-kilogramme bars of gold. They used to challenge their workers to pick one up using only one hand. 'If you can hold it, it's yours,' they'd joke. But, of course, no one could lift something that was at the same time so slippery, heavy and wide. There were economic successes, even enormous ones, but since the horrors of the famine I couldn't bring myself to care.

In 1937, more awful events came to us. People began to disappear without a trace. Kazakhs used to call this *undemes* - the stillness. A man would live honestly and peacefully, working hard to build a new Soviet life and feed his family. Then, he would disappear as if the ground had swallowed him. A short while later, the rumours would begin: it turned out he wasn't quite who he seemed. He wasn't one of us. He was working against the Soviet system; a saboteur or a spy for America or Japan. People were aghast that these characters could have committed such deeds without anyone noticing. The most absurd thing about these stories was that people believed everything that was written in the newspapers. Newspapers were seen as a symbol of truth; no one could even imagine they would lie. But they turned these honest men - who yesterday were your friends, colleagues, brothers - into foreign elements; into the harshest and most dangerous thing: an 'enemy of the people.'

To begin with, they killed the most well-known individuals and the descendants of prominent families. The Kazakh people were like wild kulan horses rounded up in a pen. As soon as the horses were trapped with nowhere to escape, the hunters caught them.

If you didn't want to live in the new Soviet world, you were called an enemy of the people and shot. If you fought and worked to build this world, you could still be shot. All of the Alash Orda were purged, even those who became loyal to the new leaders. We couldn't understand how this could be, but the hideous truth soon came to the surface. The killing machine had a specific goal: to eradicate the Ka-

A HUNDRED YEARS ON THE STEPPE

zakh nation. The awful result of those dark years was that almost all strong-minded and talented Kazakhs were murdered. The system made more and more people disappear. The newspapers warned that there were many enemies of the people inside the country and that every Soviet citizen should be vigilant.

When they started to come for those who'd made only the slightest mistakes, people began to question the motives behind the messages. Murmurs began, but no one dared to raise their voice. Fear was everywhere, and it consumed and overwhelmed everyone. Every person lived with the fear of being arrested. We all knew that at any moment we could be arrested for nothing and sent for twenty-five-years in Kolyma, Magadan or the Siberian taiga; or worse, be quickly shot and disposed of. Everybody knew who was behind this.

The most frightening thing was that every town, district, village and labour body was obliged to seek out and eradicate the enemies of the people living among them. If a district didn't neutralise all the so-called opportunists, Trotskyists, nationalists and Islamists, Japanese, American and German spies, then its political standing fell and those behind the repression would come for the leaders in charge of that district. So they all tried to uncover as many enemies of the people as possible. This brought about mass surveillance and an army of informants.

For the Kazakh people, these years were like a conveyor belt leading to a meat grinder, constantly pulling in fresh meat. The conveyor belt never stopped. It was relentless, merciless, and destroyed everything that fell into its metal teeth. People did everything they could to jump off the belt; they became extremely cunning and evasive.

Kazakhs are emotional people; we show love for one another. Through all the cruelties we have suffered, we've preserved our humanity. Even when we are close to death, we don't lose our sense of honour and dignity. So, during these years, people risked their lives to save each other. The repressions were useful to some people, though. Those cruel and dark days awoke their worst instincts, and they enjoyed sending their brothers into the meat grinder.

There is a misguided notion that the Kazakhs betrayed each other and informed the authorities that their clansmen were enemies of the people. Certainly, there were such people, but if we think about the situation now, the truth is clear. The killing machine was never satisfied; it always demanded more bodies. It ground people up without mercy, and we have to understand that the blame should always lie with those who built this machine. Most of the time, illiterate people were tricked or forced into signing letters incriminating one another. The methods the authorities used were crude and nasty, but poor people had no way of escaping from them.

Put yourself in that position. You are summoned for questioning, but to begin with, you're only a witness. Experienced interrogators take you into a dark cell, surround you, threaten and hurt you. In adjacent cells, you can hear others who have been arrested screaming in agony. In that cell, you would sign whatever they wanted. Often, they wouldn't even have to lay hands on you. 'If you don't admit

A HUNDRED YEARS ON THE STEPPE 91

this man is a Japanese spy, he'll say that you are,' they'd cajole. 'So, choose while you still can: him or you.' Or: 'You can be a witness and work with us, or we'll shoot you as an enemy of the people. Think about your children. How will they live with the shame that their father was an enemy of the people?' This was usually enough to break a person, and the NKVD made sure that the informant and his victim never saw each other again. Later on, most informants were killed too, so the methods used on them were not disseminated. Friends came to hate and blame each other for their suffering. They passed this hatred onto their children and grandchildren, so that mistrust and accusations still flow through our people to this day.

The psychological impact of those years was obvious: people believed every word they heard and read, especially if it concerned them personally and came from their leaders. It's a surprising fact about our people that they can believe anything that's said about them, no matter who says it, where it's said or whether it was really said at all. It's enough for someone just to say: 'That person said this and that about you,' and they'll believe it without checking. They will even reply, 'Oh, I expected that from him; I knew he didn't like me.' That's to say, even before the repressions people didn't trust each other. The years of the purges stirred up a feeling of suspicion that was already lying dormant in our subconscious. And I think that this suspicion still lives there.

The repressions annihilated every nationality. They even murdered Russian communists. When they came for Timofei Maidaikin, the district's chief enlistment officer, we were stunned.

Temirtas, the son of the great singer Birzhan-sal worked in one of the mines. He was a very strong boy, and so tall that when he sat on a horse, his feet touched the ground. Temirtas was kind, trusting, and fair. Whenever he saw someone being treated badly, he'd always stand up for them. He'd been much respected since the day he single-handedly fought off a group of Russian settlers after they overstepped and horribly insulted a Kazakh family. His superiors at the mine didn't like him, though, so they put him on a list and then waited for the right time to get rid of him.

Temirtas played the dombra and knew all of his father's songs. Before Birzhan-sal passed away, he made a promise that he'd keep his requiem alive. Everyone on the steppe knew these intimate melodies about life and death. Even whilst he was still alive, Temirtas had become a legend because of the great songs whose legacy he carried. But when the repressions started, the Soviet powers sent the son of the beloved singer and all of his family to Siberia. After Stalin died and those who'd been exiled gradually began to return, I met Temirtas's son, Mukhamedkali. I was already an old man when he told me that his father and the rest of his family had died in a gulag. He was the only one able to return to their homeland.

One poor teacher was imprisoned for ten years. His crime was that he'd sewed himself some underpants out of a piece of red fabric. It was his awful luck that a criminal investigator had come to the village, an old Bolshevik from Leningrad now with the NKVD. His new job was to seek

A HUNDRED YEARS ON THE STEPPE

out enemies of the people on the steppe whilst his superiors breathed down his neck. So, he and his armed henchmen called at the school. The teacher gave them all something to eat and drink and the men were about to leave, but before they left both the investigator and the teacher needed to use the toilet. That's when the NKVD man noticed that the poor teacher's underpants were red. 'Oh, you son of a bitch!' he railed. 'Now I've got you. The red flag of this great country, signifying the noble blood of our workers, and some backward Alash Orda thinks he can cover his arse with it!' The investigator got to work. It turned out that the man's vest was made from white cotton, and only his underpants were red. 'You pig!' the NKVD man ranted with this new ammunition to hand. 'So, the Whites are closer to your heart and you placed them above us, putting the Reds in the most shameful, filthy, stinking place!' The teacher pleaded that he hadn't done it on purpose; he'd simply made them from the only piece of fabric he could find. The teacher turned white with fear; the commissar punched him in the face, and off he went to Siberia.

That night, all the villagers burnt their red underpants; and all because the red flag was sacred. Communist propagandists used to claim that the colour signified the blood of the workers and peasants that was spilt in the fight to build the Soviet dream. Everyone has red blood, though, and it's terrifying to see rivers of it no matter what dream it's spilt for.

The son of one man in the village, a boy of about seven loved to draw. One day, he wanted to draw a portrait of the Great Leader, Stalin that he'd seen in a book. He didn't know how to draw facial features, so the lad improvised, tracing a copy from a book which he inadvertently defaced in the process. If the wrong person had seen the result, a smudged and ugly picture of the Leader with lines across his face, then another enemy of the people would have been found, and the boy would never have seen his father again. Happily for us, the boy's drawing and the book were found by a young history teacher who brought them in trembling hands to me. At first, I was scared too to touch them, but then I calmed down.

'Who else has seen this?' I asked.

'No one,' the young teacher replied.

'You understand what will happen to all of us if any of *them* sees it?' I asked.

The young man shivered and shook his head like a horse with a fly on its nose.

'Then you haven't seen anything. It never existed. Understood?'

My calmness gave him strength.

'Understood,' he replied emphatically.

That evening, I smuggled the cursed book and portrait home and threw them into the fire. I watched as the 'Great Leader and Father of All Nations' in full military uniform burned under a heap of dry birch twigs. His face formed a monstrous grimace as it went black. It looked like he was laughing at me. I shivered and my chest tightened. I could only breathe again once he'd disappeared completely.

Eventually, the truth sank in. The slaves of the White

A HUNDRED YEARS ON THE STEPPE

Tsar had become the slaves of the Red Tsar. The colour and the slogans were different, but the rest remained the same. We'd been subjects of the Russian Empire, and we still were. There would be no independence.

I wonder now what would have happened to our people if we'd all come together as one nation to rise up, first against the tsarist colonists, and then against the Soviets. Probably, our brave horsemen would have died heroically in battles between crossbows and guns, and the Kazakhs would have been wiped from the face of the Earth. Many years after these events, I came to understand our uneasy philosophy for protecting ourselves and surviving: we may have bowed down to our rulers and danced to their tune, but inside we stayed proud of our faith, our culture and our language. Most importantly, we didn't give away our souls.

I worked for the Soviet powers and the Communist Party. I helped those who stood on pedestals to write fiery speeches calling on the masses to embrace communism and work towards a utopian socialist future. In the evenings, though, I would read the Quran, the hadiths of the Prophet, stories of Muslim saints, and the legends and parables that my ancestors told. This was the reality of my life, and I was proud of it.

The Spies' Nest

Eventually, my time came. During this period, the arrest of a new enemy of the people, a visit from men in black jackets in a black van was not unusual. Many people, including Communist Party workers kept a little case with their toiletries and a change of clothes under their desks. People used to say that even the judges, prosecutors and the NKVD men themselves were ready to swap their offices for a prison cell at a moment's notice. Without exception, a sentence hung over all our heads. It was like the sword of Damocles, the threat of arrest and then, at the Troika's behest, either years in prison or a bullet in the head. My suitcase was packed, but I never imagined they'd take me the way they did.

It was during a literature lesson that they took me from my classroom. My students were reading *From the Mountain* by Johann Wolfgang von Goethe, which Lermontov had translated into Russian, and Abay translated into Kazakh.

The magical poems about nature in this brilliant translation had caught the children's imagination, but the mood was shattered when the doors burst open and two men in black leather jackets stormed in. My students fell silent, and my blood ran cold.

'Teacher Asanbai Amanzholovich Bektemirov?' one of the men barked, staring at me quizzically.

'Yes,' I replied, almost in a whisper, my mouth so dry that my tongue couldn't move.

'And what are we reading?' the man sarcastically asked the children.

'Goethe and Lermontov translated by Abay!,' answered the bravest student.

'I might have known,' he said snidely, turning sharply to face me. 'You're studying a German. So, I suppose you're

A HUNDRED YEARS ON THE STEPPE

spying for Germany as well?'

'Of course not; this is literature. He's one of the great poets,' I choked.

'We'll see about that. But we are here on another matter. Teacher Asanbai Amanzholovich Bektemirov, you are under arrest.'

He looked at me coldly. Fighting the terror in my chest, I tried to remain as calm as possible in front of my students, who were watching in horror.

'Children, don't worry,' I said. 'This is just a misunderstanding. I haven't done anything wrong. As soon as my comrades and I clear everything up, we'll continue our lesson. I'll see you soon.'

'Goodbye, Asanbai Amanzholovich, *agai*. Come back as soon as you can,' the children chorused.

I was ashamed that the children had seen this. They respected me, and they had to watch as I was marched out of the classroom like a criminal.

We walked out of the school. Those few familiar steps along the corridor drained every ounce of my strength. When the doors closed behind me, I imagined it would be forever.

The black van was hidden in the shade of some trees. I was being escorted into the back seat when one of the girls from my class ran out of the school towards us.

'Agai! Teacher!' she cried out.

We turned to face her. She was holding a pen in her hand.

'Agai; you forgot your pen,' she said, thrusting it towards me.

I was in shock and could barely control my hands. The commissar pushed me in the chest.

'He doesn't need it anymore. Keep it,' he said roughly to the little girl.

The girl began to cry as we got into the car. Out of the window, I saw Khalima running towards us. She was six months pregnant. She was struggling to lift her legs but almost managed to run in front of the car. I tried to get out, but the commissar shoved me again.

'Sit down; we're going,' he barked.

As the driver started the car and we sped away, I lost control of myself.

'I'll be back soon! I haven't done anything wrong! Tell everyone!' I screamed through the half-open window.

The last thing I saw behind me was Khalima and the girl holding each other, both in tears.

When we arrived at the NKVD station, I was taken to be interrogated. The officer was a Russian of about my age. He informed me that I was suspected of agitating against the authorities.

'Do you know the song "Tau ishinde"?' he asked.

'Yes; it's a love song.'

'And do you know who wrote it?'

'No,' I lied.

'Of course, you know. It was written by Saken Seifullin, an enemy of the people.'

'But the song isn't about enemies of the people. Everyone knows it, and everyone likes it.'

A HUNDRED YEARS ON THE STEPPE   *99*

'That was before. Now, no one can like it. They can forget the song and the singer; they don't exist anymore. Do you know that song is against the law, you cretin, or are you too stupid to understand? Get it into your head that a song written by an enemy of the people is against the law and people who sing it are lackeys of the imperialists.'

The officer took a breath and glared at me. I looked him straight in the eye.

'So, do you confess that you sang that song knowing full well it's the work of an enemy?' he shouted in a demented voice.

'No,' I replied.

My body had gone cold.

'I say you did, you say you didn't, so one of us is lying. Answer me - which one of us is right?'

'I'm not lying. We didn't know it was an enemy song.'

'So, you're saying I'm lying?' he said, becoming ever more livid. 'How dare you accuse me, a conscientious Soviet comrade and officer of the NKVD of lying?'

'I didn't say that.'

'No, you didn't say it, but that's what you think. Are you accusing me, you scum?'

He threw himself on me and pounded his fists into my head until I collapsed on the floor. I don't know long I lay half-conscious before he dragged me up by the collar, threw me onto a chair and gave me a glass of water.

'Okay,' he said calmly. 'Now, go and think until tomorrow; and think carefully. If you give me the right information, I'll help you get out of this shit. If not, you can die in the labour camps.'

The man was a bloodthirsty psychopath.

I was taken to a cell and locked behind a heavy iron door. I lay on the stone floor; I had no strength to stand.

'Get up, son, and lift your head,' said a quiet, old voice. 'In this life, you must keep fighting, no matter what happens to you.'

The man helped me to my feet, and I sat on a bunk. We introduced ourselves, and I almost jumped when he told me his name. It was Zhakezhan-bi, the renowned judge and public speaker. Now labelled a class enemy and repressor of the Kazakh nation, my cellmate was well respected among our people. Many stories were told about him. In 1916, he'd given five hundred of his thoroughbred horses to a group of tsarist officers in return for five hundred young men from his town who'd been conscripted. In so doing, he saved many young Kazakh boys from certain death. From that day, people - myself included - spoke his name with reverence. Now, our fates had brought us together in a prison cell.

Zhakezhan-bi told me that when the dispossessions began, his relatives convinced him to flee. He secretly took his family to Russia, to a backwater town near Omsk. Meanwhile, his friends spread a rumour that he was on his way to China. Whilst the authorities were looking for him in the east, he hid in the north under an assumed name. Still, he couldn't avoid the nest of Soviet spies, and so he'd ended up here.

'Any war, especially a political one, requires a quick mind, wisdom and cunning,' the old man said to me. 'No-

A HUNDRED YEARS ON THE STEPPE 101

mads of the steppe, children of the skies, brothers of wandering clouds and shimmering stars live honestly and openly. They open their hearts to people, tell everyone their secrets, and live without cynicism. They never cheat anyone, so they don't think anyone would ever cheat them. And this is what they get as a result. Because life is a battle, and a battle means war, you must cheat your enemy in any way you can. If you don't, you'll be the one who's cheated. So, I implore you, when it's a matter of life and death and the fate of our nation, cheat everyone everywhere. Make your enemy think you're his closest friend and believe in this lie to the bottom of your heart. There's no need to invite bullets to enter your chest. Play the game and cheat any way you want, but you must find a way to survive this mayhem and fight to save our nation. You should never shoot your own people, but if the enemy demands you do so and places a gun to your head, then in the name of future victories shoot even your own brother. Here is my advice to you: when they interrogate you, tell them you were led astray by the frivolous ideas of the Alash Orda. Make it sound as if you denounce their talk of independence and self-determination. Most importantly, beg them to forgive you for your stupidity. Say you're ready to work with them to free the country from enemies.'

'So, why don't you do this?' I asked, taken aback.

'They won't believe me. I'm too big a fish for them. I won't get out of here alive. But you are young and still have your life to live. Even if they don't believe you, they still need young recruits. They want to show the world that the Kazakhs are fighting the nationalists themselves; that youngsters from the steppe support the Soviet regime and the masses are with them. So, they're going to make you work with them whilst keeping a close eye on you, of course. Try to keep them happy and make a good impression on them. Everything you do to oppose them, do it in secret.'

I understood him. I had heard similar words from Malai ata, and life had taught me the same lessons.

I thanked the aksakal.

'I will be forever in your debt,' I said.

He sighed deeply.

'If you're thanking me from your heart,' he replied slowly, 'then your debt is already paid. I've also owed my life to the kindness of others, both young and old, but many of them I wasn't able to pay back. I've also helped others as much as I could, and many of them couldn't return my kindness. This is how life is; you can't wait for your reward. Kindness is passed from person to person like a baton in a relay. The next time you're kind to someone, consider that you've been kind to me.'

Zhakezhan-bi's words gave me strength. I was ready to fight. The next morning when they came for me, I said goodbye to him. They marched me down a long dark corridor, shoving me from side to side. By the time we got to the big grey interrogation room, I'd completely lost my bearings and could barely stand. My bones hurt and there was a din in my head as the officer marched in.

'Do you believe in God?' he asked.

I didn't reply.

'Of course, you do. All you sons of bitches believe in

A HUNDRED YEARS ON THE STEPPE 103

God. So, where is he? Where is your Allah? Show me. If he exists, then where is he now? How could he allow such awful things to happen in this world? So, he doesn't exist. Or he used to, but he left.'

Laughing hysterically, he wiped his bloodshot eyes and began to rummage through a pile of papers. His words had made me so angry that I wanted to cut his throat, but I kept my composure. *Why does the Almighty allow such awful things to happen in this world?* I thought. *Why does he let godless psychopaths drown half the world in blood whilst shouting about fairness?*

'You don't need to look for him anymore,' the investigator said, more calmly this time. 'Life is a blank canvass now, and we are its new painters. First, we're going to turn the old world into dust; then, we'll build a fair society and create a new life for everyone. You shouldn't look for an imaginary god in the clouds. You should find powerful friends here on Earth. Do you agree with me?'

I kept silent. It was the best protection.

'If you aren't with us, you're against us!' he bellowed, becoming aggressive again. 'And you don't make small talk with your enemies, you shoot them. So, it's time to decide whether you're a friend or an enemy.'

People were either your friends or your enemies. Everything was black and white, although, as a Bolshevik, the NKVD man probably saw things in red and white instead. No other colours and shades existed to him, and this made him even more terrifying.

My investigator walked towards me and placed his

hand on my shoulder.

'There are only two ways out of here: with a bullet in your head or with a ticket to Siberia. Which one do you want?'

I shook my head.

'Neither,' I replied. 'I don't deserve to be treated this way by the fairest people .'

'Don't try to be funny,' he snorted.

'What difference does it make? If I'm going to die, I'd rather die laughing than in tears.'

'Bravo, little Kazakh warrior; it's noble of you to try to be a hero, but you're being stupid. Now, listen to what I'm about to tell you. There is a third way out of here.'

He took a sip of water, but it didn't seem to satiate his thirst.

'Let's have a real drink,' he said; 'something to take the edge off this shitty morning.'

Without waiting for my answer, he took out a bottle filled with a cloudy liquid and filled two tumblers with it.

'I made it myself,' he said, handing me one of the tumblers.

I still had a small hope of salvation, and to refuse the drink would have been suicide. I'd only ever drunk alcohol twice before: once with the Red soldiers to celebrate the death of the Whites, and once with the White officers toasting the Tsar. We had to drink - if we'd refused the drunken men could have shot the whole village. So, I'd joined in their toasts to save myself and my family.

I swallowed the liquid in one big gulp. The officer did

A HUNDRED YEARS ON THE STEPPE

105

the same, and then lit a cigarette. Blowing the smoke noisily out of his mouth, he offered me one. I smoked it quietly. The cigarette felt like a lifeline.

'You know, I like you. You're a strong, uncomplicated Kazakh - a real proletarian. So, you were naive and lost your way a little; it could have happened to anyone. What good would killing you do? No, we need to re-educate you and get you back on the right track. That's the Bolshevik thing to do. So, let's think about what to do now.'

He blew his cigarette smoke into my face.

'Become a secret agent for the NKVD,' he said. 'If you work for us, your life will become much easier.'

I had expected all sorts of things from him, but not that. My mind froze. I burnt myself on the cigarette and began to sweat through my shirt. *I can get out of here alive*, I thought. That was the most important thing. Everything else could wait.

But still, I kept silent.

'Why aren't you saying anything? What is there to think about? Do you want to carry on suffering and be a hero? That isn't how it works here. You could be dead before I finish this cigarette. Everyone who leaves here alive and unharmed has to work for us; we don't just let people go. What they tell people afterwards, that they proved their innocence or made a heartfelt apology to gain their freedom, it's all lies for the masses to swallow.'

He walked around the cell and stood behind me. I could feel his breath on my neck. I wanted to stand up and punch him in the face, break his neck and tear his throat out, but I kept sitting silently.

'Your people have inflicted harm on the Soviet powers,' he continued, changing his tone. 'The fact that you and a few of your breed work honestly and are loyal to us isn't going to do you any favours. One Salim is enough to put all of your backs to the wall.'

My arms and legs went numb. Satisfied with my look of terror, he returned to his chair. Thoughts flew into my head: *Have they really caught Salim? If so, where is he? Is he dead or alive?* But, of course, I couldn't ask.

The uzunkulak had brought rumours that Salim had joined the Basmachi and fought against the Red Army on the hot sands of Central Asia. In the 1930s, we heard that he'd led an uprising against collectivisation. Once this uprising had been crushed, he disappeared into the ensuing chaos, perhaps going into hiding in the Turkmen Desert with rebels from Mangystau. After that, the uzunkulak lost trace of him. Following the famine of 1932, there was no more news. We thought he'd either died of hunger, been killed in battle, or fled abroad to Afghanistan or Iran.

'Your little brother is famous on the steppe,' the officer spat venomously. 'They say he's the saviour of your people, a resurrected warrior sent to punish the godless Russians. They say he has us Soviet workers in his sights. Unfortunately, in all these tall stories we hear, there's a grain of truth; he has indeed killed a few of us over the years. The time has come to deal with him, and you can help us do it. So, choose which one of you dies, you or him.'

He banged his fist on the table. This was my chance.

A HUNDRED YEARS ON THE STEPPE 107

Without saying a word, I nodded. My interrogator beamed an ugly smile. He filled the tumblers with more moonshine, and we drank, this time to seal our deal.

I had made my mind up: it was pointless to argue with the killing machine, even more so to disobey it. I knew what would happen if I acted like the hero in a lowbrow novel and shouted: 'No! I'll live according to my principles. I'm an honest man and will remain so until I die. I'd rather die in a fight with my head held high than live on my knees deceiving myself and others.' They'd simply shoot me then and there, and that would be that. So, I decided to be cunning.

A Necessary Evil

This is how my life took an unexpected turn. Now, I was thinking not only about how to keep myself alive but also, as much as was possible, how to warn people and keep my innocent countrymen away from the metal teeth of the NKVD's killing machine.

Learning harsh lessons in those years, I'd noticed something about these interrogators and officers. They liked to play with their victims, leading them slowly into dangerous traps. They would criticise the authorities themselves for one reason or another; perhaps saying they disagreed with how a leader had acted on a certain issue. This was a provocation; they were waiting for their prey to relax, think this was an open exchange of views and add their opinion to the conversation. Then, bang! The interrogator had enough and the victim's fate was sealed. Such ruthlessness made my blood boil. I wanted to attack those vile officers, but at the same time I wanted to go onto the steppe and cry out: 'Oh, my brothers, why are you so trusting and naive? They're trying to set you up, so keep your mouths closed.'

As I could do neither, I vowed to help my people in a very small but tangible way. I began to inform on the informers before they could carry out their dastardly deeds. To this day, as the sun sets on my life, I don't regret what I did. Of course, it would've been better if none of this had ever happened; if we could have lived our whole lives as the angels we were when we were children. As we now know, though, life gives us difficult choices to make. Morals and religions impress on us ideals for how we should live our lives, but there are no ideals in reality. We are human, mortal, and we should only talk about what really happened and how a person behaved in these moments. The Almighty gave us this life to experience both suffering and happiness; for us to think, act, express ourselves and break the rules and fight. People are not angels, so they should be accepted as they are. My life, my story is far from ideal, but it is real, and because of that my story is dear to me.

Sometime later, the investigator called me in to question me.

'Make me happy,' he said sternly. 'Don't disappoint me this time.'

I understood his threat all too well. I didn't want him to lose his temper, but I decided to keep playing the role of the simpleton.

A HUNDRED YEARS ON THE STEPPE

'I'll always try to make you happy,' I chimed. 'Come, visit my family. We'll sacrifice our fattest ram, eat a feast of *beshbarmak* and drink vodka together.'

He laughed patronisingly.

'There will be time for your feast later. Your ram can stay in the pasture for now. I'm hungry for something else. Bring me some enemies.'

'There aren't any,' I said uneasily.

'What do you mean there aren't any?'

'We've run out. They've all been caught and shot.'

'Don't be an idiot,' he snarled. 'For a start, you haven't caught anyone yet. Secondly, enemies of the people are everywhere. Vodka can run out, but there will always be enemies.'

'But there are no more in our district,' I said, refusing to back down. 'They've really all been caught. All those who remain are law-abiding devotees of Marx, Lenin and Stalin.'

'You know what, Asanbai,' the officer said, 'look at it this way. A group of people is called a society, but when one of them stands out or distances himself from the others then he becomes an enemy of the people. It's types like this we need to catch.'

I realised that my act wasn't working, but I persevered.

'I'm beginning to understand you,' I said slowly, 'but don't we have to seek out those types in a way so that innocent comrades, true Soviet people don't get hurt?'

'Keep looking,' he said, smiling murderously. 'You can find a needle in a haystack if you look hard enough. And those Soviet comrades you mentioned... I don't trust any of your people. You're all foreigners. You're all potential enemies of the regime, and if it was my choice I'd send the lot of you to the camps. Then everyone would be happy and we'd live in peace. That's probably what's going to happen in the end, but in the meantime, we have to deal with individuals. By this time next week, I want you to bring me an enemy. If you fail, you can take his place. As luck would have it, I'm only one short of my target.'

I feigned fear and nodded my head, in which I'd already come up with an idea. All I needed to do was take care of some details before carrying out my plan. The NKVD man, unsuspecting, looked pleased with himself as he lit another cigarette.

It was jarring to hear him talk of a target. People had heard rumours that each region and district was handed down a plan from above stating how many enemies of the people they needed to catch. If this target was not met, it meant that the comrades at the NKVD were not doing their jobs, and they were arrested themselves. So, each district tried to meet their targets in time or even exceed them. Now, I had to be part of this monstrous plan myself, and meet it at any price.

An old acquaintance of mine was an activist turned informant. Everyone in his neighbourhood hated him, but many, including NKVD officers, were scared of him; and with good reason. His ratting out had sent many people to the labour camps or worse. I decided the time had come to dispose of this awful man by using his own methods against him. I worked out every step of my trap to the last detail

A HUNDRED YEARS ON THE STEPPE   *111*

and carefully began the operation. First, I sent the heads of the district and regional NKVD several *domalak aryz* - anonymous tip-offs - which brought their attention to the subversive activities this man had been connected with. I wrote that he was overstepping his boundaries in his work, which was damaging the reputation of the Soviet authorities in the eyes of the public. I knew this man was one of the tithe collectors who'd taken the last scraps of food from poor villages, bringing about the famine on the steppe.

I also came to the conclusion that the investigator needed to be dealt with as well. Firstly, he was up to his elbows in the blood of innocent people whom he'd tossed into the meat grinder. He'd inflicted much cruelty on our people and taken much pleasure in doing so. His methods may have been subtle, but he'd spread fear and horror throughout the territory he covered. People were so scared of him, they were afraid to make a sound. He made my blood boil. Often, I'd thought about doing to him what he'd done to so many others if only I had the chance, and this idea lingered in the back of my mind. Our land needed to be rid of this murderer, so I began to write anonymous letters to the NKVD about him too.

Of course, I understood that freeing myself from the killing machine would not be easy and may even prove to be impossible. I knew what I was doing, though, and my conscience was clear. If my death was inevitable, I would have my vengeance in advance. It would take a miracle to save me.

And then, that miracle happened.

At exactly this time, they removed Yezhov, the head of the People's Commissariat for Internal Affairs. He was arrested as an enemy of the people and shot. Beria became the new chief, and there was another purge in the ranks of the NKVD. This provided an opportunity to punish Yezhov's accomplices, which included my minder, the chief investigator and the vile informant.

My *domalak aryz* probably got mixed in with other more dramatic events, and a short while later, the investigator and the informant were both arrested. We began to hear rumours that the Troika had ordered them to be shot. Once these two real enemies of the people had been disposed of with one cynical move, I could breathe again. No one ever contacted me about what had happened.

War

Soon after that the war began, and I was forgotten about. Despite my age - I 'd turned forty - the orders came from above that I should 'volunteer' to join the ranks on the front of what became known as the Great Patriotic War.

I remember every detail of my last evening at home. Khalima boiled some meat and baked a round of *lepyoshka* flatbreads. We sat in silence with the children. Everyone was miserable. Our three sons and two daughters were distraught; it felt like they'd grown up overnight and understood everything. My mother quietly read a prayer and hugged me. Her eyes were full of sadness. I hugged each of

A HUNDRED YEARS ON THE STEPPE

the children and ordered them to look after each other. On the doorstep, Khalima handed me a knapsack of food and, for the first time, hugged me in front of our family as she tried to hide her tears.

'Take care of yourself,' she whispered. 'Come back alive... Whatever you do, just come home. We'll be waiting and praying for you.'

My heart was filled with anguish, but there was no other way. I went to war.

There was a short military training course, and then, a few weeks later, I was sent to the front. A stream of people with bags on their backs and rifles over their shoulders walked to nowhere in particular. Only the commanders would check the way using a compass and confirm with someone over the radio. After a few days, it became clear that we were lost and were walking through a forest in unknown territory. I marched with the rest as if sleepwalking, but my thoughts drifted someplace else. I looked at my fellow soldiers and thought: *These men are walking together, but each has his own life. Each is carrying his fate on his shoulders. What are they thinking about? Each man has his own story, and at any moment that story could end.*

Various thoughts came into my head, each more frightening than the last. Looking at the line of soldiers, I suddenly thought: *These men are the walking dead: today they are alive, but they could die tomorrow. These soldiers are good men, but they're walking to where they'll kill or be killed. This is the cruel truth of war from which no one can escape. This is all happening so we can be victorious over our enemy, but is that really what life is about, to win by destroying others?* This rhetorical question made my head hurt. In despair, I thought about shooting all those around me down to my last bullet or charging at an enemy gun.

Two parts of a war are frightening: the first time you go into battle and when you go back to the front after being hospitalised. Everything else you get used to. No one thinks they'll come out alive. After a while, as bullets fly past your head and missiles explode a few paces away, what's more important to you is eating your lunch before it gets cold.

The first time I came under fire from German artillery, I was on duty on my post. Sentries are not permitted to leave their positions without authorisation, but I was standing in such a way that kept me out of the line of fire. Shells were flying overhead or exploding close by. Suddenly, there was an explosion a few metres away, and something heavy fell on me. I had time to think this was the end, but no, I was still alive but I couldn't move. I was buried up to my neck in soil. When my colleagues dug me out, the commander congratulated me.

'Good work; you didn't leave your post.'

He didn't know that I'd just frozen in fear.

This fright helped me get used to being in a war. There is nowhere to hide; they shoot at you, and you shoot at them. It's not a nice feeling to be shot at, bullets whistling past the side of your helmet. When the Germans began their intensive fire, so hard that we couldn't lift our heads, I would push myself into the ground; there the earth felt warm and soft. I wanted to sink into the ground, dissolve into the soil

A HUNDRED YEARS ON THE STEPPE 115

and escape from the horror we humans had created.

I used to watch in the mornings as heavy trucks carrying young soldiers set off for the front. I'd see these trucks returning in the evenings carrying their bodies, their blood dripping onto the wheels. As the wheels turned, they would churn the human blood and the dirt from the roads together, spreading this repulsive mixture into the ground. The sight made me so sick that I almost fainted. None of us wanted to die, but none of us thought we'd make it home alive from this hell.

I remember the first time I saw someone die in this war. The Germans were advancing, and we were lying in the trenches and shooting back. Next to me was a young Russian boy, Sasha.

'Got one!' he yelled triumphantly as his bullet tore into a German soldier.

Then Sasha gave another cry, this time in agony, and fell on his side. I ran to him and lifted his head. He looked at me with his eyes wide open.

'Asanbai; Asanbai,' he murmured.

Blood was trickling down his face and onto his chest. I held his head in my hands and looked into his eyes.

'Sasha! No!' I screamed.

He shivered, and then he died.

When the shooting quietened down, we buried him as best we could. Sometimes, I still hear his voice. What did he want to say to me, this young man who didn't want to die but knew he would?

After that came many more deaths: heroic, terrifying,

and senseless. I hadn't realised that a person can get used to death. In some battles, we'd be shooting on the move, and in the melee, we'd step on corpses from both sides. We'd look down and see we were up to our knees in blood. In these moments, some soldiers went mad and tried to kill every living thing around them.

At the very start of the war, we retreated towards the middle of the country. The Germans had better weapons and more modern equipment. We thought the end was near while still carrying a tiny hope we would win. We had to win, and for the sake of this victory rank-and-file Soviet soldiers and officers showed incredible bravery. Men sacrificed themselves to save their compatriots. I lost count of how many times my life was saved, or how many I saved myself.

We froze in the winter in those snow-filled trenches. Sitting by a warm fire now, I don't know how we survived. Sometimes, as we shivered from cold, we would dream about our next hot meal; then the enemy fire would begin again. The pain from cold and hunger are bad enough without shells exploding around you. If they hit the food supplies, then the hot soup and porridge would become just a dream again.

When the course of the war changed and the Soviet Army began to take control, our spirits lifted. We joked that death was running from us now, but really, she stayed with us and kept taking from us.

Once, during a period of calm, a special agent came to visit me in the trenches. I was wary of him, but it became clear that he often spoke with the soldiers. The other men seemed nervous talking to him and clearly didn't like him. No one could say as much, though, and just listened to him. His body language gave away the fact that he thought he was doing much more important work than us. He didn't accuse anyone of espionage and didn't arrest anyone, but he returned every time orders came from above to speed up the search for enemy spies and dangerous elements. Some soldiers and officers were sent to the disciplinary battalion, and others, it was said, were simply shot on the spot. It was another sickening detail in an already sickening war.

The agent came to talk to me. He was friendly, unassuming, and offered me a cigarette. Only then did my intuition, honed during my childhood on the steppe, tell me that something was wrong. I answered his questions briefly and as vaguely as possible, pretending that I was hanging intently on his every word. My heart was thumping. I was frightened that the special agents had gotten the scent of Salim. If they had, nothing would save me. I made up my mind not to tell them anything; to die at the feet of this agent if I had to.

The man suggested we go for a walk, and I had to obey him. I tried to bring my gun, but he told me not to. We walked away from the front lines. Leaning against a burnt-out truck, he got down to business. There was something sinister in his voice. It turned out that someone had told him about some things I'd said to my fellow soldiers about the senselessness of war. It was true that I'd lost my composure and told them exactly what I thought.

'How can people kill each other on such a vast scale?'

I'd shouted after one of the most horrific battles.

'What are you talking about? Do you think the Germans are people too?' they replied.

'What are they then?' I asked.

'They're not humans; they're fascists, and our duty is to destroy as many of them as possible.'

'That's what we think, and they think the same about us. So, what does this mean, that humans have been put on this Earth just to kill one another? I just can't understand such cruelty.'

'Enough of this crap! You've taken too many blows to the head.'

The other soldiers wanted me to shut up, and eventually I did, but these thoughts stayed with me.

So, Stalin is sitting in the Kremlin with the fate of humanity in his hands. Hitler is in the Reichstag plotting more death and destruction. Churchill, puffing on a cigar and knocking back another bottle of expensive Cognac, is working on his latest great plan for England. Across the ocean, Franklin Roosevelt is looking for ways in which America can take over the world. And Asanbai Bektemirov, son of the humble Amanzhol, is leaning on a burnt-out tank in order to hide from a hail of bullets waiting to return fire tomorrow with an old rifle. In whose name, for whose sake, are these simple Soviet and German people shooting at each other?

Whilst I was torturing myself, I realised that someone had informed on me, and analysing my words the agent had interpreted them as a call to unite with the Germans.

'You're initiating conversations under the guise of a hu-

A HUNDRED YEARS ON THE STEPPE

manitarian, but your real aim is to demoralise the troops with your ideology, to sow the seeds of doubt in their heads about the worthiness of our cause,' he said. 'This is ideological subversion, provocation.'

'No!' I cried out, either from fear or anger at the accusation. 'I've never doubted the worth of our part in this war. I know the fascists have invaded our country and raided our territories. I know they're an occupying force and that fighting against them, protecting our motherland, is the duty of every citizen of the Soviet Union.'

'You say you know,' the agent snarled. 'It's words like these you need to be saying in the trenches, instead of snivelling.'

He glared at me icily before continuing with a second accusation which was even more serious. Following a battle in which we'd suffered heavy losses, I'd criticised our commanders for forcing the soldiers to run into an attack on enemy territory in broad daylight.

'The Germans were firing at will from their concrete block-houses and bunkers, and a senseless number of our men were picked off,' I'd said, livid at the commanders' readiness to sacrifice so many lives.

This, too, had been reported to the counterintelligence department.

'You son of a bitch! So you're questioning Soviet military tactics, are you?' the agent shouted so loudly that the birds which had made a nest on the truck flew away. 'How many times have heroic Russian soldiers thrown themselves into a hail of bullets and come out with casualties? And now

120   *Bayangali Alimzhanov*

an urchin like you dares to question us.'

'I'm not saying our soldiers aren't heroes,' I replied firmly, sure that this would end badly for me. 'I'm simply against the unjustified loss of so many lives.'

'If a soldier dies bravely in the name of his motherland, then that's the very essence of this patriotic war.'

'Even better if he comes home victorious,' I countered.

Refusing to back down, I found myself reaching for the handle of my knife. I was ready to kill the agent and go into hiding in the forest. He'd read my thoughts, however, and took out his revolver and put it to my forehead.

'You are arrested as a traitor to your country! Hands above your head! The court-martial will deal with you.'

This was the end. The best I could hope for was being sent to the disciplinary battalion. I raised my hands, but I was still thinking of a way to get them on the agent's revolver. Then, there was an explosion, and I blacked out. When I came to sometime later, I was dizzy, bleeding, and realised I'd taken a blow to the head. Wrapping a cloth tightly around my head, I looked around. The agent was on the floor, a mutilated corpse.

The field medics came and rushed me to the infirmary. From there, I was taken to the military hospital. It turned out that the shell had exploded behind the agent's back as I stood facing him. His body had shielded me from the blast. The man who was about to seal my fate ended up saving my life. It felt like a miracle, except for the fact that some shrapnel had hit my right temple and got stuck there. The doctors tried for a week to dislodge it, but in the end, they

A HUNDRED YEARS ON THE STEPPE 121

had to leave it there. Most importantly, though, I was left alone: the accusations against me died with the agent.

I spent a week in the military hospital thanking the Almighty and reading prayers for the souls of my ancestors, Maral Ishan and Salyk Mullah. The pain in my head gradually became tolerable, and for once I could sleep and rest in comfort. After the trenches, a hospital bed felt like heaven. The warm food brought so much pleasure that I could have lain there and fattened up until the war was over. I wrote a few letters to my family, read newspapers and listened to the radio. Sometimes the pain from my wound flared up, and the doctors gave me medicines which lessened the pain for a while. In any case, the piece of shrapnel was embedded too deep inside my head to be removed, and the doctors didn't have time to do anything more what with so many wounded men being brought in from the front lines.

I was discharged and sent back to the trenches, but as soon as I returned the pain in my head became unbearable. The field medics couldn't do anything about the shrapnel in my skull, so they took me back to the hospital where the military doctors decided to send me away from the war zone for treatment. After lunch, I was meant to receive all the necessary documents and leave, but during lunch, the voice of Levitan came on the radio reading Stalin's order to send all wounded soldiers who were able to stand and hold a gun back to the front. And that was that.

A few days later, I began to feel a horrid itch in my temple that I couldn't get rid of. One day, whilst I was eating lunch, I brought my head down to a finish a bowl of porridge and something fell into it. There was a piece of a German shell in the bowl. It was about a centimetre long, thin and plain; this piece of high-quality German steel capable of killing and causing indescribable agony was now sitting motionless in front of me. My head began to hurt less without the fragment of metal inside it, and I wanted to live again, but the shrapnel that had torn my heart to pieces would stay with me for the rest of my life. What was I doing running at enemy tanks and rifles in the name of the Soviets and Stalin? I hated Stalin, and I hated Hitler even more. My soul was being held over two fires and being burnt by both of them.

One day, I was walking through a forest with a comrade. It was quiet and reasonably safe away from the front line. We were going towards the command centre when I tripped and almost fell. Annoyed, I looked down and saw what I'd caught my foot on. A shell had exploded and brought down part of a great pine tree. One big branch, almost broken away from the trunk but still joined to the tree, lay on the ground. I could see that a truck had driven over it as the branch had been pressed into the earth. Lying on the ground, though, the branch had continued to grow, reaching towards the sun. *A few years from now, this will be a big tree itself,* I thought. This wonder of nature touched me and I kept staring at it, trying to find some secret meaning. There was a beautiful calm in the forest. Leaves rustled and the birds were singing as if there was no war. I called out to my comrade, but he didn't reply. While I'd been lingering by the fallen tree, he'd walked on ahead. I couldn't see or hear him anymore, and although he couldn't have got too far I

A HUNDRED YEARS ON THE STEPPE   123

became worried, and calling out to him I ran in the direction he'd gone. But the forest was silent.

The comrade disappeared without a trace. The command centre raised an alarm and searched the entire forest for him, but they didn't find him. The next morning, investigators reported that on the day he disappeared a group of German soldiers on a reconnaissance mission had crossed our lines. It's likely they captured my comrade. If so, that fallen fir tree saved my life.

To get back from the command centre, we had to walk all night. Exhausted, when dawn came we found an abandoned building and lay down to sleep. I had a dream. In this dream, my mother was giving me freshly baked naan. I bit into the warm bread and chewed while my mother stroked my hair. Then I woke up. It was light. I remembered the words of the wise aksakals: 'The last dream before morning is the prophetic one. The dream won't happen as you see it, but how you interpret it. So don't tell anyone about your dreams - especially those who don't wish you well. Your dreams are only for you to see.' I quietly prayed to Allah and held on tightly to the thought that it was my fate to come home alive and taste my mother's bread again. This warmed my heart. There was only a little anxiety mixed in with the happiness: *If I come home to my family and eat one piece of bread with them and then die straight away, I will be happy with my fate*, I thought.

A noise shook me out of my daydream. The seven of us fell to the floor and looked around. We saw a group of German soldiers circling the building. There were about fifty of them armed with machine guns. We knew straight away they were headed for our territory. Our commander, Ivan, quickly ordered us to attack, counting on our ability to ambush them. We took our positions and lay in wait. As soon as they came close enough, we opened fire with all our guns and hurled our grenades. The Germans had no time to react; the explosions engulfed them in an instant. A few of them managed to return fire, but they couldn't see us and didn't even shoot in our direction. We killed all of them apart from two, who we took captive.

The commanders at the control centre were delighted and called us heroes. We learnt that by killing those men we'd foiled a secret operation. We were all recommended for medals, and Ivan and I were put forward for the title of Hero of the Soviet Union. In the mayhem that followed, though, everyone soon forgot about these medals. Maybe the letters burned along with the commanders. After the war, my children enquired at the military commissariat, but no such documents were found.

In my three years on the front lines, I witnessed a lot: the bravery of some and the dirty tricks of others, the ingenuity of soldiers and the petty tyranny of commanders. There were times when men sacrificed their lives for a respected, humane commander. At other times, soldiers would put bullets into the backs of cruel commanders before dying in battle themselves whilst crying: 'For the motherland!' I also saw soldiers with half of their torsos blown off throw themselves with their last ounce of strength at a German tank with a grenade in their hand.

A HUNDRED YEARS ON THE STEPPE

What amazed me the most was the patriotism of the Soviet troops. Young men of different nationalities, including Kazakhs, went forward into battle as one. Most of this generation had been born under the Soviet regime and were brought up with the spirit of Bolshevism. They hadn't seen what we'd seen; they didn't know what we knew, and they believed in the ideas of socialism and internationalism. Their actions deserve the greatest respect, and I put aside the pain in my heart to walk shoulder to shoulder with them in the fight against fascism. Sometimes I asked myself: *Who are you, Asanbai Bektemirov, son of Amanzhol, a proud Soviet or a Kazakh nationalist dedicated to the future of his nation?* I had no answer, and with a heavy sigh I resigned myself to my fate. Fate is always a mystery.

I'll tell you two more stories from the war. Once, we were sitting in a forest eating lunch. It was completely quiet; the only sound was the murmuring of the leaves in the breeze. Suddenly, one of our comrades slowly fell onto his side. He was dead. We hadn't heard any shot or explosion. We then realised that something had fallen onto his head, a single discarded machine gun bullet from an aeroplane flying overhead. This was the man's fate: a soldier who'd survived the most terrible of battles and attacked enemy trenches died in a quiet forest whilst eating lunch.

On another occasion, we were attacked by German pilots who fired on our positions with large-calibre machine guns. We ran for cover and watched as the bullets flew over our heads. Then, something unbelievable happened. Somehow, one captain who was returning from the command centre found himself in a field in full view and came under fire from above. He tried to run into the forest to hide. I don't know whether the pilot wanted to torment him or if he'd run out of bullets, but he flew down so low that our captain was almost close enough to touch the plane. As the plane closed in, the captain did a somersault, landed on his back and fired at the pilot with his revolver. He hit the German in the head, and the plane crashed to the ground and exploded. Inspired by our man, Soviet soldiers began to shoot at other low-flying German planes and brought several more down. The captain was congratulated ecstatically by the commanders, and we later learnt he'd been presented with a military award.

Now, over half a century later, the world is only just beginning to come to terms with this awful war. It goes without saying that a war that shook and changed the world is ambiguous and controversial. That's why there are so many different opinions, fair and biased, subjective and objective. One thing I believe with absolute certainty, though, is that every time that the leaders in this war acted without conscience, they would answer to history and to the Almighty.

The blood of the soldiers that was spilt in this war is pure and sacred. We fought fairly to protect our country from the fascist occupiers. We couldn't help it that our country was ruled by a tyrant and his henchmen. That is another question altogether. Our soldiers gave their lives for our motherland, not for its rulers.

The cruel meeting of two ideologies wore people down; it took away their warmth and humanity. A person could

A HUNDRED YEARS ON THE STEPPE

still remain a person, though; some people couldn't be broken. People showed incredible levels of bravery, sacrificing themselves to protect their motherland and singing as they died. Soldiers loved folk and Soviet songs. They didn't just sing the old favourites either, but wrote new ones. I remember that the whole front line used to sing "Zhas Kazakh" – Young Kazakh. The song has a touching backstory.

A Kazakh called Tulegen Tokhtarov who died in battle was posthumously awarded the title of Hero of the Soviet Union. An incredibly brave and skilled soldier, the young man accomplished many outstanding feats during his short life. One of the first to use an automatic machine gun, he once attacked a troop of Nazis and killed thirty-six enemy soldiers single-handedly. Another time, in the middle of a battle he ran out of bullets and was badly wounded. He took several bullets to the stomach, and his internal organs lay frozen on the snow. Despite his agony, he placed a hand over his lacerated stomach, got to his feet and threw himself at the German officer who'd shot him. He hit him on the head with his gun so hard that the officer fell dead. Tokhtarov fell on top of him and died too. His death shook his regiment, and their field medic, the composer Ramazan Yelebayev wrote the song "Zhas Kazakh" in his honour. Born out of the flames of war, this song brought the soldiers of the front lines together and became the hymn of all Kazakh soldiers.

Covered in snow, our vast steppe drips with blood;
The grey sky is howling and churning out death.
Protecting his country from war, like a lion,
The young Kazakh jumps on his enemy and kills him.

How cruelly his young soul leaves this world.

We later learnt that Ramazan Yelebayev had also died soon after, but "Zhas Kazakh" has lived on and people know it to this day. I learnt even later that Yelebayev also came from the Kerey Clan and that he'd been born in the village of Kudukagash where Salim and I had travelled to see our sister Mariyam and listen to Altyn-apa's stories. What a small world. He left the village when he was young and went to study and work in Alma-Ata. We were never able to meet in this life, but I always think of him when I hear that song.

A Test of Humanity

The commander of our regiment, Sergeant Ivan Petrov was experienced and skilled. We became close straight away. He was a simple man, but had performed many acts of bravery and slit many enemy throats. We would often talk in the calm before combat or on long marches. He would take out his tobacco pouch with such ceremony that it seemed there was nothing in life more important to him. He would deftly roll his cigarettes between his battle-hardened fingers and take deep drags of the precious tobacco. To us, this bitter aroma was the best smell on Earth. Blowing out rings of smoke together, we forgot about the war and lost ourselves in daydreams.

Once, Ivan and I were part of a reconnaissance mission through tracts of a forest in neutral territory away from the front lines. Things in the forest were never clear, though, and

A HUNDRED YEARS ON THE STEPPE 129

at any moment we could have come under fire or stepped on a mine. This is why soldiers on both sides tried to avoid going there. We were always one step away from enemy territory, and sometimes one step from death.

We ended up crossing the line into German territory. Camouflaged like leopards, we crept through the thick bushes towards our goal, finding and counting the number of German forces in this area. We'd done this many times before. Everything was as usual until a bone-chilling call rang out:

'*Hände hoch*!'

The cry was like a punch to the gut; my vision went black, and I froze like a statue. The thought came into my head that this was the end.

'I said hands up!' the command came again, this time in Russian.

'Don't shoot! Allies!' I cried, stepping forward sure that these were our soldiers who'd mistaken us for German intruders.

'Allies, allies! We're all Soviets! Come here!' the voice came again as I saw the silhouettes of two men.

'I'm coming,' I replied and walked towards them with my hands in the air.

Then, the voice came again, and this time it stunned me.

'Asanbai? Hey, is that you, Asanbai?' the voice said in Kazakh.

The voice was painfully familiar, but I was in no state to recognise it. The man then shouted something in German, probably to warn his partner, and he ran towards me.

It was Salim.

'*Bauyrym* - my brother!' he cried.

'Salim!' I replied, and we embraced each other as tears ran down my cheeks.

I don't know what Ivan and the German thought. They both stayed lying on the ground with their guns trained on each other, and, I'm sure, on us.

This is how fate plays with us; two brothers, after almost twenty years apart, embracing on the front lines of a war with guns aimed at them.

We sat under a big tree. To begin with, we were too overcome with emotion to speak. After a while, we talked about our lives. Salim asked about our mother.

'A year ago, she was alive and well at home with her grandchildren,' I said. 'Now, I don't know. There haven't been any more letters, but then we all thought you'd died.'

'You can see I'm alive and well,' he replied. 'I went over to the Germans from Vlasov's Army. One order from the General and now we're all here.'

'Come and join us!' I burst out.

'And who is "us"?' he replied tetchily. 'Are you already calling these people your own? I hope you haven't forgotten how many of ours they killed.'

'Fine, now is not the time for politics,' I said. 'Let's go home.'

'No one is going to let us go home. They'll kill me. You just shoot that Russian and come with us.'

'No, brother; I began this mission with Ivan and I'll

A HUNDRED YEARS ON THE STEPPE   *131*

return with him. Let's take your German captive and you come with us. It's reckless, but they'll forgive us.'

'I'm not going to ask for anyone's forgiveness. I've been hurt too much by the Soviets, and I've done nothing wrong.'

'But you can't deny the truth: almost the whole Kazakh nation is fighting for the Soviet Union against Nazi Germany.'

'That's both a pity and very painful. Fighting in the name of what, a foreign empire? For a psychopath who wants to take over the world?'

'You used to hate Marx and Engels. Now you love Hitler and Goebbels?' I asked.

'I hate them too,' Salim whispered with an amused smirk; 'but understand one thing: the German people haven't done anything to the Kazakh nation. It isn't they who murdered our people with famine. It isn't they who oppressed us and cut our way of life to pieces. The regime you're fighting for, who you might give your life for, are the ones who killed our Kazakh leaders. It was evil, and our peoples' blindness, naivety and fear of punishment has made them run in front of German bullets shouting: "For Stalin! For the motherland!" How can you give your life for that bloodthirsty monster? How can a country of Bolsheviks be our homeland? Tell me, what meaning do you find in your war? I mean yours, Asanbai. For whom are you ready to die?'

'Defending the Soviet Union is protecting our land, our home. Okay, let's stop arguing. Better you tell me where you've been all these years.'

Salim calmed down and told me what he'd done with

his life.

'After the Alash Orda was defeated, I hid from the Reds in the far south of the steppe. Then, we rose up again against the Soviets, but they sent hit squads, well-armed and experienced from their battles against the Whites. We clashed a few times on the steppe, but we were barely armed and they killed a lot of us. Many of our bravest horsemen fell to their guns without even challenging them in combat. There was nothing we could do. We were completely defeated, and those of us who survived scattered across the steppe. Our only comfort was that some of our warriors managed to pick off a few enemies. I killed three Red Army men and a commander with an old five-bore rifle. Then, I went south, changed my name and hid among the Turkmen in the Karakum Desert. Our losses weren't in vain, though. After our uprisings, the local Soviet authorities changed their tactics and came to treat the Kazakhs more carefully.'

'And how did you end up here?'

'I'm a "volunteer," like you, Salim said, smiling ruefully. 'I came with the Turkmen using my new name.'

'Did you at least manage to get married? Do you have a family?'

'Yes, two children, a son and a daughter. They're growing up in the Karakum among the black sands.'

As we talked about home and our loved ones, we heard gunfire close by. We hugged each other tightly and said goodbye. Salim disappeared into the forest, and I ran back to Ivan. He was angry.

'Who was that?'

A HUNDRED YEARS ON THE STEPPE   *133*

'An old comrade, a countryman,' I lied. 'He lost his way and went over to the enemy with General Vlasov.'

'Why did you let him go? This looks like treachery.'

'Nonsense,' I replied. 'I just haven't turned into such an animal that I'd shoot an old friend.'

'How can you call him a friend? He is a traitor, and nothing more. You should have killed him.'

'And why didn't you shoot him? You had him in your sights.'

'I was ready to, but I knew that his fascist partner had you in his sights. If I'd killed him, that man would have killed you.'

'Well, fair enough then.'

I looked at my compatriot. I wanted to tell him the truth, but I couldn't. The war had taught me to stay silent.

Ivan sighed gruffly.

'Fuck them all anyway!' he barked.

We went back to our regiment, but my thoughts were far away. I was in shock after my chance meeting with Salim, partly because of who he'd become. This is how war throws people around and churns them out. I couldn't judge Salim, but I couldn't understand him either. I only prayed with all my heart that he could stay alive. I wanted to go back to our village after the war was over and meet my brothers there. We would sit by the fire under a starlit sky and open our hearts to each other. My heart was breaking. I prayed for myself too.

Despite all our suffering and losses, our army began to win the war and forced the enemy out of our land. We were fighting on the Ukrainian front under the command of Marshal Zhukov. We travelled through Russian towns, freed Ukraine, and from there entered Europe. But all good luck comes to an end.

In November 1944, deep into autumn, we went into Nazi territory to capture some of their troops. There were five of us, commanded by Ivan. In the silence of night, we crept across enemy lines, located their weapons, and waited to ambush some German soldiers as soon as they left their barracks. We saw fires coming from German trenches. Then we heard steps; two men were coming towards us. We tensed up before all hell broke loose. One of our men sneezed loudly. The Germans sprang to attention and began to yell: '*Achtung! Russo! Achtung!*' There was the noise of dozens of shells flying through the sky, and then the shooting began. All of their attacks were on target, and two of my comrades were killed. The three of us that were left had to retreat.

'Get down!' Ivan screamed and threw me to the ground.

There was another explosion. When I came to I checked myself and found no injuries. I saw that Ivan was lying next to me, covering my back with his body and breathing very heavily. I understood that he was wounded and gently shook him.

'Ivan, let's get out of here.'

'No, leave me here. Goodbye, Asanbai. Farewell, and forgive me if I ever harmed you,' Ivan gasped as he fought for breath.

'No, we're going together.'

'Leave; that's an order,' he wheezed, wincing as he pre-

A HUNDRED YEARS ON THE STEPPE

pared a grenade.

We had to obey every word our commander said to us. We had no choice but to run.

We couldn't get far before the explosion came. We guessed that the fatally wounded Ivan had set off the grenade as soon as the German soldiers found him in order to take them with him. Our commander died heroically. When he threw me to the ground, he saved my life.

We couldn't escape, though. A bullet killed my last remaining comrade. I thought my end had come too, as hiding behind a large rock I waited for the German soldiers. There was no fear, just a sense of unhappiness that I'd leave this world so far from my home without being able to see my mother, my wife and my children one last time. I thought about them and longed so much to live and to go home. I saw my Khalima in front of my eyes and heard again the last words she said to me before I went to war: 'Come back alive...'

I hated this war, this murder and the sight of people destroying each other. My broken heart screamed out to everyone who lusted for power over this Earth and who were ready to use the blood and suffering of innocent people to achieve it.

'This isn't fair. War is senseless; war has no victors,' I hissed, but no one heard me, and that hurt even more.

No one would care that Asanbai Bektemirov, son of the kindest and most peaceful nation on the planet would die along with Russian soldiers on foreign soil and his body would rot in a field far from home. No one would care how

I died or what for. This hurt me most of all. I whispered a prayer, '*La ilaha ilallah*,' and only one thought remained: to avenge the deaths of my compatriots, especially Ivan, and as I left this world to take as many as I could with me. My ancestors, the nomads, used to show the greatest respect to the warriors who did not die in vain: 'Heroes are those who take an enemy with them,' they said. I don't know how many enemies I shot with my last round, but I think I caught a few.

The Germans soon surrounded me, shouting: 'Surrender! *Hände hoch!*'

With no bullets left, all I had was a bayonet and one grenade. I don't know what would've happened next if I hadn't felt a gun on the back of my head and heard the order in fluent Russian:

'Drop your weapon. Hands up; I advise you to surrender now.'

The enemy was experienced. I threw my gun on the ground.

At first, I thought I must be hallucinating when I heard the men speaking Russian and Kazakh, but then I understood: these were the soldiers of the Russian Liberation Army and the Turkestan Legion. They were serving the Germans, and in doing so had saved me from certain death.

The Germans interrogated me, but what military secrets could a simple trench soldier have known? They already knew where our troops were located and where the front lines were. I couldn't tell them anything new. A German officer pointed his gun at me, but a Kazakh from the Turkestan Legion told him to keep me alive so I could serve

A HUNDRED YEARS ON THE STEPPE 137

with them. The German stood down. One life made no difference to them, so they sent me to a prisoner of war camp.

Here, my fate took a sharp turn once again. It had transpired that my life was saved by enemies of the Soviets, traitors to the motherland; but what now? If I came across them again, my duty as a Soviet soldier would have been to kill them, but how does a man kill someone who saved his life? This is a part of history that can never be rationalised.

The legionnaire, Mazhit told me that the Turkestan Legion was organised by Mustafa Chokayev, a well-known political figure and former member of the Alash Orda who escaped to Paris during Stalin's purges. The Legion took prisoners of war from Muslim and Turkic nations, Kazakhs, Uzbeks, Kyrgyz, Turkmen, Tatars, Bashkirs, Azeris and others. Mazhit whispered that Mustafa Chokayev's goal was not so much to serve the Third Reich and fight against the Soviet Union, but to save the men he shared a culture and religion with from death at the hands of fascists. Although he died at the start of the war under mysterious circumstances, the Turkestan Legion he created did save many of our compatriots.

'You know, it's thanks to him that you're alive,' Mazhit said, slapping me on the shoulder.

I gave him a prayer of thanks.

Every year on March 9th, Victory Day, I read the Quran and pray for the souls of those who died in the Great War; and every year on the anniversary of Mustafa Chokayev's death, I pray for him and for Mazhit. What a contradiction life can be. I tried to keep my humanity as all hell broke loose around me, but I don't know whether I was able to.

As they took me to the PoW camp, Mazhit told me that most Russian and Kazakh prisoners don't want to serve in the Russian Liberation Army or the Turkestan Legion. Life in the camp was insufferable, however, and unable to cope with the inhumane conditions, some of them agree to serve the Germans instead. Given edible food, some stayed in their ranks until the end, but others, as soon as they ended up at the front, would defect back to their own army. Sometimes, groups of them would desert together; so the Germans tried to keep the Turkestan Legion as far away from the Soviet front as possible. Now, therefore, the Legion was mostly deployed elsewhere, largely in France.

Mazhit spoke to me about many things, but as the years have passed I've forgotten most of them. One thing I could never forget, though, was that he told me he'd saved me because all Kazakhs are brothers. He also advised me to be cooperative, not to draw attention to myself, and to tolerate all the miseries of the camp.

'It would be even better if you joined us in the Turkestan Legion,' he added. 'You wouldn't be on your own. Our brothers will greet you with open arms. You'll live as a soldier of the Wehrmacht - well, maybe we're below them, but it's still infinitely better than life in the camp, that's for sure. Anyway, what are you going to miss in that Russian colony? It's idiotic to fight for them.'

'How many of you are there?' I enquired quietly, not daring to argue with the man who'd saved me.

'Maybe a thousand in total,' answered Mazhit.

A HUNDRED YEARS ON THE STEPPE   *139*

'And how many of us Kazakhs are there? Millions! And the front lines are awash with our blood. We risk our lives and only hope to see our families again. This war is about the Kazakh nation too, whether we want it to be or not. This is a tragedy for the Kazakh people and all other nations that have been swallowed up by the Soviet Union. I'm sorry, but I can't go with you. I'll be forever grateful that you saved me, but remember, for a proud Kazakh betraying your country is worse than death.'

'I'll try to understand, Asanbai,' Mazhit said softly; 'but you remember this: we too only want what's best for all Kazakhs. Think some more and maybe you'll change your mind.'

I didn't reply, and the man from Turkestan didn't try to persuade me anymore. He only said that time would tell. I wanted so much to ask him about Salim, but I bit my tongue. I was afraid that I'd put his life in danger. As we said goodbye Mazhit said that he'd come back for me, but he never did. I don't know what happened to him.

I spent almost six months in the Germans' camp. In the beginning, it was unbearable, but, as the Kazakhs say, after three days a man even gets used to a coffin. No one knows exactly how many Soviet prisoners of war there were here; probably several thousand from all parts of the Union. We lived underground in horribly crowded stone cells. The low grey ceiling, iron bunk-beds and tiny windows drove all of us mad. We had no idea where we were, and we were treated like slaves. They fed us just enough so we had the strength to work, and they made us work from dawn to dusk, mainly digging and building some kind of reinforced walls. We assumed they were bunkers and came to the conclusion that the Germans were struggling and were being forced to retreat. We thought our own soldiers would be here soon, but we didn't know whether we'd still be alive by the time they arrived. Many men, starving, died from fatigue.

After several months of hard, sometimes back-breaking work, the prisoners had turned into skeletons. The guards used to shoot those who fainted during a shift and couldn't get back up. I needed every last drop of endurance my life had given me to survive the punishment and humiliation. At times, my spade felt so heavy I couldn't lift it and I didn't have the strength to take one step. Once, I fell from exhaustion on the cold earth; I heard the click of a guard loading his pistol and somehow found the will to get back to my feet. When the guard put his gun back in his pocket, I said prayers to the Almighty and to my ancestors, Maral Ishan and Salyk Mullah.

Captivity is the most humiliating fate a person can experience. I only survived because I was so desperate to live, to see my children, my mother, my wife and my homeland. It didn't depend on me, though. The Germans could have shot any of us at any moment. This happened very rarely, however, because to them we were more useful as slave labourers.

Many Soviet soldiers lived bravely through these punishments and stayed loyal to their army. There were others, though, who couldn't cope with the suffering and were pressured or threatened into joining the ranks of the Russian

A HUNDRED YEARS ON THE STEPPE

Liberation Army and the Turkestan Legion. Sometimes, I wonder what would have become of me if I'd let myself be forced into joining the Turkestan Legion. Could I have shot at a Soviet soldier? I was against the tsarist raiders, the revolutionary Reds and the Whites because they came to my land armed with weapons. I hated all of them, but I could never have shot at a Russian soldier. In this war, we were all brothers; all friends. Kazakhs, Russians, all nationalities that came from this vast territory united as equals to defend our shared motherland, the USSR. In protecting her, we were defending our own land. Despite all the pain and suffering that they'd brought to the Kazakh people, I could never have tried to harm a Russian soldier with whom I'd fought against fascism. I told myself that it was better to live with my cruel fate than to become a traitor.

America and the Village

With each passing day, the end of the war drew closer. At night, we heard the sound of gunfire and bombs exploding. We shook in our cells, afraid that we'd be killed by friendly fire. One night we felt the tremors from fierce fighting nearby. We didn't dare close our eyes, no matter how exhausted we were, and only slept for a few minutes before dawn. The next morning, no one made us get up for work. We thought the guards had forgotten us. Only the next day did we hear footsteps above us. When the doors to our cells were opened and soldiers came in, they were not ours. It was the Americans.

They wanted to take us prisoners of war to mysterious, faraway America.

'Guys, come with us and live in freedom,' they said. 'If you go back home, Stalin will only have you shot.'

There were several among us who preferred to go to America with them rather than return to the USSR. Indeed, it would have been wonderful to board a great ship and cross the ocean; to float for days on end, to lie on the deck and feel the warm breeze on my skin, look up at the stars in the bright night sky, enjoy being at peace again and go back to my daydreams. Something inside me, however, wouldn't let me go. My longing for my homeland was greater than my desire for the American dream and stronger than my fear of Stalin's gulags.

What would have happened if I'd sailed across the Atlantic? I couldn't have stayed on the ocean staring up at the stars for the rest of my life. I would've had to go onto dry land eventually, and that land would have been America. Then, I would've wanted to turn the ship around and sail back home.

In my head, I heard Salim's voice: 'So, where is your homeland? Do we even have one? Do you want to call a place ruled by a bloodthirsty tyrant home?' I don't remember when these questioning voices in my head began to disturb me. Perhaps they began in the turbulent years of the 1920s. They filled my head, these painful, harrowing questions, some accusing me, others encouraging me. These voices were my teachers as well as my torturers.

A HUNDRED YEARS ON THE STEPPE

My homeland was calling me: my village, my family. I could hear the voices of my mother, Khalima and my children: 'Come back alive... Whatever you do, just come home.' I didn't know whether my grandchildren's generation would understand me. Maybe they'd call me an idiot for refusing a free ticket to America, the land of dreams, sailing across the ocean towards green dollars and freedom. And for what: to stay in the dirt and the harsh reality of Soviet life? The best I could hope for at home was a miserable existence on a collective state-owned farm. Perhaps this generation wouldn't understand our deep attachment to our homeland, to the vast steppe and the smell of wormwood and purple sage. You have to grow up on the steppe to understand it. I missed my home so much that the prospect of freedom and the American dream couldn't tempt me.

I made my mind up to return to my heroic and spiteful, kind and cruel, honest and villainous county and decided to accept whatever awaited me there. There was hope of a pardon. A rumour spread amongst the prisoners that Stalin had given an order to exonerate all Soviet soldiers who'd been taken prisoner if before their capture they'd fought for the motherland. If that was true, then I had nothing to worry about. I'd served on the front lines for three years, been heavily wounded twice and been awarded military medals. They said that the order had been announced by the generals and had been broadcast on the radio and in the newspapers. When they heard this, many soldiers went home. Only many years later did I read that Stalin really did issue such a decree, but it didn't apply to everyone. Many soldiers were indeed forgiven, but others, for their temerity in being captured, were sent to the Soviet labour camps.

I wasn't forgiven.

Gulag

Back in our homeland, soldiers who'd been captured by the Germans were given a frosty reception. We were interrogated, and then the authorities decided what to do with us. Some were allowed to go home, some were forced to stay in the army, and many were sent to labour camps in Siberia. That was my fate for the next ten years. It was my reward for being wounded three times on the front lines. My Order of the Red Star and medal for bravery were taken away.

The accusations against me were grotesque: 'Why did you go to the camp instead of dying a heroic death like a true Soviet soldier?' Of course, I couldn't speak my mind in front of the judges and tell them that I didn't want to die for the sake of those tyrants, and they should be grateful that I fought at all.

The judges didn't take long to hand down their sentence. Those six months in the PoW camp meant more than the three years I'd spent on the front lines. My crime was, as they portrayed it, that I'd gone to the camp voluntarily. I'd wanted to work for the Germans after giving in to pressure from the Turkestan Legion. Of course, they wouldn't listen to a word I said.

So, they packed me into a crowded wagon with oth-

A HUNDRED YEARS ON THE STEPPE 145

er unfortunate souls and sent me to the ends of the Earth. There, we were put into trucks. We had no idea where we were going. After a gruelling journey, we were told that we'd arrived in the town of Susuman. The name was easy to remember as it reminded me of two Kazakh words, *su* - water, and *susu* - to flow. I later learnt that the Susuman River, which flows into nearby Kolyma, used to be called Kukhuman, which means snowdrift. So water really did flow there.

The prisoners who'd been here for a while said that this camp was in the far north, further even than Magadan. It was close to Oymyakon, and everyone knew Oymyakon was the coldest place on Earth. The name sounds like the Kazakh *Oi meken*, meaning low ground.

The climate in Susuman was incredibly harsh; in winter it fell to sixty degrees below zero. People froze, became sick and often died from the strain on their bodies. Those who died were quickly buried with nothing but a number on their graves. When you see something like that, it drives you to stay alive; otherwise, no one would ever find you. Rumours went around the gulag that we were close to what was known as the 'Valley of Death.' Any mention of this place made the prisoners shudder. The fear of death tore at every man. At the tiniest slip, any of us could disappear. People didn't only die of the cold, but at the hands of the thugs too. The guards had given up any pretence of subtlety. If anyone got on the wrong side of them, they'd have them shot for 'trying to escape.' No one could do anything. We just had to survive these inhumane conditions, knowing they'd been made for humans, by humans.

For all its horrors, life in the labour camp was in some ways better than on the front line. First of all, we weren't shot at or bombarded every day and night. Secondly, there was at least some kind of law and order, however cruel it was. The chance of surviving here was higher than it was during the war.

I was miserable at first, but gradually I began to get used to my new life. I accepted my fate. Days in the camp passed slowly. It was interesting to note how all the months and years were the same; how the same grey day seemed to last forever. But when this time came to an end, looking back, it didn't seem like such an eternity.

The first five years passed quietly with little except for tough work, threats from the guards and frequent fights between the prisoners. In Susuman, they mined for gold, and it was said that the mines were some of the richest on Earth. I was lucky; I worked as a timber cutter. Chopping wood was easier than breaking rocks. We lived in long, low barracks made of stone and wood with metal fences built by the prisoners themselves. They fed us not out of generosity, but because we couldn't work otherwise. Hot prison broth seemed delicious after a day of painful drudgery.

The only events that livened up our days were the stories that the men in the camp - political prisoners, prisoners of war and criminals of many nationalities - would tell, and the loud arguments they'd have. These conversations entertained us, annoyed us, made our blood boil or made us think. I heard a thousand opinions about politics and politicians and came to the conclusion that politics is an in-

A HUNDRED YEARS ON THE STEPPE 147

furiating subject. A politician thinks one thing, says another, does a third and hopes for a fourth whilst enquiring about a fifth. In the end, the sixth thing happens. Behind each political step, there are so many cunning tricks that ordinary people could never make sense of. I decided never to join in conversations about politics. As a Kazakh proverb goes: 'A man who is silent saves himself from misfortune.'

I tried not to draw attention to myself, never got into fights, and followed the guard's orders. Only one thing gave me the strength and patience to continue: the thought of going home. I would often hear the voice of my beloved Khalima: 'Come back alive... Whatever you do, just come home. We'll be waiting and praying for you.'

All people have differences; for some reason, we can never live peacefully for long, even if we're suffering together. One day, one of the criminals in the camp barked at me to bring him some water. Subordinating yourself to another prisoner meant losing your authority, though, so I refused. He shot a hostile look at me and walked away. After all the hurt of the war, I couldn't stand the thought of having another foe and having to fight again, but it didn't depend solely upon me. Now, I had another problem to deal with.

In the spring of 1950, a new supervisor arrived. His name was Tarasko. This unusual name was easy to remember. We never used his first name; we just called him Captain Tarasko, or, behind his back, 'the Ukrainian.' The man was a closed book. No one knew anything about him. Some said he was a war hero, others that he came from the interior ministry. It was whispered that he was a former secret agent with a pile of skeletons in his closet.

The war had left Tarasko an invalid. He limped severely on his right leg and had lost his left arm. They said he was caught in the fire from a German tank, was blown up by a shell, and when he landed, the tank ran over his arm. Before losing consciousness, he managed to throw a grenade and destroy the tank. After leaving the military hospital he was discharged from the army, but he didn't want to stop serving, so they sent him here. He was strict, harsh, but fair. A tall brute of a man, he kept the prisoners in check. Sometimes, I felt that he still harboured loftier ambitions than this.

Every day, he watched over us as we worked in the forest. Then, one day, something happened that turned my life around. We were chopping down trees as usual. In a hurry to finish their work, the two men who operated the sawmill cranked up the power. A tall pine began to slowly fall to the ground. I stood back, gazing at the top of the great tree and the sky and clouds beyond it. As the falling tree gathered speed, my intuition told me that it was about to fall on Tarasko. He had his back turned to the tree and couldn't see anything. Suddenly, I found myself jumping at Tarasko and shoving him out of the way. We fell on the ground together and landed with a thump at the same time as the huge pine came down and crashed onto the forest floor with an almighty force. A cloud of pine needles rained over us like shrapnel. For a few moments, we lay there without moving, two former soldiers trained to expect further explosions. Then, coming to our senses, we rose to our feet. The other prisoners looked at us with shock on their weather-beaten

A HUNDRED YEARS ON THE STEPPE

faces. I shivered.

The prison guards ran towards Tarasko, but he waved them away. Limping even more heavily than usual, he approached me.

'Thank you,' he said. 'You're a real man.'

He patted me on the shoulder and shook my hand. The warmth in his eyes expressed his gratitude more eloquently than any words. I was extremely shaken, and, trying to hide my emotions, walked away towards my compatriots. They didn't say a word to me and kept on working angrily. Only the criminal who I'd offended in the barracks acknowledged me, eyeing me with a piercing glare.

That night, replaying what had happened in my head over and over again, I couldn't sleep. I couldn't find any explanation for having acted so recklessly. Why had I done it? My instinct for self-preservation should have stopped me from jumping under an enormous falling tree. I was a convict, unfairly imprisoned by the Soviet regime. I'd defended this country as a soldier and was prepared to sacrifice my life for it, and the rulers had sent me to a gulag. I shouldn't have wanted to save an officer of that regime. What made me do it? Did I really still feel human compassion after all that I'd endured, or was it a simple sense of solidarity with a fellow soldier? I could have died or been left disabled, and I was desperate to stay alive now the blood and fire of war was behind me.

For half the night, I tossed and turned on my straw mattress, torturing myself with these questions to which I could find no answer. In the morning, though, it came to me: I'd thrown myself under the tree to save the supervisor out of simple human kindness. There had been no great idea and no thoughts of personal gain. A person was in trouble, and I could help him.

It turned out that not everyone liked what I'd done. The next day in the forest, I stepped away from the other prisoners to relieve myself. As I was walking back towards the group, the convict stopped me. He'd obviously been waiting to get me on my own.

'Why did you save the guard?' he asked aggressively.

'I saved a man,' I replied as softly as possible. 'He's a soldier, just like I was. He lived through the war too. Now, he should be able to go home, not have a tree take his life.'

'No,' he hissed, his eyes filled with such hatred that I began to shake. 'You saved our enemy, and that means you're our enemy as well. Fate was about to give that piece of shit the punishment he deserved, and you, you little bitch, got in the way. You wanted to suck up to him, did you? I've been watching you since you arrived here. I always knew you were scum. I've been waiting to knock you out. You couldn't avoid me forever in a place like this. Did you think you were going to hide up the Ukrainian's arse? No; you're not going to get away that easily. The choice is yours. Do away with him and we're even, or you'll see me again, and I'll have my knife this time. You've got a day to correct your mistake, you little bitch. The clock starts now.'

The convict disappeared as quickly as he came. I couldn't explain anything to him. I hoped his threat was just bravado, and the next time I saw him I could ask him to lis-

A HUNDRED YEARS ON THE STEPPE 151

ten to me and we could resolve our differences in a humane fashion. But that isn't what happened.

The next day, when we'd nearly finished our work, a young prisoner approached and asked me to step away from the gang so we could speak. I shivered again, but I had no way out. I brought the thick tree branch that was in my hands with me and watched him carefully as we walked. When we'd walked about a hundred paces, he disappeared. Then, the convict appeared in front of me.

Without a word, he took a big knife out of his boot and threw himself at me. I didn't flinch; I'd expected this moment to come. Jumping away from his slashing blade, I raised the tree branch above my head. The convict came at me again with the knife. He was as strong as a bull and as ferocious as a bear. I waited for the right split-second moment to make my move, then, with all my strength, I brought the log down on the huge man's skull. He lurched and fell to the ground dead. After I had checked that he was dead, I felt sick. As soon as I caught my breath, I went back to work.

The next day, Tarasko pulled me to one side. We sat on the stump of a tree and smoked. The Ukrainian coughed and looked around nervously.

'Old man,' he whispered, 'you need to get out of here. The sooner the better, otherwise they're going to kill you. These things are never forgiven. I reported what happened as an accident, but you can't fool the prisoners. They're going to transfer me out of here soon, and I won't be around to protect you.'

There was no sense in pretending not to understand. He knew everything and he genuinely wanted to help.

'But where can I go?' I asked.

'Wherever you can; just as far away from here as possible,' he said, his voice faltering. 'It won't be easy. It will be extremely dangerous, maybe fatal, but at least it will give you a chance to survive. I'll help you as much as I can. We'll think up a story. If you get stopped and questioned, I'll back you up. I'll steal you some rations. Go and get ready. Head south-east and the stars will show you the way.'

'I know; I'm a nomad,' I said.

'So, get to your next home. The taiga isn't the steppe, though. This is something very different that you'll have to cope with.'

We both understood that he'd repaid my kindness. Touched by his gesture, I shook his hand warmly and looked into his eyes. They were full of sorrow. I sighed and thought to myself: *O, humanity! What are we all doing in this world?*

The Test

In June 1950, after nearly five years in a labour camp, I managed to escape with the help of the guard. Tarasko had thought of something that couldn't fail. Two days after our conversation, he took me and some other prisoners to Khandyga. Prisoners at Susuman would often travel to Khandyga in a convoy flanked by guards to do chores such as transporting petrol, but this was the first time I'd been

A HUNDRED YEARS ON THE STEPPE 153

ordered to go. Tarasko whispered to me that it would get me one kilometre closer to home. From there it would only be another five thousand kilometres to my village, or seven thousand if I chose to take a safer route.

The town of Khandyga stood by the Aldan River and was one of the first towns in Russia's Far North to mine for gold. The name Khandyga sounded like the Kazakh words *Kan doga* – blood-stained bow. We travelled in American Studebakers. These heavy, powerful all-terrain vehicles had been given to the country by America during the war and were now mainly used at Siberian mines. I was alone in the boot of the last truck, with Tarasko in the front. I don't remember how far we travelled, but it felt as if the rough road would never end. Finally, just before dawn, our truck came to a stop, and

Tarasko took me to one side.

'We're outside Khandyga,' he said quietly. 'There is the River Aldan, and here is your story: we stopped to go to the toilet, but the driver left without you. You tried to walk back to the camp, but it got dark and you got lost and ended up in the middle of the taiga. I will take care of what will happen when they find you're missing. Farewell!'

He handed me a knapsack filled with bread and jam, matches and a knife, pointed in the direction of the forest, and limped back into the truck.

So, Captain Tarasko, war hero and bane of the prisoners sent me on my way home through the taiga. The way was long, unknown, and fraught with danger. We had both risked our lives. What possessed Tarasko to do this, how he managed to engineer my escape and how he would explain my disappearance, only he knew. I prayed for him to be as lucky as I'd been and marched into the forest. As I set off, intoxicated by my freedom, I could barely feel the ground beneath my feet. Shortly, though, the reality of the situation sank in. There was nothing around me apart from trees. I began to worry. I thought nothing could scare a man who'd lived through a war, but the vast, unknown taiga frightened me. Loneliness tormented me, but there was no other way out.

I was leaning on a tree, resting and regaining my composure when two armed soldiers appeared walking straight towards me. I closed my eyes. How I wished I could turn into a pine tree and live peacefully in the forest far from people. I stood and waited for them to take me, but they walked straight past. They hadn't seen me. I felt neither alive nor dead; it was as if I'd become a ghost. A surge of adrenaline rushed through me, and I started to walk again. For the rest of my days I've often thought about that mysterious occurrence. I thank Allah and recite prayers to my ancestors, Maral Ishan and Salyk Mullah.

I walked for a long time. When I became exhausted, I stopped to rest. I ate a mouthful of bread, smoked a cigarette and had a nap.

'Hey, you!' came a rasping, threatening voice. 'Are you lost?'

I went cold, thinking the gulag guards had caught me.

Two men came from behind the trees, a powerfully built man and a chubby boy.

A HUNDRED YEARS ON THE STEPPE   *155*

'Don't worry,' one of them said. 'We're on your side.'

I took a breath.

'Pakhan,' the muscular man introduced himself, holding out his hand, 'and this is Baklan.'

The pair were ordinary criminals. They'd escaped from a different prison and seeing me in the forest they'd been following me for a while. Once they were sure I was alone, they'd decided to join me. Though I was wary of them, I was glad to have the company.

We walked on together. Pakhan knew his way through the taiga, but it wasn't easy as there was nothing here except trees. When starting out I'd admired their beauty, but after two days of monotony I began to pray for an open space. The taiga didn't want to release me, though. We walked for several days, maybe even for several weeks as time lost all meaning. We ran out of rations, and our strength deserted us. In one place, we found edible plants and some berries, but those only took the edge off our hunger. Eventually, our hunger began to overwhelm us. Feeling once more as I had during the famine of 1932, I thought about my countrymen who'd died on the steppe and how they'd suffered in their final days. My head was numb and my mouth was dry. I could only think about one thing: *Stay alive. Stay alive no matter what...*

I don't know how far we walked, or where. Exhausted, we stopped and lay down on the forest floor. Pakhan took out a tobacco pouch. We sat for ages in silence as we smoked. The cigarettes soothed us, and the smoke wrapped around us as if concealing us from the bleakness of our situation.

'You know, Asanbai,' Pakhan said in a rasping voice, 'not everyone can get out of here.'

He fell silent again and stared at me as if waiting for me to say something. I shivered. There had been something sinister and cruel in his voice.

'Two full stomachs are better than three hungry ones,' he continued, gesturing towards Baklan and looking like a predator. 'One of us can save the others; and if he doesn't volunteer to do it, we can encourage him.'

'Encourage him to do what?' I asked, although I already knew what he meant.

'Encourage him to save us! There is no other way. Are you with me?'

I felt my head begin to nod.

The big man spat on the butt of his cigarette and trod it into the earth. I did the same. I realised then why Pakhan had taken the chubby boy with him. He didn't just need a partner in crime when he escaped, but meals when his rations ran out. Horror consumed me. Pakhan was creeping up on Baklan, and I was following him.

Weak from exhaustion and hunger, Baklan was lying on his back, his blue eyes staring up at the sky. Pakhan crept up to his companion as silently as a panther, and in an instant wrapped a shoelace around his neck. Baklan jumped up and instinctively began to struggle. With all the strength he had left, he got onto his knees and tried to break free from the noose, but Pakhan was stronger and wouldn't let go. By the time I reached him, Baklan had collapsed onto

A HUNDRED YEARS ON THE STEPPE

his side. The big man took out a knife the size of his hand and put it against the boy's neck. Baklan grasped for the knife in desperation, but he was much weaker than Pakhan. I stood motionless, not knowing what to do.

'What are you doing?' Pakhan barked. 'Help me cut up our steak!'

The big man was breathing heavily. Hunger had taken most of his strength. I didn't know what to do. Even though I was dying of hunger, I couldn't cut up a person. But there was no other option. In confusion, I went towards Baklan and our eyes met. The look on the face of this twenty-year-old boy was a mixture of fear and hope. No, I couldn't kill him. In desperation, I grabbed Pakhan's hand and tried to force it away from the boy's neck. The thug screamed in pain and dropped the knife.

Freed, Baklan climbed to his feet and scrambled away. Pakhan tried to run after him, but I held him back, and Baklan slowly disappeared into the forest. Pakhan swore violently, then picked up the knife and threw himself at me. I quickly pulled out my own knife. A fight to the death had begun.

Exhausted from the punishing walk and overwhelming hunger, more wild animals than men, we used the last of our strength to try to kill each other. For both of us, it was our last chance to stay alive. What a contradiction the human mind is: we stand facing our death and still we try to rip out another man's throat. What else can you do when faced with a bloodthirsty bandit waving a knife, intent on killing and eating you?

To avoid being killed, I had to kill. I wielded my knife as best I could, but Pakhan was an experienced fighter. His knife flashed quickly in front of my face. He was a little taller than me, much more powerful, and about ten years younger. I was ready, though. At the start of the fight we both managed to knock the knives from each other's hand. After landing several blows with our fists, we wrestled each other, and both had each other in a stranglehold. And that's how we stayed. I don't know how long this battle lasted, but it felt, and still feels, like an eternity. Trembling with anger and fatigue, neither of us had another ounce of energy. Our mouths frothed with hate. We both knew that whichever of us was the first to fall would be knifed to death.

My head began to cloud over from tension and weakness. The pine trees swam in front of my eyes and the ground shook. The criminal was about to keel over, though. His face twitching with impotent rage, he collapsed like a sack on the ground. I staggered back and saw Baklan. He'd cracked Pakhan across the temple with a pine log. I slumped to the ground. Baklan grabbed Pakhan's knife and cut his throat. Blood streamed out. The big man grunted and convulsed a few times before remaining still.

Baklan lit a fire. The scent of smoke and burning leaves revived us. I sat by the flames and stared off into the distance. In front of me was the unknown and most likely starvation, and next to me were a fire and a heap of meat. Without looking at me, Baklan walked up to the corpse. First, he ransacked the pockets and rucksack. He found a little tobacco, a box of matches and a packet of salt. He looked back at me.

A HUNDRED YEARS ON THE STEPPE

Without words, we understood what the salt was for. Baklan gave a sinister grin and began to cut up the body.

I had seen a lot of bloodshed and death. I'd walked over dead bodies in battle, my boots sloshing in blood. But this was different. Now, I had to eat a man's flesh to stay alive.

The taiga suffocated me with its silence. The hunger had consumed me and taken over my mind. A dead man had ceased to be a man and was simply a piece of meat. I tried to imagine that we were cutting up an animal. The voice in my head said: *Just cut it up and eat it - there is no other choice. Cannibals kill people out of necessity in order to stay alive. In this respect, they're like any person who kills livestock and eats it. When compared to kings, tsars, führers, presidents and generals who send people to their death, even the most enthusiastic cannibal is an angel.*

I took out my knife and stared at the corpse. *Which part do I begin with?* I thought. *Maybe I could cut the hand off?* Then, in front of my eyes appeared that poor little girl in the deserted village all those years ago. I staggered back in shock. I was desperate to escape, to run away and not look back, but I had no strength to move. Something was still drawing me towards Pakhan, the freshly killed man whose body was still warm.

Now, Baklan had the look of a predator in his eyes. Pakhan had planned to cut him up and eat him if they ever became famished, but he'd been handed the opposite fate. I couldn't do it. I prayed to the Almighty and begged the souls of my ancestors for help. I knew I had to get away from Baklan. The hunger had turned us into animals, and eventually, one of us would kill the other. I stood up and walked away.

'Are you insane?' yelled Baklan as I disappeared into the forest. 'You're going to die of starvation! Come back and we'll save ourselves together.'

I kept walking.

'Go to hell then!'

I took a final look behind me. As Baklan continued to hack parts off the corpse, I thought I heard the sound of him crying.

I don't know how long I kept stumbling through the taiga before I eventually reached a clearing. I was weak and delirious. I think some ancient spirits guided me, and wouldn't let me fall. I was completely lost. I'd seen nothing but pine trees for weeks. The voices in my head told me that the trees were waiting, uncaring, for me to fall under one of them and remain there forever. My vision failed, and I almost lost consciousness. Occasionally, I would come to my senses for a few moments before falling back into a trance. I thought it was the end. I prayed to Allah as I prepared to die, but still I kept staggering on.

The Beauty of Fate

Suddenly, I saw a person walking towards me. Where they came from was a mystery. They walked lightly as if floating over the soft grass of the forest floor. They were dressed in white, and their coat looked like the quilted *chapans* that Kazakhs wear. I tried to call out to them, but not

A HUNDRED YEARS ON THE STEPPE

a sound came out of my throat. I was afraid they would disappear again before they saw me. Trying to keep them in my sights, I walked with all the strength I had, but my legs were weak and I fell. When I got up, they'd gone. The last time I saw them, they were walking between two great pines. I staggered on in that direction.

Then, I saw a hare. I tried to bring myself to my senses and began to creep up on it, but how could I catch it? Then I realised: the hare was caught in a trap. If there was a trap, this meant there were people nearby. At that moment, though, I didn't care about that. I quickly snatched the frightened hare, whispered a prayer for it, and sliced it open. I lit a fire, cooked the hare over it, and began to eat.

It was the most delicious meat I had ever tasted. As I chewed on the hare, I remembered the famine on the steppe and the man who'd died just before he could reach the frozen marmot. I could have suffered the same fate. My mind couldn't fathom how I could have come across a trapped hare in the depths of the taiga. I silently offered a prayer of thanks to the Almighty and to the souls of my ancestors. This couldn't have simply been another piece of good fortune. So many times, I'd been seconds from death only be saved by a miracle. I felt warm again.

After I'd eaten the hare, I fell into a deep sleep. I don't know how long I slept for, but I woke to a stabbing sensation in my chest. Opening my eyes, I saw a woman standing over me with a rifle. At first, I thought she was a hallucination, but she was real.

'Who are you?' she shouted in Russian.

I looked up at her without answering. I knew I was saved.

'Answer me, old man. I said who are you?'

She put the rifle to my chest again.

'I surrender,' I finally spluttered.

She asked me more questions: who I was, where I was from, what was I doing here? When she had her answers, she took me with her. We walked for a long time through tracks in the taiga and eventually arrived in a small settlement. The place was made up of old and abandoned wooden huts. Most of them were falling to pieces. We entered a hut which I assumed was her home, and she made a strange-tasting herbal tea.

'Drink it; it will restore your health,' she said.

'Thank you. You've saved my life,' I murmured.

'Those who are saved save the ones who saved them. I should say thank you to you.'

Her name was Tatyana. She was a beautiful woman with long blonde hair. She said she was forty-years-old. She was large, but she moved gracefully. We talked and got to know each other.

Tatyana told me how she'd ended up here. In 1938, during Stalin's purges, she and her husband found themselves under surveillance. In fear of being arrested, they'd escaped from Omsk to stay with her grandmother in a tiny Siberian village.

'A year later,' she told me, 'we learnt that NKVD spies had found out where we were. My grandmother told us to escape into the taiga. She knew that in this part of northern

A HUNDRED YEARS ON THE STEPPE

Siberia there are a handful of settlements and told us to live there for a few years until times changed for the better. We packed some of our belongings, left our son and daughter with her, and escaped from Beria's claws. When the officers came for us, my grandmother told them we'd gone to pick mushrooms and never come back; that we'd probably gotten lost. Well, who would search for two enemies of the people this deep into the taiga? There just weren't enough NKVD men to catch everyone.

'We walked through the forest for an eternity - over a hundred kilometres. We had some food and a gun with ammunition. Finally, we came across this village of Old Believers. They'd gone into the taiga in the last century to escape religious persecution under the Tsar. The old women told us that their community had lived here for over a century completely cutoff from the rest of Russia. By the time we arrived there were very few of them left, a few huts and only nine people. As time went by, they all died apart from one old lady.'

Tatyana paused for a while before telling me that last autumn her husband had died suddenly. In the spring, the old lady died too. Tatyana was left on her own, surrounded only by the taiga.

'I'm Russian, and my husband was Russian,' she said. 'Our families were Christian, but at school and the institute they beat into us that God doesn't exist; that there's only a holy ghost who has always existed and transforms into different states. At home, my grandmother would always say: "Everything that happens is the will of God". So, what faith do you think I can have now? I don't follow Christianity in the same way that others do, but I believe that there is a Creator. They put a spell on us with their Soviet atheism mixed with materialism. I'm the result.'

Looking into a hand mirror in Tatyana's living room, I understood why she'd called me an old man. I couldn't remember when I'd last looked in a mirror. I was appalled at my reflection. Gaunt, rough, grey, wrinkled; the handsome face I was born with was gone. I was only fifty, however, and didn't think of myself as an old man.

For the first few days, I slept like a baby. I hadn't slept so much since the military hospital. The silence of the taiga, the clean air and the calm of the hut were everything an exhausted man could wish for. Here, there was no war, no gulag, no spies, no cannibals, and no one to control me. There just weren't any people. I came to think about this only later. When I arrived, all I wanted was to rest and forget; to forget and rest. This place was a blessing; a gift from Allah. After so many years of hellish punishment, I was surrounded by nature, silence and calm.

I took my time to recover. My situation hadn't changed, though. I was running from one life-threatening danger towards another. Even if I found my way out of the taiga and ended up in a town, I would still be questioned by the authorities. Staying forever in the comfort of the pine forest was almost the perfect way to save myself.

For years, I'd dreamt of peace. I'd been desperate to run away, fly away, across the ocean, into the clouds, anywhere that I didn't have to see the human madness, bloodshed and

A HUNDRED YEARS ON THE STEPPE

torture. I wanted to hide from the Soviet authorities, from society, and now I was in the depths of the taiga. The fresh air was giving me renewed vigour, and the calm of the forest soothed my soul. It felt as if time didn't pass here. The pine-log hut became my home, with a warm, kind woman next to me. Still, I couldn't find true peace, though, and, as always, I thought about my homeland and my family.

Tatyana and I would often talk for hours. We told each other about our lives, about all we'd seen and how we'd suffered. We became close and came to love one another. Gradually, I began to recover, but I still hadn't healed completely. Winter was closing in and we had to prepare, so I went to look over the tools we had. There were axes, crowbars and spades which were rusted but still usable. Tatyana also had the rifle with a few bullets.

'I've never shot an animal with it. We saved our bullets in case we needed them for something else,' she told me.

The first thing we did was to harvest the wheat and potatoes. We put all our food reserves into the cellar. The Old Believers had been very careful with their grain, and there was plenty of it leftover from previous years. There wasn't much variety in our meals. Tatyana could cook a few different dishes with the same ingredients. She baked bread and cooked potatoes. Very occasionally, a hare would walk into our trap and we'd eat what felt like a feast.

One of Tatyana's most nutritious ingredients was wheat that'd been left to germinate. I could never have guessed that wheat could give me so much energy. I got used to the lack of salt, sugar, butter and tea. Tatyana would tell me that it was even a blessing. People used to believe that not eating sweet or fatty foods and not using salt or oil was the secret to a long and healthy life. I took this as my chance to rid my body of anything harmful and become healthy again.

Tatyana's grandmother had been an expert in Siberian herbs. She knew natural treatments for every ailment there was, and Tatyana had written down as many as she could remember. She taught me about the life-giving powers of Siberia's plants. We shared a love of nature. She said that the taiga contained so many nutritious and healthy organisms that a person could never die of hunger here.

'Everything around us is healthy, but only in the correct measure,' she told me, 'otherwise your medicine becomes your poison.'

Tatyana even found medicinal vines growing on the pine trees and made potions out of cedar wood. She paid attention to every blade of grass, every nut and berry, and made sure there were enough in our cellar to see us through the winter. To someone who was raised among nomadic animal breeders, this was all unbelievable.

'Kazakhs have never eaten grass. It's our horses, camels and cows, sheep and goats who eat the grass, and we get the nutrients through their meat. You're feeding me like I used to feed our horses,' I joked one day.

A radiant smile shone on Tatyana's face, and it became warmer in the hut.

'Men break things and women put them back together,' I said.

'Women are like fire: they either give warmth or they

A HUNDRED YEARS ON THE STEPPE

167

burn,' she replied.

The woman who saved my life didn't only heal me; she opened up a new world to me and showed me a new way of life. She found that I was suffering from diseases I didn't even know I had.

'War, the gulag, eating the same gruel for years in constant anxiety: punishment like this would've ruined anyone's body. How did any of you even survive?' she exclaimed. 'I suppose it's survival of the fittest. You spent your childhood in nature, eating natural foods, always running and riding horses. Your blood and your soul are pure, and the nomads' faith and peacefulness have given you a spiritual strength that's helped you overcome these twists of fate.'

Tatyana was convinced that a person should think seriously about his health and should try to eat and live healthily. I began to learn how to live well with the right food, breathing, exercise and stillness of mind. I remembered the golden rule passed down through generations for centuries but which our generation had forgotten: everything has to be in the right measure. I stopped smoking, not only because I ran out of tobacco but because Tatyana described so vividly how unhealthy it was. I soon forgot about nicotine.

Then winter came. I remember the first day of winter on the taiga. The snow fell in big, soft flakes. It felt as if purity itself was falling onto the forest. There was a surprising silence. I held out my hands and snowflakes melted on my calloused palms. I remembered the steppe near Kokshetau where I'd seen snow for the first time. I wondered if my mother, my children, my wife, relatives and neighbours were also standing in the snow. Snow is the same for everyone - people of all races, young and old, communists and fascists, religious people and bandits - we all love to feel it fall onto our skin. Everyone feels it differently, but it's something we all have in common. Mother Nature treats everyone the same, but people treat her very differently.

Taiga snow is special. As she crunches under your feet, it feels as if she's talking to you. This voice invigorates you, gives you strength and lets you know you're not alone on the endless taiga. This voice is like a book that's yet to be written.

'Winters are long here,' said Tatyana. 'You've never seen so much snow; it gets as high as the roof. There are no storms, though. The taiga doesn't let them in. There's a beautiful silence, but the cold is cruel.'

After a few weeks, the cold had all of the taiga in its excruciating grip. The forest floor was covered in a blanket of pure white snow. The pine trees froze over and began to creak; their branches broke and fell to the ground.

At night, we would look up at the star-filled sky. Because of the total darkness all around, from here the stars looked brighter, bigger and closer than they had in other places I'd been. Sometimes, a meteorite flew by, cutting through the dark blue sky. At those moments, we felt connected to something great and mysterious.

We enjoyed living. I wanted to just live and to remain human. To stop ourselves from getting bored or going mad, we made plans for what we'd do each day. We told each other things about what we'd seen and lived through. Some-

A HUNDRED YEARS ON THE STEPPE

169

times, when there was nothing much to say, we'd keep a story going for as long as possible. These stories relaxed and entertained us, and we laughed contentedly.

We made an ice rink and skated as we had when we were children. We reminisced about childhood, forgetting about reality for a few moments and becoming as children once more. As well as being fun, it was good for our bodies and minds. We laughed like children too. I needed this therapy. Long years spent in constant anxiety fighting for my life had taken a heavy toll on my nervous system. In the war and the gulag, I hadn't noticed my shattered nerves; there just wasn't time between events - each more harrowing than the last - to think about what was happening. Now, with the terrors behind me, now that everything was calm they started to torment me again. Everything I'd been through passed in front of my eyes; I had nightmares about the famine, the purges, the agonies of the war and the inhumane cruelty of the gulag.

At night, I heard the explosions of the war again. I shouted in my sleep and often woke from nightmares. Tatyana would comfort me. I was lucky to be with her. She understood my suffering and helped me with her kind words and herbal remedies. The pain had penetrated into me so deeply, however, that no medicine could make it go away. When I told the story of my life - the death squads of the tsarist regime coming to the Kazakh villages, 'Little October,' the famine inflicted on my people, the repressions of 1937, the horror of the war, the torture of the labour camp, Tatyana's eyes filled with tears. As I let everything out, though, I began to feel better.

With only an old rifle and a few bullets in the hut, I thought about making some new weapons for hunting and protecting ourselves. I made two bows - one for each of us - and fashioned arrows from branches. We enjoyed shooting them, sending them with a hiss into a snowdrift or tree trunk. The bows and arrows were too flimsy to kill a bear or even a wolf, so we settled for hares and birds. Most importantly, it helped to pass the time. Days felt different on the taiga; time passed more slowly. We spent most of our time outside, exploring the forest and finding new paths through it.

Tatyana said that God must have sent me. If I hadn't arrived, she didn't think she would have survived such a brutal winter. I told her about the Tatyana that everyone on the steppe knew, the character from Pushkin's *Eugene Onegin* that our great poet Abai had translated.

'You can be my Tatyana,' I told her. 'You're unique too.' She blushed.

Through the long winter nights, we told each other stories, legends, parables, everything we knew. Often, we'd tell the same stories many times, but it helped us to stay sane.

'When I leave here, I'll take you with me,' I told her earnestly.

'What then? How will I live there?' asked the woman who'd healed me.

'What do you mean? You'll be my wife and heal people.'

'But you have your beloved Khalima.'

A HUNDRED YEARS ON THE STEPPE

'And you will be my *tokal* - my second wife.'

Tatyana didn't take me seriously. She couldn't understand and laughed at me.

'No, that's madness; I won't agree to that. Better you stay here with me,' she said. 'If you love me, you'll stay.'

'I love you, that's why I'll take you with me; but nothing could make me stay here.'

'How can you love me? What about Khalima?'

'I love you both.'

'I don't understand. How can you love two women at the same time?'

'If you were a man you'd understand,' I laughed. 'Look: lions have a pride; stallions have a herd. Nature has it right; it's we humans who've broken the rules.'

'Don't try to persuade me; I won't agree to it.'

We embraced and we could hear each other's hearts beating.

I loved lighting the oven; it gave our uneventful life some colour. First, I took the wood shavings that had dried overnight and placed them inside; then, I placed some logs on top. As the fire warmed, I sat by the oven and watched. The flames flickered, and the wood crackled before everything caught fire. I had seen a lot of fire in my life - you could say that I'd been burnt by it - but this fire was different. It was peaceful. Watching the flames rise I thought of my home and missed my family.

In the spring, we tried to get out of the taiga and find a settlement with people in it. We packed some food for the journey, and an axe just in case. But we never found anything, and always had to turn back.

I spent almost three years in the taiga. For three long winters, we lived far away from people, just the two of us. I always believed that I would leave, though. I didn't want to see out my days so far from home. My only goal, my dream was to reach my homeland again, to step inside my home once more, to see my mother, children, wife and relatives, and share with them a piece of *baursak* bread. Then I could die contented. I only wanted to say goodbye to my family and for my grave to be on the steppe where I grew up. Nothing scared me anymore, not the NKVD men, spies or enemy soldiers... I was going home. The call of home grew louder and louder until it consumed my healed soul.

As soon as summer came, we set off on our long journey. It was a dangerous one as the taiga was wild and vast, but we had to try as neither of us could live there any longer. Day after day, we walked almost without stopping, using the sun and the stars to guide us. We travelled for several weeks, and then, at long last, we stepped out of the taiga. After a few more days, we reached the village where Tatyana's grandmother lived. She was still alive, and although she was almost ninety, she was still healthy and active. Tatyana's children had grown up. Seeing each other again after fourteen years, they laughed and cried. There were tears in my eyes too.

I stayed with them for a week, but it was time for us to say goodbye. Tatyana's grandmother and children thanked me for saving her, and I thanked them for the same.

Tatyana walked me to the edge of the village. For a long

A HUNDRED YEARS ON THE STEPPE

173

time we couldn't bring ourselves to say goodbye. As I walked away, I looked back and saw that she was still watching me. We waved to each other one last time. We both knew we'd never see each other again.

Life is made up of meetings and separations, and we humans are at the mercy of our interconnected fates. My journey home took another whole year. I roamed between train stations, slept in remote villages and crossed the steppe. On the way, I found out that Stalin had died. My soul became lighter. It felt like an omen that my dream would come true.

The Blessing

When I arrived home to my village among the sheep stones, no one recognised me. Even I didn't know who I'd become; was I a war hero or a criminal?

When I left to go to war, I was a forty-year-old man; I returned to the village as an old man of fifty-four. Many of my clansmen had died or left. Everyone had suffered their own tragedy. The wounds from the war were still bleeding, and people had no time for outsiders like me.

It was evening when I arrived home. Khalima was baking baursak on the stove with her back to the door. She didn't hear me enter. I spoke her name softly. Khalima looked at me and froze. Then, she ran to embrace me and began to cry. She cried for a long time, and so did I. The children came in, overwhelmed with happiness.

Time had moved on, though. My mother had died four

years ago at the age of seventy-two. Even as I became a soldier and then an old man, I always felt like a child for as long as my mother was alive. Upon learning of her death, I felt my age.

'She always had faith that you'd come home,' Khalima said, comforting me as best she could. 'She was worried as we didn't hear anything after the war ended. She thought something awful had happened to you, but she told me that in a dream she saw you were alive. She used to pray to Allah for you and Salim. She asked the Almighty to keep the two of you safe and to take her instead.'

I told Khalima about walking through the taiga on the verge of death. We worked out that my mother had died at about the same time Tatyana saved me. We agreed that this period hadn't been easy for any of us. Then, I read a passage from the Quran and dedicated it to the souls of my parents, my family, ancestors, and Maral Ishan and Salyk Mullah.

For a while after I returned, I needed to stay in Koitas. The village among the sheep stones was hidden away in the depths of the steppe, and the nearest town, Stepnyak, was almost two hundred kilometres away. We were on the border of another region, Pavlodar, but there were only a handful of other settlements within several hundred kilometres. Koitas was half-forgotten, even by the Soviet authorities, so people were mainly able to hold on to their old way of life. Most people still kept livestock.

The village was quiet and peaceful. There were no secret agents terrorising the steppe anymore, searching for enemies of the people. Life had softened again, and we didn't feel the

A HUNDRED YEARS ON THE STEPPE 175

hands of the authorities around our necks. After the death of Stalin, a new era dawned. His death saved millions of people, including me.

Khalima gave me the passport of my cousin, Takhtauikhan, who'd died at the start of the war. His death was never recorded; the authorities thought he was still alive, and no one was looking for him. I felt calmer knowing I could show his documents if I was ever found, though no one was looking for me anymore. I kept having been in a gulag and escaping from it from nosey villagers. Instead, I said that after the war I'd been involved in more battles with the Japanese, and then recovered from my injuries in a military hospital.

When I returned, Khalima was forty-seven. She'd raised five children on her own and suffered alone through these painful years. Our children had all grown up and got married. Our home was full of grandchildren, and their sweet voices filled our hearts.

Many of our clansmen didn't come home from the war. Some died before they had a chance to raise families and didn't leave any descendants. Their widows carried their tragic fate and tried to conceal their grief.

My cousin Karimzhan's daughter-in-law, twenty-three-year-old Rakhiya was left with three children but wouldn't hear a word about remarrying. Her husband had worked for the government before serving on the front lines, where he disappeared without a trace. Later, we found out that he'd been killed in 1942. Rakhiya told her relatives that she'd always love her husband, though, and wouldn't let anyone else be a father to his children. This loving, honourable woman became as cold as ice as she raised her children alone.

The widow of another of our cousins, a lovely girl called Nagima waited nine years for her husband, the father of her two children to come home. I discovered that Khalima, unable to break the poor girl's heart, had hidden the notice of his death which had arrived in May 1945 on the eve of the end of the war. It was only after I returned in 1954 that we told Nagima about her husband's death. She cried uncontrollably for her beloved husband and refused to believe he was gone. The fact that I'd also disappeared for nine years gave her hope. It was agonising to see her anguish.

After a while, people began to talk about this beautiful and charming woman who was only thirty-four. Some widowed men started to ask for her hand, but she never accepted. Kazakh widows never marry men from different clans in case their children are taken away from their land. Under the law of the steppe, if a woman's husband dies, then a year after the end of the mourning period she had to marry her husband's brother. If the husband had more than one brother, then she could choose which of them to live with. If the husband had no brothers, then one of his close family would marry her. This rule was strict but fair. Families cared about the children who would continue their bloodline.

One day, Nagima's relatives visited us and gave us a choice: either one of the men in our family would marry her or they would take her. What an ultimatum. All the men of a similar age to Nagima had died during the terrible past few decades, however, and only I remained. The other men were much younger than the widow and had been brought

A HUNDRED YEARS ON THE STEPPE   *177*

up under socialism with a very different understanding of life. We had no one to become a husband to Nagima that our ancestors would have approved of. On the other hand, we didn't want to leave her to raise two children on her own. Our ancestors wouldn't have forgiven us for that, either. So, Khalima decided that the correct course of action was for me to marry Nagima.

It was painful to acknowledge that I was the only man left in our family. I was already old and had my own children. Also, having more than one wife was a crime in the Soviet Union.

'No one will know that we're breaking the law,' Khalima said firmly.

So, I married Nagima in secret. We didn't go to a registry office; the mullah pronounced us husband and wife under Sharia law. Besides, officially Asanbai Bektemirov was only Khalima's husband; Nagima had married my dead cousin, Takhtauikhan.

Kazakhs had lost the right to live according to our traditions. We were forced to live under a law that was completely foreign to us. How could one people dictate their laws to another? There was nothing we could do; we had to live like this.

My eldest son, Kabdosh was born in 1927. After him came two more sons and two daughters. They had lived through our nation's tragedies: the famine of 1932, the repressions of 1937, and the most awful war humankind had ever known. When I left home to go to war, Kabdosh was fourteen; our youngest son was only three. He was born in

1938, the year I was first arrested. They had such a burden placed on their small shoulders, but they coped. When I came home, the children excitedly told me about what they'd been through.

During the war, many people of various nationalities including a lot of Volga Germans were deported to the Kazakh steppe. Several German families ended up in our village. The men were sent to the gulags as enemies of the people, and only the women and children remained. The Kazakhs helped them to settle in any way they could.

So, whilst I was fighting a war against the Germans, my relatives were making friends with them. Among them was a little girl called Polina. As she grew older, she became tall and beautiful, and Kabdosh fell madly in love with her. Everyone in our family was against their marriage as she wasn't Kazakh or Muslim, and, most importantly, she was German. As no one in the village approved of this handsome young horse breeder's choice, Kabdosh got into a lot of arguments. Fate had the last word, though. Polina fell pregnant, and after that everyone had to find a compromise. The village's aksakals decided that if Polina were to convert to Islam, she could be a daughter-in-law to our family. We invited Absalyam-hajji to convert her, and Polina took a new name - Mariyam. After this, Absalyam-hajji conducted their wedding ceremony, and Kabdosh and Mariyam became husband and wife.

I wanted to keep my distance from Germans and Russians, but fate had other ideas in making Mariyam a mother to Kazakhs; ten of them, in fact - five sons and five daugh-

A HUNDRED YEARS ON THE STEPPE   *179*

ters. They lived on the steppe in the summer and in a yurt in the winter. She helped my son in his work as a horse breeder. With their children, they grazed hundreds of horses on the steppe near Kenashchi, won awards for their work and became known throughout the Republic. Mariyam would milk the mares, and their kumis was the best in the region.

One day, a young Kazakh girl was sent by the management of the collective farm to help them. When Mariyam saw how she milked the mares, she called out in Kazakh: 'Look at her. She does it standing up, like Germans and Russians!' After that, the Kazakhs in the village claimed her as one of their own. She spoke in Kazakh with an attractive German accent. The eldest of our daughters-in-law, she showed us great respect, calling me 'ata' and Khalima 'apa.' To begin with, I was cold with her as I couldn't look past what the Germans had done to me. Time is the best healer, though, and Mariyam's kindness and her love for our grandchildren melted my heart. Mariyam became a wonderful part of our family.

Mariyam's maiden name was Sauer, and using this the Kazakhs made up a song for her: '*Sauer - sauyr boldy, barinen tauyr boldy, nemys - kazak bauyr boldy*'; which is to say: 'Sauer has come, like spring in April; she is the best of all, and now the Kazakhs and Germans are brothers.'

In 1955, an order came from the Supreme Soviet of the USSR giving an amnesty to all Soviet soldiers who'd been sent to the prison camps for being captured by the Germans. I was pardoned and officially became a war invalid. My military awards were returned, and I was granted a pension.

Now, feeling completely free, I began the peaceful autumn of my life.

In 1960, we moved back to Stepnyak. At this time, Kazakhstan began to heavily develop its lands that had either never been cultivated or had become fallow. This was a controversial step. The new collective farms helped the steppe to prosper, but as a result, more outsiders flooded into the nation. Tractors replaced wooden ploughs, which again changed the traditional Kazakh way of life and dragged us further into the Soviet mess.

Meanwhile, Kazakhs became a minority in our land. In our region, we made up only a third of the population among the new settlers: Russians, Ukrainians, Belarusians and other peoples of the Soviet Union. The five agricultural regions of Kazakhstan were merged into one territory, and its administrative centre, the town of Akmolinsk was renamed Tselinograd. This zone didn't want to be associated with the Kazakh Soviet Republic, and the chairman of the Council of Ministers of the Kazakh Republic, Zhumabek Tashenov had to force the territory's leadership to accept the authority of the republic in which it was located.

The First Secretary of the Soviet Union, Nikita Khrushchev declared: 'We have done with a plough what the Tsar couldn't do with a gun.'

Stories spread through the republic about this fearless patriot, Tashenov. They said that Khrushchev invited him to Moscow, where he tried to charm him with talk of friendship between nations and the united territory of the Soviet Union. He then suggested that the new agricultural zone in Ka-

A HUNDRED YEARS ON THE STEPPE   *181*

zakhstan become a part of Russia. Tashenov tactfully replied that Kazakhstan was a republic in its own right, and under its constitution, its territory could not be divided. Khrushchev became irritated and pointed out that everything in the republics is the property of the USSR. Becoming even more irate, he ordered Tashenov to accept his dictate or he would be removed from his post with immediate effect. Tashenov stood firm though, pointing out that issuing such a command was in contradiction of the law.

Khrushchev was a harsh character, and when he lost his temper, he was frightening. He threatened Tashenov, saying: 'We don't need permission from a republic; we can make decisions at the highest level in Moscow.' Tashenov refused to stand down, replying: 'If you proceed I'll take you to the international court in the Hague.'

There was nothing Khrushchev could do. He wasn't able to steal Kazakh land, but he did remove Tashenov from his position in retaliation. Tashenov, however, became a national hero, and no amount of Communist propaganda could diminish his legend.

During the Khrushchev years, a command came from above that each Kazakh family was only allowed to own one horse or cow and three sheep. More heavy clouds gathered over the steppe, casting the shadow of the past over our people. In fear, some people killed all their animals, ate all of the meat at once and prayed that the future would be kind to them. Others registered animals in the names of relatives who didn't have any livestock of their own. We hid one cow with Rakhiya, who lived nearby.

One day, an inspector came to the village on a bicycle to count people's animals. He was Russian and had clearly been drinking. When we showed him our yard, he diligently wrote down every head in a fat leather notebook, then said goodbye and cycled away. Our grandchildren were playing in a neighbour's yard, and he walked up to them.

'Excuse me, do you have any cows?' he asked.

The children were very confused that an important inspector, and a Russian one at that, had spoken to them with such respect.

'Cows? Yes, yes of course!' they shouted, trying to be helpful.

They led the man towards the barn where we'd hidden the extra cow, but his path was blocked by Rakhiya, who pretended she couldn't speak Russian.

'There no cow, there no cow,' she said, waving her hands and refusing to let the man into the barn.

Then, the cow started to moo. Still, Rakhiya didn't flinch.

'I said there no cow, there no cow!'

Quite what the inspector thought as he nodded his head and left the homestead on his bicycle no one will ever know, but we do know that he didn't record our cow in his notepad and left us alone.

I also remember Khrushchev's time for the queues and fights for loaves of bread in the shop. The queues began very early in the morning. When the doors opened, people burst into the shop and literally fought to get to the bread aisle. The biggest and strongest customers got to the front of the

A HUNDRED YEARS ON THE STEPPE

183

line, but were only allowed to take two loaves each. There was only ever enough bread for half of the customers, and the rest would leave swearing under their breath.

One day, my granddaughter volunteered to go for bread and ended up in the middle of a thick, bad-tempered crowd of villagers. They nearly crushed her, and she came home shaken and in tears. After that, we never went out for bread again and instead began to bake our own.

Although Stepnyak called itself a town, it was more like a collection of many villages. The part of Stepnyak that we moved to was called Bulakbasy, which means the source of a well. There were also neighbourhoods called Abai, Irmovka, Kazaul, Zhoke ayak-Dzhukayak, Kapai, Kirpichnyi sarai ('the brick barn'), Shankhai, Tsentr, Oktyabr ('October'), Pervomaika and Konnyi dvor ('the stable'). By the 1960s, the gold mining here had slowed down, but the conveyor elevator was still working, and put to other uses, its ventilators could be heard from everywhere, especially at harvest time.

One of the largest buildings in Stepnyak was the House of Culture. It was an interesting piece of architecture, all stone and bricks; its main part had two storeys and there was a smaller part with three storeys and a high roof. The house was built in the1930s with no expense spared. They used to say that less than twelve months after it was finished, a crack was found in one wall and the engineer was sentenced to twenty years. The House of Culture is still standing, though. Nowadays, it's a concert hall and a cinema.

The public baths in Stepnyak were in the centre of town. This old, low and warm building was divided into two

184   *Bayangali Alimzhanov*

sections, the steam pools and a hairdresser's. It worked every day to a strict schedule. The best thing about the baths was they sold a wonderful fizzy drink called *mors*; men would refresh themselves with glass tumblers filled with its golden bubbles. I've never tasted anything so delicious as that drink.

The stadium hosted football matches in the region's championship, which was usually won by the team from the Stepnyak car garage. Their opponents were the youth athletic club, another garage, and some teams from the collective farms. The matches were uncompromising, and the stadium was always full.

People lived, worked and looked forward with hope to the golden future we'd been promised under communism. We lived in bunkhouses constructed in the 1930s or 40s. These bunkhouses were a status symbol; the height of socialist construction. They were an embodiment of a socialist living space, and their solid stone walls felt immovable. Our grandchildren were born in these houses; for them, it was home. We thought we'd stay there until the new world arrived.

There was a little bedroom, a kitchen, a narrow corridor, and nothing else. Now, I remember how cramped it was, but at the time it felt almost too good to be true. One building would house several families. Our neighbours were mostly gold miners. None of us could hope to receive permission to live in separate accommodation.

Each apartment had a large stove in the centre which in the bitter cold of winter emitted the heat that kept people alive. People lived in peace, even happily. After all the suffer-

A HUNDRED YEARS ON THE STEPPE

ing, famine and repressions, war and bread rations, the period under Brezhnev when life stagnated was a kind of heaven for most people. On freezing days, the sight of grey smoke drifting into the clear blue sky was enough to warm our hearts. Some years later, people, including our family, were allowed to expand their living spaces by turning two apartments into one. Then, we had a whole fifty square metres.

I had many friends of other nationalities, including Nikolai, a Russian, and Leon, a German. Nikolai drove a cargo truck made by ZIS - the Stalin Automotive Plant - then a ZIL, the 'L' standing for Lenin. Leon was a welder and a handyman. We lived in the same building. Fate had laughed at me again, putting my family between Russians and Germans.

Nikolai Borisovich Nesterov was from a simple Russian family. He fought for the entire duration of the war, was wounded twice and was awarded military medals. He was a giant of a man and very strong, but at the same time he was quiet and even-tempered. His big blue eyes radiated kindness; I used to enjoy our conversations and respectful disagreements. Nikolai knew how to listen, was genuine and tolerant, and would never turn a disagreement into an argument. Despite our very different opinions and the raw emotion of some of our debates, he was always a good friend to me.

Nikolai was twenty-one years younger than me and treated me as an elder. This didn't prevent us from being friends, though, and I treated Nikolai and Leon as I used to treat my younger brothers. I'd sometimes jokingly call him Nikolai the Third. He hated it to begin with, but then got used to it, and sometimes when he'd been drinking he'd introduce himself to people that way.

I used to love the fermented cabbage pies that his wife, Lyuba, made for my family. She was like a woman from a Russian fairy tale: cheerful, respected by all, a wonderful housewife, confident and strong, and she always spoke the truth. Lyuba loved having guests visit, but if anyone over-filled their glass and became boisterous, she'd soon put them in their place. As a former soldier, Nikolai knew to stand to attention when she spoke. They had three children, a boy and two girls.

Leon Vilbert was a distant relative of my German daughter-in-law, Mariyam. He went by the nickname "Leike," and was an interesting character. He was about thirty years my junior and spoke Kazakh almost fluently. Germans learnt our language better than anyone but spoke it in a curious way with a strong accent.

One day, a guest came to visit him. When his Kazakh neighbours asked him who it was, he ummed and ahhed before finally mumbling: '*Oi, algi katyndyky katyn!*' – 'That stupid woman!' It turned out that his guest was one of his wife's cousins from Belarus. The Kazakhs made light-hearted fun of Leike as he complained about her in his idiosyncratic Kazakh.

Leike's surname, Vilvert reminded us of the word 'velvet,' so we called him Leike Velvet. His favourite German saying was: 'Words are silver, but silence is golden.' Nations all around the world have similar phrases. Nikolai told us

A HUNDRED YEARS ON THE STEPPE 187

that Russians also say 'Silence is golden,' whilst Kazakhs say: '*Az soz - altyn, kop soz – komir*' – 'A few words are like gold; too many words are like coal.' This wisdom helps all of us in life, especially in public, but in private we chatted as much as we wanted in our blend of Kazakh, Russian and German.

Leike had grown up in a Kazakh village, whilst Nikolai had been in Kazakhstan for many years and understood us even though he couldn't speak much. Thanks to Leike, I enthusiastically added to the few German words I'd learnt during the war; it was, after all, also the language of Goethe.

Leike and Nikolai, the welder and the driver, were in demand. One fixed things that broke in people's homes and the other drove people when they needed to leave town. Once, Leike told us that an old lady had asked him to fix some very important items for her. He arrived at her home weighed down with all his welding equipment. In her apartment, the lady brought out an aluminium dish and a tea mug. Leike respectfully explained to her that objects such as these couldn't be welded. The old lady, just as courteously, said she couldn't believe that such a master, and a German one at that, couldn't mend such simple things. Leike patiently suggested that her mug could still be used for holding flowers, and put some nails in the holes to fix it. The old lady was delighted.

Leike's wife, Zoya, was Belarusian. They had four children, two sons and two daughters, all of whom spoke Kazakh. Both my neighbours loved our kumis and *kazy-karta* - a dish made from horsemeat. Their children, and later their grandchildren came to love the dried curd that we used to make, called *kurt*. Whenever there was a celebration, Nikolai would take us to the bathhouse, and always brought along some vodka and our favourite snacks.

I drank vodka for the first time in the 1920s, all those decades ago. During the war, we soldiers would have a big glass of it whenever we could; it made it easier to cope in the freezing trenches, and less frightening when we came under fire. However, I had to remember the words of the Greek poet, Solon: 'All in good measure,' because vodka can punish you for drinking to excess. The truth was, though, that vodka was our friend, our vaccine and our drug. We drank vodka to take the edge off the pain in our hearts and to heighten our joys.

We would spend half a day at the bathhouse. We loved to sit in the changing room after a bath and swap stories, tell jokes - even political ones - and laugh at the stupidities of life. We went to the bathhouse more often in winter. The hot steam after the freezing cold of the street was an indescribable pleasure, and it felt just as good to embrace the cold once again after a morning in the baths.

The bathhouse was more than just a place to wash; it was a place where we hid from the tyranny of the Soviet world. There, we could speak openly about what was troubling our souls. Sitting in a little old wooden cabin, we imagined that our words were making the Kremlin shake. The 1960s were known as Khrushchev's Thaw, and we all felt a little freer. The Kazakh people, for so long one of the many victims of Stalin's personality cult, began to lift their heads.

I remember how, one day in the middle of the 1960s,

A HUNDRED YEARS ON THE STEPPE

the people in Bulakbasy, our neighbourhood in Stepnyak, performed the *tasattyk* - a ritual where Muslims sacrifice a sheep or cow and pray to the Almighty for the rain that will give them a good harvest. Everyone came to the ceremony. The meat was being cooked; the aksakals had taken their place on top of the hill, and in the middle of them, Absalyam-hajji and the other mullahs were reading the Quran. Absalyam-hajji was twelve years older than me - almost eighty. His real name was Gabdusalyam, an Arabic name, but we'd turned this into something Kazakh. Twice he'd made the pilgrimage to Mecca on foot.

Absalyam's life story was astounding. Sometime in the 1930s, a friend had come to his house and asked him to hide a knapsack. He did so without even asking what was inside. It transpired that the bag was filled with gold which had been stolen from a mine. The authorities soon arrested the thief, and when they forced him to confess he told them the gold was with the hajji. They came to search Absalyam's house and found the gold wrapped in the cloth bag. Absalyam-hajji was arrested as an accomplice and was thrown in prison. The Soviet authorities were relieved to have gotten rid of a troublesome mullah. None of them realised at the time they were actually saving his life, because soon after this incident the repressions began and most religious figures were shot or sent to the gulags. Absalyam-hajji just went to a normal prison like an ordinary criminal, though, and then he came home.

They came for him many times after that, trying to force him to give up his faith. Absalyam-hajji would never relent, and taking all the punishments they doled out with dignity, he became a religious leader in our region. His followers were not only Kazakhs, but all Muslims living on the steppe: Tatars, Ingush and Balkars. They knew of his ancestors from the Kerey Clan who were also well-known hajjis.

Taking the opportunity now the cruel era of repressions was supposedly over, Absalyam-hajji had decided to help the dry earth of the steppe prepare for its harvest and in doing so to teach his countrymen about the ancient ritual of tasattyk. In a loud voice, he was speaking about the power and gentleness of Allah, when three members of the police force rode towards us on motorbikes. His congregation were afraid; the past still cast a shadow over everyone. The officers were Kazakhs, and seeing so many aksakals gathered around Absalyam-hajji, their expressions softened. They walked up to the crowd and politely introduced themselves. The men couldn't admit the real reason for their visit and instead said their superiors had sent them to investigate some smoke coming from the hill. The aksakals assured them they would be careful and wouldn't let the fire get out of control. Offered a piece of their *kurbandyk* - meat from the sacrificed animals -- the officers thanked the aksakals and hurried away.

We completed the tasattyk, gave thanks to the Almighty, and ate the meat. This event shook not just our region, but the entire republic. Sacrificing animals to Allah and praying publicly was insolence in a country run by the Communist Party. Times had changed since Stalin, and Absalyam-hajji, a respected figure, could not be openly punished, but others responsible for this controversy were questioned. They

A HUNDRED YEARS ON THE STEPPE 191

explained themselves as best they could and pointed out the undeniable fact that after this ceremony the rains had indeed come. The party leaders were just as happy about the effect this would have on crops, and so were lenient on the organisers.

Under their father's guidance, Absalyam-hajji's two sons - who also worked as drivers - began to practice *namaz*. When the district's party committee found out about this, its Secretary for Ideological Matters summoned the brothers to his office and mercilessly attempted to indoctrinate them. He reminded them of Marx's warning, that religion is the opiate of the masses, and threatened them to sober up before their addiction became too serious.

'If Lenin said that god doesn't exist then he doesn't exist!' the man spat bluntly. 'The Communist Party is continuing the great work of the Leader. We communists are atheists and have no desire to tolerate a god or so-called holy spirits. If you don't stop indoctrinating the population with your religious poison,' he concluded, smashing his fist down to emphasise the importance of what he was saying to the brothers, 'you'll be expelled from the region within twenty-four hours.'

The boys went to their father and told him exactly what had happened. The wise old man, who knew what it was to experience persecution and punishment, told his sons to hide their faith until it was truly safe again.

So in those years, people tried to live in peace. They worked, raised their families, and tolerated the humiliations that came from above. Slowly but surely, our language and culture, religion and traditions flowed into the hearts of these children. This was our nation's battle for survival. For example, when Kazakh schoolchildren swore they were telling the truth, they'd say they were 'as honest as a pioneer' or even 'as honest as Lenin and Stalin.' This was what Soviet schools had taught them, but children are children, and often they weren't telling the truth. When they absolutely had to tell the truth; when they really had to keep a promise, they would swear to Allah. This is when we knew they were being honest; no child would break this oath.

We used to keep precious items that belonged to our ancestors in wooden boxes fastened with metal locks. There were trinkets in silver and sometimes in gold, handmade by masters from the steppe and further east. There were coins from the Tsar's time that had become faded, and women's jewellery - silver rings and bracelets. Women fastened them to their clothes, or made little holes in them and wore them as necklaces. Very rarely, old Kazakh *apas* would have letters and manuscripts written in faded Arabic script, and little books with yellowed pages produced a century ago by the publishing house in Kazan. It was rarer still to find bigger books. I once found a copy of Rabzuga's *Qisas Al-Anbiya*, printed in Kazan at the end of the nineteenth century.

These yellowed pages took me back to my childhood, and Altyn-apa telling us stories and parables in the winter hut as the snowstorms howled outside. I read the stories of the prophets to my grandchildren and great-grandchildren, so that they, pupils of an atheist school could learn about the lives of our ancestors, and feel their own place in our

A HUNDRED YEARS ON THE STEPPE 193

ancient history.

One infamous troublemaker used to write anonymous letters of complaint to the authorities. No one was safe from him. In the 1930s, he was an NKVD informant; everyone in the neighbourhood knew how malicious he was. Some of us were scared of him and treated him with respect, whilst others tried to avoid him altogether. So, this troublemaker began to write letters to those authorities telling them that the Kazakh elders in our district were performing *sundet* - circumcisions - on our young men. To prove that he was right, he even followed these boys to the public baths. Those who he couldn't find in the baths, he approached on their way home from school, and waved a caramel toffee under their noses with the words: 'Show me your willy, and I'll give you a sweet.' The children thought: 'What an idiot. Look as much as you want, just give us the caramel.' This is how the horrid man collected his evidence.

What a scandal this caused. A committee was sent to Stepnyak from the Kokshetau Region's Communist Party. They summoned all the district's leaders to deal with the matter, and the chief inspector began to throw his weight around.

'Comrades, what is going on here? The Party has given you responsible posts, and what have you been doing? We are erasing all relics of the past, all types of nationalism and re-ligious fanaticism, and destroying all signs of dissent against Marxism and Leninism. And you are allowing children in this district to be circumcised! You're setting the population a bad example by performing this uncivilised Muslim act on your children. It's not compatible with our new Soviet morals; it contradicts communist ideology. There is no way we can tolerate this. You must stop these circumcisions and cut out this barbaric practice.'

'Comrade Inspector,' the leader of the district committee retorted, 'who are you to tell our families what to cut and what not to cut?'

Everyone burst out giggling. The inspector lost his composure and looked to the horrid informant for support. He was looking elsewhere, however, because at that moment the First Secretary of the district's Communist Party, Alpysbai Zhakupov, stood up. A former soldier who'd been wounded on the front lines, a powerful man in the mould of a Kazakh warrior with military medals on his chest, he began to pull his trousers down. The whole room turned pale with shock.

'Come here, comrade, our anonymous truth-seeker, and take your trousers down before I take them down for you. And you, Comrade Chief Inspector, and you, respected members of the committee, take your trousers down and show everyone. Only, look carefully. Together now...'

At this, the inspector came to his senses and tried to pacify the angry Zhakupov. The informant almost fell off his chair in panic. Zhakupov kept his trousers on, but he didn't relent.

'It is no secret that all Kazakhs are circumcised, and this has never stopped us from working for the benefit of our country. The leaders of the region and the republic should first look at themselves in the mirror. Then they should think about whether the Communist Party and the Soviet Union

A HUNDRED YEARS ON THE STEPPE   *195*

have any problems greater than Kazakh boys being circumcised. Our people are united with the other nations of the Soviet Union in working towards glory, gathering our harvest and making the whole territory richer. We're too busy to look under people's underpants. Does it really matter that we circumcise our children?'

So, in the bluntest way possible, Zhakupov stood up against the accusations. Thoroughly embarrassed, the committee went back to Kokshetau having failed to accomplish their task. There must have been at least some sensible people in the Communist Party because that was the end of the controversy. People laughed at the stupidity of the Soviet ideologists and continued to live and work, educating and circumcising their children, Alpysbai Zhakupov, the First Secretary of the district for twenty years, became a hero.

At this time, they tried to do away with our music. The dombra, an ancient two-stringed mandolin, had been with Kazakhs for centuries, during happy times and painful ones, but suddenly it got on the wrong side of the Soviet authorities. It was thought of as an undesirable link to the past, and we were made to understand that playing our traditional music was against the law. So the dombra came to only ever be played in secret; then it disappeared altogether. Imagine that, in the homeland of the great singer and composer, Birzhan-sal. In the town where he's buried, by the mid-1960s children didn't know what a dombra sounded like. To teach my grandchildren, I made a dombra by gluing together some simple pieces of dried wood, and made its thin strings from a goat's intestines. This was my protest against the Soviet authorities. A few years later, some patriotic Kazakhs helped the dombra to be heard again.

Reliving the hundred years of my life, I always come back to the thought that even when we live under tyranny and unfairness, life has good moments as well as bad. If you ask me whether there has been more kindness or cruelty, it would be difficult to answer, and whether there have been more good or bad people along the way, it's impossible to say. A person can be a saviour in one moment, and a killer in the next. This is life, this is humanity, and we can't change it. We should accept people as they are and try to be the kindest person we can be.

Maybe I'm wrong, but I'm certain of one thing: judging a whole era, or defining such a complicated place as the Soviet Union which was home to so many nationalities is impossible. It just can't be done objectively; you can't fit such a vast picture into a small frame. The life a man lived can't be understood by looking at how he was judged by others. This era had everything: pieces that were good, pieces that were wonderful and spiritual, but it also had parts that were bad, wretched and abhorrent. History is rarely so subtle.

The 1970s were a period when life became less harsh. People were hungry and poor, but they could live humanely. I sometimes think that these years were a gift to the Soviet people, who'd suffered so much in the decades that came before. People could finally rest. The chance to work in peace, receive a stable wage and have a better standard of living brought joy to people. In the evenings, everyone watched their black-and-white televisions, taking their thoughts

A HUNDRED YEARS ON THE STEPPE   *197*

away into the distance, distracting them from reality.

For some reason, the years from Brezhnev's rule to the beginning of Perestroika and the fall of the USSR are now known as the period of stagnation. People also used to say it was the period of overeating! If only we could count how many hours each citizen of the Soviet Union spent eating and drinking. We would eat at every opportunity. Many people held their special occasions around a kitchen table, which was always filled with food. At mealtimes, we would talk for hours about everything and everyone. It's how we freed our hearts from the iron bars that the dictatorship had locked them behind. This so-called period of stagnation deserves more attention. They criticise it now in various ways, but at the time we were happy.

Rumours used to circulate about the leaders' antics. The tricks that were concealed behind political slogans are a whole story in themselves. They used to say that such-and-such was a good orator, or a very educated person. That meant that he was good at pulling the wool over people's eyes; and memorising a few well-chosen quotes helped him to gain authority in the eyes of party members or the naive masses.

Public life was relatively free. We could be ourselves and we were always ready to help one another. No one accepted money for favours. It became shameful to take money, especially from your fellow countrymen. Instead, we would return favours. It was an unwritten law of the period of stagnation; a code of honour. If a man gave a neighbour a lift somewhere or fixed his bicycle, he would expect a bottle of something at least. Disagreements between people would often turn into heated arguments and even fistfights, but the next day they would drink together to make up. Funnily enough, people always had sufficient money for a bottle of vodka.

Nikolai, Leon and I were good friends, and also acted as each other's moral compass. If a Kazakh had disgraced himself somewhere, they would make fun of me for it. Then, I would get my own back if a Russian or German, Ukrainian or Belarusian did something wrong. We'd act as representatives of our nations: 'You should be ashamed! What would the Russians say if they found out?'; 'Stop it! The Germans will make fun of me!' We'd also often hear other Russians and Germans saying things like: 'Don't embarrass our people. What will the Kazakhs think of us if you do that?'

Even the most shameless who didn't care what their countrymen thought about them were embarrassed to show themselves in a bad light to other nationalities. We were open with one another: we gave people the freedom to say what was on their minds and told the truth to their faces. We often joked and sometimes teased people, but there was never any malice. We weren't soft on each other and argued a lot, but there were no enemies among us. We lived together, shared our happiness and our pains, borrowed bread and salt, and never stopped making fun of each other.

Sometimes, when we'd been drinking, Nikolai and Leon teased me for having two wives.

Khalima and I lived in the bunkhouse with our youngest son, Aigali, his wife, Bayan and our grandchildren. Nagi-

A HUNDRED YEARS ON THE STEPPE

199

ma lived nearby in a plain, weather-worn old house. Her eldest son and daughter - the children of our brother who died in the war - lived and worked in Kokshetau. Two years after our marriage, Nagima gave me another son, who lived with her. Our families were always close.

'Asanbai must be in heaven: two wives on the same street and beauty wherever he turns,' joked Nikolai. 'Asanbai, which one is sweeter, your first wife or your tokal?'

'It depends,' I'd reply in the same tone. 'Sometimes a man wants something sweet, and sometimes he wants something savoury. So the older one satisfies me, and the younger one makes everything a bit sweeter. Sometimes, it's the other way around.'

Their laughs echoed around the wooden baths.

'You know, Kazakhs had the right idea. They can have four wives and make four villages' worth of children, and no one complains,' said Nikolai, only half-joking now. 'There's no need for them to turn their heads. And what do we do?'

'We marry one woman, swear we'll be faithful, and still sin,' said Leon, thinking aloud.

'Who's stopping you living like us?' I replied. 'Get yourselves a second wife!'

'Oi, Asanbai, if only we could,' my friends sighed.

'You think you're too old?' I asked, pretending to not understand. 'Nikolai, you're only fifty; and Leike, you're barely forty.'

'It isn't us, it's the law,' Nikolai sighed.

'He's right,' said Leike. 'Firstly, no one would let us have a second wife - not the law, not our wives, not our society - no one!'

'And secondly, they say it's uncivilised,' added Nikolai.

'Who decided what's civilised? For you, it isn't, but for us it is. The problems begin when one country forces another to live under its rules. What's wrong with each nation living in its own way? Does it harm a Russian or a German if a Kazakh has four wives to continue his bloodline? If no one minds, then where is the harm?'

'We don't mind.'

'And we wouldn't mind having it ourselves!' replied my neighbours.

'You know why they made having several wives illegal? They wanted to stop Kazakhs from multiplying. It wasn't enough for them to murder so many of us, they had to stop our nation from renewing itself.'

'No, Asanbai, it isn't that,' said Nikolai. 'It's the opposite: the Soviet authorities have given Central Asian women their freedom!'

'What freedom? From whom?'

'It's true, Asanbai; they gave women equality and freedom,' said Leon.

'A woman can be equal to a man in the eyes of the government; but she can't be equal under the laws of nature.'

My neighbours even turned such a serious conversation into a joke.

Jokes gave us strength; a healthy sense of humour saved us from depression. Even while unimaginable events were taking place around us, there was always something to joke about.

A HUNDRED YEARS ON THE STEPPE   *201*

Once, after an alcoholic lunch some mid-ranking district officials managed to lose control of their car and get stuck in a tree. This was in the centre of town on the street named after Lenin, close to the Communist party office, the police station, and opposite the clinic. People said that when the firemen rescued them, they were singing songs about astronauts. Then the gossip started. The uzunkulak was everywhere, even during times of strict censorship. It transpired that the town's chief specialist on construction was awarded a new car, a sturdy Moskvich, and was celebrating the gift with friends. He was a Kazakh, which gave my friends an opportunity to make fun of me. That evening, as we were sitting in front of our building admiring the sunset, they congratulated me on my compatriot becoming the first Kazakh in space.

'Well done, the Kazakhs,' said Nikolai. 'You've caught up with America, and not even they would've thought of something like that.'

'Only two creatures could take off on Lenin Street and land in a tree: a goose and a Kazakh,' added Leike Velvet.

I told them they were just jealous.

'What can a Kazakh do if you're not allowed to fly into space from your own base in Baikonur?'

The next day it got more interesting still: we found out that the Kazakh's fellow 'astronauts' were a German and a Russian, and the man at the wheel was the Russian. I didn't let my neighbours forget.

'See, it's always your fault, the foreigners. Our poor Kazakh, the simple soul, sat between them to try to stop another accident from happening. This is what happens when you put a Russian in charge and let a German give directions.'

Then we opened another bottle.

Every Easter, our neighbours would bring us painted eggs, and when it was *ait*, they came to us to have *lepyoshka* bread with sour cream. I remember one time the most clearly. I had been in Kokshetau, and went to the market. A Russian woman was selling beautiful little round bread rolls covered with white cream. As I asked her if they were fresh, she nodded, and then gave me a strange look. I bought a lot of them, and when I got home, I gave them to my daughter-in-law, Bayan to put on the table for our guests. We sat down with some tea and were about to tuck into the cream rolls when Aigali and Bayan started to giggle. They told me that they were *kulichi* - Russian Easter cakes. They'd travelled too far for us to throw them away, so with a spoon, I smudged the crosses that had been drawn onto them with cream, and then said a prayer. The cakes were then Muslim, and all of us laughed at me, the absent-minded old aksakal.

There is no need to reduce the friendship between nations into a slogan, and it isn't right to ignore differences or pretend that problems don't exist. You can not like a person, but you can't hate all of his countrymen because of him, and you can't be a true friend to someone if you don't respect his culture. You can fight against the politics of another country, but that doesn't mean you have to hate all the people who live in it. It isn't their fault; and they aren't responsible for the pain that their leaders cause.

History has shown many times that she is unpredict-

A HUNDRED YEARS ON THE STEPPE

able, however, and life is not always this simple. So, once more, frightening rumours began to disturb our quiet and peaceful lives. Each day words blew through our streets like a snowstorm about the Soviet Union having sent troops into Afghanistan and starting a war with America and the Afghans. We were shocked and scared. How could this be? Why, what for? We asked each other these questions, but none of us knew the answer. We began to hear that they would send soldiers stationed in Turkmenistan to fight this war. At that time, two of my grandsons were serving in Kushka, and they could end up at the front in this hot, distant, unknown country. Worried sick, I prayed for them.

Our people used to say that the Pashtun tribe in Afghanistan were warlike and had never been defeated. Everyone, especially those of us whose children were in the army, was afraid. We weren't given any official information, and because of that, the rumours were even more terrifying. After a while, the first awful news began to filter through: we learnt of boys from our district who had died. Their bodies were brought home in zinc coffins, and as we weren't allowed to open them, that is how they were buried. Sometimes wounded soldiers would come back. Thanks to Allah, my grandsons returned home when their service ended.

One of our young neighbours from Stepnyak, Bulakbasy Madai was crippled in the war. His brigade was ambushed, and in the battle that ensued, a Pashtun mine blew off one of his legs. Reinforcements arrived for the Soviets, and the Afghans retreated. The wounded Madai was taken away by field medics. Finding him clinging tenuously to life, the doctors sent him to the military hospital where they amputated his left leg. Miraculously, Madai survived. They made him a prosthetic leg, and as soon as he learnt to walk again, he went to teach in a village school. A while later, he married and had children. Horribly burnt by the flames of war, Madai coped manfully with his trauma. I couldn't believe that after the tragedy of the Second World War, humanity was ready once more to shoot at itself.

The Absurd Made Real

Ten or fifteen years after the campaign to develop Kazakhstan's unused land and take it away from the country, they came for the Kazakh language. At the end of the 1960s and the start of the 1970s, they gradually began to close all the schools which taught in Kazakh, claiming that there weren't enough children attending them. So children had to go to Russian-speaking schools. All levels of the Soviet hierarchy openly stated that the Kazakh language had no future; soon everything would be in Russian. Parents were told their children's future would be in a Russian world, and if they didn't speak it, they wouldn't get anywhere in life; they could forget about a career. In all workplaces and universities, and in all other parts of public life, people spoke and wrote only in Russian. Even in villages where only Kazakhs lived, solely Russian schools remained. In Stepnyak, the only town in the region, of the six Kazakh schools only Abai middle school survived. The most awful consequence

A HUNDRED YEARS ON THE STEPPE   *205*

of this chauvinistic and dictatorial policy was that children who'd grown up in Kazakh-speaking homes and schools until the age of seven couldn't understand classes in Russian. A whole generation of children struggled with their education. Those who understood that this was a political move were angry. Some protested but could do nothing to prevent the powerful machine of the Soviet state.

Both open and disguised, attacks on the Kazakhs' religion, language and culture multiplied. They banned Ramadan, our period of fasting and observing *namaz*. They published articles attacking our religion in the newspapers. Kazakh family names and place names disappeared as they thought up new names for towns, villages and streets that meant nothing to us. Often, these were renamed after people who had no relation at all to the country. We knew this was also part of the Soviet drive to Russify and assimilate us. It made our blood boil and we couldn't hide our anger, but no one listened.

The first time I met a Kazakh who didn't know our mother tongue, I couldn't believe it. I thought he was playing a trick on me. When it became clear that he really didn't know a word of Kazakh, I thought the world had turned upside down. It was so unnatural, so ridiculous. I thought that just as horses neigh and dogs bark, so Kazakhs speak Kazakh, Russians speak Russian, and Germans speak German. I had naively thought that a person is born with his mother tongue inside him.

All Kazakhs could do was stew in silence. Sometimes, I would argue with Nikolai, and Leon would take my side.

He used to joke that during the war, Kazakhs and Russians fought side by side against the Germans, but now the Kazakh and the German were attacking the Russian. We quarrelled about ideas of nationhood most of all. Nikolai argued that our country was the USSR, which had its own template for a fair society and friendship between nations.

'Friendship, yes,' I replied, 'but there isn't equality; and if there isn't equality, then there's no fairness either.'

Nikolai continued to contend that the progress the Soviet Union had made in recent years wouldn't have been possible without its national policies.

'Look how many towns and collective farms they've built on the empty steppe,' he said. 'You'd have to be blind not to see them. And how many Kazakhs have received higher education and got good jobs? How can you doubt that Russia has played a positive role in the lives of the peoples of the USSR, including Kazakhs?'

'No! This doesn't give Russia the right to swallow up other nations. You can't talk about progress without also talking about aggression and repression.'

'Don't be so dramatic! No one has swallowed anyone up, and no one is going to.'

'Look around, you, Nikolai. Under the constitution, every nation has the right to self-determination. Where is it for us?'

'Then this means no one wants self-determination. All nations see their future within the USSR together.'

'No, it means no one is letting us determine our future. Soviet ideologists accused the Alash Orda and Kazakh pa-

A HUNDRED YEARS ON THE STEPPE

triots of nationalism. They destroyed us for it. Did you ever stop to think what this nationalism meant? What they wanted that was so wrong? All they ever wanted was for our people to be free and treated equally. We Kazakhs are a peaceful nation, and all we want is to protect ourselves as a people and live in peace with the other nations. We're the kindest people on this Earth. We don't try to take over or destroy other people; all we want is to be able to live our own way. If that's nationalism, then fine, call it that.'

It was clear from Nikolai's face that he didn't like my words, but he listened without interrupting.

'Every nation has the right to educate its' children in their mother tongue,' I continued. 'But now all the schools only teach in Russian. Everything the Kazakh Republic does is in Russian. The Party is even claiming that we're choosing not to send our children to Kazakh schools. How utterly shameless! This is one country swallowing up another. When one people are artificially transformed into another, how can we talk about equality and fairness? Do you understand?'

But Nikolai didn't understand.

The Party and its ideologists had promoted the idea of all nations coming together, and the propaganda programme had bitten deep. University courses were on such pseudo-sciences as dialectic and historical materialism and academic communism, which no one understood. The propaganda about the Soviet nation coming together as brothers was heard everywhere, and, at first, it seemed to be the right thing for all.

'It's perfect,' people would say. 'All of humanity living

as one. No nations, no nationalists, and no more problems.'

And what language will this united Soviet people speak? No one even asked that question. Of course, it would be the language of the majority: Russian. Is that fair? No one thought about that either, but instead tried to make it happen as soon as possible, using the Central Committee's chauvinist ideas. People quickly began to forget their mother tongue, customs and traditions; they educated their children in Russian and brought them up as Soviet citizens. In other words, they danced to the tune of the Communist Party.

'If the Central Committee says that's how it's going to be, then that's how it's going to be,' they reasoned. 'It has to be this way. If the Committee wants us to become one nation, then that's what we'll do.'

This so-called 'assimilation' gathered pace. We hated it and we rebelled against this deplorable Russification, only we couldn't do it openly. At that time, behind the Iron Curtain and with strict censorship, there wasn't a single publication that would write anything critical of the Communist Party. At home, though, we continued to raise our children and grandchildren in the traditions of our nation. We did everything we could to help them understand that they were Kazakhs and had to remain Kazakhs.

'Why divide people into nationalities when we're all part of the Soviet nation,' Nikolai would argue. 'What difference does it make what language we speak as long as we understand each other?'

His words hurt me, even more so as he spoke from his

A HUNDRED YEARS ON THE STEPPE

209

heart.

'At the start of this century, I fought against the Russians,' I told him. First, it was the Tsar's gangs, then the Reds and the Whites; all of them Russian. Then, I fought side-by-side with the Russians against fascist Germany. I spilt my own blood and killed people to defend Russian land. Now, I want to live peacefully with you as my neighbours. So, why don't you let me live in peace? Don't you have enough already? Why are you interfering with my language? Why do you want to destroy our culture and swallow us up? You say it makes no difference what language the Soviet people speak. You say that because you're sure all nations are going to speak your language. How would you feel if they made you forget Russian? I'd like to see you what you'd say then. All nations love their mother tongue and want to protect and create their own culture. That is all we want to do, to keep our nation alive. It hurts us deeply when we see our young people, brainwashed with communist ideas, wanting to live as people from another nation.'

Nikolai looked distraught.

'Forgive me, Asanbai,' he finally said. 'I honestly didn't know this meant so much to you.'

Friendship can only exist between equals. If we're not prepared to tell one another the truth, then there can be no real friendship, no understanding between us. I didn't want to deceive my neighbour.

'You say that those above, the Communist Party, have given a lot to the people of the Soviet Union, including us Kazakhs. Yes, this is true. Tell me honestly, though, what would this matter if my language and culture died and my nation became another Russia? Then what would my life be for?'

I looked at him, and Nikolai lowered his head.

'I understand you now,' he said unexpectedly. 'Only now... I didn't think before that this was so important to you. Now, I'm going to learn to speak your language.'

'But we have spoken Kazakh for years,' said Leike, who'd been silent until now, as he filled our tumblers with more vodka.

'Thank you for finally understanding, but what good does it do if a handful of Russians speak Kazakh, and the Kazakhs themselves all forget it?'

'I can't do anything more for you, and I really regret that,' Nikolai said, sighing deeply and sinking his tumbler in one gulp.

I did the same. We both felt uncomfortable and tried to change the subject.

'You'll still never be able to drink like us Russians,' Nikolai laughed, biting on some cheese.

The conversation was over and instead, we bet on who could drink more: the Kazakh, the German or the Russian. We downed every last drop of our medicine and spoke as friends again. We decided against going to the shop for another bottle. Leon and I both knew that Nikolai was right, and we could never out-drink him.

The policy of merging nations into one continued, and in the 1980s the clouds gathered over Abai Middle School in Stepnyak. In 1985, the authorities threatened to close it,

A HUNDRED YEARS ON THE STEPPE

claiming a lack of students, and this time there really weren't many. The school's director, Ospanov and the teachers came to me to ask me to speak with the heads of the district committee. I went there, angry.

Their new Secretary for Ideological Matters, Zygmund Zbignievovich Kachanowski was a Pole. His name was difficult for Kazakh villagers to pronounce, so they called him either Zigzag or Kochan. He was a very compliant person. He would never argue with anyone, and never said no to anyone. We thought he didn't know the word. Kachanowski tried to never harm anyone. He wasn't one for coercion or threats and was honest and fair insofar as the Communist Party allowed.

When I walked into his office, he gave me a broad smile and rose from his chair to show his respect to an eighty-five-year-old man, and cried out:

'Good day; please, sit down,' he cried.

I gave him a curt 'hello,' and stayed standing in the middle of his office.

He looked at me with surprise. It was probably the first time he'd seen me in such a foul mood. Pounding my walking stick on the floor, I barely tried to conceal my anger.

'Zygmund Zbignievovich Kachanowski, why do you hate Kazakhs so much? What have we ever done to you?'

My words cut him like a *kindzhal* knife. Zigzag became flustered, his right eye started to twitch, and his left one closed entirely.

'Asanbai Amanzholovich, whatever could you mean? You know me. You know how much I respect I have. Kazakhs helped my people during the dark years. I was born here and have lived with Kazakhs my entire life. I'm almost a Kazakh myself...'

'Then why are you closing our schools?'

'That isn't me; you know that,' Kachanowski said, pointing his index finger at the ceiling.

'So, who then; Ivanov, Petrov, Sidorov? They all say the same thing: "We aren't the ones closing the Kazakh schools. We respect the Kazakh people." So tell me, and be honest: if you all respect Kazakhs so much, then why don't you let us live on our own land and teach our children in their own language?'

Zygmund Zbignievovich turned red and nervously rubbed his palms together.

'Grandfather Asanbai, please understand us,' he pleaded, which softened my rage. 'It's a sign of the times, an order from above. It's the decision of the Communist Party and the government.'

Being reminded of the Communist Party and the Soviet authorities brought to mind the cruel commissars from the years of the repressions, who in the name of a class war and a fair society had killed so many of my people. This was a continuation of the same policy. We both knew that the same political goal, to colonise and Russify the steppe was behind the closure of our schools.

'So, you say it's a sign of the times? And who brought in these times? Who created this sign?'

'But you yourselves want your children to go to Russian schools. Nowadays, in the country of the Soviets, no

A HUNDRED YEARS ON THE STEPPE   *213*

one can take a step forward without the Russian language. As painful as it is to admit, a fact is a fact: your language as well as mine have no future.'

'No! Kazakhs don't want and have never wanted to lose their language and merge with other nations. We've been forced into a situation where we have to study a foreign language.'

'There's no need to be so dramatic. Almost all nations of the USSR are leaving their languages behind; they're becoming more like the Russians. My own children have almost forgotten Polish. It's upsetting, of course, but what can we do?'

'Listen, Zygmund Zbignievovich, you have all of Poland. Your people have a homeland where your people's language and culture are protected. If I don't have Kazakhstan, I have nothing else, do you understand?'

I never imagined that I'd make a political speech in the office of the Secretary for Ideological Matters of my town's Communist Party headquarters. It was, however, a matter of life and death for my mother tongue, and, therefore, for my nation. If he had had the chance, every Kazakh would have done the same.

Something good came of our conversation. Almost whispering, Zigzag told me that all was not lost. If the school's first grade could enrol seven more pupils before the new academic year began in two weeks and the other classes could find a few more children between them, then under the law, they wouldn't be able to close the school.

'So, get busy, Grandfather Asanbai. Do it quietly, and

I will help you.'

We started to look for children. We went to visit relatives and acquaintances living in the collective farms where the Kazakh schools used to be and asked them to send their children to Abai Middle School in Stepnyak. We found enough pupils to fill the missing places in all of the classes.

The story wasn't a completely happy one, though. In many villages and farms, there was already no Kazakh school. In Kenashchi, where my son Kabdosh lived, almost ninety percent of the population were Kazakhs, but the school was Russian. All of Kabdosh and Mariyam's ten children studied in Russian. In the village of Birsuat, which was where my eldest daughter, Maike, lived on the Vostochny Kolkhoz, the school was also Russian, so her eight children learnt in Russian too. Imagine that, children growing up in a Kazakh family, speaking Kazakh at home, and then, at the age of seven, they have to begin a completely different life. It's true that they also kept their mother tongue, but most of them could only speak it, not read and write. This was a drama that turned into a national tragedy. When they were young, all my children studied in Kazakh; but my grandchildren and great-grandchildren went to Russian schools as there were no Kazakh schools where they lived. I, their grandfather and great-grandfather, the head of our family, couldn't do anything about it. All that it was within my power to do was to talk to them in our mother tongue and tell them about our culture, history and traditions. At least my family know their own language, even if only to speak it.

A HUNDRED YEARS ON THE STEPPE   *215*

Against the odds, all five of my youngest son Aigali's children, who lived with me, went to the Kazakh school in Stepnyak. My second son, Temrybek, who was a literature and language teacher, lived in the village of Saule, which was entirely Kazakh. The school there was Kazakh too, almost everyone played the dombra, and four of my grandchildren went to singing lessons. My youngest daughter was not so lucky, though. She lived and worked in the town of Petropavlovsk. Her husband had grown up among Russians, gone to a Russian school, and barely knew our language, customs and traditions. They had three children, and each of them spoke only Russian. I complained about this a lot and had strong words with my daughter and son-in-law, but to no avail. They would only shrug and say: 'It's a sign of the times. We live in a Russian environment, and we just don't need Kazakh. We understand we should know our mother tongue and keep our culture, but there's nothing we can do.'

Time went by, and the policy of merging nations sucked everyone in. Convincing those living in the district's only town to send their children to a Kazakh school became harder and harder until it was impossible.

I remember visiting every home where there were children about to start school. I went with the school director, Ospanov, and two Kazakh language teachers. The parents greeted us happily with Kazakh hospitality, but when we explained why we'd come, their faces turned to stone. We had wonderful conversations with the young parents, but also disagreements. The mums and dads - who were already Russified - didn't want to listen to us.

An honest communist and a Kazakh patriot, Mr Ospanov was an emotional person. Even at party meetings, he struggled to hide his concerns about the fate of our language. He spoke passionately to the parents, and appealing to their sense of patriotism, he asked and sometimes even demanded that they send their child to the Kazakh school.

'The future of our mother tongue is at stake,' he reasoned. 'Please, send one of your children to save the nation.'

'The Kazakh language doesn't have a future,' one young mother looked him in the eye and told him. 'Soon everything will be in Russian. I don't want to harm my son by filling his head with useless things. I have the right to choose where I educate my child.'

That girl hurt me as much as the fascist guards in the prisoner of war camp or the twisted criminals in Susuman. Ospanov turned red with fury, but he kept silent. He knew that arguing was futile. We understood that these Russified young parents, the victims of the Soviets' colonial policies had already begun to carry out the programme their generation was tasked with: to tear up the roots of our nation. A feeling of hopelessness suffocated us.

In two houses, though, luck was kinder to us. After listening to Ospanov's emotional speech, the parents, who had studied at Abai School themselves, agreed to send their boys there. So, against the odds we'd found six pupils, but we still needed a seventh and time was running out. Serendipity saved me again.

I was sitting in front of the barracks one day, worrying about the problem at hand, when someone said hello to me

A HUNDRED YEARS ON THE STEPPE   *217*

in Kazakh. I looked up to see Gerold, Leike's seven-year-old son. He'd come to play with one of my great-grandchildren. Seeing his bright face, it dawned on me: why not invite this little boy, who already spoke Kazakh fluently, to join our school? As I chatted with him, he replied so beautifully it was a joy to listen to him. I asked him if he'd like to study at a Kazakh school. The offer made him very happy, and he agreed straight away. He told me some of the Russian-speaking boys who were set to be his classmates had picked fights with him whilst they were playing football, and now he didn't want to be in their class. My great-grandson, who was also about to start school, had stood up for him. They'd been neighbours since birth and had grown up together. I had found my seventh pupil; now all I needed to do was convince Leike and Zoya.

I went up to speak to them. My friend Leike had not forgotten the kindness Kazakhs had shown to the Germans during difficult times and was soon deep in thought. When he gave me his answer the next day, he made me the happiest man on Earth. He'd also not forgotten whose books had helped him to learn Kazakh; when he realised the only middle school in the country to carry the name of the great poet Abai was in danger of closing forever, he swore in anger at the Soviet authorities and the Kazakhs who'd helped them. Zoya, who spoke Kazakh well but with an accent, signed up Gerold at the Abai School. This is how, without ceremony or fuss, we knew they wanted to help our people in a time of crisis.

'So, now Goethe is translating Abai,' I smiled, remembering the 1930s.

Gerold grew up to be an idol for Kazakhs. Besides speaking perfect Kazakh, he got good grades and knew many of our poems by heart. His classmates used to call him *bilgir* - the genius. Even the eldest teachers used to call him by a pet name, Gereke. Gerold finished his studies in the 1990s and became a well-known television presenter in independent Kazakhstan.

In the late 1980s, they announced Perestroika, and an order came from the Central Committee to fight against drunkenness. Our favourite tipples began to disappear from the shops. When this happened, people began to make vodka at home and sell it on the black market. It was hard to get your hands on good vodka when guests came to visit or just for yourself, but Nikolai the Third found the answer.

'We'll drink like we always have,' he exclaimed; 'we just need to be clever about it.'

This is how the three of us began making our own underground *samogon*. Nikolai brought us leftover wheat in his truck, and when we had enough, we carefully distilled it into wort. I provided the sugar, and Leon, the master handyman, made all the equipment from scrap metal. I remember the first time we made distilled spirits; before then I'd never seen it done. Nikolai and Leike did most of the work, and I was their cover. No police officer would dare to push an eighty-five-year-old war veteran aside to get into the building. We kept our new hobby completely secret, and in the dead of night one night, our first drops dripped out of the barrel.

'The first of many,' smiled Nikolai with a deep sense of

A HUNDRED YEARS ON THE STEPPE

satisfaction. 'Let's see how strong it is.'

We three neighbours poured ourselves half a tumbler of samogon, and each grabbed a pickled cucumber. I'll never forget that delicious, burning first sip. In my hundred years, I've never been able to try even a drop of whisky, but they told me it had roughly the same taste. I thought our samogon, made from our wheat, our equipment and our sweat, was the best spirit I'd ever drunk. It was also our secret rebellion against the Party's despotism. Not everyone could take the risks we did, however. Punishments for samogon were harsh; they could even put you in prison. So, we didn't risk making it very often, and when we did, we made enough to last a few months.

Many people were struggling, and everyone found their own form of escape. During the Perestroika years, trying to get something to drink was both a comedy and a tragedy. Laying our hands on vodka was the nation's biggest problem, and the people that had some could call the shots. They'd be the first to be brought their coal, firewood, hay and straw. It was a very Soviet paradox: they wanted to get vodka out of people's lives, and instead, our lives came to revolve around it.

The district committee had decided there could be a case of vodka at each funeral. Funerals are a serious matter, and the authorities couldn't ignore their own traditions. This precious case was only provided if you presented the death certificate of a close relative. However, this privilege didn't apply to Muslim citizens. They said vodka wasn't required at Muslim funerals, but there were people who thought differently. Raised in the spirit of Soviet internationalism, they felt they were being discriminated against because of their religion. Some complained to the department that handled funerals that as well as the other necessary items they wanted their case of vodka. If the authorities wanted them to assimilate, then they'd assimilate. When the department refused, they went to see Zygmund Zbignievovich Kachanowski.

'My son is getting married,' one Kazakh woman told him. 'My husband and I have worked on a collective farm all our lives; surely we've earned just one favour from above? So, please help us to get a case of vodka for his wedding. We're entitled to it. Oh, and another for the death of my father-in-law. We didn't claim it last year.'

'How are you entitled to it?' Zigzag utterly in exasperation.

'It's the law. Everyone is entitled to it!' the fiery woman shot back.

'There's no such law; we just try to help people through difficult times,' Kochan tried to explain, his left eye closed and his right eye quivering.

'So, help us,' the relentless woman continued, 'and don't discriminate against people.'

'But you're Kazakhs; Muslims! You don't drink vodka at your funerals.'

'What we do at our funerals is none of your business. Rules are rules: my father-in-law died, so you have to give us a case of vodka.'

Zygmund Zbignievovich was helpless. It had probably been centuries since a Pole had come up against such

A HUNDRED YEARS ON THE STEPPE

an immovable object. He tried to explain, but the woman wouldn't stop.

'When our neighbour Natasha's brother-in-law died, they gave her the vodka straight away.'

'But they're Russian,' said the distraught Zygmund Zbignievovich.

'Oh, so it's like that? If a Russian dies, you help his family, and if one of us dies, you don't? So non-Russians can't commemorate their loved ones? You call that fair?'

The apoplectic woman kept on blaming Kachanowski, a proud communist, for dividing Soviet citizens by their religion and nationality.

'I'm going to write to the regional committee about you. The Communist Party will understand that we're a united nation under the Soviets. This means we can have the same customs, and you can't stop us!'

I can only imagine how Zigzag felt upon hearing those words. He was terrified of letters being sent to his superiors. He called the Chairman of the Funerals Committee and asked for the woman to receive two cases of vodka, one for her son's wedding, and the other because her father-in-law had died. Victorious, the woman rushed out of his office to collect her bounty; Kachanowski poured himself a glass of water and slumped in his chair.

This is how the issue of vodka often took on a political and national dimension. Pressured by the circumstances, Zigzag was as flexible as he could be whilst encouraging people to follow only their own ancestors' customs. Whenever he felt there was no escape from pushy citizens, especially women, however, he tactfully gave in to their demands. People didn't really understand Perestroika and the attempts to stop people drinking. They didn't know why the government had taken these steps, and it became the stuff of intrigue as to what this was really about.

Time moved on relentlessly. Unbeknown to us, big changes were on the horizon. In December 1986 in Alma-Ata, which was then the capital of Kazakhstan, events took place which reverberated throughout the Soviet Union. Moscow decided to remove the head of the republic, the Kazakh, Kunayev, and replace him with a Russian, Kolbin. People erupted in anger. Young Kazakhs, mostly students and manual workers, gathered in the town's central square to voice their disapproval. This was something unheard of: a mass open protest against a decision of the Communist Party's Central Committee, and therefore against the Soviet Union. It shook the country's totalitarian system to its foundations.

The young Kazakhs demanded from the Central Committee and the Soviet government that each nation should be governed by one of its own. That was to say, the leader of Kazakhstan should be a Kazakh. The authorities didn't care about the voice of the people, however. Internal military forces drove away the unarmed protestors who'd gathered to oppose the tyranny of the Kremlin. Then, the retaliation came: students were excluded from their universities, and some were sent to prison.

In remote parts of the republic, we didn't know anything about this. The steppe relied on rumours. As the

A HUNDRED YEARS ON THE STEPPE 223

official agencies said nothing, the uzunkulak was our only source of information. The authorities went so far as to silence anyone who spoke or asked questions about it. Parents struggled to find out what had happened to their children. Phone lines and postal deliveries were shut down. It seemed that the authorities were extremely worried and were trying to save themselves.

The rumours became more and more frightening. They said they'd sent troops into Alma-Ata, and that soldiers were beating demonstrators with shovels and using water-cannons on them. They said the students who'd been killed or badly beaten were carried out of the town in trucks and dumped on garbage heaps, left to their fate in the freezing night. Many people were killed or maimed. Others were thrown into dark basements and prison cells, where they were beaten unconscious and tortured. Alma-Ata's Communist Party committees gave secret orders to employers to arm their non-Kazakh workers with iron bars, so they were ready to attack the Kazakh youth. Witnesses said they were given these bars while they were working. No one knows how many of them were used to spill the blood of these unarmed students. We later learnt that some details had been exaggerated, but they all had a measure of truth to them.

Articles appeared in the Communist newspapers calling these events riots and accused the young Kazakhs of hooliganism and nationalism. They claimed the students were high on drugs and alcohol. It was clear the authorities were trying to cut down the first shoots of freedom and democracy.

I was sick with worry; these protests brought back to me the events of 1916, when young Kazakhs rose up against the brutality of Tsarism and went up against guns and cannons armed with nothing more than birch sticks. Then too they'd died in an uneven battle. My heart was breaking again as I prayed for our young people.

There was nothing we could do, though; no one would listen to us. Many Soviet patriots, brainwashed by the words of Lenin and the propaganda of the Communist Party, believed the official versions of events and openly accused young people. Some of these accusers were themselves Kazakhs. According to them, the students had fallen for the provocation of foreign elements, the enemies of Soviet society. They were trying to gnaw away at the foundations of our country and tear apart the nations that had united as friends within the Soviet Union.

In a kitchen in Stepnyak, three neighbours quietly discussed these events before taking the debate to the bathhouse. Nikolai and Leike were shocked by the sudden appearance of Kazakh nationalism.

'Kazakhs always used to be internationalists. What has got into them all of a sudden?' Nikolai asked.

'Always such tolerant people, and then this,' Leike shrugged.

'We've been tolerant for decades. Something had to give,' I said to my friends as calmly as I could. 'The feelings my poor people have had to suppress for so long are all coming to the surface.'

I explained everything to my neighbours. I didn't hide

A HUNDRED YEARS ON THE STEPPE 225

the fact that I supported the young protestors. In my eyes, the methods the Soviet authorities were using to silence them were almost as cruel as the bloodthirsty dictators had been before them.

'But that's what they need; that's what we should be doing with people who are against us!' exclaimed Nikolai. 'This is politics, not ballet.'

'Then your politics go against your own people. It's chauvinism bordering on despotism!' I shouted. 'How can it be so easy for you to kill your country's young people, to punish them and crush them?'

'What were they rioting for? They didn't have to go so far,' my neighbour replied.

'Ask yourself instead, why you had to take it so far!' I snapped at him. 'There's a reason why you did this. Your national policy has problems, and one day you're going to have to answer for them.'

'To who? 'snarled Nikolai.

'To history... to your God... to your own conscience for goodness' sake!'

My neighbours had upset me. I told them about the crimes that had been committed on the steppe before they were born. They listened in silence, but when I got to the famine, Nikolai interrupted me.

'Listen, if it had really been such a catastrophe, then we would have heard about it. So, if we don't know about this famine, it can't have been as bad as you say.'

Logic like that would knock any man over, but I kept my composure and continued my tale of what I'd seen and lived through during that time.

'So, why don't we know about it?' he asked. 'If we don't know about it, that means it didn't happen.'

'Is that what you think?' I shouted, losing my temper. 'That if you don't know about something then it doesn't exist? Is that it?'

'Yes; I don't believe you,' he replied bluntly.

'Everything then was hidden; the authorities covered everything up. It's a historical fact and there are documents to prove it. The whole Kazakh nation knows about it and still talks about it.'

'I don't believe you,' Nikolai said coldly, and took a sip of water.

You can't change someone's mind when they're so convinced that they're right. He really didn't know anything about the famine of 1932. He'd never heard about it. Neither did he know about the cruelties that the tsarist forces and the Soviets had put us through. Leike didn't know either.

I lost my voice telling my friends about tragedies Kazakhs had suffered on our beloved steppe. They listened carefully, but I sensed that they didn't always believe me. Explaining to them, a Russian and a German, what our nation had been through, I suddenly realised it just wasn't so important to them. Experiences that are real to us just seemed like old stories to them. I understood a simple, but cruel truth: one people's tragedy is just a tale to others. One man's suffering is another man's statistic.

'Why are you rambling on like this? I've had enough of

A HUNDRED YEARS ON THE STEPPE

227

talking about this,' snapped Nikolai.

'Let me finish so you can know the truth and accept it like men,' I said, calmly but firmly. 'Hidden grudges lead to resentment, to lies and a lack of trust. We need to tell the whole truth about events that have happened throughout history and learn from them so we can move on. The history of war must teach us to live in peace. The history of hatred must teach us to be friends. It's time to put an end to the falsehoods and speculation about the war between Kazakhs, Russians and Germans...'

'Fine, I understand,' interrupted Nikolai, 'but this is all in the past. We're at peace now, so let's just be grateful for that.'

'What peace? What gratitude?' I cried. 'Haven't you even heard about the nuclear tests in Semipalatinsk?'

'So what? It's a necessity. We need a bomb to defend ourselves.'

'And is this the way to defend ourselves? Where else, what government would subject their people to nuclear tests and risk condemning them to painful deaths and horrible illnesses? Haven't they damaged this Earth enough over the past few decades?'

Leike sat in sullen silence. At this time, we weren't supposed to talk about Semipalatinsk.

'I think so too,' Nikolai scratched his head and said sadly. 'A bomb... an atomic one doesn't choose nationalities; it's a nightmare for everyone.'

'No one will be able to hide from it,' added Leike. 'A nuclear test on the steppe is a crime.'

We all became afraid, and in the difficult moment vodka once again came to our aid. With tumblers to hand, we sat in the baths releasing our anger by whipping each other's backs with birch leaves.

That reminds me of another story I told my friends that day.

'Once, during the war, we were on a reconnaissance mission and crept up to an old farmstead. After making sure there were no Germans around, we knocked on the door of the farthest hut. The owner was delighted and terrified at the same time. He told us that later that day some German soldiers were coming to use his banya. We hid in the forest behind the hut and waited.

That evening, the Germans came on their motorbikes, talking and laughing noisily. Then they went into the banya, leaving one man to stand guard. We waited for a little longer and then began to creep closer. My compatriots quickly shot the guard and took their positions, whilst Ivan and I went into the bathhouse. The soldiers had left their clothes and weapons at the entrance. Ivan, our brave commander, slammed open the door to the steam room. Seeing us, the naked Germans panicked. Ivan grabbed one of them and threw him towards me. I killed him and put on his overcoat. Before I left, I looked at the other Germans. They were frozen in terror and staring at us. It was as if they didn't know what was happening. Ordinary human faces, hot steam and the smell of birch leaves all reminded me of my old life, but the next moment, Ivan threw a grenade into the steam room, slammed the door shut, and we ran. There was a mas-

A HUNDRED YEARS ON THE STEPPE 229

sive explosion, and the banya was engulfed in flames and smoke. *It's an awful way to die; but what else could I do?* I thought, comforting myself. Still, this day has stuck in my mind, and I can't forget it.

'Once, we went over the front lines,' Nikolai said gloomily, but then he fell silent and stared at the wall. It was clear he was finding it difficult to speak.

'No, I have to say this. I've never told anyone before, but it's time,' he continued in a quiet voice. 'Once, we went over the front lines into fascist territory and found the ditch where they kept their weapons. The machine guns were camouflaged under leaves and grass. We lay flat on the ground. We waited and watched, but it was completely silent. Then, we saw a German sleeping. My commander ordered me to kill him. I crept up to him and saw that he was only a young lad. I took my knife out to stick it into his throat, but I couldn't do it. I don't know what got into me, but my hand wouldn't move. He was sleeping so peacefully, so sweetly. I told myself: You cursed fascist; you've invaded our land and killed innocent people, but I still couldn't bring myself to kill this boy. So what could I do? An order was an order, and I had to carry it out. If you don't kill your enemy, he will kill you… I put my knife to the chest of the young German and pushed it in as hard as I could. The blade jagged through his young body like a knife through butter. The boy opened his eyes wide and stared at me. I couldn't look away from such innocent eyes. He died before he could say a word. My comrades came to me, and we carried on with our mission, but that boy has stayed with me forever. I can go months without thinking about him, but then I'll see his eyes again, and I won't sleep for days.'

All three of us became miserable, but vodka helped numb the pain as it always did. We couldn't do anything now; it had already happened. This had been our fate.

'It's strange,' said Leike. 'We're friends now and live happily together, but what would've happened if we'd met on the front lines? What if we'd been in opposite trenches? We would have shot at each other without a second thought, wouldn't we?'

We all sat in silence and imagined what might have been.

'What could we have done?' Nikolai said softly. 'Orders were orders, remember?'

'So, what about our friendship? Would we shoot each other now if some psychopath told us to?' replied Leike. 'Our descendants would say that our people were all pigs, Nazis, chauvinists.'

'Enough of that!' I cried. 'You can't blame a whole nation for a few people's sins. Life has taught me time and time again that there are no bad nations; every nation is made up of good and bad people. There are no bad nations, but there are bad politics. There are no bad people, but there are bad actions. People's bad actions come from a bad education, not their nationality.'

'I understand you, Asanbai; you're right,' said Leike. 'Once, in the autumn of 1944, some Kazakhs nearly killed me.'

Nikolai and I were shocked.

A HUNDRED YEARS ON THE STEPPE

'Yes, the same kind Kazakhs who took us in and helped us to settle here. What happened there was a notice pinned to a house that a soldier had been killed in action. His relatives were mourning their boy, and the whole village, including the people who'd been deported here, shared their pain. A few days later, two brothers of the boy who died, fourteen or fifteen-year-old boys, a year or two older than me, saw me out on the steppe while they were looking for their cows. They swore at me and insulted me, calling me a fascist and a murderer. I told them I was no fascist and was just a German. They said that all Germans were fascists and murderers, that we were a lower race.'

'That's what I'm talking about,' I said. 'When a man hates another man, it's a drama, but when a nation hates another nation, it's a tragedy. Nothing good ever comes of hatred.'

'Hurt by their brother's death, the boys threw themselves at me. They were bigger and stronger, pushed me to the ground and punched me and kicked me. I don't know if they wanted to kill me, but they would have crippled me for sure. Then, we heard a scream from behind us, and as the brothers turned around, I staggered to my feet and tried to limp away. The boys moved to attack me again, but by then, someone was standing between us. It was Batima-apa, your mother, Asanbai. She shouted at the boys, and they didn't dare to make her any angrier. She told them there was a reason why we'd arrived on the steppe, and it wasn't because we'd chosen to.

"'This war isn't their fault," Batima told them. "Not all Germans are fascists, and it isn't Leike's fault your brother was killed. So think about that, make up, and learn to live together."

'The brothers left me alone after that. That's how your mother saved me.'

I was touched by Leike's story. Nikolai also lowered his head.

'You know, Leike,' I said. 'At about the same time as that, in November 1944 I ended up in the prisoner of war camp. A German officer who wanted to shoot me was standing a few paces away toying with his automatic pistol. I prayed under my breath. Then, for some reason I'll never know, he threw his gun up in the air, caught it in one hand, put it back in its holster and walked away. I can't explain it, but I think there's a connection between these two events that we can't understand. In saving you, my mother probably saved me too. Her kindness to you found its way into the German officer and saved my life.'

'It could be,' said Nikolai.

We sat without talking for a while, remembering the events of those distant years. Then, as always, we drank to forget them.

One day, Zoya came to me to ask a surprising favour. She was very nervous, and her words tumbled out of her mouth all at once. A colour television had appeared in the shop, and her children really wanted it. Colour televisions weren't easy to come by. Firstly, these magical screens were expensive, and secondly, you needed to be on a list to re-

A HUNDRED YEARS ON THE STEPPE

ceive one, a list on which priority was given to veterans of the Great War. Zoya's idea was simple: I would go to the department in charge of consumer goods, they would sign a form for me, and I would take this form to the shop and collect the wonderful new television. I would then give it to Leike, and that same evening the whole building, our three families, could sit together and watch programmes from Moscow, drinking together and sharing plates of cucumbers. Zoya's request made me uncomfortable, but I couldn't upset a kind neighbour and the mother of Gerold, our little genius.

The head of the department for consumer goods greeted me warmly and listened carefully to my words.

'Who could deserve this colourful miracle more than you?' he said.

Without delay, he called the shop and told them to sell me their only colour television.

When I arrived at the shop, a small group of women had gathered there. They weren't pleased to see me, greeted me begrudgingly, and watched eagle-eyed to see what would happen next. I felt uncomfortable again. Reluctantly, the shopkeeper gave me the television in its box.

'There she is,' he said. 'Seven hundred and fifty-five roubles. Take it now and pay me tomorrow.'

I took the television and started to walk out of the shop, when I heard a shy voice behind me:

'Why do you only give the good items to the veterans?'

More people soon joined in.

'I've had enough of these veterans. They're taking

234   *Bayangali Alimzhanov*

everything!'

'And we're left with crumbs.'

'It's as if young people don't exist.'

I was stunned by such a crude attack, but the women hadn't finished and they turned to me.

'Do we deserve a colour television less than you?'

'It'd be all right if you were buying it for yourself, but why use your age to help your neighbours?'

'You should be ashamed of yourself!'

Weighed down by the television, I left the shop as quickly as I could. As I walked, I could still hear the angry crowd behind me.

'They've lost their conscience completely.'

'Or lost their minds!'

I hadn't been in such a hurry since I'd had to escape from German bullets. I wanted to run away and hide in a corner under my big sheepskin overcoat. My conscience began to torture me. How had I, a respected aksakal, become the target of such an ugly row? Then, an interesting idea came to me. Who loses his mind first: someone who is very bright, or someone with no mind at all? If you have no mind, then what do you have to lose? So, intelligent people must lose their minds first. I kept thinking about this, laughing at myself, and probably, without noticing, I was losing my mind. I couldn't let that happen.

I told my neighbours I'd decided to go back on Zoya's plan. They were upset, but they understood.

But then, my favourite daughter-in-law Bayan came in. She'd thought everything through with perfect logic. Why

A HUNDRED YEARS ON THE STEPPE

235

should the permission from the Department for Consumer Goods go to waste? Our neighbours may not have been eligible for that television, but I had every right to buy it. My children gently pleaded with me not to give up the colour television and to keep it for myself as I was able to do. We could then sell the old black-and-white one. Once again, I gave in.

That wasn't the end of the story, though, as there was another war veteran in the neighbourhood. Many years ago, he'd moved to Stepnyak from the village of Tassu. After he was refused a television by the department that had given me mine, he went straight to Zygmund Zbignievovich Kachanowski. Zigzag, of course, listened to him and promised to help. He was nervous; leaving a war veteran without household items could get him into more trouble.

In the shop, we bumped into Zigzag. He was looking very worried indeed.

'This is very uncomfortable. I'm afraid they won't understand us,' he said pointing his index finger at the ceiling, his left eye flickering and his right eye closed.

This is how I avoided being caught up in a scandal, which I'd always hated and tried my whole life to avoid. I've always thought that bickering and taunting, especially over petty things was beneath human dignity. I'd lived my life without bothering about petty things and was always happy to leave expensive items to those who lusted after them. This case was different, though, women from two families wanted this television, and we, the poor veterans, had ended up in the middle of them.

I've never understood how people can fight over mere household items. I always laughed to myself at those who'd make a scene at the Department for Consumer Goods in order to get their hands on some imported junk or spend all day waiting in a queue for some sought-after furniture or clothes. But this was reality for us. *Back then, in the war, we ate bread together and took bullets together. Now, we're fighting with each other over this rubbish? Did we keep our nation alive so we could argue about televisions?* I thought. I felt ill.

I found the only logical way out of the dilemma: I gave up my colour television voluntarily. The other veteran, who was twenty years younger than me, was thrilled, and so was Kachanowski. My son and daughter-in-law sulked for a couple of days, but I think people respected me for my decision.

'Well done, ata. You did the right thing.'

It was nice to hear these words and my soul felt lighter.

Sometimes I felt as if my life was a lottery. Sometimes I had big wins, but I suffered losses as well. For all the ups and down, though, it was my life, and I loved it.

I don't remember exactly when, but around this time the authorities started to give away Zaporozhets cars to war veterans, but not to all of them, of course. There were a lot of very complicated conditions. Reading the rules for qualifying for one was like finding your way out of a labyrinth. As soon as you got your hopes up, the Minotaur would appear from behind a corner and knock you down. A few old veterans were lucky, though, and were given a shiny Zaporozhets to drive home in.

With Victory Day approaching, Aigali and Bayan

A HUNDRED YEARS ON THE STEPPE 237

wouldn't let go of the idea of me - that's to say us - having a car. At the time, having your own car was such a rarity that most people didn't even dream of it. I knew that I probably wouldn't be allowed one.

In those days, official documents were worshipped; once a representative of the Soviet authorities had put their signature and stamp on a piece of paper, no one could challenge a single word of it. Bayan had to go through an ordeal just to change a little mistake in her passport. She was born in a shepherd's hut in a winter pasture a very long way from Stepnyak, and it was several weeks before her father could go to apply for all her documents. At the passport office, he proudly said that his daughter had been born on the last day of the second month of winter. When the secretary recorded the date, she wrote down, of all things, the 30th of February! Bayan finished school, received her passport, enrolled in medical school, received her degree, registered as a nurse and worked in a hospital, and through all this, no one noticed that her date of birth doesn't exist. When Aigali was preparing to marry her, the registry office refused to change the document, and issued a marriage certificate with Bayan's date of birth recorded as the 30th of February. Everyone understood that this was absurd, but her documents were Soviet, so they were sacred.

It was only after Perestroika that her passport was changed, and a real date of birth, the 28th of February was included. My son used to joke that they should have put the 29th of February so he'd only have to buy her presents once every four years. We laughed, but the Soviet phrase, 'Not allowed' was a fearful one. Whenever it was said to us, no one dared to ask any more questions.

My son and daughter-in-law wouldn't stop talking about the car. Aigali got upset with me, and Bayan looked at me crossly.

'Father,' Aigali said. 'Do you really not care that your children and grandchildren have to go everywhere on foot? You defended the country in the war and spilt your blood for us. They should give you ten cars.'

'I wasn't fighting for a car.'

'Yes, I know that. But the government is giving cars to deserving veterans; why do you refuse to claim yours?'

Aigali's blood was boiling. Bayan listened to us silently, and every so often puffed out her cheeks softly as if blowing on her husband's fire to provide it with oxygen.

'But you know that I won't be allowed,' I said, exasperated and feeling that I was losing the argument.

'It depends on how you look at it. Maybe you will,' Bayan's sweet voice joined the conversation.

I treated her like she was my own daughter. She was brought up in a lovely Kazakh family, inherited all their best traditions, and was always loving towards us. Her work ethic was phenomenal; when she was working, we could never stop her, and she'd never rest until she'd finished. She was the mother to five of my grandchildren and was an integral part of our family. For her, I was almost ready to put myself through all the medical examinations that I'd need to pass before I asked for this Zaporozhets.

'She's right!' exclaimed my son.

A HUNDRED YEARS ON THE STEPPE

'Remember the old man from Tassu? They gave him a car,' Bayan continued, 'and yet you say you won't be allowed one. It wasn't in the war that he got his limp.'

'Yes, everyone knows that. Years after the war he got drunk one night and crashed his motorcycle,' my son said. 'But twenty years later there are almost no witnesses left, so the man found some relatives in high places that changed his medical notes. Now, he's riding around in a Zap. How are you less deserving? You've given more for our motherland. You were almost named as a Hero of the Soviet Union. Why should you have to walk everywhere in your old age?'

'You're both right,' I agreed 'but what can I do? I'm sure they won't al…'

'Just agree to go for the health check. We'll take care of the rest,' Aigali said animatedly. 'These days it's easy to get people to "allow" you things.'

'What do you mean?'

'We've found some people who can help us get the car. You just go for your examination; then they'll do what needs to be done.'

'Stop that right now! Don't you dare even think of such a thing,' I shouted. 'I didn't spill my blood in the war to get things for free. I'm not paying a bribe to get that car.'

Aigali ground his teeth. He didn't say anything, but I knew what he wanted to tell me: 'Father, you're an idiot. You lived as an idiot, and you'll die as one.'

Bayan cried as she cleared the table. Aigali left the room.

Left on my own, I rest my head on my goose-feather pillow alone with my thoughts. At least, in acting honestly,

I'd honoured the memory of the men I fought with.

Suddenly, I heard Salim's voice in my head:

'Honest, you say? To whom? To the cruel Soviet powers who drowned our steppe in blood and killed millions of our innocent people?'

'Maybe the conscience of the politicians was dirty,' I answered him, 'but the blood of the soldiers who died in that war is sacred.'

We all felt bad after that argument. We tried to heal each other's hurt feelings, but some resentment remained. Aigali was the most upset, especially when he had to go somewhere.

'So, old man,' he'd say, 'who shall we ask to drive us to the village today? Maybe the man from Tassu? Of course, if we had a Zaporozhets like him we could drive ourselves.'

I felt guilty, especially to Bayan, who I loved like a daughter. She never said anything, but before every journey I felt as if she was angry with me.

Eventually, I gave in again and let my ecstatic son and daughter-in-law take me to Kokshetau, where the doctors examined me. I admit that I was scared, and was angry with myself for letting them win, but they treated me well. They checked me all over, whispered to each other, scratched their heads, and then told me their findings.

'Ata, you've served your country ten times over, and have had enough illnesses to put down five men. It'd be fair if everyone like you received a car, but, unfortunately, you're not allowed. You see, your wounds don't fall into the right category. If you'd hurt your leg, for example, it would be a

A HUNDRED YEARS ON THE STEPPE
241

different matter. Please forgive us.'

I had my answer. Feeling ashamed of myself, I didn't say a word on the way home.

'What a stupid rule!' cried Bayan. 'If someone has an injured leg, they give him a car, but if he has a wound in his head, he's not allowed. Your head is more important than your leg.'

'Father, why didn't you think of that when you were fighting? Why did you put your head in front of that bullet and not your leg?'

We laughed.

Soon, fate helped us out again. I won a car in the lottery!

Offers to play the republic's lottery, a thirty-kopeck ticket and a chance to win money and prizes were sent to us relentlessly by post, usually on the same day as we received our pensions. Every month, for the fun of it, I bought a ticket. I'd carefully place the ticket in my big leather wallet and keep it safe until the results were announced. Khalima and Nagima would both laugh at me each time I didn't win anything. My grandchildren were fascinated by the beautiful tickets. They used to collect them and pretend they were money. Still, I hoped that one day I'd win - more than anything to see the look on my wives' faces. With each successive disappointment, I hoped more and more.

One day, I went to the post office to collect my pension. There was a small queue of other pensioners, and in front of me was the old man from Tassu who'd claimed the colour television. After he'd got his money and was about to place the notes in his wallet, the woman at the desk called to him:

'And the lottery? You've forgotten to play the lottery,'

The old man seemed annoyed by the suggestion, but he bought a ticket nonetheless, and handed over all of his kopecks.

'There aren't enough kopecks here,' the woman said. 'You'll have to change a rouble.'

'I still remember the sound as she poured a handful of five-kopeck coins onto the desk in front of her. The old man looked at his money forlornly; he clearly didn't want to sacrifice a crisp red ten-rouble note for all that copper.'

He lost his temper and shouted at the woman.

'What the hell do I need your lottery for? I've had enough; every month you try to make me play, and I've never won a kopeck!'

He threw his lottery ticket back at her.

'Please understand,' the woman, herself almost a pensioner, replied firmly; 'I'm not doing it for myself. They give us targets, and we have to meet them. Who else apart from you is going to buy one? We give you your pension and you love us, but if we ask for just a little something in return, you shout at us; it isn't fair.'

The woman looked hurt and put the ticket to one side. The old man swept the remaining kopecks from the wooden desk into his wallet and left the post office jangling and muttering to himself. I felt bad for the woman, who for years had cheerfully counted out our pensions for us. After she'd given me my money, I addressed to her warmly.

A HUNDRED YEARS ON THE STEPPE 243

'Two tickets this time, please.'

The smile came back to her face as she gave me two beautiful pieces of paper, one of which was the ticket that the rude man from Tassu hadn't taken.

'Good luck,' she said. 'I hope you win the car to spite that cheapskate.'

I did, with the very same ticket.

The car, a Moskvich, was not just a way to travel; it was an enviable status symbol. In it, we travelled thousands of kilometres on the dusty roads of the steppe.

In the 1990s, the rouble began to fall in value. To begin with, no one could believe that the rouble, which we all thought was unshakeable, could lose its value. It happened, though, and those who kept their money in banks lost their savings in a matter of weeks. I remember how one livestock farmer who'd saved for decades to buy himself a car went to Zigzag for help. He'd saved up twenty-two thousand roubles and was on the waiting list to finally receive his Zhiguli. As soon as he got to the top of the list, inflation took hold, and his savings lost most of their value.

Trying to be kind, Zigzag offered him a big refrigerator which was on sale at the department for household items for twenty-two thousand roubles. The farmer was beside himself with anger

'Is that a joke? I've worked all these years for a car, not a fridge; so give me my car! He barked.

Zigzag replied that he couldn't; the prices for cars had become unthinkably high. The farmer didn't believe that the Communist Party and the Soviet authorities couldn't regulate prices and could let the rouble sink so low. He didn't take the refrigerator, expecting the rouble to recover soon; two weeks later, the fridge cost one hundred and sixty thousand roubles. This is how people who'd worked honestly for years lost their savings. Nearly everyone suffered in this way. Our people, despite being so tolerant, had to suffer this too. The fall of the rouble was the warning that big changes were about to happen.

At this time, the first Kazakh went into space. It was a celebration for us, a moment we'd waited thirty years for. Beginning with Gagarin, dozens of Soviet cosmonauts had flown into space from Baikonur on the Kazakh steppe. There hadn't been a single Kazakh among them. We complained, dreamt, and waited for justice. When the time came, when Tokhtar Aubakirov flew to the heavens he took the soul of the Kazakh people with him. As well as being the first Kazakh astronaut, he was the USSR's last. Even more interestingly, he flew with a Russian, Aleksandr Volkov, and an Austrian, Franz Fibeck. My neighbours loved this, and we drank several tumblers to them as we bathed and dreamt of flying into space ourselves.

A little while later there was a celebration in the town dedicated to the flight of our first astronaut. They invited me to attend on behalf of Stepnyak's veterans.

'We'll write this event into the town's archives;' Kachanowski told me, 'and, of course, we'll mention you.'

'You write down everything that happens in the district?' I asked, having never heard about the archive before.

Zigzag gave a knowing smile and pointed his index fin-

A HUNDRED YEARS ON THE STEPPE 245

ger at the ceiling.

'No, not everything, my dear Asanbai,' he said. 'We only write down what we think is important and necessary.'

'What events do you think are important and necessary?' I asked.

Zigzag looked nervous again.

'It isn't up to me; it's the district Party committee. The most important events are ones that leaders from Moscow and from the regional committees attend.'

'So, events that don't have anything to do with the Communist Party aren't important?' I scoffed.

I could feel my pulse racing.

'Well, how can I put it,' Zigzag mumbled evasively. 'Of course, there are some events that Party officials don't come to, and we still include them in the archive. But when the real leaders come…' Zigzag looked carefully around, raised his index finger to the ceiling again, and said, almost in a whisper, 'that's the archive we want.'

Later that night, I thought for a long time about what Zygmund Zbignievich Kachanowski had told me. It had opened my eyes, because as the archive was compiled so our history was written, and as far as Kazakh history was concerned, the Soviet regime was a continuation of the Tsarist era. They had the same method: only what the Tsarist leadership and then the Communists thought was important was included in archives and became part of our written history. That's why there's nothing in these archives about my forefathers during Tsarist times, or other talented or heroic Kazakhs from the Soviet period. Our archives were created with the strict instruction that our colonisers write our history for us. Of course, I don't deny that the documents in the archives are true and important, but this is only one truth. Another truth is that the real lives of the Kazakh people weren't of interest. You won't read about life as it was lived it in any archives.

This is why our people have always recorded our history ourselves, passing down the stories of our ancestors' lives from generation to generation. I'm tortured by those historians who believe everything that's written on paper is a historical fact and everything that isn't is just a story. If we would only think and analyse, then we'd understand that what's written in history books was once just a story too. But who wrote it? When did they write it? And is what they wrote true? What if it isn't? Even worse, what if the person who told the story lied, made mistakes or missed out facts? Then believing the archived documents and learning about history from them is impossible; it isn't objective.

Time went on and more interesting materials were added to our archives. There were more tumultuous political events, each one bigger than the last. The USSR was falling apart: one after another the Soviet republics which had been brothers announced their independence. We woke up each day frightened of what would happen next.

A HUNDRED YEARS ON THE STEPPE 247

Independence

On a freezing December evening in 1991, we learnt that our motherland, Kazakhstan had received its independence. When we heard this news on the television, at first we couldn't believe our ears. I lowered myself quietly onto the floor; I probably sat down to stop myself from falling. I felt incredible tiredness and a spiritual serenity. I knew that a great historical event had occurred; a new country had been born, and the dream of all Kazakhs for the last three centuries had come true. My soul, so damaged throughout my life, was flooded with soft but profound happiness.

The next day, I invited Nikolai and Lyuba, Leike and Zoya for dinner. Khalima and Nagima sat next to me, whilst my great-grandchildren played and entertained our guests. I'd asked Aigali to buy a big bottle of Russian vodka and Bayan prepared a Kazakh meal of horsemeat. I was ninety-one, Nikolai was seventy and Leon was sixty. We were all old, but to me, they'd always been young men. Nikolai had put on weight and his hair had turned grey. The doctors had told him he had some serious illnesses.

'Asanbai, I have gastritis, pancreatitis, esophagitis, bronchitis and arthritis,' he used to laugh about his condition. 'I know one of those means dog in Kazakh, and I feel like one of them is trying to chase me off your land.'

'It's just the German bullets and the trench food coming back to haunt you,' I replied. 'You should know that Kazakh dogs never bite our guests.'

On this day, though. It felt as if Nikolai the Third was

finding it hard to laugh. His mind was elsewhere, and he didn't even congratulate me on our independence.

'What's wrong with you? Another headache, or has Lyuba been arguing with you?' I tried to cheer him up as I opened another bottle.

'Well...' he mumbled, wiping the sweat from his forehead with a handkerchief.

'You haven't heard the news?' I asked as I filled his tumbler.

'What, who have they arrested now?' he asked, distracted.

'Not that; can you believe they've freed us?' I said excitedly.

'Kazakhstan has become an independent country,' Leike explained, 'and I was the first to congratulate Asanbai. My kind neighbour, my friend for life is now a citizen of the Republic of Kazakhstan!'

'I'm a citizen of the Soviet Union' barked Nikolai.

'You don't seem very happy that we've received our independence.' I said to my old friend.

Nikolai, the Russian settler, the proud worker, the dedicated communist was silent for a long time.

'I'm not, if you want the truth,' he finally said. 'To break up such a big and powerful country... You can't drive a car if the wheels have fallen off.'

'But every man should be the boss in his own home, shouldn't he?'

'Of course,' Nikolai replied.

'So, every nation should have its own government.

A HUNDRED YEARS ON THE STEPPE   *249*

What's so bad about that? Isn't it natural?'

Nikolai didn't reply; he just took a deep drag of his cigarette. Heavy thoughts filled his head as the tobacco smoke filled his lungs.

'You're our friend,' I continued. 'Kazakhstan is your home, so why are you torturing yourself like Tsar Nikolai before his abdication? We're going to live together the way we always have, in peace. The only difference is that now we're equal citizens in a new, independent country, Kazakhstan! So, let's drink. Russia's control is finished, and so should this bottle of their vodka be.'

Nikolai wasn't laughing.

'If it's happened, then it's happened,' he said sadly, holding out his massive fist. 'But we had you like *this* for three centuries, and now it's gone. It's an insult to my country.'

'Well, in that case... for three hundred years we Kazakhs had Mother Russia under our control. Maybe you don't know about that either, and will say that it never happened.'

Nikolai grunted.

'There was a time when our ancestors ruled over Muscovy and the whole of the great country they called *Rus*. The Golden Horde of Batu Khan contained our ancestors from all the Kazakh clans. Then, for three hundred years the Kazakhs were subjects of the Russian Empire. History repeats itself. So, it's a draw now, three hundred all. I think we can call it quits.'

Leike applauded.

Nikolai's face turned crimson. Then, he burst out

laughing.

'I think that's enough of ruling over each other,' I said. 'Let's live as friends, equals and good neighbours. What do you think? In any case, the Kazakhs can't live without the Russians, and you can't live without us. How many millennia have we spent next to each other; how many thousand kilometres of border and how many stories connect us?'

'We're all for friendship,' Nikolai said.

After getting our grievances off our chests, we, the two neighbours along with Leike drank a toast to the friendship between nations. A treaty on Russo-Kazakh-German friendship was signed.

'You know what, neighbours?' I said, looking at the half-empty bottle of vodka. 'I'm giving this up. The Soviets taught us to drink, and as they're leaving, let this habit go with them.'

'Well, how many times have I told you that you could never out-drink us?' laughed Nikolai.

'And I'm glad,' I replied, pouring the rest of the vodka into our glasses. 'So, this is my last drink, to see Soviet power and the Communist Party on their way.'

The next day, I began to read the Quran. I decided to help the town with its application to build a mosque.

A new era had arrived, the era of our independence. Being an independent country, a free people is such happiness, but do the younger generation understand what old people like me had to go through to get here? People who don't know what it's like to live under another's thumb can be surprised by our elation, but those who have experienced

A HUNDRED YEARS ON THE STEPPE

it will understand. What a joy it is to follow Allah and no one else. What a joy it is to speak our own language and create our own culture. Despite the awful difficulties, the grandfathers and grandmothers, fathers and mothers have passed the best of Kazakhstan to the next generation, and the people who wanted to combine many different countries into an artificial country have been overthrown. This has been our nation's victory.

Now, I often think about how precious it is, how unique to be guided by your grandparents. I think that grandfathers and grandmothers have an obligation to teach their grandchildren and great-grandchildren about all the good things life has taught them; about everything in their nation's soul that is kind and special. When we sign up for our pensions, we can still be useful. When we grow old and have grandchildren and great-grandchildren to teach, that's when the happiest time of our lives begins.

We all need an objective history unspoilt by other's interests. However harsh and frightening the seventy-three years of the Soviet Union were, they are part of our history too. Through everything, life went on: people lived, worked, hurt, laughed, loved, and raised several generations. The talented among us achieved a lot during this time, so no one should simply attempt to erase this part of history. Nor should they believe all the stories that biased academics have been known to tell. History doesn't care who might enjoy reading about her. History should be accepted the way that she really is. We should analyse her, try to understand her, and explain her to others and learn from her, not bully her

252   *Bayangali Alimzhanov*

or ignore her.

Nikolai Borisovich Nesterov told us a touching story:

'Once in battle, an enemy shell exploded nearby. I was seriously wounded and my uniform caught fire. I thought it was the end. Suddenly, I felt someone carrying me. I saw that it was my comrade, Satur Rakhimov. He was a Tajik and spoke Russian badly. He was carrying me whilst the Germans kept firing at us. By the time we reached our trench, I'd lost consciousness. I woke up in a military hospital. I never saw Satur again. After the war, I often thought about him. I wanted to see him and thank him, but I couldn't find him. I had no address and no other information. Then, one day I dreamt about him and heard his voice. In the dream, he told me his address. I woke up and quickly scribbled it down. I sent a letter to that address, and he replied! I found him, and we became like brothers. I went to see him, and he was overjoyed to see me. Then, he came to visit me. That's our story. And now, we're in different countries,' he concluded sadly.

'That doesn't stop you from being friends, though,' I said.

'That's life,' said Leike. '*So ist das leiben*,'

'True; that's life,' agreed Nikolai.

Oralman

In the summer of 1992, the first *Kurultai*, an assembly of Kazakhs was held in Alma-Ata. Kazakhs returned to their

A HUNDRED YEARS ON THE STEPPE
253

homeland from all over the world. We called them *oralman* - 'those who returned.'

I participated in the Kurultai as part of a delegation from our region. They put white yurts in the grounds of the National Exhibition Centre, the VDNK, and the new President of the Republic of Kazakhstan, Nursultan Nazarbayev, spoke passionately to a crowd of Kazakhs living in many countries. There was also a speech by an aksakal from Turkey, Khalifa Altai, the first man to translate the Quran into Kazakh, who reminded us that in the face of incredible hardships, Kazakhs had migrated all the way from Altai to Anatolia. Those unforgettable days of the first Kurultai were filled with emotional words and tears of joy.

In the group of Kazakhs from Turkey, I saw a grey-bearded old man who could barely walk, hunched over a wooden walking stick. As he passed me, the old man's eyes lit up.

'Asanbai? Asanbai, older brother!'

I couldn't place the man's face, but I recognised his voice. It was Salim! We embraced, and wouldn't leave each other's arms. The man helping him to walk was one of his sons. We talked for hours, not only listening intently but interrupting each other with tales of our own adventures.

'I came here under another name, the one I took on when I left. I'm probably still thought of as a war criminal here,' Salim told me.

As he said those words, he looked around warily. I smiled; I knew how hard it was to break these habits.

He told me that at the end of the war he went to Turkey, where he stayed. He married a Kazakh woman and had two more sons and two daughters. Now, he had grandchildren and great-grandchildren but had never been reunited with the children he had in the Karakum Desert before the war.

When the Kurultai was over, I took Salim and his son home to meet my family. He spent a day with us, and we stayed up all night. I still remember everything that he told me.

'I often dream about the home we grew up in, our parents, brothers and sisters, and all of our neighbours,' he said. 'In my dreams, I'm still a child running across the endless steppe through the blooming flowers. Then, I'm older and riding my favourite gelding with the wind blowing in my face. Then, suddenly, I'm in the military clothes which I've spent so much of my long life wearing. They're covered in blood. Then, I'm a boy again, and my horse is galloping, taking me away from the horror.'

As he spoke, it felt as if we were small children once more, racing our horses on the steppe with our friends.

'As I've gotten older, I've dreamt more and more about our sister, Khalilya and the officer I killed in that duel. I see Khalilya with tears running down her face, begging me to let him live. I still shoot him, and then I wake up in a cold sweat. Asanbai, do you think we should have let them go together?'

I couldn't answer. This memory still tortured me too. I can still see Khalilya's lovely face and the outline of that officer.

'I regret that in my life I've had to kill people,' he continued. 'In my youth, I deluded myself. I told myself they

A HUNDRED YEARS ON THE STEPPE 255

weren't really people, they were bloodthirsty enemies. But as time has passed, I've come to realise that we're all people; that we don't have to shoot at each other, that we can understand each other and live in peace. I can't change the past, though. Brother, we've been dealt a harsh fate. I don't know why life has played such cruel tricks on us. Now, in my final years, I'm asking the souls of those I've killed to forgive me.'

The next day, Aigali took us for a ride in the Moskvich, across the steppe where we grew up, back to Kenashchi. As dusk fell, we went to the old cemetery in the village of Bulakbasy in Stepnyak. This is where our ancestors are buried. We sat on the grass under a statue of Birzhan-sal and read prayers.

'You haven't asked what happened to my back,' said Salim. 'One evening, when I was already over seventy, I went for a walk in a park. It was a quiet, warm spring evening. Suddenly, I heard gunfire, screaming, and the sound of police sirens. Before I knew what was happening, I'd been hit in the back. I don't know how; I just remember writhing on the ground in agony. They took me to the hospital and operated on me. That's how I damaged my spine. Apparently, some boys from a radical group had gathered in the centre of town to protest about the authorities, and government forces opened fire on them. It felt as if one of the bullets I'd fired during the war had come back to haunt me.

Salim sighed deeply.

'You know what I'd like to say as my very last words before I die? I'd shout at the whole world: "People, don't ever shoot at one another!"'

I listened to Salim without interrupting. My little brother looked ancient now, but I could still see the carefree troublemaker I'd shared my happy childhood with at our parents' home. It was hard to believe he'd grown up to be a warrior and a sniper. What he was telling me now came from his heart, and the words were hurting him. I understood them; they were close to my heart too. Sometimes, I wanted to shout at all of humanity to stop killing each other.

Tired from talking so much, Salim rested for a while and filled his lungs with the steppe's aromatic air.

'Brother,' he continued, 'if only you knew how often I've prayed to the Almighty to let me visit my homeland one last time; to walk on the steppe, see my family and loved ones, and read the Quran at our ancestors' graves. Then, I could die happy. You understand me, how this longing for home has eaten away at my soul through all these years I've been away. Now, I'm happy and infinitely grateful to Allah that he has written into my fate that I can kiss this earth and stay inside her forever.'

I listened to his every word without understanding what he was doing. Salim quietly recited a prayer and then rolled gently to the ground. He opened his arms to embrace the grass and lay there serenely.

After a few moments, I realised he was gone.

And so, Salim, my brother and my hero, reached the end of his challenging life at the age of ninety. We laid him to rest at our ancestors' cemetery, close to Birzhan-sal.

A few years later, all of his children came to live in their homeland, Kazakhstan.

A HUNDRED YEARS ON THE STEPPE   *257*

A Moment and an Eternity

The new era brought with it new problems, but that's another story for the next generation to tell. *They didn't let me live peacefully; they can at least let me die peacefully*, I once thought to myself. Elections were taking place, and different candidates were bothering me. All I wanted to do was live happily with my grandchildren and great-grandchildren.

In the first few years of Kazakhstan's independence, we went through many difficulties. The old ways fell apart, and the new ways were only just beginning. The economy was struggling, and people were in a rebellious mood. Most of all, communism had been replaced by capitalism. People changed, and their relationships did too, but we stayed calm through all the difficulties and looked to the future with hope. We understood that freedom and independence were the most important things. We wouldn't have exchanged them for anything in the world.

There were still those who were unhappy that our formerly 'Soviet,' but actually colonised republic had become a free country. Their voices were everywhere. Without a hint of shame, chauvinistic political figures began dragging our people through the mud. As long as we'd been slaves, Kazakhs had always been good; now we were free, we were suddenly bad. Where we could, we stood up for ourselves, often angrily. Those moments were appreciated by the leaders of other nations, who thanked the Kazakhs and wished us well with our independence.

Leike once spoke on the radio and talked emotionally

and animatedly in our defence:

'Without the Kazakhs, we would all have died of hunger or cold in the 1940s. You should be ashamed of yourselves for talking down this kind, I would say the kindest nation on earth. Through all their hardships they've cared for so many people, not thinking about their nationality or religion. They've taken us in, fed us, clothed us, and often saved our lives. I'll always be on the Kazakhs' side.'

We were very grateful to him for those words.

Soon after this, we moved out of our bunkhouse. People used to say they were built by Japanese and German prisoners of war and those who Stalin sent here. They built them well. The demolition crew began to knock them down, but they couldn't complete the job. They took the roofs off, and somehow tore down the top parts of the metre-thick walls, but they couldn't remove the foundations. They still sit there, the ruins looking frightening as the sun sets over them or the moon illuminates them. Why demolish them when they were so well-built and were a readymade home for young couples? Were our new leaders "building a new world" again? Couldn't they just have built more new homes without destroying what belonged to our generation? C'est la vie.

We said goodbye to the bunkhouse and moved into our separate homes. We were still neighbours, though, Asanbai Bektemirov in the middle, the Russian, Nikolai Nesterov on the right, and the German, Leon Vilvert on the left.

I love standing by the river and watching the water flow. Time, like the river, flows without stopping, washing

A HUNDRED YEARS ON THE STEPPE

259

away every moment into the eternity that comes after. What is our life, a moment or an eternity?

At the start of our lives when we were young and innocent, we revered the rich landowners. We must be grateful to the rich Kazakhs for never letting their fellow clansmen fall into the iron grip of famine. Some of them were good people, some were bad, but the fact is that when these landowners were around no one died of hunger. They couldn't die; even if the landowner was greedy and didn't want to share his food with his poor relatives, he wasn't able to because his animals grazed on the steppe, and you can't hide a herd of horses or a flock of sheep in your pocket. When hunger forced the nomads to get back on their horses, no one could stop them from going hunting. So, it was easier for everyone if they simply shared their food. Even during extremely harsh winters when most of the livestock were wiped out people didn't die from hunger because there were still enough animals to survive on.

Then, the revolution came and everything was turned upside down. Now, people were told that the landowners were their enemies. The rich were either dispossessed or killed. For the next seventy years, all of my adult life, we were brainwashed into thinking that rich people were oppressors, bloodsuckers, and enemies of humanity. We were told that poor people were the best, the most intelligent, the kindest. Several generations of Soviet people were raised to believe this was the only acceptable point of view.

Now, everything has turned upside down again. We live under capitalism, which we fought against for our whole lives. Society is one again divided into rich and poor. People strive to become wealthy no matter the cost. Wealth has become the only thing that's valued.

Somehow, life shows us that in every part of history and at every twist of fate she will never conform to our understanding or our rules; instead, she flows like a river on her own winding path, and no one knows where she's going. No one is able to predict the future, much less decide her. Maybe that's what makes life so interesting.

People usually divide the world into what is familiar and what is foreign. We did this too. We were taught to believe that the poor were good, and the rich were the worst; but our fairy tales used to end with the phrase: 'they became rich and lived happily ever after.' All people secretly dream about the same thing: to have enough and not want for anything. Then, young Soviet romantics led by the Bolsheviks took this dream and ruined it. They divided the world into enemies of the people and those who extinguish them. Time and time again, we conceived of new enemies and divided the world into the familiar and the foreign. We didn't know, didn't understand that people can also be neutral. 'If you're not with us, you're against us!' went the battle cry of the revolution. The world was divided into two enemy camps: the capitalists and the socialists. Then, there were fascists and anti-fascists. The distance between these opposites was so great that anyone who tried to narrow it or build a bridge could fall into the chasm and disappear.

The wise aksakal, Zhakezhan-bi told me long ago during the bloodshed of 1937, that it's easier to live if you be-

A HUNDRED YEARS ON THE STEPPE

long to a group. Then you know what is familiar, and what is foreign. Keep close to your own kind and don't worry about everyone else. When you're lying in a trench, you know who your own are, and you know who and where your enemy is, and you can shoot at him without emotion. It's a primitive philosophy, but it's pragmatic. The people who find it hardest to live are those who understand that there's no such thing as 'us' and 'them;' there is only humanity. These people don't stand with anyone. Their life is a misery, and they're attacked from all sides.

At the time, I didn't fully comprehend this. Only at the end of my long life, after a lifetime of shock and suffering did I start to understand the wisdom of living life as a human; that everyone living on this Earth is our brother or sister, and there's no need to divide them into 'us' and 'them,' familiar and foreign, friends and enemies, and fight others because of this. This is a complicated thing, though, and perhaps beyond the ability of many people to grasp. Maybe you only really get there when you're my age.

I don't know how many times I've wanted to leave this world; just quietly and peacefully fly away from this mortal coil and experience everlasting calm. In the most painful moments, this thought has often come to me. I've always tried to chase her away, though, and put every last ounce of my strength into my life, as full of suffering as it has been. I'm a hundred years old. I know it's hard for you to understand me.

There's a paradox. When enemy shells were exploding all around us, we clung tightly to the ground, trying to sink into it and praying to the Almighty. In those moments, we were desperate to live, but when the Soviets shredded our nerves and tortured our hearts, we were ready to kill them and then kill ourselves.

I sometimes wonder how many people I killed during the war. I don't know; it was painful and impossible to count. They shot at me, and I shot at them. If I fired about ten bullets at the enemy trenches every day for a thousand days, then that's ten thousand bullets. Ninety kilogrammes of deadly bullets, all manufactured in the town of Shymkent in Kazakhstan. If I missed my target ninety-nine percent of the time, I would still have taken a hundred lives. And what if I hit my target, a person, more than one percent of the time? It's frightening to even think of. The cruellest rule in any war is to kill your enemy when you can, because if you don't kill him, he'll kill you. This was especially true of what became known as the Great Patriotic War. Soviet and German soldiers murdered each other furiously and mercilessly. Through the bloodshed my only thought was to kill as many enemies as possible, so that I might stay alive. I was a good marksman too; for every hundred bullets I fired, I would have hit my target sixty or seventy times. At the end of my life, thinking about this tortures me. The only comfort I have is that this was a sacred war. We were defending our nation; the fascists had invaded our land. This thought may justify what we did, but the flashbacks are still terrible. When we were ripping out each other's throats and disembowelling each other, what was happening to our souls? Where did our faith and our humanity go?

A HUNDRED YEARS ON THE STEPPE 263

Life and death are always together. You don't think about this when you're young, and if you ever do muse upon the fragility of life, you quickly chase these thoughts away. As you get older, though, your soul becomes stronger and wiser, and you learn to calmly consider the meaning of life and death.

Whenever I find myself frightened by uncertainty or chaos, only my faith can comfort my soul. I'm always drawn to the Almighty. When a man has faith, he can live through blood and tears, suffering and humiliation, because the Almighty will lead him to the light. If a person can remain a person no matter what hand fate deals him, then that is his victory. If he slips, then that is his tragedy.

I think I've told you everything I wanted to. I can leave you alone now. Death isn't frightening when she comes at the right time. Wise men say that a person doesn't die; he passes into another state, another dimension. We hope that death is a continuation of life; a second birth into an unknown world.

When a person lives as long as I have, he probably begins to think of his death as a second birth - a birth into a new, secret world. No one can know for certain. It's a blessing when a person dies naturally and is ready to pass into the next world, but it's a tragedy when a young life is taken away. It's a tragedy for all of humanity when people kill each other in their hundreds, thousands and millions. My mind refuses to understand it. My soul can't accept it.

Sometimes, I feel that my hundred years have passed in just one day. It's as if it was only yesterday that I was small, the happiest boy on Earth. Now, I'm as ancient as the peak of a mountain, a century old and preparing to fly away to my everlasting calm. At other times, it feels as if my life has been a long, twisting and torturous road into the unknown. Either way, this has been my life and I love the way she has been. It's probably only those of us who're a hundred that can say at the end of our journeys that life feels short. It feels very different when everything is still ahead of you.

Sometimes, it can feel as if one day, even one hour can last for an eternity. It surprises me when young people say that life goes by so fast. Why fill your young head full of crazy thoughts and weigh your soul down with torment and doubt when you still have your whole life to live? Enjoy this life. Live it with faith and with hope, with love and with kindness, and make the most of the time you have. Then, we will see what comes next.

I believe that there is a higher meaning in all of this which we can't understand. I believe that it's this mystery that makes life so wonderful.

I read somewhere when I was younger that they asked philosophers and writers, idealists and realists, atheists and abstract artists, materialists and moralists theoretical questions, such as 'Does God exist?', 'Does your soul live forever?' and 'Is life eternal?' If the answer is no, then what's the meaning of all of this? History, civilisation, all of human progress has no meaning if in the end we just disappear.

I remember the words my mother said when I was a child. She told me that when a baby cries as it is being born, it's crying from sorrow: I have been born, so I'm going to die. It seems that we live so we can die, and every day is another step towards our inevitable death. What we build today will one day be ruins, and if the end of the world comes, then the troubles that humanity has caused for centuries suddenly mean nothing.

These are probably the most important and the most difficult questions for humanity, but there are no answers to them in this life. No one has been able to answer them, and no one ever will. No one can know what eternity looks like. No one can hold a soul in their hands. So, don't punish yourself; just believe in the Almighty and live your life well.

Be a human, and please, never humiliate and kill people. This has been my life. These are my words to you.

LET ME LIVE!
A Package Instead of a Bomb

General Yang Lee Mzhanba ordered the special operation to commence in three hours. The large-scale bombardment of the city would decide the outcome of the battle. Usually, after such a devastating assault, very few would be left alive.

It's cruel, but it's necessary, the smart, slender fifty-year-old military leader and skilled politician thought to himself, as leaning back tiredly in his big chair, he breathed in the thick smoke from the expensive cigar in his mouth.

Swiftly and silently, like a trained leopard, an adjutant entered carrying an unexpected and strange package.

'We checked it, Sir... It's safe to open,' said the handler. 'We received the package from an unknown, classified professional.'

The general casually glanced at the attached letter which had been typed and printed off.

'To the General-politician, Yang Lee Mzhanba, from a fighter of conscience for worldwide justice,' he read. 'Are you Sir, perchance, a fantasist? Do you gain pleasure spewing out your nonsense? You, the head of the dastardly left radicals. You, who hides behind absurd slogans and manipulates recruits and subjects into a life-erasing fate.'

After those few opening lines, his countenance became stern. With an unwavering seriousness, the general began reading the rest of the letter sent by the mysterious stranger. Accurately assessing the situation, the adjunct quietly withdrew.

An Absurd War

Mr Yang Lee Mzhanba.

You shouldn't be surprised by my letter.

Yes, I am a sworn enemy of you and others like you, but sometimes it can prove quite useful to listen to the bitter truths of your enemies rather than the sugar-coated platitudes of fake friends.

I never imagined that I would write to you and send a package instead of a bomb. The irony of this fate is what's most amusing: here I am pouring out my wounded soul

A HUNDRED YEARS ON THE STEPPE 267

onto this paper for the eyes of my mortal enemy. Why? Be patient and read my letter through to the end, and maybe then you will understand everything.

I won't powder your brains with intellectual frills or inspiring, poetic literature which, let's be honest, no one really understands. The meaning and feelings of writers always get lost in an endless stream of words. It might sound surprising, but it's a fact - all the so-called highly educated critics would consider this unbearable chatter an example of high literature. They don't understand that the modern world is now in the age of computers and lightning-fast communication, and that people simply do not have the time or the desire to even leaf through thick volumes or to delve into detailed descriptions of the meaning of life, historical figures or the petty spiritual experiences of bloated and hollow characters. Or are they now going to start judging people's tastes? Yes, well, I pay them no mind, and in the spirit of the people, I will tell you everything simply and wisely.

Naturally, I will not tell you my real name, and, to be honest, I'm tired of making up fake names. (Although you have been hiding under a made-up, mysterious name for your entire life. We all know that Yang Lee Mzhanba is a pseudonym, and, let's be honest, you've probably forgotten your real name.)

I hate lies with a passion. It's better to hide some details and honestly tell the true story of my suffering soul than make crap up. Actually, I think that the story of a person's life is not just the facts written in their biography, it's a story of the movement of their soul.

I won't tell you about my past. The last thing I want is for your unrighteous, unbridled and absurd anger to be directed at my innocent relatives. The only thing I can say is that I have a lot of mixed blood, both Eastern and Western. I am a normal, educated person, a free citizen of a highly developed democratic state. You don't need to know which country I was born in or where I live. Such a cunning character as yourself could probably calculate a missile attack on my quarter given even the slightest hint. My profession and everyday details of my life are not important either. I will not say anything about my religion so as not to arouse suspicions that I am promoting a certain belief, or worse still, fighting for it. No, the meaning and essence of my struggle is different.

According to the signs of the zodiac, I am a Libra, born in the Year of the Horse. I love justice and honesty without giving these matters a second thought. The injustices which I have observed ever since childhood have hurt my heart. Over the years, these sufferings and experiences have hardened me, but my soul had remained the same. The injustices and violence of this world permeated the essence of my being, slowly eradicating any patience that I had left. Even the bombings in the Far East ruthlessly tore me apart, and I began hating the torturers that wore patriotic stripes upon their shoulders more and more.

And then they drafted me into the army. For days we underwent medical examinations, running from one doctor to another. It was uncomfortable and unbearable to stand butt-naked in front of strangers who all stood neatly dressed

A HUNDRED YEARS ON THE STEPPE

and staring. It was autumn; there was still no heating and in the huge, empty, draughty semi-basement corridors of the military department we were chilled to our very bones. But the cold floors and the colonel paid no mind to our suffering. At that moment, I hated all of those military tyrants. Could they not conduct these examinations of conscripts in humane conditions without mocking our young pride? I became outraged, and the colonel, having cursed at me in more ways than one, sent me to a psychiatrist.

The psychiatrist was a strange man. He had a kind of damp, haggard, dull look in his eyes.

'What do you see in your dreams?' he asked me.

Enthusiastically, I began to pour out my experiences and fantastic dreams, because no one had ever asked me about them so sympathetically, much less listened so attentively.

'Do you fly to the moon in your dreams?' he interrupted to ask unexpectedly.

'I do,' I replied. 'I even fly past the moon and walk on Mars, Jupiter and Saturn.'

His jaw dropped.

'Do you... embrace beautiful women in your dreams?' he haltingly continued.

'There isn't any skirt on Jupiter,' I snapped; 'and you can't get laid on Saturn either! But yes,' I added, 'the Martians... I dream of naked, pretty Martians... and till morning they caress me.'

'All right,' the psychiatrist said, writing something down. 'Do you fight in your dreams?'

'Yes, I fight,' I replied enthusiastically.

'With whom?' he asked with intense interest.

'With those who do evil.'

'Do you shoot them?'

'No, I don't shoot them; I blow them up!'

He wrote in his file that I am a psychopath.

Personally I think that psychiatrists themselves are psychopaths because as they constantly communicate with the mentally ill, they probably slowly become like their patients. Similar poles attract, as the ancients said, and in a mental hospital, of course, spiritual health cannot be gained. But despite being diagnosed as abnormal and unfit for military service, shortly thereafter, strange as it may seem, I was drafted again. They trained us and sent us to a distant land to face an invincible enemy in an unknown country in an incomprehensible and unjust conflict. I spent a terrible five-hundred-and-fifty-four days breathing in the iron smell of blood, fire and smoke. It finally hardened and convinced me that we, the people, the masses are a tool, a pawn and a toy in a big political game.

From the very beginning, I suffered in this bloodbath, but it was through this mental anguish that I came to realise that war is a meaningless meat-grinder and that we humans are fuel for the life of that monstrous killing machine. I have seen many deaths. Initially, we justified our being here as fulfilling our duty to our homeland, but that didn't comfort or relieve our souls.

Once, we decided to pose this sacramental question directly to our commander, an experienced major, a man

A HUNDRED YEARS ON THE STEPPE

broken to the bone marrow, a man of war that lined us up in the hangar among the stony cliffs.

'War is something placed by nature itself into human genes!' he barked. 'Every man seeks to suppress, subdue, and in the case of resistance, to destroy their competitors and plant their seed. One nation always seeks dominance over another. Life is a struggle and the law, the goal of any struggle is the humiliation or destruction of the enemy. In this fight, only the strong survive. Don't lie to yourself with big ideas about equality, peace or the union of nations. You just need to shoot, because if you don't pull the trigger first, they'll shoot you. If you don't kill, they'll kill you.

'Maybe you think they're innocent people, how can you kill them? At the beginning of my career, I thought that too. I wept when my comrades wiped out an entire village; but when they suddenly shot and killed my friends from the ashes of their smouldering homes, I realised that such pity was useless. My friends were cut down in the blink of an eye. So, don't think of your enemies as people. Imagine them as a target on a training ground and shoot. Man is just a pile of meat and nothing more. Yes, a man is just a bunch of meat, bones, blood and shit, and he's only alive whilst his body is whole. Try to keep yourself together in your bag of skin, because if it breaks...

'And don't entertain any thoughts about your soul being immortal, that there is another world, that there is eternity. None of that is true; it's just comforting lies, an illusion, call it what you will, it's still bullshit. I can say for certain that I've seen many deaths, but I've never seen immortality. Meat scattered around, splattered everywhere; I've seen enough blood in my time, but I've never seen a soul. Here it is, the meaningless, terrible thing known as life, no more than a transient game.'

The commander burst out laughing so hard that his laughter echoed, shaking the mountains. He laughed hysterically until suddenly, his laughter stopped abruptly. We really didn't understand anything. We just stood there as a terrible whistling rang through the hangar and the explosion of a missile stunned us. The next thing we saw was the commander's body slowly falling to the ground. He had been decapitated. To this day it seems to me that the headless body of our commander wanders through the gorges of these foreign mountains unable to find peace. Sometimes, in a dream, my ears are hurt by the echoing of his hysterical laughter.

It took a long time for us to come to our senses. His last words left a bitter aftertaste, raising the most important question of our lives: what if he was right? How can one be, how can one live knowing that there is no immortality of the soul and that there is no eternity? Doesn't the entire history of humanity and civilisation lose its meaning? What's the point of it all; what's the point of anything anymore? Why bother to fight and suffer, or even to live? These incomprehensible, inexplicable feelings and questions have pressed upon me ever since.

Following the death of the commander, day and night another question haunted me: why are we here and what is the point in this massacre? Why do we, healthy, strong

A HUNDRED YEARS ON THE STEPPE   *273*

young men, instead of enjoying our lives come here to kill innocent people who are completely unknown to us? Why do we refuse to allow these people to live in their homeland as they see fit? My friends and I didn't want to be here at all but had been forced to take up arms and sent to a distant land to destroy the lives of total strangers. What gave anyone the right to toy with our and other people's destinies? Some try to explain this as a political necessity, as the needs of the state, but such reasoning is false and this injustice must be corrected. A universal law must be adopted according to which no one - not a single king, lord, emperor, president, commander or ruler would have the right to order his troops to invade a foreign country. Yes, no one should have the right to start a war, to murder people and destroy nations, and that's it, period. Protecting one's homeland, however, is a completely different and sacred affair.

From these questions, I found no peace in my wakeful state or in dreams. In the whistling of every bullet, in every explosion, in the moans of wounded soldiers and the last breath of a perishing soul, the same answer always sounded out: it is senseless and absurd. There is no reason; it's pointless.

One day, after the cessation of a particularly bloody battle, we stumbled upon a wounded enemy combatant. He lay near a huge block of grey stone. Bullets fired by an automatic had pierced through his chest. Our men were ready to tear him to pieces in retaliation for our dead friends, but I managed to dissuade them. The orderly gave him water and bandaged his wound. It was clear that he was suffering a great deal, but he did his best to hide it stoically. It was immediately evident that he was a religious man and was waiting with dignity is waiting for the happy moment when he would be raised up into eternity. The orderly knew the native language and exchanged a few words with him, asking why he fought against us and shot at our soldiers knowing that he would lose and inevitably die. Wouldn't it have been better to submit to us and live in peace? These words brought the wounded soldier to life. His eyes sparkled, and he began to speak abruptly but confidently, spitting blood from between his teeth.

'We did not come to you to fight,' he said. 'We are simply defending our country; that is all. We just want to live in our native land... independently and in our own way where all are equal... and for this, you want to break us... to destroy us, but we won't let that happen. How could you possibly understand any of it? What would you do if a stranger came into your home with a weapon and demanded that you become his slave? You'd shoot him as we shoot you in the name of justice. You're fighting for the order and rules which you invented, but whilst for you, it's order, to us it's slavery. We're fighting for our conscience, from freedom and equality... Ultimately, we're all killers. Do you hear me... are you ashamed of your deeds, or do you have no conscience at all?'

With these words he perished. We buried his body under a pile of stones and hurriedly left the area, but I couldn't escape from his words about conscience and justice which resonated deep in my soul. Even now, after so many years, I can clearly hear the hoarse voice of this stranger just a day

A HUNDRED YEARS ON THE STEPPE

prior , had become connected to the meaning of my inner self in an instant.

Me - A Cripple

When my time came, I didn't even understand how it had happened. There was a fierce firefight. I was shooting blindly at the enemy when suddenly there was a dazzling flash and everything disappeared.

I woke up in the hospital. My whole body was permeated with intolerable pain. I wanted to roll over onto my side, but I couldn't move. My legs wouldn't obey me. *Must be a bit numb, I guess*, I thought. *It's alright; it'll pass in no time.*

But it didn't pass. Slowly, I began to feel around with my hands and couldn't find my leg.

Covered in a cold sweat and terrified, I began to feel for my other leg but it wasn't there either.

I cried out in shock. The doctors and nurses who came running administered an anaesthetic injection to calm me down.

'It's a miracle that you survived,' one said. 'We literally pulled you back from the next world.'

They explained that a mine had exploded. I had been found lying by a blood-stained armoured personnel carrier. Everyone else was dead. Initially, I had been counted amongst the corpses, and only later had an orderly seen some subtle signs of life. Then came the helicopter, the hospital - a cripple.

I was at once hollow and petrified. I'd never experienced such emptiness. I didn't want to live, and I didn't want to die. I felt half-dead and half-alive. It was impossible to imagine myself in the real world, in a busy downtown in this condition. To me, it seemed that everything was over, that I'd been crushed and thrown into a ditch or a landfill, call it what you will. Burning with pain, I tormented myself with questions: why had I found myself in this position; why me and not others? In reality, others didn't care about my suffering, passing my wheelchair without paying any attention, talking loudly and laughing. Some, throwing a cursory glance, quickly averted their eyes: I didn't think they felt sorry for the disabled man before them; they were healthy, happy and simply displeased to have to look upon such a freak. I gazed back at them with a sense of rage. It pained me to see all these healthy people. Angrily, I thought about how unfair it was that I was a cripple and they weren't. In my heart, I wanted everyone to be crippled. *Then it will be fair*, I thought; *then no one will look down on me or have to feel sorry for little old me.* I despised myself and what I'd become. The world had made me disabled, and I hated it for that.

Sometimes, I thought about how great it would be to install a large-calibre machine gun in the very centre of the megalopolis and snap everyone's legs or to blow them up, not sparing a single soul so that everyone on Earth would become as disabled as I was. *That's how I'll get revenge for my lost youth and my trampled dreams*, I thought. Over time though, having become accustomed to my fate I calmed

A HUNDRED YEARS ON THE STEPPE
277

down, for I clearly understood that the nations and their people had nothing to do with it. I closed myself off and hid away from people. The wheelchair became my fortress, my cover.

I began to read lengthy books about life and death concerned with ruminations on the frailty of being and the meaning of life. It is what's written and not what is said that gets to the truth of these issues. Man comes from a state of non-being; a state to which he inevitably returns. The world is heading into the abyss. The end of the world will come, and everything will be over, centuries of history and civilisations turning to dust and ashes. Ultimately, there is no point in this deceptive process called life, so what difference does it make how we live? Be it lived out in a shack or a golden palace, the inexorable flight of time will extinguish every life.

These thoughts cast such a terrible melancholy over me that sometimes I contemplated suicide. The niggling worm of doubt enraged me, however, and prevented me from carrying out the deed. But let's leave the topic of eternity alone for a while. We came into this world, and we must live with dignity as human beings. Regardless of the length of time allotted to us by the creator, destiny, the cosmos, nature, call it what you will, no one truly knows the essence of this mysterious force. This is the life given to us, our path which we have to follow to its conclusion, and then we'll see. And despite the questions that arise, we are still able to use our conscience to guide our decisions. Therefore, it still matters how and where you tread your path. If you object to these words, imagine yourself for a moment as a helpless, disabled person sitting in a wheelchair amidst the bustle of this world. No, General Yang Lee Mzhanba, of course, you don't have the slightest desire to change your command post, your comfortable chair is everything compared to my little cramped wheelchair. In all fairness, though, you should sit next to me, your former soldier and comrade-in-arms, and drink the bitter cup of fate to the bottom as we realise we are both trapped in our seats.

So, I lived and thought painfully and obsessively about justice and conscience. I asked myself a cruel question: how can such supposedly civilised, highly educated politicians create intolerable, flagrant injustices without a twinge of remorse? In asking this, I became convinced that I must fight against all the unjust and dishonest people on this Earth.

I cannot say exactly when it began. Probably, I was born with it, because as far as I can remember it was always with me. I still find it difficult to define in a single word or phrase. It's a strange mixed feeling, some vague concept that doesn't fit into any normal framework of human behaviour or psyche. As far back as I can remember, I have always reacted strongly against any manifestation of injustice or dishonesty regardless of whether these actions were directed at me or against others. I became infuriated by any injustice and would lose my temper at the verbal dirt people spit at each other. Instantly, I wanted to punish such actions, and the punishment in my mind often went to extremes. In a fit of pique, I unconditionally destroyed such people in my mind, craving for God to punish them so they would disap-

A HUNDRED YEARS ON THE STEPPE

pear into a void. In the name of justice, though, I must note that those who committed an injustice against someone and then sincerely repented and asked for forgiveness aroused in me a sense of sympathy, and I forgave them in my heart.

We had a commander who was unbearably picky. We soldiers secretly hated him. He always tried to emphasise his superiority, his chest gleaming with medals and stars. Proud to the bone, in the sweltering heat, he drove the soldiers till their sweat had completely washed their bodies. Those who tried to argue, he swore at and punished. Day after day, I tried to suppress my sense of humiliation and burning hatred. I wanted to kill him and scatter his ashes in the wind. I thought long and hard about how to shoot him with a captured machine gun at the first opportunity during a battle. Of course, it was just a manifestation of my thirst for justice, and, naturally, I wouldn't follow through with these schemes.

The day eventually came when he was mortally wounded by a sudden spray of bullets. He lay on his back bleeding profusely and stared unblinkingly at the cloudless sky. There was such anguish in his eyes that it made me shudder. I gazed upon him, sympathising with all my heart. Noticing me, he quietly called me over. I knelt beside him and he squeezed my hand tight and smiled amiably. That was the first time I'd ever seen him smile.

'Well, I've done my part. I guess I'll be there soon,' he whispered, looking to the heavens. 'Ask the boys to forgive me for my tough demands. Without this, it's impossible for me to leave without regrets. Please understand and forgive me. And live, you and the boys must live.'

I remember nodding in response. My heart melted and any trace of hostility I harboured towards him faded away. Now, I sincerely regret what I thought about doing to him and wish that he had survived. He, it turned out, was also a man, our comrade, our brave comrade. We commemorated him with kind words and were even a little ashamed of having wanted him dead. Herein lies the problem with life: it's ambiguous and illogical, it does not fit into any tidy frame.

I always wanted to climb to the highest point in the world, to scale Mount Everest and cry out from the depths of my soul for all of humanity; for humanity specifically, not for separate states and people. People of the world, why do you do evil unto each other? Why are bullets constantly flying, inflicting physical and spiritual wounds? Why do we kill each other in senseless wars? Why do one people want to enslave another, invade foreign lands and enforce their rules, oppress and exploit? Stop; live and let others live. After all, the fates of all people are interconnected. We all have only one ark - the planet Earth in the boundless ocean of space, and she, good mother Earth may not be able to bear the brunt of all the negativity that comes from humanity. True friendship can blossom only between equals, and real freedom begins with respect for the freedom of others. Truly happy people can only exist when everyone is happy.

Of course, I understood perfectly well that all these thoughts amounted to were noble impulses. Life and history speak to their polar opposite. This perplexed me though. Was this really the immutable, tragic path of humanity

A HUNDRED YEARS ON THE STEPPE

281

with no possible alternative? Perhaps we're not trying hard enough.

After much agonising, emotional turmoil and struggle, I made a firm and final decision to cleanse the world of filth and fight mercilessly for justice. But how? Destroy the bastards? Kill the murderers and scumbags? I freely admit I wanted to do just that. In my unbridled fantasy, I invented various new weapons and methods of dealing with villains of all types. But what's the point in such a fight? After all, then you yourself become a monster, an enemy of humanity, a murderer. But what could I do about my wounded soul which was so eager for retribution and wished all villains the same misfortune? Yes, for a long time I was tormented by this question.

Hate and Conscience

One day, I was attempting to cross the road in my wheelchair, but barely had time. The traffic light began to blink and a driver waiting impatiently for the light to turn green sped straight at me. I came within inches of being mown down as the brakes screeched.

'What are you doing? You good for nothing crippled cunt!' the driver roared.

Turning around, I saw the face of an obese man distorted with anger.

'Get out of my way you pathetic half-life. Your place is in the garbage!' the irritated fat man bellowed, breathing heavily.

I carried on moving to the other side, but the insults made me lose control and I, swearing at the bastard, spat in his direction as I rolled on.

Suddenly, someone grabbed my throat from behind and squeezed it so that I began to choke. My vision became blurry, and I started to lose consciousness. As I was about to do so, my attacker loosened his grip and tipped over my wheelchair. Gasping for air, I grabbed the railing at the side of the road. The passers-by didn't interfere in proceedings, everyone acting as if they hadn't seen anything until the voice of a woman rang out.

'How dare you! Get away from him!'

Writhing on the ground, I saw the driver raise his fists and approach my rescuer, a slim middle-aged woman. I was seething with rage and helplessness. The woman calmly retreated a few steps, pulled a can out of her purse and sprayed it directly into the fat man's face. He didn't understand what had happened, and slowly, like a limp bag, settled on the sidewalk in a foetal position.

'We have to hurry and get out of here,' the woman said as she helped me back into my chair. 'People have become so brutal... completely lost their minds. They should be ashamed of themselves. Their behaviour is inhumane. If only these people gave a little more thought to their actions, the world would be a far better place.'

'Give him a kick in the head, please, for me,' I asked her.

She looked down at the pointed toes of her shoes and shook her head emphatically.

A HUNDRED YEARS ON THE STEPPE

'No, if I did that I'd be no different from that scumbag. Revenge and hatred never lead to anything good. Remember that and take care of yourself.'

I thanked the brave, kind woman, and she, waving goodbye, went on her way. Her words, though, remained with me.

I thought for a long time about what had happened and about the human condition in general. Remorse is the worst punishment. Conscience is a tricky thing. It lives somewhere in the depths of our souls. It cannot be seen with the eyes; you cannot grab it with your hands and throw it out. You can't run or hide from it. It can't be corroded or cured with antibiotics. Once it awakens, it torments people tirelessly for the atrocities they have committed. It is true that you can drown it for a while with drinks and drugs, but that's just a deception, a temporary measure which in the end reaps its own vengeance. No one can help us defeat it. When a person is left alone with their conscience, it slowly but surely gnaws at the soul if one does not repent sincerely and apologise to those against whom their evil acts were directed. If a sinner doesn't start performing good deeds, eventually they wither in the body of regret.

Analysing the situation, I came to the conclusion that this had been no accident. Fate taught me a lesson and pointed out the way. The event highlighted my helplessness and insecurity. I began to think about everything in close detail, asking myself what I should do. I must decide and act, but where should I start? Thus, I decided to start with myself, to eradicate the killer in my soul. After a long and trying mental struggle, instead of poison, I chose medicine. It was my great victory, and he who defeats himself wins everything. My spiritual and intellectual search led me to the perfect method with which to combat evil: the awakening of the conscience.

How to achieve this was the question. What if these feelings were tucked away and completely suppressed? And what if such feelings had never existed at all?

I began to study chemistry, cybernetics, electronics and nanotechnology with particular zeal. I also leaned on biology, where I gained a lot of useful knowledge and ideas on bacteriological and genetic weapons. I didn't join any organisations or share my ideas with anyone. I became a lone wolf, strict, fair, free and completely clandestine.

I invented a unique device that forcibly arouses the conscience of man and ensures that he who is affected by it becomes ashamed of their misdeeds. Such an inconspicuous small transmitter directs H-particles. They are omnipotent in alliance with Substance X, which I discovered during my research. A tiny amount of Substance X must first be inserted into the blood, followed shortly by the H-particles. The results are instantaneous. In the brain, the central nervous system, the inner body, the soul, aura, chakras, vital centre, call it what you will, a powerful command signal is sent: *'Shame on you! What have you done? Stop it! This is unfair! Think before you commit these deeds! Think hard about the consequences! Don't be so unscrupulous!'*

You can literally watch as the person changes before your eyes. They become ashamed of their misdeeds. They

A HUNDRED YEARS ON THE STEPPE   *285*

repent, suffer severe torments of the conscience, refute all evil intentions and begin to act for good. The only disadvantage of this device is that a person who has undergone such treatment will experience remorse for all their crimes, even minor ones, and will be ashamed of the smallest transgressions in the future. Still, this is a small price to pay. Better to be ashamed of yourself than destroy and humiliate others.

So, I set myself a goal. Methodically, I set about tracking down the most dangerous members of society and awakening their consciences. You may say that it's immoral to plague a person with remorse for the rest of their life. That may be. But it is better that they suffer than shamelessly destroy their own kind.

I also thought about how my wheelchair was completely defenceless against any encroachment by boors or monsters. Thus, I created a wonderful wheelchair, my fortress. It was kindly made for me at a military factory by a master of his craft according to my designs, and all for a tolerable price. It is a four-wheel drive, about one and a half metres long and about a metre wide, with elegant steering, hand pedals and brakes, glass windows and a movable thin but durable awning which protects me from rain and the burning rays of the sun. The back of the chair is high and completely protects the head. The wheels are wide with solid hard rubber treads, meaning there's no need to inflate the tyres or be afraid of punctures. A soft, lightweight, comfortable chair, it can be reclined into a horizontal position and turned into a bed if desired.

Inside the metal case are many caches of different sizes, the purpose of which are known only to me. Ingenious devices are securely hidden everywhere. It has three more batteries for forty-eight hours of operation. In case of fatigue, or simply if I want to, I can turn on the batteries and my wheelchair moves at a speed of forty kilometres an hour, and in the course of this movement, the batteries recharge. The wheelchair is not afraid of the impenetrable darkness of night; two small but powerful headlights illuminate its path. In addition, there are two seats. Well, I couldn't leave a pretty girl who wished to visit me behind on the roadside. Yes, not just a wheelchair, more like a little BMP. But this is not all: it was unsinkable! If necessary, it could sail like a boat.

I named my wheelchair the Yangalibus, firstly, because it imitated the legendary Nautilus, and secondly, so that I would always remember who put me in this wheelchair. The name Yangalibus meant that the real creator of this vehicle was the general Yang Lee Mzhanba. The manufacturers attached a metal plate with an engraved inscription in Latin right on the door.

Yangalibus does not attack anyone; it defends itself smartly and gracefully. If someone attacks the chair, it reacts instantly, its defences work automatically, and it fights back. The violence of the aggressor is turned against them and they get what they deserve.

At first, two sergeants and a captain of the police road service were fooled by the Yangalibus as it was such a strange vehicle. They stopped me in a busy downtown area, pulled me aside and spent quite some time trying to understand what type of transport this was.

A HUNDRED YEARS ON THE STEPPE 287

'Oh this is wonderful,' the captain said as he goggled. 'What is this mini-car, wheelchair, quad bike or carriage-looking thing? What should I even classify it as? It doesn't fit into any category in the road traffic technical manual. There's no such thing anywhere here.'

'Now there is,' I offered in a restrained manner. 'You'll need to expand the manual.'

'Don't worry, that's something we can easily do,' replied the captain. 'But you just need to decide where you want to drive this thing; on the sidewalk, like a wheelchair, or on the road, like a vehicle?'

It was a reasonable question which could have been resolved, but the officer began to measure the chair in order to determine the status of the Yangalibus and the legal designation of this indeterminate vehicle. I got sick of it all and had to awaken their consciences, after which they apologised profusely and set about drafting the documents of legal registration. As a result of their efforts, my Yangalibus received exclusive rights to move freely along the roads, pavements and rivers of the country. Suddenly becoming extremely compassionate, the police officers even offered to secure the rights of free flight for my stroller-fortress, but even the Yangalibus had its limits.

Thus, my Yangalibus became a legitimate and unique means of transportation and even residence. Like Captain Nemo ploughing the oceans on his Nautilus, I moved among people in my Yangalibus. Of course, it never occurred to anyone that this young disabled man planned to turn the world around. On the contrary, people felt sorry for me. Some even almost guiltily tried their best to help me, taking the handles and pushing it along. Even the generals of the world could not have guessed that in this way I transformed the consciousness of one hundred and thirty-seven people. When the person I needed to enlighten stood before me, all I needed to do was pull the handle of my Yangalibus, using the "Borgia Ring" technique to insert the micro-particle Substance X into their bloodstream. Then, I sent in particle H, and *voilà*, the villain burned with shame, reproached themselves for all their atrocities and suffered, suffered horribly until they repented and stood on the path of the righteous. Attempting to cleanse themselves of their sins, the former criminal then began to do good deeds.

Fate handed me a pair of crutches for support, and I decided to squeeze the maximum benefit out of them. They became weapons for me. I had placed a special order for a pair of folding tubular crutches which could be lengthened or shortened as necessary with one tube sliding into the other. They could be used as a club, and, as the tips of the inner tube were pointed, turned into a spear. There were many holes in the crutches in which various cunning devices for attack or defence were hidden, which I will not discuss for obvious reasons.

So, for about five years, I smarted and fought. It took a lot of effort to walk with prosthetic legs, yet I adapted myself so that I could dance and nobody would suspect that I was disabled. Without the wheelchair and crutches it was difficult, though, so I used those almost all the time, especially when I alone.

A HUNDRED YEARS ON THE STEPPE

It may sound paradoxical, but the concussion I suffered at the hands of the thug who tipped me from my chair worked in my favour. I kept the relevant medical certificate with me at all times, and at the slightest hint of misunderstandings, especially with the police, I presented it and would immediately be left alone. What can you possibly want from a cripple? The best way to shirk responsibility from the burden of social etiquette is to be psychologically inadequate, mentally ill, as they say - crazy. It was the perfect mask. Imagine having no responsibility for your actions and misdeeds. People either pity you, are afraid of you or keep their distance, so you can act with impunity. True, there is a danger that you can run into the "same" kind of person as yourself, but usually crazy people quickly find a common language, sometimes even instinctively understanding one another.

The most important discovery I made, one which gave me exceptional strength of mind, is that disabled people do not consider themselves irrelevant. The body may be crippled, but the soul is not. The soul cannot become disabled. You do not understand this, Mr Yang Lee Mzhanba, for you never, not even for an instant, thought about the fate of the victims of your military campaigns or your delusions. If you thought about those tens, hundreds of thousands, millions of destinies crippled by war, you would understand that the one who is truly crippled is you. Yes, yes, you can call it what you like, but souls capable of committing such atrocities are truly the insane ones, souls such as yours, Mr Yang Lee Mzhanba.

Sometimes it seems to me that all people are to some extent crazy and that the whole world is a kind of madhouse in which my sick soul races about. In spite of everything, though, I wandered through this world in my Yangalibus, like Captain Ahab scouring the ocean in search of his white whale. In fairness, it was not the gargantuan white whale which came to ruin the heroic captain, baring its huge mouth. Moby Dick was a harmless creature no different to the monster which guides my fate. I walk alone among people as a living reproach, a victim and a witness to humanity's cruelty and madness, and I awaken people's consciences, sometimes by my appearance alone. With those who sleep too well, I awaken their conscience through violence.

Villainous Mastermind

The first time I applied my method was to my eccentric friend, Janus, with whom I grew up and studied. He was a dreamer who wanted to make great discoveries and go down in the annals of history as an unequalled genius. His sanctimonious behaviour offended me. We argued a lot and always ended up fighting. Over the years, though, I came to terms with his personality, only occasionally objecting to his pretentious and deranged ideas. Let him be as delusional as he wishes, I decided, because I'm not obliged to share his burden. He was detached from reality and utterly hopeless. His entire life was driven by the need to discover something which would stun the whole world. Looking back on his

A HUNDRED YEARS ON THE STEPPE 291

emotionally-charged verbiage, it sometimes seems to me that all the crazy ideas of today originally belonged to him; but then he had appropriated and twisted them to his ends, for he was also a born plagiarist.

One day, Janus boasted that he had invented something that would allow people to cultivate ten yields of crops a year. In the heat of his bluster, he told me that he planned to process seeds with unique compounds of radiation, bacteria and other chemical elements which would result in giant mutant fruits. He would conquer the entire market with his cheap fresh fruit and vegetables. The most important thing, though, was a psychogenic substance which would be embedded in these fruits and vegetables at the cellular level. The people consuming these products would gradually become quiet, faceless, obedient slaves who would execute any command given by the producer of this substance; that is him, of course. Thus he would become a dictator, ruling over the entire planet. If anyone should resist, he would simply send a signal that would instantly kill them.

I shuddered at the abhorrent fantasy of my fanatical friend, but I didn't believe in the reality of his scheme and thought that he was just being delirious as usual. My doubts served to provoke Janus, however, and he set about proving to me that what he was doing was not only right but also true. It got to the point where he took me to his secret laboratory, where two homeless people were living in aviaries and eating these fruits. In order to convince me, he sent a signal from his equipment and the homeless duo began to slowly and theatrically undress until they stood there stark naked. Then, as if everything was completely normal and there was no audience, they began to copulate openly. I could not watch and turned away. Seeing my disgust, my friend grinned triumphantly.

'Now do you understand the genius of my discovery?' he exclaimed in ecstasy. 'People pay for their slavery, degradation, illness and eventual death with their own money. I will become the richest man on Earth and conquer the planet without a single shot being fired.'

'But you'll destroy mankind,' I countered in horror.

'Does mankind even need to exist? We only need people for profit and as slaves,' Janus screamed and laughed hysterically. 'Actually, I love people for their naivety and stupidity, because they let themselves be deceived so easily, becoming the dutiful slaves of those who control them.'

I became cold with fear for the fate of the world. A deadly hatred of Janus and his discovery spread through my veins. Then a thought struck me like a bolt of lightning. This was the occasion to test my device and deliver the world from this filth. I would destroy the enemy of mankind and his discovery.

Without anyone noticing, I took my secret weapon from Yangalibus' cache and used it on all those present. Once injected with Substance X, Janus and the two homeless people froze. Then, from a tiny transmitter, I sent H-particles into them, and immediately everything changed. Oh, how I wish you could have seen it. At first, they shuddered from the torments of their consciences, which had been suppressed so deeply. Janus took his curly hair in both hands and ripped it

A HUNDRED YEARS ON THE STEPPE

from his skull. The homeless couple quickly got dressed and then writhed on the ground as if wanting the earth to swallow them. Decisively, Janus set fire to the laboratory and the fruit along with all documentation regarding the project and began to pray to the Lord Almighty. The consequence of my actions was that with their consciences restored, Janus and the two vagrants joined a religion. It turns out that genius and villainy are only compatible once the subject has lost their conscience and sense of morality.

So, in case you think that I'm just some mad experimental torturer, that's how I crossed the line for the first time and became a fighter for justice and the saviour of mankind. After all, using that same logic, you generals could be called murderous terrorists who experiment not only on individuals but entire nations. Is it not true that you are destroying entire neighbourhoods and villages under the guise of defeating evil? But beneath the rubble caused by your bombing and artillery strikes lie the bodies of countless innocent civilians. The worst thing about your war, though, is not the weapons but you, for the shells did not choose where to fall. Innocent people are dying in great numbers, but unlike you, I punish the perpetrators of humanity's misfortunes, delivering precise calculated blows and, albeit forcibly, turning them into conscientious and peaceful citizens.

An Alternative

I understood that the task I had assigned myself was, by and large, a task befitting a madman. All the same, the concrete benefit of my actions justifies the extravagant impulses. True, an action aimed at protecting justice, even if sometimes insane, is better than indifference.

I had discovered an alternative worth pondering on. An amazing thing is the world of thoughts, and the deeper one immerses oneself, the more amazing, sometimes even paradoxical, are the things that open up. Here, look around you. For some people, the idea of a fighter for justice, conscience and morality is that of an advocate for the people who actively criticises the authorities as the culprit which is responsible for all the ills in society. This lacks specificity, however, and these so-called fighters for the people who battle against the authorities often quietly co-operate with other representatives of that same government, receiving dividends from them on the one hand, and plaudits from the people on the other. What an alternative; what a paradox.

Love on a Train

Once, I was travelling in a double compartment of a fast luxury train. The road was long, so I had chosen the train specifically in order to rest from the hustle and bustle and get a good sleep on the way. Then, suddenly, she walked in... beautiful, surprisingly charming. We greeted each other, and

A HUNDRED YEARS ON THE STEPPE 295

she turned to face the conductor.

'For some reason, there aren't any female compartment carts on this train. What do you think I should do, maybe swap with someone?' she asked.

The conductor shrugged and my fellow traveller shuffled her feet.

'Are you worried about something?' I asked in a friendly tone. 'Did I scare you? I'm sorry; you seem so nervous that I'm worried I might have spooked you in some way.'

She laughed.

'My name is Zhanmila Tokanato,' she quietly said.

Such a sweet, rare name was instantly etched in my memory: Zhanmila Tokanato.

Adhering to my rules of secrecy, I had to give my fake name.

Zhanmila was an international political and military journalist. We got to talking, and the conversation turned to freedom of speech.

'What do you mean by free speech?' I asked with a deliberately naive look.

'A citizen of a free, democratic country should have complete freedom of speech. That is, they should have the right to express their thoughts and feelings openly, publicly, and to say what they consider to be right and necessary. To put it simply, they can say what they want,' the correspondent stated clearly.

'Do you think that a person is free to say and do what they want, anything that comes into their mind regardless of how their words or actions will affect others? And what if this freedom of theirs violates the rights of others? Can a person be free to insult, humiliate and mock others? And what if absolute freedom of speech awakens hatred and anger?'

Zhanmila listened to me carefully without interrupting. Her bright eyes expressed sympathy and understanding. I felt that my thoughts had resonated with her so I wanted to speak my mind to such an empathetic companion. I hadn't spoken this enthusiastically for a very long time, and thus the words flowed continuously from my mouth.

'Why do you play with words as if they were games when words can blow up cities?' I asked frankly. 'Wouldn't it be better to be sensitive and to speak and write in harmony with reason and morality in mind? You journalists must soothe the world and not set fire to it by adding fuel to the fire that is conflict. The Earth is already burning, yet in pursuit of popular headlines, some of your colleagues are ready to see it charred to a crisp. Tell me honestly, do you think it's blasphemous to draw and publish caricatures of the Prophet Mohammed? I believe it's not just blasphemous and shameless, but a crime against humanity because this is the kindling of inter-religious enmity. Surely no one has the right to make fun of or insult the religious beliefs of others. What will be the consequences?'

Zhanmila looked at me with piercing eyes.

'I agree with you,' she said with sadness in her voice.

Her benevolence inspired me more than ever.

'Why don't we try to live by the motto of the ancient sage, Solon, and "Pursue worthy goals"? After all, the truth

A HUNDRED YEARS ON THE STEPPE   *297*

is that an overdose turns the medicine into poison.'

'Sometimes it seems to me that mankind has the tendency to run from one extreme to another,' she said meaningfully.

'There is only one absolute freedom that does not harm anyone,' I replied, 'and that is freedom of conscience.'

'Is it really so?' she asked. 'Are there any generally accepted norms of morality? Does absolute freedom of conscience mean licentiousness and rampant shamelessness?' she said, unexpectedly introducing a new direction to our conversation.

'No, no, no! I think it's the opposite. Freedom of conscience restrains and protects people from committing shameful acts,' I retorted with fervour. 'We are all created by love; love is life, but what makes it so beautiful is its mysteries. Think about it, what self-respecting person would allow themselves to fornicate in public?'

She considered this and shook her head, her hair swaying from side to side and taking my feelings with it.

'But then why is this done on screen in front of millions of viewers? That is shamelessness. We humiliated, trampled on women are stripped in public and show them in the most shameless poses.'

Zhanmila sighed softly, and we fell silent for a moment. Of course, I could not restrain myself and continued to talk about a different aspect of conscience.

'When you write about the war, do you think it's just?' I asked. 'When your government sends its modern, powerful army, trained to kill and armed to the teeth to enslave and destroy small nations, what do you write about it? You wish to inspire young soldiers with your articles, wanting them to return home soon victorious, and for mothers to wave their sons off to war wanting the same, right?'

'Should they be wishing for something else?' she asked drily.

'Are you not aware that they are giving their blessing for their sons to kill, making other mothers mourn their children's deaths? Victory is a hollow when that victory is the death of another nation. Do you really believe in and admire the military, political journalist Zhanmila Tokanato?'

The sardonic expression faded from her face to be replaced by a look of sadness.

If I confessed my truth, I thought, *it would be easier on my soul.*

Whether I liked or not, our conversation eventually had to return to the relationship between men and women.

'A Muslim came to the prophet Muhammad and said that he was divorcing his wife,' I said, deciding to change the subject.

Instantly, Zhanmila's interest piqued.

'"She's a really crooked character," he said. "She's incorrigible, and I can't take it anymore."

The Prophet smiled radiantly and replied, "The Lord above created woman from the rib of a man. This rib is crooked. Do not try to straighten it or it will break. Use it wisely as it is."

The disciple laughed. Understanding the profound meaning of the words of the prophet, he reconciled with

A HUNDRED YEARS ON THE STEPPE

his wife and dealt with her calmly. So, women are beautiful in their natural curvature. Just don't try to bend them anymore.'

Zhanmila laughed heartily and at that moment she became even more beautiful.

'Equality between a man and a woman is provided by nature itself. They are like two halves without which the other cannot exist. Each is beautiful in its place, that is, a man must remain a man, and a woman must be a woman. Then everything will be in harmony. But when a woman begins to act like a man or vice versa, the natural order is disturbed.'

'I will try to stay in my place,' she replied with humour, and I realised that she liked my ideas.

Night had fallen long ago without either of us noticing. It was time to rest, so I went to perform my ablutions. When I returned, she was already in bed. I dimmed the light and began to fiddle with the kettle and some glasses.

'I hope you're not planning anything?' Zhanmila asked in a sing-song manner.

'Of course not; I have the best intention that humankind has ever had since its appearance on the Earth,' I answered half in jest.

She looked at me in surprise.

'I want you...' I continued.

The girl froze.

'I want you to enjoy the treat of coffee in bed,' I said, finishing my thought.

'But coffee is only served in the morning,' she laughed.

'I can't wait that long.' I answered cheerfully.

'Coffee at night! Then I won't be able to sleep.'

'And what if I want you not to sleep?'

Zhanmila took the cup, and we drank the coffee together.

'Not a goodnight,' I wished her and turned off the light.

She laughed softly, and I laughed too. Intoxicated with love, we silently and affectionately embraced. We kissed for a long time, holding each other ever closer and closer. Here I was in the sweetest, happiest moment of my life, but still I had to drink from the bitter cup of fate. As always, I had to remove my prosthetic legs. Hurriedly, I got rid of them and hugged Zhanmila once more. She understood everything but didn't look or say a word, just hugging me even tighter and eagerly reciprocating my kisses.

The next day, she disembarked before me. We exchanged phone numbers and agreed to meet again.

My soul sang, and seized with joy, after a while, I called her. I wanted to hear her melodious, tender voice again, to share the tender feelings I had for her, but her phone was disconnected. *Maybe she's got no reception?* I thought. Impatient, I began calling her every hour, but to no avail. I became anxious. In the end, she would have to have seen my calls. Doubts began to creep into my heart. Was she avoiding me? Yes, most likely, because why would she, a beautiful, blossoming girl see a cripple like me. Had it just been one night of fleeting passion? I consoled myself, telling myself that it didn't matter, but it was a flimsy piece of self-deception. In fact, I realised that I loved her. I was worried about her; maybe something bad had happened? You never know what can happen in these turbulent times.

Upon arrival in my city, I began to actively seek the name Zhanmila Tokanato in all the newspapers and on the internet, but it never appeared. Had she just disappeared? She left me bewildered, crushed under the weight of unanswered questions. Like a sip of pure spring water in the muddy stream of life or oxygen to the lungs of a patient, she had refreshed my soul and revived my dying feelings, and then she was gone.

Intuition

Heaven has gifted me with exceptional intuition, and years of intense struggle with the enemies of humanity have perfected it. I can feel the intentions of the mercilessness from a distance and feel the hidden danger and aggression with my gut, ears and eyes. Without fail, I can identify the thug or the fellow in a crowd.

One day at dusk, I was sitting in my wheelchair-fortress on an embankment. People were hurrying home after work, too busy to pay any mind to me. I was moving quietly, gently pressing the hand pedal and admiring the horizon which was still reddish just after sunset, when suddenly, on an intuitive level, I felt the presence of a very dangerous person nearby. Concealing my excitement, I calmly began to look around and, thanks to my well-developed lateral vision, saw a brigand walking a little behind me. As he overtook, staring down at me, I understood from his posture and gait that he represented a force for evil. Without delay, I called out to him, asking for assistance. At first, he scowled, but then he slowly walked towards me. His steps were incredibly heavy. As he approached, I met him with a meek look and politely asked him if he would help push the stroller onto the sidewalk. Apparently, he was not a complete scumbag yet as he assented to assist. As he took the handle of Yangalibus, my Borgia ring did its work and I sent H-particles of conscience into him.

'You're disabled, was it war or what?' he asked compassionately a few seconds later. 'Perhaps the result of an unfortunate accident?'

'Cannon fodder,' I replied; 'the result of meaningless slaughter.'

'Oh,' he said warmly, 'you know what? Let's have a drink of whiskey together and talk heart to heart; what do you say?'

His tone was almost pleading, so how I could refuse?

We sat by the shore of that night and drank and talked frankly for a long time, frankly. More precisely, he poured out his soul, which is quite natural for a person under the influence of my process. I listened and smirked to myself, enjoying another victory over a villain. It turned out he was going to blow up the station, and at that moment he was terribly ashamed. Greatly agitated, he talked about his atrocities and swore that he would never fire a single shot, plant another bomb or even harm a fly.

'That's it,' he said with remorse, 'I don't want to fight any more, let alone kill. I swear I'll try to atone.'

A HUNDRED YEARS ON THE STEPPE   *303*

With these words, my new acquaintance took off his light long cloak and unbuckled his heavy belt on which there were placed a neat row of explosives devices. Reeling it out, he stepped into the water and threw it all into the sea as far as possible from the shore. With a splash and a gurgle, the sea swallowed the deadly weapon. We both breathed a sigh of relief and clicked our glasses as the water neutralised the monstrous device.

Cleaning Company

I set up a kind of cleaning company on the internet. In a rather odd but comprehensible way, I advertised my services: 'To all who desire justice. Write to me about those who deserve punishment for any crimes and are in need of spiritual cleansing. Click here right now to begin.'

So reports about those who would spoil the world and were in need of the torture of conscience began to flow in. I was thrown into a fever, shivering from the human thirst for justice and hatred of their fellow man. There were so many reports that at a rough calculation even if I cleansed hundreds of people a day it would have taken several lifetimes to sate this thirst for justice. It seemed the whole world needed cleansing, a fact to which some respondents attested. Maybe that's what I needed to do: an indiscriminate cleansing. After all, everyone has something to be ashamed of. We, that is, all of humanity have long been mired in sin.

The respondents wrote excitedly, one even suggesting

that I create a 'Bomb of Conscience Awakening' and detonate it in the stratosphere so that its particles would envelop the entire globe. In principle, the idea was not bad. In fact, if as a result of such a bomb people came to see the light and live according to their conscience then we would praise the explosion. The catch, of course, was the irreversible nature of the process of purification. It would be ideal if a person was a little ashamed of their misdeeds, correcting their path and living calmly, but it doesn't work like that. Her Majesty, Conscience herself would eventually drive everyone insane, constantly torturing humanity for its actions. Therefore, I couldn't allow this to happen; my own conscience wouldn't allow me to deal with absolute strangers so shamelessly and ruthlessly. On the other hand, however, it would hardly be possible to achieve great success utilising an artisanal method. Still, better little by little than nothing at all. So, asking myself the moral questions, restraining myself so that I didn't accidentally let the genie out of the bottle, I continued to deliver precise blows.

What have I not experienced in these ten years of intense struggle? I have seen a lot and met many people. Among my patients there have been people of completely different worldviews, religions, educations and character whose life experiences were wildly divergent. They all had one similar trait, though: there was no sense of justice and no conscience. They believed that their actions were just and could argue endlessly about the concept of justice, and listening to them, one might think they were right, but they were acting according to an absent conscience. Once the

A HUNDRED YEARS ON THE STEPPE

verbal husks were discarded, it became clear that every villain believes their convictions stand up to moral scrutiny. To any rational human it is clear that invading foreign lands and killing people is a crime, but these figures it was impossible to convince. So, with a light heart, I forcibly aroused their consciences, and the changes in their behaviour were very interesting to watch.

One patient was a drug lord of sorts who sold counterfeit medicines which poisoned people, intensifying their illnesses. Such people, playing with the fate of others, deserve to be ashamed. Having curbed my rage, I quietly and imperceptibly impacted him with the H-particles of conscience, and how he changed! He admitted that his medicines never cured anyone and were produced in such a way that people would become addicted to his drugs. The money of the sick fuelled the lavish lifestyle of this drug lord. After meeting with my linctus, however, he gave away his fortune and became a Holy man.

On another occasion, I finally got to a professor of bacteriology whom I had been pursuing for some time. What he told me after the awakening of his conscience cannot be conveyed without a shudder. It transpires that many of the bacteria which cause the most dangerous diseases and threaten all of humanity were invented by scientists commissioned by political and military departments for the purpose of the mass destruction of the enemy nations. With his conscience awoken, the professor now resides in an insane asylum.

Everyone knows that chemical waste, gases and the harmful detritus produced by factories poison the air, water and land, that carbon dioxide is a dense, suffocating ring that has enveloped the entire planet; that there are gaps in the ozone holes gape. We do not stop to think about the consequences of our unbridled, criminal actions and, it seems, are not ashamed that we are destroying nature and poisoning the world. Well, I poison the poisoners of the world with healing particles of shame. One such character shut down their most harmful plant and donated its profits to an environmental group.

Of course, such a mass epiphany among magnates, oligarchs, politicians and military figures could not go unnoticed. Society was shocked. Like an epidemic, one by one important people began to repent publically and call upon their companions and comrades to do likewise. An investigation began at the highest level, and you, General Yang Lee Mzhanba took up the case. You began interrogating people, asking them where, when and from whom they had contracted the disease. Yes, it was dubbed a psychic infection, the awakening of the conscience.

A Cheater's Revelation

Politicians always lie. Even now they continue to lie, and society willingly believes their lies. If anything, society thirsts for deceit. Sweet lies adorn the harsh reality of being. Lies and flattery are like twin brothers. Aggressive flattery

A HUNDRED YEARS ON THE STEPPE

is identical to magic. The attacker's desire always lies on the surface of their character. Most of the attacked are clearly susceptible to absurd flattery. Looking for praise, they trust the words of the aggressor without giving the matter a second thought. In moderation, flattery is a pleasant thing, but when it goes beyond the boundaries of the rational and becomes a way of life, it melds together with political activity and becomes a truly dangerous tragi-comedy.

Lies are contagious, and humanity always gives in to the sweet temptation of believing in them. Given this immutable fact, sometimes you have to ask yourself the question: why bother to fight lies and flattery if it's pleasant and useful for people to lie to themselves? What is the point in revealing the bitter truth when lies and flattery taste so sweet? Well, firstly these untruths should be contrary to human nature, and secondly, when lies are brought into the political arena it is a danger to the nation. Therefore, every patriot, every figure who loves freedom and justice, every decent person simply must always expose lies.

One day, I managed to influence the president of a big, strong state. Oh, I can imagine your face right now, Mr Yang Lee Mzhanba! You're probably grinning and suspected me of lying myself. *Where has this flight of fancy taken this poor man*, that's what you're probably thinking? *In order to get to the president of any country, you'd need to overcome so many guards. What you're saying is absurd!*

No, that's where you're wrong, General. He, the President himself, came to me. I almost cried out I was so shocked. During the festivities held in honour of the Day of Freedom, the President walked down the capital's main street surrounded by his retinue and guards. People waved their hands and threw flowers, and he, at his discretion approached the crowd and shook hands with some loyal subjects from time to time. Suddenly, he looked at me, sitting in my Yangalibus. Our eyes met, we smiled at each other and he approached me. He shook my hand and began to talk about improving welfare for the poor and his concern for their fate as citizens. He smelt of expensive cologne and wine. Perhaps he was being sincere at that moment, but, of course, it was his favourite PR move masterfully disguised.

Such things always enrage me, but at that moment I almost lost my temper. I wanted to blurt out insults, but instead, I smiled and nodded my head. Of course, I had something of my own on my own mind, so I asked him to take a picture with me. The president slightly in front of me - as befitted his inflated sense of self - and placed his right hand on the handle of my wheelchair. I calculated everything precisely. Such an experienced politician who is madly in love with his popularity would never pass up the opportunity to show off his credentials by posing with a cripple. It's ironic that a man whose decree has thrown thousands of men into the very mouth of a fiery volcano now stood there presenting himself as a friend and guardian of all the disabled people broken by the war. But he was mistaken, probably for the first time in his political career. He had been deceiving others all his life, but here, unexpectedly, he was doomed to fail. The "Borgia Ring" mercilessly did its job. As he was saying goodbye, his expression changed, and he suddenly

A HUNDRED YEARS ON THE STEPPE   *309*

burst into tears.

'Forgive me, soldier,' he said in a trembling voice; 'forgive us politicians, devourers of nations.'

I realised I had hit the target. He shook my hand tightly with both hands for a long time, and there was so much warmth in his grip that it seemed to me that he could warm the hardened hearts of every person on this planet. His retinue quietly led him away, and I looked forward to the completion of this story.

Soon the president addressed the people on the air with truth and sincerity for the first time. He repented, saying he was ashamed of his cruel deeds and asking for forgiveness.

'In protecting and pursuing the national interest of my country, I constantly suppressed and infringed upon the interests of other nation,' he said. 'That was both unfair and shameless. Of course, you need to think about your national interests, but not to the detriment of others, for in this world we all call home everything is interconnected. All states and nations should come together, link arms and think about the future of the globe and the fate of life on this planet.

Some people build for all of their lives, and then someone comes along and instantly erases it all from the face of the Earth. No, this is monstrous. How can we allow this?' he lamented mournfully.

The whole audience was in shock. What could have made the president say these things and why now? The people were exulted - our leader had finally seen the light and grown spiritually.

The president was hastily dismissed. Taking the cause

upon himself, he began to zigzag around the world calling on other powerful people to find their compassion and take up the path of justice. Everyone agreed, nodded their heads and hastily expressed their support, but behind his back, they laughed at him and continued to commit their unscrupulous acts.

A Conspiracy

Mr Yang Lee Mzhanba, you must have smirked to yourself at the word 'conspiracy,' but you were wrong to do so. The fact is that, by and large, the whole world has been living according to the laws of conspiracy for a considerable amount of time. To some extent, all people wear disguises, are secretive, wary of each other and live in their own mental palaces. They either do not or choose not to notice what's happening around them. At first, I stuck out like a sore finger, but I soon realised that it was easier to hide amongst people in a huge metropolis than in a gaping cave in the mountains. I studied the art of disguise, taking inspiration from wherever I could find it. I studied the struggle between the East and West from code-cracking to espionage. I studied the strategies of the special forces of leading military powers. Heaven has gifted me with a sparkling imagination, and I myself came up with several methods so ingenious that my own mother wouldn't recognise. I used all the effective techniques of stage makeup and didn't shun capes, masks and wigs. My most important discoveries, however,

A HUNDRED YEARS ON THE STEPPE 311

were related to secrets from antiquity aimed at influencing people, a wealth of knowledge which I will not divulge.

So, having armed myself with scientific and practical knowledge, charged with the energies of the cosmos I easily passed unnoticed among police officers, detectives of all stripes and millions of others doing everything I considered necessary for the triumph of justice. Your hair would stand on end if I wrote in detail about the process of implementing my acts of retribution, but this is not necessary. After all, then they could become a kind of textbook for the true enemies of humanity, and that would be really scary.

Many Agents

One day, I was travelling on a train with a very strange person. He chatted incessantly for the entire day although no one asked him a thing. Immediately upon laying his eyes on me, he began to speak openly. It seemed he had accumulated a lot of secrets, and I noted how often people share intimate secrets with complete strangers on a train.

'Humanity has created so many dangerous things that it's no longer necessary to manufacture new weapons of mass destruction,' he said. 'Any beneficial discovery can be manipulated to cause harm. An overdose of the drug becomes a poison.

'There are impostors everywhere, especially when they strive for autocracy and become lost in their sense of self-worth. This is our immense field of action. In one exorbitantly ambitious country, they were going to build a district of soaring skyscrapers. Despite the true state of affairs, their leadership suffered from delusions of grandeur and wanted to rise above the rest of the world. We could not allow this, so we infiltrated our own builders into the team. During the construction, there were frequent accidents, so in the end, these idiot's edifices crumbled into the sand and they got ruins instead of their gleaming megalopolis.

'In another country, at the preparation stage for the construction of very important state facilities, we permeated the building materials with chemicals hidden under a thin layer of paint which slowly but surely would have a negative impact on the health and psyche of the inhabitants of these buildings. As a result, without knowing it they became our obedient slaves. Radioactive substances are often added to the foundation of new homes, and these cranks, losing their minds in pursuit of profit, don't even bother to check the safety of the building materials.

'There are still many ingenious methods of sabotage. They're particularly effective in countries which have forgotten one wise saying: "You can trust, but always double-check." Often, we flood such countries with unhealthy goods and industrial waste. The multilayer paints of our toys, dishes and household utensils also perform strategic tasks: systematically the effects of these chemical elements on the health of the people send those countries to hell. We also supply genetically modified products at very low prices. Our fruit and vegetables are grown on nitrates, stuffed with bio-additives and treated with all sorts of toxic chemicals which undermine health and bring illness and early death to our competitors. Falling over themselves to make a quick buck, the businessmen of these countries lap up all this cheap, smelly trash, buying them in bulk to sell to their compatriots, never for a moment thinking of the harmful consequences. They leap at the sight of these brilliant trinkets, forgetting the ancient wisdom: "Free cheese can only lead to a mousetrap." So, we conquer their homelands with our strategic warrior-goods.'

Listening to him, I realised that fate had delivered unto me the most dangerous type of person. I carried out my attack quickly and imperceptibly. He fell silent, buried his face in his pillow and wept plaintively. Disembarking at my station, I headed home; but what I had heard left me anxious at heart. How should I deal with this evil? What should I do?

Morality - The Fate of a Loser

At first glance, many successful careers are built on injustice. Despite the fact that losers speak the most frequently about conscience and morality, I'm certainly not a moralist, whimpering in envy at the successes of others. Still, if you look around, you'll see that the most moral accusers in society are simply embittered people who haven't achieved significant successes in their lives.

He who is dizzy from the heights of power, wealth and glory, though, will in most cases simply stop caring about others. They can even believe that conscience is the biggest obstacle to success. There is a deal of truth in it; in order to move up the steep, slippery steps of governance and business, one often has to step over conscience and justice. Once they slip, though, such figures begin to blow hard about their moral indignity and how shamelessly they were treated. I'm not a supporter of such a hypocritical moralism, but there are things that cannot stay silent, and the bloodshed you've cost, Mr Yang Lee Mzhanba, is one such example.

Almighty Weapons

Several years into my struggle, I finally realised that I couldn't overcome all the villains utilising such a straight-forward, simple method. Thus, I decided to create a weapon of mass destruction, my 'Bomb of Conscience Awakening.' So, after a long and intense period of research, I finally discovered a combination of $X + Y + H$ substances. The essence of this extremely powerful weapon is that it is airborne. Once one-hundred grams of the Y-Substance is added to the X -tablets, an immediate reaction occurs and the new compound dissolves imperceptibly into the air. To deliver the H-particle from the transmitter is a mere trifle, and it has the power to hit the population of a whole metropolis, but it is not entirely safe. Imagine what would happen if all at once every inhabitant of a city of millions began to see clearly and feel ashamed. They would stop everything and give themselves over to remorse day and night. Truthfully,

A HUNDRED YEARS ON THE STEPPE 315

no one knows what the consequences would be. So, I decided to first conduct an experiment on those, how to put it delicately, who most deserve it, that is to say, on politicians.

After several attempts, I managed to get into the parliament building. I was helped by one of the guards, whom I implored to help poor little me access the toilet. He pushed Yangalibus through the control passage until we reached the lavatory at which juncture I thanked him and said that I could handle the rest myself. By this time, quite a few members of the government were gathered together with the senators.

Taking protective steps, I quickly prepared the secret mixture, and it seeped its way into the ventilation ducts. Then I sent in the H-particles and calmly headed for the exit. What happened next was something quite unimaginable. Without exception, everyone in attendance began to publicly repent for their dark deeds, crimes and misconduct until finally, they all resigned.

A few weeks later, acting upon information leaked by some of those to whom I'd returned their conscience, I figured out who the dealers of the most dangerous weapons were. Posing as a representative of rich clients fighting on another continent, I came to them. Masterfully playing this role, I passed all the checks without a hitch. Blindfolding me, they snaked from left to right down long corridors before eventually delivering me to a secret underground warehouse, where, removing the blindfold from my eyes, they began to show me their wares. There wasn't a weapon in the world you couldn't find here. These ranged from the usual small arms and grenades, all neatly laid out, to nuclear devices.

I began to make my choice, selecting a cache worth hundreds of millions of dollars. For the sake of curiosity, I asked as to the capabilities of these shiny creations of human hands. The merchants - and there were many of them - burst out laughing in unison, shaking the warehouse. Still chortling, the bald, bespectacled leader, replied that the arsenal I had chosen was enough to turn half of a city to ashes, and only the ruins of an archaeological site would remain in the other. Internally shuddering in horror, I feigned laugher and asked about the safety of this storage facility.

'Are you not afraid that an accidental explosion or chemical leak could occur? How dangerous would that be for our country?'

Amused by my naivety, the leader smiled condescendingly. Eager to show off his vast knowledge, he lectured me on the reliability of the reinforced concrete armoured storage located deep underground in a mountain range far from any metropolis.

'In this place, even a massive explosion would be like a buffalo trying to headbutt down a baobab tree,' he exclaimed. 'And even if for some reason or other a catastrophe did occur inside, everything would remain forever in the arms of the earth. In addition, some crucial components have not been assembled yet; but don't worry they'll be connected before your shipment leaves. We have a reliable channel under the patronage...'

The leader abruptly stopped talking, closed his eyes and

respectfully pointed his finger towards the Heavens. Everyone bowed their heads meaningfully, and I did likewise. I had to act now because there would be no other such opportunity. Taking the components from my crutches and artificial limbs, I released a dose of substance X + Y and then sent the H-particles into them. Thus, I transformed everyone. They drove me back to the city, but before leaving the warehouse was blown up, leaving the weapons in a cold black grave forever.

Luck

It was following this event that I decided to transform you, Mr Yang Lee Mzhanba, along with your battalion and the city you occupied. I drove to the top of a forested hill on the outskirts of your city from there the majestic metropolis was in full view. For a moment, I even admired its beauty. Returning to the task at hand, I pulled a jar wrapped in a newspaper from my bag and prepared to attack. It was then that a miracle happened. Unravelling the newspaper in which the jar was wrapped, I saw a familiar name typed in bold print: Zhanmila Tokanato. It was an incredible moment. I scanned through the lines of her article about peace and war, intelligence and conscience, and there at the bottom was her email address.

My head was spinning. She had written it for me. How much time I had wasted searching in vain for her, and she, it transpired, was living and working on the other side of the world.

I did not hesitate in abandoning my plan to attack the city and instantly went to look for her. On that same day, we met.

Sincere Feelings

We sat in the booth of a restaurant and talked in hushed tones. We were immensely glad to see each other. We loved each other and were happy, our wounded souls nurtured by the peace and tranquillity we found when together. We ate delicious dishes with great delight and talked about what we'd experienced since the moment we'd parted. It turned out that she'd accidentally dropped her cell-phone in a river, losing my contact details. Obviously, her search through the annuls of the Union of Persons with Disabilities proved unsuccessful. Burning with shame but counting on her understanding, I admitted that in the luxury cabin of the fast train I had introduced myself using a fictitious name. She pouted playfully, shook her head and made a small fist, threatening me so merrily that I had an irresistible urge to hug her and kiss her pretty face.

'Don't blame yourself for the fictitious name,' she said, assuaging my guilt. 'The fact is that Zhanmila Tokanato is also a pen-name of such. I'll tell you my real name later, at home. I'll whisper it in your ear if you promise to forget it immediately and never call me by it.'

I nodded dumbly as happy as if I was in seventh heaven.

'You will always remain Zhanmila Tokanato to me,' I

A HUNDRED YEARS ON THE STEPPE

replied.

She laughed cheerfully, and we embraced.

Fair Fight

Suddenly, the door of our booth swung open and four men burst in. We were alarmed and looked enquiringly at the intruders. The men were obviously quite tipsy, with terrible faces that expressed nothing but arrogance.

'Scram; this is our favourite booth,' a ruffian bellowed.

I recognised him immediately. It was the so-called "Muscle Monster," the former Olympic champion and world record holder in weightlifting. When he lost his title at the next Olympics, he had left weightlifting behind and retrained as a professional mixed martial arts fighter. With his physical prowess, it hadn't taken long for him to become a champion in that sport. Spoiled by an excess of honours and the adulation of a subservient society, he had become incredibly proud and arrogant. Imagining himself a celebrity of the highest order, he looked down on everyone.

'Who are you compared to me, you insignificant worm?' he spat.

'I respect you,' I replied as respectfully as possible, 'but unfortunately, I can't give you this booth because I invited a girl and we really like it here.'

'Well, okay, if the girl likes it here so much, she can stay with us,' laughed the Muscle Monster, the others giggling obediently at his joke. 'But you'd better wheel yourself out of here, and your chair best not even squeak.'

'You may be a champion and a celebrity, but that doesn't give you the right to humiliate others,' I objected, trying to reason with the drunkards.

'How dare you speak like that to a champion, the pride of the whole country?' his entourage shouted indignantly.

'He may be a champion, but I'm not so sure he's the pride of the country,' I said sarcastically, feeling a surge of anger and contempt for these boors. 'What are you really so proud of anyway?'

'For a person who says they respect me, you clearly don't know much, you worm. I lifted two-hundred-and-fifty-kilograms, and the whole world applauded me.'

As the door of the booth was open, our quarrels had attracted the attention of passers-by, and hearing the words of the Muscle Monster many began to applaud him.

'The world made a mistake,' I said calmly, 'because you are no use to anyone.'

'But they're proud of me. My strength is unique, and it's the property of mankind!' he yelled, almost lacerating his vocal cords. 'No one can lift weights like I can.'

'Any camel can lift several times more than you without any training and it doesn't ask for rewards or require applause. The strength of a camel is far more useful to people.'

I still don't know why I said this, or, in general, where such thoughts came from. Probably, in the heat of the quarrel, this truth dawned on me, or perhaps the accumulated resentment from my ruined youth or envy of these minions of fate escaped from me.

A HUNDRED YEARS ON THE STEPPE 321

Of course, my hasty words didn't go down well with the champion who turned blue with rage and challenged me to a duel, a fight to the death one on one. This healthy athlete publicly mocked me by challenging me to a 'fair fight' whilst smiling sardonically, and the audience applauded. We have a strange concept of honesty. If we look at it purely and humanly then what kind of honest fight can there be between a professionally trained fighter and a simple man? If an athlete, or worse, a special agent, an assassin trained for years who has turned his body into a weapon faces off with a regular person and snaps his neck or punctures his chest with one blow, is that a 'fair fight'? Why must the regular person who has honesty and dignity be doomed to inevitable death? Going against this kind of monster would be tantamount to suicide, but to refuse under any pretext, even my disability would be shameful. Here was the terrible choice which lay before me, and realising this the boor flaunted his prowess, triumphantly pumping his muscles in front of these idolising idiots whose brains have been snapped by the modern world.

I was indignant at such a brazen intrusion into my life, but I remembered the teachings of Miyamoto Musashi, that the rising spirit is weak, but the falling spirit is also weak and, therefore, the middle is the heart of all positions. Pulling myself together, I calmly said to the thug:

'I offer you a worthy draw and a fair world.'

He laughed wildly and everyone laughed with him. They scoffed at me. Sensing easy prey, the predator decided to play up for his audience, like Charysh the Noyon (a warrior-prince among the Dzungars) had before a fight with young Khan Ablai.

Well, how could there be a tie between you and me, huh?' he shouted at the top of his lungs. 'You might as well curl up into a ball and crawl out of here before I break all of your bones.'

I barely held my tongue. The girls in the gathering crowd squealed in delight and the guys cheered. Indignant but calm, my sweet partner looked at me expressively.

'Honey, let's go home,' she said, pronouncing each word slowly and clearly. 'Don't mess with this monster. I need you alive.'

I was touched. There is a stereotype, especially in literature and cinema which has pervaded the public consciousness, that women provoke men to perform incredible, sometimes crazy actions which are then assessed as a manifestation of love. Yet my beloved wanted only one thing, to protect me from my inexorable death.

She took my hand and tried to lead me out of there, but the big man abruptly grabbed her so that she cried out in pain.

'Will you fight or leave her for me?' he muttered through his teeth, his eyes wild and bloodshot.

'All right,' I replied, looking up at his beastly face distorted with anger, and we left the booth.

As we made our exit I managed to land a couple of blows on his hands, the like of which would cause an incredible amount of pain and shock for any normal person and render them unable to fight. This athlete's body was like

A HUNDRED YEARS ON THE STEPPE 323

stone, though, and realising the extent of his wild power I was horrified. My arms are strong and the force of my punches could have split thick boards in half, yet to him they were nothing.

Deciding to change my tactics, I attempted to overwhelm him with my 'cobra strike,' but he easily evaded it. I immediately unleashed a lightning fast 'cobra back strike,' but even this he managed to deflect like an iron wall, as grabbing my hand he began to confidently topple me to the ground. After fiercely resisting for as long as I could, I succumbed and fell. The crowd was buzzing with excitement as the monster leant over me, grabbing my neck with his powerful hands and squeezing as if trying to break it. Enjoying himself, the thug cried out to the audience:

'Look at what I am! Look how easily I can break this man!'

The situation was becoming dangerous for me, but this stupid strongman could not defeat the cunning cripple he held in his grasp for nature has endowed me with the perfect weapon: intelligence. Feigning defeat under his onslaught, I simply waited for the moment to perform my 'tiger strike.' In the heat of battle, he didn't even see my counterattack, and after a moment he dropped unconscious. Throwing off the huge sack of meat, I punched him in the face a couple of times and jabbed him with the particles of conscience.

The crowd fell silent. In tears, Zhanmila rushed to me, and holding hands we swiftly made our exit. Waking up, the bully began to rise, but falling backwards he covered his head with his hands and sobbed. His awakened conscience had crushed him, and he burned with shame for his filthy words and disgusting deeds. *Well, what happened was supposed to happen*, I thought, *and from now on this thug will suffer from his remorse forever.* This was a purer form of justice than life imprisonment or the death penalty for he would live quieter than water and lower than the grass under the cloud of humiliation for the rest of his days.

We left unmolested and meandered in silence, our hands clasped tightly together. I have not left Zhanmila's side since. These years have been the happiest of my life. We had a son, and then a daughter. By the way, Zhanmila told me the secret of her real name and the story of her life, which, of course, will not be disseminated here. Take your time, Mr General Yang Lee Mzhanba, soon everything will become clear. After all, you believe that secrets cannot be kept from you. But I know something you don't because believe it or not, we've actually met before.

Agony

To this day I still shudder at the memory of our first battle. Sometimes I even dream of my dead comrades. At the very beginning of the war, we were ambushed. Tons of explosives fell on us, and amidst the fire and smoke, the roar of explosions was deafening. Everything became mixed up in this bloody kaleidoscope, and as we lay submerged beneath debris in this strange land, our only desire was to survive by any means necessary.

Suddenly, a terrible cry drowned out the sound of the

A HUNDRED YEARS ON THE STEPPE   *325*

machine guns. This cry was one I will never forget. The wounded soldier was staggering in our direction. His left hand was covered in blood and hanging by a tendon, his whole arm having been smashed to smithereens and almost ripped from his shoulder by an explosion. Two orderlies rushed to help him, but they immediately fell dead from the bullets of snipers. With them, the soldier's last hope for salvation also perished. We watched him and prayed helplessly as he stumbled towards a stone block our commanders were defending, before falling to ground from loss of blood. Led by a general, the commanders went to aid him. The young soldier barely got to his feet, and, in desperation, cut off his dangling hand with a knife and flung it at the general with a loud cry. Somersaulting several meters up in the air, the bloody hand struck the general's clean-shaven face.

We were dumbfounded and looked on with wide eyes, but the general didn't even blink. It seemed to me that he took this slap in the face for granted. A spray of blood covered his face and uniform, but he didn't show the slightest sign of disgust. It was evident that this general had a heart of stone and iron nerves and had waded across many bloody rivers. Muttering something to his officers, he saluted the dying soldier before quickly flying away in his armoured helicopter.

Soon, reinforcements arrived, and we ousted our fierce enemy from the gorge. Then we learned the name of this strange general: Yang Lee Mzhanba. Yes, it was you, General. A legend among seasoned warriors, we had heard you praised for your courage and ruthlessness. We had heard you spoken of as the stronghold of our hopes and the master strategist of our victories. We young educated people also understood, though, that it was you, with your recklessness and shameless cunning, who had led us into this meaningless massacre.

When that young soldier died, your image as a hero was shaken. We had believed in our commanders, but when for the first time before our eyes in the presence of Yang Lee Mzhanba himself, those savages managed to murder that soldier and the medical personnel, we realised that we too could be defeated and no one could save us from death. With this understanding, all the cruelty and madness of the war were felt more acutely. If I were conscious when my legs were torn off, then I would have thrown them in your face. Well, now I don't have bleeding legs, but there's another more sophisticated weapon which I'll plunge into your heart.

Either Or

For centuries, saints and sages have tried to teach humanity about the power of the mind, to guide them to the true path. Literature and art have worked to cleanse the souls of people and awaken the good in them. Still, people have failed to grasp the most simple of truths – one should not kill any living thing, let alone their own species.

Great thinkers and poets have always laboured under the yoke of a sense of guilt. They have suffered in their

A HUNDRED YEARS ON THE STEPPE 327

spiritual quests, reflecting on mortality and the eternal meaning of life. It seems to me, though, that the main cause of their anguish lies elsewhere.

It has always been the case that powerful nations or states have conquered smaller ones and unscrupulously oppressed and humiliated them, sometimes even mercilessly exterminating their people. There are plenty of examples. This bloodshed also torments the conquering nation, and poets and philosophers, indeed all highly conscious and sensitive people are the collective mind of their nations. Herein lies an intricate truth: politicians cause trouble, and the poets suffer.

But the blood and tears of innocents murdered do not disappear without a trace; they return to the guilty, demanding retribution. Can you really blame the oppressed, humiliated or enslaved for cursing at their torturers? Perhaps that is why there is no peace in this world.

I think and hurt, but I can't understand why a handful of people, sometimes even a single person makes political decisions that bring misery to the world. Why do nations allow the reins of power to fall into the hands of dictators? I tried to comprehend the history of mankind in a slightly different way, from the standpoint of morality, conscience and justice, but it left me shuddering at the acts of vaunted historical figures.

Even today, a strange pursuit of leadership is in fashion. I think that it should be simple: all people should be their own leaders, and if no one was suppressed there would be peace and harmony on Earth. Yet in advertising and campaigns, everyone is led to the attitude that to be a person with power over others is the pinnacle and is to be aspired to. What will happen if all the multibillionaires decide to strive headlong only towards this goal? When you decide to become a leader, do you bother to ask if the people assent, and if they do not will you subjugate them? And then if you meet other leaders whose sociopathic personalities are the same as yours, trouble cannot be avoided.

Many times I spoke at ease with influential politicians of all stripes, and as a result of these conversations, I came to some general conclusions which were are far from encouraging. Some of these politicians were decent people, and the guiding thread of their politics was the greater good for the benefit of their societies. It sounds reasonable, right? But if one 'looks into the root,' as Kozma Prutkov said, then it becomes a terrifying thing indeed because this greater good can trample upon the concepts of humanity and justice. What if what is useful to your country is inhumane in relation to another? A politician once frankly told me, 'If what is useful to us is inhumane, and that which is humane is useless, we choose the benefits.' This attitude is monstrous, and as far as I can I have attacked such people with H-particles. Unfortunately, though, you can't re-educate everyone.

It's no less frightening when the many seek the benefits of servility. One day, I found out that one such dictator had built a bacteriological plant in the centre of a peaceful metropolis. On another whim, he'd decided to bury the nation's radioactive waste at the bottom of a clear deep lake. The worst thing was that no one had opposed these deci-

A HUNDRED YEARS ON THE STEPPE 329

sions. That I could not get to this leader was such a disappointment.

The further humanity develops, the more terrible its deadly arsenal becomes. Now, as these weapons are scattered between nations, there is no question of whom to defeat or how. The question is will humanity, in the pursuit of profit and world domination destroy the globe, or together, in peace and harmony, save it? There is no third way, General Yang Lee Mzhanba.

Quite Exceptional

Of course, like every nation, every person considers themselves exceptional, and this is natural. It's pointless to dispute this, as it's impossible to prove otherwise, and indeed, every person, every nation is unique and beautiful in its own way. In considering yourself exceptional, though, grant this right to others as well, that is, agree you should treat others as the chosen, most beloved creatures of the Almighty just like you. There is no need to prove your exceptionality to others, and certainly not by force.

Everyone lived in peace and harmony until the goddess of discord, Eris, threw a golden apple to the three goddesses, Hera, Aphrodite and Athena, which bore the inscription: 'For the most beautiful one.' Then everything went to hell. A war ensued, many soldiers died and Troy was destroyed. People may have forgotten this instructive and tragic story, but this apple of discord from ancient times haunts humanity to this day, changing only its shape. The people of Earth continue to fight over transient material wealth, their exorbitant ambitions and stupid pride, brutally destroying each other.

The pursuit of greatness is not so bad if you follow a path of honesty and justice, but when you exalt yourself, building your greatness upon the destruction of others, that is criminal. If you rise up by trampling upon others, you end up standing on the bones of those who you destroyed.

What about a person who has honour and dignity when other countries colonise his, dictate its conditions, destroy its national cultural values, language, literature and traditions, and oppress and insult the religious freedoms of its people? Even worse, when political, spiritual and psychological pressure turns into violence and whole families within small nations are subject to the fire and sword of the strong? Naturally, a person who has undergone such trials and persecution since childhood objectively becomes a conscientious terrorist and indiscriminately sets about reaping vengeance on the representatives of the nation which tortured his. Evil begets evil - this is well known - but why should peaceful people suffer because of the exorbitant ambitions of a handful of aggressors?

Once, I tried to ask this question of two figures I'd found online. I met them according to the agreed schedule, asked them to push my stroller, and they reluctantly complied with my request. The first one I attacked accurately and efficiently, but the second one was crafty. Noticing something suspicious, he jerked back before moving men-

A HUNDRED YEARS ON THE STEPPE

acingly towards me. The handles of Yangalibus were located on both sides of the back of the chair, like half-arcs in the upper corners deliberately placed so that only one person could hold them. This was designed as such so that if necessary I could stop the stroller abruptly and trigger my device from the rear. On this occasion, though, the first hooligan took one handle with his left hand and the second with his right. I had made a small mistake, and it almost cost me my life, but the elusive and unsinkable, brisk and dexterous Yangalibus helped me out. Just as the bastard was just about to strike me, I hit the afterburners and my faithful chair rushed away into the alley, my would-be assailant falling hopelessly behind.

Having driven quite far, I crossed to the other side of the avenue and took a breath, but this spot wasn't great. The notorious thug began to catch up with me in his car. That was fun! Imagine, Mr Yang Lee Mzhanba, an inveterate big-time thug in broad daylight in a jeep in a modern city chasing a war veteran in a wheelchair. Of course, the car was faster at times, but my stroller was ahead overall. It dived briskly into the narrow alleys, turning deftly turned around the corners and passing where a larger vehicle could not.

Plea

At first, I prayed to the Almighty that he would punish all the guilty parties. I wanted so badly for those who had these crimes to pay with their lives so much. There was no other measure of justice for me. After an epiphany, though, I began to pray that He would make them pay by awakening their conscience.

I really want to ask you in front of the whole world: 'Shame on you, General, how do you feel about having destroyed people's lives? Do you feel ashamed; or maybe you not ashamed at all and will continue to bring misfortune, death and ruin? Then you are a monster who will be forever damned.'

Justice and conscience? They are the main enemies of civilisation. They are a brake on progress which does not allow people to grow. They interfere with life. Conscience, reason, justice and politics are incompatible things, is what you're probably thinking to yourself considering the naive idiot who wrote this. Do not rush to conclusions, though, for the time will come when you will have to answer for everything. Sometimes it is useful, General Yang Lee Mzhanba, to see yourself through the eyes of the people that you subjugated even though you thought you had built a paradise for them on Earth for them until the hour of their freedom arrives.

Do I Have Permission to Live?

The truth is beautiful as long as it does not concern us. We all love the truth about others.

As soon as our truth begins to be revealed, however, we try with all our strength to drown it out, to furiously rebel against it and drive it back. It is an unsinkable thing, though.

A HUNDRED YEARS ON THE STEPPE

As with all previous generations of the human race, you and I will have to admit to the truth, no matter how bitter it is. Our struggle which you took upon yourself for the destruction and enslavement of our own kind seems senseless, cruel, and wild. Why then does enlightenment not come to all people at the same time? Why can they not declare peace and allow all to live as they please? Indeed, no material or military interests - including oil - have any meaning when placed next to human blood and tears.

> Live people
> Live happily, gleefully
> With faith and hope
> Towards love we lope.
> The tormented people
> By bloody hate,
> Desperate soldiers left crippled,
> Firing straight;
> Send them home
> So their souls don't roam.
> What's found
> Is left crowned;
> A lone pilgrim
> Buries the axe of war,
> Follows the path of the world,
> Otherwise, we swore
> For the times and peoples,
> The thread that links them schisms.
> Oh, the people,
> We brothers of conscience
> Ask as one steeple

334 *Bayangali Alimzhanov*

Let others live with their spirits.
Mr General, Sir!
Let me live!
I grant you permission!

Alogism

How do people solve these problems amidst the bustling rhythms of their everyday lives?

Once, in the market, I saw a blind man. He stood at the side of a busy aisle with a crumpled cap outstretched. Most passers-by didn't pay any attention to him, but some compassionate folk casually threw coins into his hat. Suddenly, a middle-aged fellow who was clearly inebriated came up to the blind man and led him away into a dark corner. I was passing by in my Yangalibus and unwittingly witnessed the incident. The man rustled a piece of paper in front of the blind man's nose.

'Here, I'll give you this banknote and take your change,' he said in a hoarse voice.

With these words, he poured the entire contents of the cap into his pocket, replacing it with a discoloured, worthless piece of paper. I immediately realised that the blind man was being deceived and boiling with rage I rushed to his aid.

'Stop, you bastard; give him back the money!' I cried.

The man looked down on me, grinned mockingly and made to leave. Quickly catching up with the crook in my carriage, I speared him in the ass with my miraculous se-

A HUNDRED YEARS ON THE STEPPE

rum with all my strength. The man froze, then slowly turned around with a detached look etched on his face and hit himself on the forehead with all his might. Making some strange growling sound, he went up to the blind man and placed the contents of his pocket in the cap. Hugging the blind man, he wept uncontrollably. The blind man was confused at first, but after a moment he began to gently pat his assailant on the shoulder.

I, of course, understood all too well what was happening, and sighing, I quietly left.

Ours and Theirs

How easy it is to divide the world into ours and theirs, and, as long as 'our' people don't end up devastated we are happy. This is a falsehood, though, Mr Yang Lee Mzhanba. It has never been the case throughout history and is impossible in the modern world. There is no ours or theirs, there is one ship, the planet Earth in the ocean of space, and our common task is to save it. It is surprising, in my opinion, that I, an unhappy cripple scorched by the flames of war, worry about the fate of Mother Earth, and you, a highly educated, so to speak, politician and general, do not pay any mind to this at all.

You may think: *Now I'll launch a rocket to distant lands, smash its people to pieces and establish a new world order*, but Mr Yang Lee Mzhanba, you are mistaken. These volleys will return to you like boomerangs. You may be taking aim at someone else, Mr General, but you'll end up destroying 'ours.' Such is the supreme justice of the Almighty, God's punishment, karma.

If we impartially study the history of humanity from this standpoint, then we begin to understand that the violence committed by one country or people against another is always returned with an even greater force.

The Hunt

I began to hunt for people who wanted to awaken their conscience and sense of justice. It was thus that many scientists abandoned their research into fantastical new weapons of mass destruction and went to live in monasteries. Some even lost their minds, ending up in psychiatric hospitals. Pleased with my progress, I began to search for a mysterious force which could affect the minds of all these brilliant scientists, but it proved to be elusive. My thinking was far beyond the reach of your powerful agency, Mr General.

Your Excellency

I want to ask you a direct question, Mr Yang Lee Mzhanba. Of course, I will not be able to hear the answer but you can at least answer it yourself, honestly and directly. Is your "greatness," your "power" built upon the humiliation of others? Have you exalted yourself by belittling others? Is it that

A HUNDRED YEARS ON THE STEPPE 337

the lower the insects beneath your feet, the higher you seem to be? And by humiliating others, are you humiliating yourself? Is your power trained upon the destruction of others? Because by destroying others, you destroy yourself.

It would be very interesting to hear your response, but I believe the answers are in the questions themselves and everything will become clear even without a public revelation. Now, I will help you understand why I ask these questions.

Once, I hunted down a terrorist who was part of one of the many radical international organisations. For over a decade the Special Services had been tracking them across the two hemispheres but had been unable to calculate their whereabouts and eliminate them. I managed to sniff out their trail thanks to my intuition and indefatigable imagination.

Sometimes during my perambulations, I thought about how to find them, and one day it suddenly dawned on me: they're looking for this character in the wrong places; they've looked for them all over the globe but not in their own home. Could they really be living here as an absolutely law-abiding, normal citizen, and even working at a responsible government post? Looking closely at all the likely suspects in the government and analysing the path and scale of atrocities committed by Mr X, I reached some logical conclusions. Like a chess grandmaster who was always ten steps ahead, Mr X considered everything, calculating both their own and their opponent's moves. They knew their enemies well and felt invincible, but could not know that a cunning war cripple had begun to hunt them down in his wheelchair-fortress, Yangalibus.

So, I began to wait for my suspects near the exit of the government building every evening when they finished work. I wasn't certain who it was, but I knew that they were here and were one of seven officials I'd singled out. In any case, as they all had plenty to be ashamed of, I'd decided to target all seven. Most importantly, if I could 'eliminate' Mr X then all my actions would be justified.

'All warfare is based on deception,' wrote Sun Tzu. 'Hence, when we are able to attack, we must seem unable; when using our forces, we must appear inactive; when we are near, we must make the enemy believe we are far away; when far away, we must make him believe we are near... If you know the enemy and know yourself, you need not fear the result of a hundred battles.'

I have mastered this programme of the great commander and sage to perfection. It has almost always brought me the desired victory. When the first suspect exited the building, I calmly waited for him in my amazing Yangalibus. No one could pass by my miracle stroller without paying due attention. So, when the high-ranking statesman passed me, his eyes were involuntarily drawn to Yangalibus. As he reached the closest point in his trajectory, I dropped the previously prepared crutch, which, as I said, was a multi-purpose weapon. When bent down, picked up the crutch and politely handed it to me, the "Borgia Ring" struck. Silently, with a nod of the head, I thanked him and dealt an inconspicuous blow with the H-particles. Everything went fine. My work

A HUNDRED YEARS ON THE STEPPE   *339*

was done, and I calmly waited for the result.

The official took several steps forward then stopped abruptly, firmly grabbing his large, well-groomed head in both hands. He cried out and stumbled back to the place where the blow had been struck. Seeing me, he was very happy and began to pour out his soul, vehemently reproaching himself. From his story, it became clear that he had been recruited by foreign intelligence during his studies abroad. It transpired that he was not a spy and did not pass on national and military secrets. His mission was to lobby for the economic interests of the country that recruited him in our state. Now, with his awakened conscience gnawing at him, he decided to go to the prime minister and confess.

In this way, six of my seven targets looked at my Yangalibus, lifted my multifunctional crutch and were dosed. Each confessed to such crimes and sins that I could never have imagined in my wildest fantasies.

The second official to approach was a well-known figure with a slightly drawn physiognomy. I often saw him on television, always smiling and smug. This most respectable gentleman whom our people exalted and called one of the country's outstanding patriots, it turned out, had been pursuing a shadowy goal throughout his career. He freely admitted that he'd shamelessly lied to the public, sowing the dubious seeds of discord and distrust between different regions of the country. Aside from undermining the integrity of the nation, he was a secret patron of the propagation of violence and sex in the cinema and on television. It was with his support that extravagant young directors had stripped cute young girls on screen, seducing them with money and promises of fame into revealing their bodies in sex scenes. Such acts were aimed at undermining the moral foundations of the nation and corrupting the youth. All of this was done at the instructions of his powerful foreign patrons. Now, with his conscience awakened, there was nothing left of the usual mask of the nobleman as he left, hunched over and staggering strangely. A day later, he appeared on national television, spoke frankly about his atrocities, publically repented and urged filmmakers to be conscientious.

The third figure had embezzled vast sums of money from the state. He was not a very prominent figure, tried not to speak publicly, avoided reporters at all costs and did not give interviews. To the extent that he was known, it was as a master of evasion. It was this that led me to the idea that not everything was clean with this fellow. Once again, my innate rare intuition did not fail me. After my attack, he voluntarily confessed to the prosecutor.

The fourth suspect left a lasting impression on me. Seeing me, he slowed his pace and looked guilty at my glorious Yangalibus. When I dropped the crutch, he was genuinely saddened and with a particular sensitivity rushed to pick it up. *What good company this government is,* I thought, grinning to myself; *they make a person disabled and then pity them.* Holding my crutch, the official's eyes slowly began to fill with tears. It turned out that under the guise of privatisation he'd appropriated for himself just about everything that could be appropriated and it had all been completely legal. What a paradox - you can rob your country under the cover

A HUNDRED YEARS ON THE STEPPE 341

of the law. He'd quietly smuggled his massive wealth abroad, had several mansions, villas and cottages in different places and was preparing to leave his homeland. Now, admitting that for his entire time spent in a public office he'd been swindling the country, he left, swearing to return all of his ill-gotten gains to the state.

The fifth character I'd noted as being suspicious passed me proudly with his head held high. Not even out of the corner of his eye did he look at me. Arrogance and pride spilt from his every pore. I'd heard that he was a narcissist and that nothing but himself interested him, but when I saw him with my own eyes, his smug, contemptuous expression, all the mixed blood of the East and West boiled up in me and I almost threw my spear-crutch straight into his broad back. Instead, I threw a crutch on the sidewalk with a roar, but still, he didn't even look back towards the sound. Choking with anger, I breathed quickly.

'Hey, Mr self-admirer, come here!' I called after him sharply.

Such rough words hit him like a hammer on the crown of his head. He shuddered, turned nervously and looked at me in bewilderment.

'Well, pick up the crutch and hand it to me,' I said, 'otherwise you will become like me.'

My calculation was accurate. Having been showered with an excess of attention and false praise, the mannequin shell crumbled from his face at such an impudent intrusion into his cardboard world. Obediently, he raised the crutch, and the H-particles did their job. Seconds later there was no longer any trace of his arrogance; he sobbed in a boy-ish way and began to pour out his soul. What he had done was the harmless game of a spoiled child rather than that of a real shark, but it was a very funny, crazy and incomprehensible game. This nouveau riche Narcissus made money on everything he had ever done. He performed no tasks for free. He took bribes in the form of gifts; each of his services carrying its own distinct fee. Deciding that since he loves himself, it must mean that everyone loves him, our Narcissus concluded that this love should be expressed in the form of brand new greenback bills.

Concluding that the presence of such a popular high-ranking official at any celebration would raise the prestige of the celebration, Narcissus made himself available for hire for birthdays, weddings, etc. He would attend as the guest of honour if he was presented with an envelope stuffed with cash. Speeches and toasts cost more, of course, and if the beautiful Narcissus was to speak from the heart, then the price would be exorbitant. Essentially, he had been selling his soul, but my device put a stop to that.

The sixth was a golden lady, a businesswoman. The hammered knock of her high heels echoed with clear confidence in the silence of the evening among the tall buildings, like the clattering hoofs of a mountain gazelle in a deep canyon. She cast a quick glance in my direction, this sweet, inaccessible stranger passing so majestically that for a moment I forgot why I was waiting for her. I was almost a little ashamed that I suspected her of some dark affairs, but all my research had led to her and so I acted according to my

A HUNDRED YEARS ON THE STEPPE   *343*

scheme.

The sound of the crutch falling caused her to turn, and with feminine responsiveness, she tenderly handed it back to me. After the H-attack, unlike the men she didn't hastily unload her sins, but lingered near me pensively, eventually speaking in a hushed, bewitching voice. Utilising sophisticated methods of slander, trickery and lies, she'd skilfully pitted male politicians and businessmen against each other. As a result, they hated, framed and imprisoned each other, which had ultimately led to a weakening of the country's potential elite. Now, repenting earnestly, she announced her intention to right the situation.

That's it, Mr General: honoured figures that held senior government positions were not who they claimed to be. Now, all at once they had admitted their guilt, and for the rest of their lives, they'd experience remorse necessary for the cleansing of the soul. I am grateful to fate and heaven that they instructed me not to destroy people, but to shame them. Yes, indeed, how much blood and sin would have been on me if I had killed all the perpetrators.

Finally, late in the evening, I got to the seventh candidate. He was somehow unprepossessing, and I, tiring and indulging my thoughts about the universal essence of being, like a Sufi sitting alone in a trance, missed his presence. Yes, he would have passed me by if not for a chance event. As the Chinese sages say, though, 'randomness is not accidental.'

Slender, with glasses, looking like a music teacher, he swiftly turned on his heels. My phone had started ringing, and my special ringtone had caught the attention of the suspect. My beloved Zhanmila was calling, but I couldn't answer as the "musician" had already approached me.

'Excuse me, please,' he said, very politely. 'What sort of music is that? Where did you get it? I've never heard anything like it before.'

'It's a dombra piece,' I replied, 'a symphony; a song of the ancient nomads of the feather grass steppes.'

'Can I listen closer?' he asked.

I could not have foreseen that this incredible opportunity would fall right into my lap.

'Please do,' I replied, but, of course, I was in no hurry to hand him my phone and politely asked him to move Yangalibus a little to the side.

When he took the handles of the stroller, the "Borgia Ring" sent a portion of H-particles into him. He swayed slightly, shook his head, his face cringing before softening. Literally a moment later he started to make several phone calls frantically cancelling some serious business. Then he took hold of the handles of Yangalibus and rolled me to the riverbank. Seeing how carefully, even gently, he treated an unhappy disabled person, no one would have believed this was one of the most dangerous terrorists on the planet. Taking me to a deserted place, he began to unburden his criminal soul. Goosebumps ran down my back as I listened.

The "musician" had planned to simultaneously blow up several train stations around the country. With his conscience awakened, he experienced an incredible shock and came to the conclusion that his bloody struggle was meaningless. With ardour, he spoke excitedly and abruptly. It was

A HUNDRED YEARS ON THE STEPPE 345

getting late. I'd begun to fret and was looking for an excuse to get rid of this man when my beloved Zhanmila came running.

Worried that I hadn't answered her call, she and our children came by taxi to the very place where I often hunted my clients. Of course, she didn't know about this and thought I just came here to take in the scenery. Now, the children made a merry noise and rushed to hug me as Zhanmila looked upon me with joy.

It was here by the riverbank that something incredible happened. Whilst we were busy enjoying ourselves, I hadn't even noticed that the terrorist had disappeared somewhere. Suddenly, he returned in a beautiful red limousine. Shedding tears, he gave me the keys to his limo. I tried to refuse, but he just left the car and went off on foot. I didn't need it for obvious reasons, but what can you do? So it happened that Zhanmila fell in love with the car of a former-terrorist. She decided that this was a gift from a kind gentleman to a disabled war veteran, a sign of respect for his service in the name of the fatherland.

The happy Zhanmila approached the limousine, gracefully opened the door, turned to me and shook her head so that her long hair floated in the air like waves. She did this for me, and I was pleased to look at her, my head spinning with tenderness. She felt my happiness as she got into the glorious car. Planting our daughter next to her, she smiled at me and my son, waved her hand and slowly drove off along the riverbank for several hundred meters.

It was then that the explosion thundered. My son and

I froze in terror. The car shattered into pieces. Zhanmila and my daughter were dead. This was not like an explosion in an action movie; this was your bomb, General Yang Lee Mzhanba! They died together, Mother and Daughter. They were your...-

At this point, the corner of the page was bent over, and since these words were written at the very bottom of the page, the tiny bend covered a few letters. General Yang Lee Mzhanba eagerly began to unfurl the paper with the tip of a pen and, having read it, gasped for air.

... - daughter and granddaughter!

Not believing his eyes, he stared at these words and read them again.

They were your daughter and granddaughter!

These words coldly and cruelly reported the terrible news, turning the life of a successful warrior and politician into a tragedy in the blink of an eye.

General Yang Lee Mzhanba was shocked. Everything swam before my eyes. He noticed a faint, barely perceptible strange smell, but did not pay any attention to it. Putting the letter aside, he sat silently for a long time. So that's why his beloved daughter was missing.

He began to cry. Wiping his tears away, he stared at his watch. There was a quarter of an hour left before the attack. General Yang Lee Mzhanba stood resolutely and gave the command: 'Cancel the operation!'

Standing there, he felt terribly ashamed.

31.07.2013 - 30.07.2015

A HUNDRED YEARS ON THE STEPPE

Great Legends of the Steppe
Khan Ablai and His Horsemen

A Tale for Children and Youths

A Note from the Author

A historical figure, Wali-ullah Abul-Mansur, known as Khan Ablai, was a great Khan of the Kazakhs during the 18th century. This story is based on the traditions and legends of the Kazakh people recorded by Chokan Valikhanov, Mashkhur-Zhusup Kopeev, Shakarim Khudayberdiev and other prominent Kazakh ethnographers. It is also a work of art in itself, which allowed the author some liberties in the interpretation and understanding of events in that distant era.

Carelessness

It was the first half of the eighteenth century. These were turbulent times. For over a hundredyears a war had been raging between the Kazakh Khanate and the Dzungarian Horde. This ancient city in the depths of the southern outskirts of the Great Steppe, however, did not know of the war and lived its own isolated life...

The gentle rays of the rising sun awakened Ablai the Hanzad (Kazakh prince). Joyfully stretching, the happy boy basked in the warmth of his soft bed for a long time. He was twelveyearsold. His growing body radiated strength and health, and a clear mind and spiritual purity shone in his large black eyes.

The city had awoken long ago and its streets were in the full swing. The Hanzad loved this ancient city which was governed by his father, Vali the Beautiful - as the residents called him due to his good character and noble appearance.

Ablai's mother entered the room. Like all mothers, she loved her children very much, and like all children, Ablai believed that she loved him more than anyone. For him, she was extraordinary, the most wonderful mother in the world. When she pressed him to her chest, gently stroking his head, the Hanzad forgot about everything in the world and felt like a very small child as he purred with happiness.

'May Allah watch over you,' she whispered softly.

The Hanzad quickly packed up and set out for the city. A day of studying at a madrasah with bearded sages, reading in a library and exercises in martial arts led by Oraz Atalyk flew by in an instant.

Tired from the hustle and bustle of the day, the Hanzad drank a cup of kumis and went to bed. He could not sleep, though, so by the light of a copper lamp he began to read

A HUNDRED YEARS ON THE STEPPE 349

an old manuscript on government and military affairs in the Chagatai language, penned on the parchment in beautiful Arabic script. The thoughts of ancient political figures and military strategists took hold of the boy, so that the Hanzad imagined himself an outstanding ruler and commander, vividly picturing how he would have acted wisely in various historical circumstances. To these imaginings he fell asleep, floating on the waves of his unbridled childhood fantasies.

Attack

The predawn sweet dreams of the city were broken by the booming clatter of hooves, wild cries and the clang of weapons. Thousands and thousands of horsemen roared around the city like a fierce tornado, turning their deadly gaze on every single street and alley. It was a hurricane of death; the Dzungarian invaders struck suddenly and treacherously.

The residents of the city offered fierce resistance. Half-asleep, Ablai pulled on his clothes and grabbed a dagger, but he did not dare run out into the street where the massacre was occurring. Having cut down a handful of brave men, the Dzungarians were already breaking into houses. An unbearable, heart-breaking noise filled the air, crying, moans and the curses of the dying civilians mixed with the wild battle cries of jubilant Dzungars.

Suddenly, the confused boy saw a huge shadow in the doorway moving straight towards him. *This is the end*, the boy thought, dumbfounded and instantly covered with cold sweat.

As the silhouette approached him, the Hanzad jumped up and tore the dagger from its scabbard.

'Ablajan! Aynalayin!' the shadow said as the sunlight revealed his face. 'Glory to Allah, you are alive!'

It was the good, faithful servant of Khan Vali, Oraz Atalyk who addressed the boy in a kindred way, not as it should be according to the etiquette, '*Taxir*' (your majesty). Ablai grabbed his strong hand.

'What happened? What should we do?' the boy exclaimed in fear.

'It's awful, my Hanzad. We were taken by surprise. Probably there were Dzungar scouts already in the city and they opened the gates for them. Many of our people have perished.'

'Where are Mother and Father? My brothers, are they alive?'

'I don't know,' Oraz said in a low, mournful voice. 'It's impossible to escape from this slaughter. You have to hide well, but not here. They will come here soon. Quickly, come with me!'

With these words, he ushered Ablai to the exit. At that very moment, an enemy arrow whistled past and pierced the wall where the boy had just been standing.

'The Almighty saved you,' Oraz exclaimed. 'Inshallah, you shall be saved.'

The Hanzad was moved by Oraz' emotions, but he didn't show it, only muttering the word, 'Amen.'

A HUNDRED YEARS ON THE STEPPE   *351*

Bumping into corpses in the dark, they made their way by touch through a secret passage, exiting in a gloomy backstreet. It was light, but the dawn was heavy. The boy's heart was beating furiously, and he wanted to dive back into the safety of his warm downy bed. Blood was being spilt all around, though, arrows whistling and sabres sparkling. Clutching Oraz' hand, the Hanzad clenched his teeth and walked firmly behind him.

Crossing the street, they were creeping through the backyard of a teahouse when two horsemen emerged from the twilight and rushed towards them. Big and brave, Oraz thrust out his right hand at lightning speed, and his short sharp knife pierced the throat of the first rider. The boy saw clearly how the enemy spasmed, choking on his own blood after falling from his horse. This was the first death Ablai had ever seen, and it shocked him to his core.

At full gallop, the second horseman knocked Oraz' blade from his hand. Jumping deftly, Oraz' pulled another from the horseman's saddle and threw the dagger into his opponent's throat. A spray of scarlet blood gushed from the deep wound and sprayed over Oraz.

With the sound of voices and hooves rising, Ablai realised that more enemies were approaching. For a moment, he and Oraz froze in anticipation of the end.

Fury

Suddenly, Oraz saw an inverted black cauldron, and a plan dawned on him.

'Listen, my Hanzad,' he whispered, 'I'll hide you under this black cauldron. Perhaps the enemies will not notice.'

Ablai grinned.

'Me? Under the cauldron?'

'Since ancient times cauldrons such as these have been considered sacred among the Kazakhs. The Almighty has brought us here in our hour of trial.'

With these words, Oraz raised the edge of cauldron and hid Ablai underneath it.

'I'll be right here,' he whispered goodbye. 'The most important thing is peace.'

'Oh, how small the world is,' Ablai sighed bitterly, crouching under the cauldron; 'and how cruel fate can be.'

Last night, he had gazed up the heavens for a long time. His thoughts soared to the distant stars, and he felt himself the sovereign of the world. Now, the bottom of an inverted cauldron had become his heavenly vault. Last night, he had laid in a lush, soft bed, yet this morning he was lying on the bare, cold earth, hiding in an old black cauldron. He didn't even own this cramped area; at any moment the powerful Dzungars could overturn the cauldron, and then the end would come.

Gradually, his unhappy thoughts began to dissipate. It was quite spacious under the cauldron. He could turn from side to side or lie on his back bending his legs. Somewhere

A HUNDRED YEARS ON THE STEPPE

between the uneven ground and the edges of the cauldron there were cracks, and light and the sounds of a fierce battle were breaking through.

'Damned dogs; you'll never win!'

'They will avenge us!'

Judging by the voices, several Kazakh soldiers were still fighting desperately on the street.

'Ha, ha! Who will avenge you?' the cries of Dzungars rang out. 'Who are you hoping for? No one is left alive. We slaughtered the Khan's whole family and all the sultans too. The great Noyon Charysh ordered us to exterminate everyone; so goodbye!'

Soon, the noise of the battle died down. It was all over. Several arrows clanged across the cauldron. Ablai's heart pounded wildly with fear and rage. He wanted to jump out and scream: 'Me! I will avenge everyone!' He wanted to rush at the enemy and cut them limb from limb. He wanted so badly to grab this leader, Charysh, and tear off his head. He clearly realised, though, that he was powerless to do anything and that it would be pointless to thrust his small dagger in the faces in the horde of Dzungars. His young soul was torn asunder; his father, mother, brothers and sisters, all of his relatives were dead. He was alone and he must survive.

Sensing that the Dzungars were nearby and could detect him at any moment, he became frightened. He pressed himself low to the ground, afraid to even breathe freely. These moments of torment dragged on seemingly interminably until silence eventually reigned.

Exhausted, the boy fell asleep. He woke to the light

touch of someone's hand. It was dark already, but Ablai recognised that it was Oraz who had lifted the cauldron.

'I have been with you the whole time, my Hanzad,' Oraz whispered softly. 'I lay like a dead man between the corpses. Now, we must get out of here; we must go to the steppe.'

They didn't even think about horses, firstly, as it would be impossible to procure them without getting into a fight, and secondly, because their enemies would notice the riders immediately. Therefore, on foot they dissolved into the darkness, picking their way through the ruined city.

No matter how cunning Oraz was, however, he couldn't avoid the enemy. On the outskirts of the city where the steppe began, three horsemen appeared out of nowhere.

'You must flee. Farewell, my Hanzad,' Oraz whispered with fervour and hurried to confront them.

Not even noticing the child slipping away around a corner, the Dzungars chased after the bigger man.

Stumbling and falling, the Hanzad finally found himself on the open steppe. The unimpeded wind invigorated the fugitive, and he breathed freely. The mystery of the endless dark distance both powerfully attracted him and at the same time sent a shiver down his spine.

No One

As he wandered, the fact that he was all alone on the Great Steppe struck the boy. He was all alone, without a

A HUNDRED YEARS ON THE STEPPE   *355*

mother or a father, with no one and nothing, poor and hungry in the dark night. He felt uneasy. The moon looked down at him impassively from its heavenly height before bashfully hiding behind thick clouds. Distant stars sparkled bright and cold, not warming his soul as they had before. He had lost everything, absolutely everything, his relatives, loved ones, peace and comfort, wealth and honour. He had lost his future.

Before it had seemed that everything was clear: the Khan's son would grow up to sit on the throne of his father and rule the country fairly and justly. If only he was grown up now, then all of this would have come to pass. People cannot foresee the vicissitudes of fate, though. Now, deprived of everything in an instant, he had become a nameless vagrant. He would have to wander through this vast ocean of life as a man without a clan or a tribe. Revealing your name and origin would be very dangerous in these parts, and who would believe him anyway?

Falling face down, the Hanzad clutched at the grey steppe and wept bitterly, all the while trying to quieten himself so that no enemies would hear him. At any moment a red-hot arrow could fly out of the darkness and cut the thin thread of the boy's life, a life which for him had lost all meaning. His wounded soul wanted to fly like a bird and dissolve into the air. This was neither a dream nor a fairy tale, however. This was a cruel life from which there was no escape.

Maybe I should kill myself, he reflected, clutching the silver handle of his dagger, his heavy thoughts nailing him to the feather grass. *What would that achieve, though, inglorious, shameful death in these bushes? What kind of nonsense am I thinking? No, I'll never take my own life. I am a man, a Hanzad, and I will fight until my very last breath for my inheritance, for freedom, for glory and for the throne. But how should I fight? What should I do?* These cruel questions burned little Ablai's soul, but first of all, he reasoned, I must just concentrate on surviving.

Ablai had learnt a lot in the court of Khan Vali in the glorious city filled with scientists and craftsmen. Under the guidance of Oraz Atalyk and other experienced tutors, he had studied religion, philosophy and languages. He knew how to play the dombra and the kobyz. He knew how to handle weapons and had learnt how to communicate with and manage people. The irony was that he had not been taught simple survival skills. For all his knowledge, he couldn't procure food or navigate the terrain in the dark. Even in the daylight, he couldn't make a fire, find water or build a shelter. He couldn't live in the steppe as a simple nomad for these lessons were not taught to a boy meant to live the life of a royal.

'Oh, how hard it is for me,' Ablai sighed to himself, 'and no one will help me.'

Fortunately, he had been born with a brave heart.

'Why should anyone help you?' he argued with himself. 'No, don't rely on others; you must learn to help yourself. Was it easy for my great ancestor Genghis Khan when he lived as an orphan among his persecutors? Genghis Khan withstood the trials of fate and rose to power, and I too will rise.'

A HUNDRED YEARS ON THE STEPPE 357

Getting to his feet, the Hanzad headed north in the direction of Temirkazyk. Under the stars, he walked all night, farther and farther from the smouldering city of his birth.

Death

During the hours of daylight, it was too dangerous to walk in the open steppe. Therefore, the exhausted and hungry boy hid in a deep ravine overgrown with jusan and feather grass. Although his hunger and thirst tormented him, he was so tired that he soon fell asleep.

Some hours later, the Hanzad woke in alarm. The evening was falling and a distant, obscure hum was being carried on the air across the steppe. The buzzing grew louder and soon Ablai could hear the clatter of hoofs and the cries of people. Shortly a band of horsemen appeared from behind a hill and swiftly swept through the ravine. At first, with a childish naivety, Ablai thought that it was a *baiga* (a long-distance horse race) or *kokpar* (an equestrian game), and his heart was filled with excitement. Upon closer inspection, however, he realised that it was not a baiga but a massacre.

Chasing a lone horseman, a large group of warriors were gaining ground on him. The quickest of his pursuers almost nailed him with a long spear, but the fugitive, deftly dodging its point, swiftly slashed at his assailant with his sabre and the wounded spearman fell from his horse. An instant later, the fugitive approached the place where the Hanzad was hiding. The white tulpar (a noble breed of horse) was wounded, stained with blood and, it seems, was completely exhausted. Overtaking him, his attackers surrounded him, and the fugitive sharply implored his horse to meet his enemies head-on.

The Dzungar pursuers stopped dead in their tracks. Flashing with his huge *aldaspan* (sabre), the voice of the lone warrior thundered, shaking the steppe with his war cry: '*Zhekpezhek! Zhekpezhek!*' Aware of the power and fury of the driven Kazakh warrior, the Dzungarian warriors backed away and looked at each other. Ablai clearly saw and heard everything, for they were no more than the throwing distance of a lasso from him. Lying motionless, he was thankful that the grasses of his native steppe sheltered him in this ancient ravine.

'Well, Dzungarian devils,' the lone horseman cried, 'are there no worthy warriors among you? Are you not the brave wolves of the Khong Tayijii (crown prince) Galdan Tseren, but a pack of pathetic dogs?'

A fully armed Dzungarian warrior with a large shield seated on a bay stallion came forth. The Dzungars shouted, cheering on the *Sherik* (high-ranking warrior). His quiver empty and with no other weapon besides his aldaspan and shield, the lone Kazakh faced him. The Sherik threw his spear, but the white horse of the Kazakh darted forward. The whistle of the aldaspan was heard, and the Dzungar softly sank into the feather grass. Seeing his demise, his comrades in arms visibly drooped before, as if conspiring, they rushed in unison at the lone brave man. The Kazakh was strong

A HUNDRED YEARS ON THE STEPPE

and fought well, and a few more enemies fell at his hands, but the devils flew upon him delivering lightning-quick blows. Soon, the Kazakh's chain-mail was torn to shreds like old rags, blood seeping through where it had been ripped asunder. Like a flock of hungry hyenas, the Dzungar warriors rushed at the wounded lion, and it seemed that he was about to collapse along with his pure white horse, but the warrior stood firm, slaughtering several more of his enemies.

Suddenly, a loud cry rose above the noise, and everyone froze. No one had noticed the appearance of a huge warrior on a jet black horse. His black cloak fluttered, giving him a mysterious, eerie air, and his horse seemed to be made of cast black iron. A thick, long tuft like a boa constrictor encircled the warrior's powerful neck, his impudent eyes expressing a sharp temper and courage. Approaching the warring men, he spoke in a thunderous voice.

'Well, moon-like Oirot (an ancient tribe, the root of the Mongols and Kalmyks), messing around with this Kazakh dog are you? I can't wait for you to bring me his head.'

The newcomer surveyed the bodies strewn across the battlefield and whistled.

'Pah!' he spat. 'Looks like I've come upon a real warrior. Oh, how lucky I am. I love to snap the necks of these stupid firebrands and cut off their heads. Ha, ha.'

Throwing up their spears, the Dzungars honoured their leader.

'You'd better think about your own filthy head,' the defiant Kazakh shouted. 'You'll never be able to wash away the blood of innocent victims from it. The curses of the people will drive you into the ground.'

Filled with anger and hatred, the Dzungar leader unleashed a bloodcurdling laugh.

'We'll see whose head rolls in the feather grass,' he roared, circling the Kazakh.

His face tanned by the steppe winds and the fierce sun; his slanting eyes were bloodshot. His horse began to rear up, pounding the ground with its huge hooves, biting its lip and trying to tear off its bridle.

'Hai! Hai! Let's duel!' the Dzungar yelled, his words reverberating across the steppe. 'I, Charysh the Noyon, the great warrior of the proud Oirot and nephew of the sun-like Galdan Tseren challenge you, Kazakh, to an honest fight to the death. If you defeat me, I swear my warriors will allow you to live.'

Ablai almost gasped as the Dzungars parted to make space for impending battle; so this was Charysh the Noyon himself!

'Honour is the law of the steppe to which every nobleman must adhere,' thought the Hanzad, 'but this honesty is relative when one is full of strength and the other is a wounded warrior on an exhausted tulpar; how is this a fair fight?

But the Kazakh batyr accepted the challenge with dignity.

'Aruah, spirit of the ancestors; Aruah!' he exclaimed, spurring his horse.

As if by some miracle, sensing a decisive battle the exhausted white tulpar changed before Ablai's eyes. It was a true warhorse. With fierce screams of wild unbridled pas-

A HUNDRED YEARS ON THE STEPPE 361

sion, the two complete strangers pounced upon each other. Their first meeting in this mortal world where all people should be brothers brought grief. They did not have a personal history and hailed from different nations. They could have been sitting around a fire, peacefully sharing food and kind words, decorating the world with kindness. What great friends they could have been. But no, they thirsted for blood, and all because of the desire of some to dominate others. The Kazakh was a thousand times more righteous because he was defending his homeland, his freedom, honour and independence. And the Dzungar was a thousand times more wrong, for he wanted to conquer a foreign land, to enslave another people.

Without pausing for thought the warriors delivered furious blows with their steely blades. It seemed to Ablai that they were surely about to kill each other. He closed his eyes. His young soul was indignant, opposed to this violence, but the real world dictated its cruel conditions. He wanted to jump out and help the lone warrior, but some force preventing him from moving. He was aware that his time had not yet come. He could only silently observe and commit the event to memory.

The sun was already setting over the horizon. Matching the blood of the battle, like an inexplicable horror the red sky seemed ominous. Realising he could not defeat the enemy with his sabre, Charysh the Noyon took a long spear and, at full gallop, thrust it into the chest of the white tulpar. The noble animal staggered, quietly neighed and collapsed to the ground dead. The Kazakh managed to jump from his falling steed, but as he did so Charysh ran him through the chest with his spear.

To the cheers of his soldiers, Charysh the Noyon dismounted from his horse and raised the bloody warrior on his spear high above his head.

'Hai, hai, Kazakh; how are you feeling now, huh?' taunted the monster, his sarcastic question greeted with roaring laughter by his men. Slowly, the warrior opened his eyes.

'Damned Dzungarian dog,' he said hoarsely but distinctly with his final breath; 'I'm still taller than you.'

Stupefied, Charysh the Noyon lowered the body of the deceased to the ground.

'Bury him,' he commanded with a hollow voice. 'He is worthy of respect.'

The Dzungars buried their own warriors and the Kazakh warrior separately, with Charysh the Noyon claiming the brave man's aldaspan as his prize. Ablai cried quietly in his hiding place. Only when the Dzungars hid disappeared over the horizon and night had fallen did he come out of his hiding place and go to the grave. After reciting a prayer, the Hanzad sat for a long time at the grave of the unknown warrior. The shocked child experienced deep, previously unknown feelings. Something inexplicable was happening inside him.

The light of the clear moon was spreading generously over the steppe. A rare white cloud slowly floated away into the distance, and it seemed to Ablai that this was the soul of the warrior.

A HUNDRED YEARS ON THE STEPPE   363

He felt a kinship with the stranger. His heart was filled with sadness as he lifted his hands to heaven and spoke an oath.

'I, Ablai, son of Khan Vali swear never to be afraid of anyone or anything,' he vowed. 'I will make sacrifices to fight for the freedom and happiness of my people. Amen! Allah Akbar.'

Running his hands over his face, he resolutely stood up and strode firmly towards dangers and adventures, towards his fate.

Atalyk

By the evening of his second day in the steppe, the Hanzad began to feel that someone was sneaking around, relentlessly following him. Not even the slightest rustle was heard, but the Hanzad knew he was in the grip of someone's piercing gaze.

'It is not enough to be brave,' he whispered the instructions of Oraz Atalyk to himself, 'you have to be cunning.'

Heeding this advice, therefore, outwardly he remained calm and walked as normal.

The sun had set. At dusk, the silhouettes on the steppe were transformed into ambiguous forms. Caught in the grass, even last year's tumbleweeds could seem like predatory beasts.

Suddenly, growling and jumping out in front of the boy, one of them came to life. It was a huge, furry shaggy creature, like a *Zheztyrnak* or a *Zhalmauyz* (variations of a monster in Kazakh folktales which eats people). Ablai immediately pulled out a dagger from his scabbard and prepared for battle. Clutching the hilt of the dagger tightly, he vigilantly watched his enemy. Roaring menacingly, the creature circled him.

Though unfamiliar with each other, when two divine creatures meet on the vast steppe it seems they cannot disperse peacefully and must immediately decide the question of life or death. The creature circled the Hanzad for a long time in the darkness, but not daring to face the damask dagger, slowly it began to retreat. Finally, it disappeared from sight and dissolved into the night.

Ablai sighed in relief and sheathed the dagger. He could not relax, though, because this was only the beginning. The monster was unlikely to leave him alone and probably wanted to take him by surprise. Aware of every bush, every rustle, Ablai decided to push on.

Shortly, he built his camp on a low hill which afforded him an unobstructed view. It would be impossible to sneak up on him here; he just had to stay alert. Exhausted by hunger and the shock of recent events, though, Ablai soon fell asleep. When he started and woke up, above him stood a huge monster. Ablai jumped up and pulled out a dagger.

'Hey Aynalayin, before you act look who you're trying to strike,' the mysterious creature said in a familiar voice.

It was Oraz Atalyk.

The Hanzad's joy knew no bounds, and they hugged each other tightly.

A HUNDRED YEARS ON THE STEPPE

'I already mourned for you,' Ablai finally said as he came to his senses.

'That means I will live long,' laughed Oraz.

'So, the monster, the Zheztyrnak or Zhalmauyz, was it you?'

'Yes, I wanted to look at you and to test you; to see if these events had hardened you or not.'

'How did I do?' Ablai asked with a trace of irony.

'Not bad, not bad. For starters, your sight and reactions are great,' Oraz replied before beginning to tell his story enthusiastically. 'Oh, you should see how I blew away those marauders. Our land is dear, and it helps us. I know every corner and every yard, so I can hide anywhere. They don't know the way, though, so they ended up bumbling around blindly until at midnight I chased them through the backstreets and the ruins. They were completely exhausted, and I picked them off one by one.'

In turn, the Hanzad excitedly talked of his adventures, withholding only his oath. The words he had spoken unto the heavens were the purpose and meaning of his life, and because of this, except for the Almighty, no one should know them. Oraz eagerly hung onto every word uttered by his master and was pleasantly surprised at the change in his intonation. Chatting animatedly, they ate the last handful of kurut (a dried fermented milk product), which Oraz had produced from his pocket, and set off. Like a lonely sailboat in a raging ocean, they still had a long way to travel across the boundless steppe in these troubled times.

Shaggy

Several years passed. Ablai the Hanzad and Oraz Atalyk roamed the steppe, hiding from the Dzungars, who had conquered a considerable swathe of the Kazakh lands. The fugitives found temporary shelter in scattered villages. The law of the steppe - the hospitality of nomads - saved them from starvation. Having thus lived through long painful days, they finally arrived to the supreme Bey (political ruler under the Khan) of the Big Zhuz Tribe, where they were accepted. As this region was under the yoke of the Dzungarian invaders, Ablai hid his name and origin, calling himself Sabalak, which literally means 'Shaggy.'

Hardening, the duo strove to become invisible to all around them, but one shrewd man noticed at first glance that 'Shaggy' didn't look like an ordinary shepherd. After observing the youth for some time, the man came to the Hanzad's camp.

'You, Sabalak, are no ordinary person; that's what my heart tells me. Both in appearance and in demeanour it's clear that you belong to a noble clan. If the Dzungars notice you, and here it is quite likely, they will not leave you alone. I fear for your life. It would be better for you to go to Saryarka (literally 'Golden Ridge' - a place on the central-north border of Kazakhstan) where you would be free of the Dzungars.'

Presenting him with two horses, he sent him along with Oraz to Saryarka.

In Saryarka, Ablai became a herder for Dauletkeldy Bey

A HUNDRED YEARS ON THE STEPPE 367

from the Argyn family of the Atigay guard. He and Oraz lived quietly, looked after the horses and rode freely across the wide expanses, learning and improving their martial arts skills. From the very first day, however, Dauletkeldy Bey noticed something special about his young herder and decided to monitor him closely.

'This boy is no an ordinary person,' he noted to his wife. 'He is always calm; he does not laugh frivolously, does not get annoyed and does not pay any attention to petty household squabbles. He is always thoughtful and asks for nothing. If he doesn't find anything suitable to sit on, he will take off his outer clothing, spread it on the ground and sit on it. Most importantly, when he sleeps, light spreads over him. Be polite to him, my wife. Even if he should inadvertently anger us, the spirits are supporting him.'

So, they respected Sabalak-Ablai and Oraz, fed and clothed them well. The years passed, and soon Ablai grew up to be nineteenyearsold.

Truth

On one occasion, a free singer of the great steppe, Bukhar the Zhyrau (poet, philosopher and storyteller) stopped when he met the lonely young herder. He was alone, his clothes and horse harness modest but solid.

The young herdsmen met the Zhyrau with great joy. Seating him in a place of honour, they treated the bearer of the ancient nomadic traditions to boiled meat and kumis.

Ablai spoke to the Zhyrau, who had a pleasant, melodious voice and often quoted verse. Even his simple speech flowed like a song, and his voice changed tone depending on what was being said. He put a piece of his essence into his tales, and each word fascinated the audience. His words carried his audience high into the sky, and his listeners involuntarily turned their eyes to the cosmic sacraments of the heavens.

'Oh, how many Khans I've seen; how many sultans I've met,' he said. 'I've seen the Dzungars, the *Urusuts* (Russians) and the *Shurshuts* (Chinese). So many different people, many worthy of respect, and a lot of scum. Almost all, though, share one thirst, one indefatigable desire: power, glory and wealth. They need to cover the Earth, seize all the wealth and conquer the whole world. Why is this and in the name of what? Is this really the meaning of human life? Would it not be better for everyone to live on their land and improve their own lives? I cannot comprehend the reasons why people destroy each other. No matter how learned men explain it, my soul will never grasp it. If people mercilessly destroy each other and tear apart the poor land, will it not be ravished? Won't the sun fade and the bloody moon sink into oblivion? And then what will happen to my people, what will happen to this world?'

The Zhyrau fell into silent reflection. He went into himself or maybe flew away with his thoughts. Inspired and wearied by the soulful words of the great poet, the herdsmen slowly dispersed. Only Ablai did not move from his place. The wise words of the Zhyrau struck the young Hanzad's heart and sunk deep into his soul.

A HUNDRED YEARS ON THE STEPPE

369

'What do you need, young one?' Bukhar the Zhyrau asked him.

'I want to hear the rest of your speech,' Ablai calmly replied.

'Oh, curious herdsman,' the Zhyrau started warmly, 'you will be a great man, for not everyone is able to listen, much less listen to such words let alone yearn for more. Sometimes, I want to climb to the top of the highest mountain and shout to the whole world: "Oh people, do not come to foreign lands with murder in your hearts! Do not shed a single drop of blood in search of power, wealth and glory. Do not enslave other nations, but live peacefully and happily in your native lands. There is enough sun and earth for everyone.'

Bukhar the Zhyrau lowered his voice.

'Am I just amusing myself with the hope that if people hear these words they'll understand, stop their warring and peace and happiness will reign?' he asked. 'Am I just pathetic... naive?'

'You are wise!' exclaimed young Ablai.

'Yes, Aynalayin, there is no truth better than this. The trouble is that since ancient times everyone has known it and yet done the opposite. The Almighty gave all nations his lands and indicated that they should live freely and do only good deeds.'

After saying goodbye to the Zhyrau , for a long time the pleasant voice of the sage still sounded in the ears of the young man: 'A real man should always be ready to fight and die for his people, but this must also be done wisely... True freedom begins with respect for the freedom of others… The slave is not free, that much is clear; but the master is also not free from his slave. They are tethered to each other with a single chain… Man is free, but he is not free to insult, humiliate and destroy others… When a person lives for the good of his people, he becomes great.'

Ablai remembered these and many other words spoken by Bukhar the Zhyrau for the rest of his life.

Name

The following year, word reached Saryarka that Khan Abilmambet was launching a war of liberation against the Dzungars, and warriors from all over the Kazakh steppe were gathering under his banner. Ablai-Sabalak went to Dauletkeldy Bey and asked for his permission to join the campaign.

'Son, you are only twenty-years-old. Is it not better to quietly graze horses, eat meat and drink kumis in a cosy yurt than head out to a bloody slaughter?' the wise Bey asked searchingly.

'It is better to die a *jigit* (brave equestrian) than to stay away from the fluttering banner of battle and a cavalry shaking the ground,' Ablai replied.

Hearing these words, the Dauletkeldy Bey gave his blessing.

Avalanche

Like black clouds spewing thunder and lightning, two armies approached each other. Their helmets, chain-mail, spears and sabres sparkling, the best sons of two fraternal peoples had come to kill each other. People were screaming, the neighing of their horses sounding like twisted laughter. The dust from hundreds of thousands of hooves soared up, blotting out the sky.

For each of these armies, the war had a different meaning. The Dzungarian Noyons, Zaysans (nobility) and Sheriks had come to conquer the Kazakh lands and plunder its riches. They were invaders, bringing death and ruin. The Kazakh Khans, Beys, sardars (commanders) and warriors had come to defend their freedom and their native land, and as their purpose was nobler, they were stronger in spirit and ready to fight to the death. The sky was their advocate, and the Earth supported them.

Two armies of seasoned warriors were ready to clash and mingle into a bloody ball.

'Wait!' the sharp cry of the Bogembai warrior, the chief commander of the Kazakhs thundered to the horizon, momentarily stopping the avalanche of angry lions.

The battle banners of the clans waved with renewed vigour and the fierce cry of the Kazakh and Dzungarian armies shook the steppe.

'Zhekpezhek! Fight!'
'Zhekpezhek! Duel!'
The first Dzungar stampeded forward on a tall black

horse. Together, they seemed like an impermeable rock. The warrior's huge, powerful muscles were bursting with steel chain-mail, his large head concealed in a helmet which resembled an inverted black cauldron. Burning like fire, only his slanting eyes were visible. A long, thick *aidar* (male braid) like a lasso hung over his broad shoulders, emphasising his power and confidence. Looking at this giant effortlessly twirl his deadly spear, the Kazakhs collectively held their breath.

'Hai, hai, Kazakhs; do you think you're equal to us?' he bellowed. 'That is the mistake that will seal your fate. You will kneel under our banner or we will destroy you, Ha, ha!' he goaded, his furious laughter shaking the steppe.

Circling in front of the Kazakh army, he pranced on his black horse. Shuddering at his laughter, the Kazakh soldiers seethed with rage. In their ranks were many experienced warriors, but no one had stepped forth to face with this monster as it seemed to be a one-way trip to hell.

Ablai recognised the horseman immediately: it was Charysh. His name had been terrorising the steppe for years. Legends had circulated that Charysh was invincible and had killed many powerful heroes.

An elderly Bogembai of the Kanzhigaly was about to accept the challenge, but Khan Abilmambet restrained him.

'Sardar, you are not allowed to accept the duel. You are our chief commander and must manage the army through to the end of the battle.'

A young man stepped forward. Full of horror and reverence, a whisper spread through the ranks of the troops:

A HUNDRED YEARS ON THE STEPPE 373

"Look! An *algadai* (kamikaze warrior); look!"

He had to hold out as long as possible so others could learn the best techniques with which to take on the beast that stood before them.

Prepared to face his fate, dressed in light chain-mail and riding a nimble horse, the young warrior slowly approached the huge Dzungar. Instantly, Charysh unleashed a flurry of sophisticated spear attacks, but the young warrior was cunning and deftly dodged and avoided blows. Matching its master, the skilfully manoeuvred horse kept the young warrior safe from the sharp Kalmyk spear. Warming to his task, Charysh finally planted his long sabre hit straight into his opponent's head. He fell dead from his horse, but the Kazakhs who had keenly observed the fight had now learnt how Charysh wielded his spear and sabre.

Metamorphosis

Upon seeing his comrade fall, Ablai could no longer restrain himself and rushed forward to ask the Bogembai for his blessing.

'Son, you are still quite young, are you sure?' exclaimed the Bogembai.

'*Bata, bata*! Bless me!' Ablai implored, raising his hands to the heavens.

Seeing his determination, the Bogembai felt the strength of the young man's spirit and gave his blessing.

'Oh, Allah, in the name of justice and for the sake of the

salvation of our native land and the liberation of our people, we entreat you,' the Bogembai said. 'Help our horseman, give him strength and victory. Son,' he concluded, turning to Ablai, 'may Allah and the almighty spirits of our ancestors be with you. Amen.'

'Amen!' Ablai and the entire army echoed.

The legendary Bogembai handed Ablai his sharpest sabre, helped him onto his battle tulpar, Narkyzyl, and Ablai galloped off to the most decisive battle of his life.

Charysh the Noyon abruptly turned his black horse and met Ablai ready for combat. He looked upon Ablai with his deadly, piercing gaze, wanting to melt him with the fire in his bloodshot eyes. Ablai remained calm, however, reflecting this monstrous gaze with a steely determination to secure vengeance. Charysh flinched, but his words remained firm.

'Pah!' he spat 'Have the Kazakhs already reached the point of sending a little boy to his death? Do they really think that I, the victorious Charysh the Noyon, will stoop to the point of fighting this young lad? Go back to your parents and learn from your mullah, child. Maybe you can return when you're a grownup.'

Unable to speak he was so enraged, Ablai prepared for battle.

'Very well,' Charysh said, shaking his head. 'If you so wish I will snap your neck like a partridge.'

Collecting his thoughts, Ablai rushed at the formidable Dzungarian.

'Ablai! Ablai!,' he cried involuntarily, some unknown force filling his chest as a wave-like feeling of indescribably

A HUNDRED YEARS ON THE STEPPE 375

hot power lifted him.

Repelling Charysh' first terrible blow with his spear, he pushed Narkyzyl forward, and, still shouting his cry, unleashed a sharp swing of the sabre belonging to the glorious Bogembai to the Noyon's head. The two warhorses whistled past each other, and, as Ablai turned Narkyzyl, he heard the victorious cry of thousands of Kazakh troops: 'Ablai! Ablai!' It was only then that he saw the body of the Charysh sliding from his horse and his decapitated head rolling away into the feather grass of the long-suffering steppe.

Without stopping, at full gallop he turned his horse towards the Dzungarian army.

'Ablai!' he cried so loudly that heaven and earth rattled; 'the Kazakhs will be victorious!'

'Ablai! Ablai! Ablai!' his army chanted so that it seemed as if the spirits of the great ancestors of all Kazakhs had been revived and embodied in a single name.

Like peals of thunder, his name rang out, becoming in an instant a sacred word for the Kazakh people. The mighty Dzungars tried to scream their battle cries in response, but they could not utter a word. As if on wings, Ablai and his army flew at the petrified hordes before them.

After the victory, Ablai was called before the Khan, the Beys and the commanders.

'Young one, who are you?' asked Khan Abilmambet. 'Why did you fight with the name "Ablai" on your lips?'

'I am the son of Khan Vali the Beautiful. I was named Ablai after the moniker of my grandfather who was called this by the people for his invincibility in battle and prowess in military affairs. I screamed his name today, calling on his spirit for help,' the Hanzad answered.

The well-worn *aksakals* (revered elders) were touched by his story.

'I had heard that the youngest son of Khan Vali was alive but missing,' Khan Abilmambet said after giving the matter some thought. 'But, as the saying goes, "a steel dagger will not lie at the bottom of the bag." And now the time has come when the name of a worthy descendant of noble Khan Vali will light up the steppe with his glories. Bless him, aksakals, and we will elect him Khan!'

The gathered nobles blessed Ablai unanimously, raising the newly made Khan on the ceremonial white felt. Thus, at the age of twenty, the heroic and legendary reign of Khan Ablai began. His horde was founded in the north, in beautiful Kokshetau, the pearl of the Kazakh steppe.

Zhelbe

Khong Tayijii Galdan Tseren silently sat on a hill, turning his heavy gaze to the boundless steppe. A continuous wind blew, and the waves of sand led to gloomy thoughts about what lay beyond the horizon. For years now, he had been suffering greatly from the death of his beloved nephew, the son of his elder sister, the great warrior Charysh.

'I still cannot believe that he was killed in a duel, the Khong Tayijii said with pain. 'No one should have been able to defeat Charysh in a fair fight. He learnt all the battle

A HUNDRED YEARS ON THE STEPPE   *377*

techniques of the Mongols and Kalmyks and mastered all the weapons of the ancient Oirot and Chinese.'

Bowing his head in reverence to the crown prince, Zhelbe the Noyon recounted the events once more. Each time he did so, he experienced the acute bitterness of loss and a renewed surge of anger.

'Charysh the Noyon cut down a Kazakh warrior in a duel... And then this Ablai appeared. We didn't really understand what was happening. The battle cry, 'Ablai' rumbled through the earth and sky. Our horses trembled and wanted to run. We could barely stay in formation. No one had ever so charged so boldly and directly at Charysh. He hit like a tornado, and the sun of the Dzungars went out. Oh, my friend Charysh.'

Frowning, Galdan Tseren listened silently.

'Though tall, this Ablai was a well-built warrior. In comparison to the great Charysh, however, he seemed like a child. Yes, and in terms of physical power and technique of handling weapons, he couldn't compete with Charysh.'

'Then why did he win? How did he win?'

'It's hard to believe, oh great Khong Tayijii, but he's no ordinary person. He's a spirit walker. It was as if he was supported by the spirits of ancient ancestors and was exalted above all others. Following that victory, the Kazakhs raised him on the white felt as a Khan. He was at the head of the charge, and, despite his youth, since then he has led many victorious campaigns, liberating many Kazakh lands from our grasp and garnering respect across the entire steppe. There are legends about his exploits.'

'Yes, I heard,' Galdan Tseren said dryly.' I also know that he's negotiating with both the Urusuts and the Shurshuts. He is cunning and a danger to us. He must not be allowed to achieve his goals. How long ago did I tell you to deliver him to our horde? For years now, we've been hunting him, and to what avail? Even when it seems he is about to fall into our trap, he somehow manages to miraculously escape at the last moment. The spirits protect him.'

Galdan Tseren brooded for a moment before casting a sharp glance at Zhelbe the Noyon.

'If you can't trap him, then we must capture him by force,' he snapped. 'Take thirty thousand men and trawl the entire steppe. If this Khan Ablai walks this Earth, then you must bring him to me. Bring him to me alive as a captive!'

Slave

Khan Ablai was hunting in the Ulytau Mountains with his friends Zhabek, a warrior from the Argyn Clan, and Utegen, a warrior from the Uak Clan. The hunt had tired them and, having eaten some meat they soon fell asleep, dreaming heroic dreams. It was thus that the Khong Tayijii's warriors found them. Zhelbe the Noyon thrust the point of his spear delicately into the chest of the sleeping Khan Ablai. Opening his eyes, the Khan silently looked up at the Dzungarian and understood everything.

A HUNDRED YEARS ON THE STEPPE 379

Reminiscence

When news of Ablai's captivity arrived, the Dzungars were in shock. Everyone looked upon the legendary Khan of the Kazakhs as their sworn enemy. Speculation was rife as to how the Khong Tayijii would deal with him: would they cut off his head immediately, hold him captive and humiliate and torture him, or would they bind him to the tail of his obstinate horse and let it wander across the steppe so that later accusations of killing the Khan could be rebuffed?

Khan Ablai and his loyal friends, Zhabek and Utegen were being stared at with great interest. The captives held on with dignity, though. Even on the long painful road, whilst imagining what humiliating destiny awaited them, the noble appearance and magnificent posture of the Khan did not falter. Despite their hostility, the Dzungars, especially the women, among who was the young beauty Topysh, the beloved, freedom-loving daughter of the Khong Tayijii, noted the air of greatness which this man exuded.

Galdan Tseren and several of his particularly close Noyons were the only ones who did not show respect to the captives. The Khong Tayijii ordered that Ablai's companions be shackled and sent deep into the valley to herd sheep under the supervision of the Sheriks. As for the Khan, a special fate awaited him.

'Throw him in prison and hold him there for seven days and nights with neither food nor drink. After this time has elapsed, give him a bowl of water. Then, throw a piece of lamb fat into the water. Watch him carefully,' Galdan Tseren ordered his Sheriks, 'and report to me everything you see.'

So, the Dzungars took Ablai to the dungeon, threw in an armful of hay, untied his hands and left him there. The long days and nights stretched interminably as Ablai lay motionless and waited with his eyes closed. He was tormented by the fact that he, the Khan, had been captured in his own kingdom and taken to a foreign land.

'Such carelessness,' Ablai muttered to himself. 'If I get out of here, I'll remember this bitter lesson for the rest of my life.'

At times, Ablai dissolved into a world of memories and visions, the brightest moments of his glorious, adventurous life passing before his eyes. He recalled events in which he had participated and the stories told to him by the endearing Zhyrshy. He remembered the wise words of Beys and the adventures of the great warriors, and this gave him strength. His body became weak from exhaustion, but the inner fire of his soul was unquenchable and the eyes of the Khan sparkled with unshakable determination and courage.

Once, in a battle with the Dzungars, Ablai had become separated from his army. Whilst at full gallop at the height of the skirmish his warhorse had been struck with a spear, and, without making a sound the noble animal collapsed dead in the grass. Springing to his feet, the Khan saw that he was surrounded by a large detachment of Torghuts and Durbuts (Kalmyk tribes). As they approached their sabres sparkled and a gale-force wind whistled above their heads. Resolving to meet his death with dignity, Ablai prepared for battle, but regret about all the great feats he had not yet

A HUNDRED YEARS ON THE STEPPE 381

achieved for his people gnawed at him, and he gritted his teeth in frustration and rage.

Suddenly, like a whirlwind, a rider on a blue horse flew to his side.

'*Aldiyar* (good friend),' he cried, 'get on the horse!'

Jumping to the ground, the young sweat-soaked warrior handed Ablai the bridle.

'Get on, quickly!" they implored.

'But what about you?' asked Ablai.

'The Kazakhs need a Khan like you,' the young man replied. 'If I die, another warrior will be born to replace me.'

'No; I will not leave you,' said the Khan decisively.

'Listen, what's the point in us both dying? Leave or I'll cut myself down so the Dzungars don't get you.'

His eyes flashing, the warrior abruptly bundled Ablai onto his horse and struck it with his whip. The blue horse swept through the howling wind and the ranks of Dzungars, delivering hope for the Kazakh people.

After the battle, Ablai ordered his entourage to locate the brave warrior and find out about him. It turned out that his name was Zhanibek of the Kerey Tribe. Having killed many enemies, miraculously he had managed to survive the bloody massacre. Ablai thanked the hero who had been ready to sacrifice his own life for that of his Khan, that is, for his native country.

It was said that one day in his youth, Zhanibek fell asleep on a hill, and from afar his uncle saw two blue-headed wolves fussing about him. The uncle rushed to help him, but when he arrived there weren't any wolves to be found.

The uncle concluded that it must have been the spirits of totem wolves who had chosen Zhanibek as their host. Indeed, Zhanibek was fearless and menacing like a wolf.

Once, a brave Dzungar Noyon had challenged Zhanibek to a duel. The Noyon was strong and fuelled by rage, but at the sight of Zhanibek, the Dzungarian hero wilted, became depressed and fled.

'What happened?' the Dzungars asked the Noyon.

'I don't know,' the Noyon replied, 'but when I looked at him, there were two ferocious bluewolves with fiery eyes on his shoulders gnashing their sharp fangs. Their eyes literally drilled through me, filling my soul with horror, and in that instant, I was defeated.'

Plagued by nightmares, Ablai lay in the Dzungar prison, his thoughts running through the world of heroes, legends and monsters. Vividly, he imagined the feats of Kastek, the hero of a folk legend. A fourteenyearold horse grazer, Kastek sat high on a hill peering out over the steppe. During wartime, he performed the role of lookout at the same time as his primary task.

One day, from behind an oval , Kastek saw a large army stretched out like a cloud appear. The detachment of Dzungars was marching directly on the shepherds. Kastek dispatched his younger brother to the village to warn the elders about the impending danger. Then, he got on his horse and went to meet the whole army. The fact was that if he tried to flee the Dzungars would catch him anyway and then cut down the rest of the clan. So Kastek decided to detain them in order to give his relatives time to escape and disappear

A HUNDRED YEARS ON THE STEPPE   *383*

into the steppe.

As he approached the Khong Tayijii's Sheriks, he began waving a small crooked sabre.

'Zhekpezhek! Noyons! Zaysans! I challenge you to a duel!' he cried.

The Dzungars stopped in their tracks. They were very surprised that a little boy in rags with a small sabre and no chain-mail or spear, stood there defying these seasoned descendants of the great Oirots. They hesitated and then begun chuckling at the little boy, inquiringly of each other what they should do. Waving his sabre at them, the boy did not care.

'Zhekpezhek!' he yelled.

Finally, the Noyon commander honoured the boy with a question.

'Who are you, boy, and what do you need?'

'I am Kastek the warrior from the Shapyrashty Clan,' the boy answered unwaveringly. 'I need you to leave our steppe in peace and return to your *ulus* (native land).'

The Noyon laughed out loud and his men followed suit.

'Listen, kid,' he said, 'you definitely grabbed my attention, but if we disobey you, then what?'

'Then I will challenge you to a death match.'

The Noyon sighed and shook his head.

'Listen, boy,' he said, 'I do not want your blood. Get out of our way and go home. You still have your entire life to live, to get married…'

'What home are you talking about, Noyon? Didn't you

come here to destroy it, to burn down my yurt? But I won't let you. Now leave or fight me like a man.'

The Dzungars began to get angry and were ready to tear apart the arrogant brat, but raising his hands, the Noyon stopped them.

'You are a brave warrior, boy, and I will honour you; I will fight with all my might as with a worthy hero.'

So, they came together in a deadly battle, the fourteen-year-old Kastek with his small sabre and his horse against the fully armed Noyon, decked in chain-mail and upon a powerful stallion. With a loud battle cry, the Noyon pierced the little boy through his chest with a single blow from his long spear and lifted him above his head. Appreciating the combat skills of their leader, the Dzungars rejoiced. Drenched in blood, Kastek hung lifelessly on the Kalmyk spear which protruded from his back.

'Hey boy, how are you there?' the Noyon asked.

Barely opening his eyes, Kastek spat out a mouthful of blood.

'Damn, you really showed your power,' the boy choked hoarsely. 'Now show me your strength and let me down in one fell swoop.'

The Noyon was growing uncomfortable, but laughing hysterically to hide his discomfort he smashed the blunt end of the spear upon the ground. The spear broke in two, freeing Kastek from its gory grasp and leaving him face to face with the Noyon.

'Well, how are you now?' the Noyon asked, staring at the boy.

A HUNDRED YEARS ON THE STEPPE   *385*

'This is how,' Kastek the warrior muttered softly as he thrust his little sabre deep into the throat of the Noyon.

Slaughtered with a single blow, in front of his men the Noyon crashed to the ground. The stunned Dzungars buried both heroes with honours on that hill and returned to their horde without advancing further.

Once, whilst on a campaign, Khan Ablai had met a lone rider. He was huge. Even when dismounted, he remained the same height as the horse he rode on. His name was Tursunbai of the Kerey Tribe. After talking with him at length, the Khan invited him to join his army.

'I have heard tales of you, great Khan,' Tursunbai said. 'You know, when I'm alone in the steppe, I feel huge as if I were filling the entire steppe to the horizon. Yet when I join a crowd of people, I feel very small. Therefore, I always go camping alone. With such a hero as you, though, I will go wherever you want me to.'

They rode across the steppe together for many days. Passing an old, dilapidated *mazar* (tomb or shrine) they recited prayers together but decided to leave as soon as possible for fear of disturbing the departed. As they prayed, out of the corner of his eye the Khan noticed half-decayed wooden beams protruding from one dilapidated ancient grave.

Following a long, fierce battle, they returned victorious. On the way back, the warriors were tired and hungry, so the Khan decided to make camp for the night near the ancient mazar. He ordered that a horse be killed, but in the barren steppe, firewood to cook it was nowhere to be found. Whilst his horsemen were carving the carcass, the Khan turned to

386   *Bayangali Alimzhanov*

Tursunbai the warrior.

'You know where the old cemetery is?' he asked. 'Go down there and bring back all the beams. It will be dark soon and no one will be able to find that place except for you.'

Delighted that he had the confidence of the Khan, Tursunbai set off forthwith.

The warrior rode up to the cemetery, dismounted and, after reciting a short prayer, began to labour in the pitch darkness in order to pull out the wooden partitions. When, having completely opened the grave, he began to pull out the wood, a dead man in a white shroud shouted in a terrible voice: 'Hey, do not touch my grave! Do not disturb my eternal rest!' The dark, moonless night seemed to shudder at the harrowing cry of the spirit.

Tursunbai the warrior grabbed the dead man's throat, quickly twisting his hands and pinning him down.

'So, are you dead or only half-dead?' he asked. 'If you're dead and enjoy endless slumber, instead of complaining, ask yourself, why must the living starve to death? And if you're half dead, then I will make sure you die for real this time.'

With these words, he pulled out a damask dagger and as was about to wield it purposefully when the white-robed fiend cried out in horror.

'Wait, fellow warrior, do not kill me! Khan Ablai sent me to test your courage.'

Tursunbai laughed and released him.

It turned out that Khan Ablai, having witnessed Tursunbai's fearlessness and courage in battle had wanted to test

A HUNDRED YEARS ON THE STEPPE 387

his mettle once more. Therefore, before darkness had fallen, he had sent two soldiers to the ancient mazar ordering one to wear the white shroud and hide in the grave and the other to watch what transpired from afar.

'Let's see if our new recruit will be startled or not before this spirit?' the Khan had said.

Back at the encampment, they made a fire, cooked meat, ate for glory and laughed about the "half-dead."

'Tell me, warrior,' the Khan asked Tursunbai, 'have you ever been scared in your life?'

'There was one time,' he answered. 'Once, I fell sound asleep in the steppe. Suddenly, I felt something cold slithering over me. I looked out of the corner of my eye and saw that a huge black snake had wrapped itself around my neck. I opened my mouth and bit it in half with all my strength. Its head fell in one direction, its tail in the other, and I swallowed the middle section. I guess I acted out of fear. Yes, if I hadn't been scared would I have swallowed the disgusting snake?'

Khan Ablai and his warriors laughed.

'At this point, I don't know what's scarier, the snake or how you bit into the thing and swallowed it,' the Khan said.

Now, lying on his bed of hay in the damp Dzungar dungeon, Khan Ablai smiled at his memories. At the same time, though, bitterness burned his soul. Those same nearby unreachable Dzungar warriors appeared one after another in his imagination.

Satay, the warrior of the Suan Clan, was distinguished by his good disposition. On one occasion, he came across a

Kalmyk Noyon sleeping in the steppe. For any normal man there wouldn't be much to decide, you'd either tie him up or cut him up, it was that simple. But Satay woke him like a friend, quietly, even gently. After waking up, he thought to himself, *who is he, why has he come? Well, he doesn't need to be an enemy; he can be a guest.*

'Why did you come here bearing weapons?' he asked. 'Come as a friend, a neighbour.'

Touched by such an incredible offer when he had expected to meet his downfall, the Kalmyk Noyon abandoned his hostile intentions and left in peace.

When others refused his overtures, however, Satay would lose his patience. Once events began to take a serious turn, he would become angry, the force of Satay the warrior doubling before his enemy's eyes.

The events of the glorious days he had spent as the Khan swept in a continuous succession before Ablai's eyes as he lay starving. He was amazed at the vividness and clarity of these visions; it seemed as if he was reliving his past.

Once, the Kazakh Sarbas and the Dzungarian Sheriks had come together in an open field. A great number of glorious heroes had gathered on both sides, and lost in wild fury, although completely unfamiliar with one another they were there for the sole purpose of carving each other apart. Well, that is the law of war, they consoled themselves.

The Noyons sent an ambassador to the Khan.

'We are not looking for bloodshed,' he said. 'We are not looking to needlessly kill honourable warriors. Let us come to an agreement and swear to it. Let your strongest

A HUNDRED YEARS ON THE STEPPE   *389*

warrior come and duel with ours. The side that is victorious will receive all, and the vanquished will leave with nothing.'

Together they swore to that and scheduled a decisive duel for the next day.

After consulting with the elders and commanders for some time, Ablai and Bogembai decided to have Zhanibek fight Shakshakuly, from the genus Argyn. The Kalmyks, meanwhile, had chosen a man said to have once defeated a ferocious tiger, grabbing it by the tail and swinging in the air like a kitten before smashing its head on the ground. They say the skin of this tiger still adorns the Khong Tayijii's dwelling.

When Zhanibek learnt who he was to face, he became uneasy. He didn't sleep well, and in the early hours of the morning, he had a dream about meeting the Dzungar in a battle in which the warrior knocked him from his saddle with a spear, stood on his chest and brought a sabre to his throat. Zhanibek woke in a cold sweat and decided to flee.

Before making his exit he went to the Khan's tent to forewarn him of his departure. To the surprise of Zhanibek, the Khan was waiting for him. Zhanibek told the Khan his dream.

'Allow me to leave, oh mighty Khan,' he implored. 'I have not married yet, and if I die, there will be no one to carry on my family name.'

With a click of his fingers, Ablai summoned his groom. When the groom came in, Ablai ordered him to bring his horse, Narkyzyl, which had been gifted him by Bogembai before the battle with Charysh.

'Allah, I pray to you to accept mighty Narkyzyl as a sacrifice,' the Khan said when the horse was brought before him. 'Accept my sacrifice and let the dream of Zhanibek the warrior be true as I interpret it.'

The Khan ordered his groom to slaughter the horse and distribute its meat to the soldiers. When left alone with Zhanibek, he began to explain:

'From ancient times, the Kazakhs have said that whoever is frightened in a dream rejoices in reality. Popular wisdom dictates that a dream does not come true as you see it, but as you interpret it. So, if the Dzungar defeated you in a dream, you will defeat him in reality. Drive this fear away; go to the Dzungar and victory will be yours.'

Hearing Ablai's words, Zhanibek visibly perked up. Moreover, he was shocked by the fact that the Khan had sacrificed his beloved horse for the correct interpretation of his dream. Inspired, Zhanibek went to the duel and steamed at the enemy. Surprisingly, the Dzungarian strongman looked depressed and was at a loss, falling from his steed at the first strike of the spear. Zhanibek dismounted, placed his foot on the chest of the Dzungar and was about to smite him when the Dzungar stopped him with a wave of his hands.

'Wait,' he said. 'I'm not afraid to die, but listen to me first. The dream that you saw; I had a dream too in which I killed you. It is my misfortune that my soothsayer couldn't interpret my dream correctly, but yours turned out to be strong in spirit and high in intelligence.'

It was a pity that Zhanibek had to kill such a man, but such are the ways of war. Following the agreement, the

A HUNDRED YEARS ON THE STEPPE 391

Noyons handed over their property to Khan Ablai, and he returned to his horde with bags full of riches and great fame.

Yes, these warriors are no ordinary people. Ablai had thought this before, but now, tormented in the Kalmyk dungeon, he keenly felt their patriotism. They were all connected by some invisible, mysterious, otherworldly thread, and where this energy came from was known only to the Almighty.

The great warrior of the Karakerej Clan's name was Erasyl, but his people called him "Kabanbai" for his courage and assertiveness. Despite being a commander, in bloody battles Kabanbai would ride far ahead of his army like an angry lion, bursting into the ranks of the Dzungars and scything them down mercilessly. His appearance and the clattering hooves of his warhorse, Kubas, threw the Khong Tayijii's men into a blind panic and oftentimes they fled.

During one campaign, a wide, deep river blocked the way for Kazakh militia. Seemingly, there was no way to ford it. The commander became saddened.

Will I, Kabanbai the warrior who never retreats from his enemies be defeated by this pathetic excuse for an obstacle? he mused. Irritated as he reflected on his strategy for the upcoming war, he fell into a fitful sleep during which he experienced a prophetic dream. In his dream, he saw two noble aksakals who advised him that he was the hero chosen by the Almighty. They educated him on how to live a righteous life and showed him a way to ford the river which had been lost to the ages. In the morning, he found this ford, his soldiers safely crossing the river and continuing their campaign. A rumour started amongst the people that even a stormy river would give way to Kabanbai the warrior.

Reflecting on the visible and the invisible, on that which is known and that which remains an inexplicable mystery, Khan Ablai thought of Malaysary and Olzhabay. A warrior from the Argyn family, Malaysary was an unusually large, strong and courageous man. When he was still a boy and rode a pony, a tiger attacked him and his friends. Not at all afraid, he was the first to engage the formidable predator. The tiger ripped its claws into the pony so that it toppled over, but leaping from it, Malaysary landed on the tiger's back. Grabbing the predator by the neck, he prevented it from tearing at him with its claws and fangs. As the fierce tiger growled and tried to throw off the tenacious little boy, Malaysary's father, Toktaul arrived, ripping open the beast's belly with a sharp dagger and rescuing his son. From this day forth, despite his tender age, Malaysary began to participate in skirmishes with the Dzungars. He achieved many great feats and his name became known throughout the steppe.

Once, during a ferocious battle, Malaysary was captured by the Dzungars. Greeting him with honour, the Khong Tayijii came to the conclusion that it was better not to quarrel with such a military leader, but to make peace and live in friendship. Malaysary accepted his peace proposal and promised he would send his son to the Dzungars in the Amanats. They kissed the barrel of a rifle and vowed not to fight each other anymore, saying that if either should break this oath he would be shredded by thousands of bullets.

When Malaysary returned to his village, Khan Ablai

came to him and called on him to campaign against the Dzungars.

'I will not go,' Malaysary told the Khan. 'I made an oath to the Kalmyks not to fight them and kissed the barrel of a rifle.'

'Why is your oath to the Khong Tayijii? Will you just sit here whilst your people go to war to avenge their loved ones and return kidnapped prisoners? No, you will come with us and that's final.' the Khan ordered.

Learning in advance of the Kazakh campaign, the Dzungars embedded themselves in an impenetrable fortress. Commanders from the Sary, Ulak and Malaysary Clan led the assault upon the fortress. The Dzungars met them with gunfire, and the Kazakhs were forced to retreat. Three bullets had hit the slit in Malaysary's chain-mail, but all the rest had returned without a single scratch.

After examining the serious wound in Malaysary's lower back, Ablai ordered that he be given no smoked meat and only fed lightly.

'Given where the bullets have struck him, smoked meat will break his guts,' the Khan warned.

Lying quietly in the tent, Malaysary reproached himself, thinking he had been struck by his oath which he could not keep. Still, the army of the Khan continued the besiege the fortress.

In those days, Olzhabay of the Argyn clan was an unknown young soldier in the army reserves. On one spring morning when he was tending to his horse, he heard something and turned around to see someone scuttling past.

'Where are you off to in such a hurry?' asked Olzhabay.

'Haven't you heard, Olzhabay? The hero of the Middle Zhuz is laying siege to the Dzungar fortress and will distribute riches to us soldiers. I don't want to be left without anything,' his interlocutor replied and rode on.

Is it my destiny to take down this impregnable fortress? wondered Olzhabay. Putting on his armour, he mounted his horse and galloped off. Remembering the tale of Ablai, shouting his name, he grabbed the battle flag from the Khan's hands and charged at the fortress.

'Olzhabay! Olzhabay!' the warriors chanted, and in a flash, his name became the war cry of the whole of Middle Zhuz.

Only after the battle was over did Olzhabay notice that a bullet had penetrated his hand.

On his sickbed, Malaysary bitterly regretted that he had not been able to take part in the victorious battle. One day during his recuperation, he decided that he wanted to eat meat and ordered his groom to prepare some. Remembering the orders of Khan Ablai, the groom shook his head.

'I'm sorry, mighty warrior, but I cannot fulfil your wish,' he said, bowing his head.

Malaysary threatened him, saying that if he didn't obey, he would surely kill him. The groom was frightened and rummaging through the supply boxes he found some smoked *kazy* (sausage). Cutting off a large piece, he cooked and gave it to the stricken warrior. Malaysary died the very same day.

'I kept wondering where Azrael, the angel of death

A HUNDRED YEARS ON THE STEPPE

lives,' he said with his final breath. 'It turns out that he was lying at the bottom of my supply boxes. He crept up on me.'

The hero's body was delivered to his homeland and buried with honours.

Legends about Olzhabay began to circulate. According to one story, after a difficult hike, the exhausted Olzhabay lay down in the steppe and fell soundly asleep. Awaking with a start, his heart began to pound wildly, his body went cold, goosebumps ran down his spine and he began to choke. In agony, he looked around and saw that a large yellow and white mottled snake had settled on his chest. Resolving to bite off its head, Olzhabay lay still with his mouth wide open. The snake slithered onto the ground, however, so Olzhabay got up and began to look for it. The snake was nowhere to be seen, but when he turned around a spectral figure decked in a white turban was sitting on the ground.

'Do you need something from me, ghost?' Olzhabay asked indignantly.

'First, I'm not a ghost,' the figure replied, 'I'm your destiny, your guardian spirit. I'll always be with you. I wanted to test you and crawled over your body as a snake to make sure you are a courageous warrior. Do not ever worship anyone else's spirit; call upon your own spirit: "Olzhabay, Olzhabay!" and boldly go towards the enemy. The yellow and white snake will fly ahead of you at the speed of a flying bullet. Others will also cry your name, and your enemies will flee.'

Having said this, the spirit disappeared.

Yes, all of these amazing people, the Khan thought to

himself. What a blessing that I have met so many incredible heroes and accomplished many glorious feats in the name of my people. It is a pity that the road was short-lived. One consolation is that in these ten years I've managed to accomplish things that others have not been able to given a lifetime.

Thinking on his pride, he laughed at himself self-critically. Yes, there was a time when an unexpected success had turned the head of the young Khan and left him thirsting for even greater glories. The bravest and most skilled warriors had flocked to his horde from all over the boundless steppe, leaving him feeling invincible.

He thought about his decisive campaign in the footsteps of his great ancestor, Genghis Khan, on the borderlands of the tortuous snows of Russia. Ablai wondered how his own fiery speeches had excited the minds of thousands of young men to prepare for war.

Then, one day, Bukhar the Zhyrau arrived at the horde. Ablai met him with great respect. The Zhyrau was a preoccupied individual, but he told Ablai the truth honestly, impartially, sometimes even sharply. The essence of his words boiled down to the fact that no one needed a war; that we must try to live in peace and harmony with all people.

In the beginning, Ablai was angered by his words, but remembering the conversation with Bukhar the Zhyrau when he was a herder, he calmed down and considered many things. He was struck by the openness and sincerity of the Zhyrau . His words were strong because they were truthful and full of concern for the fate of not only his native people but the whole world. Ablai honoured Bukhar the

A HUNDRED YEARS ON THE STEPPE 397

Zhyrau's words with a long and intense period of thought which led him to conclude that the world was better than any war, and from now on, wherever possible, the path of peace should be the way.

Despite the suffering and deprivation of my youth and despite this ridiculous and shameful captivity, I am a happy Khan, thought Ablai. *Yes, how many rulers are there for whose sake great heroes were ready to give their lives? So, I'm worth something to them, my people.*

Like a balm to his soul, a memory of Baygozy from Argyn Clan of Tarakty surfaced in the Khan's mind. Once, during a battle, Ablai had found himself surrounded by four warriors from the Dzungarian Khoid Clan. Shortly, many Sheriks began to arrive and encircle him. Just when all seemed lost, a strong warrior on a black horse broke through this iron ring, fearlessly fighting off the Khoids and killing several with a spear. It was Baygozy, and recognising him, the inspired Ablai began to fight with renewed vigour. The pair had held off the enemy until reinforcements arrived. Subsequently, the Khan retold this story to himself many times, reflecting on how that warrior's passion and his self-lessness had torn him from the jaws of death.

Ambivalence

Indulging in his memories and reflections, Ablai occasionally spaced out, dozed, or fell into a deep sleep. On one such occasion, a rustling woke him from his sweet slumber.

Opening his eyes, the Khan saw a woman entering his cell. She was an old but pretty Kalmyk dressed in a rich outfit which betrayed her noble birth. Ablai was extremely surprised, but met her approach silently, looking directly into her stern, sad eyes.

'I am Galdan Tserena, the sister of the Khong Tayijii and mother of the great Charysh,' she said.

'Charysh's mother?' Ablai said in surprise.

The noble lady tried to maintain an external calmness, but anger and hatred burst through with her every word.

'How dare you kill my beloved Charysh, my boy? He was very kind; but how can you savages understand?' she continued.

'He was a killer!' the Khan retorted. 'He ruthlessly destroyed whole villages of Kazakhs. He deserved to die.'

'A ruthless killer, you say? You're talking about Charysh... about a sweet, kind Noyon. He passionately loved his country and was a pillar of the horde. Only during the war was he merciless to enemies. Apart from that, he wouldn't even hurt a fly. Once, a lamb sprained its leg, so he made it a splint.

'Yes, he healed a lamb, and what does that change exactly? He cut down a whole nation; does that mean nothing to you?'

'It's war! It's inevitable,' the old woman blurted out with fervour.

You are a mother and you have a maternal heart beating in your chest, right?' continued Ablai. 'And it was probably filled with tender feelings when you sent your son off to

A HUNDRED YEARS ON THE STEPPE 399

war? To a predatory, unjust war! You prayed that he would return alive and healthy, victorious with riches and glory. And then what did your maternal heart tell you? You gave your son your blessing to kill the children of mothers like yourself. And not to kill one person, but to destroy an entire nation. Blood and suffering is the price of your hero son's glory. What gave your son the right to go to a foreign country and murder people? Who invited him? How would you feel if strangers invaded your land?'

Charysh's mother hesitated, and for a moment Ablai thought that she might be ashamed. The proud sister of the Khong Tayijii responded firmly, however.

'No one could ever invade our land. The warriors of Dzungaria would never allow it and would slaughter anyone who tried.'

Ablai did not argue with her as he understood that it would be pointless.

'I understand your beloved son died,' he continued in a conciliatory tone, 'but just for a moment spare a thought for the thousands whose lives your son destroyed. Think of all the heartbroken mothers who mourn for their children like you. Think about the grief that your son brought to our steppes.'

'You dare to say that to me?' the noble Kalmyk blurted out with deep-seated hatred. 'God damn you! May your lands be barren. God damn you so that your seeds will never be scattered!' the Kalmyk screeched with such passion that Ablai flinched and goosebumps ran down his spine.

'You wish for me to have no children?' Ablai calmly

retorted. 'Yes, it is a terrible curse; but as long as my people grow, I will be happy. The children of my people are my children.'

Charysh's mother thought for a moment.

'Well then, Khan, I hope you find yourself at a loss for words in decisive situations and unable to follow the advice of those who speak wisely.'

Ablai shook his head.

'It turns out you are a smart woman,' he answered slowly. 'Indeed, this would be the worst curse. Thank you for the lesson, though. I will always try to do the opposite and obey even a baby if there is a grain of sanity in its words. Most importantly, I return all your curses to you. I believe that no curses can harm the innocent as the Most High and Mighty will not allow it. The blessings of my people will protect me from the curses of foreign enemies.'

The old woman turned sharply and strode towards the exit. On the threshold, she turned and cast a hateful glare at Khan Ablai.

'It does not matter; I will kill you myself,' she hissed venomously.

Moribund

These seven hungry days and nights played a crucial role in Ablai's life. Surviving this, he became a wiser ruler not only of the steppe but of himself as well.

Seven days and seven nights later they served the tor-

A HUNDRED YEARS ON THE STEPPE

mented, weakened Khan a cup of water with a piece of lamb fat floating in it. Ablai sipped the water hoping to attract the fat to his mouth, but mutton fat which has cooled always floats to the other side of the bowl. Three times he tried to swallow the fat, but it would not float into his mouth.

'Previously, I could not blow the fat from the broth, and now I cannot pull it to me,' the displeased Khan exclaimed. 'Happiness has turned away from me. Go to hell!' he shouted and threw the bowl at the observant Sheriks.

Stunned by the actions of the hungry prisoner, they reported back to the Khong Tayijii.

'It looks like this Ablai really is of noble birth,' Galdan Tseren said thoughtfully. 'If he were a commoner, he would have put his hand in the bowl and eaten the fat. Therefore let's try something different. Let four warriors come to him and, exposing their sabres, say fiercely: "Your time has come; the Khong Tayijii has ordered you to be executed." Rush at him, and if he begs for mercy, cut him up, but if he doesn't startle, don't touch him and report back to me.'

Shortly, four warriors entered the dungeon and surrounded the captive Khan. Like shadows of death, they stood motionless and fixed their heavy gaze upon him. Ablai looked at them with cold disinterest as the warriors exposed their sabres and issued their heart-rending battle cry.

'Hai, hai, hai, Ablai, Khan of the Kazakhs! The hour of your death has come. Khong Tayijii had ordered that you be executed.'

All four screamed at the Khan, their sabres flashing above his head, but without even blinking an eye, Ablai sat motionless as a rock. Seeing that he did not startle, the Sheriks silently bowed to him and left.

Having felt the terrible breath of death once more, Ablai sighed and thought to himself that Almighty Allah must have a special destiny for him, and that the spirits of his ancestors were watching over him.

Throne

The Khong Tayijii ordered that Khan Ablai be brought in front of his horde. He gathered ninety of the most distinguished Kalmyks, seating them on either side of the throne.

'Let it be so that no word or glance gives away the fact that I am the Khong Tayijii,' he ordered. 'Let's see how he finds me! And do not give way to the captive Kazakh Khan. Leave only a spot at the threshold for him. If he is a commoner, then he will sit in his usual place at the threshold, but if he is truly of noble origin, then let's see what he will do.'

When Khan Ablai entered, the Kalmyk nobility dressed in their finest robes met him with proud silence. Khan Ablai greeted them with dignity and the Dzungars answered him with a heavy look. Enduring their gaze, Ablai looked around but did not see a suitable place to sit, only a place at the threshold. Khong Tayijii Galdan-Tseren was not visible, and the throne was empty. Ablai stepped confidently forward and sat on the throne of the great Khong Tayijii. The unheard-of insolence of this captive in a foreign country out-

A HUNDRED YEARS ON THE STEPPE
403

raged the Noyons and the Zaysans who exploded in a rage.

'So who will sit on this throne if not the Dzungar Khong Tayijii Galdan Tseren?' Khan Ablai answered with a smile 'If not he then it is the place of the Kazakh Khan, Ablai.'

Everyone looked at each other in confusion. Khong Tayijii Galdan Tseren stood up and went to his throne, which Ablai respectfully vacated, taking a seat at his right side.

Khong Tayijii Galdan Tseren looked mournfully at Khan Ablai.

'Where is Charysh?' he asked.

'There was a fateful battle, and it was destined that he should shed his blood before me.'

'Where is Charysh?'

'My people desired his death, and I simply fulfilled this wish. Why do you need this Charysh who has disappeared into oblivion? Surely it would be better to take care of yourself and those who are still alive.'

The Khong Tayijii pondered these words and shook his head.

'Is there anything you are sorry about, Khan Ablai?' he asked finally.

'The first thing I regret is that I did not manage to build cities and protect my nomadic people.'

'You're right,' replied the Khong Tayijii.

'Secondly, I killed Charysh in a duel which was a fair fight. I am very sorry that I was captured whilst sleeping and will die ingloriously. If we came together in an open field and I died in battle, I would have no regrets.'

'Yes,' said the Khong Tayijii.

'My third regret is that I'm the only living descendant of my ancestors and no heirs to me have yet been born. If I die, then my family name will cease to exist.'

Upon hearing these words, the Khong Tayijii suddenly felt sad.

'I am also the only one left alive of my bloodline,' he said sadly. 'I guess then you're a lot like my Amursana.'

'Ah!' Khan Ablai exclaimed joyfully.

'Why are you happy?' the Khong Tayijii asked in surprise.

'You compared me to your son, and this being the case you probably do not wish for my death,' Khan Ablai exclaimed before continuing in a calm voice. 'I think we have already shed a lot of Kazakh-Kalmyk blood. For nearly two centuries, we've been bringing each other death, suffering and ruin. And what have you achieved?! It's high time to stop and think.'

Some of the Noyons grew indignant, but the Khong Tayijii imperiously raised his hand and everyone immediately fell silent.

'The Kazakhs say that the human head is the ball of Allah. Wherever he pushes it, it will roll.' continued Ablai. 'But sometimes entire countries allow others to play with their own heads.'

Upon hearing these words, the Khong Tayijii's broad face faltered slightly and there was concern in his eyes.

Most of the Dzungarian nobility also seemed to be se-

A HUNDRED YEARS ON THE STEPPE

riously considering this statement.

'Which of today's rulers do you consider the most powerful?' the Khong Tayijii finally asked.

'The Turkish Sultans, the Russian Tsar, the Chinese Emperor, and then you, Khong Tayijii.'

'And where do you stand?' one of the Noyons piped up, unable to stand it any longer.

'We are all in harmony and friendship with the others, so as equals we stand,' Ablai smiled in response.

'We know the legends about you which circulate on the Kazakh steppe,' the Noyon continued, 'but some foreigners speak unflattering words about you. They say you are cunning, treacherous, two-faced and power-mad.'

'It's good when foreign ill-wishers blaspheme you,' laughed Ablai. 'If it were the other way around, that would be really bad. I think the first duty of a Khan should be to think about the interests of his people, not winning foreign flatterers.'

A murmur of approval rose from the Noyons; smirking thoughtfully, Galdan Tseren shook his head.

'Yes, you and I think similarly about many things. So, take some time to rest and then we will continue our conversation,' the Khong Tayijii said, bringing an end to the discussion.

Signalling to his men, the guard led away the great Kazakh Khan known as Ablai.

Dream

Ablai was transferred to a separate yurt, which after the dungeon seemed like paradise. Captivity, though, no matter how honourable is always painful, and his position left Ablai feeling more oppressed as the days went by.

One night, he dreamt that he was a boy on his horse and was playing alone in the steppe. A Kalmyk boy appeared from behind a hill also on a horse and they approached each other. The Kalmyk boy was very handsome and beautifully dressed. They smiled at each other.

'I'm Ablai. What's your name?'

'My name is Charysh. I am a Dzungar. Are you a Kazakh?'

'Yes; do you want to play?'

'Sure; what shall we play?'

'*Asyk* (a Kazakh game of skill played with bones) or baiga?'

'No, let's play war.'

'No, war is bad, but we can duel.'

They dismounted and began to fight, but Ablai accidentally hit Charysh hard in the face with his elbow and the boy cried loudly. Charysh's mother appeared so suddenly it was as if she had risen out of the earth. She hugged her son and began to console him whilst shaking her fist. Ablai became scared, but as he started to cry his mother appeared in a long white dress, surveying the scene sadly. No sooner had she appeared, however, than she vanished like a mirage.

'Where did your mother go?' Charysh asked.

A HUNDRED YEARS ON THE STEPPE

'The Dzungars killed her,' answered Ablai, and broke into tears once more. 'Oh, mother; my dear mother.'

With these words on his lips, he awoke. Through bleary eyes, he saw a woman sitting next to him. Still half-asleep, for a moment he thought that it was his mother, but no, it was the Kalmyk, Charysh's mother. Stunned by his words, she sat motionless at the side of the bed clutching the dagger she had brought to kill him. Ablai jumped up. His face darkened with rage and his eyes filled with blood. Screaming in fright, the old woman recoiled towards the exit. Guards came running upon hearing her cry, and Ablai looked upon them coldly.

'Get her out of here and don't let her in anymore,' he said. 'Tell Galdan Tseren that if he has decided to kill me, then let him do it honourably; or are there no warriors left in the whole of Dzungaria? I will not die at the hands of a madwoman.'

Hearing what had happened from his men, Galdan Tseren forbade his sister from going anywhere near the prisoner's yurt.

Envoys

Soon, envoys from the Kazakh horde arrived. Led by Kazybek the Bey, their foremost demand was the immediate release of Khan Ablai. Hailing from the Karakesek Tribe of the Argyn Clan, people called Kazybek the Bey "*Kaz dauysts*" – 'speaker like the birds' - for his clear, melodious voice. The

408   *Bayangali Alimzhanov*

Khong Tayijii accepted the envoys, and after an exchange of traditional courtesies, Kazybek got down to business.

'Great Khong Tayijii,' he began, 'the entire Kazakh steppe, the free sons of all three Zhuzes are deeply outraged by the capture of the Khan. And you understand perfectly well that the Kazakhs will not forgive you if anything happens to him. We hope for your discretion. In the name of peace between our people, you must immediately return our Khan, safe and sound.'

'Are you asking me or demanding?' Galdan Tseren replied with flashing eyes.

Kazybek the Bey looked directly at him and calmly spoke his poetic words in a firm, sonorous voice:

Oh, great Khong Tayijii,
We the Kazakhs are a peaceful people.
We act only with friendship and kindness,
We never start wars; nor do we enslave.
But to those who come to us with enmity,
We were ready to raise our sharp spears.
You are iron and I am coal;
I have simply come to meet thee.
The Kazakhs and Kalmyks can be together as brothers;
I have come to reconcile with thee.
If you growl like a panther,
Then I will roar like a lion,
Because although we want peace,
We are not afraid to fight.

The speech flowed from the wise and courageous nomad like a pure spring, his powers of recitation endowing

A HUNDRED YEARS ON THE STEPPE   *409*

them with a bewitching beauty. For a moment Galdan Tseren froze in admiration of the bird-voiced Kazybek the Bey, but pulling himself together he answered sternly and with dignity:

'You will have my decision soon.'

Decision

The Khong Tayijii Galdan Tseren was sitting in his quarters talking with his beloved daughter, Topysh, when Charysh's mother burst through the doors. She was older than Galdan Tseren and used to special privileges. Therefore, she didn't abide by the etiquette for behaviour in the palace.

'Oh, Khong Tayijii, dear brother,' she blurted as she rushed towards him. 'It's about time we ended that blood-sucking Kazakh's life!'

Like a wounded tigress, she began to silently circle the room.

'Burn him at the stake and scatter his ashes in the direction of the Kazakh steppes, or tie his limbs to four horses and loose them in four directions.'

Galdan Tseren and the beautiful Topysh listened silently to her fiery speeches. Having accomplished nothing other than letting off steam, she cooled down a little and sat on a tiger-skin rug.

'The Kazakh horse requests in the strongest possible terms the immediate release of their Khan,' said the Khong

Tayijii. 'Their envoys have made it clear that in the case of our refusal and especially if any harm should come to the Khan, they will attack Dzungaria. Both the White King of Russia and the Chinese Emperor also wish to see Ablai set free, for he is loyal to them. This Ablai is a smart one if even great empires such as those would come to his aid.'

'Besides being a mighty warrior and a worthy enemy, might the Khan not prove to be a future friend?' Topysh said, entering the conversation with fervour.

'Friend, you say?' Charysh's mother exploded. 'How dare you even think that? He's stained with the blood of my son, the great warrior of Dzungaria, and instead of taking revenge, you entertain such ludicrous thoughts. No one in Dzungaria thinks the way you do.'

'You're right sister,' said Galdan Tseren. 'By all the laws of war, he must perish. The Noyons and Zaysans want me to execute him as revenge for Charysh's death, but I can't do it. I don't know why, but some unknown, incomprehensible force is holding me back and will not allow me to make this choice.'

'Then let me choose,' Galdan Tserena said in a calm, cold tone. 'I'll execute him myself with the blessing of a llama in front of the whole world as edification to our enemies. I'll execute him cruelly and drink a cup of his blood. Maybe then my soul will find peace.'

'Alright, that's enough!' the Khong Tayijii sharply interrupted. 'Although he is a mortal enemy, he is still a Khan. Yes, he is a prisoner, but his noble blood makes him of special value. He is my captive and I will decide how to deal

A HUNDRED YEARS ON THE STEPPE

with him. Once again, I remind you not to harm a single hair on his head, you understand?'

His sister's face changed dramatically, and with surprising calmness, she accepted his words, bowed obediently and silently left the room. The beautiful Topysh looked at her father with undisguised admiration, her large black eyes sparkling with gratitude.

Ram

Charysh's mother's humility was not in vain, for she intended to arrange Ablai's death to occur in such a way that no one could blame the Dzungars for it. Secretly, she conspired with the chief of security, persuading him to feed Ablai one single product every day: meat. She knew that if a person were to eat nothing but meat, within twenty to thirty days they would die, and should the Khan die of a monotonous diet no one would blame the Dzungarians.

The chief of the guards hated the captive Khan with a passion, so he undertook this insidious plan with zeal, cancelling all other products. On the third day, Ablai refused the food and asked the security chief about his new food regime.

'From now on we will feed you only meat,' the chief brazenly replied.

Mulling it over, Ablai understood the insidious plan, but he didn't let on.

'Well then, bring me a boiled ram's head,' he said in all

seriousness.

'The head of a ram such as we throw to the dogs every day? What kind of simpleton are you? Fine, we will feed you the head of a ram.'

So, every day, the guards brought a boiled ram's head to Ablai. The chief watched him for forty days eager to bring the joyful news of his death to Charysh's mother. Instead of waning, though, the Khan began to gain in strength.

Finally, the conspirators could stand it no longer and turned to the wise llama, asking him to unravel the reason behind this phenomenon whilst concealing their true goal. The llama answered that in a ram's head there are many substances that are useful to humans. He explained to them that in the eyes, brain, tongue, ears, that is, in each part of the head there are different nutrients and even their taste was different. Then the conspirators understood too late the wisdom the Khan.

Lords

The monotonous days and months in captivity dragged on depressingly slowly. Ablai recognised that he needed to hold on and survive in the hope that someday this torment would be over. At times it became unbearable, so he hummed the old, sad tunes of the steppe to himself to pacify his soul.

At the end of summer, Ablai was brought into the palace where the Khong Tayijii sat alone.

A HUNDRED YEARS ON THE STEPPE

'What leads us to keep pushing one another?' Galdan Tseren asked in a low voice.

Ablai looked at him questioningly.

'Great empires want you destroyed by my hand, and me by yours,' Galdan Tseren continued thoughtfully. 'I have not been at peace since I came to understand this cruel truth and have been thinking about how to untie this knot of fate.'

'If we both understand this, then we should stop being tools in soiled hands,' Ablai replied in surprise.

Galdan Tseren rose from his throne and began to pace around his spacious quarters.

'In this world, there are many incomprehensible things that are not subject to our will. I think that you and I understand each other. Our people have been fighting for about two hundred years. They hate each other ferociously and our warriors crave blood and glory. Can we stop them by making them understand that this fratricidal war will only lead to more death?'

'I think if we combine our efforts, then…'

Raising a hand, the Khong Tayijii stopped Ablai and continued as if thinking aloud.

'I am standing at the very top of the mountain of power and have nowhere left to rise to. Those below, the ones who lifted me and climbed behind me without a second thought now want my place. I can either fly to heaven or jump. That is the law of power and the same fate awaits you. You know, it's strange; even though we knew this we still strove to climb the mountain,' the Khong Tayijii sighed.

'I am still young and there's a lot more I want to do for my people,' answered the Khan.

'In the name of your own glory, no less,' Galdan Tseren grinned. 'Don't be embarrassed by it, we are all ambitious. It's this desire to perpetuate our good name in history and in the memory of the people which moves us to do great things. But what is the point of all this?'

Galdan Tseren took a deep breath and surveyed his palace.

'I'm tired of blood and war,' he continued. 'I'm tired of the countless children we've massacred and families we've destroyed. I'm tired of human enmity, of all-consuming hatred, envy, betrayal and lies. If you want to, take my throne and be the lord of the Kalmyk horde.'

'Thank you, great Khong Tayijii,' Ablai replied courteously, 'but my people are Kazakhs. Only with them will I fly to great heights or fall into the abyss.'

'The people… Kazakhs… Kalmyks…' Galdan Tseren grinned. 'Why does that even mean anything? Maybe it was just a random mistake made by nature. There is only one world and there must be one sovereign ruler. The people should be as one.'

'And how does that work?'

'It's quite simple, really. It's not necessary to divide people into Dzungars, Kazakhs, Turks, Urusuts or Shurshuts. If we become a single people, then there will be peace on Earth. Do you agree?'

'I agree,' the Khan replied, his eyes sparkling mischievously, 'but then who will name this collective single human race?'

A HUNDRED YEARS ON THE STEPPE

'Well, anyone.'

'Then let's call them the United Nation of Kazakhs!'

'And why do the Kazakhs get that honour?'

'Well, it's simple, because the Kazakhs are the kindest, most sincere, best people in the world.'

'Did you hit your head in prison or something? And here I was thinking you were fair and intelligent. It turns out that you too suffer from selfishness and pride. Never will a free and proud Kalmyk obey a Kazakh.'

'I jest,' said the smirking Ablai. 'I was just testing that cranky mind of yours. As for the united people, to be honest it's great that a Kalmyk does not want to become a Kazakh; but then why should a Kazakh want to become a Dzungar, a Shurshut or an Urusut?'

Galdan Tseren grinned and shook his head.

'It's all a matter of pride,' Ablai continued in a more serious tone. "Every nation considers itself the best in this world. This is a natural feeling and there is no need to be offended by it. Let everyone think how they please as long as they don't try to prove to others by force that they're superior. All human troubles, all wars begin when one people try to assert their superiority over another. Each nation must remain on its own land in peace and harmony with all of humanity. A Kazakh, whilst remaining a Kazakh can still respect others as equals.'

'Oh, how cute and simple that sounds,' the Khong Tay-ijii chortled.

'The most simple things are usually the most truthful,' the Khan countered.

'What is the truth in this? The truth is that we, great nations, must rule over smaller nations so that peace and order reign in the world,' snapped Galdan Tseren, a note of arrogance returning to his voice.

'No, such actions serve only to shatter peace and order, sowing enmity and leading to bloodshed,' Ablai replied, angry inside but firmly in control of himself. 'If yours is truly a great nation, then show this greatness by allowing others to live in peace. Why should you conquer other countries, destroy their way of life and dictate how they should live?'

'Because this is the way in this mortal world; we are an exceptional people and a special task has been assigned to us by heaven itself,' the Khong Tayijii pontificated proudly.

'The Most High created us differently but as equals. True friendship can only exist between equals,' Ablai argued vehemently. 'I want to be friends with you, with the White King, the Emperor of the Celestial Empire, with everyone as an equal. To be equal and live in friendship - is it so hard? I am a Kazakh Khan; I do not need another country. I will be with my people. I do not recognise anyone's dominion over myself or my people.'

'Don't start digging yourself an early grave yet, Khan Ablai. You are smart and shrewd. You know perfectly well that if I get angry, I can chop off your wise head in no time.'

With these words, the Khong Tayijii's countenance darkened and his voice took on a grinding, metallic quality.

'No one would blame me for this either, because according to the law of the steppes this is what should happen as revenge for the death of Charysh. If I am able to capture

A HUNDRED YEARS ON THE STEPPE 417

the Khan of the Kazakh's from his horde and place him in captivity, then it's clear that I have the right to execute him.'

Ablai said nothing, waiting patiently the other man to conclude his tirade. Like a prowling tiger, Galdan Tseren silently paced on the skins of the predatory animals which covered the floor. After a moment, he became pacified and spoke kindly.

'For many reasons, though, I will not take this path. I respect you more than I probably should, Ablai. Our peoples should no longer fight but live in peace. We must hold on to each other to ensure we're not wiped from the face of the Earth. Recently, I have often found myself thinking that all these years of war, hatred, destruction and suffering between the Kalmyks and Kazakhs do not make any sense.'

'Oh, if only you had understood this earlier, before you invaded us,' blurted Ablai, unable to hold his tongue. 'How many more people would there be now in both Kazakhstan and Kalmykia. What did the Dzungars achieve as a result of invading my country?'

The Khong Tayijii Galdan Tseren stopped him with a sharp movement of his right hand. Sitting on his throne, he finally said the words Ablai had been hoping to hear since he had been thrown in prison two years ago.

'I have no answer to this question. But let's not blame each other, Khan Ablai. What's passed has passed. Now, you need to think about the future. I am returning you to the Kazakhs. I don't know if this will be any consolation, a payment for the many years of hostility and bloodshed between our people, but I want one thing in order to stop this fratricidal, senseless war.'

'Well?' asked Ablai. 'What is it?'

'I want you to marry my beloved daughter, Topysh. Thus, I hope that if we become related we will be able to live in peace and harmony.'

Though surprised, Khan Ablai met with this fateful decision calmly. Suddenly, he felt thoroughly exhausted, but he did not show this. He thanked the Khong Tayijii Galdan Tseren with dignity and the two embraced.

Following the liberation of Khan Ablai and the rest of Kazakh prisoners, peace reigned between the Kazakhs and the Dzungars. The curses of Charysh's mother did not come to pass. In all likelihood, the Almighty and the spirits of the ancestors did not allow them to because Ablai's cause was just. Khan Ablai lived a long life. He had thirty sons and forty daughters from many beautiful wives. He was rich and his people lived freely. His khanate was prosperous and independent. The folk legends of the Kazakhs have been extolling the heroic and happy era of Khan Ablai and the warriors of legend for several centuries. Having read this legend now, I hope you can understand why.

A HUNDRED YEARS ON THE STEPPE

A HUNDRED YEARS ON THE STEPPE

ABOUT THE AUTHOR

Bayangali Tokanovich Alimzhanov is a Kazakh poet, author, playwright, *aqyn* (improviser), zhyrshy, manaschi (performer of the epic poem, *Manas*) and Honoured Worker of Kazakhstan. The winner of the international Maldybaev prize of Kyrgyzstan, he was born on October 16th 1954 in Stepnyak in the Akmola Region and graduated from the Faculty of Philological at KazSU.

The author of over forty books, four feature films and six documentaries, he has won the Republican Grand Prize twenty-two times and the Contest of Storytellers. He has also been a prize-winner at the International Manaschi Competition.

In Kazakhstan, the collected works of Alimzhanov have been published in sixteen volumes. His works have been translated into English, Russian, Spanish, French, Arabic, Chinese, Japanese, German, Turkish, Uzbek, Kyrgyz, Karakalpak, Tatar, Bashkir, Uyghur, Udmurt and Mongolian. He writes mainly in Kazakh and Russian.

Bayangali Alimzhanov

Printed in the USA
CPSIA information can be obtained
at www.ICGtesting.com
LVHW051415230224
772657LV00001B/2